Great Britain:
French residents cross the English Channel to shop in London, taking advantage of depreciation of the British pound *(Chapter 6)*

Description of Bank of England monetary policy during the global financial crisis *(Chapter 13)*

Eastern Europe:
Analysis of Eastern European countries joining the Euro *(Chapter 21)*

Russia:
Collapse of the Soviet Union *(Chapter 1)*

Central Planning *(Chapter 3)*

China:
Ownership *(Chapter 2)*
Comparison of government revenue sources and spending priorities in China and the United States *(Chapter 11)*

China example of international trade conflicts with the U.S. *(Chapter 19)*

Europe:
Switzerland: World Trade Organization *(Chapter 4)*

Why European unemployment rates are higher than U.S. *(Chapter 7)*

Eurozone agrees to economic policy rules *(Chapter 11)*

Example of U.S. and Germany competing in strategic trade policy *(Chapter 20)*

Korea: Private property rights *(Chapter 2)*

Tokyo, Japan:
Big Mac Index *(Chapter 3)*

Toyota *(Chapter 4)*

Hong Kong:
Sudden wealth *(Chapter 18)*

Cameroon:
Central planning *(Chapter 3)*

SubSahara Africa:
Development and poverty *(Chapter 3)*

Zimbabwe:
Story of hyperinflation in Zimbabwe *(Chapter 14)*

Bahrain:
Explanation of Islamic banking *(Chapter 12)*

Ethiopia:
Fighting hunger via money or food transfers *(Chapter 17)*

India:
Central planning *(Chapter 3)*

Example of U.S. and India wheat trade to illustrate comparative advantage *(Chapter 19)*

Asia, Indonesia, Thailand, Korea, Malaysia, Philippines:
Analysis of Asian financial crisis in Indonesia, Thailand, Korea, Malaysia and the Philippines *(Chapter 18)*

Europe

Asia

Africa

Australia

MACROECONOMICS

TENTH EDITION

MACROECONOMICS

TENTH EDITION

WILLIAM BOYES
Arizona State University

MICHAEL MELVIN
Arizona State University and BlackRock

CENGAGE
Learning·

Australia • Brazil • Japan • Korea • Mexico • Singapore • Spain • United Kingdom • United States

CENGAGE
Learning®

Macroeconomics, Tenth Edition
William Boyes, Michael Melvin

Vice President, General Manager, Social Science & Qualitative Business: Erin Joyner

Product Director: Mike Worls

Product Manager: Michael Parthenakis

Content Developer: Anita Verma

Product Assistant: Mary Umbarger

Sr. Marketing Manager: John Carey

Sr. Content Project Manager: Colleen A. Farmer

Manufacturing Planner: Kevin Kluck

Production Service: Cenveo Publisher Services

Sr. Art Director: Michelle Kunkler

Internal and Cover Designer: Ramsdell Design, LLC

Cover Image: © Carsten Reisinger/ Shutterstock.com

Intellectual Property:
Analyst: Jennifer A. Nonenmacher
Project Manager: Sarah Shainwald

For product information and technology assistance, contact us at **Cengage Learning Customer & Sales Support, 1-800-354-9706**

For permission to use material from this text or product, submit all requests online at **www.cengage.com/permissions**
Further permissions questions can be emailed to
permissionrequest@cengage.com

Unless otherwise noted, all items © Cengage Learning

Library of Congress Control Number: 2014949787

ISBN: 978-1-285-85947-7

Cengage Learning
20 Channel Center Street
Boston, MA 02210
USA

Cengage Learning is a leading provider of customized learning solutions with office locations around the globe, including Singapore, the United Kingdom, Australia, Mexico, Brazil, and Japan. Locate your local office at: **www.cengage.com/global**

Cengage Learning products are represented in Canada by Nelson Education, Ltd.

To learn more about Cengage Learning Solutions, visit **www.cengage.com**

Purchase any of our products at your local college store or at our preferred online store **www.cengagebrain.com**

Printed in Mexico
Print Number: 03   Print Year: 2020

To Melissa, Katie, and Lindsey –W. B.
To Bettina, Jason, Jeremy, Anna, and Sonia –M. M.

BRIEF CONTENTS

CONTENTS

APPENDIX TO CHAPTER 9

An Algebraic Model of Aggregate Expenditures   200

CHAPTER 10

Income and Expenditures Equilibrium   203

APPENDIX TO CHAPTER 10

An Algebraic Model of Income and Expenditures Equilibrium   225

CHAPTER 11

Fiscal Policy   227

APPENDIX TO CHAPTER 11

An Algebraic Examination of the Balanced-Budget Change in Fiscal Policy   250

CHAPTER 12

Money and Banking   253

SUGGESTED OUTLINES FOR ONE-TERM COURSES*

Macroeconomic Emphasis	Microeconomic Emphasis	Balanced Micro-Macro
1. The Wealth of Nations: Ownership and Economic Freedom	1. The Wealth of Nations: Ownership and Economic Freedom	1. The Wealth of Nations: Ownership and Economic Freedom
2. Scarcity and Opportunity Costs	2. Scarcity and Opportunity Costs	2. Scarcity and Opportunity Costs
3. Markets and the Price System	3. Markets and the Price System	3. Markets and the Price System
4. The Aggregate Economy	20. Elasticity: Demand and Supply	4. The Aggregate Economy
5. National Income Accounting	21. Demand: Consumer Choice	5. National Income Accounting
6. An Introduction to the Foreign Exchange Market and the Balance of Payments	22. Supply: The Costs of Doing Business	6. An Introduction to the Foreign Exchange Market and the Balance of Payments
7. Unemployment and Inflation	23. Profit Maximization	7. Unemployment and Inflation
8. Macroeconomic Equilibrium: Aggregate Demand and Supply	24. Perfect Competition	8. Macroeconomic Equilibrium: Aggregate Demand and Supply
9. Aggregate Expenditures	25. Monopoly	11. Fiscal Policy
10. Income and Expenditures Equilibrium	26. Monopolistic Competition and Oligopoly	12. Money and Banking
11. Fiscal Policy	27. Markets and Government	13. Monetary Policy
12. Money and Banking	28. Antitrust and Regulation	19. Using Economics to Understand the World Around You
13. Monetary Policy	29. Resource Markets	20. Elasticity: Demand and Supply
14. Macroeconomic Policy: Tradeoffs, Expectations, Credibility, and Sources of Business Cycles	30. The Labor Market	21. Demand: Consumer Choice
	31. The Capital Market	22. Supply: The Costs of Doing Business
15. Macroeconomic Viewpoints: New Keynesian, Monetarist, and New Classical	32. The Land Market and Natural Resources	28. Profit Maximization
	33. Current Issues: Income, Income Distribution, Poverty, and Government Policy	29. Resource Markets
16. Economic Growth	34. World Trade Equilibrium	33. Current Issues: Income, Income Distribution, Poverty, and Government Policy
17. Development Economics	35. International Trade Restrictions	34. World Trade Equilibrium
18. Globalization		
34. World Trade Equilibrium		
35. International Trade Restrictions		
36. Exchange Rates and financial Links between Countries		

---

* Chapter numbers represent *Economics, 10th ed.* For *Macroeconomics, 10th ed.*, and *Microeconomics, 10th ed.*, see the conversion chart in the Brief Contents section.

PREFACE

In the first edition of *Macroeconomics*, we integrated a global perspective with traditional economic principles to give students a framework to understand the globally developing economic world. Events since then have made this approach even more imperative. In the 1990s, the Soviet Union disintegrated and newly independent nations emerged. Much of Latin America was turning toward free markets and away from government controls. But by 2005, several of these nations were turning back—away from free markets. Hugo Chavez and Evo Morales were guiding Venezuela and Bolivia away from free markets and toward government-run and controlled economies. Vladimir Putin was driving Russia toward more government control. Other events were making the world seem very small: North Korea was testing nuclear weapons, Somalia was embroiled in a civil war, terrorism was prevalent in nations around the world, and much of Africa remained mired in poverty. In 2007, the interconnectedness of nations was once again highlighted when the world fell into a deep recession created by the housing collapse in the United States. When economic growth returned in the summer of 2009, it was slow and unemployment remained high. In 2011 the European Union and the eurozone faced severe challenges as Greece, Portugal, Spain, Italy, and Ireland had debt burdens that were historically high. In 2014, Russia invaded Ukraine and civil war permeated Syria and much of the middle East, as well as several regions of Africa. The United States had applied tariffs to some Chinese goods and sanctions on Russia. They both retaliated with their own tariffs and embargos.

Students and instructors have embraced the idea that the economies of countries are interrelated and that this should be made clear in the study of economics. *Economics* gives students the tools they need to make connections between the economic principles they learn and the now-global world they live in.

In this edition, we continue to refine and improve the text as a teaching and learning instrument while expanding its international base by updating and adding examples related to global economics.

Changes in the Tenth Edition

The tenth edition of *Macroeconomics* has been thoroughly updated and refined taking into account the events of 2008-2014.

Revised Introductory Chapters

The introductory chapters have been reduced from 5 to 4. An emphasis on what leads to the wealth of nations occurs in chapters 1 and 2. This places current events and economic developments in perspective. Is this economy or other economies carrying out the correct actions to enhance the wealth and well-being of it citizens?

Revised Macroeconomic Coverage

The focus of this new edition has been to ensure that the information and discussion faithfully represent the latest thinking of economists on important macroeconomic phenomena. To this end, many small additions and revisions appear throughout. Larger changes of note include: many applications to the recent financial crisis and associated recession appear throughout the macro section; All data-related tables and figures are updated to be as current as possible at the time of publication. The big issues are the same as they have been for years, but economic policies have changed with the times. For instance, we now discuss central bank *forward guidance*, the idea that central banks can have beneficial effects on the economy by committing to follow policies for a stated period of time. For instance, the Federal Reserve has repeatedly stated that interest rates will stay low for a prolonged time in order to convince people to take risks funded with low-interest rate loans. Many applications to the recent financial crisis and associated recession appear throughout the macro section. In chapter 11, potential solutions to the debt crisis in the eurozone are addressed; Chapter 13 now includes a discussion of a recent Federal Reserve policymaking meeting where inflation worries were deemphasized and avoiding slower growth and recession were primary concerns; Chapter 14 contains a new example of the hyperinflation in Zimbabwe—the worst in recent times; Chapter 16 has a new example of cross-country differences in broadband usage to illustrate differences in levels of development; Chapter 35 (20 in macro text) has a new example of U.S. sugar quotas to illustrate why U.S. sugar prices are higher than the rest-of-the-world; and Chapter 36 (21 in macro text) uses the crisis in the eurozone as a lesson in how a currency union requires harmonious macro policies among member countries to survive.

The macroeconomic chapters have all been updated and many of the Economically Speaking boxes and commentaries have been revised or replaced with more current examples of economic activity around the world.

Successful Features Retained from the Ninth Edition

In addition to the considerable updating and revising we've done for the tenth edition, there are several features preserved from the previous edition that instructors have found valuable.

Enhanced Student Relevance

With all of the demands on today's students, it's no wonder that they resist spending time on a subject unless they see how the material relates to them and how they will benefit from mastering it. We incorporate features throughout the text that show economics as the relevant and necessary subject we know it to be.

Real-World Examples Students are rarely intrigued by unknown manufacturers or service companies. Our text talks about people and firms that students recognize. We describe business decisions made by McDonald's and Wal-Mart, and by the local video store or cafe. We discuss standards of living around the world, comparing the poverty of sub-Saharan Africa to the wealth of the industrial nations. We discuss policies applied to real-world economic issues. We talk about political, environmental, and other social issues. These examples grab students' interest. Reviewers have repeatedly praised the use of novel examples to convey economic concepts.

Economic Insight Boxes These brief boxes use contemporary material from current periodicals and journals to illustrate or extend the discussion in the chapter. By reserving interesting but more technical sidelights for boxes, we lessen the likelihood that students will be confused or distracted by issues that are not critical to understanding the chapter. By including excerpts from articles, we help students move from theory to real-world examples. And by including plenty of contemporary issues, we guarantee that students will see how economics relates to their own lives.

Economically Speaking Boxes The objective of the principles course is to teach students how to translate to the real world the predictions that come out of economic models, and to translate real-world events into an economic model in order to analyze and understand what lies behind the events. The Economically Speaking boxes present students with examples of this kind of analysis. Students read an article at the end of each chapter. The commentary that follows shows how the facts and events in the article translate into a specific economic model or idea, thereby demonstrating the relevance of the theory. Nearly two-thirds of the articles and commentaries are new to the tenth edition, and cover such current events as U.S. trade with China, measures of consumer confidence and what information they convey, the Federal Reserve Chair's testimony before Congress, illegal immigration, redistribution of wealth, high gasoline prices, the impact of the government's bailout of large companies, the true effects of "fair trade" coffee, dramatic improvement in the lives of hundreds of millions of people over the past twenty years.

Global Business Insight Boxes These boxes link business events and developments around the world to the economic concepts discussed in the main text of the chapters. Topics include such basic micro- and macroeconomic issues as global competition, resource pricing, and foreign exchange.

An Effective and Proven System of Teaching and Learning Aids

This text is designed to make teaching easier by enhancing student learning. Tested pedagogy motivates students, emphasizes clarity, reinforces relationships, simplifies review, and fosters critical thinking. And, as we have discovered from reviewer and user feedback, this pedagogy works.

In-Text Referencing System Sections are numbered for easy reference and to reinforce hierarchies of ideas. Numbered section heads serve as an outline of the chapter, allowing instructors flexibility in assigning reading and making it easy for students to find topics to review. Each item in the key terms list and summary at the end of the chapter refers students back to the appropriate section number.

Fundamental Questions These questions help to organize the chapter and highlight those issues that are critical to understanding. Each fundamental question also appears in the margin next to the related text discussion and, with brief answers, in the chapter summaries. A fuller discussion of and answer to each of these questions may be found in the *Study Guides* that are available as supplements to this text. The fundamental questions also serve as one of several criteria used to categorize questions in the *Test Banks*.

Preview This motivating lead-in sets the stage for the chapter. Much more so than a road map, it helps students identify real-world issues that relate to the concepts that will be presented.

Recaps Briefly listing the main points covered, a recap appears at the end of each major section within a chapter. Students are able to quickly review what they have just read before going on to the next section.

Summary The summary at the end of each chapter is organized along two dimensions. The primary organizational device is the list of fundamental questions. A brief synopsis of the discussion that helps students to answer those questions is arranged by section below each of the questions. Students are encouraged to create their own links among topics as they keep in mind the connections between the big picture and the details that make it up.

Comments Found in the text margins, these comments highlight especially important concepts, point out common mistakes, and warn students of common pitfalls. They alert students to parts of the discussion that they should read with particular care.

Key Terms Key terms appear in bold type in the text. They also appear with their definition in the margin and are listed at the end of the chapter for easy review. All key terms are included in the Glossary at the end of the text.

Friendly Appearance

Economics can be intimidating; this is why we've tried to keep *Economics 10th edition* looking friendly and inviting. The one-column design and ample white space in this text provide an accessible backdrop. More than 300 figures rely on well-developed pedagogy and consistent use of color to reinforce understanding. Striking colors were chosen to enhance readability and provide visual interest. Specific curves were assigned specific colors, and families of curves were assigned related colors.

Annotations on the art point out areas of particular concern or importance. Students can see exactly which part of a graph illustrates a shortage or a surplus, a change in consumption, or a consumer surplus. Tables that provide data from which graphs are plotted are paired with their graphs. Where appropriate, color is used to show correlations between the art and the table, and captions clearly explain what is shown in the figures and link them to the text discussion.

The color photographs not only provide visual images, but make the text appealing. These vibrant photos tell stories as well as illustrate concepts, and lengthy captions explain what is in the photos, again drawing connections between the images and the text discussion.

Thoroughly International Coverage

Students understand that they live in a global economy; they can hardly shop, watch the news, or read a newspaper without stumbling upon this basic fact. International examples are presented in every chapter but are not merely added on, as is the case with many other texts. By introducing international effects on demand and supply in Chapter 3 and then describing in a nontechnical manner the basics of the foreign exchange market and the balance of payments in Chapter 6, we are able to incorporate the international sector into the economic models and applications wherever appropriate thereafter. Because the international content is incorporated from the beginning, students develop a far more realistic picture of the national economy; as a result, they don't have to alter their thinking to allow for international factors later on. The three chapters that focus on international topics at the end of the text allow those instructors who desire to delve much more deeply into international issues to do so.

The global applicability of economics is emphasized by *using traditional economic concepts to explain international economic events and using international events to illustrate economic concepts that have traditionally been illustrated with domestic examples.* Instructors need not know the international institutions in order to introduce international examples, since the topics through which they are addressed are familiar; for example, price ceilings, price discrimination, expenditures on resources, marginal productivity theory, and others.

Uniquely international elements of the macroeconomic coverage in the text include:

- The treatment of the international sector as an economic participant and the inclusion of net exports as early as Chapter 4
- The early description of the foreign exchange market and the balance of payments in Chapter 6
- International elements in the development of aggregate demand and supply
- An entire chapter devoted to globalization

Uniquely international elements of the microeconomic coverage in the text include:

- The treatment of the international sector as an economic participant and the inclusion of net exports as early as Chapter 4
- Extensive analyses of the effects of trade barriers, tariffs, and quotas
- An examination of strategic trade

- An examination of dumping as a special case of price discrimination
- The identification of problems faced by multinational firms
- A comparison of behavior, results, and institutions among nations with respect to consumption, production, firm size, government policies toward business, labor markets, health care, income distribution, environmental policy, and other issues

  - Economic freedom around the world
  - Freedom and human development, that is, the wealth of nations
  - Importance of private property rights and rule of law

Modern Macroeconomic Organization and Content

Macroeconomics is changing and textbooks must reflect that change. We begin with the basics: GDP, unemployment, and inflation. These are the ongoing concerns of any economy, for they have a significant influence on how people feel. These are the issues that don't go away. In addition to these core topics is an easy-to-understand, descriptive introduction to the foreign exchange market and the balance of payments. We provide a critical alternative for those instructors who believe that it is no longer reasonable to relegate this material to the final chapters, where coverage may be rushed.

Armed with these basics, students are ready to delve into the richness of macroeconomic thought. Macro models and approaches have evolved over the years, and they continue to invite exciting theoretical and policy debates. The majority of the instructors we asked voiced frustration with the challenge of pulling this rich and varied material together in class, and stressed that a coherent picture of the aggregate demand and supply model was critical. We have structured the macro portion to allow for many teaching preferences while ensuring a clear delineation of the aggregate demand/aggregate supply (AD/AS) model.

To help instructors successfully present a single coherent model, we present aggregate demand and aggregate supply first in Chapter 8, immediately following the chapter on inflation and unemployment. This sequence allows for a smooth transition from business cycle fluctuations to AD/AS. The Keynesian income and expenditures model is presented in full in Chapters 9 and 10 as the fixed-price version of the AD/AS model (with a horizontal aggregate supply curve). Those who want to use the AD/AS model exclusively will have no problem moving from the Chapter 8 presentation to the fiscal policy material in Chapter 11. The policy chapters rely on the AD/AS model for analysis.

The macroeconomic policy chapters begin with a thorough presentation of fiscal policy, money and banking, and monetary policy, with international elements included. Chapter 14 covers contemporary policy issues, and various schools of thought are treated in Chapter 15, when students are ready to appreciate the differences between and can benefit from a discussion of the new Keynesian and new classical models as well as their precursors.

Part Five, "Product Markets," brings together the concepts and issues presented in the core macro chapters to explain how economies grow and what factors encourage or discourage growth. Most of the world's population live in poor countries. Growth and development are critical to those people. The material in these chapters also addresses issues of importance to industrial countries, such as the determinants of productivity growth and the benefits and costs of globalization.

Part Eight, "Issues in International Trade and Finance," provides a thorough discussion of world trade, international trade restrictions, and exchange rates and links between countries.

A Complete Teaching and Learning Package

In today's market no book is complete without a full complement of ancillaries. Those instructors who face huge lecture classes find good PowerPoint slides and a large variety of reliable test questions to be critical instructional tools. Those who teach online in distance or hybrid courses need reliable course management systems with built-in assignments and resource materials. Other instructors want plenty of options available to their students for review, application, and remediation. All of these needs are addressed in the Boyes and Melvin supplements package. And to foster the development of consistent teaching and study strategies, the ancillaries pick up pedagogical features of the text— such as the fundamental questions—wherever appropriate.

A Supplements Package Designed for Success

To access additional course material for *Boyes/Melvin 10e* visit www.cengagebrain.com. At the CengageBrain.com home page, search for the ISBN of your book using the search box at the top of the page. This will take you to the product page where these resources can be found. For additional information, contact your Cengage sales representative.

Instructor Online Resources

The Boyes and Melvin tenth edition provides a rich store of teaching resources for instructors online at the Instructors Companion site. Instructors will need to sign up at the site for a username and password to get onto the password-protected parts of the site. This site includes a variety of support materials to help you organize, plan, and deliver your lectures; assign and grade homework; and stay up-to-date with current economics news. Here you'll find a thoroughly updated set of multimedia PowerPoint slides covering key points in each chapter, with graphs, charts, and photos. You will also find IM, Test bank in pdf and other downloadable teaching and learning resources.

Instructor's Manual (IM)

Patricia Diane Nipper has produced a manual that will streamline preparation for both new and experienced faculty. Preliminary sections cover class administration, alternative syllabi, and an introduction to the use of cooperative learning in teaching the principles of economics.

The *IM* also contains a detailed chapter-by-chapter review of all the changes made in the tenth edition. This Transition Guide should help instructors more easily move from the use of the ninth edition to this new edition.

Each chapter of the *IM* contains an overview that describes the content and unique features of the chapter and the objectives that students will need to master in order to succeed with later chapters; the chapter's fundamental questions and key terms; a lecture outline with teaching strategies—general techniques and guidelines, essay topics, and other hints to enliven classes; opportunities for discussion; answers to every end-of-chapter exercise.

Cognero:

Cengage Learning Testing Powered by Cognero is a flexible, online system that allows you to:

- author, edit, and manage test bank content from multiple Cengage Learning solutions
- create multiple test versions in an instant
- deliver tests from your LMS, your classroom or wherever you want

Start right away!　Cengage Learning Testing Powered by Cognero works on any operating system or browser.

- No special installs or downloads needed
- Create tests from school, home, the coffee shop – anywhere with Internet access

What will you find?

- <u>Simplicity at every step</u>. A desktop-inspired interface features drop-down menus and familiar, intuitive tools that take you through content creation and management with ease.
- <u>Full-featured test generator</u>. Create ideal assessments with your choice of 15 question types (including true/false, multiple choice). Multi-language support, an equation editor and unlimited metadata help ensure your tests are complete and compliant.
- <u>Cross-compatible capability</u>. Import and export content into other systems.

Student Resources

MindTap

MindTap engages and empowers students to produce their best work – consistently. By seamlessly integrating course material with videos, activities, games, apps, and much more, MindTap creates a unique learning path that fosters increased comprehension and efficiency.

- MindTap delivers real-world relevance with activities and assignments that help students build critical thinking and analytic skills that will transfer to other courses and their professional lives.
- MindTap helps students stay organized and efficient with a single destination that reflects what's important to the instructor, along with the tools students need to master the content.
- MindTap empowers and motivates students with information that shows where they stand at all times – both individually and compared to the highest performers in class.
- Relevant readings, multimedia, and activities are designed to take students up the levels of learning, from basic knowledge to analysis and application.
- Personalized teaching becomes yours through a Learning Path built with key student objectives and your syllabus in mind. Control what students see and when they see it.
- Analytics and reports provide a snapshot of class progress, time in course, engagement and completion rates.
- BBC videos with assessment as the chapter activator;
- Media eReader rich in ConceptClips videos; Graphing-at-a-Glance Videos with assessment; Economically Speaking with assessment; Now you try it with assessment;
- Multiple games for student engagement;
- Global Economic Watch
- Aplia generic homework and math and graphing tutorials.
- End of chapter homework;

Aplia Online Learning Platform

- Founded in 2000 by economist and professor Paul Romer in an effort to improve his own economics courses at Stanford, Aplia is the leading online learning platform for economics.
- Aplia provides a rich online experience that gets students involved and gives instructors the tools and support they need.
- Aplia saves instructors valuable time they would otherwise spend on routine grading while giving students an easy way to stay on top of coursework with regularly scheduled assignments.

- Currently, Aplia supports college-level courses and has been used by more than 1,000,000 students at over 1,300 institutions.
- Aplia's economics students use interactive chapter assignments, tutorials, news analyses, and experiments to make economics relevant and engaging.
- Math and graphing tutorials help students overcome deficiencies in these crucial areas.
- Economics articles from top news sources challenge students to connect current events to course concepts.
- Traditional Aplia Homework Problem Sets allow students to work through the economic concepts they have learned in each chapter.
- Students can choose to "Grade it Now" on a homework problem and will receive instant feedback if an answer is correct or incorrect. The student can then choose to complete another problem to test themselves on the same concept with randomization.

The integrated Aplia courses offered for Boyes and Melvin include Math and Graphing review/tutorials, news analyses, and online homework assignments correlated to the relevant Boyes and Melvin text. In addition, a digital version of the text-media eReader is linked to the Aplia course to make it easy for students to access the text when completing assignments. Media eReader in Aplia is rich in Concept Clips videos with assessment; Graphing-at-a-Glance Videos with assessment; Economically Speaking with assessment; Now you try it with assessment;

Instructors should consult their South-Western/Cengage Learning sales representative for more information on how to use Aplia with this text.

Acknowledgments

Writing a text of this scope is a challenge that requires the expertise and efforts of many. We are grateful to our friends and colleagues who have so generously given their time, creativity, and insight to help us create a text that best meets the needs of today's students.

We'd especially like to thank the many reviewers of *Macroeconomics* listed on the following pages who weighed in on key issues throughout the development of each edition. Their comments have proved invaluable in revising this text. Unsolicited feedback from current users has also been greatly appreciated.

We would also like to thank Patricia Diane Nipper of Southside Virginia Community College for her work on the tenth and previous editions of the *Instructor's Resource Manual*. Carola Conces of UC Berkeley provided excellent research assistance in revising earlier editions and John Mondragon of UC Berkeley for this current edition.

We want to thank the many people at South-Western/Cengage Learning who devoted countless hours to making this text the best it could be, including Michael Parthenakis, Product Manager; Anita Verma, Content and Media Developer; Colleen Farmer, Senior Content Project Manager; Mary Umbarger, Product Assistant; and Chris Walz, Marketing Coordinator, who put all the pieces of the puzzle together and brought their creative talent to this text. We also thank John Carey for his skillful marketing. Thanks to Rajachitra of Cenveo for the copyediting of the manuscript.

Finally, we wish to thank our families and friends. The inspiration they provided through the conception and development of this book cannot be measured but certainly was essential.

Our students at Arizona State University continue to help us improve the text through each edition; their many questions have given us invaluable insight into how best to present this intriguing subject. It is our hope that this textbook will bring a clear understanding of economic thought to many other students as well. We welcome any feedback for improvements.

W. B. M. M.

Reviewers

Okechukwu Dennis Anyamele
Jackson State University—Jackson, MS

David Black
University of Toledo—Toledo, OH

Gary Bogner
Baker College-Muskegon—Muskegon, MI

Rick Boulware
University of South Carolina—Beaufort—Beaufort, SC

Bradley Braun
University of Central Florida—Orlando, FL

William S. Brewer
Genesee Community College—Batavia, NT

Gregory Brown
Martin Community College—Williamston, NC

Kristin Carrico
Umpqua Community College—Roseburg, OR

Jill L. Caviglia
Salisbury State University—Salisbury, MD

Mitch Charkiewicz
Central Connecticut State University—New Britain, CT

Kenny Christianson
Binghamton University—Binghamton, NT

Mike Cohick
Collin County Community—College Piano, TX

Valerie A. Collins
Colorado Mountain College—Glenwood Springs, CO

Wilfrid W. Csaplar, Jr.
Southside Virginia Community College—Keysville, VA

Bob Cunningham
Alma College—Alma, MI

Steven R. Cunningham
University of Connecticut—Storrs, CT

Stephen B. Davis
Valley City State University—Valley City, ND

Lynne Pierson Doti
Chapman University—Orange, CA

Raymond J. Egan
WA (Retired, formerly at Pierce College),—Lakewood, WA

Martha Field
Greenfield Community College—Greenfield, MA

Fred Fisher
Colorado Mountain College—Glenwood Springs, CO

Davis Folsom
University of South Carolina, Beaufort—Beaufort, SC

Kaya V.P. Ford
Northern Virginia Community College—Alexandria, VA

Bradley Garton
Laramie County Community College—Laramie, Wyoming

Omer Gokcekus
North Carolina Central University—Durham, NC

R. W. Hafer
Southern Illinois University—Edwardsville, IL

Michael Harsh
Randolph-Macon College—Ashland, VA

Arleen Hoag
Owens Community College—Toledo, OH

Calvin Hoy
County College of Morris—Randolph, NJ

Miren Ivankovic
Southern Wesleyan University—Central, SC

James Johnson
Black Hawk College—Moline, IL

Jeff Keil
Sargeant Reynolds Community College—Richmond, VA

Donna Kish-Goodling
Muhlenberg College—Allentown, PA

Ali Kutan
Southern Illinois University—Edwardsville, IL

Nikiforos Laopodis
Villa Julie College—Stevenson, MD

John D. Lathrop
New Mexico Junior College—Hobbs, NM

Paul Lockard
Black Hawk College—Moline, IL

Glenna Lunday
Western Oklahoma State College—Altus, OK

Jeff Keele
Porterville College—Porterville, CA
University at Albany, State University of
New York—Albany, NY

Thorn Smith
Hill College—Hillsboro, TX

John Somers
Portland Community College,—Sylvania
Portland, OR

John P. Speir, Jr.
The University of Hartford—West Hartford,
CT

John J. Spitzer
State University of New York College at
Brockport—Brockport, NY

Chin-Chyuan Tai
Averett University—Danville, VA

Rob Verner
Ursuline College—Pepper Pike, OH

Michele T. Villinski
DePauw University—Greencastle, IN

Larry Waldman
University of New Mexico—Albuquerque,
NM

Mark E. Wohar
University of Nebraska—Omaha, NE

Edward M. Wolfe
Piedmont College—Athens, GA

Darrel A. Young
University of Texas—Austin, TX

Girma Zelleke
Kutztown University—Kutztown, PA

Vani Kotcherlakota
University of Nebraska—Kearney, NE

Vince Marra
University of Delaware—Newark, DE

Gretchen Mester
Anne Arundel Community College—
Arnold, MD

Kenneth M. Parzych
Eastern Connecticut State University—
Willimantic, CA

Lea Templer
College of the Canyons—Santa Clarita, CA

Hal Wendling
Heartland Community College—Normal, IL

Sourushe Zandvakili
University of Cincinnati—Cincinnati, OH

CHAPTER 1

The Wealth of Nations: Ownership and Economic Freedom

Jupiter mages/Stockbyte/Getty Images

FUNDAMENTAL QUESTIONS

1. Why are some countries rich while others are dirt poor?

2. What are private property rights?

3. What is economic freedom?

Preview

The differences in wealth from one nation to another are really staggering. A map showing each nation's income appears in Figure 1. The countries shaded in dark blue on the map are the richest, followed by lighter blue, turquoise, and so on to those shaded in red, the poorest nations. A person in Malawi may have less than $1 a day to live on, while the average person in the United States has more than $40,000 per year.

The income disparity has not always existed. In 1800 it would have been hard to know whether you were living in Latin America, North America, or Europe; standards of living were not very different. By 1900, a differential between wealthy and poor nations was being created, and today the differences are huge.

top: © Carsten Reisinger/Shutterstock

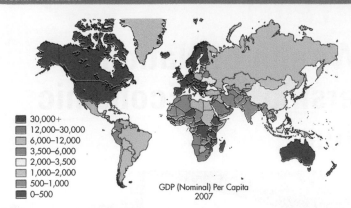

FIGURE 1 Wealth of Nations

30,000+
12,000–30,000
6,000–12,000
3,500–6,000
2,000–3,500
1,000–2,000
500–1,000
0–500

GDP (Nominal) Per Capita
2007

Wealth of nations: The countries shaded in dark blue on the map are the richest, with a per capita GDP exceeding $30,000, followed by lighter blue, turquoise, and so on to those shaded in red, the poorest nations, with a per capita GDP ranging from zero to $500.

Source: http://data.worldbank.org/indicator/NY.GDP.MKTP.CD/countries?display=map; February 9, 2012.

According to the United Nations' Food and Agriculture Organization, there are over 800 million people in the world who do not get enough to eat. Thirty percent of children in Malawi are malnourished, and more than two of every 10 will die before their fifth birthday. At the same time, the United States is rich. Even those in poverty in the United States are in the top 7 percent of all people in the world in terms of wealth.

Why have all nations not progressed like the United States has? Canada has; it is wealthy. Is it because Canada shares a 2,000-mile border with the United States? Sharing the border must not be the cause since Mexico also shares a 2,000-mile border with the United States, and its standard of living is less than half of that in the United States.

Which ones are owned and which are not? Perhaps hard to tell whether the shacks on the water are actually owned or not, but their quality and structure would suggest not. Conversely, the mansions behind the shacks are clearly taken care of and carefully constructed implying that people own them.

1-1 Ownership

Ownership is crucial for economic success. Think about how you treat a car you own compared to a car you rent. Think about buying and selling anything. Can you buy something no one owns? Can you sell something you do not own? Ownership allows trade to take place, and ownership creates an incentive to take care of what is owned.

1-1a Anecdotes about Ownership

During Mao Zedon's reign, starvation was rampant in China. When Mao died in 1976, Communist control of the country was in full force, and starvation continued. In 1978 in Xiaogang, Anhui province—the heart of China's rice-growing region—20 families held a secret meeting to find ways to combat starvation. The system that the Communists had in place across China was leading to a breakdown in food production. Everybody was collectively responsible for tilling the land, and everybody had a share in the land's output. Laborers got their rice share whether they worked hard or not, and as a result, people hardly worked.

The villagers of Xiaogang decided they would divide up the land and farm it individually with each person keeping the output of his own land. They had to keep the arrangement secret out of fear of the Communist authorities. But as rice production in Xiaogang rose dramatically, neighboring villages noticed. As other villages copied Xiaogang, their rice production increased as well. It was not long before the Communist authorities found out what the farmers were doing. But, rather than clamping down and throwing the farmers in jail, the Communist Party expanded the idea of allowing farmers to keep some of their produce. This provided the incentive to work harder and produce more.

The first colonies established in North America—Jamestown and the Virginia colony, in 1607 and 1609, respectively—failed miserably. In each case, within a year, at least half of the settlers had starved to death. The colonies had been established by profit-seeking entities, and the settlers were indentured servants recruited on the streets of London. The indentured servants had no financial stake in the outcome of the colony. Working harder or longer was of no benefit to them. Everything produced by the settlers was sent to a company store and then back to England. The people doing the work got nothing. Obviously, getting no additional reward for working harder meant the indentured servants were not going to work harder.

When representatives of the government and investors arrived in the colonies to find out why there were problems, the basic issue quickly became evident. People were not working. Why should they? The produce they raised would not keep them alive; instead, it had to go to the company store. As a result, settlers did not devote their efforts to planting and producing. Instead, they played games and loafed. Once the problem was identified, the solution was simple: Each settler was given title to a few acres of land, and only a small amount of their output was required to provide returns to investors. The colonies prospered from that point on.

1-1b Private Property Rights

These anecdotes suggest that a primary reason that some nations are rich and others poor is private ownership. It is pretty clear that systems without private ownership do not fare as well as those with such ownership. Figure 2 lists several countries and their per capita incomes in 1850, 1900, 1950, and 2000. Incomes do not differ all that much in 1850, as shown by the red bars. But for 2000 (the crosshatched bars), the differences are staggering. Countries such as India, China, Albania, Hungary, and Poland, where very little private ownership was allowed, did not fare as well as countries where private ownership was

1. Why are some countries rich while others are dirt poor?

2. What are private property rights?

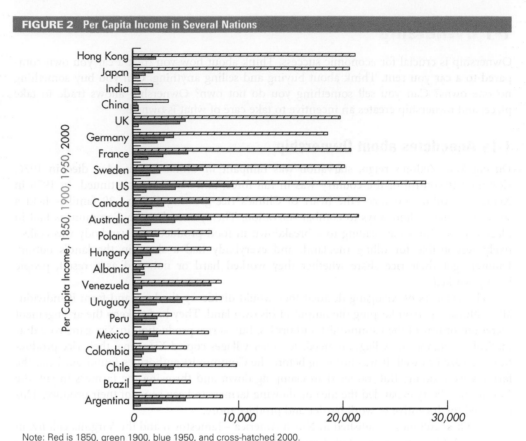

FIGURE 2 Per Capita Income in Several Nations

Note: Red is 1850, green 1900, blue 1950, and cross-hatched 2000.

Source: Data come from A. Maddison, The World Economy: Historical Statistics, OECD, 2003.

allowed. It is interesting to note that Hong Kong, which was nothing but a rock with no natural resources other than a port, was able to make itself one of the wealthiest "countries" in the world because it allowed private ownership. (If you have difficulty reading and interpreting charts, you might find the Appendix to Chapter 1 of value.)

When you own something, that something is yours to do with as you want—at least as long as you do not harm others. That this leads to success and wealth seems like a simple idea, but it is a powerful one.

private property rights
Ownership; the right to do anything you want with what you own as long as it does not harm the property of others.

This situation is known as **private property rights**. Private property rights mean that people can own things, and they can pretty much do what they want with what they own as long as they do not infringe on the private property rights of others. Private property rights exist and are relatively secure in the richest nations. People or governments cannot take your property without just compensation. In poor nations, either there are no private property rights or what private property rights do exist are not secure. If private property rights are not secure, people may damage or steal property or assault others without penalty; corruption and bribes might be necessary to carry out trades or to otherwise use so-called private property.

When private property rights are not secure, people are unlikely to be able to sell the things they own, to use them for collateral on a loan, or to pass them along to family. And they have much less incentive to improve the property because they are not assured of a return on any investments they make.

Until 1800, life everywhere was brutal and very short. The average life expectancy was only about 35 years in most nations. But something occurred around the turn of the nineteenth century that led to a rapid rise in the standard of living among Western nations. Notice in Figure 3 how the standard of living (measured as GDP per capita)[1] in the United Kingdom, the world's richest nation at that time, begins to rise only around 1800. What occurred to create the rising standard of living? The answer has to do with private property rights and the Industrial Revolution. It is a long story, but the short version is that about 1688, new laws in England enabled entrepreneurs to know that what they invented or created would benefit them, and that they would be able to retain profits and property. This system of private property rights laid the foundation for the Industrial Revolution.

FIGURE 3   GDP Per Capita in the United Kingdom, 1500–2000

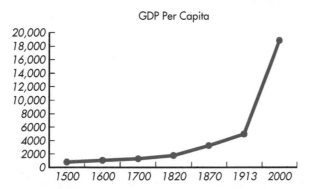

GDP Per Capita

From the beginning of humanity, living standards were bare subsistence at best. This did not improve until the tail end of the eighteenth century.

Until just recently in China, everything was owned by government; in Pakistan, Afghanistan, Bolivia, Venezuela, and other countries, no one could be sure that whatever they claimed as theirs would remain theirs. In Zimbabwe, the government takes property whenever it wants. As president since Zimbabwe gained independence, Robert Mugabe has confiscated property and given it to those he favored.

When private property rights are not universal among citizens, or when property rights are not secure, a nation will not prosper. An abundance of a natural resource such as oil may distort this fact for a while, but the abundance cannot carry over to all citizens unless private property exists. In most oil-producing nations, the resource (oil) is owned by the government, and only a very few benefit from it. But when private property rights prevail, nations prosper even without abundant resources. As noted previously, Hong Kong had nothing, no natural resources except a harbor, and it emerged as one of the wealthiest countries in the world in a just a few decades (Hong Kong is not actually a country, as it was never independent—it was developed as part of the British Empire and then reverted to China). Similarly, Singapore is wealthy, and it, like Hong Kong, is a small island without natural resources. The wealthiest nations have a system of private property rights where people can own property and be secure in their ownership. The poorest nations do not.

In Figure 4, the GDP per capita of the United States and a few Asian nations over time is presented. China and India did not begin to progress until they began allowing private ownership—about 1990 or so. Although China still allows only limited private property, those parts of the economy that have been freed have done very well. In India, private ownership is now encouraged, and India too has experienced rising standards of living. As a result of India's and China's progress in the past couple of decades, a billion people have

---

[1] GDP per capita is gross domestic product per person; GDP is the total value of output created in a country during one year.

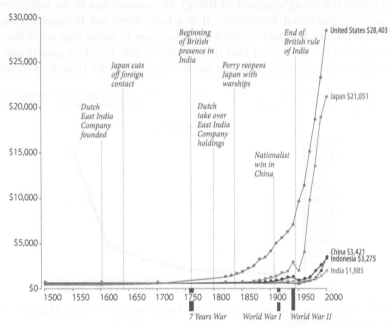

FIGURE 4   Per Capita GDP in the United States, China, India, Japan, and Indonesia

Japan began growing after the United States established a system of private property rights following World War II. China, Indonesia, and India had followed the Soviet Union in adopting communism and government-run economies. When the Soviet Union collapsed in 1989, these countries began moving toward free markets and private property rights.

Source: Catherine Mulbrandon, VisualizingEconomics.com.

risen from dire poverty with a life expectancy of less than 35 years to comfortable prosperity with a life expectancy that exceeds 72 years.

Private property may seem like a right just for the rich, but it is crucial for the poor. If people do not own property, they cannot rent it to others, subdivide it, sell it, use it for collateral, or pass it on to family. The farmers in Xiaogang who agreed to divide up the land for cultivation could not sell their land or even pass it along to family. Nevertheless, the amount of rice raised on the so-called private plots was significantly greater than when everything was communal. But it could have been so much more had the farmers owned the property.

Private property rights matter. They matter because they create incentives that enable people to improve their standards of living. When you own something, you have the incentive to take care of it—that is, you have the incentive to increase its value and to invest in it. If farmers can raise corn and that corn is theirs, they can take the corn to market and sell it. They will invest in ways to provide better quality and more abundant corn, and they will ensure that they have seeds remaining to grow more corn next year. Similarly, when you offer to work, you are taking your own labor, something you own, and exchanging it for pay. The higher the quality of your work, the more valuable you are to your employers, the more you will be paid.

When no one owns something, no one has an incentive to take care of it. Workers who were forced to work in shipbuilding factories in Gdansk, Poland, during the communist regime would show up and then loaf. They had no incentive to be productive because they received the same pay no matter what they did. When you own your own labor or property, you have the incentive to make it as valuable as possible because then you can trade for other things you want. When no one owns something, problems arise; for instance, no one owns the fish in the oceans, so no one takes care of them. Overfishing and, in some cases, extinction of species result.

1-1c Title to Property

In 1981, about 1,800 families took over a piece of wasteland in San Francisco Solano in the province of Buenos Aires, Argentina.[2] The occupants were landless citizens organized by a Catholic chapel. The Church and the squatters believed the land belonged to the state, so they assumed they could simply plop themselves down and enjoy the land. Once situated, the squatters had to resist several attempts at eviction, but eventually, the military government lost track of them.

When the military government was replaced by a democracy, the squatters brought the issue of ownership to the attention of the government, requesting that they be given the land. It was then discovered that the land was not state property; the area was composed of different tracts of land, each with a different legal owner. So the congress of the province of Buenos Aires ordered the transfer of the land from the original owners to the state in exchange for a monetary compensation. About 60 percent of the land was sold to the government, and these parcels were deeded to the squatters; legal titles secured the property of the parcels. The rest of the property was not deeded to the squatters. Either original owners could not be identified or other original owners refused to give up the land, arguing that the compensation was too low. They contested the government's compensation in the Argentine courts—a contest that continued for more than 20 years.

As a result, there are two divisions of land in the occupied region, as is illustrated in Figure 5. Some of the squatters obtained formal land rights, titles to their properties, whereas others lived in the occupied parcels without paying rent but without legal titles. Although the groups shared the same household characteristics (size of family, education, skills, health, etc.) before the government transferred ownership to some of the residents,

NOW YOU TRY IT

In college today, when you want to take a class, you must register, and if there is room available and you have taken the prerequisites you can take the class. The college owns the access to classes. What would occur if no one owned the right to sign up for a class?

FIGURE 5 Illustration of the Squatter Results in Argentina

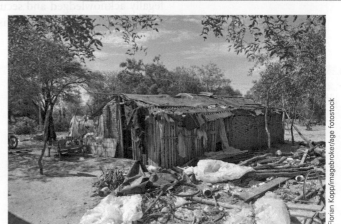

Those on the left were given title to the property. Those on the right had no title.

[2] The complete story and some empirical examinations are presented in Sebastian Galiani and Ernesto Schargrodsky, "Property Rights for the Poor: Effects of Land Titling" (Coase Institute Working Paper, August 9, 2005).

NOW YOU TRY IT

Explain why those families who acquired title to property behaved differently than those families who had no title. Explain why the houses are of different quality. Explain why those with title had fewer children and more of those children acquired an education.

and although they lived next to each other for 20 years, the outcome of their ownership arrangements was dramatically different. Owners with title invested in their properties, whereas residents without title did not. There is a significant difference in the quality of housing between the titled and untitled properties. The titled properties have been upgraded, expanded, and improved. The untitled properties remain shanties that are run down and crumbling. Not only is the housing different, but those with title have behaved differently than those without title: They had fewer children, and the children have experienced more education and better health.

While the squatters in Buenos Aires lived on their properties for several years, they could not consider themselves owners until they had titles to their property, that is, legal documents specifying all aspects of the ownership. The title to property is typically a registration with the government specifying the location of the property and who owns the property. The title allows the owner to sell the asset or to use it to obtain loans or mortgages. In the United States, when you sell or purchase property, a "title search" must be undertaken to be sure that the title is given to the correct owner.

Insecure property rights—property rights without ownership title or without security from confiscation—weaken the incentives for owners to make long-term investments and hinder the ability of owners to use their property as collateral to secure loans. Without access to credit, economic growth is hindered. In order to achieve secure property rights, a country must ensure that property rights are protected by law and that any informal, unarticulated rights are incorporated into a written, formal, legal property rights system.

Peruvian economist, Hernando de Soto has spent years examining insecure property rights systems.[3] He notes that citizens of most poor countries do not lack entrepreneurial energy nor do they lack assets. But because they have no title over these assets, they cannot use them to improve their lives. From countryside to urban shantytown, ownership is informal. Mr. Jones knows that Mr. Assalt down the road owns the farm he works, but Mr. Assalt has no title to his property. Owners like Mr. Assalt are locked out of the formal, legal economy—they have houses, crops, and businesses but no titles of ownership. Citizens lacking formal legal title to their property are unable to use their assets as collateral. They cannot get bank loans to expand their businesses or improve their properties.

Private property rights are crucial for economic success. The property rights must be legally acknowledged and secure. People have to be able to buy and sell property and to use property for collateral on loans in order to feel secure in improving the property and making other investments.

RECAP

1. Much of the economic success of nations is dependent on ownership.

2. A system of private property rights enables people to do what they want with what they own as long as they do not harm the private property of others.

3. With ownership comes the incentive to invest in or take care of the asset that is owned. With ownership comes the incentive to improve the asset that is owned.

4. Legal recognition of ownership—titles—are necessary to ensure that owned property can be freely bought and sold and used as collateral for loans.

[3] Hernando de Soto is the economist focusing most on titling. See his book *The Mystery of Capital: Why Capitalism Triumphs in the West and Fails Everywhere Else* (2000), Basic Books, New York.

1-2 Economic Freedom

Economic freedom is important to the success of a nation. **Economic freedom** refers to the degree to which private individuals can carry out voluntary exchange. People can buy or sell things without government involvement or without getting the permission of some king or commission. People can work for whom they want at a wage the employer is willing and able to pay. A communist system is the opposite of economic freedom; it is one in which there is no economic freedom.

1-2a Index of Economic Freedom

Most countries are somewhere between 100 percent economic freedom and no economic freedom. In an economically free society, individuals are free to work, produce, consume, and invest in any way they please, with that freedom both protected by the state and unconstrained by the state. In economically free societies, governments allow labor, capital, and goods to move freely, and they refrain from coercion or constraint of liberty beyond the extent necessary to protect and maintain liberty itself. Higher taxes mean less economic freedom because, in general, people have to be coerced into paying taxes. Most would not pay taxes unless they were required to. Similarly, more rules and regulations mean less economic freedom. Regulations requiring that you obtain a license to be a beautician limit some people from being beauticians. Regulations on emissions from automobiles restrict what kinds of cars people can drive. Restrictions on travel mean less economic freedom. Having to obtain a passport limits some travel. Having to go through security at airports takes time and effort. Restrictions on international trade mean less economic freedom. Japan might not allow citizens to purchase meat from elsewhere, which limits the freedom of its citizens. Even the paperwork necessary to comply with government rules and regulations means less economic freedom.

The *Wall Street Journal* and the Heritage Foundation coauthor an annual measure of economic freedom called the Index of Economic Freedom (a similar measure is provided by the Fraser Institute). The authors of the Index attempt to measure how much free, voluntary trade is affected by government. In 2008, the United States was ranked 5, the fifth most economically free country. Today it is ranked 10th. According to the Index of Economic Freedom, the United States slipped in 2010 from the group of countries called "free" to the group of countries called "mostly free" because the role of the U.S. government in the economy expanded from 2009 on. The top 10 economically freest nations are listed in Table 1.

3. *What is economic freedom?*

economic freedom
The ability to engage in voluntary trade without interference or restrictions by government or outside parties.

NOW YOU TRY IT

What is the difference between economic freedom and voluntary trade?

TABLE 1 The Ten Most Economically Free Countries in 2013			

Each year, the Heritage Foundation and the *Wall Street Journal* calculate the list of the most and least economically free nations. Shown here are the 10 most economically free countries in 2013.

World Rank	Country	Overall Score	Change From Previous
1	Hong Kong	89.9	0.2
2	Singapore	87.5	0.3
3	Australia	83.1	0.6
4	New Zealand	82.1	−0.2
5	Switzerland	81.1	−0.8
6	Canada	79.9	−0.9
7	Chile	78.3	0.9
8	Mauritius	77.0	0.8
9	Ireland	76.9	−1.8
10	United States	76.3	−1.5

Note: Definition: Free, 80–100; Mostly free, 60–79.9.

Source: http://www.heritage.org/Index/

1-2b Economic Freedom and Standards of Living

In general, the greater a nation's economic freedom, the higher its standard of living. This should make sense because if people are not free to work where they want at what they want and to purchase what they want, then they have few if any private property rights, and we know that private property rights lead to wealth. People in the unfree and repressed economies, those with few or no private property rights, average less than one-eighth of the income of people in the freest nations, as shown in Figure 6.[4]

You would expect that with more income comes a better quality of life, and in general that is true. Having more income means there is more money for health care, for better education, for living in locations more free from diseases and natural disasters, and, in general, to support a better and longer life. The Human Development Index created by the United Nations rates nations on the basis of quality of life. It is obvious in Figure 7 that, indeed, economic freedom and human development are strongly related. The "free" countries have a much higher index of human development than do the "repressed" countries.

Secure private property rights and economic freedom are the most important explanations for the wealth of nations. Bad government is important, but bad government means no or at least, few secure private property rights and very little if any economic freedom. Natural resources are important to a nation's wealth, but as noted earlier, simply having abundant natural resources is not likely to lead to national wealth. Along with the resources, private property rights and economic freedom are needed. Given that we know what leads to the wealth of nations, why isn't every country wealthy? Is there more to the story? Looking for answers to these questions is why we study economics.

FIGURE 6 Top Ten Highest Standards of Living

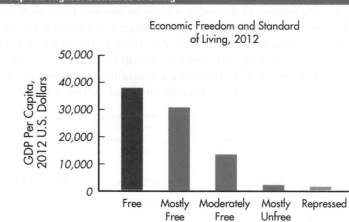

Economic Freedom and Standard of Living, 2012

Source: http://www.heritage.org/index/download

---

[4] The average Index of Economic Freedom (IEF) score for a country with GDP growth of over 10 percent is 10 percent higher than the IEF score for the countries with GDP growth of 3 percent or less. These numbers are for 2005. Libya, which had the lowest score where reliable GDP growth figures are available, had a growth rate of 3.5 percent in a year that the average growth rate was almost 5 percent. Zimbabwe, which had the second lowest IEF score, had a 6.5 percent GDP decline.

FIGURE 7 Economic Freedom and Human Development

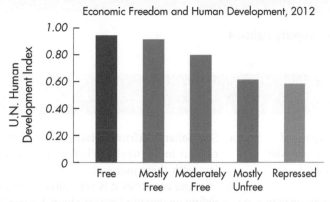

Economic Freedom and Human Development, 2012

Using the Index of Human Development constructed by the United Nations, we are able to see that economic freedom is strongly related to human development.

Source: 2011 United Nations Development Report; http://hdr.undp.org/en/; accessed February 9, 2012.

RECAP

1. Economic freedom is the ability to carry out voluntary trade. Anything that inhibits voluntary trade reduces economic freedom.

2. Economic freedom and a system of secure private property rights go hand in hand. One is necessary for the other to work.

3. Economic freedom and standards of living are positively related. The more economic freedom, the higher the standard of living.

SUMMARY

1. Why are some nations rich while others are dirt poor?

- Ownership and economic freedom are crucial elements of the success of nations.
- Without ownership, no one has an incentive to work or to improve property or themselves.
- Without ownership, nations do not progress.
- If you own something, you take care of it. If no one owns something, no one takes care of it.

2. What are private property rights?

- Private property rights mean ownership. You have the right to do what you want with what you own as long as you do not infringe on the private property rights of others.

- Secure private property rights mean that others cannot take or damage your property without just compensation. Secure property rights mean that you have a legally recognized title to the property.

3. What is economic freedom?

- Economic freedom means you can engage in voluntary transactions without interference or restrictions from government or others.
- With private property rights and economic freedom, nations progress, standards of living improve, and human development increases.
- Although factors other than ownership and economic freedom may contribute to a country's success, nothing else is as important.

KEY TERMS

economic freedom, 9   private property rights, 4

EXERCISES

1. Do you own yourself? Is this a private property right?
2. Are you allowed to put anything you want into your body? Would you say this is a violation of private property rights?
3. In Venezuela, the president confiscates land from owners and then gives the land to whom he wants. How would you describe Venezuela's private property rights?

4. Sub-Saharan Africa includes some of the poorest nations in the world. What would you say is the problem with these nations?
5. In some countries it is very difficult or impossible to define ownership because there are no "property titles." If people generally know who lives where, why does it matter whether people have titles to their property?

ECONOMICALLY SPEAKING

BILLIONAIRES URGED TO USE THEIR INFLUENCE BEYOND THE GRAVE

Craig McInnes
Vancouver Sun, CANADA & WORLD section, p. B5

The Well-Lined Pockets of the Richest Americans Represent a Tremendous Potential for Change Should They Be Emptied for the Right Cause

The ghost of Andrew Carnegie is loose in America. You know the name, even if you don't know why. It has been attached to thousands of public buildings in the U.S., Canada and around the world, from the glittering Carnegie Hall in New York to the sturdy Carnegie Centre in the Downtown Eastside, which opened in 1903 as Vancouver's Public Library.

Carnegie was a 19th-century industrialist who was born in a weaver's cottage in Scotland and grew to be the second richest man in American history, after the old baron John D. Rockefeller, before turning his vast wealth—estimated at about $300 billion in 2007 dollars—to philanthropy, including his great gift to literacy, the underwriting of some 3,000 libraries.

On Wednesday, two of the richest men of our age announced that their plan to change the world one billionaire at a time is gaining traction with 34 of the wealthiest men and women in America pledging to leave at least half of their fortunes to charity when they die.

Celebrated investor Warren Buffett and Microsoft cofounder Bill Gates launched "The Giving Pledge" campaign in June with a target of harnessing half of the immense wealth of America's tycoons for good works of their choice.

If it all came in at once, that would be a staggering $600 billion of the $1.2 trillion Forbes magazine estimates is controlled by the 400 richest individuals in the U.S.

The latest pledgers included New York Mayor Michael Bloomberg, Oracle co-founder Larry Ellison, David Rockefeller, Texas oilman T. Boone Pickens and media magnate Ted Turner.

What's interesting to me in all this is not the inevitable political argument over whether these folks are merely paying back some of what they made off the labour of common working folk, but the immense power for change that their accumulated wealth represents.

The minimum $600-billion goal represents roughly twice the total charitable contributions in the U.S. in 2008, according to the National Philanthropic Trust.

Many of the tycoons on the list have already started giving away substantial fortunes. Buffett pledged in 2006 to endow most of his holdings to the Bill and Melinda Gates Foundation, which already has a larger foreign aid budget than many sovereign states.

Even Gates's old partner in Microsoft, Paul Allen, who is better known for his toys than his charity—he owns numerous mega-yachts and two professional sports teams, the Seattle Seahawks and the Portland Trailblazers—has already given away more than $1 billion. He has also taken the pledge to give away the bulk of his estimated $13.5-billion fortune when he dies.

What will be interesting to watch in all of this is how the increasingly muscular foundations these billionaires endow choose to throw their weight around. It's not all going for building hospitals and universities. A lot of money will be spent to support political change.

So taxpayers may celebrate when private donors do the heavy lifting for the funding of hospitals, schools or libraries. They may be relieved when the wealthy step up to fund medical research or economic development in Africa. But what the deep-pocket set have accumulated in their lifetimes is not just a lot of money for good works, but tremendous influence in how the future unfolds. The adage that he (or she) who pays the piper calls the tune is still relevant.

It's not just about whose name gets carved into a building.

In British Columbia, we have long seen the effects of the funding by large donors such as the David and Lucile Packard Foundation for environmental organizations, including the Sierra Club and Greenpeace, that have been able to wage international campaigns that have had a profound effect on our resource industries.

Money buys influence and there may be a lot more on the way.

COMMENTARY

Are Bill Gates and Warren Buffett heroes for pledging to "give away" at least half their fortunes when they die? Is Bill Gates a super hero for giving away millions of dollars now through the Bill and Melinda Gates Foundation?

According to the article, the "...plan to change the world one billionaire at a time is gaining traction with 34 of the wealthiest men and women in America pledging to leave at least half of their fortunes to charity when they die."

The article also notes that "If it all came in at once, that would be a staggering $600 billion of the $1.2 trillion Forbes magazine estimates is controlled by the 400 richest individuals in the U.S."

In a free country with private property rights, people may do what they want with what they own as long as they do not trample on the private property rights of others. These richest 400 are rich primarily because they live in a free country with private property rights. They did not steal the money nor did they force others to give it to them. So why would the article state: "What's interesting to me in all this is not the inevitable political argument over whether these folks are merely paying back some of what they made off the labour of common working folk, but the immense power for change that their accumulated wealth represents"? When voluntary exchange and private property rights prevail, the money made by someone is not taken from the backs of some poor slob. Instead, the money is freely given to the wealthy person in exchange for a good or service. This is what economic freedom means. You have the choice to do what you want, to earn what you want, and to spend what you earn as you want. No one forces you to give up the money.

What immense power for change is the author referring to? If the peer pressure campaign produces $600 billion or just $6 billion, then who will decide where the money is to be used? Will the philanthropists all agree with where the money goes or do they just give it away to some anonymous committee or individual? What would happen if instead of giving the money away the donors used the money to create jobs in low-income communities or in any community? Would not jobs mean more to people than some pool of money that most will never see?

APPENDIX TO CHAPTER 1
Working with Graphs

1-1 Reading and Constructing Graphs

It is important to understand how the axes (the horizontal and vertical lines) are used and what they measure. Let us begin with the horizontal axis, the line running across the page in a horizontal direction. Notice in Figure 1(a) that the line is divided into equal segments. Each point on the line represents a quantity, or the value of the variable being measured. For example, each segment could represent 10 years, or 10,000 pounds of diamonds, or some other value. Whatever is measured, the value increases from left to right, beginning with negative values, going on to zero, which is called the origin, and then moving on to positive numbers.

A number line in the vertical direction can be constructed as well, also shown in Figure 1(a). Zero is the origin, and the numbers increase from bottom to top. Like the horizontal axis, the vertical axis is divided into equal segments; the distance between 0 and 10 is the same as the distance between 0 and −10, between 10 and 20, and so on.

Putting the horizontal and vertical lines together lets us express relationships between two variables graphically. The axes cross, or intersect, at their origins, as shown in Figure 1(a). From the common origin, movements to the right and up, in the area—called a quadrant—marked I, are combinations of positive numbers; movements to the left and down, in quadrant III, are combinations of negative numbers; movements to the right and down, in quadrant IV, are negative values on the vertical axis and positive values on the horizontal axis; and movements to the left and up, in quadrant II, are positive values on the vertical axis and negative values on the horizontal axis.

Economic data are typically positive numbers: the unemployment rate, the inflation rate, the price of something, the quantity of something produced or sold, and so on. Because economic data are usually positive numbers, the only part of the coordinate system that usually comes into play in economics is the upper right portion, quadrant I. That is why economists may simply sketch a vertical line down to the origin and then extend a horizontal line out to the right, as shown in Figure 1(b). When data are negative, the other quadrants of the coordinate system may be used.

1-1a Constructing a Graph from a Table

Now that you are familiar with the axes—that is, the coordinate system—you are ready to construct a graph using the data in the table in Figure 2. The table lists a series of possible price levels for a personal computer (PC) and the corresponding number of PCs people choose to purchase. The data are only hypothetical; they are not drawn from actual cases.

FIGURE 1   The Axes, the Coordinate System, and the Positive Quadrant

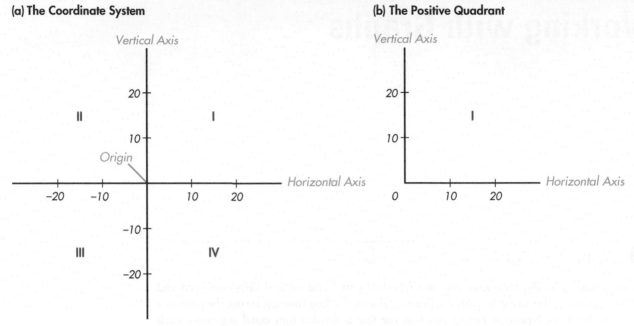

1(a) Vertical and horizontal axes. The horizontal axis has an origin, measured as zero, in the middle. Negative numbers are to the left of zero, positive numbers to the right. The vertical axis also has an origin in the middle. Positive numbers are above the origin; negative numbers are below. The horizontal and vertical axes together show the entire coordinate system. Positive numbers are in quadrant I, negative numbers in quadrant III, and combinations of negative and positive numbers in quadrants II and IV.
1(b) The positive quadrant only. Because most economic data are positive, often only the upper right quadrant, the positive quadrant, of the coordinate system is used.

The information given in the table is graphed in Figure 2. We begin by marking off and labeling the axes. The vertical axis is the list of possible price levels. We begin at zero and move up the axis at equal increments of $1,000. The horizontal axis is the number of PCs sold. We begin at zero and move out the axis at equal increments of 1,000 PCs. According to the information presented in the table, if the price is $10,000, no one buys a PC. The combination of $10,000 and zero PCs is point *A* on the graph. To plot this point, find the quantity zero on the horizontal axis (it is at the origin), and then move up the vertical axis from zero to a price level of $10,000. (Note that units in the table and on the graph are measured in thousands.) At a price of $9,000, 1,000 PCs are purchased. To plot the combination of $9,000 and 1,000 PCs, find 1,000 units on the horizontal axis and then measure up from there to a price of $9,000. This is point *B*. Point *C* represents a price of $8,000 and 2,000 PCs. Point *D* represents a price of $7,000 and 3,000 PCs. Each combination of price and PCs purchased listed in the table is plotted in Figure 2.

The final step in constructing a line graph is to connect the points that are plotted. When the points are connected, the straight line slanting downward from left to right in Figure 2 is obtained. It shows the relationship between the price of PCs and the number of PCs purchased.

1-1b Interpreting Points on a Graph

Let's use Figure 2 to demonstrate how points on a graph may be interpreted. Suppose the current price of a PC is $6,000. Are you able to tell how many PCs are being purchased at

FIGURE 2   Prices and Quantities Purchased

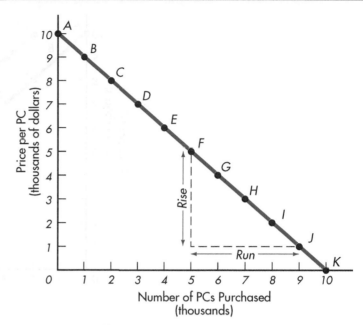

Point	Price per PC (thousands of dollars)	Number of PCs Purchased (thousands)
A	10	0
B	9	1
C	8	2
D	7	3
E	6	4
F	5	5
G	4	6
H	3	7
I	2	8
J	1	9
K	0	10

The information given in the following table is graphed here. We begin by marking off and labeling the axes. The vertical axis is the list of possible price levels. The horizontal axis is the number of PCs purchased. Beginning at zero, the axes are marked at equal increments of 1,000. According to the information presented in the table, if the price level is $10,000, no PCs are purchased. The combination of $10,000 and zero PCs is point A on the graph. At a price of $9,000, 1,000 PCs are purchased. This is point B. The final step in constructing a line graph is to connect the points that are plotted. When the points are connected, the straight line slanting downward shows the relationship between the price of PCs and the number of PCs purchased.

this price? By tracing that price level from the vertical axis over to the curve and then down to the horizontal axis, you find that 4,000 PCs are purchased. You can also find what happens to the number purchased if the price falls from $6,000 to $5,000. By tracing the price from $5,000 to the curve and then down to the horizontal axis, you discover that 5,000 PCs are purchased. Thus, according to the graph, a decrease in the price from $6,000 to $5,000 results in 1,000 more PCs being purchased.

1-1c   Shifts of Curves

Graphs can be used to illustrate the effects of a change in a variable not represented on the graph. For instance, the curve drawn in Figure 2 shows the relationship between the price of PCs and the number of PCs purchased. When this curve was drawn, the only two variables that were allowed to change were the price and the number of computers. However, it is likely that people's incomes determine their reaction to the price of computers as well. An increase in income would enable more people to purchase computers. Thus, at every price more computers would be purchased. How would this be represented? It can be seen as an outward shift of the curve, from points A, B, C, and so on, as shown in Figure 2, to A', B', C', and so on, as shown in Figure 3.

Following the shift of the curve, we can see that more PCs are purchased at each price than was the case prior to the income increase. For instance, at a price of $8,000, the increased income allows 4,000 PCs to be purchased, rather than 2,000. The important point to note is that if some variable that influences the relationship shown in a curve or line graph changes, then the entire curve or line changes; that is, it shifts.

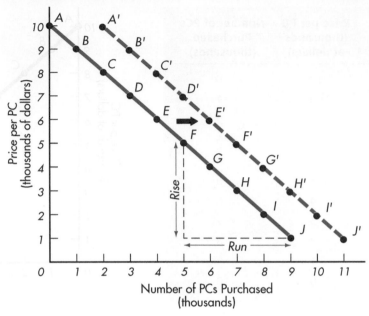

FIGURE 3 **Per Capita Income: 1850, 1900, 1950, 2000**

An increase in income allows more people to purchase T-shirts at each price. At a price of $80 for instance, 4,000 T-shirts are purchased instead of 2,000.

Source: Data are taken from A. Maddison, *The World Economy: Historical Statistics* (OECD, 2003).

SUMMARY

1. Most economic data are positive numbers, so often only the upper right quadrant of the coordinate system is used in economics.

2. Curves illustrate the relationship between two variables.

3. Curves are drawn assuming that nothing that might affect the relationship between two variables changes. When one such change occurs, the curves shift.

EXERCISES

1. Plot the data listed in the table that follows.
   a. Measure price along the vertical axis and quantity along the horizontal axis, then plot the first two columns.
   b. Show what quantity is sold when the price is $550.
   c. Directly below the graph drawn in part *a*, plot the data in columns 2 and 3. In this graph, measure quantity on the horizontal axis and total revenue on the vertical axis.
   d. What is total revenue when the price is $550? Will total revenue increase or decrease when the price is lowered?

Price	Quantity Sold	Total Revenue
$1,000	200	200,000
900	400	360,000
800	600	480,000
700	800	560,000
600	1,000	600,000
500	1,200	600,000
400	1,400	560,000
300	1,600	480,000
200	1,800	360,000
100	2,000	200,000

CHAPTER 2
Scarcity and Opportunity Costs

©Tyler Olson/Shutterstock.com

FUNDAMENTAL QUESTIONS

1. What are opportunity costs?

2. What is a production possibilities curve?

3. What are the gains from trade?

4. How do we determine who gets what?

Preview

top: © Carsten Reisinger/Shutterstock

Why are some countries rich and others poor? The primary reason is that some countries have a system of private property rights and economic freedom and others do not. But private property rights and economic freedom do not mean that everyone has everything they want. Everyone wants more of something than what they have, even the wealthy. This brings up several issues. Who decides what is available? Who decides who gets some items and who gets left out? Is it possible that everyone can have everything they want? We discuss answers to these questions in this chapter.

2-1 Scarcity, Opportunity Costs, and Voluntary Trade

scarcity
The shortage that exists when less of something is available than is wanted at a zero price.

Virtually everything is limited; there is not enough to go around. **Scarcity** refers to the idea that there is not enough of something to satisfy everyone who would like that something. People have unlimited wants—they always want more than they have or can purchase with their incomes. Whether they are wealthy or poor, what they have is never enough. Since people do not have everything they want, they must use their limited time and income to select those things they want most and forgo the rest. The choices they make and the manner in which the choices are made explain much about why the real world is what it is.

2-1a Opportunity Cost

1. What are opportunity costs?

opportunity cost
The highest-valued alternative that must be forgone when a choice is made.

Opportunity cost is the highest-valued alternative that must be forgone when a choice is made. If you have $25, you could purchase many things. Suppose you select a video game. The cost of the video game is $25, but more accurately, it is anything else that you could have purchased with $25. We say the opportunity cost of the video game is the benefit you do not enjoy from purchasing something else. Opportunity cost includes not just the dollars you give up but all costs involved with your purchase. For instance, buying used books saves money but could increase frustration and affect your grades. The book might be missing pages, unreadable in spots, or out of date. The full or opportunity cost of the used book is the price you paid for the used copy plus the frustration of having an incomplete book.

An attorney in Scottsdale, Arizona, is paid $325 an hour to write contracts. The attorney loves Ralph Lauren dress shirts and can get them for $100 at Nordstrom in Scottsdale or, when they are available, for $50 at the outlet mall in Casa Grande. He likes to purchase just one or two shirts at a time and usually buys them at Nordstrom, taking 15 minutes out of his lunch time to go to the store. Is this smart? Well, he figures he could spend two hours driving to Casa Grande and back and save $50 per shirt. But this also means he is not writing contracts and charging $325 per hour during those two hours. The real cost of the $50 saved on a single shirt in Casa Grande is the amount that the attorney would give up in income, $325 per hour less the $50 savings on each shirt, plus the cost of the additional gas used.

NOW YOU TRY IT

Suppose you decided to attend a school where the tuition and other expenses add up to $4,290 per year. Are these your total costs?

When economists refer to costs, it is opportunity costs they are measuring. The cost of anything is what must be given up to get that item. Every human activity responds to costs in one way or another. When the cost of something falls, typically that something becomes more attractive to us, all else being the same.[1] For instance, when the cost of text messaging phone service dropped, more of us signed up for the service. Conversely, when the cost of something rises, and all else remains unchanged, we tend to use less of it. When photo radar machines were placed on the freeways, the cost of speeding went up because the likelihood of getting caught speeding dramatically increased. As a result, the amount of speeding dropped—average speeds went from 78 to 65 virtually overnight.

2-1b Trade-Offs

trade-off
The giving up of one good or activity in order to obtain some other good or activity.

Life is a continuous sequence of decisions, and every single decision involves choosing one thing over another or trading off something for something else. A **trade-off** means a sacrifice—giving up one good or activity in order to obtain some other good or activity. Because your income is scarce, if you purchase one thing you have to forgo other things. Because your time is limited, if you decide to attend a football game you are forgoing time spent studying or sleeping. You trade off time at studying for time spent at the football game.

[1] Notice the phrase "all else being the same." The idea is that we are examining just one thing at a time—cost falls. It would be very, very difficult to ask what our attitude toward something is when cost falls, quality declines, color changes, our income decreases, and on and on. Thus, a common assumption, so common it is often not mentioned or written, is to allow only one thing to change.

ECONOMIC INSIGHT

A Tricky Question on Opportunity Costs

A few years ago, a problem similar to the following was given to economists at their annual convention. Only a small percentage came up with the right answer.

You have won a free ticket for a concert by a popular performer we will call A (the ticket has no resale value). Another performer you also like, B, is putting on a concert at the same time and that is your next-best alternative activity (and vice versa). A ticket for B's concert is $40. On any given day, you would be willing to pay up to $50 for B's ticket. You decide to attend A's concert. Based on this information, what is your opportunity cost of going to A's concert?

a. $40
b. $50
c. $0
d. $10
e. $60

You chose to go to the free concert, so you value that ticket at least equal to how much you value a ticket to B's concert. You would have been willing to pay $50 for B's concert but would have had to pay $40, so the net benefit you would have received is $10. It is this you give up to attend A's concert.

Each decision is a **marginal** decision. By marginal, economists mean additional or incremental or next unit. For instance, each term you must decide whether or not to register for college. You could work full time and not attend college, attend college and not work, or work part time and attend college. The time you devote to college will decrease as you devote more time to work. You trade off hours spent at work for hours spent in college; in other words, you compare the benefits you think you will get from going to college *this term* with the costs of college *this term*. You decide to spend the next hour studying by comparing the benefits you expect to receive from an additional hour of studying to the costs of not studying for that hour.

marginal
Additional, incremental

2-1c The Production Possibilities Curve

Trade-offs can be illustrated in a graph known as the **production possibilities curve (PPC)**. The production possibilities curve shows all possible combinations of quantities of goods and services that can be produced when the existing resources are used *fully and efficiently*. Figure 1 shows a production possibilities curve for the production of defense goods and services and nondefense goods and services by a nation. Defense goods and services include guns, ships, bombs, personnel, and so forth that are used for national defense. Nondefense goods and services include education, housing, health care, and food that are not used for national defense. All societies allocate their scarce resources in order to produce some combination of defense and nondefense goods and services. Because resources are scarce, a nation cannot produce as much of everything as it wants. When it produces more health care, it cannot produce as much education or automobiles; when it devotes more of its resources to the military area, fewer resources are available to devote to health care.

In Figure 1, units of defense goods and services are measured on the vertical axis, and units of nondefense goods and services are measured on the horizontal axis. If all resources are allocated to producing defense goods and services, then 200 million units can be produced, but there will be no production of nondefense goods and services. The combination of 200 million units of defense goods and services and zero units of nondefense goods and

2. What is a production possibilities curve?

production possibilities curve (PPC)
A graphical representation showing all possible combinations of quantities of goods and services that can be produced using the existing resources fully and efficiently.

FIGURE 1 The Production Possibilities Curve

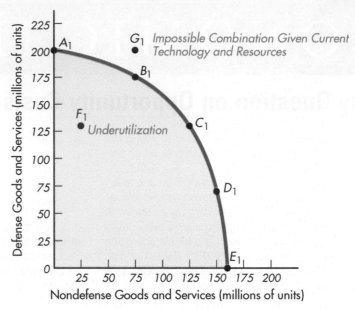

With a limited amount of resources, only certain combinations of defense and nondefense goods and services can be produced. The maximum amounts that can be produced, given various tradeoffs, are represented by points A_1 through E_1. Point F_1 lies inside the curve and represents the underutilization of resources. More of one type of goods could be produced without producing less of the other, or more of both types could be produced. Point G_1 represents an impossible combination. There are insufficient resources to produce quantities lying beyond the curve.

NOW YOU TRY IT

Using a production possibilities curve, illustrate the trade-offs facing many societies between a larger safety net (such as more welfare, more food stamps, or more unemployment compensation) and better transportation facilities.

services is point A_1, a point on the vertical axis. At 175 million units of defense goods and services, 75 million units of nondefense goods and services can be produced (point B_1). Point C_1 represents 125 million units of nondefense goods and services and 130 million units of defense goods. Point D_1 represents 150 million units of nondefense goods and services and 70 million units of defense goods and services. Point E_1, a point on the horizontal axis, shows the combination of no production of defense goods and services and 160 million units of nondefense goods and services.

2-1c-1 Points Inside the Production Possibilities Curve Suppose a nation produces 130 million units of defense goods and services and 25 million units of nondefense goods and services. That combination, point F_1 in Figure 1, lies inside the production possibilities curve. A point lying inside the production possibilities curve indicates that resources are not being fully or efficiently used. If the existing work force is employed only 20 hours per week, it is not being fully used. If two workers are used when one would be sufficient—say, two people in each Domino's Pizza delivery car—then resources are not being used efficiently. If there are resources available for use, society can move from point F_1 to a point on the PPC, such as point C_1. The move would gain 100 million units of nondefense goods and services with no loss of defense goods and services.

During recessions, unemployment rises and other resources are not fully and efficiently used. A point inside a nation's PPC could represent recession. This would be represented as a point inside the PPC, such as F_1. Should the economy expand, and resources become more fully and efficiently used, this would be represented as a move out from a point such as F_1 to a point on the PPC, such as point C_1.

2-1c-2 Points Outside the Production Possibilities Curve Point G_1 in Figure 1 represents the production of 200 million units of defense goods and services and 75 million units of nondefense goods and services. Point G_1, however, represents the use of more resources than are available—it lies outside the production possibilities curve. Unless more resources can be obtained and/or the quality of resources improved (for example, through technological change) so that the nation can produce more with the same quantity of resources, there is no way that the society can currently produce 200 million units of defense goods and 75 million units of nondefense goods.

2-1c-3 Shifts of the Production Possibilities Curve If a nation obtains more resources or if the existing resources become more efficient, everything else the same, then the PPC shifts outward. Suppose a country discovers new sources of oil within its borders and is able to greatly increase its production of oil without using more resources. Then some resources could be allocated to other uses, and the country would be able to increase production of all types of goods and services and have as much or more oil.

Figure 2 shows the production possibilities curve before (PPC_1) and after (PPC_2) the discovery of oil. PPC_1 is based on the data given in Figure 1. PPC_2 is based on the data given in Figure 2, which shows the increase in production of goods and services that result from the increase in oil supplies. The first combination of goods and services on PPC_2, point A_2, is 220 million units of defense goods and zero units of nondefense goods. The second point, B_2, is a combination of 200 million units of defense goods and 75 million units of nondefense goods. C_2 through F_2 are the combinations shown in Figure 2. Connecting these points yields the bowed-out curve PPC_2. Because of the availability of new supplies of oil, the nation can increase production of all goods, as shown by the *shift* from PPC_1 to PPC_2. A comparison of the two curves shows that more goods and services for both defense and nondefense are possible along PPC_2 than along PPC_1.

The outward shift of the PPC can be the result of an increase in the quantity of resources, but it also can occur because the quality of resources improves. Economists call an

---

FIGURE 2 A Shift of the Production Possibilities Curve

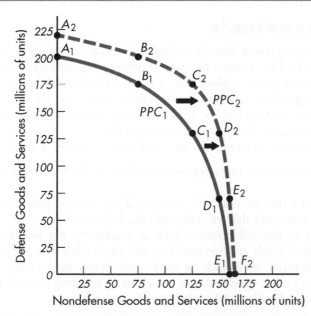

Whenever everything else is not constant, the curve shifts. In this case, an increase in the quantity of a resource enables the society to produce more of both types of goods. The curve shifts out, away from the origin.

increase in the quality of resources an increase in the productivity of resources. Consider a technological breakthrough that improves the speed with which data are transmitted. Following this breakthrough, it might require fewer people and machines to do the same amount of work, and it might take less time to produce the same quantity and quality of goods. Each quality improvement in resources is illustrated as an outward shift of the PPC.

R E C A P

1. Opportunity costs are the benefits that are forgone as a result of a choice. When you choose one thing, you must give up—forgo—others. Opportunity cost is the highest valued alternative.

2. The production possibilities curve (PPC) illustrates the concept of opportunity cost. Each point on the PPC means that every other point is a forgone opportunity.

3. The PPC represents all combinations of goods and services that can be produced using limited resources efficiently to their full capabilities.

4. Points inside the PPC represent the underutilization, unemployment, or inefficient use of resources—more goods and services could be produced by using the limited resources more fully or efficiently.

5. Points outside the PPC represent combinations of goods and services that are unattainable given the resource limitations.

6. If more resources are obtained or a technological change or innovation occurs, the PPC shifts out.

2-2 Output and Resources

Societies, like individuals, face scarcities and must make choices. A nation cannot produce as much of everything as it wants. When it produces more health care, it must forgo the production of some education, automobiles, or military hardware. The items it has to forgo constitute the opportunity cost of its action.

2-2a Resources and Income

resources
Goods used to produce other goods, i.e., land, labor, and capital.

labor
The physical and intellectual services of people, including the training, education, and abilities of the individuals in a society.

capital
Products such as machinery and equipment that are used in production.

land
All natural resources, such as minerals, timber, and water, as well as the land itself.

financial capital
The source of funds used to purchase capital (bonds, stocks)

Goods and services are scarce because resources are scarce. **Resources** are goods used to produce other goods. For instance, to make chocolate chip cookies we need flour, sugar, chocolate chips, butter, our own labor, and an oven. To distinguish between the ingredients of a good and the good itself, we call the ingredients resources. (Resources are also called *factors of production* and *inputs*; the terms are interchangeable.) The ingredients of the cookies are the resources, and the cookies are the goods.

Economists have classified resources into three general categories: land, labor, and capital.

1. **Land** includes all natural resources, such as minerals, timber, and water, as well as the land itself.
2. **Labor** refers to the physical and intellectual services of people and includes the training, education, and abilities of the individuals in a society.
3. **Capital** refers to physical products such as machinery and buildings that are used to produce other goods and services. You will more often hear the term *capital* used to refer to financial items such as stocks and bonds than to the physical capital. Economists try to distinguish between these two by referring to funds used to purchase the physical capital as **financial capital**.

Goods and services are scarce because resources are scarce. Only a couple of dozen chocolate chip cookies can be made from one 12-ounce bag of chocolate chips. Only so many wells can be dug on 100 acres of land having oil and natural gas under it.

Only so many iPads can be produced in a year because of limitations on labor, capital, and land. When the quantity and/or the quality of resources increases, the quantity of goods and services that can be produced increases. In 1850, 75 percent of the U.S. population lived and worked on the farm. Today, less than 2 percent of the U.S. population are farmers. But, because the people, the machines, and the land have become so much more efficient and productive, these 2 percent produce far more than the 75 percent did in 1850.

Highly skilled people earn higher salaries than less skilled people. Acquiring training and experience leads to higher income. Here, two people just having graduated from College are obtaining training from a more experienced employee.

2-2b The Value of Resources

People obtain income by selling their resources or the use of their resources. For instance, people sell the use of their labor in return for wages and salaries. People rent land or apartments or sell the produce of the land. And people invest in stocks and bonds and start businesses and receive interest and profits.

The greater the value of resources, the more income that the owners of those resources earn. Resources have value when their use is in goods that have value. People can earn more income when they increase the value of their resources by making them more useful to business. A business will pay a higher salary to someone whose labor is more valuable than to someone whose labor has little value. For instance, someone with skills, such as computer skills, will earn more than someone without skills. People attend college, acquire skills and training, and obtain job experience in order to make their labor more valuable.

Location, location, location, is the mantra of increasing the value of land. If your land is located on the coast with a great view of the ocean or on a ski hill with a great view of the mountain, your land will have greater value than if your land is located somewhere without a view and without the amenities of ocean or mountains. Your land will become more valuable if oil or natural gas is discovered beneath it. Owners of land cannot move the land, but they can take care of it and find more valuable uses for it.

In 2013 Apple was the most valuable company in the world. Those who purchased shares of stock of the company years before made substantial profits. The resource, the capital that makes up Apple, had become much more valuable because Apple products had become more valuable.

Figure 3 illustrates what resources are and the income they create. It showns in the third panel, who receives the income and who purchases goods and services and the use of resources.

FIGURE 3 Flow of Resources and Income

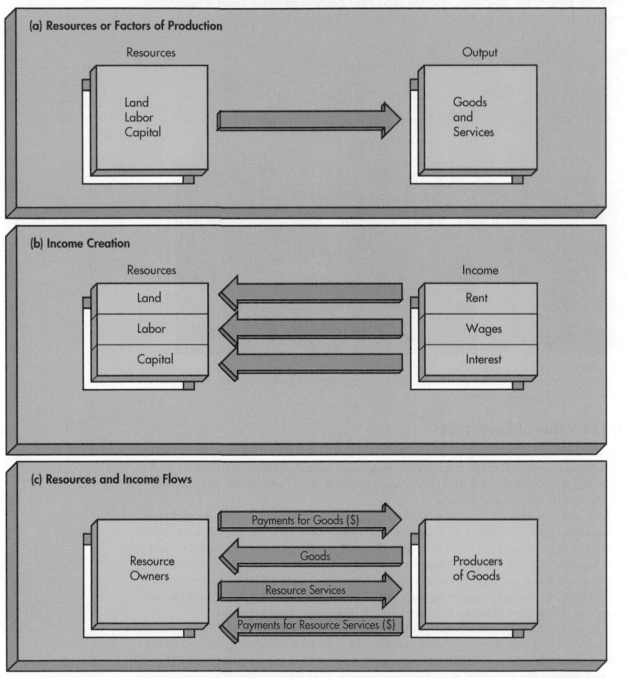

Three types of resources are used to produce goods and services: land, labor, and capital. See 3(a). The owners of resources are provided income for selling their services. Landowners are paid rent, laborers receive wages, and capital receives interest. See 3(b). Figure 3(c) links Figures 3(a) and 3(b). People use their resources to acquire income with which they purchase the goods they want. Producers use the money received from selling the goods to pay for the use of the resources in making goods. Resources and income flow between certain firms and certain resource owners as people allocate their scarce resources to best satisfy their wants.

1. Resources are the inputs into production. They are the ingredients of a product.

2. Economists classify resources into three broad categories: land, labor, and capital.

3. Capital is the machinery and buildings used in production. Financial capital is the financial means by which capital is acquired.

4. People earn income on the basis of the value of the resources they own. They are paid for working. They rent their land. They loan companies money and receive interest or they own shares of stock and receive part of the company's profits.

5. The more valuable resources are to businesses, the more income the owners of those resources earn.

2-3 Voluntary Trade and Exchange

When you walk into your local Starbucks to get a tall mocha frappuccino with whipped cream, do you wonder who told the baristas to work there, or who told the coffee growers to send their coffee beans to this particular Starbucks, or who told the dairy to provide this Starbucks with cream? Probably not. Most of us take all these things for granted. But the simple act of purchasing a drink from Starbucks includes many different exchanges. You had to obtain income; you may have sold or rented your resources (your labor, probably) for money. You then trade the money for the drink. And all the people working at the coffee shop are getting paid for their labor; the coffee growers, dairy farmers, truck drivers, and on and on all carried out trades or exchange. All of this just to get you your coffee drink.

2-3a Gains from Trade

Why do people engage in this type of voluntary trade? Because they benefit from it. People could choose to be self-sufficient—using their resources and producing what they want and need themselves— but they typically do not. Most people specialize in one or two activities for which they earn income and then purchase whatever else they want. As long as trade is voluntary, people trade only when trading benefits them. If all parties in an exchange did not anticipate to gain, then at least one of the parties would refuse to make the exchange.

We want to get the most we can with our resources; that is, earn the greatest income. Thus, we have to decide the best way to use our own scarce resources. What makes sense is for us to devote our energies to what we do best. This means that we specialize in those activities that cause us to forgo the least of other things. A plumber does plumbing and leaves teaching to the teachers. The teacher teaches and leaves electrical work to the electrician. A plumber does not do plumbing, teaching, and electrical work because doing all three would provide him less (that is, cost him more) than if he sticks to plumbing. In other words, people are better off focusing on those activities that have the lowest opportunity costs to them than in doing activities that have higher opportunity costs. This is called **comparative advantage**—focusing on activities that have the lowest opportunity costs.

2-3b Specialize Where Opportunity Costs Are Lowest

If we have a choice, we should devote our time and efforts to those activities in which we are relatively better than others. In other words, we should specialize in those activities that require us to give up the smallest amount of other things relative to others.

If we focus on one thing, how do we get the other things that we want? The answer is that we trade—we earn money and purchase goods and services. The teacher teaches, earns

Explain what the points A, B, C, and D on the following production possibilities curve illustrate.

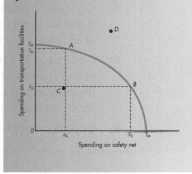

3. What are the gains from trade?

comparative advantage
An advantage derived from comparing the opportunity costs of production in two countries.

gains from trade
The difference between what can be produced and consumed without specialization and trade and with specialization and trade.

a salary, and hires a plumber to fix the sinks. This is called voluntary trade or voluntary exchange. The teacher is trading money to the plumber for the plumber's services. The teacher is trading her time to the students and getting money in return.

By specializing in the activities in which opportunity costs are lowest and then trading, everyone will end up with more than if everyone tried to produce everything. This is the **gains from trade**.

RECAP

1. Scarcity exists when people want more of an item than exists at a zero price.

2. Choices have to be made because of scarcity. People cannot have or do everything they desire all the time. Economics is the study of how people choose to use their scarce resources in an attempt to satisfy their wants.

3. Opportunity costs are the benefits that are forgone due to a choice. When you choose one thing, you must give up—forgo—others.

4. Opportunity cost is an individual concept, but it can be used to demonstrate scarcity and choice for a society as a whole.

5. Goods are produced with resources (also called factors of production and inputs). Economists have classified resources into three categories: land, labor, and capital.

6. Income comes from the ownership of resources.

7. Exchange occurs because all parties involved believe the exchange can be beneficial.

8. Opportunity cost is the amount of one good or service that must be given up to obtain one additional unit of another good or service.

9. The rule of specialization is that the individual (firm, region, or nation) will specialize in the activity in which it has the lowest opportunity cost.

10. Specialization and trade enable individuals, firms, and nations to get more than they could without specialization and trade.

11. By specializing in an activity that one does relatively better than other activities, one can trade with others and gain more than if one carried out all activities oneself. This additional amount is referred to as **gains from trade**.

2-4 Allocation Systems

4. How do we determine who gets what?

An allocation system is the process of determining who gets the goods and services and who does not. There are many different allocation systems that we might use. One is to have someone, say the government, determine who gets what, as in Cuba or Cameroon. Another is to have a first-come, first-served system, where those who arrive first get the goods and services. A third is to have a lottery, with the lucky winners getting the goods and services. A fourth is the market or price system, where those with the incomes are able to buy the goods and services. Which is best? Take the quiz on the next page, and then we will discuss allocation systems some more.

2-4a Fairness

How did you respond to the four questions in each scenario? If you are like most people, you believe that the price on the bottles of water ought to be raised and that the first patients showing up at the doctor's office ought to get service. Very few believe that the price or the market ought to be used to allocate important items like health care. Most claim that the price system is not fair. Yet none of the allocation approaches is "fair" if fairness means that everyone gets what he or she wants. In every case, someone gets the good or service and someone does not. This is what scarcity is all about—there is not enough to go around. With the market system, it is those without income or wealth who must do without. Is this fair? No. Under the first-come, first-served system, it is those who arrive later who do without. This is not fair either, since those who are slow, old, disabled, or otherwise not first to arrive will not get the goods and services. Under the government scheme, it is those who are not in favor or those who do not match up with the government's rules who do without. In the former Soviet Union, Cuba, Venezuela, Cameroon, and other government-run countries, it is the government officials who get most of the goods and services through what we call corruption, graft, and bribes. And, with a random procedure, it is those who do not have the lucky ticket or the correct number who are left out.

None of these allocation systems is fair in the sense that no one gets left out. Scarcity means that someone gets left out. Only if your measure of fair is equal opportunity is the lottery system fair. When everything is allocated by lottery, everyone has an equal chance of winning. But otherwise, life is not fair.

2-4b Incentives

Since each allocation mechanism is unfair, how do we decide which to use? One way might be by the incentives that each creates. Do the incentives lead to behavior that will improve things, increase supplies, and raise standards of living?

Allocation Quiz

I. At a sightseeing point reachable only after a strenuous hike, a firm has established a stand where bottled water is sold. The water, carried in by the employees of the firm, is sold to thirsty hikers in six-ounce bottles. The price is $1 per bottle. Typically, only 100 bottles of the water are sold each day. On a particularly hot day, however, 200 hikers each want to buy at least one bottle of water. Indicate what you think of each of the following means of distributing the water to the hikers by responding to each allocation approach with one of the following five responses:

a. Agree completely
b. Agree with slight reservation
c. Disagree
d. Strongly disagree
e. Totally unacceptable

1. Increasing the price until the quantity of bottles of water that hikers are willing and able to purchase exactly equals the number of bottles available for sale
2. Selling the water for $1 per bottle on a first-come, first-served basis
3. Having the local authority (government) buy the water for $1 per bottle and distribute it according to its own judgment
4. Selling the water for $1 per bottle following a random selection procedure or lottery

II. A physician has been providing medical services at a fee of $100 per patient and typically sees 30 patients per day. One day the flu bug has been so vicious that the number of patients attempting to visit the physician exceeds 60. Indicate what you think of each of the following means of distributing the physician's services to the sick patients by responding with one of the following five responses:

a. Agree completely
b. Agree with slight reservation
c. Disagree
d. Strongly disagree
e. Totally unacceptable

1. Raising the price until the number of patients the doctor sees is exactly equal to the number of patients who are willing and able to pay the doctor's fee
2. Selling the services for $100 per patient on a first-come, first-served basis
3. Having the local authority (government) pay the physician $100 per patient and choose who is to receive the services according to its own judgment
4. Selling the physician's services for $100 per patient following a random selection procedure or lottery

With the first-come, first-served allocation scheme, the incentive is to be first. You have no reason to improve the quality of your products or to increase the value of your resources. There is no incentive to increase the amounts of goods and services supplied. Why would anyone produce when all everyone wants is to be first? As a result, with a first-come, first-served allocation system, growth will not occur, and standards of living will not rise. A society based *solely* on first-come, first-served would die a quick death.

A government scheme provides an incentive either to be a member of government and thus help determine the allocation rules or to do exactly what the government orders you to do. There are no incentives to improve production and efficiency or to increase the quantities supplied, and thus there is no reason for the economy to grow. This type of system is a failure, as evidenced by the Soviet Union, Mao Tse-Tung's China, Cuba, and socialist systems in Latin America and Africa and in virtually every poor country in the world.

The random allocation system incentivizes you to do nothing—you simply hope that manna from heaven falls on you.

With the market system, the incentive is to acquire purchasing ability—to obtain income and wealth. This means that you must provide goods that have high value to others and provide resources that have high value to producers—to enhance your worth as an employee by acquiring education or training, and to enhance the value of the resources you own.

Very importantly, the market system also provides incentives for quantities of scarce goods to increase. In the case of the water stand in Scenario I, if the price of the water increases and the owner of the water stand is earning significant profits, others may carry or truck water to the top of the hill and sell it to thirsty hikers; the amount of water available thus increases. In the case of the doctor in Scenario II, other doctors may think that opening an office near the first might be a way to earn more; the amount of physician services available increases. Since the market system creates the incentive for the amount supplied to increase, economies grow and expand, and standards of living improve. The market system also ensures that resources are allocated where they are most highly valued. If the price of an item rises, consumers may switch to another item, or another good or service, that can serve about the same purpose. When consumers switch, production of the alternative good rises, and thus the resources used in its production must increase as well. As a result, resources are reallocated from lower-valued uses to higher-valued uses.

2-4c The Market Process: Arbitrage

When the Mazda Miata was introduced in the United States in 1990, the little sports roadster was an especially desired product in southern California. As shown in Figure 4, the suggested retail price was $13,996, the price at which it was selling in Detroit. In Los Angeles,

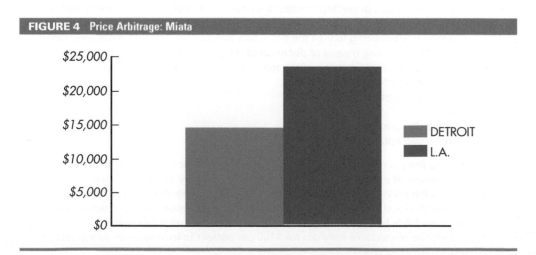

FIGURE 4 Price Arbitrage: Miata

the purchase price was nearly $25,000. Several entrepreneurs recognized the profit potential in the $10,000 price differential and sent hundreds of students to Detroit to pick up Miatas and drive them back to Los Angeles. Within a reasonably short time, the price differential between Detroit and Los Angeles was reduced. The increased sales in Detroit drove the price there up, while the increased number of Miatas being sold in Los Angeles reduced the price there. The price differential continued to decline until it was less than the cost of shipping the cars from Detroit to Los Angeles. This story of the Mazda Miata illustrates how markets work to allocate scarce goods, services, and resources. A product is purchased where its price is low and sold where its price is high. As a result, resources devoted to that product flow to where they have the highest value. The same type of situation occurred with the introduction of the Mini Cooper in 2001. The car was selling for much more in California than in New York and Chicago, so people purchased the cars in Chicago or New York and had the cars shipped to California. Similarly, there is a price differential on the BMW X5 in the United States and China. In the United States it lists for about $60,000, while in China it lists for nearly three times that much. Some people are purchasing the X5 in the United States and selling it in China.

Suppose an electronics firm is inefficient, its employees are surly, and its products are not displayed well. To attempt to earn a profit, the firm charges more than the efficiently run firm down the street. Where do customers go? Obviously, they seek out the best deal and go to the more efficient firm. The more efficient store has to get more supplies, hire more employees, acquire more space, and so on. The inefficient store lays off employees, sells used equipment, and gets rid of its inventory. The resources thus go from where they were not as highly valued to where they are most highly valued.

Why does the market process work? For a very simple reason: People are looking for the best deal—the highest-quality products at the lowest prices. So when an opportunity for a "best deal" arises, people respond to it by purchasing where the price is low and selling where the price is high.

As long as the market is free to change, it will ensure that resources are allocated to where they have the highest value and people get what they want at the lowest price. But what happens if something interferes with the market process? Each year *The Economist* magazine[1] publishes its Big Mac Index, which lists the price of a Big Mac in many different countries. Adjusting for different currencies, one year the index looked something like Figure 5.

FIGURE 5 A Big Mac Index

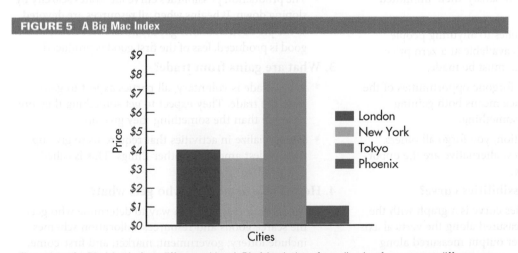

The price of a Big Mac in four different cities A Big Mac Index after adjusting for currency differences.

NOW YOU TRY IT

Suppose one sector of the economy's prices (costs) were increasing much more rapidly than the prices (costs) of all other sectors. If arbitrage were to occur, it would seem to imply that resources would flow from the slower price increase sectors to the rapid price increase sector. Explain what would happen if arbitrage did occur.

What do you bright entrepreneurs see? That's right—an arbitrage opportunity: You could load up a Boeing 747 with Big Macs in Phoenix and fly to Tokyo and sell the Big Macs for a nice profit. The larger supply in Tokyo would reduce the Tokyo price, and the greater demand in Phoenix would raise the price there. Why does that not happen? Part of the reason might be that the food is not portable; it deteriorates in the airplane. Another reason is that regulations would not allow it: Japan would not allow someone to simply land on the tarmac and beginning selling Big Macs out of a cargo hold. Arbitrage in the movement of Big Macs does not take place because regulations interfere with the market process. So, when something interferes with the market process, resources do not go to where they are most highly valued, and consumers do not get what they want at the lowest prices.

RECAP

1. Scarce goods and resources can be allocated in many different ways. Four common approaches are first-come, first-served; prices; government; and random.

2. No allocation mechanism is fair in the sense that everyone gets everything they want. This would defy the idea of scarcity. Some people will get the goods and resources and others will not.

3. The incentives each allocation system creates is a fundamental reason that markets are selected to do the allocation. Only a market system creates the incentives that lead to increasing standards of living.

SUMMARY

1. What are opportunity costs?

- Economics is the study of how people choose to allocate scarce resources to satisfy their unlimited wants.

- Scarcity is universal; it applies to anything people would like more of than is available at a zero price. Because of scarcity, choices must be made.

- Opportunity costs are the forgone opportunities of the next best alternative. Choice means both gaining something and giving up something.

- When you choose one option, you forgo all others. The benefits of the next best alternative are the opportunity costs of your choice.

2. What is a production possibilities curve?

- The production possibilities curve is a graph with the quantity of one output measured along the vertical axis and the quantity of another output measured along the horizontal axis.

- The production possibilities curve is defined by the quantity and quality of resources. With fewer resour-

ces, the curve would shift in; with more resources, the curve would shift out.

- The production possibilities curve illustrates scarcity by sloping down. It begins when all resources are devoted to the production of one good, and as more of the other good is produced, less of the first good is produced.

3. What are gains from trade?

- When trade is voluntary, all parties expect to gain from the trade. They expect to get something they prefer more than the something they give up.

- We specialize in activities that require us to give up the smallest amount of other things. This is called comparative advantage.

4. How do we determine who gets what?

- An allocation system is a way to determine who gets the scarce goods and resources. Allocation schemes include lottery; government; market; and first-come, first-served. §4

- The advantage of a market system over other allocation schemes is the incentive created by the market system. §4.b

KEY TERMS

capital, 24

comparative advantage, 27

financial capital, 24

gains from trade, 28

labor, 24

land, 24

marginal, 21

opportunity cost, 20

production possibilities curve, 21

resources, 24

scarcity, 20

trade-off, 20

EXERCISES

1. In presidential campaigns, candidates always seem to make more promises than they can fulfill: more and better health care; a better environment; only minor reductions in defense; better education; better roads, bridges, sewer systems, and water systems; and so on. What economic concept is ignored by the candidates?

2. What does the old saying "There is no such thing as a free lunch" mean? If someone invites you to a lunch and offers to pay for it, is it free for you?

3. Economics is the study of the relationship between
   a. people's unlimited wants and their scarce resources.
   b. people's limited wants and their scarce resources.
   c. people's limited wants and their infinite resources.
   d. people's limited income and their scarce resources.
   e. human behavior and limited human wants.

4. Janine is an accountant who makes $30,000 a year. Robert is a college student who makes $8,000 a year. All other things being equal, who is more likely to stand in a long line to get a cheap concert ticket?
   a. Janine; her opportunity cost is lower.
   b. Janine; her opportunity cost is higher.
   c. Robert; his opportunity cost is lower.
   d. Robert; his opportunity cost is higher.
   e. Janine; she is better able to afford the cost of the ticket.

5. Which of the following should *not* be considered an opportunity cost of attending college?
   a. money spent on living expenses that are the same whether or not you attend college
   b. lost salary
   c. business lunches
   d. interest that could have been earned on your money had you put the money into a savings account instead of spending it on tuition
   e. opportunities sacrificed in the decision to attend college

6. Exchange among people occurs because
   a. everyone involved believes they will gain.
   b. one person gains, and the others lose.
   c. only one person loses while everyone else gains.
   d. people have no other choices.
   e. the government requires it.

7. You have a comparative advantage in producing something when you
   a. have a higher opportunity cost than someone else.
   b. have a special talent.
   c. have a lower opportunity cost than someone else.
   d. have learned a useful skill.
   e. have the same opportunity cost as someone else.

Use the following table to answer study questions 8 through 11.

On a 10-acre farm, one farmer can produce these quantities of corn or wheat in Alpha and Beta.

	Corn	Wheat
Alpha	200	400
Beta	100	300

8. The opportunity cost of corn in Beta is
   a. 300 wheat.
   b. 1 wheat.
   c. 3 wheat.
   d. 100 corn.
   e. 5 corn.

9. The opportunity cost of corn in Alpha is
   a. 400 wheat.
   b. 2 wheat.
   c. 4 wheat.
   d. 100 corn.
   e. 5 corn.

10. The opportunity cost of wheat in Beta is
    a. 333 corn.
    b. 1 wheat.
    c. 3 wheat.
    d. 300 wheat.
    e. 5 corn.

11. The opportunity cost of wheat in Alpha is
    a. 400 wheat.
    b. 2 wheat.
    c. 4 wheat.
    d. 100 corn.
    e. 5 corn.

12. It is in your best interest to specialize in the area in which your opportunity costs are _____ (highest, constant, lowest).

13. A person or even a nation has a comparative advantage in those activities in which it has _____ (the highest, constant, the lowest) opportunity costs.

14. Chris works at a part-time job that pays $15 per hour. He wants a new shirt to wear next Friday night. He can buy one at the mall for $30, or he can make one (using materials he already has) with five hours of labor.

a. If Chris makes the shirt himself, how many hours will he spend on making the shirt? _____

b. If Chris works at his job and uses the money to buy a shirt, how many hours of work will it take him to earn the money to buy the shirt? _____

c. What do economists call the three hours Chris saved by working at his job and trading his money for a shirt instead of making it himself?

15. Why do most people object to the idea of using a price system to allocate human organs rather than the current donation and first-come, first-served system?

16. Which is more fair, having a board of experts decide who gets medical services or a price (market) system?

ECONOMICALLY SPEAKING

QUEUES HIT ABUJA AS FUEL SCARCITY SPREADS

Daniel Adugbo and Abbas Jimoh
Daily Trust (Abuja), February 25, 2014

Long queues resurfaced at major petrol filling stations in Abuja yesterday as residents struggled for hours to buy fuel following the unavailability of the product in some other stations.

At some petrol stations visited, our correspondents observed that the long queues of vehicles resulted in serious traffic gridlocks, especially at most NNPC stations in the city centre.

Already, other states like Lagos, Kano, Nasarawa, Katsina and Maiduguri started suffering the fuel scarcity one week ago.

Daily Trust reported last week that fuel loading reduced by 95 percent in major depots across Lagos.

Marketers have for long complained of the federal government's failure to release the subsidy payment to them which brought about the artificial scarcity recently.

Motorists spoken to expressed dismay at the development calling on the relevant government agencies to immediately step in to address the situation.

At the popular NNPC Mega Station in Central Area, the queue resulted in a traffic jam and blockage of the adjoining road.

Fuel attendants told our correspondent they had been dispensing petrol to motorists since morning and that the product was available and wondered why the long queues.

However, at Forte Oil located opposite the NNPC station, motorists could buy fuel unimpeded, as well as at Oando and Advance Link stations, as at the time our reporters visited.

But the story was different at the NNPC station located along Ngozi Okonjo-Iweala Way, Utako. One of the fuel attendants told our reporter they had been experiencing shortage of petrol supply since last week but that it got worse yesterday as they were about running out of supply with no reserve. Long queues of desperate motorists searching for fuel blocked the free flow of traffic in the entire road.

The situation was also not different at Total Filling Station, Central Area, opposite the NNPC Towers as a major traffic hold up was witnessed around the station. One of the attendants dispelled rumour of scarcity, insisting they had enough reserve to dispense to motorists.

However, checks by Daily Trust at filling stations located along Obafemi Awolowo Way, Jabi, which accommodates retail outlets of major oil marketers such as Mobil, Eterna, Conoil, Forte Oil, among others, showed similar trend.

Mobil officials told our correspondent they had already exhausted fuel for the day and would not dispense until they received fresh supply. Their inability to sell prompted long queues at Eterna Oil, Conoil and other stations located on the same road.

In the satellite towns like Suleja, Nyanya and Mararaba among others the situation was the same.

Most of the filling stations had their gates locked apparently due to the non-availability of the commodity.

Those with fuel had long queues stretching many kilometres and causing gridlock on the roads, with many motorists expressing dismay at the development.

Efforts to reach NNPC spokesman on the situation were unsuccessful.

COMMENTARY

Long lines for gas or an inability to find any fuel result not from a free market but from restrictions on the free market. According to the author of the article, "Marketers have for long complained of the federal government's failure to release the subsidy payment to them which brought about the artificial scarcity recently." So it seems that the government's interference has led to the shortage and the long lines. So why then would the people want the government to step in and correct the situation? The article notes that "Motorists spoken to expressed dismay at the develop-ment, calling on the relevant government agencies to im-mediately step in to address the situation."

One problem with government policy is that oppor-tunity costs are not considered. In this case, the short-ages and queues created by a policy were most likely not anticipated by the government agency implementing the policy.

The government intervention has created a huge inefficiency; resources are not being fully used in pro-ductive activities. Instead, people have to spend hours upon hours in lines to purchase fuel.

CHAPTER 3
The Market and Price System

© Semmick Photo /Shutterstock.com

top: © Carsten Feisinger/Shutterstock

FUNDAMENTAL QUESTIONS

1. *In a market system, who decides what goods and services are produced?*

2. *What is demand?*

3. *What is supply?*

4. *How is price determined by demand and supply?*

5. *What causes price to change?*

Preview

People (and firms and nations) can get more if they specialize in certain activities and then trade with one another to acquire the goods and services that they desire than they can if they do everything themselves. This is what we described in the chapter "Scarcity and Opportunity Costs" as gains from trade. But how does everyone get together to trade? Who decides who specializes in what, and who determines who gets what?

In some countries, the government decides who gets what and what is produced. In India until the mid-1990s, in the Soviet Union from 1917 until 1989, in China at least until 1980 and in many cases still today, and in Cuba, Venezuela, and Cameroon and other African nations today, a few government officials dictate what is produced, by whom it is produced, where it is produced, what price it sells at, and who may buy it.

A market arises when buyers and sellers exchange a well-defined good or service. In the case of a supermarket like this one, buyers purchase groceries and household items. The market occurs in a building at a specific location.

market
A place or service that enables buyers and sellers to exchange goods and services.

In most developed or industrial nations, government officials dictate what, how, for whom, and at what price a few things are produced, but for most goods and services, private individuals decide. When you walk into your supermarket to get some groceries, do you wonder who told the people working there to work there, or who told the 60,000 or so suppliers to provide their products to the store? As we said in the previous chapter, most of us take all these things for granted. Yet, it is a remarkable phenomenon—we get what we want, when we want it, and where we want it. How and why does this work? It is the market process; no one dictates what is produced, how it is produced, the price at which it sells, or who buys it. All this occurs through the self-interested behavior of individuals interacting in a **market**.

The term *market* refers to the interaction of buyers and sellers. A market may be a specific location, such as the supermarket, or it may be the exchange of particular goods or services at many different locations, such as the foreign exchange market. A market makes possible the exchange of goods and services. It may be a formally organized exchange, such as the New York Stock Exchange, or it may be loosely organized, like the market for used bicycles or automobiles. A market may be confined to one location, as in the case of a supermarket, or it may encompass a city, a state, a country, or the entire world, such as the market for foreign exchange.

In the case of the flower market, shoppers can examine the day's assortment and make their choices. This flower market does not occur at a specific location nor in a fixed building.

3-1 The Market System

Tablet sales are dominating laptop computer sales, which exceed sales of desktop PCs. Smartphones have taken over from mobile phones. A smartphone can take care of all of your handheld computing and communication needs in a single, small package. The first smartphone was called Simon; it was designed by IBM in 1992. Smartphone adoption in the United States initially lagged that of other developed areas, such as Japan or Europe, but the North American market expanded considerably beginning in 2008.

In the 1990s, people wanted mobile devices to carry out those daily tasks. The Blackberry, iPod, and other devices served various functions. By emphasizing convenience and flexibility, Nokia, Sharp, Fujitsu, and RIM grabbed a big share of the smartphone market worldwide, and Apple did well in North America. While these and a few manufacturers became successful, the star of the story is not these companies. It is the consumer. In a market system, if consumers are willing and able to pay for more powerful and flexible phones, more such phones appear. If consumers are willing and able to pay for a small phone that takes pictures and entertains you and does other tasks, such a phone will be available. Why does the consumer have such power? The name of the game for a supplier or business is profit, and the only way a business can make a profit is by satisfying consumer wants. Consumers, not politicians or business firms, ultimately determine what is to be produced. An entrepreneur or firm may introduce a new product—such as the iPod—something consumers had not thought about prior to its introduction, but once the product is introduced, the consumers determine whether that product will continue to be produced. A firm that produces a product that no consumers want will not remain in business very long, and the product will disappear. **Consumer sovereignty**—the authority of consumers to determine what is produced through their purchases of goods and services—dictates what goods and services will be produced. Firms and inventors come up with new products, but if consumers are not willing and able to purchase these products, the products will not exist for long.

1. *In a market system, who decides what goods and services are produced?*

consumer sovereignty
The authority of consumers to determine what is produced through their purchases of goods and services.

3-1a Profit and the Allocation of Resources

When a good or service seems to have the potential to generate a profit, some entrepreneur will put together the resources needed to offer that good or service for sale. If the potential profit turns into a loss, the entrepreneur may stop buying resources and turn to some other occupation or project. The resources used in the losing operation will then be available for use in an activity where they are more highly valued.

To illustrate how resources get allocated in the market system, let's look at the market for PDAs and smartphones. The PDA was introduced in the market several years before the smartphone. When consumer tastes changed, that is when people preferred to have a smartphone rather than just a PDA fewer people purchased PDAs and thus the price of them fell. Consumer tastes, not the price of PDAs, changed first.

While the market for PDAs was changing, so was the market for smartphones. The demand for smartphones increased. This demand change resulted in a higher price for smartphones.

The changing profit potential of the two markets induced existing firms to switch from PDAs to smartphones and for new firms to offer smartphones from the start. Nokia dominated the smartphone market, but Apple, which at first did not offer smartphones, had to play catch-up and begin offering its own smartphone. It did so with its iPhone. Then came the Android phones by Samsung and Motorola. Many PDA firms saw declining profits while in the smartphone business, the opposite occurred. Fewer PDAs were produced and more smartphones were produced.

Why did the production of smartphones increase while the production of PDAs declined? Not because of a government decree. Not because of the desires of the business sector, especially the owners of the smartphone manufacturers. The consumer—*consumer sovereignty*—made all this happen. Businesses that failed to respond to consumer desires and failed to provide the desired good at the lowest price failed to survive.

Smart phones are ubiquitous (everywhere) today. Tomorrow something will take their place. The market system ensures that consumers get what they want at the lowest possible price and ensures that innovation will occur.

3-1b Creative Destruction

After demand shifted to smartphones, the resources that had been used in the production of PDAs were available for use elsewhere. Some former employees were able to get jobs in the smartphone industry. Some of the equipment used in manufacturing PDAs was purchased by the smartphone firms; some of the components that previously would have gone to the PDAs were used in the smartphones. Although some former employees of the PDA business became employed in the smartphone business, others had to find entirely new positions in totally different businesses. Some of the equipment used to manufacture PDAs was sold as scrap; other equipment was sold to other manufacturers. In other words, the resources moved from an activity where their value was relatively low to an activity where they were more highly valued. No one commanded the resources to move. They moved because they could earn more in some other activity.

This same story applies in case after case after case. The Sony Walkman was replaced by Apple's iPod, and the early iPod is now contained in the iPhone. The process of new products and new firms replacing existing products and firms is called *creative destruction*. This is what the market process is all about—creating new ideas, new products, and new ways of doing things, and replacing the obsolete, costly, and inefficient. Every year *Forbes* magazine publishes a list of the 100 largest companies in terms of sales. In 1987, *Forbes* compared that year's list to the 100 largest firms in 1917. Only 39 of the 1917 group remained in business in 1987. Of the 39 that remained in business, 18 had managed to stay in the top 100. Of the 18 that stayed in the top 100, only two had performed better than the market average—Kodak and GE. Both of these have since fallen. Kodak went bankrupt and has tried to reemerge focusing on digital imagery while giving up the cameras and other products it became famous for. GE has also struggled, undertaking serious cost cutting in 2013 and turning to government subsidies. This seems an amazing change, but the pace of change has only quickened since 1987. Fewer than 25 percent of today's major corporations will continue to exist in 25 years.

In 1900, over 60 percent of the U.S. work force was employed in agriculture. Today, only about 2 percent are employed in agriculture. Yet the U.S. produces far more agricultural produce today than it did in 1900. The technology used in agriculture so increased the productivity on farms that only 3 percent of the work force is needed to produce far more than had been produced with 60 percent of the labor force. Since 57 percent of the work force that was in agriculture in 1900 is not today, where did workers go? (We are using a metaphor since people living in 1900 would not be alive today.) Since only 3 percent or less of the labor force is needed in agriculture today, others must have received training in high technology or other fields that had a greater value for them than working on the farm would have had. In a sense, jobs on the farm were destroyed, but they were destroyed by the creation of new jobs in technology or services.

Firms produce the goods and services and use the resources that enable them to generate the highest profits. If one firm does this better than others, then that firm earns a greater profit than others. Seeing that success, other firms copy or mimic the first firm. If a firm cannot be as profitable as the others, it will eventually go out of business or move to another line of business where it can be successful. In the process of firms always seeking to lower their costs and make higher profits, society finds that the goods and services that buyers want are produced in the least costly manner. Not only do consumers get the goods and services that they want and will pay for, but they get these products at the lowest possible price.

3-1c The Determination of Income

Consumer demands dictate what is produced, and the search for profit defines how goods and services are produced. For whom are the goods and services produced; that is, who gets the goods and services? In a price or market system, those who have the ability to pay for the products get the products. Your income determines your ability to pay, and a person's income comes from selling the services of the resources that person owns.

In reality, households own all resources. Everyone owns his or her own labor; some households also own land, and many also own firms or portions of firms (by owning stocks or mutual funds). When a household owns shares of stock, it owns a portion of the firm whose shares it owns. Many households own shares of stock either as direct investments or as part of their retirement funds. The firm you or your parents work for might provide a 401(k) or some other retirement plan. A portion of these plans typically own shares of stock. All firms, whether private firms or firms traded through stock markets, are owned by households in some way. Thus, if a firm acquires equipment, buildings, land, and natural resources, it is actually households that ultimately own those things. If a firm were taken apart and its parts sold off, households would end up with the money.

RECAP

1. In a market system, consumers are sovereign and decide by means of their purchases what goods and services will be produced.

2. In a market system, firms decide how to produce the goods and services that consumers want. In order to earn maximum profits, firms use the least-cost combinations of resources.

3. Income and prices determine who gets what in a market system. Income is determined by the ownership of resources.

3-2 Markets and Money

The market process refers to the way that scarce goods and services are allocated through the individual actions of buyers and sellers. The price adjusts to the actions of buyers and sellers so as to ensure that resources are used where they have the highest value—the price of the Miata in Los Angeles declines as more Miatas end up in Los Angeles. The price measures the opportunity cost—how much has to be given up in order to get something else. If you pay a dollar for a cup of coffee, then the opportunity cost of that coffee is everything else that dollar could have been used to buy. In most cases, when you buy something you exchange money for that something. There are cases where you actually exchange one good for another—you might mow someone's lawn in exchange for them taking care of your house while you are on vacation. Every market exchange is not necessarily a monetary exchange but most are.

3-2a Barter and Money Exchanges

The purpose of markets is to facilitate the exchange of goods and services between buyers and sellers. In some cases, money changes hands; in others, only goods and services are exchanged. Recall that the cost (price) of something is what must be given up to acquire a unit of that something. If the price of a gallon of milk is $2, then the cost of that gallon of milk is whatever would have been purchased with that $2. Suppose that the $2 would have been used to purchase one piece of chocolate cake. Then we could say that the cost of a gallon of milk is one piece of chocolate cake. If we simply exchanged a gallon of milk for the piece of cake, we would be engaging in **barter**. The exchange of goods and services directly, without money, is called barter. Barter occurs when a plumber fixes a leaky pipe for a lawyer in exchange for the lawyer's work on a will or when a Chinese citizen provides fresh vegetables to a U.S. visitor in exchange for a pack of U.S. cigarettes.

Most markets involve money because goods and services can be exchanged more easily with money than without it. Economists say the costs of transacting are lower with money than without it. When IBM purchases microchips from Yakamoto of Japan, IBM and Yakamoto do not exchange goods directly. Neither firm may have what the other wants. Barter requires a **double coincidence of wants**: IBM must have what Yakamoto wants, and Yakamoto must have what IBM wants. The difficulty of finding a double coincidence of wants for barter transactions is typically very high. Using money makes trading easier. To obtain the microchips, all IBM has to do is provide dollars to Yakamoto. Yakamoto is willing to accept the money, since it can spend that money to obtain the goods that it wants.

barter
The direct exchange of goods and services without the use of money.

double coincidence of wants
The situation that exists when A has what B wants and B has what A wants.

RECAP

1. Barter refers to exchanges made without the use of money.
2. Money makes it easier and less expensive to exchange goods and services.

3-3 Demand

?

2. What is demand?

A market consists of demand and supply—buyers and sellers. To understand how a price level is determined and why a price rises or falls, it is necessary to know how demand and supply function. We begin by considering demand alone, then supply, and then we put the two together. Before we begin, we discuss some economic terminology that is often confusing.

Economists distinguish between the terms **demand** and **quantity demanded**. When they refer to the *quantity demanded*, they are talking about the amount of a product that people are willing and able to purchase at a *specific* price. When they refer to *demand*, they are talking about the amount that people would be willing and able to purchase at *every possible* price. Demand is the quantities demanded at every price. Thus, the statement that "the demand for U.S. white wine rose following an increase in the price of French white wine" means that at each price for U.S. white wine, more people were willing and able to purchase U.S. white wine. They switched from the French wine to the U.S. wine. And the statement that "the quantity demanded of white wine fell as the price of white wine rose" means that people were willing and able to purchase less white wine because the price of the wine rose.

3-3a The Law of Demand

Consumers and merchants know that if you lower the price of a good or service without altering its quality or quantity, people will beat a path to your doorway. This simple truth is referred to as the **law of demand**.

According to the law of demand, people purchase more of something when the price of that item falls. More formally, the law of demand states that the quantity of some item that people are willing and able to purchase during a particular period of time decreases as the price rises, and vice versa.

The more formal definition of the law of demand can be broken down into five phrases:

1. The quantity of a well-defined good or service that
2. people are willing and able to purchase
3. during a particular period of time
4. decreases as the price of that good or service rises and increases as the price falls,
5. everything else held constant.

The first phrase ensures that we are referring to the same item, that we are not mixing different goods. A watch is a commodity that is defined and distinguished from other goods by several characteristics: quality, color, and design of the watch face, to name a few. The law of demand applies to a well-defined good, in this case, a watch. If one of the characteristics should change, the good would no longer be well defined—in fact, it would be a different good. A Rolex watch is different from a Timex watch; Polo brand golf shirts are different goods from generic brand golf shirts; Mercedes-Benz automobiles are different goods from Saturn automobiles.

The second phrase indicates that not only must people *want* to purchase some good, but they must be *able* to purchase that good in order for their wants to be counted as part of demand. For example, Sue would love to buy a membership in the Paradise Valley Country Club, but because the membership costs $35,000, she is not able to purchase the membership. Though she is willing, she is not able. At a price of $5,000, however, she is willing and able to purchase the membership.

The third phrase points out that the demand for any good is defined for a specific period of time. Without reference to a time period, a demand relationship would not make any sense. For instance, the statement that "at a price of $3 per Happy Meal, 13 million Happy Meals are demanded" provides no useful information. Are the 13 million meals sold in one week or one year? Think of demand as a rate of purchase at each possible price over a period of time—two per month, one per day, and so on.

The fourth phrase points out that price and quantity demanded move in opposite directions; that is, as the price rises, the quantity demanded falls, and as the price falls, the quantity demanded rises.

Demand is a measure of the relationship between the price and quantity demanded of a particular good or service when the determinants of demand do not change. The **determinants of demand** are income, tastes, prices of related goods and services, expectations, and the

demand
The amount of a product that people are willing and able to purchase at each possible price during a given period of time, everything else held constant.

quantity demanded
The amount of a product that people are willing and able to purchase at a specific price.

law of demand
The quantity of a well-defined good or service that people are willing and able to purchase during a particular period of time decreases as the price of that good or service rises and increases as the price falls, everything else held constant.

determinants of demand
Factors other than the price of the good that influence demand—income, tastes, prices of related goods and services, expectations, and number of buyers.

number of buyers. If any one of these items changes, demand changes. The final phrase, everything else held constant, ensures that the determinants of demand do not change. We are focusing on the relationship between price and quantity demanded—everything else held constant.

3-3b The Demand Schedule

demand schedule
A table or list of prices and the corresponding quantities demanded for a particular good or service.

A **demand schedule** is a table or list of prices and the corresponding quantities demanded for a particular good or service. Consider the demand for access time to online games. Console games made their debut in the 1970s, but it has been in the first decade of this century in which the growth of online games or interactive console games has really exploded. There are different formats and ways to download games and access networks, but let us deal with a simple setting wherein you can purchase access to a network featuring games such as World of Warcraft on a weekly basis. The table in Figure 1 is a demand schedule for hours of access to the games. It shows the number of hours per week that a consumer named Bob would be willing and able to buy at each price during a month, everything else held constant.

FIGURE 1   Bob's Demand Schedule and Demand Curve for Hours of Access per Week

Combination	Price per Hour (constant quality units)	Quantity Demanded per Week (constant quality units)
A	$5	10
B	$4	20
C	$3	30
D	$2	40
E	$1	50

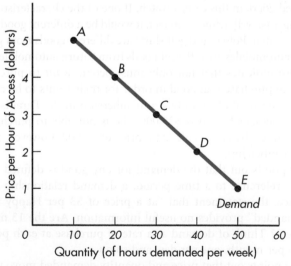

The number of hours of access to online games that Bob is willing and able to buy at each price during the week is listed in the table, or the demand schedule. The demand curve is derived from the combinations given in the demand schedule. The price–quantity combination of $5 per hour and 10 hours is point A. The combination of $4 per hour and 20 hours is point B. Each combination is plotted, and the points are connected to form the demand curve.

As the price of the access time gets higher relative to the prices of other goods, Bob would be willing and able to purchase fewer access hours.

At a price of $5 per hour, Bob indicates that he will purchase only 10 hours during the week. At a price of $4, Bob tells us that he will purchase 20 hours during the week. As the price drops from $5 to $4 to $3 to $2 and to $1, Bob is willing and able to purchase more access time. At a price of $1, Bob would purchase 50 hours of access for the week.

3-3c The Demand Curve

A **demand curve** is a graph of the demand schedule. The demand curve shown in Figure 1 is plotted from the information given in the demand schedule. The price per hour of access time (price per unit) is measured on the vertical axis, and the number of hours of access per week (quantity per unit of time) is measured on the horizontal axis. The demand curve slopes downward because of the inverse relationship between the price and the quantity that Bob is willing and able to purchase. Point A in Figure 1 corresponds to combination A in the table: a price of $5 and 10 hours per week demanded. Similarly, points B, C, D, and E in Figure 1 represent the corresponding combinations in the table. The line connecting these points is Bob's demand curve for hours of access to a network game.

All demand curves slope down because of the law of demand: As price falls, quantity demanded increases. The demand curves for bread, electricity, automobiles, colleges, labor services, health care, and any other good or service you can think of slope down. You might be saying to yourself, "That's not true. When the price of some rock concerts goes up, more people want to attend the concert. As the ticket price goes up, going to the concert becomes more prestigious, and the quantity demanded actually rises." To avoid confusion in such circumstances, we say "everything else held constant." With this statement, we are assuming that tastes do not change and that, therefore, the goods *cannot* become more prestigious as the price changes. Similarly, we do not allow the quality or the brand name of a product to change as we define the demand schedule or demand curve. We concentrate on the one quality or the one brand; so when we say that the price of a good has risen, we are talking about a good that is identical at all prices.

demand curve
A graph of a demand schedule that measures price on the vertical axis and quantity demanded on the horizontal axis.

3-3d From Individual Demand Curves to a Market Curve

Bob's demand curve for hours of access to a network game is plotted in Figure 1. Unless Bob is the only person who plays the game, his demand curve is not the total or market demand curve. Market demand is derived by adding up the quantities that everyone is willing and able to purchase at each price—the sum of all individual demands. The market demand curve is the horizontal sum of all individual demand curves of all consumers in the market. The table in Figure 2 lists the demand schedules of three individuals, Bob, Maria, and Liu. If these three were the only consumers in the market, then the market demand would be the sum of their individual demands, shown as the last column of the table.

Bob's, Maria's, and Liu's demand schedules are plotted as individual demand curves in Figure 2(a). In Figure 2(b), their individual demand curves have been added together to obtain the market demand curve for hours of access per week to a network game. (Notice that we add in a horizontal direction—that is, we add the quantities at each price, not the prices at each quantity.) At a price of $5, we add the quantity that Bob would be willing and able to buy, 10, to the quantity that Maria would be willing and able to buy, 5, to the quantity that Liu would be willing and able to buy, 15, to get the market quantity demanded of 30. At a price of $4, we add the quantities that each of the consumers is willing and able to buy to get the total quantity demanded of 48. At all prices, then, we add the quantities demanded by each individual consumer to get the total, or market quantity, demanded.

When speaking of the demand curve or demand schedule, we are using constant-quality units. The quality of a good does not change as the price changes along a demand curve.

FIGURE 2 The Market Demand Schedule and Demand Curve

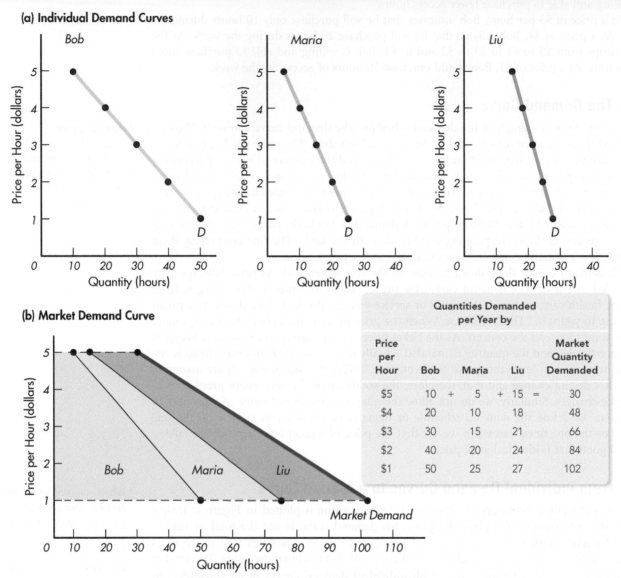

(a) Individual Demand Curves

Bob

Maria

Liu

(b) Market Demand Curve

Bob

Maria

Liu

Market Demand

Price per Hour	Quantities Demanded per Year by			Market Quantity Demanded
	Bob	Maria	Liu	
$5	10 +	5 +	15 =	30
$4	20	10	18	48
$3	30	15	21	66
$2	40	20	24	84
$1	50	25	27	102

The market is defined to consist of three individuals: Bob, Maria, and Liu. Their demand schedules are listed in the table and plotted as the individual demand curves shown in Figure 2(a). By adding the quantities that each demands at every price, we obtain the market demand curve shown in Figure 2(b). At a price of $1, we add Bob's quantity demanded of 50 to Maria's quantity demanded of 25 to Liu's quantity demanded of 27 to obtain the market quantity demanded of 102. At a price of $2, we add Bob's 40 to Maria's 20 to Liu's 24 to obtain the market quantity demanded of 84. To obtain the market demand curve, for every price we sum the quantities demanded by each market participant.

3-3e Changes in Demand and Changes in Quantity Demanded

When one of the determinants of demand—income, tastes, prices of related goods, expectations, or number of buyers—is allowed to change, the demand for a good or service changes as well. What does it mean to say that demand changes? Demand is the entire demand schedule, or demand curve. When we say that demand changes, we are referring to a change in the quantities demanded at each and every price.

FIGURE 3 An Increase and a Decrease in Demand

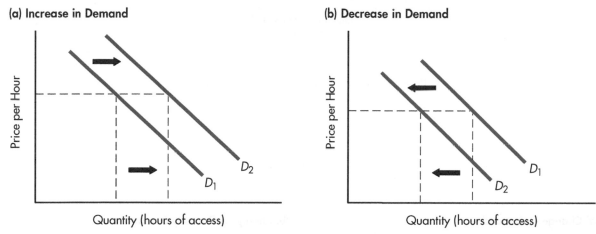

(a) Increase in Demand

Price per Hour

Quantity (hours of access)

D_2

D_1

(b) Decrease in Demand

Price per Hour

Quantity (hours of access)

D_1

D_2

In Figure 3(a), an increase in demand occurs due to an increase in income. The consumer is willing and able to purchase more at *every price*. This change is expressed as a rightward shift of the demand curve from D_1 to D_2. Figure 3(b) shows a decrease in demand due to a decrease in income. The consumer is willing to purchase less at *every price*. This is illustrated as a leftward shift of demand from D_1 to D_2.

For example, if Bob's income rises, then he is willing and able to purchase more access time for the network game. At each and every price, the number of hours of access time that Bob is willing and able to buy each week rises. An increase in demand is expressed by a rightward shift of the demand curve, such as that shown in Figure 3(a) in the move from D_1 to D_2. Conversely, if Bob's income declined, then he would be willing and able to purchase less access time. This decrease in demand is expressed as a leftward shift of the demand curve, as shown in Figure 3(b) in the move from D_1 to D_2.

A change in demand is represented by a shift of the demand curve.

When the price of a good or service is the only factor that changes, the quantity demanded changes, but the demand curve does not shift. Instead, as the price of the access time is decreased (increased), everything else held constant, the quantity that people are willing and able to purchase increases (decreases). This change is merely a movement from one point on the demand curve to another point on the same demand curve, not a shift of the demand curve. A *change in the quantity demanded* is the phrase that economists use to describe the change in the quantities of a particular good or service that people are willing and able to purchase as the price of that good or service changes. A change in the quantity demanded, from point *A* to point *B* on the demand curve, is shown in Figure 4(b). Compare this to a change in demand illustrated by the shift of the entire curve as shown in Figure 4(a).

A change in the quantity demanded is a movement along the demand curve. A change in the demand is a shift of the demand curve.

The demand curve shifts when income, tastes, prices of related goods, expectations, or the number of buyers changes. Let's consider how each of these determinants of demand affects the demand curve.

3-3e-1 Income The demand for any good or service depends on income. For most goods and services, the higher someone's income is, with everything else the same, the more that person can purchase at any given price. These are called **normal goods**. The increase in Bob's income causes his demand to increase. This change is shown in Figure 4(a) by the shift to the right from the curve labeled D_1 to the curve labeled D_2. Increased income means a greater ability to purchase goods and services. At every price, more hours of access time are demanded along curve D_2 than along curve D_1; this is an increase in demand.

normal goods
Goods for which demand increases as income increases.

For some goods and services, however, the amount demanded declines as income rises, everything else the same. The reason could be that these are goods or services that people

FIGURE 4 **A Change in Demand and a Change in the Quantity Demanded**

Price per Hour	Quantities Demanded per Week	
	Before	After
$5	10	15
$4	20	25
$3	30	35
$2	40	45
$1	50	55

(a) Change in Demand

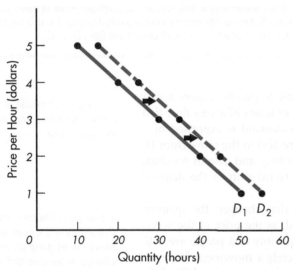

(b) Change in Quantity Demanded

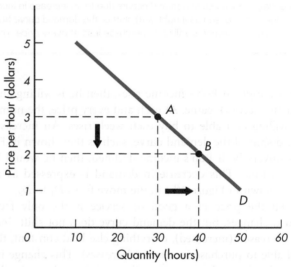

According to the table, Bob's demand for access time has increased by five hours at each price. In Figure 4(a), this change is shown as a shift of the demand curve from D_1 to D_2. Figure 4(b) shows a change in the quantity demanded. The change in quantity demanded is an increase in the quantity that consumers are willing and able to purchase at a lower price. It is shown as a movement along the demand curve from point A to point B.

---

use only when their incomes are declining—such as bankruptcy services. In addition, people might not like the good or service as well as they like a more expensive good or service, so when their income rises, they purchase the more expensive items. These types of items are called **inferior goods**.

inferior goods
Goods for which demand decreases as income increases.

3-3e-2 Tastes The demand for any good or service depends on individuals' tastes and preferences. When the iPod came out in 2000, it became an instant success. The Sony Walkman lost market share and essentially disappeared. Tastes changed toward the more mobile iPod and, more importantly, toward the more powerful iPod. Thousands of songs could be stored on an iPod, while the Walkman was constrained by the size of the CD. The iPhone incorporates the iPod into a mobile phone, and it too has been a huge success. Consumers no longer demand the old fixed-line phones but instead want more capabilities in their mobile phones and MP3 devices; their tastes have changed.

3-3e-3 Prices of Related Goods and Services

Goods and services may be related in two ways. **Substitute goods** can be used in place of each other, so that as the cost of one rises, everything else the same, people will buy more of the other. Bread and crackers, BMWs and Acuras, movie downloads and theater movies, universities and community colleges, electricity and natural gas, and time used to access network games and time used for other activities are, more or less, pairs of substitutes. As the price of entertainment venues rises, everything else held constant, the demand for access time for network games will rise; the demand curve for access time will shift to the right.

Complementary goods are goods that are used together, and so as the price of one rises, everything else the same, consumers buy less of it but also buy less of the complementary good. Bread and margarine, beer and peanuts, cameras and film, shoes and socks, CDs and CD players, a computer or game board and access to network games, and iPods and iTunes are examples of pairs of complementary goods. As the price of a machine on which to play network games rises, people purchase less access time to those network games. The demand curve for a complementary good shifts to the left when the price of the related good increases.

substitute goods
Goods that can be used in place of each other; as the price of one rises, the demand for the other rises.

complementary goods
Goods that are used together; as the price of one rises, the demand for the other falls.

3-3e-4 Expectations

Expectations about future events can have an effect on demand today. People make purchases today because they expect their income level to be a certain amount in the future, or because they expect the price of certain items to be higher in the future. You might buy running shoes today if you expect the price of those shoes to be higher tomorrow. You might buy your airline ticket home now rather than wait until semester break if you expect the price to be higher next month.

3-3e-5 Number of Buyers

Market demand consists of the sum of the demands of all individuals. The more individuals there are with income to spend, the greater the market demand is likely to be. For example, the populations of Florida and Arizona are much larger during the winter than they are during the summer. The demand for any particular good or service in Arizona and Florida rises (the demand curve shifts to the right) during the winter and falls (the demand curve shifts to the left) during the summer.

NOW YOU TRY IT

List four events that would cause the demand curve to shift out.

RECAP

1. According to the law of demand, as the price of any good or service rises (falls), the quantity demanded of that good or service falls (rises), during a specific period of time, everything else held constant.

2. A demand schedule is a listing of the quantity demanded at each price.

3. The demand curve is a downward-sloping line plotted using the values in the demand schedule.

4. Market demand is the sum of all individual demands.

5. Demand changes when one of the determinants of demand changes. A demand change is illustrated as a shift of the demand curve.

6. The determinants of demand are income, tastes, prices of related goods and services, expectations, and number of buyers.

7. The quantity demanded changes when the price of the good or service changes. This is a change from one point on the demand curve to another point on the same demand curve.

3-4 Supply

Why do students get discounts at movie theaters? Demand *and* supply. Why do restaurants offer early bird specials? Demand *and* supply. Why is the price of hotel accommodations in Phoenix higher in the winter than in the summer? Demand *and* supply. Why is the price of beef higher in

3. What is supply?

Japan than in the United States? Demand *and* supply. Both demand and supply determine price; neither demand nor supply alone determines price. We just discussed demand; we now discuss supply.

3-4a The Law of Supply

supply
The amount of a good or service that producers are willing and able to offer for sale at each possible price during a period of time, everything else held constant.

Just as demand is the relation between the price and the quantity demanded of a good or service, supply is the relation between the price and the quantity supplied. **Supply** is the amount of the good or service that producers are willing and able to offer for sale at each possible price during a period of time, everything else held constant. **Quantity supplied** is the amount of the good or service that producers are willing and able to offer for sale at a *specific* price during a period of time, everything else held constant. According to the **law of supply**, as the price of a good or service rises, the quantity supplied rises, and vice versa.

The formal statement of the law of supply consists of five phrases:

quantity supplied
The amount that sellers are willing and able to offer at a given price during a particular period of time, everything else held constant.

1. The quantity of a well-defined good or service that
2. producers are willing and able to offer for sale
3. during a particular period of time that
4. increases as the price of the good or service increases and decreases as the price decreases,
5. everything else held constant.

The first phrase is the same as the first phrase in the law of demand. The second phrase indicates that producers must not only *want* to offer the product for sale but be *able* to offer the product. The third phrase points out that the quantities producers will offer for sale depend on the period of time being considered. The fourth phrase points out that more will be supplied at higher than at lower prices. The final phrase ensures that the **determinants of supply** do not change. The determinants of supply are those factors other than the price of the good or service that influence the willingness and ability of producers to offer their goods and services for sale—the prices of resources used to produce the product, technology and productivity, expectations of producers, the number of producers in the market, and the prices of related goods and services. If any one of these should change, supply changes.

law of supply
The quantity of a well-defined good or service that producers are willing and able to offer for sale during a particular period of time increases as the price of the good or service increases and decreases as the price decreases, everything else held constant.

3-4b The Supply Schedule and Supply Curve

determinants of supply
Factors other than the price of the good that influence supply—prices of resources, technology and productivity, expectations of producers, number of producers, and the prices of related goods and services.

A **supply schedule** is a table or list of the prices and the corresponding quantities supplied of a good or service. The table in Figure 5 presents a single firm's supply schedule for access to network games. (We will assume that three firms offer access to the same network games.) The schedule lists the quantities that each firm is willing and able to supply at each price, everything else held constant. As the price increases, the firm is willing and able to offer more access time to the network games.

A **supply curve** is a graph of the supply schedule. Figure 5 shows Aber's supply curve of access time to the network games. The price and quantity combinations given in the supply schedule correspond to the points on the curve. For instance, combination A in the table corresponds to point A on the curve; combination B in the table corresponds to point B on the curve, and so on for each price–quantity combination.

supply schedule
A table or list of prices and the corresponding quantities supplied of a particular good or service.

The supply curve slopes upward. This means that a supplier is willing and able to offer more for sale at higher prices than it is at lower prices. This should make sense—if prices rise, everything else held constant, the supplier will earn more profits. Higher profits create the incentive for the supplier to offer more for sale.

supply curve
A graph of a supply schedule that measures price on the vertical axis and quantity supplied on the horizontal axis.

3-4c From Individual Supply Curves to the Market Supply

To derive market supply, the quantities that each producer supplies at each price are added together, just as the quantities demanded by each consumer are added together to get market demand. The table in Figure 6 lists the supply schedules of three firms that sell access to network games: Aber, Broadband, and Courage. The supply schedules are plotted in

FIGURE 5 Aber's Supply Schedule and Supply Curve of Access Time to Network Games

Combination	Price per Hour (constant quality units)	Quantity Supplied per Week (constant quality units)
A	$5	60
B	$4	50
C	$3	40
D	$2	30
E	$1	20

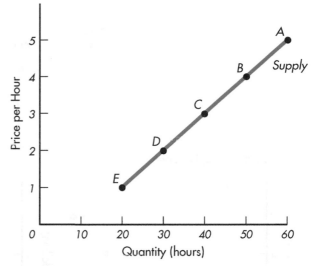

The quantity that Aber is willing and able to offer for sale at each price is listed in the supply schedule and shown on the supply curve. At point A, the price is $5 per hour and the quantity supplied is 60 hours. The combination of $4 per hour and 50 hours is point B. Each price–quantity combination is plotted, and the points are connected to form the supply curve.

Figure 6(a). Then in Figure 6(b) the individual supply curves have been added together (in a horizontal direction) to obtain the market supply curve. At a price of $5, the quantity supplied by Aber is 60, the quantity supplied by Broadband is 30, and the quantity supplied by Courage is 12. This means a total quantity supplied in the market of 102. At a price of $4, the quantities supplied are 50, 25, and 9, for a total market quantity supplied of 84. The market supply schedule is the last column in the table. The graph of the price and quantity combinations listed in this column is the market supply curve. The market supply curve slopes up because each of the individual supply curves has a positive slope. The market supply curve tells us that the quantity supplied in the market increases as the price rises.

3-4d Changes in Supply and Changes in Quantity Supplied

When we draw the supply curve, we allow only the price and quantity supplied of the good or service that we are discussing to change. Everything else that might affect supply is assumed not to change. If any of the determinants of supply—the prices of resources used to produce the product, technology and productivity, expectations of producers, the number of producers in the market, and the prices of related goods and services—changes, the supply schedule changes and the supply curve shifts.

A change in the quantity supplied is a movement along the supply curve. A change in the supply is a shift of the supply curve.

3-4d-1 Prices of Resources If labor costs rise, higher prices will be necessary to induce each store to offer as many hours of access as it did before the cost of the resource rose. The higher cost of resources causes a decrease in supply, meaning a leftward shift of the supply curve, from S_1 to S_2 in Figure 7(a). Compare point B on curve S_2 with point A on curve S_1. Both points correspond to a price of $3, but along curve S_1, sellers are willing to offer 66 hours of access time, whereas curve S_2 indicates that sellers will offer only 57 hours of access time.

3-4d-2 Technology and Productivity If resources are used more efficiently in the production of a good or service, more of that good or service can be supplied for the same cost, or the original quantity supplied can be produced for a lower cost. As a result, the supply curve shifts to the right, as in Figure 7(b).

FIGURE 6   The Market Supply Schedule and Curve of Access Time to Network Games

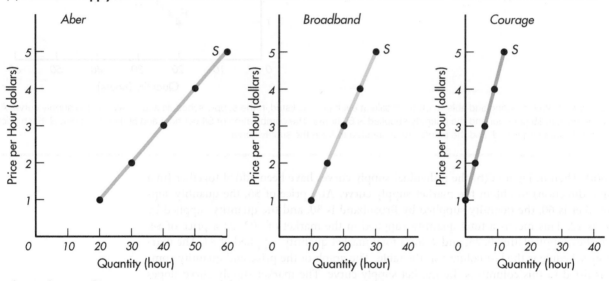

Price per Hour	Quantities Supplied per Year by						Market Quantity Supplied
	Aber		Broadband		Courage		
$5	60	+	30	+	12	=	102
$4	50		25		9		84
$3	40		20		6		66
$2	30		15		3		48
$1	20		10		0		30

(a) Individual Supply Curves

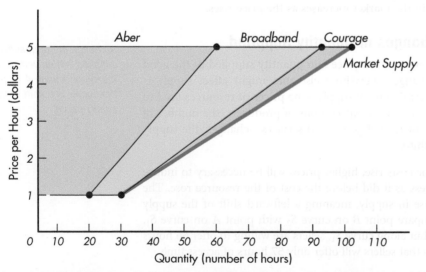

(b) Market Supply Curve

The market supply is derived by summing the quantities that each supplier is willing and able to offer for sale at each price. In this example, there are three producers: The supply schedules of each are listed in the table and plotted as the individual supply curves shown in Figure 6(a). By adding the quantities supplied at each price, we obtain the market supply curve shown in Figure 6(b). For instance, at a price of $5, Aber offers 60 units, Broadband 30 units, and Courage 12 units, for a market supply quantity of 102. The market supply curve reflects the quantities that each producer is able and willing to supply at each price.

FIGURE 7 A Shift of the Supply Curve

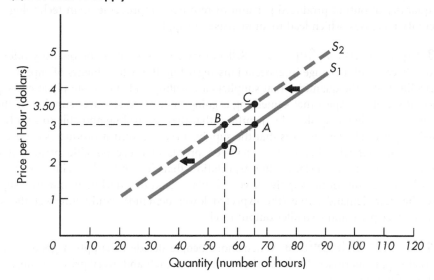

(a) Decrease in Supply

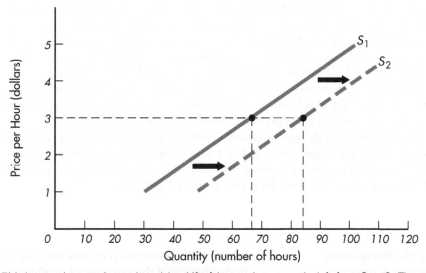

(b) Increase in Supply

Figure 7(a) shows a decrease in supply and the shift of the supply curve to the left, from S_1 to S_2. The decrease is caused by a change in one of the determinants of access time to network games—an increase in the price of labor. Because of the increased price of labor, producers are willing and able to offer fewer access hours at each price than they were before the cost of labor rose. Supply curve S_2 shows that at a price of $3 per hour of access, suppliers will offer 57 hours. That is 9 hours less than the 66 hours at $3 per access hour indicated by supply curve S_1. Conversely, to offer a given quantity, producers must receive a higher price per access hour than they previously were getting: $3.50 per hour for 66 hours (on supply curve S_2) instead of $3 per hour (on supply curve S_1). Figure 7(b) shows an increase in supply. A technological improvement or an increase in productivity causes the supply curve to shift to the right, from S_1 to S_2. At each price, a higher quantity is offered for sale. At a price of $3, 66 hours were offered, but with the shift of the supply curve, the quantity of hours for sale at $3 apiece increases to 84. Conversely, producers can reduce prices for a given quantity—for example, charging $2 per hour for 66 hours.

The move from horse-drawn plows to tractors or from mainframe computers to personal computers meant that each worker was able to produce more. The increase in output produced by each unit of a resource is called a *productivity increase*. **Productivity** is defined as the quantity of output produced per unit of resource. Improvements in technology cause productivity increases, which lead to an increase in supply.

productivity
The quantity of output produced per unit of resource.

3-4d-3 Expectations of Suppliers

Sellers may choose to alter the quantity offered for sale today because of a change in expectations regarding the determinants of supply. A supply curve illustrates the quantities that suppliers are willing and able to supply at every possible price. If suppliers expect that something is going to occur to resource supplies or the cost of resources, then they may alter the quantities that they are willing and able to supply at every possible price. The key point is that the supply curve will shift if producers expect something to occur that will alter their anticipated profits at every possible price, not just a change in one price. For instance, the expectation that demand will decline in the future does not lead to a shift of the supply curve; it leads instead to a decline in quantity supplied, because the new demand curve (the expected lower demand) would intersect the supply curve at a lower price and a smaller output level.

3-4d-4 Number of Suppliers

When more people decide to supply a good or service, the market supply increases. More is offered for sale at each and every price, causing a rightward shift of the supply curve.

3-4d-5 Prices of Related Goods or Services

The opportunity cost of producing and selling any good or service is the forgone opportunity to produce any other good or service. If the price of an alternative good changes, then the opportunity cost of producing a particular good changes. This could cause the supply curve to change. For instance, if McDonald's can offer hamburgers or salads with equal ease, an increase in the price of salads could lead the manager to offer more salads and fewer hamburgers. The supply curve of salads would shift to the right, and the supply curve of hamburgers would shift to the left.

A *change in supply* occurs when the quantity supplied at each and every price changes or there is a shift in the supply curve—like the shift from S_1 to S_2 in Figure 8(a). A change in one of the determinants of supply brings about a change in supply.

When only the price changes, a greater or smaller quantity is supplied. This is shown as a movement along the supply curve, not as a shift of the curve. A change in price is said to cause a *change in the quantity supplied*. An increase in quantity supplied is shown in the move from point *A* to point *B* on the supply curve of Figure 8(b).

NOW YOU TRY IT

List four things that would cause the supply curve to shift out.

Is this a change in quantity supplied or a change in supply?

RECAP

1. According to the law of supply, the quantity supplied of any good or service is directly related to the price of the good or service during a specific period of time, everything else held constant.
2. Market supply is found by adding together the quantities supplied at each price by every producer in the market.
3. Supply changes if the prices of relevant resources change, if technology or productivity changes, if producers' expectations change, if the number of producers changes, or if the prices of related goods and services change.
4. Changes in supply are reflected in shifts of the supply curve. Changes in the quantity supplied are reflected in movements along the supply curve.

FIGURE 8 A Change in Supply and a Change in the Quantity Supplied

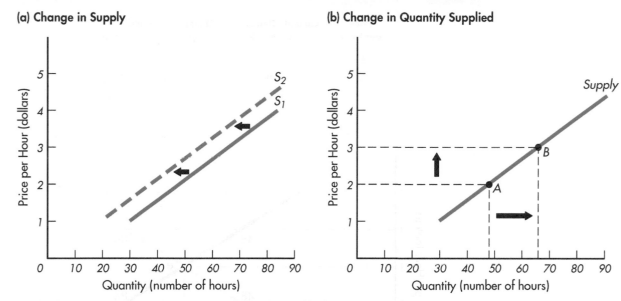

(a) Change in Supply

(b) Change in Quantity Supplied

In Figure 8(a), the quantities that producers are willing and able to offer for sale at every price decrease, causing a leftward shift of the supply curve from S_1 to S_2. In Figure 8(b), the quantities that producers are willing and able to offer for sale increase, because of an increase in the price of the good, causing a movement along the supply curve from point A to point B.

3-5 Equilibrium: Putting Demand and Supply Together

The demand curve shows the quantity of a good or service that buyers are willing and able to purchase at each price. The supply curve shows the quantity that producers are willing and able to offer for sale at each price. Only where the two curves intersect is the quantity supplied equal to the quantity demanded. This intersection is the point of **equilibrium**. Equilibrium is a pedagogical device; that is, it is used for teaching or educational purposes. In reality, demand and supply are changing all the time, so the market process is always working; there is not really a static, constant equilibrium price and quantity. Nevertheless, because prices and quantities are always moving toward an equilibrium, the concept is well worth considering. And in our analyses and discussions, we will focus on an equilibrium point in order to illustrate the effects of some change in either demand or supply.

3-5a Determination of Equilibrium

Figure 9 brings together the market demand and market supply curves for access hours to network games. The supply and demand schedules are listed in the table, and the curves are plotted in the graph in Figure 9. Notice that the curves intersect at only one point, labeled e, a price of $3 and a quantity of 66. The intersection point is the equilibrium price, the only price at which the quantity demanded and quantity supplied are the same. You can see that at any other price, the quantity demanded and quantity supplied are not the same. This is called **disequilibrium**.

Whenever the price is greater than the equilibrium price, a **surplus** arises. For example, at $4, the quantity of hours of access demanded is 48, and the quantity supplied is 84. Thus, at $4 per hour, there is a surplus of 36 hours—that is, 36 hours supplied are not purchased. Conversely, whenever the price is below the equilibrium price, the quantity demanded is

4. How is price determined by demand and supply?

equilibrium
The price and quantity at which quantity demanded and quantity supplied are equal.

disequilibrium
Prices at which quantity demanded and quantity supplied are not equal at a particular price.

surplus
A quantity supplied that is larger than the quantity demanded at a given price; it occurs whenever the price is greater than the equilibrium price.

FIGURE 9 Equilibrium

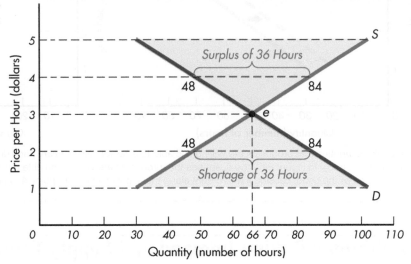

Price per Hour	Quantity Demanded per Week	Quantity Supplied per Week	Status
$5	30	102	Surplus of 72
$4	48	84	Surplus of 36
$3	66	66	Equilibrium
$2	84	48	Shortage of 36
$1	102	30	Shortage of 72

Equilibrium is established at the point where the quantity that suppliers are willing and able to offer for sale is the same as the quantity that buyers are willing and able to purchase. Here, equilibrium occurs at the price of $3 per hour and a quantity of 66 hours per week. It is shown as point *e*, at the intersection of the demand and supply curves. At prices above $3, the quantity supplied is greater than the quantity demanded, and the result is a surplus. At prices below $3, the quantity supplied is less than the quantity demanded, and the result is a shortage. The area shaded tan shows all prices at which there is a surplus—where quantity supplied is greater than the quantity demanded. The amount of the surplus is measured in a horizontal direction at each price. The area shaded blue represents all prices at which a shortage exists—where the quantity demanded is greater than the quantity supplied. The amount of the shortage is measured in a horizontal direction at each price.

shortage
A quantity supplied that is smaller than the quantity demanded at a given price; it occurs whenever the price is less than the equilibrium price.

Note that a shortage is not the same thing as scarcity.

greater than the quantity supplied, and there is a **shortage**. For instance, if the price is $2 per hour of access, consumers will want and be able to pay for more hours of access than are available. As shown in the table in Figure 9, the quantity demanded at a price of $2 is 84, but the quantity supplied is only 48. There is a shortage of 36 hours of access at the price of $2.

Neither a surplus nor a shortage will exist for long if the price of the product is free to change. Suppliers who are stuck with hours of access not being purchased will lower the price and reduce the quantities they are offering for sale in order to eliminate a surplus. Conversely, suppliers who cannot supply enough hours to meet demand and who have consumers on hold or losing connection will raise the price to eliminate a shortage. Surpluses lead to decreases in the price and the quantity supplied and increases in the quantity demanded. Shortages lead to increases in the price and the quantity supplied and decreases in the quantity demanded.

A shortage exists only when the quantity that people are willing and able to purchase at a particular price is more than the quantity supplied *at that price*. Scarcity occurs when more is wanted at a zero price than is available.

3-5b Changes in the Equilibrium Price: Demand Shifts

Equilibrium is the combination of price and quantity at which the quantities demanded and supplied are the same. Once an equilibrium is achieved, there is no incentive for suppliers or consumers to move away from it. An equilibrium price changes only when demand and/or supply changes—that is, when the determinants of demand or the determinants of supply change.

Let us consider a change in demand and what it means for the equilibrium price. Suppose that experiments on rats show that playing network games causes brain damage. As a result, a large segment of the human population decides not to purchase access time to the games. Suppliers experience a decrease in the number of customers willing and able to pay for access, as shown in Figure 10 by a leftward shift of the demand curve, from curve D_1 to curve D_2.

Once the demand curve has shifted, the original equilibrium price of $3 per hour of access per week at point e_1 is no longer equilibrium. At a price of $3, the quantity supplied is still 66, but the quantity demanded has declined to 48 (look at the demand curve D_2 at a price of $3). There is, therefore, a surplus of 18 hours of access time per week at the price of $3.

With a surplus comes downward pressure on the price. This downward pressure occurs because producers acquire fewer hours of access for purchase and reduce the price in an attempt to sell those hours not being used. Suppliers continue reducing the price and the quantity available until consumers purchase all the hours that the sellers have available, or until a new equilibrium is established. That new equilibrium occurs at point e_2 with a price of $2.50 and a quantity of 57.

The decrease in demand is represented by the leftward shift of the demand curve. A decrease in demand results in a lower equilibrium price and a lower equilibrium quantity as

5. *What causes price to change?*

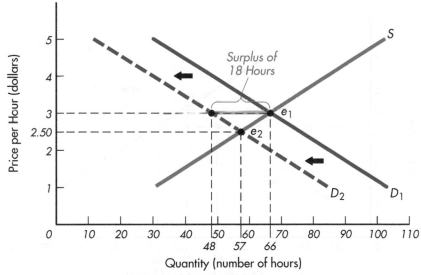

FIGURE 10 **The Effects of a Shift of the Demand Curve**

The initial equilibrium price ($3 per hour of access time) and quantity (66 hours of access time) are established at point e_1, where the initial demand and supply curves intersect. A change in the tastes for access hours to the network games causes demand to decrease, and the demand curve shifts to the left. At $3 per hour of access, the initial quantity supplied, 66 hours, is now greater than the quantity demanded, 48 hours. The surplus of 18 hours causes suppliers to reduce the amount of hours of access offered and to lower the price. The market reaches a new equilibrium, at point e_2, $2.50 per hour and 57 hours per week.

long as there is no change in supply. Conversely, an increase in demand would be represented as a rightward shift of the demand curve and would result in a higher equilibrium price and a higher equilibrium quantity as long as there is no change in supply.

3-5c Changes in the Equilibrium Price: Supply Shifts

The equilibrium price and quantity may be altered by a change in supply as well. If the price of relevant resources, technology and productivity, the expectations of suppliers, the number of suppliers, or the prices of related products change, supply changes.

Let us consider an example. Suppose a tax is imposed on all Internet access and that this tax increases the cost for the network game suppliers to provide access time. This is represented by a leftward shift of the supply curve in Figure 11.

The leftward shift of the supply curve, from curve S_1 to curve S_2, leads to a new equilibrium price and quantity. At the original equilibrium price of $3 at point e_1, 66 hours of access are supplied. After the shift in the supply curve, 48 hours are supplied at a price of $3 per hour, and there is a shortage of 18 hours per week. The shortage puts upward pressure on price. As the price rises, consumers decrease the quantities that they are willing and able to purchase, and suppliers increase the quantities that they are willing and able to supply. Eventually, a new equilibrium price and quantity is established at $3.50 and 57 hours of access each week at point e_2.

The decrease in supply is represented by the leftward shift of the supply curve. A decrease in supply with no change in demand results in a higher price and a lower quantity. Conversely, an increase in supply would be represented as a rightward shift of the supply curve. An increase in supply with no change in demand would result in a lower price and a higher quantity.

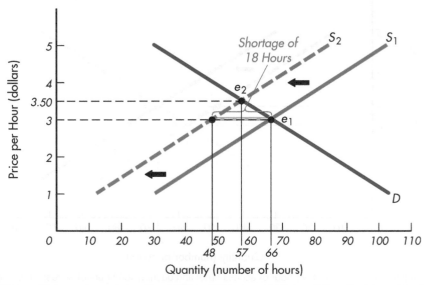

FIGURE 11   The Effects of a Shift of the Supply Curve

The initial equilibrium price and quantity are $3 and 66 hours, at point e_1. When the Internet tax is imposed, suppliers' costs have risen, and so they are willing and able to offer fewer hours for sale at each price. The result is a leftward (upward) shift of the supply curve, from S_1 to S_2. At the old price of $3, the quantity demanded is still 66, but the quantity supplied falls to 48. The shortage is 18 hours of access time. The shortage leads to a new equilibrium, e_2, the intersection between curves S_2 and D, which is $3.50 per hour of access time and 57 hours of access time.

1. Equilibrium occurs when the quantity demanded and the quantity supplied are equal: It is the price–quantity combination where the demand and supply curves intersect.

2. A price that is above the equilibrium price creates a surplus. Producers are willing and able to offer more for sale than buyers are willing and able to purchase.

3. A price that is below the equilibrium price leads to a shortage, because buyers are willing and able to purchase more than producers are willing and able to offer for sale.

4. When demand changes, price and quantity change in the same direction—both rise as demand increases, and both fall as demand decreases.

5. When supply changes, price and quantity change, but not in the same direction. When supply increases, price falls and quantity rises. When supply decreases, price rises and quantity falls.

6. When both demand and supply change, the direction of the change in price and quantity depends on the relative sizes of the changes of demand and supply.

SUMMARY

1. In a market system, who decides what goods and services are produced?

- The consumer decides what is produced. If a business does not provide what consumers want, the business will not remain in business. §3-1

- While a firm or inventer may come up with something new and innovative, if the consumer is not willing and able to buy it, the good or service will disappear. §3-1

2. What is demand?

- Demand is the quantities that buyers are willing and able to buy at alternative prices. §3-3

- The quantity demanded is a specific amount at one price. §3-3

- The law of demand states that as the price of a well-defined commodity rises (falls), the quantity demanded during a given period of time will fall (rise), everything else held constant. §3-3a

- Demand will change when one of the determinants of demand changes, that is, when income, tastes, prices of related goods and services, expectations, or number of buyers changes. A demand change is illustrated as a shift of the demand curve. §3-3e

3. What is supply?

- Supply is the quantities that sellers will offer for sale at alternative prices. §3-4a

- The quantity supplied is the amount that sellers offer for sale at one price. §3-4a

- The law of supply states that as the price of a well-defined commodity rises (falls), the quantity supplied during a given period of time will rise (fall), everything else held constant. §3-4a

- Supply changes when one of the determinants of supply changes, that is, when prices of resources, technology and productivity, expectations of producers, the number of producers, or the prices of related goods or services change. A supply change is illustrated as a shift of the supply curve. §3-4d

4. How is price determined by demand and supply?

- Together, demand and supply determine the equilibrium price and quantity. §3-5

5. What causes price to change?

- A price that is above equilibrium creates a surplus, which leads to a lower price. A price that is below equilibrium creates a shortage, which leads to a higher price. §3-5a

- A change in demand or a change in supply (a shift of either curve) will cause the equilibrium price and quantity to change. §3-5b, 3-5c

- Markets are not always in equilibrium, but when they are not, surpluses or shortages arise and force the price to move them toward equilibrium. §3-5c

KEY TERMS

barter, 42
complementary goods, 49
consumer sovereignty, 39
demand, 43
demand curve, 45
demand schedule, 44
determinants of demand, 43
determinants of supply, 50
disequilibrium, 55

double coincidence of wants, 42
equilibrium, 55
inferior goods, 47
law of demand, 42
law of supply, 50
market, 36
normal goods, 47
productivity, 54
quantity demanded, 43

quantity supplied, 50
shortage, 56
substitute goods, 49
supply, 50
supply curve, 50
supply schedule, 50
surplus, 55

EXERCISES

1. Illustrate each of the following events using a demand and supply diagram for bananas.
   a. Reports surface that imported bananas are infected with a deadly virus.
   b. Consumers' incomes drop.
   c. The price of bananas rises.
   d. The price of oranges falls.
   e. Consumers expect the price of bananas to decrease in the future.
2. Answer true or false, and if the statement is false, change it to make it true. Illustrate your answers on a demand and supply graph.
   a. An increase in demand is represented by a movement up the demand curve.
   b. An increase in supply is represented by a movement up the supply curve.
   c. An increase in demand without any changes in supply will cause the price to rise.
   d. An increase in supply without any changes in demand will cause the price to rise.
3. Using the following schedule, define the equilibrium price and quantity. Describe the situation at a price of $10. What will occur? Describe the situation at a price of $2. What will occur?

Price	Quantity Demanded	Quantity Supplied
$ 1	500	100
$ 2	400	120
$ 3	350	150
$ 4	320	200
$ 5	300	300

Price	Quantity Demanded	Quantity Supplied
$ 6	275	410
$ 7	260	500
$ 8	230	650
$ 9	200	800
$10	150	975

4. Suppose the government imposed a minimum price of $7 in the schedule of exercise 3. What would occur? Illustrate.
5. A common feature of skiing is waiting in lift lines. Does the existence of lift lines mean that the price is not working to allocate the scarce resource? If so, what should be done about it?
6. Why are barter systems less common than the use of currency?
7. A severe drought in California has resulted in a nearly 30 percent reduction in the quantity of citrus grown and produced in California. Explain what effect this event might have on the Florida citrus market.
8. The prices of the Ralph Lauren Polo line of clothing are considerably higher than those of comparable-quality lines. Yet this line sells more than a J. C. Penney brand line of clothing. Does this violate the law of demand?
9. In December, the price of Christmas trees rises and the quantity of trees sold rises. Is this a violation of the law of demand?
10. In recent years, the price of artificial Christmas trees has fallen while the quality has risen. What impact has this event had on the price of cut Christmas trees?
11. Many restaurants do not take reservations. You simply arrive and wait your turn. If you arrive at 7:30 in the

evening, you have at least an hour wait. Notwithstanding that fact, a few people arrive, speak quietly with the maitre d', hand him some money, and are promptly seated. At some restaurants that do take reservations, there is a month wait for a Saturday evening, three weeks for a Friday evening, two weeks for Tuesday through Thursday, and virtually no wait for Sunday or Monday evening. How do you explain these events using demand and supply?

12. Evaluate the following statement: "The demand for U.S. oranges has increased because the quantity of U.S. oranges demanded in Japan has risen."

13. In December 1992, the federal government began requiring that all packaged foods display information about fat content and other ingredients on food packages. The displays had to be verified by independent laboratories. The price of an evaluation of a food product could run as high as $20,000. What impact do you think this law had on the market for meat?

14. Draw a PPC. Which combination shown by the PPC will be produced? How is this combination determined? Does the combination that is produced depend on how goods and services are allocated?

15. The price of oil increased to more than $100 per barrel following the turmoil in the Mideast in 2011. Illustrate, using a market for oil, why the price rose.

ECONOMICALLY SPEAKING

CAPITALISM NEEDS TO BE RESTRAINED

Julie Delegal
Florida Times-Union (Jacksonville) March 18, 2013

Pollster Matt Towery's divisive drivel over the right's obsession with the deficit is belied by reputable economists.

Complaining about how poorly some bankers are doing in the aftermath of the worst economic downturn since the Great Depression makes no sense; neither does characterizing money appropriated by acts of governance as "artificial."

Bridges and roads are as real as any Wall Street banker, and our citizens are smart enough to make the distinction between stimulatory domestic spending and long-term structural deficit reform—both of which must be undertaken now.

Republican President Dwight D. Eisenhower's launch of the interstate highway system was certainly far from "artificial." He extended New Deal policies into his own postwar presidency and knew, unlike his present day GOP successors, that lowering taxes wasn't the cure for every economic ailment.

There is a balance to be struck between national economic health and unfettered business interests. Government has, can and should play an appropriate role in preserving our nation's economic health.

No Room for Partisans

Capitalism is a force on this earth that left untouched would work in a certain way—but that doesn't mean we shouldn't try to harness or change it for the betterment of human beings. For example, NASA harnesses science to escape its bounds of gravity to explore our universe.

We also use science to create medicines to heal the sick.

Capitalism can be used to serve the human race as a force for good. When it's working well, its tide lifts all boats.

But the force has a dark side: Unfettered capitalism brought us slavery, sweatshops, unsafe workplaces, child labor, discrimination, Joe Camel and the housing collapse.

These harms are overcome—in the United States at least—by another market force that some ideologues tend to forget: morality born of natural law.

Pure and unfettered capitalism has no place in the civilized world, and it causes unnecessary death, injury and human rights violations in the less-civilized world.

Avoid Reckless Action

Towery apparently wants citizens to believe that our tradition of consensus-born governance is merely some worthless, interloping barrier to human progress.

Perhaps he'd tell us that our infrastructure and educational needs aren't fundamental to equal opportunity or to the long-term health of our nation.

He'd apparently prefer reckless, across-the-board budget cuts over plans to stimulate our economy while simultaneously addressing our structural deficit.

That kind of thinking gives a pass to congressional gridlock and would ultimately yield a self-fulfilling prophecy of economic failure. The American people know better.

Citizens should call their Congress members and tell them to do their job: Pass a budget that addresses both our infrastructure needs and our long-term structural budget deficit, including common sense approaches to raising revenue.

The refusal to even look at the revenue column makes no economic sense and harms our national interests.

Julie Delegal is a Jacksonville writer.

COMMENTARY

Perhaps the most important statement in the article is: "There is a balance to be struck between national economic health and unfettered business interests. Government has, can and should play an appropriate role in preserving our nation's economic health." Why is there a trade-off between national economic health and unfettered business interests? As discussed in the chapter, unfettered free markets generate more economic health than any intervention in the free market would.

The article states that "Capitalism can be used to serve the human race as a force for good. When it's working well, its tide lifts all boats.

But the force has a dark side: Unfettered capitalism brought us slavery, sweatshops, unsafe workplaces, child labor, discrimination, Joe Camel and the housing collapse." The author has this so wrong. All these dark developments were the result of government interfering in free markets.

Private property rights (especially where people own their own bodies and minds) is required to have unfettered capitalism. The unfettered market system requires voluntary exchange. So, if there are sweatshops, unsafe workplaces, child labor, then people have chosen to work in these places and at these ages. They choose these because the next best alternative is not as good for them. "Joe Camel" is an advertisement for Camel cigarettes. People are given the choice–choose to smoke or not, choose to become addicted to smoking or not. Even if people generally did not know smoking cigarettes was addictive, they had the choice to engage in it or not. Once addicted, the choice to quit was made much more difficult, but it was still a choice that could be made.

Finally, discrimination cannot exist in a competitive free-market system. If firms hire only green people even though all people are equally productive, the green people become very expensive and everyone else very inexpensive. As a result, the profit motive will induce some firm to hire other than green people and sell the same product at a lower price. Pretty soon, no firm can afford to discriminate in favor of green people.

CHAPTER 4
The Aggregate Economy

Dimas Ardian/Bloomberg/Contributor/Getty Images

FUNDAMENTAL QUESTIONS

1. What is the private sector?

2. What is a household, and what is household income and spending?

3. What is a business firm, and what is business spending?

4. How does the international sector affect the economy?

5. What is the public sector? What is public sector spending?

6. How do the private and public sectors interact?

Preview

If there is a point on which most economists agree, it is that trade among nations makes the world better off. When a firm or an individual buys a good or a service produced more cheaply abroad, the firm or individual benefits. The good is cheaper, thereby leaving them with more income to spend elsewhere; the product may better fit their needs than similar domestic offerings; or the good may not be available domestically. The foreign producer also benefits by making more sales than it could selling solely in its own market and by earning foreign exchange (currency) that can be used by itself or others in the country to purchase foreign-made products.

top: © Carsten Reisinger/Shutterstock

microeconomics
The study of economics using the individual – individual consumer, individual firm.

macroeconomics
The study of economics using aggregate sectors – households, businesses, government, and the foreign sector.

1. What is the private sector?

private sector
Households, businesses, and the international sector.

public sector
The government.

NOW YOU TRY IT

What is the difference between the "private" sector and the "public" sector?

household
One or more persons who occupy a unit of housing.

consumption
Household spending.

2. What is a household, and what is household income and spending?

When we discuss international trade, it is not typically the individual buyer or seller we are talking about. It is, instead, the country as a whole or specific sectors of economies such as the household, business, or government sector. When economists examine individual markets, individual buyers, and individual sellers, they are engaging in **microeconomics**. When they look at how the aggregate sectors of the economy and other economies interact, they are involved with **macroeconomics**. In this chapter we introduce the aggregate sectors of an economy.

4-1 The Private Sector

Buyers and sellers of goods and services and resource owners are linked together in an economy and across economies. For every dollar someone spends, someone else receives a dollar as income. For instance, suppose you decide to buy a new Toyota, so you go to a Toyota dealer and exchange money for the car. The Toyota dealer has rented land and buildings and hired workers in order to make cars available to you and other members of the public. The employees earn incomes paid by the Toyota dealer and then use those incomes to buy food from the grocery store. This transaction generates revenue for the grocery store, which hires workers and pays them incomes that they then use to buy groceries and Toyotas.

Your Toyota may have been manufactured in Japan and then shipped to the United States before it was sold by the local Toyota dealer. Your purchase of the Toyota thus creates revenue for both the local dealer and the manufacturer, which pays autoworkers to assemble the cars. When you buy your Toyota, you pay a sales tax, which the government uses to support its expenditures on police, fire protection, national defense, the legal system, and other services. In short, many people in different areas of the economy are involved in what seems to be a single transaction.

The aggregate sectors involved are the household sector, the business sector, and the foreign sector. We classify the buyers and the resource owners into the household sector; the sellers or business firms are the business sector; households and firms in other countries, who may also be buyers and sellers of this country's goods and services, are the international sector. These three sectors—households, business firms, and the international firms and consumers—constitute the **private sector** of the economy. The private sector refers to any part of the economy that is not part of government. The **public sector** refers to the government, government spending and taxing, and government-sponsored and government-run entities. The relative sizes of private and public sectors vary from economy to economy. The market economies tend to have smaller public sectors relative to the total economy than do the more socialist or centrally planned economies.

4-1a Households

A **household** consists of one or more persons who occupy a unit of housing. The unit of housing may be a house, an apartment, or even a single room, as long as it constitutes separate living quarters. A household may consist of a single person, related family members, like a father, mother, and children, or it may comprise unrelated individuals, like three college students sharing an apartment. The person in whose name the house or apartment is owned or rented is called the householder.

Household spending is called **consumption**. Household spending (also called consumer spending) per year in the United States is shown in Figure 1, along with household income. The pattern is generally one of steady increase, but you can see that from the second quarter 2008 to the second quarter 2010, real household expenditures actually declined. (A quarter

FIGURE 1 Consumption or household spending and income

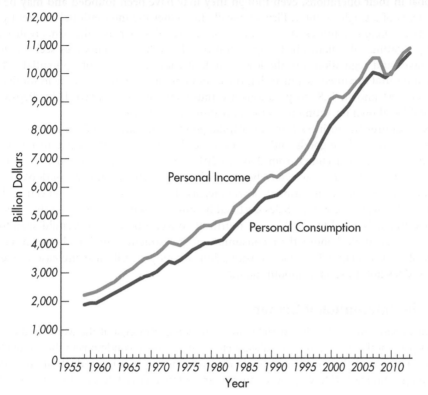

Household spending is the largest of the aggregate sectors in the economy. The primary determinant of the spending is income.

Source: *U.S. Department of Commerce, Bureau of Economic Analysis;* www.census.gov.

refers to three months.) This was a period of financial crisis and recession. As income declined, so did consumption.

Spending by the household sector is the largest component—constituting about 70 percent of total spending in the economy.

4-1b Business Firms

A **business firm** is a business organization controlled by a single management. The terms *company, enterprise,* and *business* are used interchangeably with *firm.*

Firms are organized as sole proprietorships, partnerships, or corporations. A **sole proprietorship** is a business owned by one person. This type of firm may be a one-person operation or a large enterprise with many employees. In either case, the owner receives all the profits and is responsible for all the debts incurred by the business.

A **partnership** is a business owned by two or more persons who share both the profits of the business and the responsibility for the firm's losses. The partners can be individuals, estates, or other businesses.

A **corporation** is a business whose identity in the eyes of the law is distinct from the identity of its owners. For instance, the owners are not responsible for the debts of the corporation. This is referred to as limited liability. The liabilities of the corporation are limited to the extent that an owner's own assets cannot be taken to pay the liabilities of the corporation. In fact, a corporation is an economic entity that, like a person, can own property and borrow money in its own name.

business firm
A business organization controlled by a single management.

sole proprietorship
A business owned by one person who receives all the profits and is responsible for all the debts incurred by the business.

partnership
A business with two or more owners who share the firm's profits and losses.

3. What is a business firm, and what is business spending?

corporation
A legal entity owned by shareholders whose liability for the firm's losses is limited to the value of the stock they own.

A firm may refer to a business at a single location or a worldwide business. Many firms are global in their operations, even though they may have been founded and may be owned by residents of a single country. Firms typically first enter the international market by selling products to foreign countries. As revenues from these sales increase, the firms realize advantages by locating subsidiaries in foreign countries. In addition, companies seek the location where taxes and regulations are the lowest and, of course, where profit potential is highest. A **multinational business** is a firm that owns and operates producing units in foreign countries. The best-known U.S. corporations are multinational firms. Ford, IBM, PepsiCo, and McDonald's all own operating units in many different countries.

Expenditures by business firms for capital goods—machines, tools, and buildings—that will be used to produce goods and services are called **investment**. Notice in Figure 2 that investment spending declined from 2007 to 2010; businesses had reduced expenditures on capital goods in 2007 through 2009 because sales had declined and the outlook for future sales was not very good. Investment slowly increased from 2009 to 2013, reflecting the slow growth of the overall economy. Sales declined because households were spending less.

Investment is equal to roughly one-fourth of consumption, or household spending, but fluctuates a great deal more than consumption. Investment spending between 1959 and 2013 is shown in Figure 2. Unlike consumption, which generally just increases, investment rises but does not do so in a smooth manner.

4-1c The International Sector

Economic conditions in the United States affect conditions throughout the world, and conditions in other parts of the world have a significant effect on economic conditions in the United States.

The nations of the world may be divided into two categories: industrial countries and developing countries. (Developing countries are often referred to as emerging markets or

multinational business
A firm that owns and operates producing units in foreign countries.

investment
Spending on capital goods to be used in producing goods and services.

NOW YOU TRY IT

Why do you think that investment fluctuates more than consumption?

4. *How does the international sector affect the economy?*

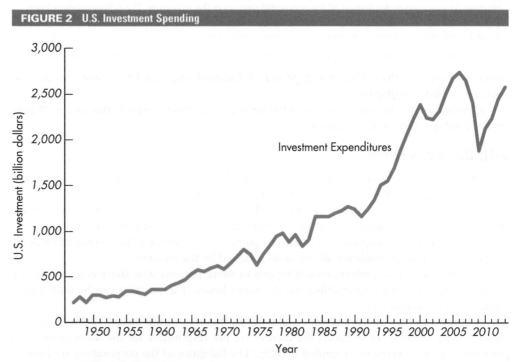

FIGURE 2   U.S. Investment Spending

Business expenditures on capital goods have been increasing erratically since 1959.
Source: *Economic Report of the President, 2010.*

LDCs, less-developed countries.) Developing countries greatly outnumber industrial countries (see Figure 3). The World Bank (an international organization that makes loans to developing countries) groups countries according to per capita income (income per person). Low-income economies are those with per capita incomes of less than $1,000. Middle-income economies have per capita annual incomes of $1,000–$10,000. High-income economies—oil exporters and industrial market economies—are distinguished from the middle-income economies and have per capita incomes of greater than $10,000. Some countries are not members of the World Bank and so are not categorized, and information about a few small countries is so limited that the World Bank is unable to classify them.

It is readily apparent from Figure 3 that low-income economies are heavily concentrated in Africa and Asia. As we discussed in the first chapter, an important question in economics is: Why are some countries rich and others poor? Why are poor countries concentrated in Africa and Asia with some in Latin America?

FIGURE 3 World Economic Development

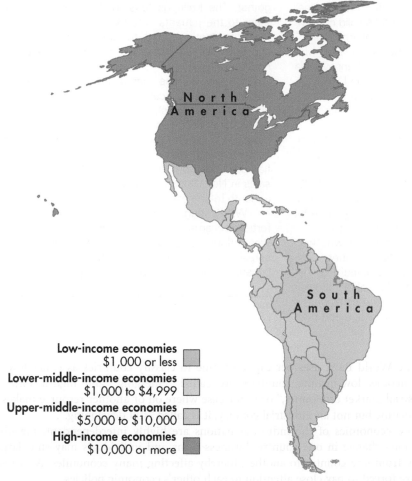

Low-income economies
$1,000 or less

Lower-middle-income economies
$1,000 to $4,999

Upper-middle-income economies
$5,000 to $10,000

High-income economies
$10,000 or more

The colors on the map identify low-income, middle-income, and high-income economies. Countries have been placed in each group on the basis of GNP per capita and, in some instances, other distinguishing economic characteristics.

Source: World Bank; http://nebula.worldbank.org/website/GNIwdi/viewer.htm.

ECONOMIC INSIGHT

The Successful Entrepreneur

Sometimes It's Better to Be Lucky Than Good

Entrepreneurs do not always develop an abstract idea into reality when starting a new firm. Sometimes people stumble onto a good thing by accident and then are clever enough and willing to take the necessary risk to turn their lucky find into a commercial success.

In 1875, a Philadelphia pharmacist on his honeymoon tasted tea made from an innkeeper's old family recipe. The tea, made from 16 wild roots and berries, was so delicious that the pharmacist asked the innkeeper's wife for the recipe. When he returned to his pharmacy, he created a solid concentrate of the drink that could be sold for home consumption.

The pharmacist was Charles Hires, a devout Quaker, who intended to sell "Hires Herb Tea" to hard-drinking Pennsylvania coal miners as a nonalcoholic alternative to beer and whiskey. A friend of Hires suggested that miners would not drink anything called "tea" and recommended that he call his drink "root beer."

The initial response to Hires Root Beer was so enthusiastic that Hires soon began nationwide distribution. The yellow box of root beer extract became a familiar sight in homes and drugstore fountains across the United States. By 1895, Hires, who started with a $3,000 loan, was operating a business valued at half a million dollars (a lot of money in 1895) and bottling ready-to-drink root beer across the country.

Hires, of course, is not the only entrepreneur who was clever enough to turn a lucky discovery into a business success. In 1894, in Battle Creek, Michigan, a sanitarium handyman named Will Kellogg was helping his older brother prepare wheat meal to serve to patients in the sanitarium's dining room. The two men would boil wheat dough and then run it through rollers to produce thin sheets of meal. One day they left a batch of the dough out overnight. The next day, when the dough was run through the rollers, it broke up into flakes instead of forming a sheet.

By letting the dough stand overnight, the Kelloggs had allowed moisture to be distributed evenly to each individual wheat berry. When the dough went through the rollers, the berries formed separate flakes instead of binding together. The Kelloggs toasted the wheat flakes and served them to the patients. They were an immediate success. In fact, the brothers had to start a mail-order flaked-cereal business because patients wanted flaked cereal for their households.

Kellogg saw the market potential of the discovery and started his own cereal company (his brother refused to join him in the business). He was a great promoter who used innovations like four-color magazine ads and free-sample promotions. In New York City, he offered a free box of corn flakes to every woman who winked at her grocer on a specified day. The promotion was considered risqué, but Kellogg's sales in New York increased from two railroad cars of cereal a month to one car a day.

Will Kellogg, a poorly paid sanitarium worker in his mid-forties, became a daring entrepreneur after his mistake with wheat flour led to the discovery of a way to produce flaked cereal. He became one of the richest men in America because of his entrepreneurial ability.

Source: From FUCINI. ENTREPRENEURS. 1985 Gale, a part of Cengage Learning, Inc.

The World Bank uses per capita income to classify countries as either low income or high income; low-income countries are called "emerging" and high-income are called "industrial market economies," or in the case where oil or another resource makes a country high income but not an industrial country, it is called "still developing.".

The economies of the industrial nations are highly interdependent, meaning that as conditions change in one country, business firms and individuals may shift large sums of money from one country to another, thereby affecting many economies. As a result, countries are forced to pay close attention to each other's economic policies.

The United States tends to buy primary products such as agricultural produce and minerals from the developing countries and manufactured products from the industrial nations. Products that a country buys from another country are called **imports**. Products that a country sells to another country are called **exports**. The United States tends to sell, or *export*, manufactured goods to all countries.

imports
Products that a country buys from other countries.

exports
Products that a country sells to other countries.

"The best and brightest are leaving." Statements like this are heard in many nations throughout the world. The best trained and most innovative people in many countries find their opportunities greater in the United States. As a result, they leave their countries to gain citizenship in the United States. But it is not easy for people to move from one country to another. The flow of goods and services among nations—international trade—occurs more readily than does the flow of workers.

The economic activity of the United States with the rest of the world includes U.S. spending on foreign goods and foreign spending on U.S. goods. Figure 4 shows how U.S. exports and imports are spread over different countries. Notice that the largest trading partners with the United States are Canada, Mexico, China, and Western Europe.

FIGURE 4 **Direction of U.S. Trade**

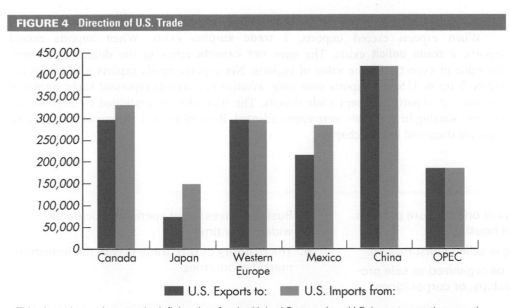

This chart shows that a trade deficit exists for the United States, since U.S. imports greatly exceed U.S. exports. The chart also shows that the largest trading partners with the U.S. are Western Europe, Japan, Canada, Mexico, and China.

Source: *Economic Report of the President, 2010*; www.census.gov/foreign-trade/Press-Release/current_press_release/exh14a.xls.

FIGURE 5   Net Exports

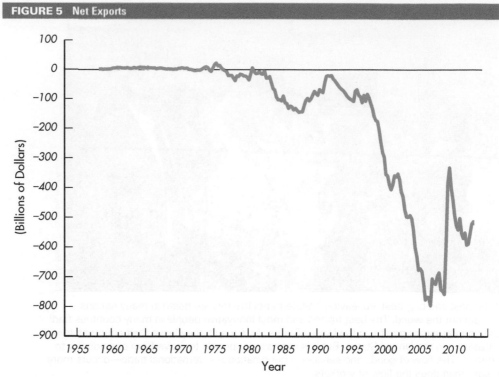

U.S. Exports are sales of U.S. goods and services to other countries. U.S. Imports are purchases by the United States of goods and services from other countries. Exports minus Imports is Net Exports. Negative net exports means that imports exceed exports or that the United States has a trade deficit.

Source: U.S. Department of Commerce: Bureau of Economic Analysis

trade surplus
The situation that exists when imports are less than exports.

trade deficit
The situation that exists when imports exceed exports.

net exports
The difference between the value of exports and the value of imports.

When exports exceed imports, a **trade surplus** exists. When imports exceed exports, a **trade deficit** exists. The term **net exports** refers to the difference between the value of exports and the value of imports: Net exports equals exports minus imports. Figure 5 traces U.S. net exports over time. Positive net exports represent trade surpluses; negative net exports represent trade deficits. The trade deficits (indicated by negative net exports) starting in the 1980s were unprecedented. Reasons for this pattern of international trade are discussed in later chapters.

RECAP

1. A household consists of one or more persons who occupy a unit of housing.
2. Household spending is called consumption.
3. Business firms may be organized as sole proprietorships, partnerships, or corporations.
4. Business investment spending fluctuates widely over time.
5. The majority of U.S. trade is with the industrial market economies.

4-2 The Public Sector

When we refer to the public sector, it is government that we are talking about. Government in the United States consists of federal, state, and local government. In the United States, government's influence is extensive. From conception to death, individuals are affected by the activities of the government. Many mothers receive prenatal care through government programs. We are born in hospitals that are subsidized or run by the government. We are delivered by doctors who received training in subsidized colleges. Our births are recorded on certificates filed with the government. Ninety percent of students attend public schools as opposed to private schools. Many people live in housing that is directly subsidized by the government or have mortgages that are insured by the government. Most people, at one time or another, put savings into accounts that are insured by the government. Virtually all of us, at some time in our lives, receive money from the government—from student loan programs, unemployment compensation, disability insurance, food stamps, social security, or Medicare. We drive on government roads, recreate on government lands, and fish in government waters.

5. What is the public sector? What is public sector spending?

4-2a Growth of Government

The United States was founded as a *republic*, meaning that government is divided between the federal level and state and local levels. Local government includes county, regional, and municipal units. Each level affects us through its taxing and spending decisions and its laws regulating behavior. In 1900, the federal government was a small player. States had the power—called states' rights—because the country's founders believed that government closest to the people

The United States Capitol is where the Senate and House of Representatives meet. The Capitol represents the public sector—government. Thomas Jefferson insisted the legislative building be called the "Capitol" rather than "Congress House." He thought "Capitol" represented the shining city on a hill. The word *capitol* comes from Latin, meaning city on a hill.

could be constrained better than a federal government. But soon after the country's founding, people began to demand more federal government and less states' rights.

From 1789 until 1930 government grew, but compared to what has occurred since 1930, that growth was minimal. The number of people employed by the local, state, and federal governments combined grew from 3 million in 1930 to more than 18 million today; there are now more people employed in government than in manufacturing. Annual expenditures by the federal government rose from $3 billion in 1930 to $4.5 trillion today. In 1929, government spending constituted less than 2.5 percent of total spending in the economy. Today it is around 35 percent, as shown in Figure 6.

4-2b Government Spending

transfer payments
Income transferred by the government from a citizen who is earning income to another citizen.

Federal, state, and local government spending for goods and services as a percent of the total spending in the economy is shown in Figure 6. Total government spending is larger than investment spending but smaller than consumption. In addition to purchasing goods and services, government also takes money from some taxpayers and gives it to others. This is called a **transfer payment**. In 2013, total expenditures of federal, state, and local government for goods and services were about $6.5 trillion. In this same year, transfer payments made by the federal government were about $2.5 trillion. Federal government transfer payments are shown in Figure 7.

The magnitude of federal government spending relative to federal government revenue from taxes has become an important issue in recent years. The federal budget (revenue less

---

FIGURE 6   Government Spending

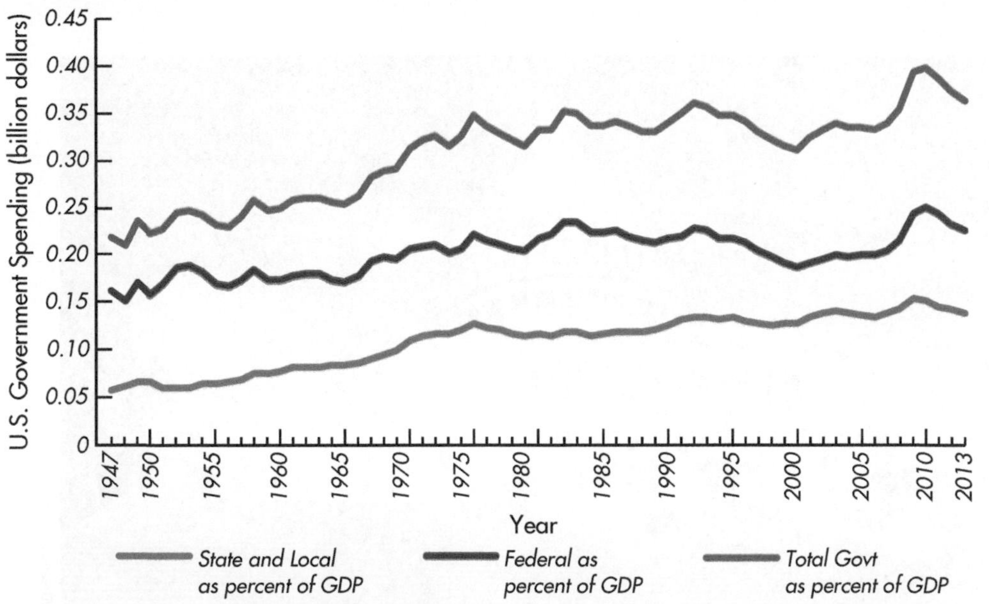

Total Government Spending—federal, state, and local divided by gross domestic product (GDP)—the total spending of all sectors in the economy as a percent of total GDP.
In 1929, government spending constituted less than 2.5 percent of total spending in the economy. Today it is around 37 percent.

Source: U.S. Department of Commerce: Bureau of Economic Analysis retrieved from Federal Reserve Bank of St. Louis. FRED data retrieval.

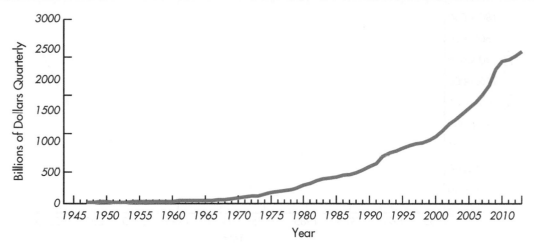

FIGURE 7 Federal Government and Total Government Transfer Payments

Transfer payments are payments made by government that do not purchase anything. They are funds transferred from one group to another group.

Source: U.S. Department of Commerce: Bureau of Economic Analysis

spending) was roughly balanced until the early 1970s. The budget is a measure of spending and revenue. A balanced budget occurs when federal spending is approximately equal to federal revenue. This was the case through the 1950s and 1960s.

If federal government spending is less than tax revenue, a **budget surplus** exists. The federal government deficit and surplus are shown in Figure 8. By the early 1980s, federal government spending was much larger than revenue, so a large **budget deficit** existed. The federal budget deficit grew very rapidly to about $290 billion by the early 1990s before

budget surplus
The excess that results when government spending is less than tax revenue.

budget deficit
The shortage that results when government spending is greater than tax revenue.

FIGURE 8 Federal Government Surplus or Deficit.

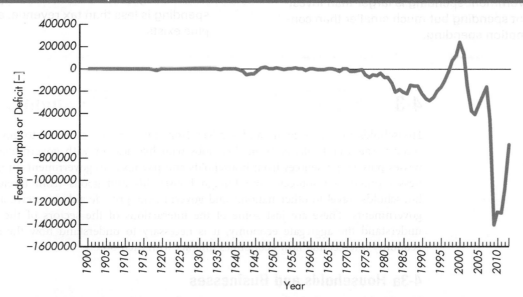

The difference between federal government expenditures and tax revenues is the surplus or deficit. Since 1930 the government has run a deficit in all but 3 years.

Source: Data are from the Economic Report of the President, 2010.

FIGURE 9 Total Government Debt

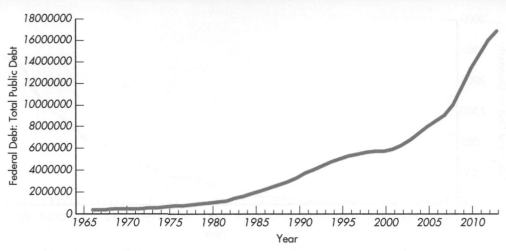

When the federal government borrows in order to finance its deficits, it creates public debt. The total public debt has risen to about $17 trillion today.

beginning to drop and turning to surplus by 1998. After four years of surpluses, a deficit was again realized in 2002, and the deficit has grown since then. It exploded during the period 2008 to 2013. Since the deficit rose, so too did government debt; when the federal government spends more than it takes in, it must borrow. Debt is the accumulation of deficits; each deficit adds to the debt. The total debt of the U.S. federal government exceeds $17 trillion. The federal government debt is shown in Figure 9.

RECAP

1. The public sector refers to government.
2. Government spending is larger than investment spending but much smaller than consumption spending.

3. When government spending exceeds tax revenue, a budget deficit exists. When government spending is less than tax revenue, a budget surplus exists.

4-3 Interaction Among Sectors and Economies

Households purchase goods and services from businesses, pay taxes to government, and receive wages and salaries from their jobs with business or with government, while businesses purchase resources from households and pay taxes to government. In addition, businesses purchase resources from foreign households and goods from foreign businesses, households travel to other nations, and governments provide aid or receive aid from other governments. These are just some of the interactions of the sectors of the economy. To understand the aggregate economy, it is necessary to understand how the sectors of the economy interact and how economies interact with each other.

4-3a Households and Businesses

Households own all the basic resources, or factors of production, in the economy. Household members own land and provide labor, and they are the stockholders, proprietors, and partners who own business firms. Businesses, governments, and foreign businesses employ the services of resources in order to produce goods and services. Households receive wages, salaries, and benefits for their services. This is their income.

What do households do with the income they receive? They spend most of it, they pay taxes, and they often save some. When households save, they do so in different ways. The most common way is to deposit their savings in banks and credit unions. The banks and credit unions are called **financial intermediaries** because they lie between the household saver and the borrower. Households may also put money into pension funds, through what are called 401(k) funds or IRAs. These funds may be stocks and bonds as well as cash. Financial intermediaries use the deposits from savers to make loans to borrowers. Households borrow money to purchase homes, cars, and other items. Businesses borrow money to purchase machines, equipment, and buildings, and to hire labor. So the money that is saved by households reenters the economy in the form of business and household spending.

financial intermediaries
Institutions that accept deposits from savers and make loans to borrowers.

4-3b Government

The government sector buys goods and services from businesses and hires labor from households. It pays for these things with money it collects in taxes and with loans it undertakes—its debt. The government uses the resource services and final goods and services to carry out its many activities—everything from national defense to subsidies for solar companies and welfare and unemployment compensation.

6. How do the private and public sectors interact?

4-3c The International Sector

Foreign countries also affect and are affected by the household, business, and government sectors of the home country. We typically buy a foreign-made product from a local business firm rather than directly from the foreign producer. For instance, glancing at products in retail stores, we can see "Made in China" or "Made in Mexico" on many of the products. Yet you purchase these from U.S. firms using dollars. The business firm purchases the items from the foreign countries. Even in some "Made in America" products you are purchasing foreign products and services. For instance, when you purchase an iPod, you are purchasing a product that has parts from Japan, the Philippines, Taiwan, and China, as well as the United States. This makes it difficult to accurately measure the relative values of goods and services purchased and sold from one country to another. About 30 to 40 percent of the iPod's price is actually counted as an import (purchase of a Chinese good by the United States) from China to the United States. Nevertheless, we attempt to provide some measures of the extent of trade among nations with exports (sales) and imports (purchases).

As mentioned previously, net exports is the difference between exports of goods from one country and imports of goods by that country. Net exports of the home country may be either positive (a trade surplus) or negative (a trade deficit). When net exports are positive, there is a net flow of goods from the firms of the home country to foreign countries and a net flow of money from foreign countries to the firms of the home country. When net exports are negative, the opposite occurs. A trade deficit involves net flows of goods from foreign countries to the firms of the home country and net money flows from the domestic firms to the foreign countries. As an example, the United States has been a negative net exporter with China, so Chinese goods have flowed to the United States while U.S. dollars have flowed to China. If exports and imports are equal, net exports are zero because the value of exports is offset by the value of imports.

NOW YOU TRY IT

Total spending in the economy consists of what? Total income in the economy consists of what?

4-3d Macroeconomics

What goes on in one sector affects what occurs in other sectors, and what goes on in one economy often affects what goes on in other economies. This is essentially what we study in macroeconomics. For instance, when the government increases taxes on the business sector, the business sector might reduce employment and purchases of resources from the private sector. This lowers the income of the private sector and thus reduces their spending and saving. When the government increases its deficit (increases spending more than revenue), it might have to finance that debt by selling bonds to the financial intermediaries. This could reduce the amount of money the intermediaries have to lend to households and businesses. Foreigners and foreign governments might purchase the bonds the government sells, and this could affect spending and income in the foreign countries.

Should the home country place a tax on foreign goods and services, households and businesses would reduce spending on foreign goods and increase spending on domestic goods, or those not subject to the higher tax. This could lead to retaliation by other countries, thereby reducing the home country's sales to foreign businesses and households, or it could lead to higher prices domestically. In macroeconomics we will examine these and many other issues.

RECAP

1. Domestic households, firms, and government interact among themselves and with households, firms, and government in other countries.

2. Households get government services and pay taxes; they provide resource services and receive income.

3. Firms sell goods and services to government and receive income.

4. Firms buy resources and receive goods from firms in other countries.

SUMMARY

1. What is the private sector?

- The private sector refers to the household, business, and nongovernmental international sectors. §4-1
- The public sector refers to government. §4-1

2. What is a household, and what is household income and spending?

- A household consists of one or more persons who occupy a unit of housing. §4-1a
- Household spending is called consumption and is the largest component of spending in the economy. §4-1a

3. What is a business firm, and what is business spending?

- A business firm is a business organization controlled by a single management. §4-1b
- Businesses may be organized as sole proprietorships, partnerships, or corporations. §4-1b
- Business investment spending—the expenditure by business firms for capital goods—fluctuates a great deal over time. §4-1b

4. How does the international sector affect the economy?

- The international trade of the United States occurs predominantly with the other industrial economies. §4-1c
- Exports are products sold to the rest of the world. Imports are products bought from the rest of the world. §4-1c
- Exports minus imports equal net exports. Positive net exports mean that exports are greater than imports and that a trade surplus exists. Negative net exports mean that imports exceed exports and that a trade deficit exists. §4-1c

5. What is the public sector? What is public sector spending?

- The public sector refers to all levels of government—federal, state, and local. §4-2
- When a government spends more than it receives in taxes, the government runs a deficit; when it receives more than it spends, it runs a surplus. §4-2a

6. How do the private and public sectors interact?

- Government interacts with both households and firms. Households get government services and pay taxes; they provide resource services and receive income. Firms sell goods and services to government and receive income. §4-3a

KEY TERMS

budget deficit, 75
budget surplus, 75
business firm, 67
consumption, 66
corporation, 67
exports, 70
financial intermediaries, 77

household, 66
imports, 70
investment, 68
macroeconomics, 66
microeconomics, 66
multinational business, 68
net exports, 72

partnership, 67
private sector, 66
public sector, 66
sole proprietorship, 67
trade deficit, 72
trade surplus, 72
transfer payments, 74

EXERCISES

1. Is a family a household? Is a household a family?
2. Which sector (households, business, or international) spends the most? Which sector spends the least? Which sector has the most volatility of spending?
3. What does it mean if net exports are negative?
4. People sometimes argue that imports should be limited by government policy. Suppose a government quota on the quantity of sugar imported to the United States occurs. What is likely to happen to the price of sugar in the United States and in the rest of the world?
5. Suppose there are three countries in the world. Country A exports $11 million worth of goods to Country B and $5 million worth of goods to Country C; Country B exports $3 million worth of goods to Country A and $6 million worth of goods to Country C; and Country C exports $4 million worth of goods to Country A and $1 million worth of goods to Country B.
   a. What are the net exports of countries A, B, and C?
   b. Which country is running a trade deficit? A trade surplus?

6. List the four sectors of the economy along with the type of spending associated with each sector. Order the types of spending in terms of magnitude, and give an example of each kind of spending.
7. Using the interconnection between sectors of the economy, explain the effects of imposing an increase in taxes on the household sector.
8. Can a household spend more than it earns? How? Can the government spend more than it receives in tax revenues? How? What is the difference between households running deficits and governments running deficits, or are there any? What is the ratio of government spending to GDP? What is the ratio of payments on the debt (interest payments) to GDP? (You may find this at **www.gpoaccess.gov/eop/tables11.html**.)
9. See if you can find the ratio of debt to GDP for several developed nations. Who has the highest ratio?

ECONOMICALLY SPEAKING

2014 ECONOMIC REPORT OF THE PRESIDENT, PP. 29–30, CHAPTER 1

As part of the budget deal, Congress also agreed on discretionary funding levels for the remainder of FY 2014 and all of FY 2015, offering a way to avoid another counterproductive shutdown. Earlier this year, Congress passed appropriations bills for FY 2014 consistent with these spending levels and also extended the debt limit into 2015. As fiscal headwinds ease at the Federal level, State and local governments are also showing encouraging signs. After shedding more than 700,000 jobs from 2009 to 2012, State and local governments added 32,000 jobs in 2013.

p. 56, Chapter 2: 2014 EROP

Consumer Spending

Real consumer spending grew about 2 percent during each of the past three years. With consumer spending constituting 68 percent of GDP, that stability explains much of the stability of the growth of aggregate demand during those three years. Yet the stability of consumption growth during 2013 results from several offsetting developments.

pp. 58–59

Business Investment

Business Fixed Investment. Real business fixed investment grew moderately, 3.0 percent during the four quarters of 2013, down from a 5.0 percent increase during 2012. The slower pace of business investment during 2013 was concentrated in structures and equipment investment, while investment in intellectual property products grew faster in 2013 than the year earlier. Investment in nonresidential structures declined 0.2 percent following robust growth of 9.2 percent during 2012. Investment in equipment slowed to 3.8 percent, following a 4.5 percent increase in 2012. In contrast, investment in intellectual property products picked up to 4.0 percent during 2013 from 2.9 percent in 2012.

pp. 62–63

State and Local Governments

Although State and local governments continued to experience fiscal pressure in 2013, the four-year contraction in the sector—measured in terms of both purchases (consumption and investment) and employment— finally appears to have ended. State and local purchases, which had generally declined for 13 quarters through the first quarter of 2013, ended the year at a higher level than in the first quarter, marking its first increase over three quarters since 2009. The cumulative decline in State and local purchases during this recovery contrasts with the usual experience during recoveries (Figure 2-10). In a typical recovery, growth in State and local government bolsters the economic recovery. In contrast, declines in State and local government have been a headwind to private-sector growth and hiring during the first four years of this recovery.

International Trade

In 2013, U.S. exports of goods and services to the world averaged nearly $189 billion a month and imports averaged nearly $229 billion a month (Figure 2-12). Exports accounted for 13.5 percent of U.S. production (GDP) in 2013, the same as in 2011 and 2012.

The U.S. trade deficit, the excess of the Nation's imports over its exports, averaged nearly $40 billion a month in 2013.

COMMENTARY

The Economic Report of the President is an annual report created by the President's Council of Economic Advisers (CEA). The report is a summary of developments in the U.S. economy over the past year. The report is macroeconomic in nature, reporting developments by major sector: federal and state and local governments, households, businesses, and the foreign sector. The report not only presents data but also interprets the data. Typically, the report by a Democratic ((shouldn't this be Democrat? We are referring to the party not the election procedure) administration will be focused more on the benefits of government, while the report from a Republican administration will emphasize individual initiatives. Yet, the CEA of both parties devotes most of the report to discussing recent past developments and expected future developments in the various sectors.

CHAPTER 5
National Income Accounting

©TungCheung/Shutterstock.com

top: © Carsten Reisinger/Shutterstock

FUNDAMENTAL QUESTIONS

1. How is the total output of an economy measured?

2. Who produces the nation's goods and services?

3. Who purchases the goods and services produced?

4. Who receives the income from the production of goods and services?

5. What is the difference between nominal and real GDP?

6. What is a price index?

Preview

The Korean economy grew at an average rate of 3.9 percent per year from 2000 to 2012. This compares with an average rate of 1.6 percent per year for the United States over the same period. Still, the U.S. economy is much larger than the Korean economy—in fact, it is larger than the economies of the 50 largest developing countries combined. The size of an economy cannot be compared across countries without common standards of measurement. National income accounting provides these standards. Economists use this system to evaluate the economic condition of a country and to compare conditions across time and across countries.

A national economy is a complex arrangement of many different buyers and sellers—households, businesses, and government units—and of their interactions with the rest of the world. To assess the economic health of a country or to compare the performance of an economy from year to year, economists must be able to measure national output and real gross domestic product (GDP). Without these data, policymakers cannot evaluate their economic policies. For instance, in the United States, real GDP fell in 1980, 1981, and 1982, and again in 1990–1991, 2001, and 2008–2009. This drop in real GDP was accompanied by widespread job losses and a general decline in the economic health of the country. As this information became known, political and economic debate centered on economic policies, on what should be done to stimulate the economy. Without real GDP statistics, policymakers would not have known that there were problems, let alone how to go about fixing them.

5-1 Measures of Output and Income

1. How is the total output of an economy measured?

national income accounting
The framework that summarizes and categorizes productive activity in an economy over a specific period of time, typically a year.

In this chapter, we discuss GDP, real GDP, and other measures of national productive activity by making use of the **national income accounting** system used by all countries. National income accounting provides a framework for discussing macroeconomics. Figure 1 reproduces the circular flow diagram you saw in the chapter "The Aggregate Economy." The lines connecting the various sectors of the economy represent flows of goods and services and of money expenditures (income). National income accounting is the process of counting the value of the flows between sectors and then summing them to find the total value of the economic activity in an economy. National income accounting fills in the dollar values in the circular flow.

National income accounting measures the output of an entire economy as well as the flows between sectors. It summarizes the level of production in an economy over a specific period of time, typically a year. In practice, the process *estimates* the amount of activity that occurs. It is beyond the capability of government officials to count every transaction that takes place in a modern economy. Still, national income accounting generates useful and fairly accurate measures of economic activity in most countries, especially wealthy industrial countries that have comprehensive accounting systems.

The most common measure of a nation's output is GDP.

5-1a Gross Domestic Product

Modern economies produce an amazing variety of goods and services. To measure an economy's total production, economists combine the quantities of oranges, golf balls, automobiles, and all the other goods and services produced into a single measure of output. Of course, simply adding up the number of things produced—the number of oranges, golf balls, and automobiles—does not reveal the *value* of what is being produced. If a nation produces 1 million more oranges and 1 million fewer automobiles this year than it did last year, the total number of things produced remains the same. But because automobiles are much more valuable than oranges, the value of the nation's output has dropped substantially. Prices reflect the value of goods and services in the market, so economists use the money value of things to create a measure of total output, a measure that is more meaningful than the sum of the units produced.

gross domestic product (GDP)
The market value of all final goods and services produced in a year within a country.

The most common measure of a nation's output is gross domestic product. **Gross domestic product (GDP)** is the market value of all final goods and services produced in a year within a country's borders. A closer look at three parts of this definition—*market value*, *final goods and services*, and *produced in a year*—will make clear what the GDP does and does not include.

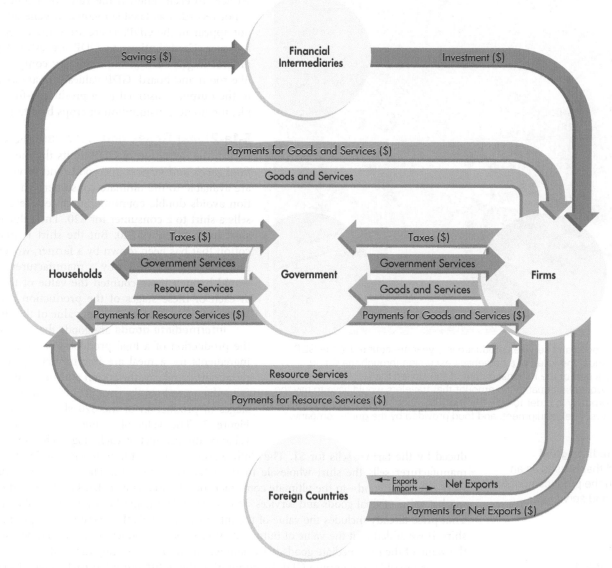

The value of national output equals expenditures plus income. If the domestic economy has positive net exports (a trade surplus), goods and services flow out of the domestic firms toward the foreign countries and money payments flow from the foreign countries to the domestic firms. If the domestic economy has negative net exports (a trade deficit), just the reverse is true.

5-1a-1 Market Value The *market value* of final goods and services is their value at market price. The process of determining market value is straightforward when prices are known and transactions are observable. However, there are cases in which prices are not known and transactions are not observable. For instance, illegal drug transactions are not reported to the government, which means that they are not included in GDP statistics. In fact, almost any activity that is not traded in a market is not included. For example, production that takes place in households, such as homemakers' services, is not counted, nor are unreported barter and cash transactions. For instance, if a lawyer has a sick dog and a veterinarian needs some legal advice, by trading services and not reporting the activity to the tax

All final goods and services produced in a year are counted in the GDP. For instance, the value of a horseback excursion through the Grand Canyon is part of the national output of the United States. The value of the trip would be equal to the amount that travelers would have to pay the guide company in order to take the trip. This price would reflect the value of the personnel, equipment, and food provided by the guide company.

Tony Gervis/Robert Harding World Imagery/Getty Images

intermediate good
A good that is used as an input in the production of final goods and services.

value added
The difference between the value of output and the value of the intermediate goods used in the production of that output.

authorities, each can avoid taxation on the income that would have been reported had they sold their services to each other. If the value of a transaction is not recorded as taxable income, it generally does not appear in the GDP. There are some exceptions, however. Contributions to GDP are estimated for *in-kind wages*, such as nonmonetary compensation like room and board. GDP values also are assigned to the output consumed by a producer—for example, the home consumption of crops by a farmer.

5-1a-2 Final Goods and Services

The second part of the definition of GDP limits the measure to *final goods and services*, the goods and services that are available to the ultimate consumer. This limitation avoids double counting. Suppose a retail store sells a shirt to a consumer for $20. The value of the shirt in the GDP is $20. But the shirt is made of cotton that has been grown by a farmer, woven at a mill, and cut and sewn by a manufacturer. What would happen if we counted the value of the shirt at each of these stages of the production process? We would overstate the market value of the shirt.

Intermediate goods are goods that are used in the production of a final product. For instance, the ingredients for a meal are intermediate goods to a restaurant. Similarly, the cotton and the cloth are intermediate goods in the production of the shirt. The stages of production of the $20 shirt are shown in Figure 2. The value-of-output axis measures the value of the product at each stage. The cotton produced by the farmer sells for $1. The cloth woven by the textile mill sells for $5. The shirt manufacturer sells the shirt wholesale to the retail store for $12. The retail store sells the shirt—the final good—to the ultimate consumer for $20. Remember that GDP is based on the market value of final goods and services. In our example, the market value of the shirt is $20. That price already includes the value of the intermediate goods that were used to produce the shirt. If we added to it the value of output at every stage of production, we would be counting the value of the intermediate goods twice, and we would be overstating the GDP.

It is possible to compute GDP by computing the **value added** at each stage of production. Value added is the difference between the value of output and the value of the intermediate goods used in the production of that output. In Figure 2, the value added by each stage of production is listed at the right. The farmer adds $1 to the value of the shirt. The mill takes the cotton worth $1 and produces cloth worth $5, adding $4 to the value of the shirt. The manufacturer uses $5 worth of cloth to produce a shirt that it sells for $12, so the manufacturer adds $7 to the shirt's value. Finally, the retail store adds $8 to the value of the shirt: It pays the manufacturer $12 for the shirt and sells it to the consumer for $20. The sum of the value added at each stage of production is $20. The total value added, then, is equal to the market value of the final product.

Economists can thus compute GDP using two methods. The final goods and services method uses the market value of the final good or service; the value-added method uses the value added at each stage of production. Both methods count the value of intermediate goods only once. This is an important distinction: GDP is not based on the market value of *all* goods and services, but on the market value of all *final* goods and services.

| FIGURE 2 | Stages of Production and Value Added in Shirt Manufacturing |

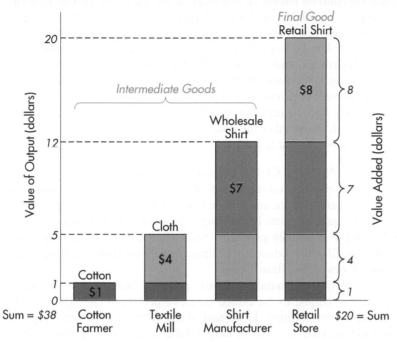

A cotton farmer sells cotton to a textile mill for $1, adding $1 to the value of the final shirt. The textile mill sells cloth to a shirt manufacturer for $5, adding $4 to the value of the final shirt. The manufacturer sells the shirt wholesale to the retail store for $12, adding $7 to the value of the final shirt. The retail store sells the final shirt to a consumer for $20, adding $8 to the value of the final shirt. The sum of the prices received at each stage of production equals $38, which is greater than the price of the final shirt. The sum of the value added at each stage of production equals $20, which equals the market value of the shirt.

inventory
The stock of unsold goods held by a firm.

5-1a-3 Produced in a Year GDP measures the value of the output *produced in a year*. The value of goods produced last year is counted in last year's GDP; the value of goods produced this year is counted in this year's GDP. The year of production, not the year of sale, determines the allocation to GDP. Although the value of last year's goods is not counted in this year's GDP, the value of services involved in the sale is. This year's GDP does not include the value of a house built last year, but it does include the value of the real estate broker's fee; it does not include the value of a used car, but it does include the income earned by the used-car dealer in the sale of that car.

To determine the value of goods produced in a year but not sold in that year, economists calculate changes in inventory. **Inventory** is a firm's stock of unsold goods. If a shirt that is produced this year remains on the retail store's shelf at the end of the year, it increases the value of the store's inventory. A $20 shirt increases that value by $20. Changes in inventory allow economists to count goods in the year in which they are produced, whether or not they are sold.

Changes in inventory can be planned or unplanned. A store may want a cushion above expected sales (*planned inventory changes*), or it may not be able to sell all the goods that it expected to sell when it placed the order (*unplanned inventory changes*). For instance, suppose Jeremy owns a surfboard shop, and he always wants to keep 10 more surfboards than he expects to sell. He does this so that in case business is surprisingly good, he does not have to turn away customers and lose those sales to his competitors. At the beginning of the year,

NOW YOU TRY IT

Use the following information to find the value of:

a.	GDP	**d.**	NI
b.	GNP	**e.**	PI
c.	NNP	**f.**	DPI

Consumption	$600
Gross investment	$100
Government spending	$200
Net exports	$100
Income earned but not received	$ 20
Income received but not earned	$ 30
Personal taxes	$200
Capital consumption allowance	$230
Receipts of factor income from the rest of the world	$ 50
Payments of factor income to the rest of the world	$ 50
Indirect business taxes	$ 90
Statistical Discrepancy	$ 0

Jeremy has 10 surfboards, and he then builds as many new boards during the year as he expects to sell. He *plans* on having an inventory at the end of the year of 10 surfboards. Suppose Jeremy expects to sell 100 surfboards during the year, so he builds 100 new boards. If business is surprisingly poor and he sells only 80 surfboards, how do we count the 20 new boards that he made but did not sell? We count the change in his inventory. He started the year with 10 surfboards and ends the year with 20 more unsold boards, for a year-end inventory of 30. The change in inventory of 20 (equal to the ending inventory of 30 minus the starting inventory of 10) represents output that is counted in GDP. In Jeremy's case, the inventory change is unplanned, since he expected to sell the 20 extra surfboards that he has in his shop at the end of the year. But whether the inventory change is planned or unplanned, changes in inventory will count output that is produced but not sold in a given year.

5-1a-4 GDP as Output

The GDP is a measure of the market value of a nation's total output in a year. Remember that economists divide the economy into four sectors: households, businesses, government, and the international sector. Figure 1 shows how the total value of economic activity equals the sum of the output produced in each sector. Figure 3 indicates where the U.S. GDP is actually produced. Since GDP counts the output produced in the United States, U.S. GDP is produced in business firms, households, and government located within the boundaries of the United States.

Not unexpectedly in a capitalist country, privately owned businesses account for the largest percentage of output: In the United States, 76 percent of the GDP is produced by private firms. Government produces 12 percent of the GDP, and households produce 12 percent. Figure 3 defines GDP in terms of output: GDP is the value of final goods and services produced in a year by domestic households, businesses, and government units. Even if some of the firms producing in the United States are foreign owned, the output that they produce in the United States is counted in the U.S. GDP.

5-1a-5 GDP as Expenditures

The circular flow diagram in Figure 1 shows not only the output of goods and services from each sector but also the payments for goods and services. Here we look at GDP in terms of what each sector pays for the goods and services that it purchases.

The dollar value of total expenditures—the sum of the amount that each sector spends on final goods and services—equals the dollar value of output. In the chapter "The Aggregate Economy," you learned that household spending is called *consumption*. Households spend their income on goods and services to be consumed. Business spending is called *investment*.

2. *Who produces the nation's goods and services?*

GDP is the value of final goods and services produced by domestic households, businesses, and government.

3. *Who purchases the goods and services produced?*

FIGURE 3 **U.S. Gross Domestic Product by Sector (billion dollars)**

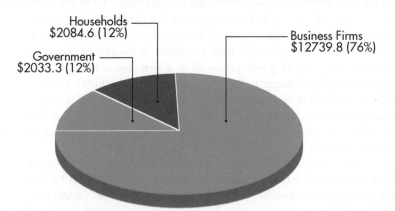

Households
$2084.6 (12%)

Government
$2033.3 (12%)

Business Firms
$12739.8 (76%)

Business firms produce 76 percent of the U.S. GDP. Government produces 12 percent; households, 12 percent.

Source: Bureau of Economic Analysis, Q3 2013, www.bea.gov, Table 1.3.5

Investment is spending on capital goods that will be used to produce other goods and services. The other two components of total spending are *government spending* and *net exports*. Net exports are the value of *exports* (goods and services sold to the rest of the world) minus the value of *imports* (goods and services bought from the rest of the world).

GDP = consumption + investment + government spending + net exports

Or, in the shorter form commonly used by economists,

$$GDP = C + I + G + X$$

where X is net exports.

$GDP = C + I + G + X$

Figure 4 shows the U.S. GDP in terms of total expenditures. Consumption, or household spending, accounts for 68 percent of national expenditures. Government spending represents 19 percent of expenditures, and business investment represents 16 percent. Net exports are negative (−3 percent), which means that imports exceeded exports. To determine total national expenditures on domestic output, the value of imports, or spending on foreign output, is subtracted from total expenditures.

5-1a-6 GDP as Income The total value of output can be calculated by adding up the expenditures of each sector. And because one sector's expenditures are another's income, the total value of output can also be computed by adding up the income of all sectors.

Business firms use factors of production to produce goods and services. Remember that the income earned by factors of production is classified as wages, interest, rent, and profits. *Wages* are payments to labor, including fringe benefits, social security contributions, and retirement payments. *Interest* is the net interest paid by businesses to households plus the net interest received from foreigners (the interest that they pay us minus the interest that we pay them). *Rent* is income earned from selling the use of real property (houses, shops, and farms). Finally, *profits* are the sum of corporate profits plus proprietors' income (income from sole proprietorships and partnerships).

Figure 5 shows the U.S. GDP in terms of income. Notice that wages account for 53 percent of the GDP. Interest and profits account for 4 and 10 percent of the GDP, respectively. Proprietors' income accounts for 8 percent. Rent (4 percent) is very small in comparison. *Net factor income from abroad* is income received from U.S.-owned resources located in other countries minus income paid to foreign-owned resources located in the United States. Since U.S. GDP refers only to income earned within U.S. borders, we must add income payments from the rest of the world and subtract income payments to the rest of the world to arrive at GDP (1 percent).

4. *Who receives the income from the production of goods and services?*

FIGURE 4 U.S. Gross Domestic Product as Expenditures (trillion dollars)

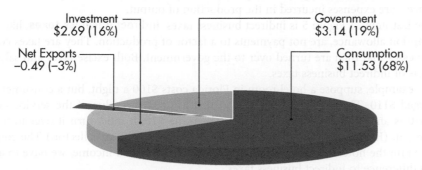

Consumption by households accounts for 68 percent of the GDP, followed by government spending at 19 percent, investment by business firms at 16 percent, and net exports at −3 percent.

Source: U.S. Bureau of Economic Analysis, Q3 2013, www.bea.gov, Table 1.1.5

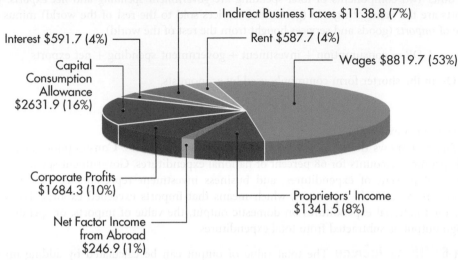

FIGURE 5   U.S. Gross Domestic Product as Income Received (billion dollars)

Indirect Business Taxes $1138.8 (7%)

Interest $591.7 (4%)

Rent $587.7 (4%)

Capital Consumption Allowance $2631.9 (16%)

Wages $8819.7 (53%)

Corporate Profits $1684.3 (10%)

Proprietors' Income $1341.5 (8%)

Net Factor Income from Abroad $246.9 (1%)

The largest component of income is wages, at 53 percent. Profits represent 10 percent; interest, 4 percent; proprietors' income, 8 percent; and rent, 4 percent. Capital consumption allowance (16 percent) and indirect business taxes (7 percent) are not income received but still must be added; net factor income from abroad must be added (1 percent). (Note: Percentages do not always equal 100 percent).

Source: U.S. Bureau of Economic Analysis, third quarter 2013; www.bea.gov.

capital consumption allowance
The estimated value of depreciation plus the value of accidental damage to capital stock.

depreciation
A reduction in the value of capital goods over time as a result of their use in production.

indirect business tax
A tax that is collected by businesses for a government agency.

The GDP as income is equal to the sum of wages, interest, rent, and profits, less net factor income from abroad, plus capital consumption allowance and indirect business taxes.

Figure 5 also includes two income categories that we have not discussed: capital consumption allowance and indirect business taxes. **Capital consumption allowance** is not a money payment to a factor of production; it is the estimated value of capital goods used up or worn out in production plus the value of accidental damage to capital goods. The value of accidental damage is relatively small, so it is common to hear economists refer to capital consumption allowance as **depreciation**. Machines and other capital goods wear out over time. The reduction in the value of the capital stock as a result of its being used up or worn out over time is called depreciation. A depreciating capital good loses value each year of its useful life until its value is zero.

Even though capital consumption allowance does not represent income received by a factor of production, it must be accounted for in GDP as income. If it were not, the value of GDP measured as output would be higher than the value of GDP measured as income. Depreciation is a kind of resource payment, part of the total payment to the owners of capital. All of the income categories—wages, interest, rent, profits, and capital consumption allowance—are expenses incurred in the production of output.

The last item in Figure 5 is indirect business taxes. **Indirect business taxes**, like capital consumption allowance, are not payments to a factor of production. They are taxes collected by businesses that then are turned over to the government. Both excise taxes and sales taxes are forms of indirect business taxes.

For example, suppose a hotel room in Florida costs $100 a night, but a consumer would be charged $110. The hotel receives $100 of that $110 as the value of the service sold; the other $10 is an excise tax. The hotel cannot keep the $10; it must turn it over to the state government. (In effect, the hotel is acting as the government's tax collector.) The consumer spends $110; the hotel earns $100. To balance expenditures and income, we have to allocate the $10 difference to indirect business taxes.

To summarize, GDP measured as income includes the four payments to the factors of production: wages, interest, rent, and profits. These income items represent expenses incurred in the production of GDP. From these we must subtract net factor income from abroad and then add two nonincome items—capital consumption allowance and indirect business taxes—to find real GDP.

GDP = wages + interest + rent + profits − net factor income from abroad + capital consumption allowance + indirect business taxes

The GDP is the total value of output produced in a year, the total value of expenditures made to purchase that output, and the total value of income received by the factors of production. Because all three are measures of the same thing—GDP—all must be equal.

5-1b Other Measures of Output and Income

GDP is the most commonly used measure of a nation's output, but it is not the only measure. Economists rely on a number of other measures as well in analyzing the performance of components of an economy.

5-1b-1 Gross National Product

Gross national product (GNP) equals GDP plus receipts of factor income from the rest of the world minus payments of factor income to the rest of the world. If we add to GDP the value of income earned by U.S. residents from factors of production located outside the United States and subtract the value of income earned by foreign residents from factors of production located inside the United States, we have a measure of the value of output produced by U.S.-owned resources—GNP.

Figure 6 shows the national income accounts in the United States. The figure begins with the GDP and then shows the calculations necessary to obtain the GNP and other measures of national output. In 2013, the U.S. GNP was $16,907.9 billion.

5-1b-2 Net National Product

Net national product (NNP) equals GNP minus capital consumption allowance. The NNP measures the value of goods and services produced in a year less the value of capital goods that became obsolete or were used up during the year. Because NNP includes only net additions to a nation's capital, it is a better measure of the expansion or contraction of current output than is GNP. Remember how we previously defined GDP in terms of expenditures:

GDP = consumption + investment + government spending + net exports

The investment measure in GDP (and GNP) is called **gross investment**. Gross investment is total investment, which includes investment expenditures required to replace capital goods consumed in current production. The NNP does not include investment expenditures required to replace worn-out capital goods; it includes only net investment. **Net investment** is equal to gross investment minus capital consumption allowance. Net investment measures business spending over and above that required to replace worn-out capital goods.

Figure 6 shows that in 2013 the U.S. NNP was $14,276 billion. This means that the U.S. economy produced over $14 trillion worth of goods and services above those required to replace capital stock that had depreciated. Over $1.61 trillion in capital was "worn out" in 2013.

5-1b-3 National Income

National income (NI) equals the NNP plus or minus a small adjustment called "statistical discrepancy." The NI captures the costs of the factors of production used in producing output. Remember that GDP includes a nonincome expense item: capital consumption allowance. Subtracting this plus the statistical discrepancy from the GDP leaves the income payments that actually go to resources.

Because the NNP equals the GNP minus capital consumption allowance, we can subtract the statistical discrepancy from the NNP to find NI, as shown in Figure 6. This measure helps economists analyze how the costs of (or payments received by) resources change.

gross national product (GNP)
Gross domestic product plus receipts of factor income from the rest of the world minus payments of factor income to the rest of the world.

net national product (NNP)
Gross national product minus capital consumption allowance.

gross investment
Total investment, including investment expenditures required to replace capital goods consumed in current production.

net investment
Gross investment minus capital consumption allowance.

national income (NI)
Net national product plus or minus statistical discrepancy.

FIGURE 6 U.S. National Income Accounts, 2013 (billion dollars)

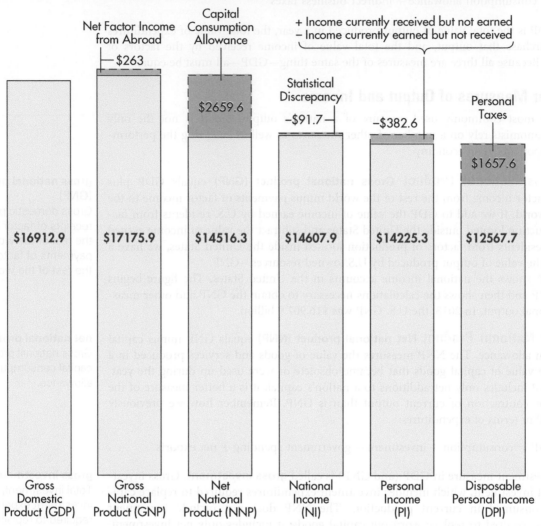

Gross domestic product plus receipts of factor income from the rest of the world minus payments of factor income to the rest of the world equals gross national product. Gross national product minus capital consumption allowance equals net national product. Net national product minus statistical discrepancy equals national income. National income plus income currently received but not earned (transfer payments, personal interest, dividend income) minus income currently earned but not received (retained corporate profits, net interest, social security taxes) equals personal income. Personal income minus personal taxes equals disposable personal income.

Source: Bureau of Economic Analysis, third quarter 2013; www.bea.gov

personal income (PI)
National income plus income currently received but not earned, minus income currently earned but not received.

transfer payment
Income transferred by the government from a citizen who is earning income to another citizen.

5-1b-4 Personal Income **Personal income (PI)** is national income adjusted for income that is received but not earned in the current year and income that is earned but not received in the current year. Social security and welfare benefits are examples of income that is received but not earned in the current year. As you learned in the chapter "The Aggregate Economy," these are called **transfer payments**. Transfer payments represent income transferred from one citizen who is earning income to another citizen, who may not be. The government transfers income by taxing one group of citizens and using the tax payments to fund the income for another group. An example of income that is currently earned but not received is profits that are retained by a corporation to finance current needs rather than paid out to stockholders. Another is social security (FICA) taxes, which are deducted from workers' paychecks.

5-1b-5 Disposable Personal Income Disposable personal income (DPI) equals personal income minus personal taxes—income taxes, excise and real estate taxes on personal property, and other personal taxes. DPI is the income that individuals have at their disposal for spending or saving. The sum of consumption spending plus saving must equal disposable personal income.

disposable personal income (DPI)
Personal income minus personal taxes.

RECAP

1. Gross domestic product (GDP) is the market value of all final goods and services produced in an economy in a year.

2. The GDP can be calculated by summing the market value of all final goods and services produced in a year, by summing the value added at each stage of production, by adding total expenditures on goods and services (GDP = consumption + investment + government spending + net exports), and by using the total income earned in the production of goods and services (GDP = wages + interest + rent + profits), subtracting net factor income from abroad, and adding depreciation and indirect business taxes.

3. Other measures of output and income include gross national product (GNP),

net national product (NNP), national income (NI), personal income (PI), and disposable personal income (DPI).

National Income Accounts

GDP = consumption + investment + government spending + net exports

GNP = GDP + receipts of factor income from the rest of the world — payments of factor income to the rest of the world

NNP = GNP − capital consumption allowance

NI = NNP − statistical discrepancy

PI = NI − income earned but not received + income received but not earned

DPI = PI − personal taxes

5-2 Nominal and Real Measures

The GDP is the market value of all final goods and services produced within a country in a year. Value is measured in money terms, so the U.S. GDP is reported in dollars, the German GDP in euro, the Mexican GDP in pesos, and so on. Market value is the product of two elements: the money price and the quantity produced.

5-2a Nominal and Real GDP

Nominal GDP measures output in terms of its current dollar value. **Real GDP** is adjusted for changing price levels. In 1980, the U.S. GDP was $2,790 billion; in 2013, it was $16,857 billion—an increase of 504 percent. Does this mean that the United States produced 504 percent more goods and services in 2013 than it did in 1980? If the numbers reported are for nominal GDP, we cannot be sure. Nominal GDP cannot tell us whether the economy produced more goods and services, because nominal GDP changes both when prices change *and* when quantity changes.

Real GDP measures output in constant prices. This allows economists to identify the changes in the actual production of final goods and services: Real GDP measures the quantity of goods and services produced after eliminating the influence of price changes contained in nominal GDP. In 1980, real GDP calculated using chained-dollar estimates in the United States was $6,376 billion; in 2013, it was $15,790 billion, an increase of just 247 percent. A large part of the 504 percent increase in nominal GDP reflects increased prices, not increased output.

5. What is the difference between nominal and real GDP?

nominal GDP
A measure of national output based on the current prices of goods and services.

real GDP
A measure of the quantity of final goods and services produced, obtained by eliminating the influence of price changes from the nominal GDP statistics.

Because we prefer more goods and services to higher prices, it is better to have nominal GDP rise because of higher output than because of higher prices. We want nominal GDP to increase as a result of an increase in real GDP.

Consider a simple example that illustrates the difference between nominal GDP and real GDP. Suppose a hypothetical economy produces just three goods: oranges, coconuts, and pizzas. The dollar value of output in three different years is listed in Figure 7.

As shown in Figure 7, in year 1, 100 oranges were produced at $.50 per orange, 300 coconuts at $1 per coconut, and 2,000 pizzas at $8 per pizza. The total dollar value of output in year 1 is $16,350. In year 2, prices remain constant at the year 1 values, but the quantity of each good has increased by 10 percent. The dollar value of output in year 2 is $17,985, 10 percent higher than the value of output in year 1. In year 3, the quantity of each good

FIGURE 7   Prices and Quantities in a Hypothetical Economy

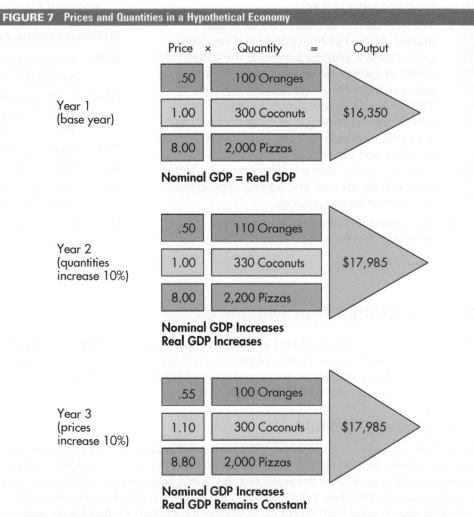

In year 1, total output was $16,350. In year 2, prices remained constant but quantities produced increased by 10 percent, resulting in a higher output of $17,985. With prices constant, we can say that both nominal GDP and real GDP increased from year 1 to year 2. In year 3, quantities produced returned to the year 1 level but prices increased by 10 percent, resulting in the same increased output as in year 2, $17,985. Production has not changed from year 1 to year 3, however, so although nominal GDP has increased, real GDP has remained constant.

is back at the year 1 level, but prices have increased by 10 percent. Oranges now cost $.55, coconuts $1.10, and pizzas $8.80. The dollar value of output in year 3 is $17,985.

Notice that the dollar value of output ($17,985) in years 2 and 3 is 10 percent higher than the dollar value in year 1. But there is a difference here. In year 2, the increase in output is due entirely to an increase in the production of the three goods. In year 3, the increase is due entirely to an increase in the prices of the goods.

Because prices did not change between years 1 and 2, the increase in nominal GDP is entirely accounted for by an increase in real output, or real GDP. In years 1 and 3, the actual quantities produced did not change, which means that real GDP was constant; only nominal GDP was higher, a product only of higher prices.

Figure 8 plots the growth rate of real GDP for several of the industrial countries. One can see in the figure that the countries show somewhat different patterns of real GDP growth over time. For instance, over the period beginning in the mid-1990s, real GDP grew at a slower pace in Japan than in the other countries. Most of the countries had fairly fast rates of GDP growth in the late 1990s, only to experience a falling growth rate in the early 2000s followed by a pickup in growth, and then the most recent downturn associated with the global recession. Following the deep recession where countries experienced negative growth rates, all of the countries grew in 2010.

5-2b Price Indexes

The total dollar value of output or income is equal to price multiplied by the quantity of goods and services produced:

$$\text{Dollar value of output} = \text{price} \times \text{quantity}$$

6. What is a price index?

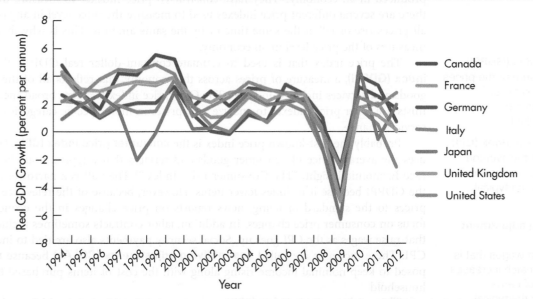

FIGURE 8 Real GDP Growth in Some Industrial Countries

Real GDP grew at a fast pace in the late 1990s in most countries depicted in the figure, only to fall dramatically in 2001 and 2002. Japan has experienced slower growth of real GDP over this period than the other countries. Note how severe the drop in real GDP growth was during the financial crisis of 2008–2009.

Source: OECD.Stat

By dividing the dollar value of output by price, you can determine the quantity of goods and services produced:

$$\text{Quantity} = \frac{\text{dollar value of output}}{\text{price}}$$

price index
A measure of the average price level in an economy.

In macroeconomics, a **price index** is a measure of the average level of prices in an economy; it shows how prices, on average, have changed. Prices of individual goods can rise and fall relative to one another, but a price index shows the general trend in prices across the economy.

The value of the price index in any particular year indicates how prices have changed relative to the base year.

5-2b-1 Base Year

The example in Figure 7 provides a simple introduction to price indexes. The first step is to pick a **base year**, the year against which other years are measured. Any year can serve as the base year. Suppose we pick year 1 in Figure 7. The value of the price index in year 1, the base year, is defined to be 100. This simply means that prices in year 1 are 100 percent of prices in year 1 (100 percent of 1 is 1). In the example, year 2 prices are equal to year 1 prices, so the price index is equal to 100 in year 2 as well. In year 3, every price has risen 10 percent relative to the base-year (year 1) prices, so the price index is 10 percent higher in year 3, or 110. The value of the price index in any particular year indicates how prices have changed relative to the base year. A value of 110 indicates that prices are 110 percent of base-year prices, or that the average price level has increased 10 percent.

base year
The year against which other years are measured.

Price index in any year = 100 ± percentage change in prices from the base year

5-2b-2 Types of Price Indexes

The price of a single good is easy to determine. But how do economists determine a single measure of the prices of the millions of goods and services produced in an economy? They have constructed price indexes to measure the price level; there are several different price indexes used to measure the price level in any economy. Not all prices rise or fall at the same time or by the same amount. This is why there are several measures of the price level in an economy.

GDP price index (GDPPI)
A broad measure of the prices of goods and services included in the gross domestic product.

The price index that is used to estimate constant-dollar real GDP is the **GDP price index (GDPPI)**, a measure of prices across the economy that reflects all of the categories of goods and services included in GDP. The GDP price index is a very broad measure. Economists use other price indexes to analyze how prices in more specific categories of goods and services change.

consumer price index (CPI)
A measure of the average price of goods and services purchased by the typical household.

Probably the best-known price index is the **consumer price index (CPI)**. The CPI measures the average price of consumer goods and services that a typical household purchases. (See Economic Insight, "The Consumer Price Index.") The CPI is a narrower measure than the GDPPI because it includes fewer items. However, because of the relevance of consumer prices to the standard of living, news reports on price changes in the economy typically focus on consumer price changes. In addition, labor contracts sometimes include provisions that raise wages as the CPI goes up. Social security payments also are tied to increases in the CPI. These increases are called **cost-of-living adjustments (COLAs)** because they are supposed to keep nominal income rising along with the cost of items purchased by the typical household.

cost-of-living adjustment (COLA)
An increase in wages that is designed to match increases in the prices of items purchased by the typical household.

producer price index (PPI)
A measure of average prices received by producers.

The **producer price index (PPI)** measures average prices received by producers. At one time this price index was known as the *wholesale price index (WPI)*. Because the PPI measures price changes at an earlier stage of production than the CPI, it can indicate a coming change in the CPI. If producer input costs are rising, we can expect the price of goods produced to go up as well.

ECONOMIC INSIGHT

The Consumer Price Index

The CPI is calculated by the Department of Labor using price surveys taken in 87 U.S. cities. Although the CPI often is called a *cost-of-living index*, it is not. The CPI represents the cost of a fixed market basket of goods purchased by a hypothetical household, not a real one.

In fact, no household consumes the exact market basket used to estimate the CPI. As relative prices change, households alter their spending patterns. But the CPI market basket changes only every two years. This is due in part to the high cost of surveying the public to determine spending patterns. Then, too, individual households have different tastes and spend different portions of their budgets on the various components of household spending (housing, food, clothing,

transportation, medical care, and so on). Only a household that spends exactly the same portion of its income on each item counted in the CPI would find the CPI representative of its cost of living.

The Department of Labor surveys spending in eight major areas. The figure shows these areas and the percentage of the typical household budget devoted to each area. If you kept track of your spending over the course of several months, you probably would find that you spend much more than the typical household on some items and much less on others. In other words, the CPI is not a very good measure of *your* cost of living.

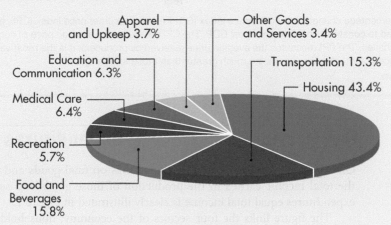

- Apparel and Upkeep 3.7%
- Education and Communication 6.3%
- Medical Care 6.4%
- Recreation 5.7%
- Food and Beverages 15.8%
- Other Goods and Services 3.4%
- Transportation 15.3%
- Housing 43.4%

Source: Data from *Bureau of Labor Statistics.*

Figure 9 illustrates how the three different measures of prices have changed over time. Notice that the PPI is more volatile than the GDPPI or the CPI. This is because there are smaller fluctuations in the equilibrium prices of final goods than in those of intermediate goods.

RECAP

1. Nominal GDP is measured using current dollars.
2. Real GDP measures output with price effects removed.
3. The GDP price index, the consumer price index, and the producer price index are all measures of the level of prices in an economy.

FIGURE 9 The GDP Price Index, the CPI, and the PPI

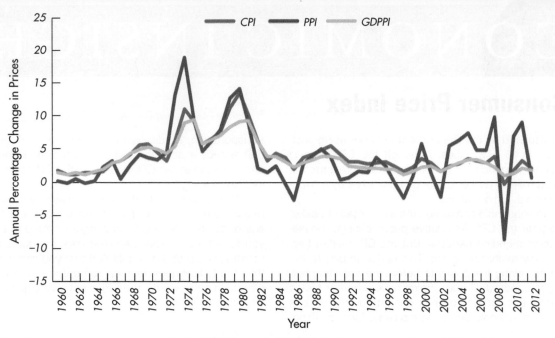

The graph plots the annual percentage change in the GDP price index (GDPPI), the consumer price index (CPI), and the producer price index (PPI). The GDPPI is used to construct constant-dollar real GDP. The CPI measures the average price of consumer goods and services that a typical household purchases. The PPI measures the average price received by producers; it is the most variable of the three because fluctuations in equilibrium prices of intermediate goods are much greater than those for final goods.

Source: www.bls.gov and www.bea.gov.

5-3 Flows of Income and Expenditures

GDP is both a measure of total expenditures on final goods and services and a measure of the total income earned in the production of those goods and services. The idea that total expenditures equal total income is clearly illustrated in Figure 1.

The figure links the four sectors of the economy: households, firms, government, and foreign countries. The arrows between the sectors indicate the direction of the flows. Gold arrows with dollar signs represent money flows; blue-green arrows without dollar signs represent flows of real goods and services. The money flows are both income and expenditures. For instance, household expenditures for goods and services from business firms are represented by the gold arrow at the top of the diagram. Household income from firms is represented by the gold arrow flowing from firms to households at the bottom of the diagram. Because one sector's expenditures are another sector's income, the total expenditures on goods and services must be the same as the total income from selling goods and services, and those must both be equal to the total value of the goods and services produced.

RECAP

1. Total spending on final goods and services equals the total income received from producing those goods and services.

2. The circular flow model shows that one sector's expenditures become the income of other sectors.

SUMMARY

1. How is the total output of an economy measured?

- National income accounting is the system that economists use to measure both the output of an economy and the flows between sectors of that economy. §5-1

- Gross domestic product (GDP) is the market value of all final goods and services produced in a year in a country. §5-1a

- GDP also equals the value added at each stage of production. §5-1a

2. Who produces the nation's goods and services?

- GDP as output equals the sum of the output of households, business firms, and government within the country. Business firms produce 75 percent of the U.S. GDP. §5-1a

3. Who purchases the goods and services produced?

- The GDP as expenditures equals the sum of consumption plus investment plus government spending plus net exports. In the United States, consumption accounts for roughly two-thirds of total expenditures. §5-1a

4. Who receives the income from the production of goods and services?

- The GDP as income equals the sum of wages, interest, rent, profits, proprietors' income, capital consumption allowance, and indirect business taxes less net factor income from abroad. Wages account for about 60 percent of the total. §5-1a

- Capital consumption allowance is the estimated value of depreciation plus the value of accidental damage to capital stock. §5-1a

- Other measures of national output include gross national product (GNP), net national product (NNP), national income (NI), personal income (PI), and disposable personal income (DPI). §5-1b

5. What is the difference between nominal and real GDP?

- Nominal GDP measures output in terms of its current dollar value, including the effects of price changes; real GDP measures output after eliminating the effects of price changes. §5-2a

6. What is a price index?

- A price index is a measure of the average level of prices across an economy. §5-2b

- The GDP price index is a measure of the prices of all the goods and services included in the GDP. §5-2b

- The consumer price index (CPI) measures the average price of goods and services consumed by the typical household. §5-2b

- The producer price index (PPI) measures average prices received by producers (wholesale prices). §5-2b

- Total expenditures on final goods and services equal total income. §5-3

KEY TERMS

base year, 96
capital consumption allowance, 90
consumer price index (CPI), 96
cost-of-living adjustments (COLAs), 96
depreciation, 90
disposable personal income (DPI), 93
GDP price index (GDPPI), 96
gross domestic product (GDP), 84

gross investment, 91
gross national product (GNP), 91
indirect business taxes, 90
intermediate good, 86
inventory, 87
national income (NI), 91
national income accounting, 84
net investment, 91
net national product (NNP), 91

nominal GDP, 93
personal income (PI), 92
price index, 96
producer price index (PPI), 96
real GDP, 93
transfer payments, 92
value added, 86

EXERCISES

1. The following table lists the stages in the production of a personal computer. What is the value of the computer in GDP?

Stage	Value Added
Components manufacture	$ 100
Assembly	$ 250
Wholesaler	$ 500
Retailer	$ 1,850

2. What is the difference between GDP and each of the following?
   a. Gross national product
   b. Net national product
   c. National income
   d. Personal income
   e. Disposable personal income

3.

	Year I		Year 2	
	Quantity	Price	Quantity	Price
Oranges	100	$5	150	$5
Pears	100	$3	75	$4

   a. What is the growth rate of constant-dollar real GDP using year 1 as the base year?
   b. What is the growth rate of constant-dollar real GDP using year 2 as the base year?

4. Why do total expenditures on final goods and services equal total income in the economy?

5. Why do we not measure national output by simply counting the total number of goods and services produced each year?

6. Why is the CPI not a useful measure of *your* cost of living?

Use the following national income accounting information to answer exercises 7–11:

Consumption	$ 400
Imports	$ 10
Net investment	$ 20
Government purchases	$ 100
Exports	$ 20
Capital consumption allowance	$ 20
Statistical discrepancy	$ 6
Receipts of factor income from the rest of the world	$ 10
Payments of factor income to the rest of the world	$ 13

7. What is the GDP for this economy?
8. What is the GNP for this economy?
9. What is the NNP for this economy?
10. What is the national income for this economy?
11. What is the gross investment in this economy?
12. Indirect business taxes and capital consumption allowance are not income, yet they are included in the calculation of GDP as income received. Why do we add these two nonincome components to the other components of income (like wages, rent, interest, profits, and net factor income from abroad) to find GDP?
13. Why has nominal GDP increased faster than real GDP in the United States over time? What would it mean if an economy had real GDP increasing faster than nominal GDP?
14. We usually discuss GDP in terms of what is included in the definition. What is *not* included in GDP? Why are these things excluded?15. If a surfboard is produced this year but not sold until next year, how is it counted in this year's GDP and not next year's?

ECONOMICALLY SPEAKING

HIDING IN THE SHADOWS: THE GROWTH OF THE UNDERGROUND ECONOMY

International Monetary Fund, March 2002

A factory worker has a second job driving an unlicensed taxi at night; a plumber fixes a broken water pipe for a client, gets paid in cash, but doesn't declare his earnings to the tax collector; a drug dealer brokers a sale with a prospective customer on a street corner. These are all examples of the underground or shadow economy—activities, both legal and illegal, that add up to trillions of dollars a year that take place "off the books," out of the gaze of tax-men and government statisticians.

Although crime and shadow economic activities have long been a fact of life—and are now increasing around the world—almost all societies try to control their growth, because a prospering shadow economy makes official statistics (on unemployment, official labor force, income, consumption) unreliable. Policies and programs that are framed on the basis of unreliable statistics may be inappropriate and self-defeating ...

Also called the underground, informal, or parallel economy, the shadow economy includes not only illegal activities but also unreported income from the production of legal goods and services, either from monetary or barter transactions. Hence, the shadow economy comprises all economic activities that would generally be taxable were they reported to the tax authorities.

Estimating the size of the shadow economy is difficult. After all, people engaged in underground activities do their best to avoid detection. But policymakers and government administrators need information about how many people are active in the shadow economy, how often underground activities occur, and the size of these activities so that they can make appropriate decisions on resource allocation.

Table 1 shows average estimates for the three main country groups—developing countries, transition economies, and 21 advanced economies, the last all members of the Organization for Economic Cooperation and Development (OECD). The comparisons among countries remain somewhat crude because they are based on different estimation methods.

The ranges reflect the different estimation methods used by different sources.

Countries with relatively low tax rates, fewer laws and regulations, and a well-established rule of law tend to have smaller shadow economies.

Macroeconomic and microeconomic modeling studies based on data for several countries suggest that the major driving forces behind the size and growth of the shadow economy are an increasing burden of tax and social security payments, combined with rising restrictions in the official labor market. Wage rates in the official economy also play a role ...

Shadow economies tend to be smaller in countries where government institutions are strong and efficient. Indeed, some studies have found that it is not higher taxes per se that increase the size of the shadow economy, but ineffectual and discretionary application of the tax system and regulations by governments.

TABLE 1 Shadow Economy as Percent of Official GDP, 1988–2000

Country Group	Percent of GDP
Developing	35–44
Transition	21–30
OECD	14–16

Source: Friedrich Schneider with Dominik Enste, *Hiding in the Shadows: The Growth of the Underground Economy, Economic Issues,* No. 30, International Monetary Fund, March 2002.

COMMENTARY

I n this chapter, we learned about different measures of macroeconomic performance. It is important to have accurate measures in order to formulate appropriate policy. Bad data on economic performance could result in policymakers attempting to fix problems that do not really exist or failing to address problems that have not been identified. However, it is not easy to measure the performance of an economy. This article indicates a particular type of problem that exists in every economy: the underground economy.

The presence of a large and active underground economy means that the official GDP figure is missing much of the economic activity that occurs. As indicated in the article, this is more than just illegal activity, like dealing in illicit drugs. Perfectly legal activities that are conducted "off the books" are also missed in the official GDP accounting. So if a carpenter performs work for someone, is paid in cash, and never reports the transaction as income to be taxed, this activity is part of the underground economy. Although the carpenter was engaged in productive activity, it will not be counted, and so the official GDP measure will underestimate the true amount of production undertaken in a year.

This article serves as a reminder that, although government officials may do the best job they can of counting economic activity, they will never be able to count everything. As shown in Table 1 of the article, the problems are worse for developing countries and those countries that are in transition from socialism than for the industrial countries (referred to as OECD countries in the table). Yet even in the industrial countries, it is estimated that between 14 and 16 percent of GDP takes place in the underground economy.

CHAPTER 6

An Introduction to the Foreign Exchange Market and the Balance of Payments

FUNDAMENTAL QUESTIONS

1. *How do individuals of one nation trade money with individuals of another nation?*

2. *How do changes in exchange rates affect international trade?*

3. *How do nations record their transactions with the rest of the world?*

Preview

In the chapter "National Income Accounting," you learned that gross domestic product equals the sum of consumption, investment, government spending, and net exports (GDP = $C + I + G + X$). Net exports (X) are one key measure of a nation's transactions with other countries, a principal link between a nation's GDP and developments in the rest of the world. In this chapter, we extend the macroeconomic accounting framework to include more detail on a nation's international transactions. This extension is known as balance of payments accounting.

International transactions have grown rapidly in recent years as the economies of the world have become increasingly interrelated. Improvements in transportation and communication, and global markets for goods and services, have created a community of world economies. Products made in one country are sold in the world market, where they compete against products from other nations. Europeans purchase stocks listed on the New York Stock Exchange; Americans purchase bonds issued in Japan.

Different countries use different monies. When goods and services are exchanged across international borders, national monies also are traded. To make buying and selling decisions in the global marketplace, people must be able to compare prices across countries, to compare prices quoted in Japanese yen with those quoted in Mexican pesos. This chapter begins with a look at how national monies are priced and traded in the foreign exchange market.

6-1 The Foreign Exchange Market

1. How do individuals of one nation trade money with individuals of another nation?

foreign exchange
Currency and bank deposits that are denominated in foreign money.

foreign exchange market
A global market in which people trade one currency for another.

Foreign exchange is foreign money, including paper money and bank deposits like checking accounts, that is denominated in foreign currency. When someone with U.S. dollars wants to trade those dollars for Japanese yen, the trade takes place in the **foreign exchange market**, a global market in which people trade one currency for another. Many financial markets are located in a specific geographic location. For instance, the New York Stock Exchange is a specific location in New York City where stocks are bought and sold. The Commodity Exchange is a specific location in New York City where contracts to deliver agricultural and metal commodities are bought and sold. The foreign exchange market is not in a single geographic location, however. Trading occurs all over the world, electronically and by telephone. Most of the activity involves large banks in New York, London, and other financial centers. A foreign exchange trader at Citigroup in New York can buy or sell currencies with a trader at Barclays Bank in London by calling the other trader on the telephone or exchanging computer messages.

Only tourism and a few other transactions in the foreign exchange market involve an actual movement of currency. The great majority of transactions involve the buying and selling of bank deposits denominated in foreign currency. A bank deposit can be a checking account that a firm or individual writes checks against to make payments to others, or it can be an interest-earning savings account with no check-writing privileges. Currency notes, like dollar bills, are used in a relatively small fraction of transactions. When a large corporation or a government buys foreign currency, it buys a bank deposit denominated in the foreign currency. Still, all exchanges in the market require that monies have a price.

6-1a Exchange Rates

exchange rate
The price of one country's money in terms of another country's money.

An **exchange rate** is the price of one country's money in terms of another country's money. Exchange rates are needed to compare prices quoted in two different currencies. Suppose a shirt that has been manufactured in Canada sells for 20 U.S. dollars in Seattle, Washington, and for 25 Canadian dollars in Vancouver, British Columbia. Where would you get the better buy? Unless you know the exchange rate between U.S. and Canadian dollars, you cannot tell. The exchange rate allows you to convert the foreign currency price into its domestic currency equivalent, which then can be compared to the domestic price.

Table 1 lists exchange rates for December 2, 2013. The rates are quoted in U.S. dollars per unit of foreign currency in the second column, and in units of foreign currency per U.S. dollar in the last column. For instance, the Canadian dollar was selling for $.94, or about 94 U.S. cents. The same day, the U.S. dollar was selling for 1.06 Canadian dollars (1 U.S. dollar would buy 1.06 Canadian dollars).

TABLE 1 Exchange Rates, December 2, 2013		
Country	**U.S.$ per Currency**	**Currency per U.S.$**
Argentina (peso)	0.165	6.16
Australia (dollar)	0.910	1.10
Britain (pound)	1.64	0.61
Canada (dollar)	0.94	1.06
China (renminbi)	0.16	6.09
Israel (shekel)	0.28	3.53
Japan (yen)	0.0097	103.09
Mexico (peso)	0.076	13.20
New Zealand (dollar)	0.82	1.22
Russia (ruble)	0.03	33.22
Singapore (dollar)	0.80	1.26
Switzerland (franc)	1.10	0.91
EU (euro)	1.36	0.74

Note: The second column lists U.S. dollars per unit of foreign currency, or how much one unit of foreign currency is worth in U.S. dollars. On this day, you could get about 94 U.S. cents for 1 Canadian dollar. The third column lists units of foreign currency per U.S. dollar, or how much 1 U.S. dollar is worth in foreign currency. On the same day, you could get about 1.06 Canadian dollars for 1 U.S. dollar.

If you know the price of a currency in U.S. dollars, you can find the price of the U.S. dollar in that currency by taking the reciprocal. To find the reciprocal of a number, write it as a fraction and then turn the fraction upside down. Let's say that 1 British pound sells for 2 U.S. dollars. In fraction form, 2 is 2/1. The reciprocal of 2/1 is 1/2, or 0.5. So 1 U.S. dollar sells for .5 British pound. The table shows that the actual dollar price of the pound on December 2, 2013, was 1.64. The *reciprocal exchange rate*—the number of pounds per dollar—is .61 (1/1.64), which was the pound price of 1 dollar that day.

Let us go back to comparing the price of the Canadian shirt in Seattle and in Vancouver. The International Standards Organization (ISO) symbol for the U.S. dollar is USD. The symbol for the Canadian dollar is CAD. (Table 2 lists the symbols for a number of currencies.) The shirt sells for USD20 in Seattle and CAD25 in Vancouver. Suppose the exchange rate between the U.S. dollar and the Canadian dollar is 0.8. This means that CAD1 costs 0.8 U.S. dollar, or 80 U.S. cents. To find the domestic currency value of a foreign currency price, multiply the foreign currency price by the exchange rate:

Domestic currency value = foreign currency price × exchange rate

In our example, the U.S. dollar is the domestic currency:

U.S. dollar value = CAD25 × 0.8 = USD20

If we multiply the price of the shirt in Canadian dollars (CAD25) by the exchange rate (0.8), we find the U.S. dollar value ($20). After adjusting for the exchange rate, then, we can see that the shirt sells for the same price in both countries when the price is measured in a single currency.

The euro is the common currency of the following western European countries: Austria, Belgium, Cyprus, Estonia, Finland, France, Germany, Greece, Ireland, Italy, Latvia, Luxembourg, Malta, Netherlands, Portugal, Slovakia, Slovenia, and Spain. The Global Business Insight "The Euro" provides more discussion.

NOW YOU TRY IT

You travel to Mexico and find that your lunch costs 80 pesos. The exchange rate is 10 pesos per dollar.

a. What is the cost of 1 peso in terms of U.S. dollars?

b. How much does your lunch cost in U.S. dollars?

Find the reciprocal of a number by writing it as a fraction and then turning the fraction upside down. In other words, make the numerator the denominator and the denominator the numerator

TABLE 2   **International Currency Symbols, Selected Countries**

Country	Currency	ISO Symbol
Australia	Dollar	AUD
Canada	Dollar	CAD
China	Yuan	CNY
Denmark	Krone	DKK
India	Rupee	INR
Iran	Rial	IRR
Japan	Yen	JPY
Kuwait	Dinar	KWD
Mexico	Peso	MXN
Norway	Krone	NOK
Russia	Ruble	RUB
Saudi Arabia	Riyal	SAR
Singapore	Dollar	SGD
South Africa	Rand	ZAR
Sweden	Krona	SEK
Switzerland	Franc	CHF
United Kingdom	Pound	GBP
United States	Dollar	USD
Venezuela	Bolivar	VEB
European Union	Euro	EUR

Because different countries use different currencies, international business requires the exchange of monies in the foreign exchange market.

GLOBAL BUSINESS INSIGHT

Active Trading Around the World

It is often said that the foreign exchange market never closes, since trading can take place in different parts of the world as time passes. However, people in each region tend to work certain normal business hours, and so each major foreign exchange trading location has fairly regular hours during which active trading occurs. The accompanying figure shows the normal hours of active trading in each major trading region. The times are in *Greenwich Mean Time*, or *GMT*, which is the time in London. For instance, we see that active trading in London opens at 0800. This is 8 a.m. in London. Active trading stops in London at 1600, which is 4 p.m. in London. (In many parts of the world, a 24-hour clock registers time from 0000 to 1200 in the morning, where 1200 is noon. Then in the afternoon, time starts to count up from 1200. So 1 p.m. is 1300, 2 p.m. is 1400, and so on.)

The figure shows trading in New York as opening at 1200, or noon in London. Eastern time in the United States

is five hours behind London time (as seen by the −5 for that region of the world at the bottom of the figure), so that when it is noon in London, it is five hours earlier, or 7 a.m., in New York. Note that active trading in London closes at 1600 and active trading in New York opens at 1200, so London and New York trading overlap for four hours each day. Similarly, the figure shows that trading in New York also overlaps with trading in Frankfurt, Germany. However, there is no overlap of trading in North America with trading in Asia, as Asian trading centers open after trading has ended in North America and close before trading begins in North America. There is a short overlap of Asian trading with European trading. This figure reminds us that the world of foreign exchange trading, and that of business in general, tends to be conducted during regular business hours in each region.

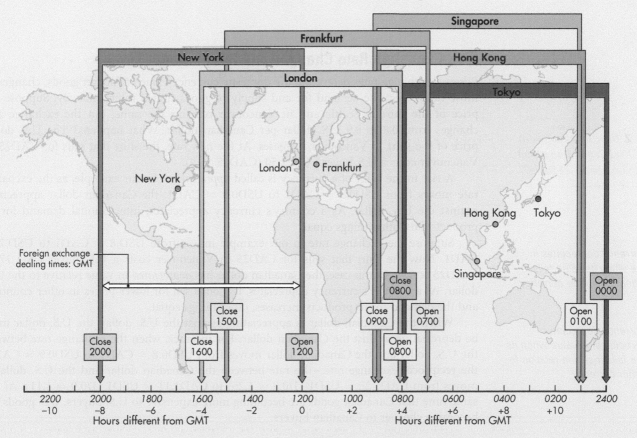

GLOBAL BUSINESS INSIGHT

The Euro

The euro began trading in January 1999 and for more than three years circulated jointly with the national currencies of the original 12 countries that adopted the euro. The former currencies of these countries are the Austrian schilling, Belgian franc, Finnish markka, French franc, German mark, Greek drachma, Irish pound, Italian lira, Luxembourg franc, Netherlands guilder, Portuguese escudo, and Spanish peseta. Prior to the beginning of the euro, the value of each of the "legacy currencies" of the euro area was fixed in terms of the euro. For instance, 1 euro was equal to 40.3399 Belgian francs or 1.95583 German marks. In February 2002, the former monies of each of the euroarea countries were withdrawn from circulation, and now only the euro is used in the 12-country area. Since that time, the following countries have joined the euroarea and replaced their domestic currencies with the euro: Cyprus, Estonia, Latvia, Malta, Slovenia, and Slovakia.

Euro coins are available in the following denominations: 1, 2, 5, 10, 20, and 50 cents and 1 and 2 euro. One side of each coin has an image that is common in all euro-land countries. The other side has a design that is individualized for each country. For instance, a 2-euro coin has a common side with a big number 2 placed over a map of Europe. But the reverse side differs across countries. In Germany, the 2-euro coin has an eagle surrounded by a ring of stars, while in Spain, the 2-euro coin has a portrait of the Spanish king, Carlos I. However, even though each country can issue its own coins, the coins are all usable in any euro-land country. You could receive French coins in Paris and then spend them in Rome. Euro currency or banknotes are available in the following denominations: 5, 10, 20, 50, 100, 200, and 500 euros. The paper money is identical in all countries.

6-1b Exchange Rate Changes and International Trade

?

2. How do changes in exchange rates affect international trade?

A currency depreciates in value when its value falls in relation to another currency

A currency depreciates (appreciates) in value when its value falls (rises) in relation to another currency

Because exchange rates determine the domestic currency value of foreign goods, changes in those rates affect the demand for and supply of goods traded internationally. Suppose the price of the shirt in Seattle and in Vancouver remains the same, but the exchange rate changes from 0.8 to 0.9 U.S. dollar per Canadian dollar. What happens? The U.S. dollar price of the shirt in Vancouver increases. At the new rate, the shirt that sells for CAD25 in Vancouver costs a U.S. buyer USD22.50 (CAD25 × .9).

A rise in the value of a currency is called *appreciation*. In our example, as the exchange rate moves from USD0.8 = CAD1 to USD0.9 = CAD1, the Canadian dollar appreciates against the U.S. dollar. As a country's currency appreciates, international demand for its products falls, other things equal.

Suppose the exchange rate in our example moves from USD.8 = CAD1 to USD.7 = CAD1. Now the shirt that sells for CAD25 in Vancouver costs a U.S. buyer USD 17.50 (CAD25 × 0.7). In this case, the Canadian dollar has *depreciated* in value relative to the U.S. dollar. As a country's currency depreciates, its goods sell for lower prices in other countries and the demand for its products increases, other things equal.

When the Canadian dollar is appreciating against the U.S. dollar, the U.S. dollar must be depreciating against the Canadian dollar. For instance, when the exchange rate between the U.S. dollar and the Canadian dollar moves from USD0.8 = CAD1 to USD0.9 = CAD1, the reciprocal exchange rate—the rate between the Canadian dollar and the U.S. dollar—moves from CAD1.25 = USD1 (1/0.8 = 1.25) to CAD1.11 = USD1 (1/0.9 = 1.11). At the same time that Canadian goods are becoming more expensive to U.S. buyers, U.S. goods are becoming cheaper to Canadian buyers.

In later chapters we look more closely at how changes in exchange rates affect international trade and at how governments use exchange rates to change their net exports.

6-2 The Balance of Payments

The U.S. economy does not operate in a vacuum. It affects and is affected by the economies of other nations. This point is brought home to Americans when newspaper headlines announce a large trade deficit and politicians denounce foreign countries for running trade surpluses against the United States. In such times, it seems as if everywhere there is talk of the balance of payments.

The **balance of payments** is a record of a country's trade in goods, services, and financial assets with the rest of the world. This record is divided into categories, or accounts, that summarize the nation's international economic transactions. For example, one category measures transactions in merchandise; another measures transactions involving financial assets (bank deposits, bonds, stocks, loans). Balance of payments data are reported quarterly for most developed countries.

Once we understand the various definitions of the balance of payments, there remains the issue of why we should care. One important reason is that balance of payments issues are often hot political topics. One cannot make sense of the political debate without an understanding of balance of payments basics. For instance, the United States is said to have a large deficit in its merchandise trade with the rest of the world. Is this bad? Some politicians will argue that a large trade deficit calls for government action, as it is harmful for a nation to buy more than it sells to the rest of the world. The economics of the balance of payments allows us to judge the value of such arguments. Some policymakers, labor leaders, and business people will argue that it is bad if a country has a trade deficit with another single country. For instance, if the United States has a trade deficit with Japan, it is common to hear calls for policy aimed at eliminating this *bilateral* trade deficit. Once again, an understanding of the economics of the trade deficit allows a proper evaluation of calls for policies aimed at eliminating bilateral trade imbalances. We will encounter references to policy issues related to the balance of payments in later chapters.

3. How do nations record their transactions with the rest of the world?

balance of payments
A record of a country's trade in goods, services, and financial assets with the rest of the world.

6-2a Accounting for International Transactions

The balance of payments is an accounting statement known as a balance sheet. A balance sheet is based on **double-entry bookkeeping**, a system in which every transaction is recorded in at least two accounts. We do not need to know the details of accounting rules to understand the balance of payments. We can simply think of transactions bringing money into a country as being positive numbers that are recorded as *credits* and transactions taking money out of a country as being negative numbers that are recorded as *debits*. Double-entry bookkeeping requires that the debit and credit entries for any transaction must balance. Suppose a U.S. tractor manufacturer sells a $50,000 tractor to a resident

double-entry bookkeeping
A system of accounting in which every transaction is recorded in at least two accounts.

of France. This transaction would have a positive effect on the U.S. balance of trade in merchandise. If a U.S. resident bought a $500 bicycle from a Japanese firm, this would have a negative effect on the U.S. balance of trade in merchandise. Of course, people buy and sell things other than merchandise. The classification of international transactions into major accounts is now considered.

6-2b Balance of Payments Accounts

The balance of payments uses several different accounts to classify transactions (see Table 3). The **current account** is the sum of the balances in the merchandise, services, income, and unilateral transfers accounts.

Merchandise This account records all transactions involving goods. The exports of goods by the United States are merchandise credits, bringing money into the United States; its imports of foreign goods are merchandise debits, taking money out of the United States. When exports (or credits) exceed imports (or debits), the merchandise account shows a **surplus**. When imports exceed exports, the account shows a **deficit**. The balance in the merchandise account is frequently referred to as the **balance of trade**.

In the third quarter of 2013, the merchandise account in the U.S. balance of payments showed a deficit of $179,457 million. This means that the merchandise credits created by U.S. exports were $179,457 million less than the merchandise debits created by U.S. imports. In other words, the United States bought more goods from other nations than it sold to them.

Services This account measures trade involving services. It includes travel and tourism, royalties, transportation costs, and insurance premiums. In Table 3, the balance on the services account was a $56,824 million surplus.

Income Both investment income and employee compensation are included here. The income earned from investments in foreign countries is a credit; the income paid on foreign-owned investments in the United States is a debit. Investment income is the return on a special kind of service: It is the value of services provided by capital in foreign countries. Compensation earned by U.S. workers abroad is a credit. Compensation earned by foreign workers in the United States is a debit. In Table 3, there is a surplus of $50,880 million in the income account.

Unilateral Transfers In a unilateral transfer, one party gives something but gets nothing in return. Gifts and retirement pensions are forms of unilateral transfers.

---

current account
The sum of the merchandise, services, income, and unilateral transfers accounts in the balance of payments.

surplus
In a balance of payments account, the amount by which credits exceed debits.

deficit
In a balance of payments account, the amount by which debits exceed credits.

balance of trade
The balance in the merchandise account in a nation's balance of payments.

TABLE 3   Simplified U.S. Balance of Payments, 2013 Third Quarter (million dollars)

Account	Net Balance
Merchandise	−$179,457
Services	$ 56,824
Income	$ 50,880
Unilateral transfers	−$ 33,143
Current account	−$104,896
Financial account	$ 40,422
Statistical discrepancy	$ 64,513

Source: Data from *Bureau of Economic Analysis.*

For instance, if a farmworker in El Centro, California, sends money to his family in Guaymas, Mexico, this is a unilateral transfer from the United States to Mexico. In Table 3, the unilateral transfers balance is a deficit of $33,143 million.

The current account is a useful measure of international transactions because it contains all of the activities involving goods and services. In the third quarter of 2013, the current account showed a deficit of $104,896 million. This means that U.S. imports of merchandise, services, investment income, and unilateral transfers were $104,896 million greater than exports of these items.

If we draw a line in the balance of payments under the current account, then all entries below the line relate to financing the movement of merchandise, services, investment income, and unilateral transfers into and out of the country. The **financial account** is where trade involving financial assets and international investment is recorded. Credits to the financial account reflect foreign purchases of U.S. financial assets or real property like land and buildings, and debits reflect U.S. purchases of foreign financial assets and real property. In Table 3, the U.S. financial account showed a surplus of $40,422 million.

financial account
The record in the balance of payments of the flow of financial assets into and out of a country.

The *statistical discrepancy* account, the last account listed in Table 3, could be called *omissions and errors*. The government cannot accurately measure all transactions that take place. Some international shipments of goods and services go uncounted or are miscounted, as do some international flows of financial assets. The statistical discrepancy account is used to correct for these omissions and errors. In Table 3, measured credits were less than measured debits, so the statistical discrepancy was $64,513 million.

Over all of the balance of payments accounts, the sum of credits must equal the sum of debits. The bottom line—the *net balance*—must be zero. It cannot show a surplus or a deficit. When people talk about a surplus or a deficit in the balance of payments, they are actually talking about a surplus or a deficit in one of the balance of payments accounts. The balance of payments itself, by definition, is always in balance, a function of double-entry bookkeeping.

6-2c The Current Account and the Financial Account

The current account reflects the movement of goods and services into and out of a country. The financial account reflects the flow of financial assets into and out of a country. In Table 3, the current account shows a deficit balance of $104,896 million. Remember that the balance of payments must *balance*. If there is a deficit in the current account, there must be a surplus in the financial account that exactly offsets that deficit.

What is important here is not the bookkeeping process, the concept that the balance of payments must balance, but rather the meaning of deficits and surpluses in the current and financial accounts. These deficits and surpluses tell us whether a country is a net borrower from or lender to the rest of the world. A deficit in the current account means that a country is running a net surplus in its financial account, and it signals that a country is a net borrower from the rest of the world. A country that is running a current account deficit must borrow from abroad an amount sufficient to finance that deficit. A financial account surplus is achieved by selling more bonds and other debts of the domestic country to the rest of the world than the country buys from the rest of the world.

In the chapter "National Income Accounting," we learned that the value of a nation's output, GDP, is equal to the sum of consumption, investment, government spending, and net exports, or $GDP = C + I + G + X$. We could rewrite this equation in terms of X as $X = GDP - C - I - G$. The X in total spending is net exports involving trade in goods and services. As can be seen in Table 3, this is the largest component of the current account. Thus, a country that is running a current account deficit will have a negative X. Since $X = GDP - C - I - G$, one can see that negative net exports or a current account deficit is consistent with domestic spending being in excess of domestic production. A country that is running a current account deficit is spending more than it produces. Such a country must borrow to cover this difference between production and spending.

Figure 1 shows the annual current account balance in the United States. The United States experienced large current account deficits in the 1980s and then again from the mid-1990s to the present. These deficits indicate that the United States consumed more than it produced. This means that the United States sold financial assets to and borrowed large amounts of money from foreign residents to finance its current account deficits. This large amount of foreign borrowing made the United States the largest debtor in the world. A *net debtor* owes more to the rest of the world than it is owed; a *net creditor* is owed more than it owes. The United States was an international net creditor from the end of World War I until the mid-1980s. The country financed its large current account deficits in the 1980s by borrowing from the rest of the world. As a result of this accumulated borrowing, in 1985 the United States became an international net debtor for the first time in almost 70 years. Since that time, the net debtor status of the United States has grown steadily.

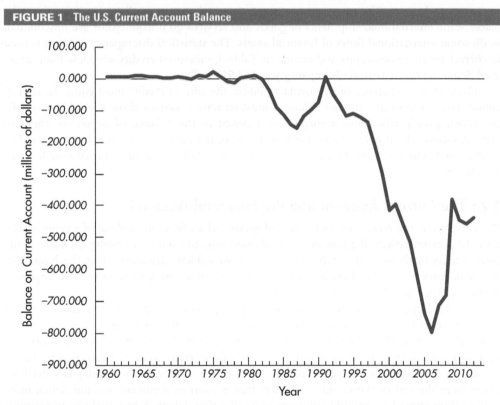

FIGURE 1 The U.S. Current Account Balance

The current account of the balance of payments is the sum of the balances in the merchandise, services, income, and unilateral transfers accounts. The United States experienced very large current account deficits in the 1980s and again more recently.

Source: Bureau of Economic Analysis.

1. The balance of payments is a record of a nation's international transactions.

2. Double-entry bookkeeping requires that every transaction be entered in at least two accounts so that credits and debits are balanced.

3. In the balance of payments, credits record activities that represent payments into the country, and debits record activities that represent payments out of the country.

4. The current account is the sum of the balances in the merchandise, services, income, and unilateral transfers accounts.

5. A surplus exists when credits exceed debits; a deficit exists when credits are less than debits.

6. The financial account is where the transactions necessary to finance the movement of merchandise, services, income, and unilateral transfers into and out of the country are recorded.

7. The net balance in the balance of payments must be zero.

SUMMARY

1. How do individuals of one nation trade money with individuals of another nation?

- Foreign exchange is currency and bank deposits that are denominated in foreign currency. §6-1

- The foreign exchange market is a global market in which people trade one currency for another. §6-1

- Exchange rates, the price of one country's money in terms of another country's money, are necessary to compare prices quoted in different currencies. §6-1a

- The value of a good in a domestic currency equals the foreign currency price times the exchange rate. §6-1a

2. How do changes in exchange rates affect international trade?

- When a domestic currency appreciates, domestic goods become more expensive to foreigners, and foreign goods become cheaper to domestic residents. §6-1b

- When a domestic currency depreciates, domestic goods become cheaper to foreigners, and foreign goods become more expensive to domestic residents. §6-1b

3. How do nations record their transactions with the rest of the world?

- The balance of payments is a record of a nation's transactions with the rest of the world. §6-2

- The balance of payments is based on double-entry bookkeeping. §6-2a

- Credits record activities that bring payments into a country; debits record activities that take payments out of a country. §6-2a

- The current account is the sum of the balances in the merchandise, services, income, and unilateral transfers accounts. §6-2b

- In a balance of payments account, a surplus is the amount by which credits exceed debits, and a deficit is the amount by which debits exceed credits. §6-2b

- The financial account reflects the transactions necessary to finance the movement of merchandise, services, income, and unilateral transfers into and out of the country. §6-2b

- The net balance in the balance of payments must be zero. §6-2b

- A deficit in the current account must be offset by a surplus in the financial account. §6-2c

- A country that shows a deficit in its current account (or a surplus in its financial account) is a net borrower. §6-2c

KEY TERMS

balance of payments, 109
balance of trade, 110
current account, 110
deficit, 110

double-entry bookkeeping, 109
exchange rate, 104
financial account, 111
foreign exchange, 104

foreign exchange market, 104
surplus, 110

EXERCISES

1. What is the price of 1 U.S. dollar in terms of each of the following currencies, given the following exchange rates?
   a. 1 euro = $1.41
   b. 1 Chinese yuan = $.15
   c. 1 Israeli shekel = $.28
   d. 1 Kuwaiti dinar = $3.60
2. A bicycle manufactured in the United States costs $200. Using the exchange rates listed in Table 1, what would the bicycle cost in each of the following countries?
   a. Argentina
   b. Britain
   c. Canada
3. The U.S. dollar price of a Swedish krona changes from $.1572 to $.1730.
   a. Has the dollar depreciated or appreciated against the krona?
   b. Has the krona appreciated or depreciated against the dollar?

Use the information in the following table on Mexico's 2007 international transactions to answer exercises 4–6 (the amounts are the U.S. dollar values in millions):

Merchandise exports	$ 271,594
Merchandise imports	$ 281,649
Services exports	$ 17,512
Services imports	$ 23,784
Income receipts	$ 7,972
Income payments	$ 26,036
Unilateral transfers	$ 24,197

4. What is the balance of trade?
5. What is the current account?

6. Did Mexico become a larger international net debtor during 2007?
7. How reasonable is it for every country to follow policies aimed at increasing net exports?
8. How did the United States become the world's largest debtor nation in the 1980s?
9. If the U.S. dollar appreciated against the Japanese yen, what would you expect to happen to U.S. net exports to Japan?
10. Suppose the U.S. dollar price of a British pound is $1.50; the dollar price of a euro is $1; a hotel room in London, England, costs 120 British pounds; and a comparable hotel room in Hanover, Germany, costs 200 euro.
    a. Which hotel room is cheaper for a U.S. tourist?
    b. What is the exchange rate between the euro and the British pound?
11. Many residents of the United States send money to relatives living in other countries. For instance, a Salvadoran farmworker who is temporarily working in San Diego, California, sends money back to his family in El Salvador. How are such transactions recorded in the balance of payments? Are they debits or credits?
12. Suppose the U.S. dollar price of the Canadian dollar is $.75. How many Canadian dollars will it take to buy a set of dishes selling for $60 in Detroit, Michigan?
13. Why is it true that if the dollar depreciates against the yen, the yen must appreciate against the dollar?
14. Why does the balance of payments contain an account called "statistical discrepancy"?
15. Use the national income identity GDP = $C + I + G + X$ to explain what a current account deficit (negative net exports) means in terms of domestic spending, production, and borrowing.

ECONOMICALLY SPEAKING

FRENCH CROSS CHANNEL TO BUY CHANEL IN LONDON

Mark Blunden
London Evening Standard, March 23, 2009

Channel-hopping shoppers are taking advantage of the weak pound and flocking to London to snap up famous French brands, retailers said today.

Chanel, Chloe and Louis Vuitton goods are proving most popular with the French shoppers, according to Selfridges.

The department store, which has a flagship shop in Oxford Street, said trade from France soared by 70 per cent in January and February compared with the same months last year. The trend held for shoppers from other countries using the euro, with trade growing by more than 40 per cent.

The pound's weakness means European customers can make big savings on purchases such as designers handbags, with a Chanel quilted leather bag costing the equivalent of £1,780 in Paris available at Selfridges for £1,525.

Euro shoppers are also snapping up British brands, with sales of Vivienne Westwood handbags up more than 50 per cent this year. Selfridges' buying director, Anne Pitcher, said: "European customers have clearly resolved not to give up on life's uplifting luxuries and are coming to London to get them at the best possible price."

Source: From **www.thisisLondon.co.uk/** standard, March 23, 2009.

COMMENTARY

Why were French shoppers traveling to London to shop? The article says that it has to do with a weak British pound. There are two elements involved in determining the price of an internationally traded good: the price in terms of the home currency of the country in which the good is produced and the exchange rate. With constant pound prices of goods in London, if the British pound depreciates in value against the euro, British goods will become cheaper to French buyers, as emphasized in the article.

If one examines how the euro value of a pound has changed in recent times, it is easy to see how the price of goods in London has changed for French residents. In early 2007, 1 pound was worth about 1.50 euro. But by early 2009, a pound was only worth about 1.05 euro. So if the prices of goods and services in London did not change at all, the prices of London goods to French shoppers fell by about a third. A luxury purse that sells for 1,000 pounds in London would have cost a French shopper about 1,500 euro in 2007 but fell in price to about 1,050 euro by 2009.

This brief article reminds us of how interdependent countries are. The story of the increase in French shoppers in London in 2009 is a good example of how the exchange rate between currencies is one of the key variables linking countries together.

CHAPTER 7
Unemployment and Inflation

FUNDAMENTAL QUESTIONS

1. What is a business cycle?

2. How is the unemployment rate defined and measured?

3. What is the cost of unemployed resources?

4. What is inflation?

5. Why is inflation a problem?

Preview

If you were graduating from college today, what would your job prospects be? In 1932, they would have been bleak. A large number of people were out of work (about one in four workers), and a large number of firms had laid off workers or gone out of business. At any given time, job opportunities depend, not only on the individual's ability and experience, but also on the current state of the economy.

Economies follow cycles of activity: Periods of expansion, in which output and employment increase, are followed by periods of contraction, in which output and

117

employment decrease. For instance, during the expansionary period of the 1990s and 2000, only 4 percent of U.S. workers had no job by 2000. But during the period of contraction of 1981–1982, 9.5 percent of U.S. workers had no job. When the economy is growing, the demand for goods and services tends to increase. To produce those goods and services, firms hire more workers. Economic expansion also has an impact on inflation: As the demand for goods and services goes up, the prices of those goods and services also tend to rise. By 2000, following several years of economic growth, consumer prices in the United States were rising by about 3 percent a year. During periods of contraction, when more people are out of work, demand for goods and services tends to fall, and there is less pressure for rising prices. During the period of the Great Depression in the 1930s in the United States, consumer prices fell by more than 5 percent in 1933. Both price increases and the fraction of workers without jobs are affected by business cycles in fairly regular ways. But their effects on individual standards of living, income, and purchasing power are much less predictable.

Why do certain events move in tandem? What are the links between unemployment and inflation? What causes the business cycle to behave as it does? What effect does government activity have on the business cycle—and on unemployment and inflation? Who is harmed by rising unemployment and inflation? Who benefits? Macroeconomics attempts to answer all of these questions.

7-1 Business Cycles

In this chapter, we describe the business cycle and examine measures of unemployment and inflation. We talk about the ways in which the business cycle, unemployment, and inflation are related. And we describe their effects on the participants in the economy.

The most widely used measure of a nation's output is gross domestic product (GDP). When we examine the value of real GDP over time, we find periods in which it rises and other periods in which it falls.

7-1a Definitions

This pattern—real GDP rising, then falling—is called a **business cycle**. The pattern occurs over and over again, but as Figure 1 shows, the pattern over time is anything but regular. Historically, the duration of business cycles and the rate at which real GDP rises or falls (indicated by the steepness of the line in Figure 1) vary considerably.

Looking at Figure 1, it is clear that the U.S. economy has experienced up-and-down swings in the years since 1959. Still, real GDP has grown at an average rate of approximately 3 percent per year over the long run. While it is important to recognize that periods of economic growth, or prosperity, are followed by periods of contraction, or **recession**, it is also important to recognize the presence of long-term economic growth despite the presence of periodic recessions. In the long run, the economy produces more goods and services. The long-run growth in the economy depends on the growth in productive resources, like land, labor, and capital, along with technological advance. Technological change increases the productivity of resources so that output increases even with a fixed amount of inputs.

1. What is a business cycle?

business cycle
Fluctuations in the economy between growth (expressed in rising real GDP) and stagnation (expressed in falling real GDP).

recession
A period in which real GDP falls.

FIGURE 1 U.S. Real GDP

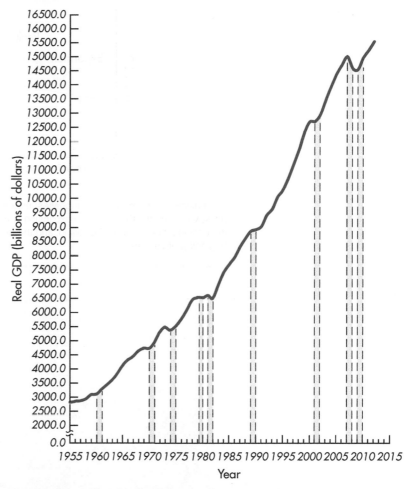

Peaks	Troughs
April 1960	February 1961
December 1969	November 1970
November 1973	March 1975
January 1980	July 1980
July 1981	November 1982
July 1990	March 1991
March 2001	November 2001
December 2007	June 2009

The shaded areas represent periods of economic contraction (recession). The table lists the dates of business cycle peaks and troughs. The peak dates indicate when contractions began; the trough dates, when expansions began.

Source: Bureau of Economic Analysis; **www.bea.gov**.

Figure 2 shows how real GDP behaves over a hypothetical business cycle and identifies the stages of the cycle. The vertical axis on the graph measures the level of real GDP; the horizontal axis measures time in years. In year 1, real GDP is growing; the economy is in the *expansion* phase, or *boom* period, of the business cycle. Growth continues until the *peak* is reached, in year 2. Real GDP begins to fall during the *contraction* phase of the cycle, which continues until year 4. The *trough* marks the end of the contraction and the start of a new expansion. Even though the economy is subject to periodic ups and downs, real GDP, the measure of a nation's output, has risen over the long term, as illustrated by the upward-sloping line labeled *Trend*.

If an economy is growing over time, why do economists worry about business cycles? Economists try to understand the causes of business cycles so that they can learn how to moderate or avoid recessions and their harmful effects on standards of living.

FIGURE 2   The Business Cycle

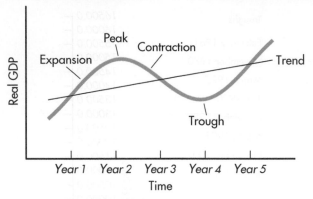

The business cycle contains four phases: the expansion (boom), when real GDP is increasing; the peak, which marks the end of an expansion and the beginning of a contraction; the contraction (recession), when real GDP is falling; and the trough, which marks the end of a contraction and the beginning of an expansion.

As real income falls, living standards go down. This 1937 photo of a Depression-era breadline indicates the paradox of the world's richest nation, as emphasized on the billboard in the background, having to offer public support to feed able-bodied workers who were out of work due to the severity of the business cycle downturn.

7-1b Historical Record

The official dating of recessions in the United States is the responsibility of the National Bureau of Economic Research (NBER), an independent research organization. The NBER has identified the shaded areas in the graph in Figure 1 as recessions and the unshaded areas as expansions. Recessions are periods between cyclical peaks and the troughs that follow them. Expansions are periods between cyclical troughs and the peaks that follow them. There have been 14 recessions since 1929. The most severe was the period between 1929 and 1933, called the Great Depression. During this period, national output fell by 25 percent. A **depression** is a prolonged period of severe economic contraction. The fact that people speak of "the Depression" when they talk about the recession that began in 1929 indicates the severity of that contraction relative to others in recent experience. There was widespread suffering during the Depression. Many people were jobless and homeless, and many firms went bankrupt.

depression
A severe, prolonged economic contraction.

The NBER defines a recession as "a period of significant decline in total output, income, employment, and trade, usually lasting from six months to a year, and marked by wide-spread contractions in many sectors of the economy." People sometimes say that a recession is defined by two consecutive quarters of declining real GDP. This informal idea of what constitutes a recession seems to be consistent with the past recessions experienced by the United States, as every recession through the 1990s has had at least two quarters of falling real GDP. However, this is not the official definition of a recession. The business cycle dating committee of the NBER generally focuses on monthly data. Close attention is paid to the following monthly data series: employment, real personal income less transfer payments, the volume of sales of the manufacturing and wholesale-retail sectors adjusted for price changes, and industrial production. The focus is not on real GDP, because it is measured only quarterly and does not permit the identification of the month in which business-cycle turning points occur.

The shaded areas represent periods of economic contraction (recession). The table lists the dates of business cycle peaks and troughs. The peak dates indicate when contractions began; the trough dates, when expansions began.

On November 28, 2008, the NBER Business Cycle Dating Committee met and determined that December 2007 was the most recent business-cycle peak. It always takes some time for the committee that dates business cycles to have enough evidence to be convinced that the data have identified the turning point in the business cycle. For instance, in determining the end of the previous recession, it was not until July 17, 2003, that the NBER announced the recession had ended in November 2001. It took more than 1.5 years to identify the trough that marked the end of the prior recent recession. On September 19, 2010, the NBER determined that a trough in business activity occurred in the U.S. economy in June 2009, marking the end of the recession that had begun in December 2007.

The business cycle contains four phases: the expansion (boom), when real GDP is increasing; the peak, which marks the end of an expansion and the beginning of a contraction; the contraction (recession), when real GDP is falling; and the trough, which marks the end of a contraction and the beginning of an expansion.

7-1c Indicators

We have been talking about the business cycle in terms of real GDP. There are a number of other variables that move in a fairly regular manner over the business cycle. These variables are classified into three categories—leading indicators, coincident indicators, and lagging indicators—depending on whether they move up or down before, at the same time as, or following a change in real GDP (see Table 1).

Leading indicators generally change before real GDP changes. As a result, economists use them to forecast changes in output. Looking at Table 1, it is easy to see how some of these leading indicators could be used to forecast future output. For instance, new building permits signal new construction. If the number of new permits issued goes up, economists

leading indicator
A variable that changes before real output changes.

TABLE 1 Indicators of the Business Cycle	
Leading Indicators	
Average workweek	New building permits
Unemployment claims	Delivery times of goods
Manufacturers' new orders	Interest rate spread
Stock prices	Money supply
New plant and equipment orders	Consumer expectations
Coincident Indicators	**Lagging Indicators**
Payroll employment	Labor cost per unit of output
Industrial production	Inventories-to-sales ratio
Personal income	Unemployment duration
Manufacturing and trade sales	Consumer credit–to–personal income ratio
	Outstanding commercial loans
	Prime interest rate
	Inflation rate for services

can expect the amount of new construction to increase. Similarly, if manufacturers receive more new orders, economists can expect more goods to be produced.

Leading indicators are not infallible, however. The link between them and future output can be tenuous. For example, leading indicators may fall one month and then rise the next, although real output rises steadily. Economists want to see several consecutive months of a new direction in the leading indicators before forecasting a change in output. Short-run movements in the indicators can be very misleading.

coincident indicator
A variable that changes at the same time as real output changes.

Coincident indicators are economic variables that tend to change at the same time as real output changes. For example, as real output increases, economists expect to see employment and sales rise. The coincident indicators listed in Table 1 have demonstrated a strong tendency over time to change along with changes in real GDP.

lagging indicator
A variable that changes after real output changes.

The final group of variables listed in Table 1, **lagging indicators**, do not change in value until after the value of real GDP has changed. For instance, as output increases, jobs are created and more workers are hired. It makes sense, then, to expect the duration of unemployment (the average length of time that workers are unemployed) to fall. The duration of unemployment is a lagging indicator. Similarly, the inflation rate for services (which measures how prices for things like dry cleaners, veterinarians, and other services change) tends to change after real GDP changes. Lagging indicators are used along with leading and coincident indicators to identify the peaks and troughs in business cycles.

RECAP

1. The business cycle is a recurring pattern of rising and falling real GDP.
2. Although all economies move through periods of expansion and contraction, the duration of the periods of expansion and recession varies.

3. Real GDP is not the only variable affected by business cycles; leading, lagging, and coincident indicators also show the effects of economic expansion and contraction.

7-2 Unemployment

Recurring periods of prosperity and recession are reflected in the nation's labor markets. In fact, this is what makes understanding the business cycle so important. If business cycles signified only a little more or a little less profit for businesses, governments would not be so anxious to forecast or to control their swings. It is the human costs of lost jobs and incomes—the inability to maintain standards of living—that make an understanding of business cycles and of the factors that affect unemployment so important.

7-2a Definition and Measurement

The **unemployment rate** is the percentage of the labor force that is not working. The rate is calculated by dividing the number of people who are unemployed by the number of people in the labor force:

$$\text{Unemployment rate} = \frac{\text{number unemployed}}{\text{number in labor force}}$$

This ratio seems simple enough, but there are several subtle issues at work here. First, the unemployment rate does not measure the percentage of the total population that is not working; it measures the percentage of the *labor force* that is not working. Who is in the labor force? Obviously, everybody who is employed is part of the labor force. But only some of those who are not currently employed are counted in the labor force.

The Bureau of Labor Statistics of the Department of Labor compiles labor data each month based on an extensive survey of U.S. households. All U.S. residents are potential members of the labor force. The Labor Department arrives at the size of the actual labor force by using this formula:

Labor force = all U.S. residents − residents under 16 years of age − institutionalized adults minus adults not looking for work

2. *How is the unemployment rate defined and measured?*

unemployment rate
The percentage of the labor force that is not working.

You are in the labor force if you are working or actively seeking work.

Agricultural harvests, like this one in Mexico, create seasonal fluctuations in the employment of labor. During the harvest period, workers are hired to help out. When the harvest has ended, many of these workers will be temporarily unemployed until the next crop requires their labor.

discouraged workers
Workers who have stopped looking for work because they believe that no one will offer them a job.

underemployment
The employment of workers in jobs that do not utilize their productive potential.

Activity in the underground economy is not included in official statistics.

So the labor force includes those adults (an adult being someone 16 or older) who are currently employed or actively seeking work. It is relatively simple to see to it that children and institutionalized adults (e.g., those in prison or in long-term care facilities) are not counted in the labor force. It is more difficult to identify and accurately measure adults who are not actively looking for work.

A person is actively seeking work if he or she is available to work, has looked for work in the past four weeks, is waiting for a recall after being laid off, or is starting a job within 30 days. Those who are not working and who meet these criteria are considered unemployed.

7-2b Interpreting the Unemployment Rate

Is the unemployment rate an accurate measure? The fact that the rate does not include those who are not actively looking for work is not necessarily a failing. Many people who are not actively looking for work—homemakers, older citizens, and students, for example—have made a decision not to work—to do housework, to retire, or to stay in school. These people rightly are not counted among the unemployed.

But there are people missing from the unemployment statistics who are not working and are not looking for work, yet they would take a job if one were offered. **Discouraged workers** have looked for work in the past year but have given up looking for work because they believe that no one will hire them. These individuals are ignored by the official unemployment rate, even though they are able to work and may have spent a long time looking for work. Estimates of the number of discouraged workers indicate that, in October 2013, 2.3 million people were not counted in the labor force yet claimed that they searched for work and were available. Of this group, 34 percent, or over 800,000 people, were considered to be discouraged workers. It is clear that the reported unemployment rate underestimates the true burden of unemployment in the economy because it ignores discouraged workers.

Discouraged workers are one source of hidden unemployment; underemployment is another. **Underemployment** is the underutilization of workers, employing them in tasks that do not fully utilize their productive potential; this includes part-time workers who would prefer full-time employment. Even if every worker has a job, substantial underemployment leaves the economy producing less than its potential GDP.

The effect of discouraged workers and underemployment is to produce an unemployment rate that *understates* actual unemployment. In contrast, the effect of the *underground economy* is to produce a rate that *overstates* actual unemployment. A sizable number of the officially unemployed are actually working. The unemployed construction worker who plays in a band at night may not report that activity because he or she wants to avoid paying taxes on his or her earnings as a musician. This person is officially unemployed but has a source of income. Many officially unemployed individuals have an alternative source of income. This means that official statistics overstate the true magnitude of unemployment. The larger the underground economy, the greater this overstatement.

We have identified two factors, discouraged workers and underemployment, that cause the official unemployment rate to underestimate true unemployment. Another factor, the underground economy, causes the official rate to overestimate the true rate of unemployment. There is no reason to expect these factors to cancel one another out, and there is no way to know for sure which is most important. The point is to remember what the official data on unemployment do and do not measure.

7-2c Types of Unemployment

Economists have identified four basic types of unemployment:

Seasonal unemployment A product of regular, recurring changes in the hiring needs of certain industries on a monthly or seasonal basis

Frictional unemployment A product of the short-term movement of workers between jobs and of first-time job seekers

Structural unemployment A product of technological change and other changes in the structure of the economy

Cyclical unemployment A product of business-cycle fluctuations

Frictional and structural unemployment are always present in a dynamic economy.

In certain industries, labor needs fluctuate throughout the year. When local crops are harvested, farms need lots of workers; the rest of the year, they do not. (Migrant farmworkers move from one region to another, following the harvests, to avoid seasonal unemployment.) Ski resort towns like Park City, Utah, are booming during the ski season, when employment peaks, but they need fewer workers during the rest of the year. In the nation as a whole, the Christmas season is a time of peak employment and low unemployment rates. To avoid confusing seasonal fluctuations in unemployment with other sources of unemployment, unemployment data are seasonally adjusted.

Frictional and structural unemployment exist in any dynamic economy. For individual workers, frictional unemployment is short term in nature. Workers quit one job and soon find another; students graduate and soon find a job. This kind of unemployment cannot be eliminated in a free society. In fact, it is a sign of efficiency in an economy when workers try to increase their income or improve their working conditions by leaving one job for another. Frictional unemployment is often called *search unemployment* because workers take time to search for a job after quitting a job or leaving school.

Frictional unemployment is short term; structural unemployment, on the other hand, can be long term. Workers who are displaced by technological change (assembly line

Snow plow drivers are needed in the peak winter season, but may be unemployed in the warmer times of year.

workers who have been replaced by machines, for example) or by a permanent reduction in the demand for an industry's output (cigar makers who have been laid off because of a decrease in demand for tobacco) may not have the necessary skills to maintain their level of income in another industry. Rather than accept a much lower salary, these workers tend to prolong their job search. Eventually they either adjust their expectations to the realities of the job market or enter the pool of discouraged workers.

Structural unemployment is very difficult for those who are unemployed. But for society as a whole, the technological advances that cause structural unemployment raise living standards by giving consumers a greater variety of goods at lower cost.

Cyclical unemployment is a result of the business cycle. When a recession occurs, cyclical unemployment increases, and when growth occurs, cyclical unemployment decreases. It is also a primary focus of macroeconomic policy. Economists believe that a greater understanding of business cycles and their causes may enable them to find ways to smooth out those cycles and swings in unemployment. Much of the analysis in future chapters is related to macroeconomic policy aimed at minimizing business-cycle fluctuations. In addition to macroeconomic policy aimed at moderating cyclical unemployment, other policy measures—for example, job training and counseling—are being used to reduce frictional and structural unemployment.

Cyclical unemployment is a product of recession.

7-2d Costs of Unemployment

The cost of unemployment is more than the obvious loss of income and status suffered by the individual who is not working. In a broader sense, society as a whole loses when resources are unemployed. Unemployed workers produce no output. So an economy with unemployment will operate inside its production possibilities curve rather than on the curve. Economists measure this lost output in terms of the *GDP gap:*

$$\text{GDP gap} = \text{potential real GDP} - \text{actual real GDP}$$

Potential real GDP is the level of output produced when nonlabor resources are fully utilized and unemployment is at its natural rate. The **natural rate of unemployment** is the unemployment rate that would exist in the absence of cyclical unemployment, so it includes seasonal, frictional, and structural unemployment. The natural rate of unemployment is not fixed; it can change over time. For instance, some economists believe that the natural rate of unemployment has risen in recent decades, a product of the influx of baby boomers and women into the labor force. As more workers move into the labor force (begin looking for jobs), frictional unemployment increases, raising the natural rate of unemployment. The natural rate of unemployment is sometimes called the "nonaccelerating inflation rate of unemployment," or NAIRU. The idea is that there would be upward pressure on wages and prices in a tight labor market in which the unemployment rate fell below the NAIRU. We will see macroeconomic models of this phenomenon in later chapters.

Potential real GDP measures what we are capable of producing at the natural rate of unemployment. If we compute potential real GDP and then subtract actual real GDP, we have a measure of the output lost as a result of unemployment, or the cost of unemployment.

The GDP gap in the United States from 1975 to 2012 is shown in Figure 3. The gap widens during recessions and narrows during expansions. As the gap widens (as the output that is not produced increases), there are fewer goods and services available, and living standards are lower than they would be at the natural rate of unemployment. Figure 3(b) is a graph of the gap between potential and real GDP, taken from Figure 3(a). During the strong expansion of the late 1990s, and more recently before the financial crisis and associated recession, the gap went to zero. Following the recession the gap widened considerably and has remained large.

3. What is the cost of unemployed resources?

potential real GDP
The output produced at the natural rate of unemployment.

natural rate of unemployment
The unemployment rate that would exist in the absence of cyclical unemployment.

FIGURE 3 The GDP Gap

(a) Potential and Real GDP

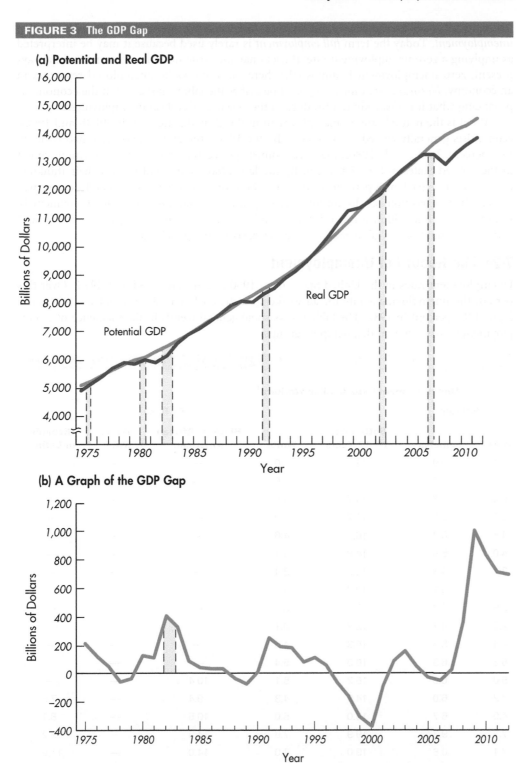

(b) A Graph of the GDP Gap

The GDP gap is the difference between what the economy can produce at the natural rate of unemployment (potential GDP) and actual output (actual GDP). When the unemployment rate is higher than the natural rate, actual GDP is less than potential GDP. The gap between potential and actual real GDP is a cost associated with unemployment. Recession years are shaded to highlight how the gap widens around recessions.

Source: Federal Reserve Bank of St. Louis; **http://research.stlouisfed.org**. All data in 2005 dollars.

Because frictional and structural unemployment are always present, the term full employment *is misleading. Today economists use the term* natural rate of unemployment *instead.*

Until recently, economists used the term *full employment* instead of *natural rate of unemployment*. Today the term *full employment* is rarely used because it may be interpreted as implying a zero unemployment rate. If frictional and structural unemployment are always present, zero unemployment is impossible; there must always be unemployed resources in an economy. *Natural rate of unemployment* describes the labor market when the economy is producing what it realistically can produce in the absence of cyclical unemployment.

What is the natural rate of unemployment in the United States? In the 1950s and 1960s, economists generally agreed on 4 percent. By the 1970s, the agreed-upon rate had gone up to 5 percent. In the early 1980s, many economists placed the natural rate of unemployment in the United States at 6 to 7 percent. By the late 1980s, some had revised their thinking, placing the rate back at 5 percent. In the late 1990s, one could have said that 4 percent was correct. In fact, economists do not know exactly what the natural rate of unemployment is. It varies over time within a range from around 4 percent to around 7 percent. It will also vary across countries, as labor markets and macroeconomic policies differ.

7-2e The Record of Unemployment

Unemployment rates in the United States from 1960 to 2012 are listed in Table 2. Over this period, the unemployment rate for all workers reached a low of 3.5 percent in 1969 and a high of 9.7 percent in 1982. The table shows some general trends in the incidence of unemployment across different demographic groups:

TABLE 2 Unemployment Rates in the United States

	Unemployment Rate, Civilian Workers[1]							
	By Gender				By Race			
Year	All Civilian Workers	Males	Females	Both Sexes 16–19 Years	White	Black or African American	Asian (NSA)	Hispanic or Latino
1960	5.5	5.4	5.9	14.7	5.0	—	—	—
1961	6.7	6.4	7.2	16.8	6.0	—	—	—
1962	5.5	5.2	6.2	14.7	4.9	—	—	—
1963	5.7	5.2	6.5	17.2	5.0	—	—	—
1964	5.2	4.6	6.2	16.2	4.6	—	—	—
1965	4.5	4.0	5.5	14.8	4.1	—	—	—
1966	3.8	3.2	4.8	12.8	3.4	—	—	—
1967	3.8	3.1	5.2	12.9	3.4	—	—	—
1968	3.6	2.9	4.8	12.7	3.2	—	—	—
1969	3.5	2.8	4.7	12.2	3.1	—	—	—
1970	4.9	4.4	5.9	15.3	4.5	—	—	—
1971	5.9	5.3	6.9	16.9	5.4	—	—	—
1972	5.6	5.0	6.6	16.2	5.1	10.4	—	—
1973	4.9	4.2	6.0	14.5	4.3	9.4	—	7.5
1974	5.6	4.9	6.7	16.0	5.0	10.5	—	8.1
1975	8.5	7.9	9.3	19.9	7.8	14.8	—	12.2
1976	7.7	7.1	8.6	19.0	7.0	14.0	—	11.5
1977	7.1	6.3	8.2	17.8	6.2	14.0	—	10.1
1978	6.1	5.3	7.2	16.4	5.2	12.8	—	9.1
1979	5.8	5.1	6.8	16.1	5.1	12.3	—	8.3
1980	7.1	6.9	7.4	17.8	6.3	14.3	—	10.1
1981	7.6	7.4	7.9	19.6	6.7	15.6	—	10.4

| TABLE 2 Unemployment Rates in the United States (*continued*) |

Unemployment Rate, Civilian Workers[1]

| | By Gender | | | | By Race | | | |
Year	All Civilian Workers	Males	Females	Both Sexes 16–19 Years	White	Black or African American	Asian (NSA)	Hispanic or Latino
1982	9.7	9.9	9.4	23.2	8.6	18.9	—	13.8
1983	9.6	9.9	9.2	22.4	8.4	19.5	—	13.7
1984	7.5	7.4	7.6	18.9	6.5	15.9	—	10.7
1985	7.2	7.0	7.4	18.6	6.2	15.1	—	10.5
1986	7.0	6.9	7.1	18.3	6.0	14.5	—	10.6
1987	6.2	6.2	6.2	16.9	5.3	13.0	—	8.8
1988	5.5	5.5	5.6	15.3	4.7	11.7	—	8.2
1989	5.3	5.2	5.4	15.0	4.5	11.4	—	8.0
1990	5.6	5.7	5.5	15.5	4.8	11.4	—	8.2
1991	6.8	7.2	6.4	18.7	6.1	12.5	—	10.0
1992	7.5	7.9	7.0	20.1	6.6	14.2	—	11.6
1993	6.9	7.2	6.6	19.0	6.1	13.0	—	10.8
1994	6.1	6.2	6.0	17.6	5.3	11.5	—	9.9
1995	5.6	5.6	5.6	17.3	4.9	10.4	—	9.3
1996	5.4	5.4	5.4	16.7	4.7	10.5	—	8.9
1997	4.9	4.9	5.0	16.0	4.2	10.0	—	7.7
1998	4.5	4.4	4.6	14.6	3.9	8.9	—	7.2
1999	4.2	4.1	4.3	13.9	3.7	8.0	—	6.4
2000	4.0	3.9	4.1	13.1	3.5	7.6	3.6	5.7
2001	4.7	4.8	4.7	14.7	4.2	8.6	4.5	6.6
2002	5.8	5.9	5.6	16.5	5.1	10.2	5.9	7.5
2003	6.0	6.3	5.7	17.5	5.2	10.8	6.0	7.7
2004	5.5	5.6	5.4	17.0	4.8	10.4	4.4	7.0
2005	5.1	5.1	5.1	16.6	4.4	10.0	4.0	6.0
2006	4.6	4.6	4.6	15.4	4.0	8.9	3.0	5.2
2007	4.6	4.7	4.5	15.7	4.1	8.3	3.2	5.6
2008	5.8	6.1	5.4	18.7	5.2	10.1	4.0	7.6
2009	9.3	10.3	8.1	24.3	8.5	14.8	7.3	12.1
2010	9.6	10.5	8.6	25.9	8.7	16	7.5	12.5
2011	8.9	9.4	8.5	24.4	7.9	15.8	7.0	11.5
2012	8.1	8.2	7.9	24	7.2	13.8	5.9	10.3

[1]Unemployed as a percentage of the civilian labor force in the group specified.

Source: Bureau of Labor Statistics; **http://data.bls.gov/**.

Teenagers have the highest unemployment rates in the economy. This makes sense because teenagers are the least-skilled segment of the labor force.

Whites have lower unemployment rates than nonwhites. Discrimination plays a role here. To the extent that discrimination extends beyond hiring practices and job opportunities for minority workers to the education that is necessary to prepare students to enter the work force, minority workers will have fewer opportunities for employment. The quality of education provided in many schools with large minority populations may not be as good as that provided in schools with large white populations. Equal opportunity programs and legislation are aimed at rectifying this inequality.

Although exact comparisons across countries are difficult to make because different countries measure unemployment in different ways, it is interesting to look at the reported unemployment rates of different countries. Table 3 lists unemployment rates for seven major industrial nations. The rates have been adjusted to match the U.S. definition of unemployment as closely as possible.

TABLE 3 Unemployment Rates in Major Industrial Countries

			Civilian Unemployment Rate (percent)				
Year	United States	Canada	Japan	France	Germany	Italy	United Kingdom
1980	7.1	7.3	2.0	6.5	2.8	4.4	6.9
1981	7.6	7.3	2.2	7.6	4.0	4.9	9.7
1982	9.7	10.7	2.4	8.3	5.6	5.4	10.8
1983	9.6	11.6	2.7	8.6	6.9	5.9	11.5
1984	7.5	10.9	2.8	10.0	7.1	5.9	11.8
1985	7.2	10.2	2.7	10.5	7.2	6.0	11.4
1986	7.0	9.3	2.8	10.6	6.6	7.5	11.4
1987	6.2	8.4	2.9	10.8	6.3	7.9	10.5
1988	5.5	7.4	2.5	10.3	6.3	7.9	8.6
1989	5.3	7.1	2.3	9.6	5.7	7.8	7.3
1990	5.6	7.7	2.1	8.6	5.0	7.0	7.1
1991	6.8	9.8	2.1	9.1	5.6	6.9	9.5
1992	7.5	10.6	2.2	10.0	6.7	7.3	10.2
1993	6.9	10.8	2.5	11.3	8.0	9.8	10.4
1994	6.1	9.6	2.9	11.9	8.5	10.7	9.5
1995	5.6	8.6	3.2	11.3	8.2	11.3	8.7
1996	5.4	8.8	3.4	11.8	9.0	11.3	8.1
1997	4.9	8.4	3.4	11.7	9.9	11.4	7.0
1998	4.5	7.7	4.1	11.2	9.3	11.5	6.3
1999	4.2	7.0	4.7	10.5	8.5	11.0	6.0
2000	4.0	6.1	4.8	9.1	7.8	10.2	5.5
2001	4.7	6.5	5.1	8.4	7.9	9.2	5.1
2002	5.8	7.0	5.4	8.8	8.6	8.7	5.2
2003	6.0	6.9	5.3	9.2	9.3	8.5	5.0
2004	5.5	6.4	4.8	9.6	10.3	8.1	4.8
2005	5.1	6.0	4.5	9.6	11.2	7.8	4.9
2006	4.6	5.5	4.2	9.5	10.4	6.9	5.5
2007	4.6	5.3	3.9	8.6	8.7	6.2	5.4
2008	5.8	5.3	4.0	7.5	7.5	6.8	5.7
2009	9.3	7.3	4.8	9.2	7.8	7.9	7.7
2010	9.6	7.1	4.8	9.5	7.1	8.5	7.9
2011	8.9	6.5	4.2	9.4	6.0	8.5	8.1
2012	8.1	6.3*	3.8*	10.0*	5.8	10.7	7.9

*Data based on first three quarters of 2012.

Source: *Economic Report of the President, 2013.*

GLOBAL BUSINESS INSIGHT

High Unemployment in Europe

The data in Table 3 indicate that European countries tend to have higher unemployment rates than other industrial countries. This is not true for all European countries, but it is certainly true for the biggest: France, Germany, Italy, and Spain. One factor that contributes to the higher unemployment rates in these countries is government policy with regard to the labor market. Countries that have policies that encourage unemployment should be expected to have more unemployed workers. In a recent speech, a British scholar gave his analysis of why Europe has such high unemployment. One story he told illustrates how government policy aimed at protecting citizens against unemployment can create the very unemployment that is the focus of its concern. In Italy, laws require parents to support their adult children who do not work, even if the children are entirely capable of working. The story goes as follows:

> *The Italian Court of Cessation ruled that a professor at Naples University, separated from his family, must continue to pay his 30-year-old son €775 per month until he can find himself suitable employment. This despite the fact that the son owns a house and possesses an investment trust fund worth €450,000. The judges said that an adult son who refused work that did not reflect his training, abilities, and personal interests could not be held to blame. In particular the judges said, "You cannot blame a young person, particularly from a well-off family, who refuses a job that does not fit his aspirations." By contrast, under UK law, a separated father would only have to support his children until they completed full-time education. (Nickell, 2002)*

The government requirement that parents support unemployed adult children encourages those children to remain unemployed.

Among men of prime working age (age 25–54), there are more who are inactive and not participating in the labor force than there are who are unemployed. The majority of these men are receiving benefits from the government, claiming disability or illness. In the 1970s, there were many fewer disabled or ill workers as a fraction of the population. But as social bene-

fits were increased and the eligibility rules were relaxed, the number of people claiming to suffer from such problems increased also. The unfortunate truth of human nature is that when you provide better support for those who truly need help, there will be more and more who do not truly need it, yet claim a need. The experience of Denmark is instructive in this regard. Denmark has generous unemployment benefits. But in the 1990s, Danish eligibility requirements were tightened, creating greater incentives for the unemployed to look for work. Danish unemployment rates fell dramatically as a result.

Yet another factor contributing to higher unemployment rates in some countries is restrictions on the ability of firms to terminate workers and the requirement that firms pay high separation costs to workers whom they do fire. The more difficult it is for firms to adjust their labor force in the face of economic fluctuations, the less likely firms are to hire new workers. If you own a business and your sales increase, you are likely to hire extra employees to meet the increased demand for your product. However, you cannot be sure that your sales will be permanently higher, so you would be very conservative about hiring new workers if you would have to pay terminated workers a large amount of money if your sales fell and you needed to lay off some of your employees. Such labor market rigidities, aimed at protecting workers from losing their jobs, create incentives against hiring, so that those who would like to work cannot get hired.

The lesson from large European countries is that government policies aimed at protecting workers from unemployment may create a bigger unemployment problem. Thus, the costs imposed on the economy in the form of taxes and reduced labor market flexibility may exceed the benefits to those who keep their jobs or receive unemployment compensation because of the programs.

Source: Stephen Nickell, "A Picture of European Unemployment: Success and Failure," speech given to CESifo Conference in Munich, December 2002, and Lars Ljungqvist and Thomas Sargent, "The European Unemployment Dilemma," *Journal of Political Economy,* 1998.

Knowing their limitations, we can still identify some important trends from the data in Table 3. In the early 1980s, both U.S. and European unemployment rates increased substantially. But in the mid-1980s, when U.S. unemployment began to fall, European unemployment remained high. The issue of high unemployment rates in Europe has become a major topic of discussion at international summit meetings and is addressed in the Global Business Insight "High Unemployment in Europe." The inflexibility of labor markets in Europe is a factor that makes the European economies more prone to slow growth. Japanese unemployment rates, like those in Europe, were much lower than U.S. and Canadian rates in the 1980s. However, by the late 1990s, Japanese rates began to approach those of the United States.

RECAP

1. The unemployment rate is the number of people unemployed as a percentage of the labor force.

2. To be in the labor force, one must either have or be looking for a job.

3. Through its failure to include discouraged workers and the output lost because of under-employment, the unemployment rate under-states real unemployment in the United States.

4. Through its failure to include activity in the underground economy, the U.S. unemploy-ment rate overstates actual unemployment.

5. Unemployment data are adjusted to eliminate seasonal fluctuations.

6. Frictional and structural unemployment are always present in a dynamic economy.

7. Cyclical unemployment is a product of recession; it can be moderated by controlling the period of contraction in the business cycle.

8. Economists measure the cost of unemployment in terms of lost output.

9. Unemployment data show that women gener-ally have higher unemployment rates than men, that teenagers have the highest unemployment rates in the economy, and that blacks and other minority groups have higher unemployment rates than whites.

7-3 Inflation

4. What is inflation?

inflation
A sustained rise in the average level of prices.

5. Why is inflation a problem?

Inflation is a sustained rise in the average level of prices. Notice the word *sustained*. Inflation does not mean a short-term increase in prices; it means that prices are rising over a pro-longed period of time. Inflation is measured by the percentage change in price level. The inflation rate in the United States was −0.36 percent in 2009. This means that, on average, the level of prices declined slightly over the year. Low inflation, or perhaps even deflation, is what one typically expects during a recession when spending falls.

7-3a Absolute versus Relative Price Changes

In the modern economy, over any given period, some prices rise faster than others. To evalu-ate the rate of inflation in a country, then, economists must know what is happening to prices on average. Here it is important to distinguish between *absolute* and *relative* price changes.

Let us look at an example using the prices of fish and beef:

	Year I	Year 2
1 pound of fish	$1	$2
1 pound of beef	$2	$4

In year 1, beef is twice as expensive as fish. This is the price of beef *relative* to the price of fish. In year 2, beef is still twice as expensive as fish. The relative prices have not changed between years 1 and 2. What has changed? The prices of both beef and fish have doubled. The *absolute* levels of all prices have gone up, but because they have increased by the same percentage, the relative prices are unchanged.

Inflation measures changes in absolute prices. In our example, all prices doubled, so the inflation rate is 100 percent. There was a 100 percent increase in the prices of beef and fish. In reality, inflation does not take place evenly throughout the economy. Prices of some goods rise faster than others, which means that relative prices are changing at the same time that absolute prices are rising. The measured inflation rate records the *average* change in absolute prices.

7-3b Effects of Inflation

To understand the effects of inflation, you have to understand what happens to the value of money in an inflationary period. The real value of money is what it can buy, its *purchasing power*:

$$\text{Real value of } \$1 = \frac{\$1}{\text{price level}}$$

The purchasing power of a dollar is the amount of goods and services it can buy.

The higher the price level, the lower the real value (or *purchasing power*) of the dollar. For instance, suppose an economy had only one good—milk. If a glass of milk sold for $.50, then $1 would buy two glasses of milk. If the price of milk rose to $1, then a dollar would buy only one glass of milk. The purchasing power, or real value, of money falls as prices rise.

Table 4 lists the real value of the dollar in selected years from 1946 to 2013. The price level in each year is measured relative to the average level of prices over the 1982–1984 period. For

TABLE 4 The Real Value of a Dollar

Year	Average Price Level[1]	Purchasing Power Power of a Dollar[2]
1946	0.195	5.13
1950	0.241	4.15
1954	0.269	3.72
1958	0.289	3.46
1962	0.302	3.31
1966	0.324	3.09
1970	0.388	2.58
1974	0.493	2.03
1978	0.652	1.53
1982	0.965	1.04
1986	1.096	0.91
1990	1.307	0.77
1994	1.482	0.67
1998	1.63	0.61
2002	1.809	0.55
2006	2.016	0.50
2008	2.153	0.46
2009	2.145	0.47
2010	2.181	0.46
2011	2.249	0.44
2012	2.296	0.44
2013	2.335	0.43

[1]Measured by the consumer price index as given at **http://www.bls.gov/cpi/**.
[2]Found by taking the reciprocal of the consumer price index (1/CPI).

instance, the 1946 value, 0.195, means that prices in 1946 were, on average, only 19.5 percent of prices in the 1982–1984 period. Notice that as prices go up, the purchasing power of the dollar falls. In 1946, a dollar bought five times as much as it bought in the early 1980s. The value 5.13 means that one could buy 5.13 times as many goods and services with a dollar in 1946 as one could buy in 1982–1984.

Prices have risen steadily in recent decades. By 2013, they had risen to more than 100 percent above the average level of prices in the 1982–1984 period. Consequently, the purchasing power of a 2013 dollar was lower. In 2013, $1 bought just 43 percent of the goods and services that one could buy with a dollar in 1982–1984.

If prices and nominal income rise by the same percentage, it might seem that inflation is not a problem. It does not matter if it takes twice as many dollars to buy fish and beef now as it did before if we have twice as many dollars of income available to buy the products. Obviously, inflation is very much a problem when a household's nominal income rises at a slower rate than prices. Inflation hurts those households whose income does not keep up with the prices of the goods they buy.

In the 1970s, the rate of inflation in the United States rose to near-record levels. Many workers believed that their incomes were lagging behind the rate of inflation, so they negotiated cost-of-living raises in their wage contracts. The typical cost-of-living raise ties salary to changes in the consumer price index. If the CPI rises 8 percent during a year, workers receive an 8 percent raise plus compensation for experience or productivity increases. As the U.S. rate of inflation fell during the 1980s, concern about cost-of-living raises subsided as well.

It is important to distinguish between expected and unexpected inflation. *Unexpectedly high inflation* redistributes income away from those who receive fixed incomes (like creditors who receive debt repayments of a fixed amount of dollars per month) and toward those who make fixed expenditures (like debtors who make fixed debt repayments per month). For example, consider a simple loan agreement:

Unexpectedly high inflation redistributes income away from those who receive fixed incomes and toward those who make fixed expenditures.

> *Maria borrows $100 from Ali, promising to repay the loan in one year at 10 percent interest. One year from now, Maria will pay Ali $110—principal of $100 plus interest of $10 (10 percent of $100, or $10).*

When Maria and Ali agree to the terms of the loan, they do so with some expected rate of inflation in mind. Suppose they both expect 5 percent inflation over the year. In other words, they expect that one year from now, it will take 5 percent more money to buy goods than it does now. Ali will need $105 to buy what $100 buys today. Because Ali will receive $110 for the principal and interest on the loan, he will gain purchasing power. However, if the inflation rate over the year turns out to be surprisingly high— say, 15 percent—then Ali will need $115 to buy what $100 buys today. He will lose purchasing power if he makes a loan at a 10 percent rate of interest.

nominal interest rate
The observed interest rate in the market.

real interest rate
The nominal interest rate minus the rate of inflation.

Real interest rates are lower than expected when inflation is higher than expected.

Economists distinguish between nominal and real interest rates when analyzing economic behavior. The **nominal interest rate** is the observed interest rate in the market and includes the effect of inflation. The **real interest rate** is the nominal interest rate minus the rate of inflation:

$$\text{Real interest rate} = \text{nominal interest rate} - \text{rate of inflation}$$

If Ali charges Maria a 10 percent nominal interest rate and the inflation rate is 5 percent, the real interest rate is 5 percent (10% − 5% = 5%). This means that Ali will earn a positive real return from the loan. However, if the inflation rate is 10 percent, the real return from a nominal interest rate of 10 percent is zero (10% − 10% = 0). The interest that Ali will receive from the loan will just compensate him for the rise in prices; he will not realize an increase in purchasing power. If the inflation rate is higher than the nominal interest rate, then the real interest rate is negative—the lender will lose purchasing power by making the loan.

Now you can see how unexpected inflation redistributes income. Borrowers and creditors agree to loan terms based on what they *expect* the rate of inflation to be over the period of the loan. If the *actual* rate of inflation turns out to be different from what was expected, then the real interest rate paid by the borrower and received by the lender will be different from what was expected. If Ali and Maria both expect a 5 percent inflation rate and agree to a 10 percent nominal interest rate for the loan, then they both expect a real interest rate of 5 percent (10% − 5% = 5%) to be paid on the loan. If the actual inflation rate turns out to be greater than 5 percent, then the real interest rate will be less than expected. Maria will get to borrow Ali's money at a lower real cost than she expected, and Ali will earn a lower real return than he expected. Unexpectedly high inflation hurts creditors and benefits borrowers because it lowers real interest rates.

Figure 4 shows the real interest rates on U.S. Treasury bills from 1970 through 2013. You can see a pronounced pattern in the graph. In the late 1970s, there was a period of negative real interest rates, followed by high positive real rates in the 1980s. The evidence suggests that nominal interest rates did not rise fast enough in the 1970s to offset high inflation. This was a time of severe strain for many creditors, including savings and loan associations and banks. These firms had lent funds at fixed nominal rates of interest. When those rates of interest turned out to be lower than the rate of inflation, the financial institutions suffered significant losses. In the early 1980s, the inflation rate dropped sharply. Because nominal interest rates did not drop nearly as fast as the rate of inflation, real interest rates were high. In this period, many debtors were hurt by the high costs of borrowing to finance business or household expenditures. More recently, real interest rates have been negative again due to the very low nominal interest rates resulting from the global recession and associated government policies.

Unexpected inflation affects more than the two parties to a loan. Any contract calling for fixed payments over some long-term period changes in value as the rate of inflation changes. For instance, a long-term contract that provides union members with 5 percent raises each

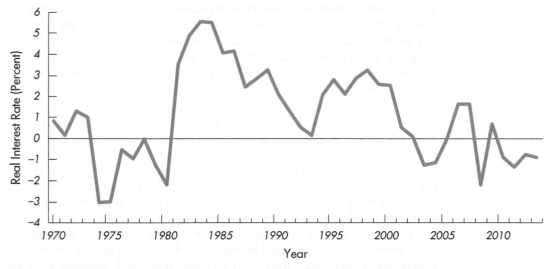

FIGURE 4 The Real Interest Rate on U.S. Treasury Bills

The real interest rate is the difference between the nominal interest rate (the interest rate actually observed) and the rate of inflation over the life of the bond. The figure shows the real interest rate in June and December for each year. For instance, in the first observation, for June 1970, a six-month Treasury bill paid the holder 6.91 percent interest. This is the nominal rate of interest. To find the real rate of interest on the bond, we subtract the rate of inflation that existed over the six months of the bond's life (June to December 1970), which was 5.17 percent. The difference between the nominal interest rate (6.91 percent) and the rate of inflation (5.17 percent) is the real interest rate, 1.74 percent. Notice that real interest rates were negative during most of the 1970s and then turned highly positive (by historical standards) in the early 1980s.

year for five years gives the workers more purchasing power if inflation is low than if it is high. Similarly, a contract to sell a product at a fixed price over a long-term period will change in value as inflation changes. Suppose a lumber company promises to supply a builder with lumber at a fixed price for a two-year period. If the rate of inflation in one year turns out to be higher than expected, the lumber company will end up selling the lumber for less profit than it had planned. Inflation raises the lumber company's costs. Usually the company would raise its prices to compensate for the higher costs. Because the company contracted to sell its goods to the builder at a fixed price, however, the builder benefits at the lumber company's expense. Again, unexpectedly high inflation redistributes real income or purchasing power away from those receiving fixed payments to those making fixed payments.

One response to the effects of unexpected inflation is to allow prices, wages, or interest rates to vary with the rate of inflation. Labor unions sometimes negotiate cost-of-living adjustments as part of new wage contracts. Financial institutions offer variable interest rates on home mortgages to reflect current market conditions. Any contract can be written to adjust dollar amounts over time as the rate of inflation changes.

7-3c Types of Inflation

Economists often classify inflation according to the source of the inflationary pressure. The most straightforward method defines inflation in terms of pressure from the demand side of the market or the supply side of the market:

Demand-pull inflation Increases in total spending that are not offset by increases in the supply of goods and services and so cause the average level of prices to rise.

Cost-push inflation Increases in production costs that cause firms to raise prices to avoid losses.

Sometimes inflation is blamed on "too many dollars chasing too few goods." This is a roundabout way of saying that the inflation stems from demand pressures. Because demand-pull inflation is a product of increased spending, it is more likely to occur in an economy that is producing at maximum capacity. If resources are fully employed, it may not be possible in the short run to increase output to meet increased demand. The result: Existing goods and services are rationed by rising prices.

Some economists claim that the rising prices in the late 1960s were a product of demand-pull inflation. They believe that increased government spending for the Vietnam War caused the level of U.S. prices to rise.

Cost-push inflation can occur in any economy, whatever its output. If prices go up because the costs of resources are rising, the rate of inflation can go up regardless of demand. For example, some economists argue that the inflation in the United States in the 1970s was largely the result of rising oil prices. This means that decreases in the oil supply (a shift to the left in the supply curve) brought about higher oil prices. Because oil is so important in the production of many goods, higher oil prices led to increases in prices throughout the economy. Cost-push inflation stems from changes in the supply side of the market.

Cost-push inflation is sometimes attributed to profit-push or wage-push pressures. *Profit-push pressures* are created by suppliers who want to increase their profit margins by raising prices faster than their costs increase. *Wage-push pressures* are created by labor unions and workers who are able to increase their wages faster than their productivity. There have been times when "greedy" businesses and unions have been blamed for periods of inflation in the United States. The problem with these "theories" is that people have always wanted to improve their economic status and always will. In this sense, people have always been greedy. But inflation has not always been a problem. Were people less greedy in the early 1980s, when inflation was low, than they were in the late 1970s, when inflation was high? Obviously, we have to look for other reasons to explain inflation. We discuss some of those reasons in later chapters.

7-3d The Inflationary Record

Many of our students, having always lived with inflation, are surprised to learn that it is a relatively new problem for the United States. From 1789, when the U.S. Constitution was ratified, until 1940, there was no particular trend in the general price level. At times prices rose, and at times they fell. The average level of prices in 1940 was approximately the same as it was in the late eighteenth century.

Since 1940, prices in the United States have gone up markedly. The price level today is eight times what it was in 1940. But the rate of growth has varied.

Annual rates of inflation for several industrial and developing nations in 2012 are shown in Table 5. Look at the diversity across countries: Rates range from deflations of −0.9 percent in Japan to 11.6 percent inflation in high-inflation nations like Tajikistan. In most cases, **hyperinflation**, an extremely high inflation rate, eventually makes a country's currency worthless and leads to the introduction of a new money. Argentina experienced hyperinflation in the 1980s. People had to carry large stacks of currency for small purchases. Cash registers and calculators ran out of digits as prices reached ridiculously high levels. After years of high inflation, Argentina replaced the old peso with the peso Argentino in June 1983. The government set the value of 1 peso Argentino equal to 10,000 old pesos (striking four zeros from all prices).

hyperinflation
An extremely high rate of inflation.

TABLE 5 Rates of Inflation for Selected Countries, 2012

Industrial	Inflation Rate (percent)
Canada	1.7
Germany	1.3
Italy	1.6
Japan	−0.9
United Kingdom	1.4
United States	2.4
Developing	
Botswana	1.3
Brazil	5.3
Egypt	10.1
Hong Kong, China	3.9
India	8.2
Israel	4.0
Mexico	3.6
Philippines	1.9
Poland	2.5
South Africa	5.5
Tajikistan	11.6
Zambia	6.2

Source: Data are average annual percentage changes in the GDP price index as reported by the World Bank; **http://databank.worldbank.org/**.

A product that had sold for 10,000 old pesos before the reform sold for 1 new peso after. But Argentina did not follow up its monetary reform with a noninflationary change in economic policy. In 1984 and 1985, the inflation rate exceeded 600 percent each year. As a result, in June 1985, the government again introduced a new currency, the austral, setting its value at 1,000 pesos Argentino. However, the economic policy associated with the introduction of the austral lowered the inflation rate only temporarily. By 1988, the inflation rate was over 300 percent, and in 1989 the inflation rate was over 3,000 percent. The rapid rise in prices associated with the austral resulted in the introduction of yet another currency, again named the peso Argentino, in January 1992, with a value equal to 10,000 australes. This new peso was fixed at a value of 1 peso per 1 U.S. dollar, and this exchange rate lasted for about 10 years because of reasonably stable inflation in Argentina. In late 2001, Argentina experienced another financial crisis brought on by large government budget deficits; the fixed rate of exchange between the peso and the dollar ended, but the peso remained the currency of Argentina.

The most dramatic hyperinflation in recent years, and one of the most dramatic ever, occurred in Zimbabwe in 2007–2008. Although the government was not forthcoming about inflation data, research[1] indicates that the price index rose from a value of 1.00 in January 2007 to 853,000,000,000,000,000,000,000 by mid-November 2008, when the price level was doubling every 24 hours. As prices rose, the government issued larger and larger units of paper money as people had to carry huge stacks of old currency to buy anything. A 100 trillion Zimbabwe dollar bill was issued in January 2009. Then in the same month, the government sanctioned the use of U.S. dollars as a substitute currency in Zimbabwe as the local currency had become essentially worthless.

Table 6 provides data on the other recent cases of hyperinflation. The Zimbabwe episode lasted 26 months until the U.S. dollar was sanctioned as a substitute currency. The hyperinflation episodes in Table 6 range in duration from only 3 months in Turkmenistan,

TABLE 6   Recent Hyperinflations

Country	Dates	Months Duration	Cumulative Inflation (percent)
Angola	Dec. 94–Jun. 96	19	62,445
Argentina	May 89–Mar. 90	11	15,167
Armenia	Oct. 93–Dec.94	15	34,158
Azerbaijan	Dec. 92–Dec. 94	25	41,742
Bolivia	Apr. 84–Sep. 85	18	97,282
Brazil	Dec. 89–Mar. 90	4	693
Congo, Dem. Rep.	Nov. 93–Sep. 94	11	69,502
Georgia	Sep. 93–Sep. 94	13	76,219
Nicaragua	Jun. 86–Mar. 91	58	11,895,866,143
Serbia	Feb. 93–Jan. 94	12	156,312,790
Tajikistan	Aug. 93–Dec. 93	9	3,636
Turkmenistan	Nov. 95–Jan. 96	3	291
Ukraine	Apr. 91–Nov. 94	44	1, 864,715

Source: Stanley Fischer, Ratna Sahay, and Carlos A. Vegh, "Modern Hyper- and High Inflations," *Journal of Economic Literature*, September 2002, pp. 837–880.

---

[1] Steve H. Hanke, "R.I.P. Zimbabwe Dollar," **www.cato.org/zimbabwe**.

when prices rose by 291 percent, to 58 months in Nicaragua, when prices rose an astounding 11,895,866,143 percent. Hyperinflation is often associated with crises that lead to new governments, new economic policies, and new monies that replace the essentially worthless old money.

In later chapters, we will see how high rates of inflation generally are caused by rapid growth of the money supply. When a central government wants to spend more than it is capable of funding through taxation or borrowing, it simply issues money to finance its budget deficit. As the money supply increases faster than the demand to hold it, spending increases and prices go up.

RECAP

1. Inflation is a sustained rise in the average level of prices.

2. The higher the price level, the lower the real value (purchasing power) of money.

3. Unexpectedly high inflation redistributes income away from those who receive fixed-dollar payments (like creditors) and toward those who make fixed-dollar payments (like debtors).

4. The real interest rate is the nominal interest rate minus the rate of inflation.

5. Demand-pull inflation is a product of increased spending; cost-push inflation reflects increased production costs.

6. Hyperinflation is a very high rate of inflation that often results in the introduction of a new currency.

SUMMARY

1. What is a business cycle?

- Business cycles are recurring changes in real GDP, in which expansion is followed by contraction. §7-1a

- The four stages of the business cycle are expansion (boom), peak, contraction (recession), and trough. §7-1a

- Leading, coincident, and lagging indicators are variables that change in relation to changes in output. §7-1c

2. How is the unemployment rate defined and measured?

- The unemployment rate is the percentage of the labor force that is not working. §7-2a

- To be in the U.S. labor force, an individual must be working or actively seeking work. §7-2a

- Unemployment can be classified as seasonal, frictional, structural, or cyclical. §7-2c

- Frictional and structural unemployment are always present in a dynamic economy; cyclical unemployment is a product of recession. §7-2c

3. What is the cost of unemployed resources?

- The GDP gap measures the output lost because of unemployment. §7-2d

4. What is inflation?

- Inflation is a sustained rise in the average level of prices. §7-3

- The higher the level of prices, the lower the purchasing power of money. §7-3b

5. Why is inflation a problem?

- Inflation becomes a problem when income rises at a slower rate than prices. §7-3b

- Unexpectedly high inflation hurts those who receive fixed-dollar payments (like creditors) and benefits those who make fixed-dollar payments (like debtors). §7-3b

- Inflation can stem from demand-pull or cost-push pressures. §7-3c

- Hyperinflation—an extremely high rate of inflation—can force a country to introduce a new currency. §7-3d

KEY TERMS

business cycle, 118
coincident indicator, 122
depression, 121
discouraged workers, 124
hyperinflation, 137

inflation, 132
lagging indicator, 122
leading indicator, 121
natural rate of unemployment, 126
nominal interest rate, 134

potential real GDP, 126
real interest rate, 134
recession, 118
underemployment, 124
unemployment rate, 123

EXERCISES

1. What is the labor force? Do you believe that the U.S. government's definition of the labor force is a good one—that it includes all the people it should include? Explain your answer.
2. List the reasons why the official unemployment rate may not reflect the true social burden of unemployment. Explain whether the official numbers overstate or understate *true* unemployment in light of each reason you discuss.
3. Suppose you are able-bodied and intelligent, but lazy. You would rather sit home and watch television than work, even though you know you could find an acceptable job if you looked.
   a. Are you officially unemployed?
   b. Are you a discouraged worker?
4. Can government do anything to reduce the number of people in the following categories? If so, what?
   a. Frictionally unemployed
   b. Structurally unemployed
   c. Cyclically unemployed
5. Does the GDP gap measure all of the costs of unemployment? Why or why not?
6. Why do teenagers have the highest unemployment rate in the economy?
7. Suppose you are currently earning $15 an hour. If the inflation rate over the current year is 10 percent and your firm provides a cost-of-living raise based on the rate of inflation, what would you expect to earn after your raise? If the cost-of-living raise is always granted on the basis of the past year's inflation, is your nominal income really keeping up with the cost of living?
8. Write an equation that defines the real interest rate. Use the equation to explain why unexpectedly high inflation redistributes income from creditors to debtors.
9. Many home mortgages in recent years have been made with variable interest rates. Typically, the interest rate is adjusted once a year on the basis of current interest

rates on government bonds. How do variable interest rate loans protect creditors from the effects of unexpected inflation?
10. The word *cycle* suggests a regular, recurring pattern of activity. Is there a regular pattern to the business cycle? Support your answer by examining the duration (number of months) of each expansion and contraction in Figure 1.
11. Using the list of leading indicators in Table 1, write a brief paragraph explaining why each variable changes before real output changes. In other words, provide an economic reason why each indicator is expected to lead the business cycle.
12. Suppose 500 people were surveyed, and of those 500, 450 were working full time. Of the 50 not working, 10 were full-time college students, 18 were retired, 5 were under 16 years of age, 7 had stopped looking for work because they believed there were no jobs for them, and 10 were actively looking for work.
    a. How many of the 500 surveyed are in the labor force?
    b. What is the unemployment rate among the 500 surveyed people?
13. Consider the following price information:

	Year 1	Year 2
Cup of coffee	$ .50	$1.00
Glass of milk	$1.00	$2.00

   a. Based on the information given, what was the inflation rate between year 1 and year 2?
   b. What happened to the price of coffee relative to that of milk between year 1 and year 2?
14. Use a supply and demand diagram to illustrate:
    a. Cost-push inflation caused by a labor union successfully negotiating for a higher wage.
    b. Demand-pull inflation caused by an increase in demand for domestic products from foreign buyers.

15. During the Bolivian hyperinflation in the 1980s, Bolivians used U.S. dollars as a substitute for the domestic currency (the peso) for many transactions. Explain how the value of money is affected by hyperinflation and the incentives to use a low-inflation currency like the dollar as a substitute for a high-inflation currency like the Bolivian peso.

16. Suppose the government raises the benefits available to unemployed workers and then discovers that the number of unemployed workers has increased substantially, although there has been no other change in the economy. How can government policies aimed at helping the unemployed actually create more unemployment?

17. Toward the end of the recent recession, the economy was characterized by a "jobless recovery"— output and hours worked were rising, but employment was not. Explain what may have been happening.

ECONOMICALLY SPEAKING
OLDER WORKERS AND THE RECESSION

Richard W. Johnson
The Urban Institute
San Diego Union-Tribune, December 8, 2008

Last week's triple dose of grim employment news stirred memories of the early 1980s. Made official on Monday, the current recession has already outlasted any downturn since 1982. Friday's sock to the solar plexus? The economy lost 533,000 jobs last month, the largest monthly decline since 1974.

It gets worse. For older workers, this recession is unprecedented. Last month, 298,000 Americans ages 65 and older were unemployed, 50 percent more than when the recession began a year ago.

During previous downturns, relatively few older Americans were counted as unemployed. Although many lost their jobs, they generally retired instead of looking for work. During the severe 1981–82 recession, seniors' unemployment rate grew by just 0.8 percentage points— only about one-fourth the increase for prime-age workers (25 to 54).

Today, however, seniors are nearly as likely as their juniors to join unemployment lines, because pink-slipped seniors can no longer afford to put their feet up. Shrinking Social Security benefits, traditional pension plans, and 401(k) balances combine with soaring health care costs to force them to keep pounding the pavement.

Rising medical expenses, which consume 15 percent of older people's budgets, can also jinx retirement. And only one in three large private employers offers retiree health benefits to supplement Medicare, compared with two in three in the 1980s. Meanwhile, Medicare's new drug benefit has barely dented seniors' out-of-pocket spending.

Whipsawed by these trends, it's no surprise that three in 10 Americans ages 65 to 69 were working or job hunting in 2007, up from two in 10 in 1982. Paychecks provided nearly one-fifth of this group's income in 2006.

The stock market shed about half its value over the past 14 months, destroying $2.8 trillion in 401(k) and individual retirement accounts and intensifying pressure on seniors to work. Older Americans have been hit hardest because those 50 and older hold nearly three-quarters of these assets.

(During the 1981–82 recession, the S&P 500 index fell by only 6 percent.)

California should do more to help. Other states already train career center staff on the special challenges older workers face, certify employers friendly to mature workers, develop the entrepreneurial skills of older dislocated workers, and create Web sites for older job-seekers.

It's also time for a federal stimulus package committing billions of dollars to rebuilding our crumbling infrastructure. That's a sure way to create jobs, some of them for seniors.

Budgets are tight. But investing in getting willing-and-able seniors back to work would boost the nation's output, spur spending, get the economy back on track and ease the recession's toll on our oldest workers, most of whom have done their bit for their families and the economy for decades.

Source: RICHARD W. JOHNSON The Urban Institute San Diego Union-Tribune, December 8, 2008

COMMENTARY

The article says that the recession in 2008 had created many more unemployed older workers than in prior recessions. Partly, this is because people retired at earlier ages in past decades but now, due to longer life expectancies as well as delayed and smaller retirement benefits, older workers remain in the labor force seeking jobs. Should we expect older workers to have an easier or tougher time finding a job than younger workers? What does economics have to say about why older workers might find it harder to find new jobs than younger workers? The answer lies in the type of knowledge that workers possess that may make them attractive to certain employers.

Many newly unemployed workers have worked for many years and have earned higher salaries than they can expect to earn in other jobs. This, of course, is the problem. If they could simply find another job that offered them comparable pay, they would not be so devastated by the prospect of losing their jobs. This raises an interesting question: If someone is highly valued at one firm and paid accordingly, why is that person not as valuable to other companies who could now hire her or him? In fact, laid-off workers with successful job histories at one firm are often unable to meet entry-level requirements at other jobs.

We can better understand the causes of the plight of many laid-off industrial workers if we consider the determinants of people's wages. Economic theory suggests that people's wages are tied to the amount they contribute to their firm, which implies that people's wages increase with their skills. We can think of two broad categories of skills: general skills that make people valuable to any firm, and more specialized skills that make people valuable to certain firms. Examples of general skills include welding, bookkeeping, and an ability to manage people. Skills that are useful to only one firm are those that are specifically tied to the product or structure of that firm. Specific knowledge of this second type is not transferable to other firms.

People who work in a particular firm for an extended period learn both general skills that make them valuable to any similar company and specific skills that make them valuable to their company only. Experienced workers who are seeking new jobs must possess or else learn general skills that make them attractive in an economy with rapid technological change.

The distinction between general and firm-specific skills suggests why the workers who are least likely to benefit from retraining are those within a few years of retirement. Older workers who must undergo on-the-job training will not be able to use their new firm-specific skills for as many years as younger workers will. It is not worthwhile for firms to hire and train workers who are near retirement.

Structural change is an integral part of a dynamic, growing economy. Dislocations are probably inevitable when large-scale structural change occurs, and these dislocations benefit some people while hurting others. Although retraining helps mitigate some of the effects of the upheaval that accompanies structural change, unfortunately it cannot solve all the problems that arise. For the economy as a whole, such change is necessary. Unfortunately, some people are always harmed when the economy undergoes structural change.

CHAPTER 8

Macroeconomic Equilibrium: Aggregate Demand and Supply

FUNDAMENTAL QUESTIONS

1. What factors affect aggregate demand?

2. What causes the aggregate demand curve to shift?

3. What factors affect aggregate supply?

4. Why does the short-run aggregate supply curve become steeper as real GDP increases?

5. Why is the long-run aggregate supply curve vertical?

6. What causes the aggregate supply curve to shift?

7. What determines the equilibrium price level and real GDP?

Preview

Total output and income in the United States have grown over time. Each generation has experienced a higher standard of living than the previous generation. Yet, as we learned in the earlier chapter, economic growth has not been steady. Economies go through periods of expansion followed by periods of contraction or recession, and such business cycles have major impacts on people's lives, incomes, and living standards.

Economic stagnation and recession throw many, often those who are already relatively poor, out of their jobs and into real poverty. Economic growth increases the number of jobs and draws people out of poverty and into the mainstream of economic progress. To understand why economies grow and why they go through cycles, we must discover why firms decide to produce more or less and why buyers decide to buy more or less. The approach we take is similar to the approach we followed in the first five chapters of the text, using demand and supply curves. In the introductory chapters we derived demand and supply curves and used them to examine questions involving the equilibrium price and quantities demanded and supplies of a single good or service. This simple yet powerful microeconomic technique of analysis has a macroeconomic counterpart: aggregate demand and aggregate supply, which are used to determine an equilibrium price level and quantity of goods and services produced for the *entire economy*. In this chapter we shall use aggregate demand and supply curves to illustrate the causes of business cycles and economic growth.

8-1 Aggregate Demand, Aggregate Supply, and Business Cycles

What causes economic growth and business cycles? We can provide some answers to this important question using aggregate demand (*AD*) and aggregate supply (*AS*) curves. Suppose we represent the economy with a simple demand and supply diagram, as shown in Figure 1. Aggregate demand represents the total spending in the economy at alternative price levels. Aggregate supply represents the total output of the economy at alternative price levels. To understand the causes of business cycles and inflation, we must understand how aggregate demand and aggregate supply cause the equilibrium price level and real GDP, the nation's output of goods and services, to change. The intersection between the *AD* and *AS* curves defines the equilibrium level of real GDP and the level of prices. The equilibrium price level is P_e, and the equilibrium level of real GDP is Y_e. This price and output level represents the level of prices and output for some particular period of time, say 2010. Once that equilibrium is

FIGURE 1   Aggregate Demand and Aggregate Supply Equilibrium

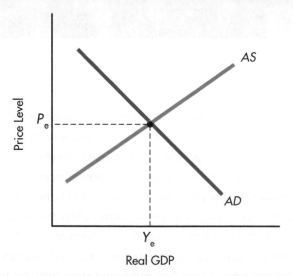

The equilibrium price level and real GDP are determined by the intersection of the *AD* and *AS* curves.

established, there is no tendency for prices and output to change until changes occur in either the aggregate demand curve or the aggregate supply curve. Let us first consider a change in aggregate demand and then look at a change in aggregate supply.

8-1a Aggregate Demand and Business Cycles

An increase in aggregate demand is illustrated by a shift of the **Aggregate Demand curve** to the right, like the shift from AD_1 to AD_2 in Figure 2. This represents a situation in which buyers are buying more at every price level. The shift causes the equilibrium level of real GDP to rise from Y_{e1} to Y_{e2}, illustrating the expansionary phase of the business cycle. As output rises, unemployment decreases. The increase in aggregate demand also leads to a higher price level, as shown by the change in the price level from P_{e1} to P_{e2}. The increase in the price level represents an example of **demand-pull inflation**, which is inflation caused by increasing demand for output.

If aggregate demand falls, like the shift from AD_1 to AD_3, then there is a lower equilibrium level of real GDP, Y_{e3}. In this case, buyers are buying *less at* every price level. The drop in real GDP caused by lower demand would represent an economic slowdown or a recession when output falls and unemployment rises.

aggregate demand curve
A curve that shows the different equilibrium levels of expenditures on domestic output at different levels of prices.

demand-pull inflation
Inflation caused by increasing demand for output.

FIGURE 2 Effects of a Change in Aggregate Demand

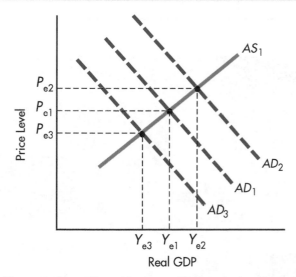

If aggregate demand increases from AD_1 to AD_2, the equilibrium price level increases to P_{e2} and the equilibrium level of real GDP rises to Y_{e2}. If aggregate demand decreases from AD_1 to AD_3, the equilibrium price level falls to P_{e3} and the equilibrium level of real GDP drops to Y_{e3}.

8-1b Aggregate Supply and Business Cycles

Changes in **aggregate supply** can also cause business cycles. Figure 3 illustrates what happens when aggregate supply changes. An increase in aggregate supply is illustrated by the shift from AS_1 to AS_2, leading to an increase in the equilibrium level of real GDP from Y_{e1} to Y_{e2}. An increase in aggregate supply comes about when firms produce more at every price level. Such an increase could result from an improvement in technology or a decrease in the costs of production.

aggregate supply curve
A curve that shows the quantity of real GDP produced at different price levels.

FIGURE 3   Effects of a Change in Aggregate Supply

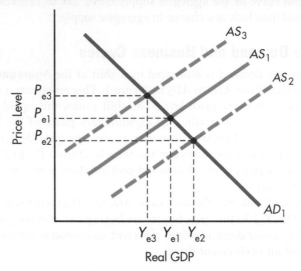

If aggregate supply increases from AS_1 to AS_2, the equilibrium price level falls from P_{e1} to P_{e2} and the equilibrium level of real GDP rises to Y_{e2}. If aggregate supply decreases from AS_1 to AS_3, the equilibrium price level rises to P_{e3} and the equilibrium level of real GDP falls to Y_{e3}.

Technology advance shifts the aggregate supply curve outward and increases output. An example of a technological advance that has increased efficiency in the airline industry is the self check-in kiosk. This allows the airlines to lower costs, as customers do not require an airline employee for assistance.

If aggregate supply decreased, as in the shift from AS_1 to AS_3, then the equilibrium level of real GDP would fall to Y_{e3} and the equilibrium price level would increase from P_{e1} to P_{e3}. A decrease in aggregate supply could be caused by higher production costs that lead producers to raise their prices. This is an example of **cost-push inflation**—where the price level rises as a result of increased costs of production and the associated decrease in aggregate supply.

cost-push inflation
Inflation caused by rising costs of production.

8-1c A Look Ahead

Business cycles result from changes in aggregate demand, from changes in aggregate supply, and from changes in both AD and AS. The degree to which real GDP declines during a recession or increases during an expansion depends on the amount by which the AD and/or AS curve shifts. The degree to which an expansion produces output growth or increased inflation depends on the shapes of the AD and AS curves. We need to consider why the curves have the shapes they do, and what causes them to shift.

The comparison we made earlier, between aggregate demand, aggregate supply, and their microeconomic counterparts, the supply and demand curves, is only superficial. As we examine the aggregate demand and supply curves, you will see that the reasons underlying the shapes and movements of AD and AS are in fact quite different from those explaining the shapes and movements of the supply and demand curves.

RECAP

1. Aggregate demand (AD) represents the total spending in the economy at alternative price levels.

2. Aggregate supply (AS) represents the total output of the economy at alternative price levels.

3. The intersection between the AD and AS curves defines the equilibrium level of real GDP and the level of prices.

4. Business cycles result from changes in AD and/or AS.

8-2 Factors that Influence Aggregate Demand

Aggregate demand is the relation between aggregate expenditures, or total spending, and the price level. Aggregate expenditures are the sum of the expenditures of each sector of the economy: households (consumption), business firms (investment), government, and the rest of the world (net exports). Each sector of the economy has different reasons for spending; for instance, household spending depends heavily on household income, whereas business spending depends on the profits that businesses expect to earn. Because each sector of the economy has a different reason for the amount of spending it undertakes, aggregate spending depends on all of these reasons. To understand aggregate demand, therefore, requires that we look at the factors that influence the expenditures of each sector of the economy.

1. What factors affect aggregate demand?

8-2a Consumption

How much households spend depends on their income, their wealth, expectations about future prices and incomes, demographics like the age distribution of the population, and taxes.

- Income: If current income rises, households purchase more goods and services.
- Wealth: Wealth is different from income. It is the value of the assets owned by a household, including homes, cars, bank deposits, stocks, and bonds. An increase in household wealth will increase consumption.

- Expectations: Expectations regarding future changes in income or wealth can affect consumption today. If households expect a recession and worry about job loss, consumption tends to fall. On the other hand, if households become more optimistic regarding future increases in income and wealth, consumption rises today.
- Demographics: Demographic change can affect consumption in several different ways. Population growth is generally associated with higher consumption for an economy. Younger households and older households generally consume more and save less than middle-aged households. Therefore, as the age distribution of a nation changes, so will consumption.
- Taxes: Higher taxes will lower the disposable income of households and decrease consumption, while lower taxes will raise disposable income and increase consumption. Government policy may change taxes and thereby bring about a change in consumption.

8-2b Investment

Investment is business spending on capital goods and inventories. In general, investment depends on the expected profitability of such spending, so any factor that could affect profitability will be a determinant of investment. Factors affecting the expected profitability of business projects include the interest rate, technology, the cost of capital goods, and capacity utilization.

- Interest rate: Investment is negatively related to the interest rate. The interest rate is the cost of borrowed funds. The greater the cost of borrowing, other things being equal, the fewer the investment projects that offer sufficient profit to be undertaken. As the interest rate falls, investment is stimulated, as the cost of financing the investment is lowered.
- Technology: New production technology stimulates investment spending, as firms are forced to adopt new production methods to stay competitive.
- Cost of capital goods: If machines and equipment purchased by firms rise in price, then the higher costs associated with investment will lower profitability, and investment will fall.
- Capacity utilization: The more excess capacity (unused capital goods) there is available, the more firms can expand production without purchasing new capital goods, and the lower investment will be. As firms approach full capacity, more investment spending will be required to expand output further.

8-2c Government Spending

Government spending may be set by government authorities independent of current income or other determinants of aggregate expenditures.

8-2d Net Exports

Net exports are equal to exports minus imports. We assume that exports are determined by conditions in the rest of the world, such as foreign income, tastes, prices, exchange rates, and government policy. Imports are determined by similar domestic factors.

- Income: As domestic income rises and consumption rises, some of this consumption includes goods produced in other countries. Therefore, as domestic income rises, imports rise and net exports fall. Similarly, as foreign income rises, foreign residents buy more domestic goods, and net exports rise.
- Prices: Other things being equal, higher (lower) foreign prices make domestic goods relatively cheaper (more expensive) and increase (decrease) net exports. Higher (lower) domestic prices make domestic goods relatively more expensive (cheaper) and decrease (increase) net exports.
- Exchange rates: Other things being equal, a depreciation of the domestic currency on the foreign exchange market will make domestic goods cheaper to foreign buyers and

NOW YOU TRY IT

What will happen to the equilibrium price level and real GDP when
1. foreign price levels rise?
2. foreign incomes fall?
3. taxes rise?
4. the use of new computers increases productivity?

make foreign goods more expensive to domestic buyers, so that net exports will rise. An appreciation of the domestic currency will have just the opposite effects.

- Government policy: Net exports may fall if foreign governments restrict the entry of domestic goods into their countries, reducing domestic exports. If the domestic government restricts imports into the domestic economy, net exports may rise.

8-2e Aggregate Expenditures

You can see how aggregate expenditures, the sum of all spending on U.S. goods and services, must depend on prices, income, and all of the other determinants discussed in the previous sections. As with the demand curve for a specific good or service, we want to classify the factors that influence spending into the price and the nonprice determinants for the aggregate demand curves. The components of aggregate expenditures that change as the price level changes will lead to movements along the aggregate demand curve—changes in quantity demanded—whereas changes in aggregate expenditures caused by nonprice effects will cause shifts of the aggregate demand curve—changes in aggregate demand. In the following section, we look first at the price effects, or movements along an aggregate demand curve. Following that discussion, we focus on the nonprice determinants of aggregate demand.

RECAP

1. Aggregate expenditures are the sum of consumption, investment, government spending, and net exports.

2. Consumption depends on household income, wealth, expectations, demographics, and taxation.

3. Investment depends on the interest rate, technology, the cost of capital goods, and capacity utilization.

4. Government spending is determined independent of current income.

5. Net exports depend on foreign and domestic incomes, prices, government policies, and exchange rates.

8-3 The Aggregate Demand Curve

When we examined the demand curves in the chapter titled "The Market and Price System," we divided our study into two parts: the movement along the curve—changes in quantity demanded—and the shifts of the curve—changes in demand. We take the same approach here in examining aggregate demand. We first look at the movements along the aggregate demand curve caused by changes in the price level. We then turn to the nonprice determinants of aggregate demand that cause shifts in the curve.

8-3a Why the Aggregate Demand Curve Slopes Downward

Aggregate demand curves are downward sloping just like the demand curves for individual goods that were shown in the chapter titled "The Market and Price System," although for different reasons. Along the demand curve for an individual good, the price of that good changes while the prices of all other goods remain constant. This means that the good in question becomes relatively more or less expensive compared to all other goods in the economy. Consumers tend to substitute a less expensive good for a more expensive good. The effect of this substitution is an inverse relationship between price and quantity demanded. As the price of a good rises, the quantity demanded falls. For the economy as a whole, however, it is not a substitution of a less expensive good for a more expensive good that causes the demand curve to slope down. Instead, the aggregate quantity demanded, or total spending, will change as the price level changes as a result of the wealth effect, the interest rate effect, and the international trade effect of a price-level change on aggregate expenditures. We will discuss each of these effects in turn.

8-3a-1 The Wealth Effect Individuals and businesses own money, stocks, bonds, and other financial assets. The purchasing power of these assets is the quantity of goods and services for which the assets can be exchanged. When the level of prices falls, the purchasing power of these assets increases, allowing households and businesses to purchase more. When prices go up, the purchasing power of financial assets falls, causing households and businesses to spend less. This is the **wealth effect** (sometimes called the *real-balance effect*) of a price change: a change in the real value of wealth that causes spending to change when the level of prices changes. *Real values* are values that have been adjusted for price-level changes. Here *real value* means "purchasing power." When the price level changes, the purchasing power of financial assets also changes. When prices rise, the real value of assets and wealth falls, and aggregate expenditures tend to fall. When prices fall, the real value of assets and wealth rises, and aggregate expenditures tend to rise.

8-3a-2 The Interest Rate Effect When the price level rises, the purchasing power of each dollar falls, which means that more money is required to buy any particular quantity of goods and services (see Figure 4). Suppose that a family of three needs $100 each week to buy food. If the price level doubles, the same quantity of food costs $200. The household must have

wealth effect
A change in the real value of wealth that causes spending to change when the level of prices changes.

FIGURE 4   The Interest Rate Effect of Price-Level Changes on Aggregate Expenditures

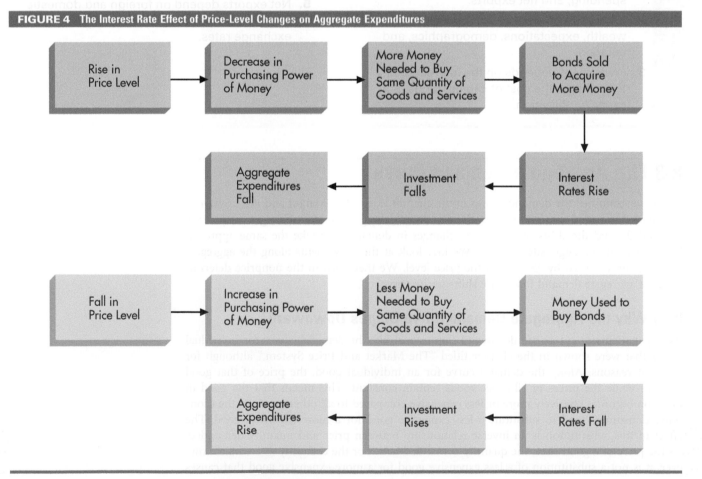

twice as much money to buy the same amount of food. Conversely, when prices fall, the family needs less money to buy food because the purchasing power of each dollar is greater.

When prices go up, people need more money. So they sell their other financial assets, such as bonds, to get that money. The increase in the supply of bonds lowers bond prices and raises interest rates. Since bonds typically pay fixed-dollar interest payments each year, as the price of a bond varies, the interest rate (or yield) will change. For instance, suppose you pay $1,000 for a bond that pays $100 a year in interest. The interest rate on this bond is found by dividing the annual interest payment by the bond price, or $100/$1,000 = 10 percent. If the price of the bond falls to $900, then the interest rate is equal to the annual interest payment (which remains fixed at $100 for the life of the bond) divided by the new price of $900: $100/$900 = 11 percent. When bond prices fall, interest rates rise, and when bond prices rise, interest rates fall.

If people want more money and they sell some of their bond holdings to raise the money, bond prices will fall and interest rates will rise. The rise in interest rates is necessary to sell the larger quantity of bonds, but it causes investment expenditures to fall, which causes aggregate expenditures to fall.

When prices fall, people need less money to purchase the same quantity of goods. So they use their money holdings to buy bonds and other financial assets. The increased demand for bonds increases bond prices and causes interest rates to fall. Lower interest rates increase investment expenditures, thereby pushing aggregate expenditures up.

Figure 4 shows the **interest rate effect**, the relationship among the price level, interest rates, and aggregate expenditures. As the price level rises, interest rates rise and aggregate expenditures fall. As the price level falls, interest rates fall and aggregate expenditures rise.

8-3a-3 The International Trade Effect

The third channel through which a price-level change affects the quantity of goods and services demanded is called the **international trade effect**. A change in the level of domestic prices can cause net exports to change. If domestic prices rise while foreign prices and the foreign exchange rate remain constant, domestic goods become more expensive in relation to foreign goods.

Suppose the United States sells oranges to Japan. If the oranges sell for $1 per pound and the yen-dollar exchange rate is 100 yen = $1, a pound of U.S. oranges costs a Japanese buyer 100 yen. What happens if the level of prices in the United States goes up 10 percent? All prices, including the price of oranges, increase 10 percent. Oranges in the United States sell for $1.10 a pound after the price increase. If the exchange rate is still 100 yen = $1, a pound of oranges now costs the Japanese buyer 110 yen (100 × 1.10). If the prices of oranges from other countries do not change, some Japanese buyers may buy oranges from those countries instead of from the United States. The increase in the level of U.S. prices makes U.S. goods more expensive relative to foreign goods and causes U.S. net exports to fall; a decrease in the level of U.S. prices makes U.S. goods cheaper in relation to foreign goods, which increases U.S. net exports.

When the price of domestic goods increases in relation to the price of foreign goods, net exports fall, causing aggregate expenditures to fall. When the price of domestic goods falls in relation to the price of foreign goods, net exports rise, causing aggregate expenditures to rise. The international trade effect of a change in the level of domestic prices causes aggregate expenditures to change in the opposite direction.

8-3a-4 The Sum of the Price-Level Effects

The aggregate demand curve (*AD*) shows how the equilibrium level of expenditures for the economy's output changes as the price level changes. In other words, the curve shows the amount that people spend at different price levels.

Figure 5 displays the typical shape of the *AD* curve. The price level is plotted on the vertical axis, and real GDP is plotted on the horizontal axis. Suppose that initially the economy

When the price level changes, the purchasing power of financial assets also changes.

interest rate effect
A change in interest rates that causes investment and therefore aggregate expenditures to change as the level of prices changes.

international trade effect
A change in aggregate expenditures resulting from a change in the domestic price level that changes the price of domestic goods relative to that of foreign goods.

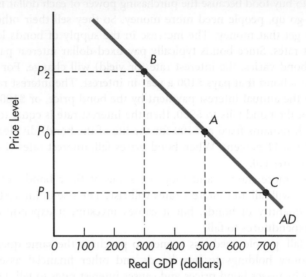

FIGURE 5   The Aggregate Demand Curve

The aggregate demand curve (*AD*) shows the level of expenditures at different price levels. At price level P_0, expenditures are $500; at P_1, they are $700; and at P_2, they are $300.

is at point *A*, with prices at P_0. At this point, spending equals $500. If prices fall to P_1, expenditures equal $700 and the economy is at point *C*. If prices rise from P_0 to P_2, expenditures equal $300 at point *B*.

Because aggregate expenditures increase when the price level decreases and decrease when the price level increases, the aggregate demand curve slopes down. The aggregate demand curve is drawn with the price level for the *entire economy* on the vertical axis. A price-level change here means that, on average, *all prices in the economy change*; there is no relative price change among domestic goods. The negative slope of the aggregate demand curve is a product of the wealth effect, the interest rate effect, and the international trade effect.

A lower domestic price level increases consumption (the wealth effect), investment (the interest rate effect), and net exports (the international trade effect). As the price level drops, aggregate expenditures rise.

A higher domestic price level reduces consumption (the wealth effect), investment (the interest rate effect), and net exports (the international trade effect). As prices rise, aggregate expenditures fall. These price effects are summarized in Figure 6.

8-3b Changes in Aggregate Demand: Nonprice Determinants

2. What causes the aggregate demand curve to shift?

The aggregate demand curve shows the level of aggregate expenditures at alternative price levels. We draw the curve by varying the price level and finding out what the resulting total expenditures are, holding all other things constant. As those "other things"— the nonprice determinants of aggregate demand—change, the aggregate demand curve shifts. The nonprice determinants of aggregate demand include all of the factors covered in the discussion of the components of expenditures—income, wealth, demographics, expectations, taxes, the interest rate (interest rates can change for reasons other than price-level changes), the cost of capital goods, capacity utilization, foreign income and price levels, exchange rates, and government policy. A change in any one of these can cause the *AD* curve to shift. In the discussions that follow, we will focus particularly on the effects of expectations, foreign income,

FIGURE 6 Why the Aggregate Demand Curve Slopes Downward

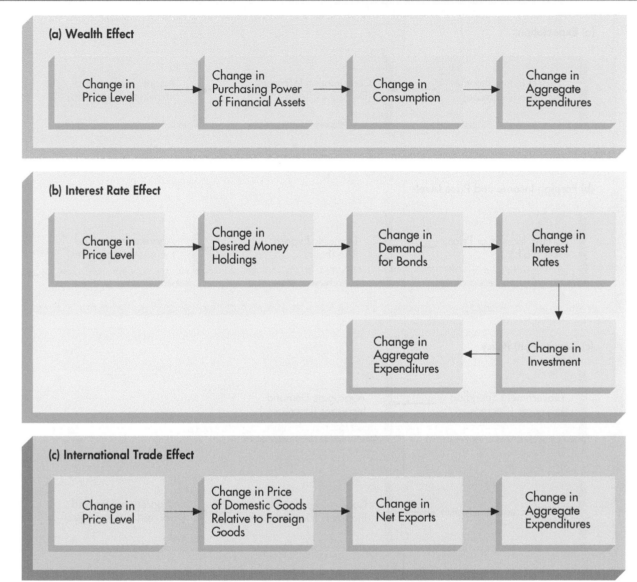

and price levels; we will also mention government policy, which will be examined in detail in the chapter on fiscal policy. Figure 7 summarizes these effects, which are discussed next.

8-3b-1 Expectations Consumption and business spending are affected by expectations. Consumption is sensitive to people's expectations of future income, prices, and wealth. For example, when people expect the economy to do well in the future, they increase their consumption today at every price level. This is reflected in a shift of the aggregate demand curve to the right, from AD_0 to AD_1, as shown in Figure 8. When aggregate demand increases, aggregate expenditures increase at every price level.

On the other hand, if people expect a recession in the near future, they tend to reduce their consumption and increase their saving in order to protect themselves against a greater likelihood of losing a job or a forced cutback in hours worked. As consumption drops,

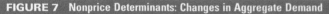

FIGURE 7 Nonprice Determinants: Changes in Aggregate Demand

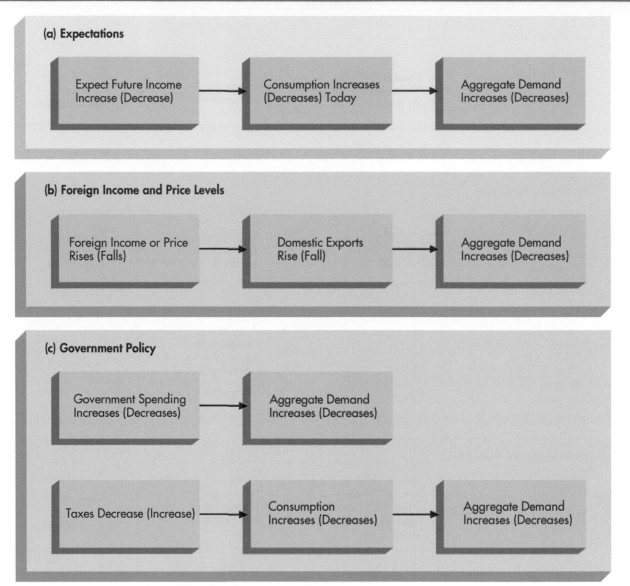

(a) Expectations

Expect Future Income Increase (Decrease) → Consumption Increases (Decreases) Today → Aggregate Demand Increases (Decreases)

(b) Foreign Income and Price Levels

Foreign Income or Price Rises (Falls) → Domestic Exports Rise (Fall) → Aggregate Demand Increases (Decreases)

(c) Government Policy

Government Spending Increases (Decreases) → Aggregate Demand Increases (Decreases)

Taxes Decrease (Increase) → Consumption Increases (Decreases) → Aggregate Demand Increases (Decreases)

aggregate demand decreases. The AD curve shifts to the left, from AD_0 to AD_2. At every price level along AD_2, planned expenditures are less than they are along AD_0.

Expectations also play an important role in investment decisions. Before undertaking a particular project, businesses forecast the likely revenues and costs associated with that project. When the profit outlook is good—say, a tax cut is on the horizon— investment and therefore aggregate demand increase. When profits are expected to fall, investment and aggregate demand decrease.

8-3b-2 Foreign Income and Price Levels When foreign income increases, so does foreign spending. Some of this increased spending is for goods produced in the domestic economy. As domestic exports increase, aggregate demand rises. Lower foreign income has just the opposite effect. As foreign income falls, foreign spending falls, including foreign spending on

FIGURE 8 Shifting the Aggregate Demand Curve

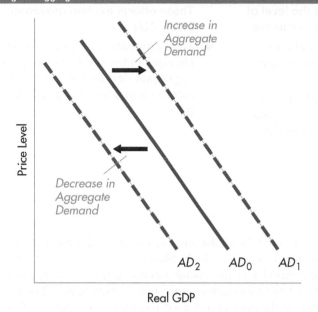

As aggregate demand increases, the *AD* curve shifts to the right, like the shift from AD_0 to AD_1. At every price level, the quantity of output demanded increases. As aggregate demand falls, the *AD* curve shifts to the left, like the shift from AD_0 to AD_2. At every price level, the quantity of output demanded falls.

Higher foreign income increases net exports and aggregate demand; lower foreign income reduces net exports and aggregate demand.

the exports of the domestic economy. Lower foreign income, then, causes domestic net exports and domestic aggregate demand to fall.

If foreign prices rise in relation to domestic prices, domestic goods become less expensive relative to foreign goods, and domestic net exports increase. This means that aggregate demand rises, or the aggregate demand curve shifts right, as the level of foreign prices rises. Conversely, when the level of foreign prices falls, domestic goods become more expensive relative to foreign goods, causing domestic net exports and aggregate demand to fall.

Let us go back to the market for oranges. Suppose U.S. growers compete with Brazilian growers for the Japanese orange market. If the level of prices in Brazil rises while the level of prices in the United States remains stable, the price of Brazilian oranges to the Japanese buyer rises in relation to the price of U.S. oranges. What happens? Exports of U.S. oranges to Japan should rise, while exports of Brazilian oranges to Japan should fall.[1]

Changes in the level of foreign prices change domestic net exports and aggregate demand in the same direction.

8-3b-3 Government Policy One of the goals of macroeconomic policy is to achieve economic growth without inflation. For GDP to increase, either *AD* or *AS* would have to change. Government economic policy can cause the aggregate demand curve to shift. An increase in government spending or a decrease in taxes will increase aggregate demand; a decrease in government spending or an increase in taxes will decrease aggregate demand. We devote an entire chapter to fiscal policy, an examination of the effect of taxes and government spending on aggregate demand. In another chapter, on monetary policy, we describe how changes in the money supply can cause the aggregate demand curve to shift.

[1] This assumes no change in exchange rates. If the Brazilian currency were to depreciate in value as Brazilian prices rose, then the cheaper exchange rate would at least partially offset the higher price and reduce the impact of the price change on exports.

1. The aggregate demand curve shows the level of aggregate expenditures at different price levels.

2. Aggregate expenditures are the sum of consumption, investment, government spending, and net exports.

3. The wealth effect, the interest rate effect, and the international trade effect are three reasons why the aggregate demand curve slopes down.

These effects explain movements along a given *AD* curve.

4. The aggregate demand curve shifts with changes in the nonprice determinants of aggregate demand: expectations, foreign income and price levels, and government policy.

8-4 Aggregate Supply

3. What factors affect aggregate supply?

The aggregate supply curve shows the quantity of real GDP produced at different price levels. The aggregate supply curve (*AS*) looks like the supply curve for an individual good, but, as with aggregate demand and the microeconomic demand curve, different factors are at work. The positive relationship between price and quantity supplied of an individual good is based on the change in the price of that good relative to the prices of all other goods. As the price of a single good rises relative to the prices of other goods, sellers are willing to offer more of the good for sale. With aggregate supply, on the other hand, we are analyzing how the amount of all goods and services produced changes as the level of prices changes. The direct relationship between prices and national output is explained by the effect of changing prices on profits, not by relative price changes.

8-4a Why the Aggregate Supply Curve Slopes Upward

Along the aggregate supply curve, everything is held fixed except the price level and the output. The price level is the price of output. The prices of resources—that is, the costs of production (wages, rent, and interest)—are assumed to be constant, at least for a short time following a change in the price level.

If the price level rises while the costs of production remain fixed, business profits go up. As profits rise, firms are willing to produce more output. As the price level rises, then, the quantity of output that firms are willing to supply increases. The result is the positively sloped aggregate supply curve shown in Figure 9.

As the price level rises from P_0 to P_1 in Figure 9, real GDP increases from \$300 to \$500. The higher the price level, the higher are profits, everything else held constant, and the greater is the quantity of output produced in the economy. Conversely, as the price level falls, the quantity of output produced falls.

8-4b Short-Run versus Long-Run Aggregate Supply

The curve in Figure 9 is a *short-run* aggregate supply curve because the costs of production are held constant. Although production costs may not rise immediately when the price level rises, eventually they will. Labor will demand higher wages to compensate for the higher cost of living; suppliers will charge more for materials. The positive slope of the *AS* curve, then, is a short-run phenomenon. How short is the short run? It is the period of time over which production costs remain constant. (In the long run, all costs change or are variable.) For the economy as a whole, the short run can be months or, at most, a few years.

FIGURE 9 Aggregate Supply

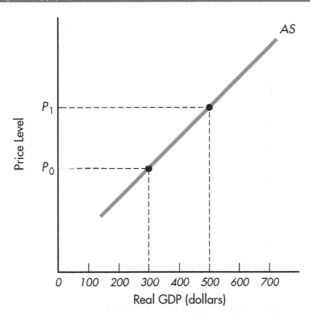

The aggregate supply curve shows the amount of real GDP produced at different price levels. The *AS* curve slopes up, indicating that the higher the price level, the greater the quantity of output produced.

8-4b-1 Short-Run Aggregate Supply Curve Figure 9 represents the general shape of the short-run aggregate supply curve. In Figure 10, you see a more realistic version of the same curve—its steepness varies. The steepness of the aggregate supply curve depends on the ability and willingness of producers to respond to price-level changes in the short run. Figure 10 shows the typical shape of the short-run aggregate supply curve.

Notice that as the level of real GDP increases in Figure 10, the *AS* curve becomes steeper. This is because each increase in output requires firms to hire more and more resources, until eventually full capacity is reached in some areas of the economy, resources are fully employed, and some firms reach maximum output. At this point, increases in the price level bring about smaller and smaller increases in output from firms as a whole. The short-run aggregate supply curve becomes increasingly steep as the economy approaches maximum output.

8-4b-2 Long-Run Aggregate Supply Curve Aggregate supply in the short run is different from aggregate supply in the long run (see Figure 11). That difference stems from the fact that, in the long run, quantities and costs of resources are not fixed. Over time, contracts expire, and wages and other resource costs adjust to current conditions. The increased flexibility of resource costs in the long run has costs rising and falling with the price level and changes the shape of the aggregate supply curve. Lack of information about economic conditions in the short run also contributes to the inflexibility of resource prices as compared to the long run. The Economic Insight "How Lack of Information in the Short Run Affects Wages in the Long Run" shows why this is true for labor, as well as for other resources.

The **long-run aggregate supply curve (*LRAS*)** is viewed by most economists as being a vertical line at the potential level of real GDP or output (Y_p), as shown in Figure 11. Remember that the potential level of real GDP is the income level that is produced in the absence of any cyclical unemployment, or when the natural rate of unemployment exists. In the long run, wages and other resource costs fully adjust to price changes. The short-run *AS* curve slopes upward because we assume that the costs of production, particularly

4. Why does the short-run aggregate supply curve become steeper as real GDP increases?

5. Why is the long-run aggregate supply curve vertical?

long-run aggregate supply curve (LRAS)
A vertical line at the potential level of real GDP.

FIGURE 10 The Shape of the Short-Run Aggregate Supply Curve

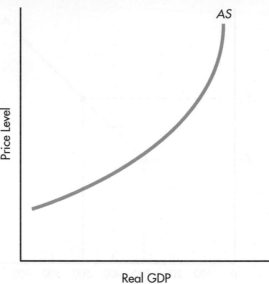

The upward-sloping aggregate supply curve occurs when the price level must rise to induce further increases in output. The curve gets steeper as real GDP increases, since the closer the economy comes to the capacity level of output, the less output will rise in response to higher prices as more and more firms reach their maximum level of output in the short run.

FIGURE 11 The Shape of the Long-Run Aggregate Supply Curve

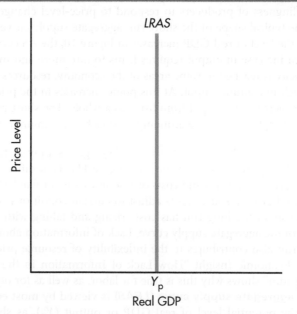

In the long run, the *AS* curve is a vertical line at the potential level of real GDP, which indicates that there is no relationship between price-level changes and the quantity of output produced.

ECONOMIC INSIGHT

How Lack of Information in the Short Run Affects Wages in the Long Run

Workers do not have perfect information. In other words, they do not know everything that occurs. This lack of information includes information about the price level. If workers form incorrect expectations regarding the price level in the short run, they may be willing to work for a different wage in the short run than in the long run. For example, if workers thought that the inflation rate would be 3 percent over the next year, they would want a smaller wage raise than if they believed that the inflation rate would be 6 percent. If, in fact, they base their wage negotiations on 3 percent inflation and accept a wage based on that inflation rate, but it turns out that the price level has increased by 6 percent, workers will then seek higher wages. In the long run, wages will reflect price-level changes.

If it cost nothing to obtain information, everyone who was interested would always know the current economic conditions. However, since there are costs of obtaining and understanding information about the economy, people will make mistakes in the short run. Both managers and employees make mistakes as a result of lack of information. Such mistakes are not caused by stupidity but by ignorance—ignorance of future as well as current economic conditions. In the long run, mistakes about the price level are recognized, and wages adjust to the known price level.

We now have two reasons why wages will be more flexible in the long run than in the short run: long-term contracts and lack of information in the short run. The same arguments could be made for other resources as well. For these two reasons, the short-run aggregate supply curve is generally upward sloping because resource prices are relatively fixed in the short run.

---

wages, do not change to offset changing prices. In the short run, then, higher prices increase producers' profits and stimulate production. In the long run, however, because the costs of production adjust completely to the change in prices, neither profits nor production increases. What we find here are higher wages and other costs of production to match the higher level of prices.

8-4c Changes in Aggregate Supply: Nonprice Determinants

The aggregate supply curve is drawn with everything but the price level and real GDP held constant. There are several things that can change and cause the aggregate supply curve to shift. The shift from AS_0 to AS_1 in Figure 12 represents an increase in aggregate supply. The AS_1 curve lies to the right of AS_0, which means that at every price level, production is higher on AS_1 than on AS_0. The shift from AS_0 to AS_2 represents a decrease in aggregate supply. The AS_2 curve lies to the left of AS_0, which means that at every price level, production along AS_2 is less than that along AS_0. The nonprice determinants of aggregate supply are resource prices, technology, and expectations. Figure 13 summarizes the nonprice determinants of aggregate supply, discussed in detail next.

6. *What causes the aggregate supply curve to shift?*

8-4c-1 Resource Prices   When the price of output changes, the costs of production do not change immediately. At first, then, a change in profits induces a change in production. Costs eventually change in response to the change in prices and production, and when they do, the aggregate supply curve shifts. When the cost of resources—labor, capital goods, and materials—falls, the aggregate supply curve shifts to the right, from AS_0 to AS_1 in Figure 12.

FIGURE 12   Changes in Aggregate Supply

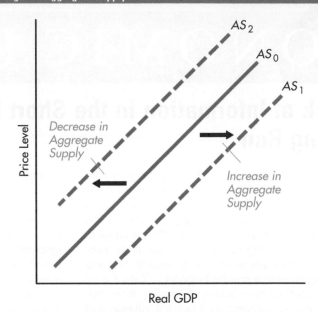

The aggregate supply curve shifts with changes in resource prices, technology, and expectations. When aggregate supply increases, the curve shifts to the right, like the shift from AS_0 to AS_1, so that at every price level more is being produced. When aggregate supply falls, the curve shifts to the left, like the shift from AS_0 to AS_2, so that at every price level less is being produced.

This means that firms are willing to produce more output at any given price level. When the cost of resources goes up, profits fall and the aggregate supply curve shifts to the left, from AS_0 to AS_2. Here, at any given level of price, firms produce less output.

Remember that the vertical axis of the aggregate supply graph represents the price level for all goods and services produced in the economy. Only those changes in resource prices that raise the costs of production across the economy have an impact on the aggregate supply curve. For example, oil is an important raw material. If a new source of oil is discovered, the price of oil falls and aggregate supply increases. However, if oil-exporting countries restrict oil supplies and the price of oil increases substantially, aggregate supply decreases, a situation that occurred in the 1970s when the Organization of Petroleum Exporting Countries (OPEC) reduced the supply of oil (see the Global Business Insight "Oil and Aggregate Supply"). If the price of only one minor resource were to change, then aggregate supply would be unlikely to change. For instance, if the price of land in Las Cruces, New Mexico, increased, we would not expect the U.S. aggregate supply curve to be affected.

8-4c-2 Technology Technological innovations allow businesses to increase the productivity of their existing resources. As new technology is adopted, the amount of output that can be produced by each unit of input increases, moving the aggregate supply curve to the right. For example, personal computers and word-processing software have allowed secretaries to produce much more output in a day than typewriters allowed.

8-4c-3 Expectations To understand how expectations can affect aggregate supply, consider the case of labor contracts. Manufacturing workers typically contract for a nominal wage based on what they and their employers expect the future level of prices to be. Because wages typically are set for at least a year, any unexpected increase in the price level during

FIGURE 13 Determinants of Aggregate Supply Shift the *AS* Curve

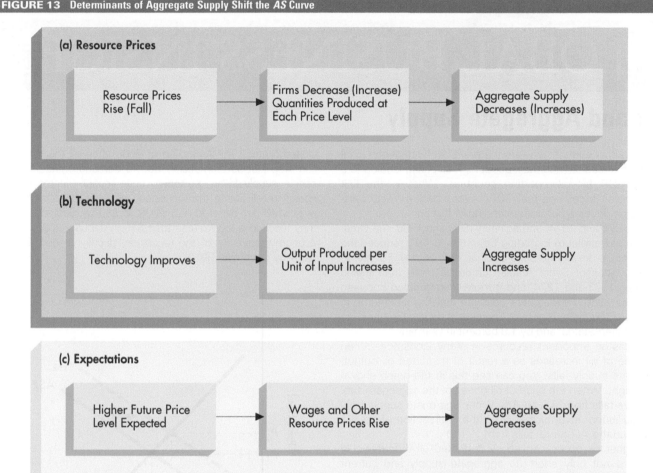

(a) Resource Prices

Resource Prices Rise (Fall) → Firms Decrease (Increase) Quantities Produced at Each Price Level → Aggregate Supply Decreases (Increases)

(b) Technology

Technology Improves → Output Produced per Unit of Input Increases → Aggregate Supply Increases

(c) Expectations

Higher Future Price Level Expected → Wages and Other Resource Prices Rise → Aggregate Supply Decreases

the year lowers real wages. Firms receive higher prices for their output, but the cost of labor stays the same. So profits and production go up.

If wages rise in anticipation of higher prices but prices do not go up, the cost of labor rises. Higher real wages caused by expectations of higher prices reduce current profits and production, moving the aggregate supply curve to the left. Other things being equal, anticipated higher prices cause aggregate supply to decrease; conversely, anticipated lower prices cause aggregate supply to increase. In this sense, expectations of price-level changes that shift aggregate supply actually bring about price-level changes.

8-4c-4 Economic Growth: Long-Run Aggregate Supply Shifts The vertical long-run aggregate supply curve, as shown in Figure 11, does not mean that the economy is forever fixed at the current level of potential real gross domestic product. Over time, as new technologies are developed and the quantity and quality of resources increase, potential output also increases, shifting both the short- and the long-run aggregate supply curves to the right. Figure 14 shows long-run economic growth by the shift in the aggregate supply curve from $LRAS$ to $LRAS_1$. The movement of the long-run aggregate supply curve to the right reflects the increase in potential real GDP from Y_p to Y_{p1}. Even though the price level has no effect on the level of output in the long run, changes in the determinants of the supply of real output in the economy do.

GLOBAL BUSINESS INSIGHT

Oil and Aggregate Supply

It seems that every few years there are big fluctuations in oil prices that lead to much talk about high oil prices leading to a fall in GDP for oil-importing countries. What is the link between oil prices and real GDP? A look back to recent history helps develop our understanding of this link.

In 1973 and 1974, and again in 1979 and 1980, the Organization of Petroleum Exporting Countries (OPEC) reduced the supply of oil, driving the price of oil up dramatically. For example, the price of Saudi Arabian crude oil more than tripled between 1973 and 1974, and it more than doubled between 1979 and 1980. Researchers estimate that the rapid jump in oil prices reduced output by 17 percent in Japan, by 7 percent in the United States, and by 1.9 percent in Germany.[†]

Oil is an important resource in many industries. When the price of oil increases as a result of restricted oil output, aggregate supply falls. You can see this in the graph shown at the right. When the price of oil goes up, the aggregate supply curve falls from AS_1 to AS_2. When aggregate supply falls, the equilibrium level of real GDP (the intersection of the AS curve and the AD curve) falls from Y_1 to Y_2.

Higher oil prices caused by restricted oil output would decrease not only short-run aggregate supply and current equilibrium real GDP, as shown in the graph, but also potential equilibrium income at the natural rate of unemployment. Unless other factors change to contribute to economic growth, the higher resource (oil) price reduces the productive capacity of the economy.

There is evidence that fluctuations in oil prices have less effect on the economy today than they did in the past.[‡] The amount of energy that goes into producing a dollar of GDP has declined over time, so oil plays a less important role in determining aggregate supply today than it did in the 1970s and earlier. This means that any given change in oil prices today will be associated with smaller shifts in the AS curve than in earlier decades.

While we have focused on the AS curve and oil prices, more recently the AD curve has entered the discussion. Unlike earlier episodes, when oil price rises were the result of restricting the supply of oil, in the mid-2000s, the price of oil was being driven higher by rising demand—particularly from China and the

United States.[§] The recession of 2008 showed that oil prices can drop just as dramatically due to demand shifts as in the earlier supply-driven episodes once supply increased. As spending fell during the recession, oil prices fell sharply from over $140 per barrel in July 2008 to $90 by September, and they reached a low of less than $40 in January 2009. As the economy grew out of the recession, prices reached $88 per barrel by December 2010.

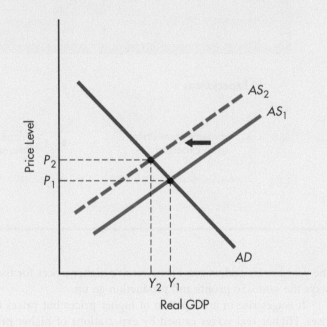

[†] These estimates were taken from Robert H. Rasche and John A. Tatom, "Energy Price Shocks, Aggregate Supply, and Monetary Policy: The Theory and the International Evidence," *Carnegie-Rochester Conference Series on Public Policy*, Vol. 14, eds. Karl Brunner and Allan H. Meltzer (North-Holland, 1981), pp. 9–93.

[‡] See Stephen P. A. Brown and Mine K. Yücel, "Oil Prices and the Economy," Federal Reserve Bank of Dallas, *Southwest Economy*, July–August 2000.

[§] See Christopher J. Neely, "Will Oil Prices Choke Growth," Federal Reserve Bank of St. Louis, *International Economic Trends*, July 2004.

FIGURE 14 Shifting the Long-Run Aggregate Supply Curve

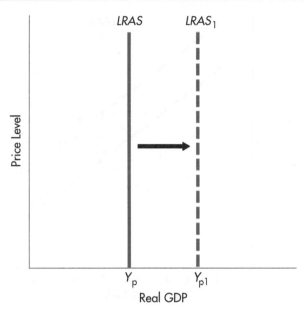

Changes in technology and the availability and quality of resources can shift the *LRAS* curve. For instance, a new technology that increases productivity would move the curve to the right, from *LRAS* to *LRAS₁*.

RECAP

1. The aggregate supply curve shows the quantity of output (real GDP) produced at different price levels.

2. The aggregate supply curve slopes up because, everything else held constant, higher prices increase producers' profits, creating an incentive to increase output.

3. The aggregate supply curve shifts with changes in resource prices, technology, and expectations.

These are nonprice determinants of aggregate supply.

4. The short-run aggregate supply curve is upward sloping, showing that increases in production are accompanied by higher prices.

5. The long-run aggregate supply curve is vertical at potential real GDP because, eventually, wages and the costs of other resources adjust fully to price-level changes.

8-5 Aggregate Demand and Supply Equilibrium

Now that we have defined the aggregate demand and aggregate supply curves separately, we can put them together to determine the equilibrium price level and real GDP.

8-5a Short-Run Equilibrium

Figure 15 shows the level of equilibrium in a hypothetical economy. Initially, the economy is in equilibrium at point 1, where *AD* and *AS* intersect. At this point, the equilibrium price level is P_1, and the equilibrium real GDP is $500. At price level P_1, the amount of output demanded is equal to the amount supplied. Suppose aggregate demand increases from AD_1 to AD_2. In the short run, aggregate supply does not change, so the new equilibrium is at the intersection of the new aggregate demand curve, AD_2, and the same aggregate supply curve,

7. What determines the equilibrium price level and real GDP?

FIGURE 15   Aggregate Demand and Supply Equilibrium

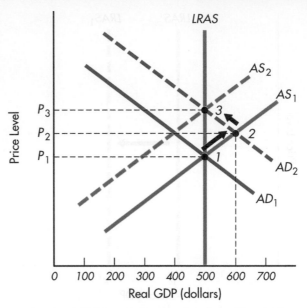

The equilibrium price level and real GDP is at the intersection of the *AD* and *AS* curves. Initially, equilibrium occurs at point *1*, where the AD_1 and AS_1 curves intersect. Here the price level is P_1 and real GDP is $500. If aggregate demand increases, moving from AD_1 to AD_2, in the short run there is a new equilibrium at point 2, where AD_2 intersects AS_1. The price level rises to P_2, and the equilibrium level of real GDP increases to $600. Over time, as wages and the costs of other resources rise in response to higher prices, aggregate supply falls, moving AS_1 to AS_2. Final equilibrium occurs at point 3, where the AS_2 curve intersects the AD_2 curve. The price level rises to P_3, but the equilibrium level of real GDP returns to its initial level, $500. In the long run, there is no relationship between prices and the equilibrium level of real GDP because the costs of resources adjust to changes in the level of prices.

AS_1, at point 2. The new equilibrium price level is P_2, and the new equilibrium real GDP is $600. Note that in the short run, the equilibrium point on the short-run aggregate supply curve can lie to the right of the long-run aggregate supply curve (*LRAS*). This is because the *LRAS* represents the potential level of real GDP, not the capacity level. It is possible to produce more than the potential level of real GDP in the short run if the unemployment rate falls below the natural rate of unemployment.

8-5b Long-Run Equilibrium

Point 2 is not a permanent equilibrium because aggregate supply decreases to AS_2 once the costs of production rise in response to higher prices. Final equilibrium is at point 3, where the price level is P_3 and real GDP is $500. Notice that equilibrium real GDP here is the same as the initial equilibrium at point 1. Points 1 and 3 both lie along the long-run aggregate supply curve (*LRAS*). The initial shock to or change in the economy was an increase in aggregate demand. The change in aggregate expenditures initially led to higher output and higher prices. Over time, however, as resource costs rise and profit falls, output falls back to its original value.

We are not saying that the level of output never changes. The long-run aggregate supply curve shifts as technology changes and new supplies of resources are obtained. But the

An increase in aggregate demand increases real GDP only temporarily.

output change that results from a change in aggregate demand is a temporary, or short-run, phenomenon. The price level eventually adjusts, and output eventually returns to the potential level.

RECAP

1. The equilibrium price level and real GDP are at the point where the aggregate demand and aggregate supply curves intersect.
2. In the short run, a shift in aggregate demand establishes a temporary equilibrium along the short-run aggregate supply curve.
3. In the long run, the short-run aggregate supply curve shifts so that changes in aggregate demand affect only the price level, not the equilibrium level of output or real GDP.

SUMMARY

1. What factors affect aggregate demand?

- Aggregate demand is the relation between aggregate expenditures and the price level. §8-2
- Aggregate demand is the sum of consumption, investment, government spending, and net exports at alternative price levels. §8-2a, 8-2b, 8-2c, 8-2d
- Aggregate expenditures change with changes in the price level because of the wealth effect, the interest rate effect, and the international trade effect. These cause a movement along the AD curve. §8-3a

2. What causes the aggregate demand curve to shift?

- The aggregate demand (AD) curve shows the level of expenditures for real GDP at different price levels. §8-3a
- Because expenditures and prices move in opposite directions, the AD curve is negatively sloped. §8-3a
- The nonprice determinants of aggregate demand include expectations, foreign income and price levels, and government policy. §8-3b

3. What factors affect aggregate supply?

- The aggregate supply curve shows the quantity of real GDP produced at different price levels. §8-4
- Movements along the AS curve are caused by changes in price. Shifts in the curve are caused by the determinants of AS. §8-4c

4. Why does the short-run aggregate supply curve become steeper as real GDP increases?

- As real GDP rises and the economy pushes closer to capacity output, the level of prices must rise to induce increased production. §8-4b

5. Why is the long-run aggregate supply curve vertical?

- The long-run aggregate supply curve is a vertical line at the potential level of real GDP. The shape of the curve indicates that higher prices have no effect on output when an economy is producing at potential real GDP. §8-4b

6. What causes the aggregate supply curve to shift?

- The nonprice determinants of aggregate supply are resource prices, technology, and expectations. §8-4c, 8-4c, 8-4c

7. What determines the equilibrium price level and real GDP?

- The equilibrium price level and real GDP are at the intersection of the aggregate demand and aggregate supply curves. §8-5a
- In the short run, a shift in aggregate demand establishes a new, but temporary, equilibrium along the short-run aggregate supply curve. §8-5a
- In the long run, the short-run aggregate supply curve shifts so that changes in aggregate demand determine the price level but not the equilibrium level of output or real GDP. §8-5b

KEY TERMS

aggregate demand curve, 147
aggregate supply curve, 147
cost-push inflation, 149

demand-pull inflation, 147
interest rate effect, 153
international trade effect, 153

long-run aggregate supply curve
(LRAS), 159
wealth effect, 152

EXERCISES

1. How is the aggregate demand curve different from the demand curve for a single good, like hamburgers?
2. Why does the aggregate demand curve slope downward? Give real-world examples of the three effects that explain the slope of the curve.
3. How does an increase in foreign income affect domestic aggregate expenditures and demand? Draw a diagram to illustrate your answer.
4. How does a decrease in foreign price levels affect domestic aggregate expenditures and demand? Draw a diagram to illustrate your answer.
5. How is the aggregate supply curve different from the supply curve for a single good, like pizza?
6. There are several determinants of aggregate supply that can cause the aggregate supply curve to shift.
   a. Describe those determinants and give an example of a change in each.
   b. Draw and label an aggregate supply diagram that illustrates the effect of the change in each determinant.
7. Draw a short-run aggregate supply curve that gets steeper as real GDP rises.
   a. Explain why the curve has this shape.
   b. Now draw a long-run aggregate supply curve that intersects a short-run AS curve. What is the relationship between short-run AS and long-run AS?
8. Draw and carefully label an aggregate demand and supply diagram with initial equilibrium at P_0 and Y_0.
   a. Using the diagram, explain what happens when aggregate demand falls.
   b. How is the short run different from the long run?
9. Draw an aggregate demand and supply diagram for Japan. In the diagram, show how each of the following affects aggregate demand and supply.
   a. The U.S. gross domestic product falls.
   b. The level of prices in Korea falls.
   c. Labor receives a large wage increase.
   d. Economists predict higher prices next year.
10. If the long-run aggregate supply curve gives the level of potential real GDP, how can the short-run aggregate

supply curve ever lie to the right of the long-run aggregate supply curve?
11. What will happen to the equilibrium price level and real GDP if:
   a. aggregate demand and aggregate supply both increase?
   b. aggregate demand increases and aggregate supply decreases?
   c. aggregate demand and aggregate supply both decrease?
   d. aggregate demand decreases and aggregate supply increases?
12. During the Great Depression, the U.S. economy experienced a falling price level and declining real GDP. Using an aggregate demand and aggregate supply diagram, illustrate and explain how this could occur.
13. Suppose aggregate demand increases, causing an increase in real GDP but no change in the price level. Using an aggregate demand and aggregate supply diagram, illustrate and explain how this could occur.
14. Suppose aggregate demand increases, causing an increase in the price level but no change in real GDP. Using an aggregate demand and aggregate supply diagram, illustrate and explain how this could occur.
15. Use an aggregate demand and aggregate supply diagram to illustrate and explain how each of the following will affect the equilibrium price level and real GDP:
   a. Consumers expect a recession.
   b. Foreign income rises.
   c. Foreign price levels fall.
   d. Government spending increases.
   e. Workers expect higher future inflation and negotiate higher wages now.
   f. Technological improvements increase productivity.
16. In the boom years of the late 1990s, it was often said that rapidly increasing stock prices were responsible for much of the rapid growth of real GDP. Explain how this could be true, using aggregate demand and aggregate supply analysis.

17. Suppose you read in the newspaper that rising oil prices would contribute to a global recession. Use aggregate demand and supply analysis to explain how high oil prices could reduce real GDP.

18. Find an article in today's news that could indicate a shift in aggregate supply and/or demand, and draw corresponding aggregate supply and demand curves.

19. From 2008 to 2009 the price level in the United States fell significantly due to the recession associated with the financial crisis. Do you think this was because of a change in aggregate supply or demand? Illustrate your answer with a graph.

20. Imagine there is a technological change which permanently makes all manufacturing workers more productive at their jobs. This means that firms will be able to produce goods at a lower cost and assume that workers will earn more in wages. Is this a shift in long-run or short-run aggregate supply or both? Is there a change in aggregate demand? Illustrate your answers with graphs.

ECONOMICALLY SPEAKING

THE CONFERENCE BOARD *CONSUMER CONFIDENCE INDEX*® INCREASES AGAIN

The Conference Board, January 28, 2014

The Conference Board *Consumer Confidence Index*®, which had rebounded in December, increased again in January. The Index now stands at 80.7 (1985 = 100), up from 77.5 in December. The Present Situation Index increased to 79.1 from 75.3. The Expectations Index increased to 81.8 from 79.0 last month. ...

"Consumer confidence advanced in January for the second consecutive month," said Lynn Franco, Director of Economic Indicators at The Conference Board. "Consumers' assessment of the present situation continues to improve, with both business conditions and the job market rated more favorably. Looking ahead six months, consumers expect the economy and their earnings to improve, but were somewhat mixed regarding the outlook for jobs. All in all, confidence appears to be back on track and rising expectations suggest the economy may pick up some momentum in the months ahead."

Consumers' assessment of overall present-day conditions continues to improve. Those claiming business conditions are "good" increased to 21.5 percent from 20.2 percent, while those claiming business conditions are "bad" edged down to 22.8 percent from 23.2 percent. Consumers' appraisal of the labor market was also more positive. Those saying jobs are "plentiful" ticked up to 12.7 percent from 11.9 percent, while those saying jobs are "hard to get" decreased slightly to 32.6 percent from 32.9 percent.

Consumers' expectations, which had improved sharply in December, increased again in January. Those expecting business conditions to improve over the next six months remained unchanged at 17.4 percent, while those anticipating business conditions to worsen decreased to 12.1 percent from 13.9 percent. Consumers' outlook for the labor market was mixed. Those expecting more jobs in the months ahead declined to 15.4 percent from 17.1 percent. However, those anticipating fewer jobs decreased to 18.3 percent from 19.4 percent. The proportion of consumers expecting their incomes to increase rose to 15.8 percent from 13.9 percent, while those anticipating a decrease in their incomes declined to 13.6 percent from 14.3 percent.

COMMENTARY

Why would a business firm want to receive reports regarding consumer confidence in the U.S. economy? The answer lies in the role of expectations as a determinant of consumption spending and therefore aggregate demand. If households are confident that incomes will rise and prosperous times are ahead, they are much more likely to spend more than if they expect a recession. By monitoring consumer confidence in the economy, we can better understand consumer spending. Since consumption accounts for about two-thirds of GDP, changes in household spending can play a big role in business-cycle fluctuations.

In terms of aggregate demand and supply analysis, if households are more optimistic about the economy's performance, then the aggregate demand curve should shift to the right, like the shift from AD_0 to AD_1 in the accompanying figure. This would increase the equilibrium level of real GDP from Y_0 to Y_1. If households are less optimistic about the economy's performance, then the aggregate demand curve should shift to the left, like the shift from AD_0 to AD_2. This would decrease the equilibrium level of real GDP from Y_0 to Y_2.

Because of the implications of shifts in consumer confidence for business-cycle fluctuations, government officials, along with businesspeople, watch the consumer confidence measures to maintain a sense of what is happening in the typical household. The two best-known surveys, the University of Michigan and Conference Board surveys, ask questions like: "Six months from now, do you think business conditions will be better, the same, or worse?" and "Would you say that you are better off or worse off financially than you were a year ago?" The answers to these questions and others are used as inputs in constructing an index of consumer confidence so that the press typically reports only how the overall index changes rather than the responses to any particular question.

Although the popular consumer confidence indexes fluctuate up and down every month, researchers have found that the monthly fluctuations are not very useful in predicting consumption or GDP. However, major shifts in the indexes or several months of rising or falling indexes may provide an early signal of forthcoming changes in consumption and GDP.

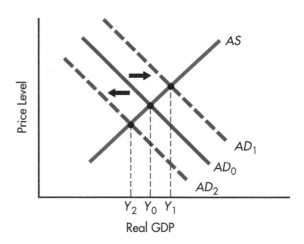

CHAPTER 9
Aggregate Expenditures

© Lewis Tse Pui Lung/Shutterstock.com

FUNDAMENTAL QUESTIONS

1. How are consumption and saving related?

2. What are the determinants of consumption?

3. What are the determinants of investment?

4. What are the determinants of government spending?

5. What are the determinants of net exports?

6. What is the aggregate expenditures function?

Preview

To understand why real GDP, unemployment, and inflation rise and fall over time, we must know what causes the aggregate demand and aggregate supply curves to shift. We cannot understand why the U.S. economy has experienced 11 recessions since 1945 or why, in the 1990s and 2000s, we witnessed the longest peacetime business-cycle expansion in modern times, or why there was a global recession in 2008–2009 unless we understand why the *AD* and *AS* curves shift. In this chapter, we examine in more detail the demand side of the economy.

top: © Carsten Reisinger/Shutterstock

In the chapter titled "Macroeconomic Equilibrium: Aggregate Demand and Supply," we discussed how the price level affects aggregate expenditures through the interest rate, international trade, and wealth effects. This chapter examines the nonprice determinants of spending and shifts in aggregate demand in greater detail and assumes that the price level is fixed. This assumption means that the aggregate supply curve is a horizontal line at the fixed-price level. This approach was used by John Maynard Keynes, who analyzed the macro economy during the Great Depression.

A fixed price level, as shown in Figure 1, suggests a situation in which unemployment and excess capacity exist. Firms can hire from this pool of unemployed labor and increase their output at no extra cost and without any pressure on the price level. It is not surprising that Keynes would rely on such a model at a time when he was surrounded by mass unemployment. He was more interested in the determination of income and output than in the problem of inflation.

With a horizontal AS curve, as shown in Figure 1, the location of the AD curve will determine the equilibrium level of real GDP, Y_e. If we understand what determines aggregate demand—consumption, investment, government spending, and net exports— we will understand what determines real GDP.

We begin our detailed examination of aggregate expenditures by discussing consumption, which accounts for approximately 68 percent of total expenditures in the U.S. economy. We then look at investment (16 percent of total expenditures), government spending (19 percent of total expenditures), and net exports (−3 percent of total expenditures).

FIGURE 1   The Fixed-Price Keynesian Model

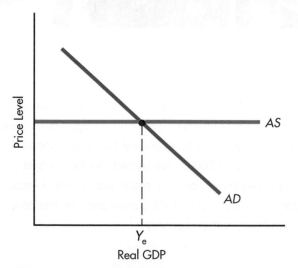

The Keynesian assumption that the price level is fixed requires a horizontal aggregate supply curve. In this case, aggregate demand will determine the equilibrium level of real GDP.

9-1 Consumption and Saving

Households can do three things with their income: They can spend it for the consumption of goods and services, they can save it, or they can pay taxes with it. Disposable income is what is left after taxes have been paid. It is the sum of consumption and saving:

Disposable income = consumption + saving

or

$$Yd = C + S$$

Disposable income is the income that households actually have available for spending after taxes. Whatever disposable income is not spent is saved.

Why are we talking about saving, which is not a component of total spending, in a chapter that sets out to discuss the components of total spending? Saving is simply "not consuming"; it is impossible to separate the incentives to save from the incentives to consume.

9-1a Saving and Savings

Before we go on, it is necessary to understand the difference between *saving* and *savings*. *Saving* occurs over a unit of time—a week, a month, a year. For instance, you might save $10 a week or $40 a month. Saving is a *flow* concept. *Savings* is an amount accumulated at a particular point in time—today, December 31, or your 65th birthday. For example, you might have savings of $2,500 on December 31. Savings is a *stock* concept.

Like saving, GDP and its components are flow concepts. They are measured by the year or quarter of the year. Consumption, investment, government spending, and net exports are also flows. Each of them is an amount spent over a period of time.

1. How are consumption and saving related?

Consumption spending is the largest component of aggregate expenditures. Households in Chichicastenango, Guatemala, come to the produce market shown here to purchase food. Their expenditures on food will be counted in the consumption and the GDP of Guatemala. If the households decide to save less and spend more, then, other things being equal, the higher consumption will raise the GDP of Guatemala.

9-1b The Consumption and Saving Functions

The primary determinant of the level of consumption over any given period is the level of disposable income. The higher the disposable income, the more households are willing and able to spend. This relationship between disposable income and consumption is called the **consumption function**. Figure 2 contains the consumption function for the United States over the long-run period from 1990 to 2012. For each year in this period, the values of disposable income and consumption are plotted in the figure. Note that Figure 2 also contains a 45-degree line. (A 45-degree line makes a graph easier to read

consumption function
The relationship between disposable income and consumption.

Saving occurs over a unit of time; it is a flow concept.

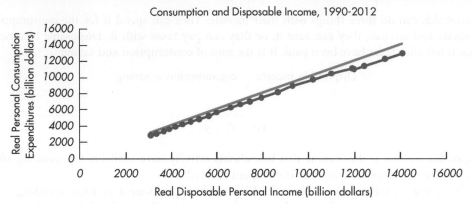

FIGURE 2   Consumption and Disposable Income, 1990–2012

Consumption and Disposable Income, 1990-2012

The figure shows the long-run consumption function for the United States. The 45-degree line shows all points at which consumption and disposable income are equal. Note that the actual consumption function lies only slightly below the 45-degree line. This indicates that consumption is less than disposable income—but not much less.

Source: www.bea.gov.

Savings are an amount accumulated at a point in time; they are a stock concept.

because every point on the line represents the same value on both axes.) This line splits the area of the figure in half and shows all points at which the value of disposable income and the value of consumption are equal. Since the actual consumption function lies below the 45-degree line, it can be seen that consumption is less than disposable income—but not much less.

The consumption function in Figure 2 is a long-run consumption function. In the short run, like this year, the relationship between consumption and disposable income may be much flatter than that shown in Figure 2. We now turn to a deeper analysis of the consumption function to better understand this important relationship.

To focus on the relationship between income and consumption, we draw a new graph, Figure 3, with income on the horizontal axis and consumption on the vertical axis. Figure 3(a) shows a hypothetical consumption function. In this economy, when disposable income is zero, consumption is $30. As disposable income rises, consumption rises. For instance, when disposable income is $100, consumption is $100.

We use C to represent consumption and Yd to represent disposable income. The line labeled C in Figure 3a is the consumption function: It represents the relationship between disposable income and consumption. The other line in the figure creates a 45-degree angle with either axis. In Figure 3a, as in Figure 2, the 45-degree line shows all the points where consumption equals disposable income.

The level of disposable income at which all disposable income is being spent occurs at the point where the consumption function (line C) crosses the 45-degree line. In the graph, C equals Yd when disposable income is $100. Consumers save a fraction of any disposable income above $100. You can see this in the graph. Saving occurs at any level of disposable income at which the consumption function lies below the 45-degree line (at which consumption is less than disposable income). The amount of saving is measured by the vertical distance between the 45-degree line and the

FIGURE 3 Disposable Income Consumption and Saving in a Hypothetical Economy

Disposable Income (Yd)	Consumption (C)	Saving (S)
$0	$30	– $30
$100	$100	$0
$200	$170	$30
$300	$240	$60
$400	$310	$90
$500	$380	$120
$600	$450	$150
$700	$570	$180

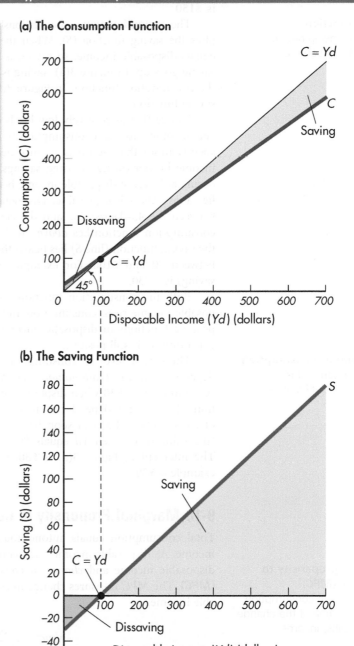

(a) The Consumption Function

(b) The Saving Function

3(a) Consumption is a positive function of disposable income: It goes up as disposable income rises. The line labeled $C = Yd$ forms a 45-degree angle at the origin. It shows all points where consumption equals disposable income. The point at which the consumption function (line C) crosses the 45-degree line—where disposable income measures $100—is the point at which consumption equals disposable income. At lower levels of disposable income, consumption is greater than disposable income; at higher levels, consumption is less than disposable income. 3(b) The saving function. Saving equals disposable income minus consumption. When consumption equals disposable income, saving is 0. At higher levels of disposable income, we find positive saving; at lower levels, we find negative saving, or dissaving.

saving function
The relationship between disposable income and saving.

dissaving
Spending financed by borrowing or using savings.

autonomous consumption
Consumption that is independent of income.

marginal propensity to consume (*MPC*)
The change in consumption as a proportion of the change in disposable income.

consumption function. If disposable income is $600, consumption is $450 and saving is $150.

The **saving function** is the relationship between disposable income and saving. Figure 3(b) plots the saving function (*S*). When the level of disposable income is at $100, consumption equals disposable income, so saving is zero. As disposable income increases beyond $100, saving goes up. In Figure 3(a), saving is the vertical distance between the 45-degree line and the consumption function. In Figure 3(b), we can read the level of saving directly from the saving function.

Notice that at relatively low levels of disposable income, consumption exceeds disposable income. How can consumption be greater than disposable income? When a household spends more than it earns in income, the household must finance the spending above income by borrowing or using savings. This is called **dissaving**. In Figure 3(a), dissaving occurs at levels of disposable income between $0 and $100, where the consumption function lies above the 45-degree line. Dissaving, like saving, is measured by the vertical distance between the 45-degree line and the consumption function, but dissaving occurs when the consumption function lies *above* the 45-degree line. In Figure 3(b), dissaving occurs when the saving function (line *S*) lies below the disposable income axis, at disposable income levels between $0 and $100. For example, when disposable income is $0, dissaving (negative saving) is −$30.

Both the consumption function and the saving function have positive slopes: As disposable income rises, consumption and saving increase. Consumption and saving, then, are positive functions of disposable income. Notice that when disposable income equals zero, consumption is still positive.

There is a level of consumption, called **autonomous consumption**, that does not depend on income. (*Autonomous* here means "independent of income.") In Figure 3(a), consumption equals $30 when disposable income equals $0. This $30 is autonomous consumption; it does not depend on income but will vary with the nonincome determinants of consumption that will soon be introduced. The intercept of the consumption function (the value of *C* when *Yd* equals $0) measures the amount of autonomous consumption. The intercept in Figure 3(a) is $30, which means that autonomous consumption in this example is $30.

9-1c Marginal Propensity to Consume and Save

Total consumption equals autonomous consumption plus the spending that depends on income. As disposable income rises, consumption rises. This relationship between *change* in disposable income and *change* in consumption is the **marginal propensity to consume** (*MPC*). The *MPC* measures change in consumption as a proportion of the change in disposable income.

$$MPC = \frac{\text{change in consumption}}{\text{change in disposable income}}$$

In Table 1, columns 1 and 2 list the consumption function data used in Figure 3. The marginal propensity to consume is shown in column 4. In our example, each time that disposable income changes by $100, consumption changes by $70. This means that consumers spend 70 percent of any extra income that they receive.

$$MPC = \frac{\$70}{\$100}$$
$$= .70$$

TABLE 1 Marginal Propensity to Consume and to Save				
Disposable Income (*Yd*)	Consumption (*C*)	Saving (*S*)	Marginal Propensity to Consume (*MPC*)	Marginal Propensity to Save (*MPS*)
$ 0	$ 30	−$ 30	–	–
$100	$100	$ 0	.70	.30
$200	$170	$ 30	.70	.30
$300	$240	$ 60	.70	.30
$400	$310	$ 90	.70	.30
$500	$380	$120	.70	.30
$600	$450	$150	.70	.30
$700	$520	$180	.70	.30

The *MPC* tells us what fractional change in income is used for consumption. The **marginal propensity to save (*MPS*)** defines the relationship between change in saving and change in disposable income. It is the change in saving divided by the change in disposable income:

$$MPS = \frac{\text{change in saving}}{\text{change in disposable income}}$$

The *MPS* in Table 1 is a constant 30 percent at all levels of income. Each time that disposable income changes by $100, saving changes by $30:

$$MPS = \frac{\$30}{\$100}$$
$$= .30$$

The *MPC* and the *MPS* will always be constant at all levels of disposable income in our examples.

Because disposable income will be either consumed or saved, the marginal propensity to consume plus the marginal propensity to save must total 1:

$$MPC + MPS = 1$$

The percentage of additional income that is not consumed must be saved. If consumers spend 70 percent of any extra income, they save 30 percent of that income.

The *MPC* and the *MPS* determine the rate of consumption and saving as disposable income changes. The *MPC* is the slope of the consumption function; the *MPS* is the slope of the saving function. Remember that the slope of a line measures the change along the vertical axis that corresponds to a change along the horizontal axis, the rise over the run (see the Appendix to titled "The Wealth of Nations: Ownership and Economic Freedom"). In the case of the consumption function, the slope is the change in consumption (the change on the vertical axis) divided by the change in disposable income (the change on the horizontal axis):

$$\text{Slope of consumption function} = \frac{\text{change in consumption}}{\text{change in disposable income}}$$
$$= MPC$$

The higher the *MPC*, the greater the fraction of any additional disposable income that consumers will spend. At an *MPC* of .70, consumers spend 70 percent of any change in disposable income;

marginal propensity to save (*MPS*)
The change in saving as a proportion of the change in disposable income.

The slope of the consumption function is the same as the MPC; the slope of the saving function is the same as the MPS.

at an *MPC* of .85, consumers want to spend 85 percent of any change in disposable income. The size of the *MPC* shows up graphically as the steepness of the consumption function. The consumption function with an *MPC* of .85 is a steeper line than the one drawn in Figure 3(a). In general, the steeper the consumption function, the larger the *MPC*. If the *MPC* is less than .70, the consumption function will be flatter than the one in the figure.

The slope of the saving function is the *MPS*:

$$\text{Slope of saving function} = \frac{\text{change in saving}}{\text{change in disposable income}}$$
$$= MPS$$

In general, the steeper the saving function, the greater the slope and the greater the *MPS*.

Figure 4(a) shows three consumption functions. Since all three consumption functions have the same intercept, autonomous consumption is the same for all. But each consumption function in Figure 4(a) has a different slope. Line C_1 has an *MPC* of .70. A larger *MPC*, .80, produces a steeper consumption function (line C_2). A smaller *MPC*, .60, produces a flatter consumption function (line C_3). The saving functions that correspond to these consumption functions are shown in Figure 4(b). Function S_1, with an *MPS* of .30, corresponds to consumption function C_1, with an *MPC* of .70 (remember: $MPS = 1 - MPC$). Function S_2 corresponds to C_2, and S_3 corresponds to C_3. The higher the *MPC* (the steeper the consumption function), the lower the *MPS* (the flatter the saving function). If people spend a greater fraction of extra income, they save a smaller fraction.

9-1d Average Propensity to Consume and Save

Suppose our interest is not in the proportion of change in disposable income that is consumed or saved, but in the proportion of disposable income that is consumed or saved. For this, we must know the average propensity to consume and the average propensity to save.

The **average propensity to consume (*APC*)** is the proportion of disposable income that is spent for consumption:

$$APC = \text{consumption/disposable income}$$

or

$$APC = \frac{C}{Yd}$$

The **average propensity to save (*APS*)** is the proportion of disposable income that is saved:

$$APC = \frac{\text{consumption}}{\text{disposable income}}$$

or

$$APS = \frac{S}{Yd}$$

Table 2 uses the consumption and saving data plotted in Figure 3. The *APC* and *APS* are shown in columns 4 and 5. When disposable income is $100, consumption is also $100, so the ratio of consumption to disposable income (*C*/*Yd*) equals 1 ($100/$100). At this point, saving equals $0, so the ratio of saving to disposable income (*S*/*Yd*) also equals 0 ($0/$100). We really do not have to compute the *APS* because we already know the *APC*. There are only two things that can be done with disposable income: spend it or save it. The percentage

average propensity to consume (*APC*)
The proportion of disposable income spent for consumption.

average propensity to save (*APS*)
The proportion of disposable income saved.

FIGURE 4   Marginal Propensity to Consume and Save

(a) Three Consumption Functions

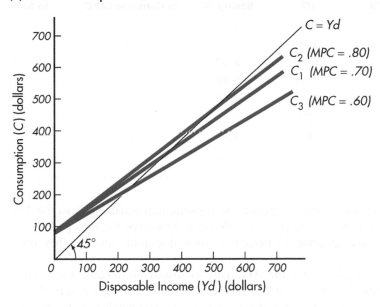

(b) Three Saving Functions

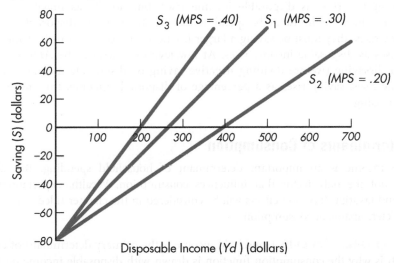

The *MPC* is the slope of the consumption function. The greater the MPC, the steeper the consumption function. The *MPS* is the slope of the saving function. The greater the *MPS*, the steeper the saving function. Because the sum of the *MPC* and the *MPS* is 1, the greater the *MPC*, the smaller the *MPS*. The steeper the consumption function, then, the flatter the saving function.

of income spent plus the percentage saved must add up to 100 percent of disposable income. This means that

$$APC + APS = 1$$

If the *APC* equals 1, then the *APS* must equal 0.

Disposable Income (Y_d)	Consumption (C)	Saving (S)	Average Propensity to Consume (APC)	Average Propensity to Save (APS)
$ 0	$ 30	$ 30	–	–
$100	$100	$ 0	1	0
$200	$170	$ 30	.85	.15
$300	$240	$ 60	.80	.20
$400	$310	$ 90	.78	.22
$500	$380	$120	.76	.24
$600	$450	$150	.75	.25
$700	$520	$180	.74	.26

TABLE 2   Average Propensity to Consume and to Save

When disposable income equals $600, consumption equals $450, so the *APC* equals .75 ($450/$600) and the *APS* equals .25 ($150/$600). As always, the *APC* plus the *APS* equals 1. If households are spending 75 percent of their disposable income, they must be saving 25 percent.

Notice in Table 2 that the *APC* falls as disposable income rises. This is because households spend only part of any change in income. In Figure 3(a), the consumption function rises more slowly than the 45-degree line. (Remember that consumption equals disposable income along the 45-degree line.) The consumption function tells us, then, that consumption rises as disposable income rises, but not by as much as disposable income rises. Because households spend a smaller fraction of disposable income as that income rises, they must be saving a larger fraction. You can see this in Table 2, where the *APS* rises as disposable income rises. At low levels of income, the *APS* is negative, a product of dissaving (we are dividing negative saving by disposable income). As disposable income rises, saving rises as a percentage of disposable income; this means that the *APS* is increasing.

9-1e Determinants of Consumption

Disposable income is an important determinant of household spending. But disposable income is not the only factor that influences consumption. Wealth, expectations, demographics, and taxation (taxation effects will be considered in the chapter titled "Fiscal Policy") are other determinants of consumption.

2. What are the determinants of consumption?

9-1e-1 Disposable Income Household income is the primary determinant of consumption, which is why the consumption function is drawn with disposable income on the horizontal axis. Household income is usually measured as current disposable income. By *current* we mean income that is received in the current period—the current period could be today, this month, this year, or whatever period we are discussing. Past income and future income certainly can affect household spending, but they do so through household wealth or expectations, not through income. Disposable income is after-tax income.

The two-dimensional graphs we have been using relate consumption only to current disposable income. A change in consumption caused by a change in disposable income is shown by *movement along* the consumption function. The effects of other variables are shown by *shifting* the intercept of the consumption function up and down as the values of these other variables change. All variables *except* disposable income change *autonomous* consumption.

Changes in taxes will affect disposable income. *If we assume that there are no taxes, then Yd equals Y, and consumption (and other expenditures) may be drawn as a function of real GDP rather than disposable income.* The chapter titled "Fiscal Policy" is devoted to an analysis of government fiscal policy, including taxation. As a result, we put off our discussion of tax effects until then; this allows us to simplify our analysis of aggregate expenditures. The discussion of the components of aggregate expenditures in the remainder of this chapter and in later chapters will be related graphically to pretax real GDP rather than to disposable income.

9-1e-2 Wealth

Wealth is the value of all the assets owned by a household. Wealth is a stock variable; it includes homes, cars, checking and savings accounts, and stocks and bonds, as well as the value of income expected in the future. As household wealth increases, households have more resources available for spending, so consumption increases at every level of real GDP. You can see this in Figure 5(a) as a shift of the consumption function from C to C_1. The autonomous increase in consumption shifts the intercept of the consumption function from \$60 to \$100, so consumption increases by \$40 at every level of real GDP. If households spend more of their current income as their wealth increases, they save less. You can see this as the downward shift of the saving function in Figure 5(b), from S to S_1. The higher level of wealth has households more willing to dissave at each income level than before. Dissaving now occurs at any level of income below \$500. During the long expansionary period of the 1990s, stock price increases made many households much wealthier and stimulated consumption.

A decrease in wealth has just the opposite effect. For instance, during the 2008 recession, property values in most areas of the United States declined. Household wealth declined as the value of real estate fell, and spending fell as a result. Here you would see an autonomous drop in consumption, like the shift from C to C_2, and an autonomous increase in saving, like the shift from S to S_2. Now at every level of real GDP, households spend \$40 less than before and save \$40 more. The intercept of the consumption function is \$20, not \$60, and the intercept of the saving function is −\$20, not −\$60. The new consumption function parallels the old one; the curves are the same vertical distance apart at every level of income. So consumption is \$40 lower at every level of income. Similarly, the saving functions are parallel because saving is \$40 greater at every level of real GDP along S_2 compared to S.

9-1e-3 Expectations

Another important determinant of consumption is consumer expectations about future income, prices, and wealth. When consumers expect a recession, when they are worried about losing their jobs or facing cutbacks in hours worked, they tend to spend less and save more. This means an autonomous decrease in consumption and an increase in saving, like the shift from C to C_2 and from S to S_2 in Figure 5. Conversely, when consumers are optimistic, we find an autonomous increase in consumption and a decrease in saving, like the shift from C to C_1 and from S to S_1 in Figure 5.

Expectations are subjective opinions; they are difficult to observe and measure. This creates problems for economists trying to analyze the effect of expectations on consumption. The Conference Board surveys households to construct its *Consumer Confidence Index*, a measure of consumer opinion regarding the outlook for the economy. Economists follow the index in order to predict how consumer spending will change. Since consumption is the largest component of GDP, changes in consumption have important implications for business cycles.

Clearly the Consumer Confidence Index is not always a reliable indicator of expansion or recession. Still, economists' increasing use of this and other measures to better understand fluctuations in consumption underscores the importance of consumer expectations in the economy (see the Economic Insight "Permanent Income, Life Cycles, and Consumption").

wealth
The value of all assets owned by a household.

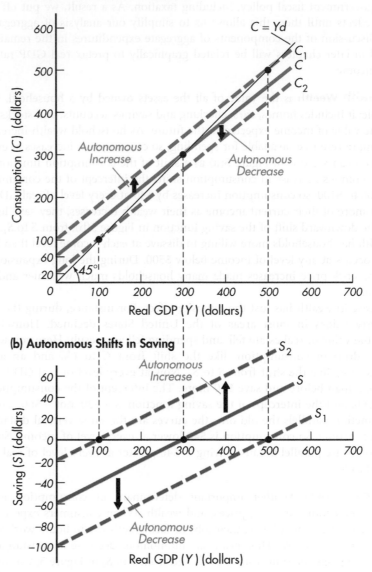

FIGURE 5   Autonomous Shifts in Consumption and in Saving

(a) Autonomous Shifts in Consumption

(b) Autonomous Shifts in Saving

Autonomous consumption is the amount of consumption that exists when real GDP is zero. It is the intercept of the consumption function. The shift from C to C_1 is an autonomous increase in consumption of $40; it moves the intercept of the consumption function from $60 to $100. The shift from C to C_2 is an autonomous decrease in consumption of $40; it moves the intercept of the consumption function from $60 to $20. Autonomous saving is the amount of saving that exists when real GDP is zero. This is the intercept of the saving function. The shift from S to S_1 is an autonomous decrease in saving of $40; it moves the intercept of the saving function from −$60 to −$100. The shift from S to S_2 is an autonomous increase in saving of $40; it moves the intercept of the saving function from −$60 to −$20. Because disposable income minus consumption equals saving, an autonomous increase in consumption is associated with an autonomous decrease in saving, and an autonomous decrease in consumption is associated with an autonomous increase in saving.

ECONOMIC INSIGHT

Permanent Income, Life Cycles, and Consumption

Studies of the consumption function over a long period of time find a function like the one labeled C_L in the graph, as we saw earlier in Figure 2. This function has a marginal propensity to consume of .90 and an intercept of 0. Consumption functions studied over a shorter period of time have lower MPCs and positive intercepts, like the function C_S in the graph, with an MPC of .60. How do we reconcile these two functions?

Economists offer two related explanations for the difference between long-run and short-run consumption behavior: the permanent income hypothesis and the life-cycle hypothesis. The fundamental idea is that people consume on the basis of their idea of what their long-run or permanent level of income is. A substantial increase in income this month does not affect consumption much in the short run unless it is perceived as a permanent increase.

Let's use point 1 on the graph as our starting point. Here disposable income is $50,000 and consumption is $45,000. Now suppose household income rises to $60,000. Initially consumption increases by 60 percent, the short-run MPC. The household moves from point 1 to point 2 along the short-run consumption function (C_S). The short-run consumption function has a lower MPC than the long-run consumption function because households do not completely adjust their spending and saving habits with short-run fluctuations in income. Once the household is convinced that $60,000 is a permanent level of income, it moves from point 2 to point 3 along the long-run consumption function. At point 3, consumption has increased by 90 percent, the long-run MPC. In the long run, households adjust fully to changes in income; in the short run, a fluctuation in income does not cause as large a fluctuation in consumption.

When income falls below the permanent income level, the household is willing to dissave or borrow to support its

normal level of consumption. When income rises above the permanent income level, the household saves at a higher rate than the long-run MPS. The lower MPC in the short run works to smooth out consumption in the long run. The household does not adjust current consumption with every up and down movement in household income.

To maintain a steady rate of consumption over time, households follow a pattern of saving over the life cycle. Saving is low when current income is low relative to permanent income (during school years, periods of unemployment, or retirement). Saving is high when current income is high relative to the lifetime average, typically during middle age.

In the long run, households adjust fully to changes in income. In the short run, in order to smooth consumption over time, they do not. This explains both the difference between the long-run and short-run consumption functions and the stability of consumption over time.

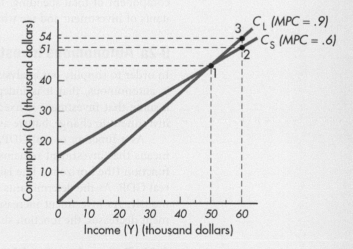

9-1e-4 Demographics Other things being equal, economists expect the level of consumption to rise with increases in population. The focus here is on both the number of people in the economy and the composition of that population. The size of the population affects the position of the consumption function; the age of the population affects the slope of the consumption function. The greater the size of the population, other things equal, the higher the intercept of the consumption function. With regard to the effect of age composition on the economy, young households typically are accumulating durable consumer goods (refrigerators, washing machines, automobiles); they have higher MPCs than older households.

1. It is impossible to separate incentives to save from incentives to consume.

2. Saving is a flow variable; savings is a stock variable.

3. Dissaving is spending financed by borrowing or using savings.

4. The marginal propensity to consume measures change in consumption as a proportion of change in disposable income.

5. The marginal propensity to save measures change in saving as a proportion of change in disposable income.

6. The MPC plus the MPS must equal 1.

7. Change in the MPC changes the slope of the consumption function; change in the MPS changes the slope of the saving function.

8. The average propensity to consume measures that portion of disposable income spent for consumption.

9. The average propensity to save measures that portion of disposable income saved.

10. The sum of the APC and the APS must equal 1.

11. The determinants of consumption include income, wealth, expectations, demographics, and taxation.

12. A change in consumption caused by a change in disposable income is shown by movement along the consumption function.

13. Changes in wealth, expectations, or population change autonomous consumption, which is shown as a shift of the consumption function.

9-2 Investment

Investment is business spending on capital goods and inventories. It is the most variable component of total spending. In this section of the chapter, we take a look at the determinants of investment and see why investment changes so much over the business cycle.

9-2a Autonomous Investment

In order to simplify our analysis of real GDP in the next chapter, we assume that investment is autonomous, that it is independent of current real GDP. This does not mean that we assume that investment is fixed at a constant amount. There are several factors that cause investment to change, but we assume that current real GDP is not one of them.

As a function of real GDP, autonomous investment is drawn as a horizontal line. This means that investment remains constant as real GDP changes. In Figure 6, the investment function (the horizontal line labeled I) indicates that investment equals $50 at every level of real GDP. As the determinants of investment change, the investment function shifts autonomously. As investment increases, the function shifts upward (e.g., from I to I_1); as investment decreases, the function shifts downward (from I to I_2).

9-2b Determinants of Investment

3. What are the determinants of investment?

Investment is business spending on capital goods and inventories. Capital goods are the buildings and equipment that businesses need to produce their products. Inventories are final goods that have not been sold. Inventories can be planned or unplanned. For example, in the fall, a retail department store wants to have enough sizes and styles of the new clothing lines to attract customers. Without a good-sized inventory, sales will suffer. The goods it buys are *planned* inventory, based on expected sales. But come February, the store wants to have as few fall clothes left unsold as possible. Goods that have not been sold at this stage are *unplanned* inventory. They are a sign that sales were not as good as expected and that the store purchased too much last year.

FIGURE 6 Investment as a Function of Income

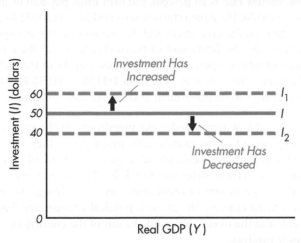

Investment is assumed to be autonomous. Because it is independent of current real GDP, it is drawn as a horizontal line. An autonomous increase in investment shifts the function upward, from I to I_1. An increase could be the product of lower interest rates, optimism in business about future sales and revenues, technological change, an investment tax credit that lowers the cost of capital goods, or a need to expand capacity because of a lack of available productive resources. An autonomous decrease in investment moves the function down, from I to I_2. The same factors that cause investment to rise can also cause it to fall when they move in the opposite direction.

Both types of inventories—planned and unplanned—are called investment. But only planned investment—capital purchases plus planned inventories—is combined with planned consumer, government, and foreign-sector spending to determine the equilibrium level of aggregate expenditures, as we will see in the next chapter. Unplanned investment and unwanted inventories do not affect the equilibrium. They are simply the leftovers of what has recently gone on in the economy. What economists are interested in are the determinants of planned investment.

9-2b-1 The Interest Rate Business investment is made in the hope of earning profits. The greater the expected profit, the greater the investment. A primary determinant of whether an investment opportunity will be profitable is the rate of interest. The interest rate is the cost of borrowed funds. Much of business spending is financed by borrowing. As the rate of interest goes up, fewer investment projects offer enough profit to warrant undertaking them. In other words, the higher the interest rate, the lower the rate of investment. As the interest rate falls, opportunities for greater profits increase and investment rises.

Let us look at a simple example. A firm can acquire a machine for $100 that will yield $120 in output. Whether the firm is willing to undertake the investment depends on whether it will earn a sufficient return on its investment. The return on an investment is the profit from the investment divided by its cost.

If the firm has to borrow $100 to make the investment, it will have to pay interest to the lender. Suppose the lender charges 10 percent interest. The firm will have to pay 10 percent of $100, or $10, interest. This raises the cost of the investment to $110, the $100 cost of the machine plus the $10 interest. The firm's return on the investment is 9 percent:

$$\text{Return on investment} = (\$120 - \$110)/\$110$$
$$= 0.09$$

As the interest rate rises, the firm's cost of borrowing also rises, and the return on investment falls. When the interest rate is 20 percent, the firm must pay $20 in interest, so the total cost of the investment is $120. Here the return is zero ([$120 – $120]/$120). The higher interest rate reduces the return on the investment and discourages investment spending.

As the interest rate falls, the firm's cost of borrowing falls and the return on the investment rises. If the interest rate is 5 percent, the firm must pay $5 in interest. The total cost of the investment is $105, and the return is 14 percent ([$120 − $105]/$105). The lower interest rate increases the return on the investment and encourages investment spending.

9-2b-2 Profit Expectations

Firms undertake investment in the expectation of earning a profit. Obviously, they cannot know exactly how much profit they will earn. So they use forecasts of revenues and costs to decide on an appropriate level of investment. It is their *expected* rate of return that actually determines their level of investment.

Many factors affect expectations of profit and, therefore, change the level of investment. Among them are new firms entering the market; political change; new laws, taxes, or subsidies from government; and the overall economic health of the country or the world as measured by gross domestic product.

9-2b-3 Other Determinants of Investment

Everything that might affect a firm's expected rate of return determines its level of investment. But three factors—technological change, the cost of capital goods, and capacity utilization—warrant special attention.

Technological Change   Technological change is often a driving force behind new investment. New products or processes can be crucial to remaining competitive in an industry. The computer industry, for example, is driven by technological change. As faster and larger-capacity memory chips are developed, computer manufacturers must utilize them in order to stay competitive.

The impact of technology on investment spending is not new. For example, the invention of the cotton gin stimulated investment spending in the early 1800s, and the introduction of the gasoline-powered tractor in 1905 created an agricultural investment boom in the early 1900s. More recently, the development of integrated circuits stimulated investment spending in the electronics industry.

One measure of the importance of technology is the commitment to research and development. Data on spending for research and development across countries are listed in Table 3. The data indicate that rich countries tend to spend a greater percentage of GDP on research and development, rely less on government financing of research and development, and have a greater fraction of the work force employed in research positions.

A commitment to research and development is a sign of the technological progress that marks the industrial nations. The industrial nations are the countries in which new technology generally originates. New technology developed in any country tends to stimulate investment spending across all nations, as firms in similar industries are forced to adopt new production methods to keep up with their competition.

Cost of Capital Goods   The cost of capital goods also affects investment spending. As capital goods become more expensive, the rate of return on investment in them drops and the amount of investment falls. One factor that can cause the cost of capital goods to change sharply is government tax policy. The U.S. government has enacted and then removed investment tax credits several times in the past. These credits allow firms to deduct part of the cost of investment from their tax bill. When the cost of investment drops, investment increases. When the cost of investment increases, the level of investment falls.

Capacity Utilization   If its existing capital stock is being used heavily, a firm has an incentive to buy more. But if much of its capital stock is standing idle, the firm has little incentive to increase that stock. Economists sometimes refer to the productive capacity of the

TABLE 3 Research and Development Expenditures as a Percentage of GDP, 2008

	% of GDP	% Government Financed	Researchers per 1,000 Workers
Australia	1.8	44.4	8.4
Canada	2.0	34.5	7.8
Finland	3.5	25.7	16.6
France	2.1	38.4	8.2
Germany	2.5	31.1	7.2
Italy	1.1	50.8	3.4
Japan	3.3	17.7	11.0
Mexico	0.5	59.1	1.2
Poland	0.6	62.7	4.5
Turkey	0.8	50.6	1.9
United Kingdom	1.8	31.3	5.9
United States	2.6	31.2	9.7

Source: Data from *OECD Factbook*, OECD, 2008.

economy as the amount of output that can be produced by businesses. In fact, the Federal Reserve constructs a measure of capacity utilization that indicates how close the economy is to capacity output.

Figure 7 plots the rate of capacity utilization in the U.S. economy. Between 1975 and 2013, U.S. industry operated at a high rate of 85 percent of capacity in 1979 and at a low rate of 68.5 percent of capacity in the recession year of 2009. We never expect to

FIGURE 7 Capacity Utilization Rates for Total U.S. Industry

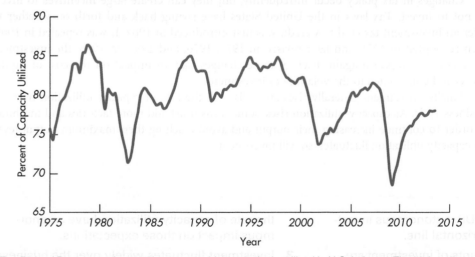

The Federal Reserve estimates the rate at which capacity is utilized in U.S. industry. The higher the rate, the greater the pressure for investment to expand productive capacity. Shaded areas represent recessions.

see 100 percent of capacity utilized for the same reasons that we never expect to see zero unemployment. There are always capital goods that are temporarily unused, just as there is frictional unemployment of labor, and there are always capital goods that are obsolete because of technological change, similar to the case of structural unemployment of labor.

When the economy is utilizing its capacity at a high rate, there is pressure to increase the production of capital goods and expand productive capacity. When capacity utilization is low—when factories and machines are sitting idle—investment tends to fall.

9-2c Volatility

We said that investment is the most variable component of total spending. What role do the determinants of investment play in that volatility?

Interest rates fluctuate widely. They are much more variable than income. Interest rates are a very important determinant of investment. Clearly, the fact that they are so variable contributes to the variability of investment.

Expectations are subjective judgments about the future. Expectations can and often do change suddenly with new information. A rumor of a technological breakthrough, a speech by the president or a powerful member of Congress, even a revised weather forecast can cause firms to reexamine their thinking about the expected profitability of an investment. In developing economies, the protection of private property rights can have a large impact on investment spending. If a business expects a change in government policy to increase the likelihood of the government's expropriating its property, obviously it is not going to undertake new investments. Conversely, if a firm believes that the government will protect private property and encourage the accumulation of wealth, it will increase its investment spending. The fact that expectations are subject to large and frequent swings contributes to the volatility of investment.

Technological change proceeds very unevenly, making it difficult to forecast. Historically we find large increases in investment when a new technology is first developed and decreases in investment once the new technology is in place. This causes investment to move up and down unevenly through time.

Changes in tax policy occur infrequently, but they can create large incentives to invest or not to invest. Tax laws in the United States have swung back and forth on whether to offer an investment tax credit. A credit was first introduced in 1962. It was repealed in 1969, then readopted in 1971, and later revised in 1975, 1976, and 1981. In 1986, the investment tax credit was repealed again. Each of these changes had an impact on the cost of capital goods and contributed to the volatility of investment.

Finally, investment generally rises and falls with the rate of capacity utilization over the business cycle. As capacity utilization rises, some firms must add more factories and machines in order to continue increasing their output and avoid reaching their maximum output level. As capacity utilization fluctuates, so will investment.

RECAP

1. As a function of real GDP, autonomous investment is drawn as a horizontal line.

2. The primary determinants of investment are the interest rate and profit expectations. Technological change, the cost of capital goods, and the rate of capacity utilization have an enormous impact on those expectations.

3. Investment fluctuates widely over the business cycle because the determinants of investment are so variable.

9-3 Government Spending

Government spending on goods and services is the second largest component of aggregate expenditures in the United States. In later chapters, we examine the behavior of government in detail. Here we focus on how the government sector fits into the aggregate expenditures–income relationship. We assume that government spending is set by government authorities at whatever level they choose, independent of current income. In other words, we assume that government spending, like investment, is autonomous.

Figure 8 depicts government expenditures as a function of real GDP. The function, labeled G, is a horizontal line. If government officials increase government expenditures, the function shifts upward, parallel to the original curve, by an amount equal to the increase in expenditures (for example, from G to G_1). If government expenditures are reduced, the function shifts downward by an amount equal to the drop in expenditures (for example, from G to G_2).

4. What are the determinants of government spending?

9-4 Net Exports

The last component of aggregate expenditures is net exports, or spending by the international sector. Net exports equal a country's exports of goods and services (what it sells to the rest of the world) minus its imports of goods and services (what it buys from the rest of the world). When net exports are positive, there is a surplus in the merchandise and services accounts. When net exports are negative, there is a deficit. The United States has had a net

5. What are the determinants of net exports?

FIGURE 8   Government Expenditures as a Function of Real GDP

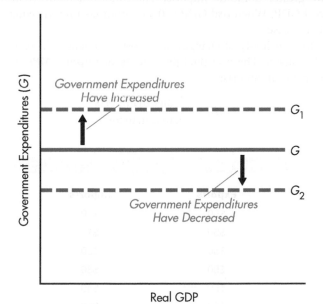

Government spending is assumed to be autonomous and set by government policy. The government spending function is the horizontal line labeled G. Autonomous increases in government spending move the function upward (for example, from G to G_1); decreases move the function downward (for example, from G to G_2).

exports deficit since 1975. This is a relatively new phenomenon; the country had run surpluses throughout the post–World War II era until that time.

9-4a Exports

We assume that exports are autonomous. There are many factors that determine the actual value of exports, among them foreign income, tastes, prices, government trade restrictions, and exchange rates. But we assume that exports are not affected by current domestic income. You see this in the second column of Table 4, where exports are $50 at each level of real GDP.

As foreign income increases, foreign consumption rises—including consumption of goods produced in other countries—so domestic exports increase at every level of domestic real GDP. Decreases in foreign income lower domestic exports at every level of domestic real GDP. Similarly, changes in tastes or government restrictions on international trade or exchange rates can cause the level of exports to shift autonomously. When tastes favor domestic goods, exports go up. When tastes change, exports go down. When foreign governments impose restrictions on international trade, domestic exports fall. When restrictions are lowered, exports rise. Finally, as discussed in the chapter titled "An Introduction to the Foreign Exchange Market and the Balance of Payments," when the domestic currency depreciates on the foreign exchange market, making domestic goods cheaper in foreign countries, exports rise. When the domestic currency appreciates on the foreign exchange market, making domestic goods more expensive in foreign countries, exports fall.

9-4b Imports

Domestic purchases from the rest of the world (imports) are also determined by tastes, trade restrictions, and exchange rates. Here domestic income plays a role, too. The greater domestic real GDP, the greater domestic imports. The import data in Table 4 show imports increasing with real GDP. When real GDP is 0, autonomous imports equal $0. As real GDP increases, imports increase.

We measure the sensitivity of changes in imports to changes in real GDP by the marginal propensity to import. The **marginal propensity to import (MPI)** is the proportion of any extra income spent on imports:

Marginal propensity to import (MPI)
The change in imports as a proportion of the change in income.

$$MPI = \frac{\text{change in imports}}{\text{change in income}}$$

TABLE 4   Hypothetical Export and Import Schedule

Real GDP	Exports	Imports	Net Exports
$ 0	$50	$ 0	$50
$100	$50	$10	$40
$200	$50	$20	$30
$300	$50	$30	$20
$400	$50	$40	$10
$500	$50	$50	$ 0
$600	$50	$60	−$10
$700	$50	$70	−$20

In Table 4, the *MPI* is .10, or 10 percent. Every time income changes by $100, imports change by $10.

How do other factors—tastes, government trade restrictions, and exchange rates—affect imports? When domestic tastes favor foreign goods, imports rise. When they do not, imports fall. When the domestic government tightens restrictions on international trade, imports fall. When those restrictions are loosened, imports rise. Finally, when the domestic currency depreciates on the foreign exchange market, making foreign goods more expensive to domestic residents, imports fall. And when the domestic currency appreciates on the foreign exchange market, lowering the price of foreign goods, imports rise.

9-4c The Net Export Function

In our hypothetical economy in Table 4, net exports are listed in the last column. They are the difference between exports and imports. Because imports rise with domestic income, the higher that income is, the lower net exports are.

The net exports function, labeled *X*, is shown in Figure 9. The downward slope of the function (given by the *MPI*) indicates that net exports fall as real GDP increases. Net exports are the only component of aggregate expenditures that can take on a negative value (saving can be negative, but it is not part of spending). Negative net exports mean that the domestic economy is importing more than it exports. The net exports function shifts with changes in foreign income, prices, tastes, government trade restrictions, and exchange rates. For example, as foreign income increases, domestic exports increase and the net exports function shifts upward.

The higher domestic income is, the lower net exports are.

FIGURE 9 Net Exports as a Function of Real GDP

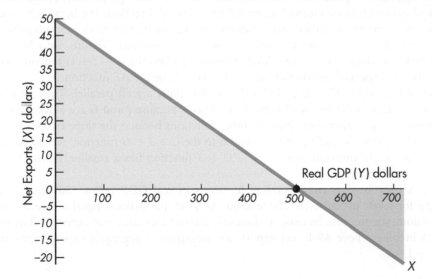

The net exports function is the downward-sloping line labeled *X*. Because exports are autonomous and imports increase with income, net exports fall as domestic real GDP rises. Notice that net exports can be positive or negative.

1. Net exports equal a country's exports minus its imports.

2. Exports are determined by foreign income, tastes, government trade restrictions, and exchange rates; they are independent of domestic real GDP.

3. Imports are a positive function of domestic real GDP; they also depend on tastes, domestic

government trade restrictions, and exchange rates.

4. The marginal propensity to import measures the change in imports as a proportion of the change in domestic income.

5. Net exports fall as domestic real GDP rises.

9-5 The Aggregate Expenditures Function

The aggregate, or total, expenditures function is the sum of the individual functions for each component of planned spending. Aggregate expenditures (AE) equal consumption (C), plus investment (I), plus government spending (G), plus net exports (X):

$$AE = C + I + G + X$$

9-5a Aggregate Expenditures Table and Function

6. What is the aggregate expenditures function?

The table in Figure 10 lists aggregate expenditures data for a hypothetical economy. Real GDP is in the first column; the individual components of aggregate expenditures are in columns 2 through 5. Aggregate expenditures, listed in column 6, are the sum of the components at each level of income.

The aggregate expenditures function (AE) can be derived graphically by summing the individual expenditure functions (Figure 10) in a vertical direction. We begin with the consumption function (C) and then add autonomous investment, $50, to the consumption function at every level of income to arrive at the $C + I$ function. To this we add constant government spending, $70, at every level of income to find the $C + I + G$ function. Finally, we add the net exports function to find $C + I + G + X$, or the AE function.

Notice that the C, $C + I$, and $C + I + G$ functions are all parallel. They all have the same slope, which is determined by the MPC. This is because I and G are autonomous. The AE function has a smaller slope than the other functions because the slope of the net exports function is negative. By adding the X function to the $C + I + G$ function, we are decreasing the slope of the AE function; the $C + I + G + X$ function has a smaller, flatter slope than the $C + I + G$ function.

The X function increases spending for levels of real GDP below $500 and decreases spending for levels of real GDP above $500. At $500, net exports equal 0 (see column 5). Because domestic imports increase as domestic income increases, net exports fall as income rises. At incomes above $500, net exports are negative, so aggregate expenditures are less than $C + I + G$.

9-5b The Next Step

Though we have also been using *aggregate demand* to refer to total spending, you can see from Figure 10 that the aggregate expenditures line slopes up, whereas the aggregate demand curve you saw in Figure 1 slopes down. In the next chapter, we will explore the formal relationship between these two related concepts when we go about determining the equilibrium level of real GDP using the AE function.

FIGURE 10 The Aggregate Expenditures Function

(1) Y	(2) C	(3) I	(4) G	(5) X	(6) AE
$0	$30	$50	$70	$50	$200
$100	$100	$50	$70	$40	$260
$200	$170	$50	$70	$30	$320
$300	$240	$50	$70	$20	$380
$400	$310	$50	$70	$10	$440
$500	$380	$50	$70	$0	$500
$600	$450	$50	$70	−$10	$560
$700	$520	$50	$70	−$20	$620

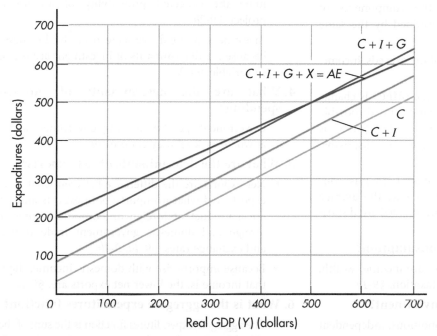

To find the aggregate expenditures function, we begin with the consumption function (labeled C) and add the investment function (I) to create the $C + I$ function. We then add the government spending function (G) to find the $C + I + G$ function. Notice that the C, $C + I$, and $C + I + G$ functions are all parallel. They have the same slope because investment and government spending are assumed to be autonomous. Because I and G do not change with income, the slopes of the $C + I$ and $C + I + G$ functions are equal to the slope of the consumption function (the MPC). Net exports are added to the $C + I + G$ function to find the aggregate expenditures function, $C + I + G + X$. The aggregate expenditures function has a smaller slope than the other functions because the slope of the net exports function is negative.

The concept of macroeconomic equilibrium points out the key role that aggregate expenditures play in determining output and income. As you will see, the equilibrium level of real GDP is that level toward which the economy automatically tends to move. Once that equilibrium is established, there is no tendency for real GDP to change unless a change in autonomous expenditures occurs. If aggregate expenditures rise, then the equilibrium level of real GDP rises. If aggregate expenditures fall, then the equilibrium level of real GDP falls. Such shifts in the AE function are associated with shifts in C, I, G, or X.

1. Aggregate expenditures are the sum of planned consumption, planned investment, planned government spending, and planned net exports at every level of real GDP.

2. Assuming that *I* and *G* are autonomous, the *C*, *C* + *I*, and *C* + *I* + *G* functions are parallel lines.

3. Net exports increase aggregate expenditures at relatively low levels of domestic real GDP and decrease aggregate expenditures at relatively high levels of domestic real GDP.

SUMMARY

1. How are consumption and saving related?

- Consumption and saving are the components of disposable income; they are determined by the same variables. §9-1

- Dissaving occurs when consumption exceeds income. §9-1b

- The marginal propensity to consume (*MPC*) is change in consumption divided by change in disposable income; the marginal propensity to save (*MPS*) is change in saving divided by change in disposable income. §9-1c

- The average propensity to consume (*APC*) is consumption divided by disposable income; the average propensity to save (*APS*) is saving divided by disposable income. §9-1d

2. What are the determinants of consumption?

- The determinants of consumption are income, wealth, expectations, demographics, and taxation. §9-1e

3. What are the determinants of investment?

- Investment is assumed to be autonomous, independent of current income. §9-2a

- The determinants of investment are the interest rate, profit expectations, technological change, the cost of capital goods, and the rate at which capacity is utilized. §9-2b

- Firms use the expected return on investment to determine the expected profitability of an investment project. §9-2b

- Investment is highly variable over the business cycle because the determinants of investment are themselves so variable. §9-2c

4. What are the determinants of government spending?

- Government spending is set by government authorities at whatever level they choose. §9-3

5. What are the determinants of net exports?

- Net exports are the difference between what a country exports and what it imports; both exports and imports are a product of foreign or domestic income, tastes, foreign and domestic government trade restrictions, and exchange rates. §9-4a, 9-4b

- Because imports rise with domestic income, the higher that income is, the lower net exports are. §9-4c

6. What is the aggregate expenditures function?

- The aggregate expenditures function is the sum of the individual functions for each component of spending. §9-5

- The slope of the aggregate expenditures function is flatter than that of the consumption function because it includes the net exports function, which has a negative slope. §9-5a

KEY TERMS

EXERCISES

1. Why do we study the consumption and saving functions together?
2. Explain the difference between a flow variable and a stock variable. Classify each of the following as a stock or a flow: income, wealth, saving, savings, consumption, investment, government expenditures, net exports, GDP.
3. Fill in the blanks in the following table:

Income	Consumption	Saving	MPC	MPS	APC	APS
$1,000	$ 400					.60
$2,000	$ 900	$1,100				
$3,000	$ 1,400			.50		
$4,000		$2,100				

4. Why is consumption so much more stable over the business cycle than investment? In formulating your answer, discuss household behavior as well as business behavior.
5. Assuming investment is autonomous, draw an investment function with income on the horizontal axis. Show how the function shifts if:
   a. The interest rate falls.
   b. An investment tax credit is repealed by Congress.
   c. A new president is expected to be a strong advocate of pro-business policies.
   d. There is a great deal of excess capacity in the economy.
6. Use the following table to answer these questions:

Y	C	I	G	X
$ 500	$500	$10	$20	$60
$ 600	$590	$10	$20	$40
$ 700	$680	$10	$20	$20
$ 800	$770	$10	$20	$ 0
$ 900	$860	$10	$20	−$20
$1,000	$950	$10	$20	−$40

   a. What is the *MPC*?
   b. What is the *MPS*?
   c. What is the *MPI*?
   d. What is the level of aggregate expenditures at each level of income?
   e. Graph the aggregate expenditures function.
7. Based on the table in exercise 6, what is the linear equation for each of the following functions?
   a. Consumption
   b. Investment
   c. Net exports
   d. Aggregate expenditures

8. Is the *AE* function the same thing as a demand curve? Why or why not?
9. What is the level of saving if:
   a. Disposable income is $500 and consumption is $450?
   b. Disposable income is $1,200 and the *APS* is .9?
   c. The *MPC* equals .9, disposable income rises from $800 to $900, and saving is originally $120 when income equals $800?
10. What is the marginal propensity to consume if:
    a. Consumption increases by $75 when disposable income rises by $100?
    b. Consumption falls by $50 when disposable income falls by $100?
    c. Saving equals $20 when disposable income equals $100 and saving equals $40 when disposable income equals $300?
11. How can the *APC* fall as income rises if the *MPC* is constant?
12. Why would economies with older populations tend to have consumption functions with greater slopes?
13. Draw a diagram and illustrate the effects of the following on the net exports function for the United States:
    a. The French government imposes restrictions on French imports of U.S. goods.
    b. The U.S. national income rises.
    c. Foreign income falls.
    d. The dollar depreciates on the foreign exchange market.
14. Why is the slope of the $C + I + G$ function different from the slope of the $C + I + G + X$ function?
15. Suppose the consumption function is $C = \$200 + 0.8Y$.
    a. What is the amount of autonomous consumption?
    b. What is the marginal propensity to consume?
    c. What would consumption equal when real GDP equals $1,000?
16. Explain why the consumption function is flatter in the short run than in the long run. Draw a diagram to illustrate your answer.

ECONOMICALLY SPEAKING

2012 TRADE GAP IS $539.5 BILLION

Bureau of Economic Analysis, March 7, 2013

The U.S. goods and services deficit decreased in 2012, according to the U.S. Bureau of Economic Analysis and the U.S. Census Bureau. The deficit decreased from $559.9 billion in 2011 to $539.5 billion (revised) in 2012, as exports increased more than imports. As a percentage of U.S. gross domestic product, the goods and services deficit was 3.4 percent in 2012, down from 3.7 percent in 2011. The goods deficit decreased from $738.4 billion in 2011 to $735.3 billion in 2012, and the services surplus increased from $178.5 billion in 2011 to $195.8 billion in 2012.

Exports

Exports of goods and services increased $91.1 billion, or 4.3 percent, in 2012 to $2,194.5 billion. Exports of goods increased $66.7 billion and exports of services increased $24.4 billion.

* The largest increases in exports of goods were in capital goods ($33.7 billion), automotive vehicles, parts, and engines ($12.9 billion), and consumer goods ($6.7 billion).
* The largest increases in exports of services were in travel ($12.4 billion), other private services ($7.8 billion), which includes items such as business, professional, and technical services, insurance services, and financial services, and passenger fares ($2.9 billion).

Imports

Imports of goods and services increased $70.8 billion, or 2.7 percent, in 2012 to $2,734.0 billion. Imports of goods increased $63.6 billion and imports of services increased $7.2 billion.

* The largest increases in imports of goods were in automotive vehicles, parts, and engines ($43.1 billion), capital goods ($37.5 billion), and other goods ($6.3 billion).
* The largest increases in imports of services were in travel ($5.0 billion), royalties and license fees ($3.4 billion), which partly reflects payments for the rights to broadcast the 2012 Summer Olympic Games, and passenger fares ($3.3 billion).

Goods by geographic area

* The goods deficit with China increased from $295.4 billion in 2011 to $315.1 billion in 2012. Exports increased $6.7 billion to $110.6 billion, while imports increased $26.3 billion to $425.6 billion.
* The goods deficit with the European Union increased from $99.9 billion in 2011 to $115.7 billion in 2012. Exports decreased $3.3 billion to $265.1 billion, while imports increased $12.5 billion to $380.8 billion.
* The goods deficit with Mexico decreased from $64.5 billion in 2011 to $61.3 billion in 2012. Exports increased $18.0 billion to $216.3 billion, while imports increased $14.8 billion to $277.7 billion.

Source: U.S. Department of Commerce.

COMMENTARY

In this chapter, we saw how net exports contribute to aggregate expenditures. Merchandise exports bring money from the rest of the world, and higher net exports mean greater aggregate expenditures. Merchandise imports involve outflows of money to foreign countries, and lower net exports mean lower aggregate expenditures.

We saw in the chapter that higher domestic real GDP leads to higher imports and lower net exports. This article points out that the U.S. net export deficit fell in 2012, a year of mild growth. As U.S. incomes grew slowly, U.S. demand for foreign goods increased, which would normally increase the deficit with the rest of the world. However this perspective ignores what is going on with incomes in the rest of the word. While incomes in the U.S. may have been growing, incomes in other countries may have been growing faster, which would increase the amount the U.S. exports to them.

In a time of falling or slowly growing incomes, international trade deficits become more politically sensitive than in good times. Because of the effect of net exports on aggregate expenditures, we often hear arguments for policies aimed at increasing exports and decreasing imports. Domestic residents are often resentful of foreign producers and blame foreign competitors for job losses in the home country. However, we must consider the circumstances and then ask if a policy aimed at increasing the national trade surplus (or decreasing the deficit) is really desirable.

Since one country's export is another's import, it is impossible for everyone to have a surplus—on a worldwide basis, the total value of exports equals the total value of imports. If someone must always have a trade deficit when others have trade surpluses, is it necessarily true that surpluses are good and deficits bad so that one country is benefiting at another's expense? In a sense, imports should be preferred to exports, since exports represent goods that are no longer available for domestic consumption and will be consumed by foreign importers. In later chapters you will learn that the benefits of free international trade include more efficient production and increased consumption. Furthermore, if trade among nations is voluntary, it is difficult to argue that deficit countries are harmed while surplus countries benefit from trade.

In general, it is not obvious whether a country is better or worse off running merchandise surpluses rather than deficits. Consider the following simple example of a world with two countries, R and P. Country R is a rich creditor country that is growing rapidly and has a net exports deficit. Country P is a poor debtor country that is growing slowly and has positive net exports. Should we prefer living conditions in P to living conditions in R based solely on the knowledge that P has a net exports surplus and R has a net exports deficit? Although this is indeed a simplistic example, there are real-world analogues of rich creditor countries with international trade deficits and poor debtor nations with international trade surpluses. The point is that you cannot analyze the balance of payments apart from other economic considerations. Deficits are not inherently bad, nor are surpluses necessarily good.

An Algebraic Model of Aggregate Expenditures

Aggregate expenditures (AE) equal consumption (C) plus investment (I) plus government spending (G) plus net exports (X). If we can develop an equation for each component of spending, we can put them together in a single model.

Consumption The consumption function can be written in general form as

$$C = C^a + cYd$$

where C^a is autonomous consumption and c is the MPC. The consumption function for the data in the chapter titled "Aggregate Expenditures" is

$$C = \$30 + .70Yd$$

as shown in Figure 1.

FIGURE 1 The Consumption Function

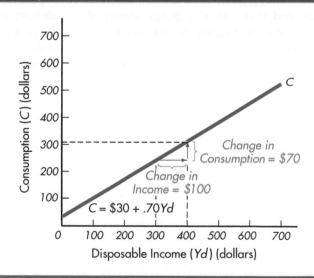

Saving The corresponding saving function is

$$S = -\$30 + .30Yd$$

as illustrated in Figure 2.

Investment Investment is autonomous at I^a, which is equal to $50.

Government Spending Government spending is autonomous at G^a, which is equal to $70.

Net Exports Exports are autonomous at EX^a and are equal to $50. Imports are given by the function

$$IM = IM^a + imY$$

where im is the *MPI*. Here, then,

$$IM = \$0 + .10Y$$

Net exports equal exports minus imports, or

$$X = \$50 - \$0 - .10Y$$
$$= \$50 - .10Y$$

as shown in Figure 3.

Aggregate Expenditures Summing the functions for the four components (and ignoring taxes, so that Yd equals Y) gives

$$AE = C^a + cY + I^a + G^a + EX^a - IM^a - imY$$
$$= \$30 + .70Y + \$50 + \$70 + \$50 - \$0 - .10Y$$
$$= \$200 + .60Y$$

as shown in Figure 4.

FIGURE 2 The Saving Function

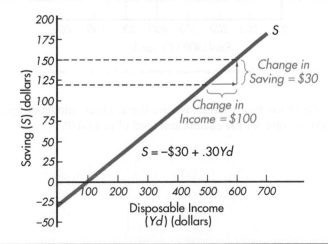

$S = -\$30 + .30Yd$

Change in Saving = $30

Change in Income = $100

FIGURE 3   The Net Exports Function

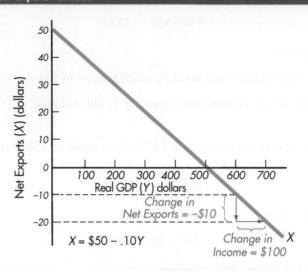

FIGURE 4   The Aggregate Expenditures Function

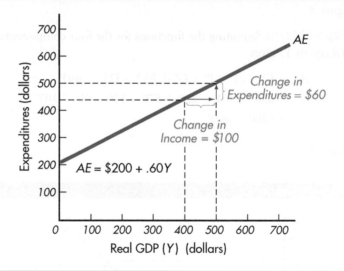

In the Appendix to the next chapter, we use the algebraic model of aggregate expenditures presented here to solve for the equilibrium level of real GDP.

CHAPTER 10
Income and Expenditures Equilibrium

Preview

What determines the level of income and expenditures, or real GDP? In the chapter titled "Macroeconomic Equilibrium: Aggregate Demand and Supply," we used aggregate demand and aggregate supply to answer this question. Then, in the chapter titled "Aggregate Expenditures," we developed the components of aggregate expenditures in more detail to provide the foundation for an additional approach to answering the question, "What determines the level of real GDP?" If you know the answer to this question, you are well on your way to understanding business cycles. Sometimes real GDP is growing and jobs are relatively easy to find; at other times real GDP is falling and large numbers of people are out of work. Macroeconomists use several models to analyze the causes of business cycles. Underlying all of these models is the concept of macroeconomic equilibrium.

FUNDAMENTAL QUESTIONS

1. What does equilibrium mean in macroeconomics?

2. How do aggregate expenditures affect income, or real GDP?

3. What are the leakages from and injections into spending?

4. Why does equilibrium real GDP change by a multiple of a change in autonomous expenditures?

5. What is the spending multiplier?

6. What is the relationship between the GDP gap and the recessionary gap?

7. How does international trade affect the size of the spending multiplier?

8. Why does the aggregate expenditures curve shift with changes in the price level?

203

Equilibrium here means what it did when we talked about supply and demand: a point of balance, a point from which there is no tendency to move. In macroeconomics, equilibrium is the level of income and expenditures that the economy tends to move toward and remain at until autonomous spending changes.

Economists have not always agreed on how an economy reaches equilibrium or on the forces that move an economy from one equilibrium to another. This last issue formed the basis of economic debate during the Great Depression of the 1930s. Before the 1930s, economists generally believed that the economy was always at or moving toward an equilibrium consistent with a high level of employed resources. The British economist John Maynard Keynes did not agree. He believed that an economy can come to rest at a level of real GDP that is too low to provide employment for all those who desire it. He also believed that certain actions are necessary to ensure that the economy rises to a level of real GDP consistent with a high level of employment. In particular, Keynes argued that government must intervene in the economy in a big way (see the Economic Insight "John Maynard Keynes").

To understand the debate that began during the 1930s and continues on various fronts today, it is necessary to understand the Keynesian view of how equilibrium real GDP is determined. This is our focus here. We have seen in the chapter titled "Macroeconomic Equilibrium: Aggregate Demand and Supply" that the aggregate demand and supply model of macroeconomic equilibrium allows the price level to fluctuate as the equilibrium level of real GDP changes. The Keynesian income-expenditures model assumes that the price level is fixed. It emphasizes aggregate expenditures without explicitly considering the supply side of the economy. This is why we considered the components of spending in detail in the chapter titled "Aggregate Expenditures"—to provide a foundation for the analysis in this chapter. The Keynesian model may be viewed as a special fixed-price case of the aggregate demand and aggregate supply model. In later chapters, we examine the relationship between equilibrium and the level of employed resources and the effect of government policy on both of these elements.

10-1 Equilibrium Income and Expenditures

Equilibrium is a point from which there is no tendency to move. People do not change their behavior when everything is consistent with what they expect. However, when plans and reality do not match, people adjust their behavior to make them match. Determining a nation's equilibrium level of income and expenditures is the process of defining the level of income and expenditures at which plans and reality are the same.

10-1a Expenditures and Income

We use the aggregate expenditures function described at the end of the chapter titled "Aggregate Expenditures" to demonstrate how equilibrium is determined. Keep in mind that the aggregate expenditures function represents *planned* expenditures at different levels of income, or real GDP. We focus on planned expenditures because they represent the amount that households, firms, government, and the foreign sector expect to spend.

1. What does equilibrium mean in macroeconomics?

2. How do aggregate expenditures affect income, or real GDP?

ECONOMIC INSIGHT

John Maynard Keynes

John Maynard Keynes (pronounced "canes") is considered by many to be the greatest economist of the twentieth century. His major work, The *General Theory of Employment, Interest, and Money*, had a profound impact on macroeconomics, both in thought and policy. Keynes was born in Cambridge, England, on June 5, 1883. He studied economics at Cambridge University, where he became a lecturer in economics in 1908. During World War I, Keynes worked for the British treasury. At the end of the war, he was the treasury's representative at the Versailles Peace Conference. He resigned from the British delegation at the conference to protest the harsh terms being imposed on the defeated countries. His resignation and the publication of *Economic Consequences of the Peace* (1919) made him an international celebrity.

In 1936, Keynes published *The General Theory*. It was a time of world recession (it has been estimated that around one-quarter of the U.S. labor force was unemployed at the height of the Depression), and policymakers were searching for ways to explain the persistent unemployment. In the book, Keynes suggested that an economy could be at equilibrium at less than potential GDP. More important, he argued that government policy could be altered to end recession. His analysis emphasized aggregate expenditures. If private expenditures were not sufficient to create equilibrium at potential GDP, government expenditures could be increased to stimulate income and output. This was a startling concept. Most economists of the time believed that government should not take an active role in the economy. With his *General Theory*, Keynes started a "revolution" in macroeconomics.

Actual expenditures always equal income and output because they reflect changes in inventories. That is, inventories automatically raise or lower investment expenditures so that actual spending equals income, which equals output, which equals real GDP. However, aggregate expenditures (which are planned spending) may not equal real GDP. What happens when planned spending and real GDP are not equal?

When planned spending on goods and services exceeds the current value of output, the production of goods and services increases. Because output equals income, the level of real GDP also increases. This is the situation for all income levels below $500 in Figure 1. At these levels, total spending is greater than real GDP, which means that more goods and services are being

Net exports equal exports minus imports. Agricultural products are important exports for many countries, like these papayas being shipped from the port of Manaus Amazonas Brazil. If sold to a U.S. importer, the papayas will represent Brazilian exports and contribute to increased GDP in Brazil by means of higher net exports.

purchased than are being produced. The only way this can happen is for goods produced in the past to be sold. When planned spending is greater than real GDP, business inventories fall.

FIGURE 1   The Equilibrium Level of Real GDP

(1) Real GDP (Y)	(2) Consumption (C)	(3) Investment (I)	(4) Government Spending (G)	(5) Net Exports (X)	(6) Aggregate Expenditures (AE)	(7) Unplanned Change in Inventories	(8) Change in Real GDP
$0	$30	$50	$70	$50	$200	−$200	Increase
$100	$100	$50	$70	$40	$260	−$160	Increase
$200	$170	$50	$70	$30	$320	−$120	Increase
$300	$240	$50	$70	$20	$380	−$80	Increase
$400	$310	$50	$70	$10	$440	−$40	Increase
$500	$380	$50	$70	$0	$500	$0	No change
$600	$450	$50	$70	−$10	$560	$40	Decrease
$700	$520	$50	$70	−$20	$620	$80	Decrease

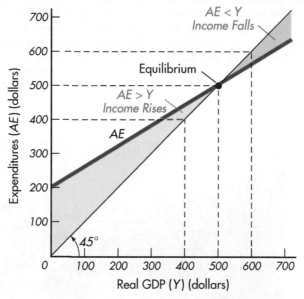

Macroeconomic equilibrium occurs where aggregate expenditures (*AE*) equal real GDP (*Y*). In the graph it is the point where the *AE* line crosses the 45-degree line, where expenditures and real GDP both equal $500. When aggregate expenditures exceed real GDP (as they do at a real GDP level of $400, for example), real GDP rises to the equilibrium level. When aggregate expenditures are less than real GDP (as they are at a real GDP level of $600, for example), real GDP falls back to the equilibrium level.

This change in inventories offsets the excess of planned expenditures over real GDP, so actual expenditures (including the unplanned change in inventories) equal real GDP. You can see this in column 7 of the table in Figure 1, where the change in inventories offsets the excess of aggregate expenditures over real GDP (the difference between columns 6 and 1).

When aggregate expenditures exceed real GDP, real GDP rises.

What happens when inventories fall? As inventories fall, manufacturers increase production to meet the demand for products. The increased production raises the level of real GDP. *When aggregate expenditures exceed real GDP, real GDP rises.*

At real GDP levels above $500 in the table, aggregate expenditures are less than income. As a result, inventories are accumulating above planned levels—more goods and services are being produced than are being purchased. As inventories rise, businesses begin to reduce the quantity of output they produce. The unplanned increase in inventories is counted as a form of investment spending so that actual expenditures equal real GDP. For example, when real GDP is $600, aggregate expenditures are only $560. The $40 of goods that are produced but not sold are measured as inventory investment. The $560 of aggregate expenditures plus the $40 of unplanned inventories equal $600, the level of real GDP. As inventories increase, firms cut production; this causes real GDP to fall. *When aggregate expenditures are less than real GDP, real GDP falls.*

There is only one level of real GDP in the table in Figure 1 at which real GDP does not change. When real GDP is $500, aggregate expenditures equal $500. The equilibrium level of real GDP (or output) is that point at which aggregate expenditures equal real GDP (or output).

When aggregate expenditures equal real GDP, planned spending equals the output produced and the income generated from producing that output. As long as planned spending is consistent with real GDP, real GDP does not change. But if planned spending is higher or lower than real GDP, real GDP does change. Equilibrium is that point at which planned spending and real GDP are equal.

The graph in Figure 1 illustrates equilibrium. The 45-degree line shows all possible points where aggregate expenditures (measured on the vertical axis) equal real GDP (measured on the horizontal axis). The equilibrium level of real GDP, then, is simply the point where the aggregate expenditures line (*AE*) crosses the 45-degree line. In the figure, equilibrium occurs where real GDP and expenditures are $500.

When the *AE* curve lies above the 45-degree line—for example, at a real GDP level of $400—aggregate expenditures are greater than real GDP. What happens? Real GDP rises to the equilibrium level, where it tends to stay. When the *AE* curve lies below the 45-degree line—at a real GDP level of $600, for example—aggregate expenditures are less than real GDP; this pushes real GDP down. Once real GDP falls to the equilibrium level ($500 in our example), it tends to stay there.

> *When aggregate expenditures are less than real GDP, real GDP falls.*

> *The equilibrium level of real GDP is where aggregate expenditures equal real GDP.*

10-1b Leakages and Injections

Equilibrium can be determined by using aggregate expenditures and real GDP, which represents income. Another way to determine equilibrium involves leakages from and injections into the income stream, the circular flow of income and expenditures.

Leakages reduce autonomous aggregate expenditures. There are three leakages in the stream from domestic income to spending: saving, taxes, and imports.

- The more households save, the less they spend. An increase in autonomous saving means a decrease in autonomous consumption, which could cause the equilibrium level of real GDP to fall (see the Economic Insight "The Paradox of Thrift").
- Taxes are an involuntary reduction in consumption. The government transfers income away from households. Higher taxes lower autonomous consumption, in the process lowering autonomous aggregate expenditures and the equilibrium level of real GDP.
- Imports are expenditures for foreign goods and services. They reduce expenditures on domestic goods and services. An autonomous increase in imports reduces net exports, causing autonomous aggregate expenditures and the equilibrium level of real GDP to fall.

For equilibrium to occur, these leakages must be offset by corresponding *injections* of spending into the domestic economy through investment, government spending, and exports.

- Household saving generates funds that businesses can borrow and spend for investment purposes.
- The taxes collected by government are used to finance government purchases of goods and services.
- Exports bring foreign expenditures into the domestic economy.

3. What are the leakages from and injections into spending?

> *Saving, taxes, and imports are leakages that reduce autonomous aggregate expenditures.*

> *Investment, government spending, and exports are injections that increase autonomous aggregate expenditures.*

ECONOMIC INSIGHT

The Paradox of Thrift

People generally believe that saving is good and more saving is better. However, if every family increased its saving, the result could be less income for the economy as a whole. In fact, increased saving could actually lower savings for all households.

An increase in saving may provide an example of the *paradox of thrift*. A *paradox* is a true proposition that seems to contradict common beliefs. We believe that we will be better off if we increase our saving, but in the aggregate, increased saving could cause the economy to be worse off. The paradox of thrift is a *fallacy of composition:* the assumption that what is true of a part is true of the whole. It often is unsafe to generalize from what is true at the micro level to what is true at the macro level.

The graph illustrates the effect of higher saving. Initial equilibrium occurs where the $S_1 + T + IM$ curve intersects the $I + G + EX$ curve, at an income of $500. Suppose saving

increases by $20 at every level of income. The $S_1 + T + IM$ curve shifts up to the $S_2 + T + IM$ curve. A new equilibrium is established at an income level of $400. The higher rate of saving causes equilibrium income to fall by $100.

Notice that the graph is drawn with a constant $I + G + EX$ line, since these are autonomous spending items that do not depend upon income. If investment increases along with saving, equilibrium income will not necessarily fall. In fact, because saving is necessary before there can be any investment, we would expect a greater demand for investment funds to induce higher saving. If increased saving is used to fund investment expenditures, the economy should grow over time to higher and higher levels of income. Only if the increased saving is not injected back into the economy is there a paradox of thrift. The fact that governments do not discourage saving suggests that the paradox of thrift generally is not a real-world problem,

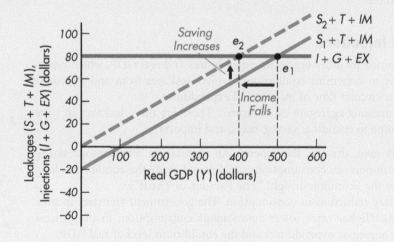

The equilibrium level of real GDP occurs where leakages equal injections.

There is no reason to expect that each injection will match its corresponding leakage—that investment will equal saving, that government spending will equal taxes, or that exports will equal imports. But for equilibrium to occur, total injections must equal total leakages.

Figure 2 shows how leakages and injections determine the equilibrium level of real GDP. Column 5 of the table lists the total leakages from aggregate expenditures: saving (S) plus taxes (T) plus imports (IM). Saving and imports both increase when real GDP increases. We assume that there are no taxes, so the total amount of leakages ($S + T + IM$) increases as real GDP increases.

FIGURE 2 Leakages, Injections, and Equilibrium Income

(1) Real GDP (Y)	(2) Saving (S)	(3) Taxes (T)	(4) Imports (IM)	(5) Leakages (S + T + IM)	(6) Investment (I)	(7) Government Spending (G)	(8) Exports (EX)	(9) Injections (I + G + EX)	(10) Change in Real GDP
$0	$30	$0	$0	−$30	$50	$70	$50	$170	Increase
$100	$0	$0	$10	$10	$50	$70	$50	$170	Increase
$200	$30	$0	$20	$50	$50	$70	$50	$170	Increase
$300	$60	$0	$30	$90	$50	$70	$50	$170	Increase
$400	$90	$0	$40	$130	$50	$70	$50	$170	Increase
$500	$120	$0	$50	$170	$50	$70	$50	$170	No change
$600	$150	$0	$60	$210	$50	$70	$50	$170	Decrease
$700	$180	$0	$70	$250	$50	$70	$50	$170	Decrease

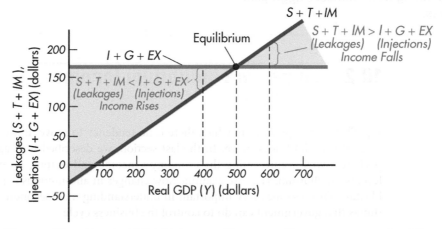

Leakages equal saving (S), taxes (T), and imports (IM). Injections equal investment (I), government spending (G), and exports (EX). Equilibrium is that point where leakages equal injections. In the graph, equilibrium is the point at which the S + T + IM curve intersects the I + G + EX curve, where real GDP (Y) equals $500. At lower levels of income, injections exceed leakages, so Y rises. At higher levels of income, leakages exceed injections, so Y falls

Column 9 lists the injections at alternative income levels. Because investment (I), government spending (G), and exports (EX) are all autonomous, total injections (I + G + EX) are constant at all levels of real GDP.

To determine the equilibrium level of real GDP, we compare leakages with injections. When injections exceed leakages, planned spending is greater than current income or output, so real GDP rises. In the table in Figure 2, this occurs for levels of real GDP under $500, so real GDP increases if it is under $500 (see the last column). When leakages exceed injections, planned spending is less than current real GDP, so real GDP falls. In Figure 2, at all levels of real GDP above $500, real GDP falls. Only when leakages equal injections is the equilibrium level of real GDP established. When real GDP equals $500, both leakages and injections equal $170, so there is no pressure for real GDP to change. The equilibrium level of real GDP occurs where leakages (S + T + IM) equal injections (I + G + EX).

Figure 2 shows the interaction of leakages and injections graphically. The equilibrium point is where the S + T + IM and I + G + EX curves intersect, at a real GDP level of $500. At higher levels of real GDP, leakages are greater than injections (the S + T + IM curve lies above the I + G + EX curve). When leakages are greater than injections, real GDP falls to the equilibrium point. At lower levels of income, injections are greater than leakages (the $I + G + EX$ curve lies above the $S + T + IM$ curve). Here real GDP rises until it reaches $500. Only at $500 is there no pressure for real GDP to change.

If you compare Figure 1 and Figure 2, you can see that it does not matter whether we use aggregate expenditures or leakages and injections—the equilibrium level of real GDP is the same.

RECAP

1. Equilibrium is a point from which there is no tendency to move.

2. When aggregate expenditures exceed real GDP, real GDP rises.

3. When aggregate expenditures are less than real GDP, real GDP falls.

4. Saving, taxes, and imports are leakages of planned spending from domestic aggregate expenditures.

5. Investment, government spending, and exports are injections of planned spending into domestic aggregate expenditures.

6. Equilibrium occurs at the level of real GDP at which aggregate expenditures equal real GDP, and leakages equal injections.

10-2 Changes in Equilibrium Income and Expenditures

Equilibrium is a point from which there is no tendency to move. But in fact, the equilibrium level of real GDP does move. In the last section, we described how aggregate expenditures push real GDP, representing the economy's income and output, up or down toward their level of equilibrium. Here we examine how changes in autonomous expenditures affect equilibrium. This becomes very important in understanding macroeconomic policy, the kinds of things that government can do to control the business cycle.

4. Why does equilibrium real GDP change by a multiple of a change in autonomous expenditures?

5. What is the spending multiplier?

Any change in autonomous expenditures is multiplied into a larger change in equilibrium real GDP.

10-2a The Spending Multiplier

Remember that equilibrium is that point where aggregate expenditures equal real GDP. If we increase autonomous expenditures, then we raise the equilibrium level of real GDP—but by how much? It seems logical to expect a one-to-one ratio: If autonomous spending increases by a dollar, equilibrium real GDP should increase by a dollar. Actually, equilibrium real GDP increases by *more* than a dollar. The change in autonomous expenditures is *multiplied* into a larger change in the equilibrium level of real GDP.

In the chapter titled "National Income Accounting," we used a circular flow diagram to show the relationship of expenditures to income. In that diagram, we saw how one sector's expenditures become another sector's income. This concept helps explain the effect of a change in autonomous expenditures on the equilibrium level of income or real GDP. If A's autonomous spending increases, then B's income rises. Then B spends part of that income in the domestic economy (the rest is saved or used to buy foreign goods), generating new income for C. In turn, C spends part of that income in the domestic economy, generating new income for D. And the rounds of increased spending and income continue. All of this is the product of A's initial autonomous increase in spending. And each round of increased spending and income affects the equilibrium level of income, or real GDP.

Let us look at an example, using Table 1. Suppose government spending goes up $20 to improve public parks. What happens to the equilibrium level of income? The autonomous increase in government spending increases the income of park employees by $20. As the income of the park employees increases, so does their consumption. For example, let us say they spend more money on hamburgers. In the process, they are increasing the income of the hamburger producers, who in turn increase their consumption.

Table 1 shows how a single change in spending generates further changes. Round 1 is the initial increase in government spending to improve public parks. That $20 expenditure increases the income of park employees by $20 (column 1). As income increases, those components of aggregate expenditures that depend on current income—consumption and net exports—also increase by some fraction of the $20.

Consumption changes by the marginal propensity to consume multiplied by the change in income; imports change by the marginal propensity to import multiplied by the change in income. To find the total effect of the initial change in spending, we must know the fraction of any change in income that is spent in the domestic economy. In the hypothetical economy we have been using, the MPC is .70 and the MPI is .10. This means that for each $1 of new income, consumption rises by $.70 and imports rise by $.10. Spending on *domestic* goods and services, then, rises by $.60. Because consumption is spending on domestic goods and services, and imports are spending on foreign goods and services, the percentage of a change in income that is spent domestically is the difference between the MPC and the MPI. If the MPC equals .70 and the MPI equals .10, then 60 percent of any change in domestic income ($MPC - MPI = .60$) is spent on domestic goods and services.

The percentage of a change in income that is spent domestically is the difference between the MPC and the MPI.

In round 1 of Table 1, the initial increase in spending on domestic goods and services of $12 (.60 × $20). Out of the $20, $6 is saved, because the marginal propensity to save is .30 (1 − MPC). The other $2 is spent on imports ($MPI = .10$). The park employees receive $20 more income. They spend $12 on hamburgers at a local restaurant, they save $6, and they spend $2 on imported coffee.

Only $12 of the workers' new income is spent on goods produced in the domestic economy, hamburgers. That $12 becomes income to the restaurant's employees and owner. When their income increases by $12, they spend 60 percent of that income ($7.20) on domestic goods (round 2, column 2). The rest of the income is saved or spent on imports.

TABLE 1 The Spending Multiplier Effect

	(1) Change in Income	(2) Change in Domestic Expenditures	(3) Change in Saving	(4) Change in Imports
Round 1	$20.00	$12.00	$ 6.00	$2.00
Round 2	12.00	7.20	3.60	1.20
Round 3	7.20	4.32	2.16	0.72
Round 4	4.32	2.59	1.30	0.43
Totals	$50.00	$30.00	$15.00	$5.00

$$\text{Column 2} = \text{column 1} \times (MPC - MPI)$$
$$\text{Column 3} = \text{column 1} \times MPS$$
$$\text{Column 4} = \text{column 1} \times MPI$$
$$\text{Multiplier} = \frac{1}{MPS + MPI}$$
$$= \frac{1}{(.30 + .10)}$$
$$= \frac{1}{.40}$$
$$= 2.50$$

Each time income increases, expenditures increase. But the increase is smaller and smaller in each new round of spending. Why? Because 30 percent of each change in income is saved and another 10 percent is spent on imports. These are leakages out of the income stream. This means that just 60 percent of the change in income is spent and passed on to others in the domestic economy as income in the next round.

To find the total effect of the initial change in spending of $20, we could keep on computing the change in income and spending round after round, and then sum the total of all rounds. The change in income and spending never reaches zero, but it becomes infinitely small.

Fortunately, we do not have to compute the increases in spending round by round to find the total increase. If we know the percentage of additional income that "leaks" from domestic consumption at each round, we can determine the total change in income, or real GDP, by finding its reciprocal. This measure is called the **spending multiplier**. The leakages are that portion of the change in income that is saved (the *MPS*) and that proportion of the change in income that is spent on imports (the *MPI*).

$$\text{Multiplier} = \frac{1}{\text{leakages}}$$
$$= \frac{1}{MPS + MPI}$$

When the *MPS* is .30 and the *MPI* is .10, the multiplier equals 2.5 (1/.4). An initial change in expenditures of $20 results in a total change in real GDP of $50, 2.5 times the original change in expenditures. The greater the leakages, the smaller the multiplier. When the *MPS* equals .35 and the *MPI* equals .15, the multiplier equals 2 (1/.50). The multiplier is smaller here because less new income is being spent in the domestic economy. The more people save, the smaller the expansionary effect on income of a change in spending. And the more people spend on imports, the smaller the expansionary effect on income of a change in spending. Notice that the multiplier would be larger in a *closed economy*, an economy that does not trade with the rest of the world. In that economy, because the *MPI* equals zero, the spending multiplier is simply equal to the reciprocal of the *MPS*.

10-2b The Spending Multiplier and Equilibrium

The spending multiplier is an extremely useful concept. It allows us to calculate how a change in autonomous expenditures affects real GDP. To better understand how changes in spending can bring about changes in equilibrium income, or real GDP, let us modify the example we used in Figure 1. In the table in Figure 3, we have increased government spending to $110. The autonomous increase in government spending raises aggregate expenditures by $40 at every level of income. Aggregate expenditures now equal real GDP at $600. The increase in government spending of $40 yields an increase in equilibrium real GDP of $100.

The graph in Figure 3 illustrates the multiplier effect and shows the change in equilibrium income when spending increases by $40. The original aggregate expenditures curve, AE_1, intersects the 45-degree line at a real GDP level of $500. A spending increase of $40 at every level of real GDP creates a new aggregate expenditures curve, AE_2, which lies $40 above the original curve. The curve AE_2 is parallel to AE_1 because the increase is in autonomous spending. The new curve, AE_2, intersects the 45-degree line at an income of $600.

In the chapter titled "Unemployment and Inflation," we introduced the concept of the natural rate of unemployment—the unemployment rate that exists in the absence of cyclical unemployment. When the economy operates at the natural rate of unemployment, the corresponding level of output (and income) is called potential real GDP. However, equilibrium does not necessarily occur at potential real GDP. Equilibrium occurs at any level of real GDP at which planned expenditures equal real GDP. Suppose that equilibrium real GDP is not at the level of potential real GDP and that government policymakers make the

spending multiplier
A measure of the change in equilibrium income or real GDP produced by a change in autonomous expenditures.

NOW YOU TRY IT

The MPS equals .20 and the MPI equals .10. If expenditures increase by $100, how much will the equilibrium level of real GDP increase?

6. What is the relationship between the GDP gap and the recessionary gap?

FIGURE 3 A Change in Equilibrium Expenditures and Income

(1) Real GDP (Y)	(2) Consumption (C)	(3) Investment (I)	(4) Government Spending (G)	(5) Net Exports (X)	(6) Aggregate Expenditures (AE)	(7) Unplanned Change in Inventories	(8) Change in Real GDP
$0	$30	$50	$110	$50	$240	−$240	Increase
$100	$100	$50	$110	$40	$300	−$200	Increase
$200	$170	$50	$110	$30	$360	−$160	Increase
$300	$240	$50	$110	$20	$440	−$120	Increase
$400	$310	$50	$110	$10	$480	−$80	Increase
$500	$380	$50	$110	$0	$540	−$40	Increase
$600	$450	$50	$110	−$10	$600	$0	No Change
$700	$520	$50	$110	−$20	$660	$40	Decrease

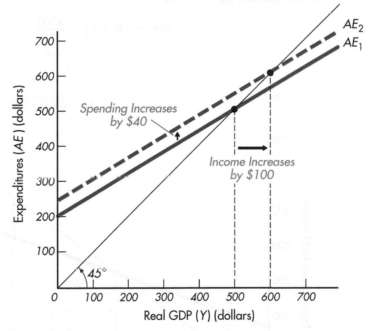

A change in aggregate expenditures (AE) causes a change in equilibrium real GDP (Y). Initially equilibrium is $500, the point at which the AE₁ curve intersects the 45-degree line. If autonomous expenditures increase by $40, the aggregate expenditures curve shifts up to AE₂. The new curve intersects the 45-degree line at a new equilibrium level of real GDP, $600. An increase in autonomous expenditures of $40, then, causes equilibrium real GDP to increase by $100.

achievement of potential real GDP an important goal. In this case, government policy is addressed toward closing the *GDP gap*, the difference between potential real GDP and actual real GDP. The nature of that policy depends on the value of the multiplier.

If we know the size of the GDP gap and we know the size of the spending multiplier, we can determine by how much spending needs to change in order to yield equilibrium at potential real GDP. Remember that the GDP gap equals potential real GDP minus actual real GDP:

$$\text{GDP gap} = \text{potential real GDP} - \text{actual real GDP}$$

When real GDP is less than potential real GDP, the GDP gap is the amount by which GDP must rise to reach its potential. Suppose potential real GDP is $500, but the economy is in equilibrium at $300. The GDP must rise by $200 to reach potential real GDP. How much must spending rise? If we know the size of the spending multiplier, we simply divide the spending multiplier into the GDP gap to determine how much spending must rise to achieve equilibrium at potential real GDP. This required change in spending is called the **recessionary gap:**

recessionary gap
The increase in expenditures required to reach potential GDP.

$$\text{Recessionary gap} = \frac{\text{GDP gap}}{\text{spending multiplier}}$$

Figure 4 shows an economy in which equilibrium real GDP (Y_e) is less than potential real GDP (Y_p). The difference between the two—the GDP gap—is $200. It is the *horizontal* distance between equilibrium real GDP and potential real GDP. The amount by which spending must rise in order for real GDP to reach a new equilibrium level of $500 is measured by the recessionary gap. The recessionary gap is the *vertical* distance between the aggregate expenditures curve and the 45-degree line at the potential real GDP level.

The recessionary gap in Figure 4 is $80:

$$\text{Recessionary gap} = \frac{\$200}{2.5}$$
$$= \$80$$

FIGURE 4   The GDP Gap and the Recessionary Gap

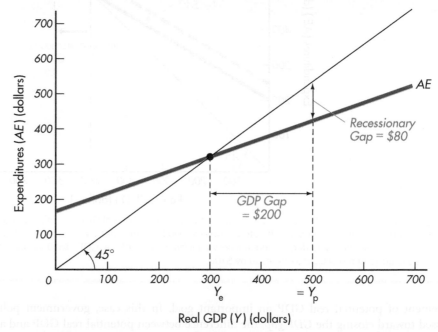

In the graph, the GDP gap is $200, the difference between potential real GDP (Y_p) of $500 and equilibrium real GDP (Y_e) of $300. The GDP gap tells us that equilibrium real GDP must rise by $200 to reach equilibrium at the potential level of real GDP. The recessionary gap indicates the amount that autonomous expenditures must rise to close the GDP gap. The recessionary gap is the vertical distance between the 45-degree line and the *AE* curve at the potential level of real GDP, or $80. If autonomous expenditures are increased by $80, the *AE* curve will move up, intersecting with the 45-degree line at $500.

With a spending multiplier of 2.5, if aggregate expenditures rise by $80, equilibrium income rises by the $200 necessary to close the GDP gap. Government policy may be addressed to closing the gap, as an increase in government expenditures of $80 would move the economy to the potential level of real GDP in this example.

$$\frac{1}{MPS + MPI}$$

10-2c Real-World Complications

Our definition of the spending multiplier is a simplification of reality. Often other factors besides the *MPS* and *MPI* determine the actual multiplier in an economy. If prices rise when spending increases, the spending multiplier will not be as large as shown here. Also, taxes (which are ignored until the chapter titled "Fiscal Policy") will reduce the size of the multiplier. Another factor is the treatment of imports. We have assumed that whatever is spent on imports is permanently lost to the domestic economy. For a country whose imports are a small fraction of the exports of its trading partners, this is a realistic assumption. But for a country whose imports are very important in determining the volume of exports of the rest of the world, this simple spending multiplier understates the true multiplier effect. To see why, let us examine how U.S. imports affect income in the rest of the world.

7. How does international trade affect the size of the spending multiplier?

10-2c-1 Foreign Repercussions of Domestic Imports
When a resident of the United States buys goods from another country, that purchase becomes income to foreign residents. If Mike in Miami buys coral jewelry from Victor in the Dominican Republic, Mike's purchase increases Victor's income. So the import of jewelry into the United States increases income in the Dominican Republic.

Imports purchased by one country can have a large effect on the level of income in other countries. For instance, Canada and Mexico are very dependent on sales to the United States, since about 80 percent of their exports go to the United States. South Africa, on the other hand, sells about 5 percent of its total exports to U.S. buyers. If U.S. imports from South Africa doubled, the effect on total South African exports and income would be small. But if imports from Canada or Mexico doubled, the effect on those countries' exports and income would be substantial.

Imports into the United States play a key role in determining the real GDP of the major U.S. trading partners. This is important because foreign income is a determinant of U.S. exports. As that income rises, U.S. exports rise (see the chapter titled "Aggregate Expenditures"). That is, foreign imports increase with foreign income, and some of those imports come from the United States. And, of course, when foreign spending on U.S. goods increases, national income in the United States rises.

The simple spending multiplier understates the true multiplier effects of increases in autonomous expenditures because of the foreign repercussions of domestic spending. Some spending on imports comes back to the domestic economy in the form of exports. This means that the chain of spending can be different from that assumed in the simple spending multiplier. Figure 5 illustrates the difference.

Figure 5(a) shows the sequence of spending when there are no foreign repercussions from domestic imports. In this case, domestic spending rises, which causes domestic income, or real GDP, to rise. Higher domestic real GDP leads to increased spending on imports as well as further increases in domestic spending, which induce further increases in real GDP, and so on, as the multiplier process works itself out. Notice, however, that the imports are simply a leakage from the spending stream.

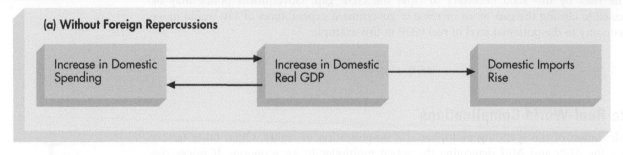

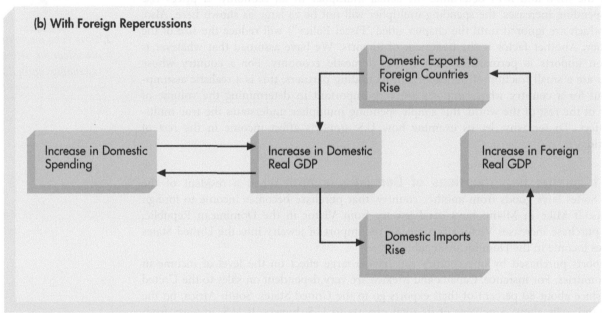

If there are no foreign repercussions from changes in domestic income or real GDP, the simple spending multiplier holds. Increases in domestic spending increase domestic income or real GDP, which causes domestic spending—including spending on foreign goods—to rise further. Here higher expenditures on domestic imports do not have any effect on domestic exports to foreign countries.

If there are foreign repercussions from changes in domestic real GDP, the simple spending multiplier underestimates the actual effect of a change in autonomous expenditures on the equilibrium level of real GDP. As (b) shows, increases in domestic spending increase domestic income, or real GDP, which causes domestic spending—including spending on foreign goods—to rise further. Here higher spending on foreign goods causes foreign real GDP to rise, and with it, spending on domestic exports. Higher domestic exports stimulate domestic real GDP further. The actual multiplier effect of an increase in domestic spending, then, is larger than it is when domestic imports have no effect on domestic exports.

In Figure 5(b), the sequence of expenditures includes the foreign repercussions of domestic imports. As before, increases in domestic spending cause domestic income, or real GDP, to rise; this, in turn, leads to more domestic spending as well as greater domestic imports. Now, however, the greater imports increase foreign income, or real GDP, which increases foreign imports of goods produced in the domestic economy. As domestic exports rise, domestic real GDP rises. This is a more realistic view of how spending and income interact to create interdependencies among nations.

The diagrams in Figure 5 show why the multiplier effect is higher with foreign repercussions than without. Rather than complicate the multiplier definition, we continue to use the simple spending multiplier. But remember that (holding prices constant and ignoring taxes) our definition underestimates the true magnitude of the multiplier's effects in open economies. In fact, the foreign repercussions of domestic imports help explain the similarity in business cycles across countries. When the United States is booming, the economies of other countries that depend on exports to the U.S. market also boom. When the United States is in recession, income in these other countries tends to fall.

10-2c-2 Multiplier Estimates Many private and public organizations have developed models that are used to analyze current economic developments and to forecast future ones. A large number of these models include foreign repercussions. From these models, we get a sense of just how much the simple multiplier can vary from the true multiplier.

An increase in U.S. autonomous expenditures has a multiplier of about 0.8. This means that if autonomous government expenditures increased by $25, U.S. equilibrium GDP would be $20 higher after one year. A multiplier less than 1 suggests important "leakages" in the operation of the economy. One such leakage stems from the openness of the U.S. economy. Thus, when there is an expansionary fiscal policy in the United States, the GDP of other countries is increased because some of that spending is on U.S. imports from the rest of the world. Estimates of spending multipliers indicate that the equilibrium level of GDP for the industrial countries taken as a whole increases by 0.4 times the change in U.S. expenditures. For developing countries, the multiplier effect is smaller, at 0.1. So increases in U.S. government spending have a bigger impact on the GDP of other industrial countries than on the GDP of developing countries. Because trade between industrial countries is much larger than the trade between industrial countries and developing countries, it is not surprising that increases in spending in one industrial country, like the United States, have a bigger impact on other industrial countries than on developing countries.

The multiplier examples we use in this chapter show autonomous government spending changing. It is important to realize that the multiplier effects apply to any change in autonomous expenditures in any sector of the economy.

RECAP

1. Any change in autonomous expenditures is multiplied into a larger change in the equilibrium level of real GDP.

2. The multiplier measures the change in equilibrium real GDP produced by a change in autonomous spending.

3. The multiplier equals

$$\frac{1}{Leakages} = \frac{1}{MPS + MPI}$$

4. The recessionary gap is the amount by which spending must increase in order to achieve equilibrium at potential real GDP. Graphically, it is measured by the vertical distance between the 45-degree line and the aggregate expenditures curve at potential real GDP.

5. The true spending multiplier may differ from the simple spending multiplier ($1/[MPS + MPI]$) because of the foreign repercussions of domestic spending. Price changes and taxes cause the simple spending multiplier to overestimate the true multiplier.

10-3 Aggregate Expenditures and Aggregate Demand

The approach to macroeconomic equilibrium presented in this chapter focuses on aggregate expenditures and income. It is called the *Keynesian model*. This model of the economy can be very useful in explaining some real-world events, but it suffers from a serious drawback: It assumes that the supply of goods and services in the economy always adjusts to aggregate expenditures, that there is no need for price changes. The Keynesian model is a *fixed-price model*.

In the real world, we find that shortages of goods and services are often met by rising prices, not just increased production. We also find that when supply increases in the face of relatively constant demand, prices may fall. In other words, prices as well as production adjust to differences between demand and supply. We introduced price as a component of macroeconomic equilibrium in the chapter titled "Macroeconomic Equilibrium: Aggregate Demand and Supply," in the aggregate demand and supply model. You may recall that aggregate expenditures represent demand when the price level is constant. This can be demonstrated by using the income and expenditures approach developed in this chapter to derive the aggregate demand curve that was introduced in the chapter on macroeconomic equilibrium.

10-3a Aggregate Expenditures and Changing Price Levels

8. Why does the aggregate expenditures curve shift with changes in the price level?

As discussed in the chapter on macroeconomic equilibrium, the *AE* curve will shift with changes in the price level because of the wealth effect, the interest rate effect, and the international trade effect. Wealth is one of the nonincome determinants of consumption. Households hold part of their wealth in financial assets like money and bonds. As the price level falls, the purchasing power of money rises and aggregate expenditures increase. As the price level rises, the purchasing power of money falls and aggregate expenditures fall.

The interest rate is a determinant of investment spending. As the price level changes, interest rates may change as households and business firms change their demand for money. The change in interest rates will then affect investment spending. For instance, when the price level rises, more money is needed to buy any given quantity of goods and services. To acquire more money, households and firms sell their nonmonetary financial assets, like bonds. The increased supply of bonds will tend to raise interest rates to attract buyers. The higher interest rates will tend to lower investment spending and aggregate expenditures. Conversely, a lower price level will tend to be associated with lower interest rates, greater investment spending, and greater aggregate expenditures.

Net exports may change, causing aggregate expenditures to change, when the domestic price level changes. If domestic prices rise while foreign prices and the exchange rate are constant, then domestic goods become more expensive relative to foreign goods, and net exports and aggregate expenditures tend to fall. If domestic prices fall while foreign prices and the exchange rate are constant, then domestic goods become cheaper relative to foreign goods, and net exports and aggregate expenditures tend to rise.

10-3b Deriving the Aggregate Demand Curve

The aggregate demand curve (*AD*) shows how the equilibrium level of expenditures changes as the price level changes. In other words, the curve shows the amount that people spend at different price levels. Let us use the example in Figure 6 to show how aggregate demand is derived from the shifting aggregate expenditures curve (*AE*).

The aggregate demand curve is derived from the *AE* curve. Figure 6(a) shows three *AE* curves, each drawn for a different price level. Suppose that the initial equilibrium occurs at point *A* on curve AE_0 with prices at P_0. At this point, equilibrium real GDP and expenditures are \$500. If prices fall to P_1, the *AE* curve shifts up to AE_1. Here equilibrium is at point C, where real GDP equals \$700. If prices rise from P_0 to P_2, the *AE* curve falls to AE_2. Here equilibrium is at point *B*, where real GDP equals \$300.

In Figure 6(b), price level is plotted on the vertical axis and real GDP is plotted on the horizontal axis. A price-level change here means that, on average, all prices in the economy change. The negative slope of the aggregate demand curve results from the effect of changing prices on wealth, interest rates, and international trade. If you move vertically down from points *A*, *B*, and *C* in Figure 6(a), you find corresponding points along the aggregate demand curve in Figure 6(b). The *AD* curve shows all of the combinations of price levels and corresponding equilibrium levels of real GDP and aggregate expenditures.

FIGURE 6 Aggregate Expenditures and Aggregate Demand

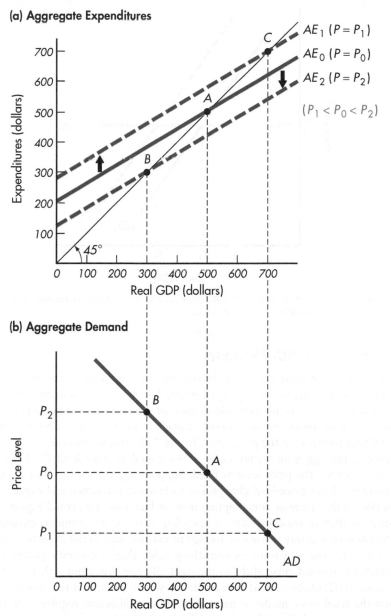

(a) Aggregate Expenditures

(b) Aggregate Demand

6(a) Changes in the price level cause the AE curve to shift. The initial curve, AE_0, is drawn at the initial level of prices, P_0. On this curve, the equilibrium level of aggregate expenditures (where expenditures equal real GDP) is $500. If the price level falls to P_1, autonomous expenditures increase, shifting the curve up to AE_1, and moving the equilibrium level of aggregate expenditures to $700. If the price level rises to P_2, autonomous expenditures fall, shifting the curve down to AE_2 and moving the equilibrium level of aggregate expenditures to $300. The aggregate demand curve (AD) in 6(b) is derived from the aggregate expenditures curves. The AD curve shows the equilibrium level of aggregate expenditures at different price levels. At price level P_0, equilibrium aggregate expenditures are $500; at P_1, they are $700; and at P_2, they are $300.

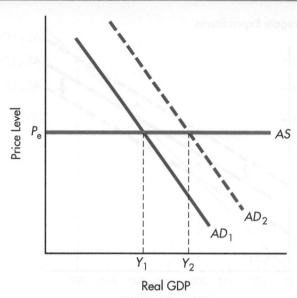

FIGURE 7 A Fixed-Price *AD–AS* Model

If the *AS* curve is horizontal, then shifts in the *AD* curve will have no effect on the equilibrium level of prices but will change the equilibrium level of real GDP.

10-3c A Fixed-Price *AD-AS* Model

The Keynesian model of fixed-price equilibrium may be considered a special case of the aggregate demand and aggregate supply equilibrium. We can define a horizontal segment of the aggregate supply curve as the Keynesian region of the curve. This represents an economy with substantial unemployment and excess capacity, so real GDP and output may be increased without pressure on the price level. Figure 7 illustrates this case.

In Figure 7, the aggregate supply curve is horizontal at price level P_e. Throughout the range of the *AS* curve, the price level is fixed. Suppose aggregate expenditures increase for some reason other than a price-level change. For instance, consumers could expect their future incomes to rise, so they increase consumption now; or business firms could expect sales to rise in the future, so they increase investment spending now; or government spending rises to improve the national highway system; or foreign prices rise, and so net exports increase. If aggregate expenditures rise as a result of something other than a domestic price-level change, then the aggregate demand curve shifts to the right, like the shift from AD_1 to AD_2 in Figure 7. This increase in *AD* causes real GDP to rise to Y_2, yet the price level remains fixed at P_e.

The Keynesian model is a fixed price model.

Because the fixed-price model of macroeconomic equilibrium requires a horizontal *AS* curve, many economists believe that this model is too restrictive and not representative of the modern economy. As a result, we will generally see the *AD–AS* model using upward-sloping *AS* curves so that price as well as real GDP fluctuates with shifts in aggregate demand.

RECAP

1. As the price level rises (falls), aggregate expenditures fall (rise).

2. Aggregate demand is the equilibrium level of aggregate expenditures at alternative price levels.

3. The Keynesian fixed-price model is represented by a horizontal aggregate supply curve.

SUMMARY

1. What does equilibrium mean in macroeconomics?

- Macroeconomic equilibrium is the point at which aggregate expenditures equal real GDP. *§10-1a*

2. How do aggregate expenditures affect income, or real GDP?

- When aggregate expenditures exceed income, or real GDP, real GDP rises; when they are less than real GDP, real GDP falls. *§10-1a*

3. What are the leakages from and injections into spending?

- Leakages are saving, taxes, and imports; injections are investment, government spending, and exports. *§10-1b*
- Equilibrium real GDP occurs where leakages equal injections. *§10-1b*

4. Why does equilibrium real GDP change by a multiple of a change in autonomous expenditures?

- The effect of a change in autonomous spending is multiplied by a spiral of increased spending and income. *§10-2a*

5. What is the spending multiplier?

- The spending multiplier equals the reciprocal of the sum of the *MPS* and the *MPI*. *§10-2a*

6. What is the relationship between the GDP gap and the recessionary gap?

- The recessionary gap is the amount by which autonomous expenditures must change to eliminate the GDP gap and reach potential GDP. *§10-2b*

7. How does international trade affect the size of the spending multiplier?

- The actual spending multiplier may be larger than the reciprocal of the sum of the *MPS* and the *MPI* because of the foreign repercussions of changes in domestic spending. *§10-2c*

8. Why does the aggregate expenditures curve shift with changes in the price level?

- The *AE* curve shifts with changes in the price level because of the wealth effect, the interest rate effect, and the international trade effect. *§10-3a*
- The Keynesian model of fixed-price equilibrium is a special case of the *AD* and *AS* equilibrium. *§10-3c*

KEY TERMS

recessionary gap, 214   spending multiplier, 212

EXERCISES

1. Explain the role of inventories in keeping actual expenditures equal to real GDP.
2. Rework Figure 1, assuming a closed economy (net exports equal zero at all levels of income). What is the equilibrium level of real GDP? What is the spending multiplier?
3. Draw a graph representing a hypothetical economy. Carefully label the two axes, the $S + T + IM$ curve, the $I + G + EX$ curve, and the equilibrium level of real GDP. Illustrate the effect of an increase in the level of autonomous saving.
4. Given the following information, what is the spending multiplier in each case?
   a. $MPC = .90$, $MPI = .10$
   b. $MPC = .90$, $MPI = .20$
   c. $MPC = .80$, $MPI = .30$
   d. $MPC = .90$, $MPI = 0$
5. Draw a graph representing a hypothetical economy in a recession. Carefully label the two axes, the 45-degree line, the *AE* curve, and the equilibrium level of real GDP. Indicate and label the GDP gap and the recessionary gap.

6. Explain the effect of foreign repercussions on the value of the spending multiplier.
7. Suppose the *MPC* is .80, the *MPI* is .10, and the income tax rate is 15 percent. What is the multiplier in this economy?

Use the information in the following table to do exercises 8-15:

Y	C	I	G	X
$100	$120	$20	$30	$10
$300	$300	$20	$30	−$10
$500	$480	$20	$30	−$30
$700	$660	$20	$30	−$50

8. What is the MPC?
9. What is the *MPI?*
10. What is the *MPS?*
11. What is the multiplier?
12. What is the equilibrium level of real GDP?

13. What is the value of autonomous consumption?
14. If government spending increases by $15, what is the new equilibrium level of real GDP?
15. What are the equations for the consumption, net exports, and aggregate expenditures functions?
16. Derive the aggregate demand curve from an aggregate expenditures diagram. Explain how aggregate demand relates to aggregate expenditures.
17. In the chapter titled "Macroeconomic Equilibrium: Aggregate Demand and Supply," the aggregate supply (*AS*) curve was upward sloping. Now, in this chapter, we have a flat *AS* curve. What are the implications for equilibrium real GDP if *AD* shifts by some amount and the *AS* curve is perfectly flat in one economy and upward sloping in another?
18. Why should the business cycles of Canada and Mexico be much like the U.S. business cycle, while those of South Africa and Turkey may differ from the U.S. pattern of economic expansion and contraction?

ECONOMICALLY SPEAKING

NAFTA AT 20: OVERVIEW AND TRADE EFFECTS

The North American Free Trade Agreement (NAFTA) entered into force on January 1, 1994.... The overall economic impact of NAFTA is difficult to measure since trade and investment trends are influenced by numerous other economic variables, such as economic growth, inflation, and currency fluctuations. The agreement may have accelerated the trade liberalization that was already taking place, but many of these changes may have taken place with or without an agreement. Nevertheless, NAFTA is significant because it was the most comprehensive free trade agreement (FTA) negotiated at the time and contained several groundbreaking provisions. A legacy of the agreement is that it has served as a template or model for the new generation of FTAs that the United States later negotiated ...

NAFTA was controversial when first proposed, mostly because it was the first FTA involving two wealthy, developed countries and a developing country. The political debate surrounding the agreement was divisive, with proponents arguing that the agreement would help generate thousands of jobs and reduce income disparity in the region, while opponents warned that the agreement would cause huge job losses in the United States as companies moved production to Mexico to lower costs. In reality, NAFTA did not cause the huge job losses feared by the critics or the large economic gains predicted by supporters. The net overall effect of NAFTA on the U.S. economy appears to have been relatively modest, primarily because trade with Canada and Mexico account for a small percentage of U.S. GDP. However, there were worker and firm adjustment costs as the three countries adjusted to more open trade and investment among their economies ...

A major challenge in assessing NAFTA is separating the effects that came as a result of the agreement from other factors. U.S. trade with Mexico and Canada was already growing prior to NAFTA and it likely would have continued to do so without an agreement ... In some sectors, trade-related effects could have been more significant, especially in those industries that were more exposed to the removal of tariff and non-tariff trade barriers, such as the textile, apparel, automotive, and agriculture industries ...

Much of the trade between the United States and its NAFTA partners occurs in the context of production sharing as manufacturers in each country work together to create goods. The expansion of trade has resulted in the creation of vertical supply relationships, especially along the U.S.-Mexico border. The flow of intermediate inputs produced in the United States and exported to Mexico and the return flow of finished products greatly increased the importance of the U.S.-Mexico border region as a production site. U.S. manufacturing industries, including automotive, electronics, appliances, and machinery, all rely on the assistance of Mexican manufacturers. One report estimates that 40% of the content of U.S. imports from Mexico and 25% of the content of U.S. imports from Canada are of U.S. origin. In comparison, U.S. imports from China are said to have only 4% U.S. content. Taken together, goods from Mexico and Canada represent about 75% of all the U.S. domestic content that returns to the United States as imports.

Source: excerpted from M.A. Villareal and I.F. Ferguson, *Congressional Research Service*, February 21, 2013

COMMENTARY

This article reemphasizes a main point made in this chapter: Countries are linked internationally, and so aggregate expenditure shifts in one country will have an impact on other nations. When other countries, like Mexico, sell goods to the United States, those exports increase Mexican GDP, since net exports is one of the components of GDP. Remembering that net exports increase with a country's GDP, we should expect net exports to vary over the business cycle. Since U.S. imports vary with U.S. GDP, slower growth in the United States tends to reduce U.S. imports, leading to lower GDP in the countries that export to the United States. Conversely, when the U.S. economy is booming, U.S. imports from Mexico will rise and stimulate GDP growth in Mexico.

The United States had a very large recession in 2008. Did the economies of the major trading partners of the United States have recessions around this time? There was a recession in Canada and Mexico that strongly coincided with the U.S. recession. In Europe, real GDP continued to grow for a while following the onset of the U.S. recession. We should expect Mexico to be greatly affected by U.S. business cycles, since about 85 percent of Mexican exports go to the United States. Australia, South Africa, Sweden, and Turkey are likely to have business cycles that are more independent of U.S. influences, since their exports to the United States as a share of their total exports are less than 10 percent.

The strength of these channels also varies with the amount of trade between countries relative to the sizes of those countries. The article mentions that many of the large economic impacts predicted by both sides of the NAFTA debate did not materialize. This is partly because the amount of trade between the countries was relatively small. However, the international links between countries should grow over time as restrictions on international trade are removed through agreements like NAFTA and as transportation and communication costs continue to fall. The future may be one in which national business cycles are increasingly interdependent, and such interdependencies will have to be given greater emphasis in national policymaking.

APPENDIX TO CHAPTER 10

An Algebraic Model of Income and Expenditures Equilibrium

Continuing the example we began in the appendix to the chapter on aggregate expenditures, if we know the equation for each component of aggregate expenditures (AE), we can solve for the equilibrium level of real GDP (Y) for the economy represented in Figure 1 of the chapter:

$$C = \$30 + .70Y$$
$$I = \$50$$
$$G = \$70$$
$$X = \$50 - .10Y$$

Summing these components, we can find the aggregate expenditures function:

$$AE = \$30 + .70Y + \$50 + \$70 + \$50 - .10Y = \$200 + .60Y$$

Given the AE function, we can solve for the equilibrium level of Y, where:

$$Y = AE$$
$$Y = \$200 + .60Y$$
$$Y - .60Y = \$200$$
$$.40Y = \$200$$
$$Y = \$200/.40$$
$$Y = \$500$$

The Spending Multiplier It is also possible to solve for the spending multiplier algebraically. We start by writing the general equations for each function, where C^a, I^a, G^a, EX^a, and IM^a represent autonomous consumption, investment, government spending, exports, and imports, respectively, and where c represents the MPC and im represents the MPI:

$$C = C^a + cY$$
$$I = I^a$$
$$G = G^a$$
$$X = EX^a - IM^a - imY$$

Now we sum the individual equations for the components of aggregate expenditures to get the aggregate expenditures function:

$$AE = C + I + G + X$$
$$= C^a + cY + I^a + G^a + EX^a - IM^a - imY$$
$$= (C^a + I^a + EX^a - IM^a) + cY - imY$$

We know that aggregate expenditures equal income. So

$$Y = (C^a + I^a + G^a + EX^a - IM^a) + cY - imY$$

Solving for Y, we first gather all of the terms involving Y on the left side of the equation:

$$Y[1 - (c - im)] = C^a + I^a + G^a + EX^a - IM^a$$

Next, we divide each side of the equation by $[1 - (c - im)]$ to get an equation for Y:

$$Y = \frac{1}{1 - (c - im)}(C^a + I^a + G^a + EX^a - IM^a)$$

A change in autonomous expenditures causes Y to change by

$$\frac{1}{1 - (c - im)}$$

times the change in expenditures. Because c is the *MPC* and *im* is the *MPI*, the multiplier can be written

$$\frac{1}{1 - (MPC - MPI)}$$

or, since $1 - MPC = $ MPS, then $1 - (MPC + MPI) = $ MPS $+$ MPI, and the spending multiplier equals

$$\frac{1}{(MPS + MPI)}$$

CHAPTER 11

Fiscal Policy

© Solaria/Shutterstock.com

top: © Carsten Reisinger/Shutterstock

FUNDAMENTAL QUESTIONS

1. How can fiscal policy eliminate a GDP gap?

2. How has U.S. fiscal policy changed over time?

3. What are the effects of budget deficits?

4. How does fiscal policy differ across countries?

Preview

Macroeconomics plays a key role in national politics. When Jimmy Carter ran for the presidency against Gerald Ford in 1976, he created a "misery index" to measure the state of the economy. The index was the sum of the inflation rate and the unemployment rate, and Carter showed that it had risen during Ford's term in office. When Ronald Reagan challenged Carter in 1980, he used the misery index to show that inflation and unemployment had gone up during the Carter years as well. The implication is that presidents are responsible for the condition of the economy. If the inflation rate or the

Fiscal policy includes government spending on the provision of goods and services as well as infrastructure. In this photo, workers create mud bricks in the desert. The bricks will be used in infrastructure construction projects. Such activities are often provided by government and funded by taxpayers.

Michael Zysman/Dreamstime.com

unemployment rate is relatively high coming into an election year, an incumbent president is open to criticism by opponents. For instance, many people believe that George Bush was defeated by Bill Clinton in 1992 because of the recession that began in 1990—a recession that was not announced as having ended in March 1991 until after the election. Clinton's 1992 campaign made economic growth a focus of its attacks on Bush, and his 1996 campaign emphasized the strength of the economy.

In 1996, a healthy economy helped Clinton defeat Bob Dole. And in the election of 2004, supporters of George W. Bush made economic growth a major focal point of their campaign against John Kerry. More recently, Barack Obama's successful campaign for president had economic issues as a leading concern with the U.S. recession beginning in 2008. This was more than just campaign rhetoric, however. By law the government *is* responsible for the macroeconomic health of the nation. The Employment Act of 1946 states:

> *It is the continuing policy and responsibility of the Federal Government to use all practical means consistent with its needs and obligations and other essential considerations of national policy to coordinate and utilize all its plans, functions, and resources for the purpose of creating and maintaining, in a manner calculated to foster and promote free competitive enterprise and the general welfare conditions under which there will be afforded useful employment opportunities, including self-employment for those able, willing, and seeking to work, and to promote maximum employment, production, and purchasing power.*

Fiscal policy is one tool that government uses to guide the economy along an expansionary path. In this chapter, we examine the role of fiscal policy—government spending and taxation—in determining the equilibrium level of income. Then we review the budget process and the history of fiscal policy in the United States. Finally, we describe the difference in fiscal policy between industrial and developing countries.

11-1 Fiscal Policy and Aggregate Demand

The GDP gap is the difference between potential real GDP and the equilibrium level of real GDP. If the government wants to close the GDP gap so that the equilibrium level of real GDP reaches its potential, it must use fiscal policy to alter aggregate expenditures and cause the aggregate demand curve to shift.

Fiscal policy is the government's policy with respect to spending and taxation. Since aggregate demand includes consumption, investment, net exports, and government spending, government spending on goods and services has a direct effect on the level of aggregate demand. Taxes affect aggregate demand indirectly by changing the disposable income of households, which alters consumption.

11-1a Shifting the Aggregate Demand Curve

Changes in government spending and taxes shift the aggregate demand curve. Remember that the aggregate demand curve represents combinations of equilibrium aggregate expenditures and alternative price levels. An increase in government spending or a decrease in taxes raises the level of expenditures at every level of prices and moves the aggregate demand curve to the right.

Figure 1 shows the increase in aggregate demand that would result from an increase in government spending or a decrease in taxes. Only if the aggregate supply curve is horizontal do prices remain fixed as aggregate demand increases. In Figure 1(a), equilibrium occurs along the horizontal segment (the Keynesian region) of the *AS* curve. If government spending increases and the price level remains constant, aggregate demand shifts from *AD* to AD_1; it increases by the horizontal distance from point *A* to point *B*. Once aggregate demand shifts, the AD_1 and *AS* curves intersect at potential real GDP, Y_p.

But Figure 1(a) is not realistic. The *AS* curve is not likely to be horizontal all the way to the level of potential real GDP; it should begin sloping up well before Y_p. And once the economy reaches the capacity level of output, the *AS* curve should become a vertical line, as shown in Figure 1(b).

If the *AS* curve slopes up before reaching the potential real GDP level, as it does in Figure 1(b), expenditures have to go up by more than the amount suggested in Figure 1(a) for the economy to reach Y_p. Why? Because when prices rise, the effect of spending on real GDP is reduced. This effect is shown in Figure 1(b). To increase the equilibrium level of real GDP from Y_e to Y_p, aggregate demand must shift by the amount from point *A* to point *C*, a larger increase than that shown in Figure 1(a), where the price level is fixed.

11-1b Multiplier Effects

Changes in government spending may have an effect on real GDP that is a multiple of the original change in government spending; a $1 change in government spending may increase real GDP by more than $1. This is because the original $1 of expenditure is spent over and over again in the economy as it passes from person to person. The government spending multiplier measures the multiple by which an increase in government spending increases real GDP. Similarly, a change in taxes may have an effect on real GDP that is a multiple of the original change in taxes. (The Appendix to this chapter provides an algebraic analysis of the government spending and tax multipliers.)

If the price level rises as real GDP increases, the multiplier effects of any given change in aggregate demand are smaller than they would be if the price level remained constant. In addition to changes in the price level modifying the effect of government spending and taxes on real GDP, there are other factors that affect how much real GDP will change following a

?

1. How can fiscal policy eliminate a GDP gap?

By varying the level of government spending, policymakers can affect the level of real GDP.

NOW YOU TRY IT

Draw AD and AS curves for a hypothetical economy, labeling the equilibrium point *e*.

a. draw a change in your diagram that illustrates the effect of lowering taxes

b. draw a change in your diagram that illustrates the effect of increasing government spending (don't worry about how it is financed)

If the price level rises as real GDP increases, the multiplier effects of any given change in aggregate demand are smaller than they would be if the price level remained constant.

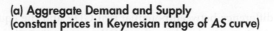

FIGURE 1   Eliminating the Recessionary Gap: Higher Prices Mean Greater Spending

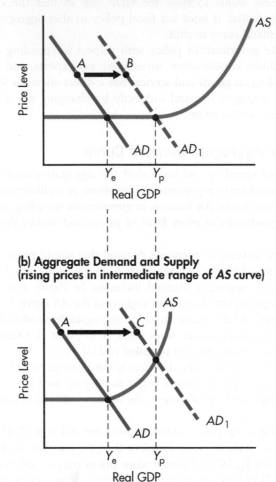

1(a) When aggregate demand increases from *AD* to *AD*₁, equilibrium real GDP increases by the full amount of the shift in demand. This is because the aggregate supply curve is horizontal over the area of the shift in aggregate demand. 1(b) In order for equilibrium real GDP to rise from Y_e to Y_p, aggregate demand must shift by more than it does in (a). In reality, the aggregate supply curve begins to slope up before potential real GDP (Y_p) is reached, as shown in (b).

change in government spending. One such factor is how the government pays for, or finances, its spending.

Government spending must be financed by some combination of taxing, borrowing, and creating money:

$$\text{Government spending} = \text{taxes} + \text{change in government debt}$$
$$+ \text{change in government-issued money}$$

In the chapter titled "Monetary Policy," we discuss the effect of financing government spending by creating money. As you will see, this source of government financing is relied on heavily in some developing countries. Here we talk about the financing problem that is relevant for industrial countries: how taxes and government debt can modify the expansionary effect of government spending on national income.

11-1c Government Spending Financed by Tax Increases

Suppose that government spending rises by $100 billion and that this expenditure is financed by a tax increase of $100 billion. Such a "balanced-budget" change in fiscal policy will cause equilibrium real GDP to rise. This is because government spending increases aggregate expenditures directly, but higher taxes lower aggregate expenditures indirectly through consumption spending. For instance, if taxes increase by $100, consumers will not cut their spending by $100, but they will cut it by some fraction, say 9/10, of the increase. If consumers spend 90 percent of a change in their disposable income, then a tax increase of $100 would lower consumption by $90. So the net effect of raising government spending and taxes by the same amount is an increase in aggregate demand, illustrated in Figure 2 as the shift from AD to AD_1. However, it may be incorrect to assume that the only thing that changes is aggregate demand. An increase in taxes may also affect aggregate supply.

Aggregate supply measures the output that producers offer for sale at different levels of prices. When taxes go up, workers have less incentive to work because their after-tax income is lower. The cost of taking a day off or extending a vacation for a few extra days is less than it is when taxes are lower and after-tax income is higher. When taxes go up, then, output can fall, causing the aggregate supply curve to shift to the left. Such supply-side effects of taxes have been emphasized by the so-called supply-side economists, as discussed in the Economic Insight "Supply-Side Economics and the Laffer Curve."

Figure 2 shows the possible effects of an increase in government spending financed by taxes. The economy is initially in equilibrium at point A, with prices at P_1 and real GDP

FIGURE 2 The Effect of Taxation on Aggregate Supply

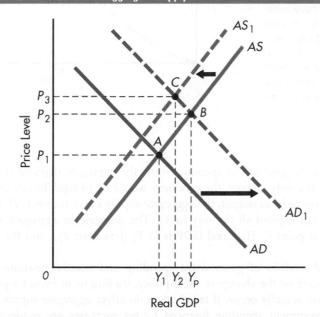

An increase in government spending shifts the aggregate demand curve from AD to AD_1, moving equilibrium from point A to point B and equilibrium real GDP from Y_1 to Y_p. If higher taxes reduce the incentive to work, aggregate supply could fall from AS to AS_1, moving equilibrium to point C and equilibrium real GDP to Y_2, a level below potential real GDP.

ECONOMIC INSIGHT

Supply-Side Economics and the Laffer Curve

The large budget deficits incurred by the U.S. government in the 1980s were in part a product of lower tax rates engineered by the Reagan administration. President Ronald Reagan's economic team took office in January 1981 hoping that lower taxes would stimulate the supply of goods and services to a level that would raise tax revenues, even though tax rates as a percentage of income had been cut. These arguments were repeated in 1995 by members of Congress pushing for tax-rate cuts. This emphasis on greater incentives to produce created by lower taxes has come to be known as *supply-side economics*.

The most widely publicized element of supply-side economics was the *Laffer curve*. The curve is drawn with the tax rate on the vertical axis and tax revenue on the horizontal axis. When the rate of taxation is zero, there is no tax revenue. As the tax rate increases, tax revenue increases up to a point. The assumption here is that there is some rate of taxation that is so high that it discourages productive activity. Once this rate is reached, tax revenue begins to fall as the rate of taxation goes up. In the graph, tax revenue is maximized at R_{max} with a tax rate of t percent. Any increase in the rate of taxation above t percent produces lower tax revenues. In the extreme case—a 100 percent tax rate—no one is willing to work because the government taxes away all income.

Critics of the supply-side tax cuts proposed by the Reagan administration argued that lower taxes would increase the budget deficit. Supply-side advocates insisted that if the United States were in the backward-bending region of the

Laffer curve (above t percent in the graph), tax cuts would actually raise, not lower, tax revenue. The evidence following the tax cuts indicates that the tax cuts did, however, contribute to a larger budget deficit, implying that the United States was not on the backward-bending portion of the Laffer curve.

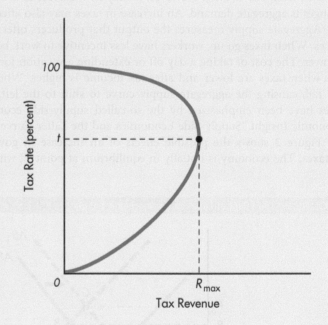

The standard analysis of government spending and taxation assumes that aggregate supply is not affected by the change in fiscal policy, leading us to expect a greater change in real GDP than may actually occur. If tax changes do affect aggregate supply, the expansionary effects of government spending financed by tax increases are moderated. The actual magnitude of this effect is the subject of debate among economists. Most argue that the evidence in the United States indicates that tax increases have a fairly small effect on aggregate supply.

at Y_1. The increase in government spending shifts the aggregate demand curve from AD to AD_1. If this were the only change, the economy would be in equilibrium at point B. But if the increase in taxes reduces output, the aggregate supply curve moves back from AS to AS_1, and output does not expand all the way to Y_p. The decrease in aggregate supply creates a new equilibrium at point C. Here real GDP is at Y_2 (less than Y_p), and the price level is P_3 (higher than P_2).

11-1d Government Spending Financed by Borrowing

The standard multiplier analysis of government spending does not differentiate among the different methods of financing that spending. Yet you just saw how taxation can offset at least part of the expansionary effect of higher government spending. Borrowing to finance government spending can also limit the increase in aggregate demand.

A government borrows funds by selling bonds to the public. These bonds represent debt that must be repaid at a future date. Debt is, in a way, a kind of substitute for current taxes. Instead of increasing current taxes to finance higher spending, the government borrows the savings of households and businesses. Of course, the debt will mature and have to be repaid. This means that taxes will have to be higher in the future in order to provide the government with the funds to pay off the debt.

Current government borrowing, then, implies higher future taxes. This can limit the expansionary effect of increased government spending. If households and businesses take higher future taxes into account, they tend to save more today so that they will be able to pay those taxes in the future. And as saving today increases, consumption today falls.

The idea that current government borrowing can reduce current nongovernment expenditures was suggested originally by the early nineteenth-century English economist David Ricardo. Ricardo recognized that government borrowing could function like increased current taxes, reducing current household and business expenditures. *Ricardian equivalence* is the principle that government spending activities financed by taxation and those financed by borrowing have the same effect on the economy. If Ricardian equivalence holds, it does not matter whether the government raises taxes or borrows more to finance increased spending. The effect is the same: Private-sector spending falls by the same amount today, and this drop in private spending will at least partially offset the expansionary effect of government spending on real GDP. Just how much private spending drops (and how far to the left the aggregate demand curve shifts) depends on the degree to which current saving increases in response to expected higher taxes. The less that people respond to the future tax liabilities arising from current government debt, the smaller the reduction in private spending.

There is substantial disagreement among economists over the extent to which current government borrowing acts like an increase in taxes. Some argue that it makes no difference whether the government raises current taxes or borrows. Others insist that the public does not base current spending on future tax liabilities. If the first group is correct, we would expect government spending financed by borrowing to have a smaller effect than if the second group is correct. Research on this issue continues, with most economists questioning the relevance of Ricardian equivalence and a small but influential group arguing its importance.

Ricardian equivalence holds if taxation and government borrowing both have the same effect on spending in the private sector.

11-1e Crowding Out

Expansionary fiscal policy can crowd out private-sector spending; that is, an increase in government spending can reduce consumption and investment. **Crowding out** is usually discussed in the context of government spending financed by borrowing rather than by taxes. We have just seen how future taxes can cause consumption to fall today, but investment can also be affected. Increases in government borrowing drive up interest rates. As interest rates go up, investment falls. This sort of indirect crowding out works through the bond market. The U.S government borrows by selling Treasury bonds or bills. Because the government is not a profit-making institution, it does not have to earn a profitable return on the money it raises by selling bonds. A corporation does, however.

crowding out
A drop in consumption or investment spending caused by discretionary changes in fiscal policy, changes in government spending and taxation that are aimed at meeting specific policy goals.

When interest rates rise, fewer corporations offer new bonds to raise investment funds because the cost of repaying the bond debt may exceed the rate of return on the investment.

Crowding out, like Ricardian equivalence, is important in principle, but economists have never demonstrated conclusively that its effects can substantially alter spending in the private sector. Still, you should be aware of the possibility in order to understand the potential shortcomings of changes in government spending and taxation.

RECAP

1. Fiscal policy refers to government spending and taxation.

2. By increasing spending or cutting taxes, a government can close the GDP gap.

3. If government spending and taxes increase by the same amount, equilibrium real GDP rises.

4. If a tax increase affects aggregate supply, then a balanced-budget change in fiscal policy will have a smaller expansionary effect on equilibrium real GDP than otherwise.

5. Current government borrowing reduces current spending in the private sector if people increase current saving in order to pay future tax liabilities.

6. Ricardian equivalence holds when taxation and government borrowing have the same effect on current spending in the private sector.

7. Increased government borrowing can crowd private borrowers out of the bond market so that investment falls.

11-2 Fiscal Policy in the United States

2. How has U.S. fiscal policy changed over time?

Our discussion of fiscal policy assumes that this policy is made at the federal level. In the modern economy, this is a reasonable assumption. This was not the case before the 1930s, however. Before the Great Depression, the federal government limited its activities largely to national defense and foreign policy and left other areas of government policy to the individual states. With the growth in the importance of the federal government in fiscal policy has come a growth in the role of the federal budget process.

When one is talking about the federal budget, the monetary amounts of the various categories of expenditures are so huge that they are often difficult to comprehend. But if you were to divide up the annual budget by the number of individual taxpayers, you would come up with an average individual statement that might make more sense, as shown in the Economic Insight "The Taxpayer's Federal Government Credit Card Statement."

The federal budget is determined as much by politics as by economics. Politicians respond to different groups of voters by supporting different government programs, regardless of the needed fiscal policy. It is the political response to constituents that tends to drive up federal budget deficits (the difference between government expenditures and tax revenues), not the need for expansionary fiscal policy. As a result, deficits have become commonplace.

11-2a The Historical Record

The U.S. government has grown dramatically since the early part of the century. Figure 3 shows federal revenues and expenditures over time. Note that expenditures were lower than revenues in the 1998–2001 period. Figure 4 places the growth of government in perspective

FIGURE 3 U.S. Government Revenues and Expenditures

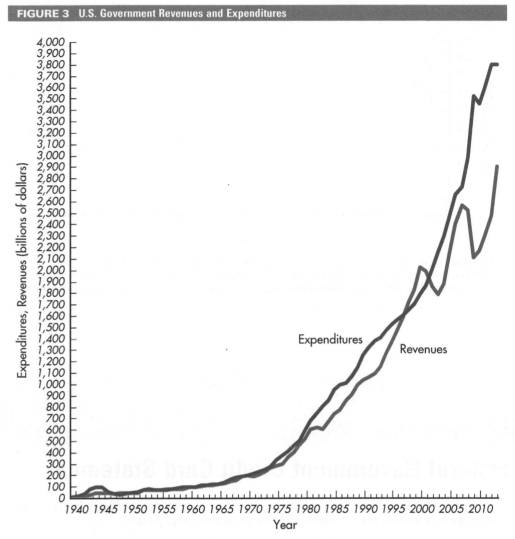

Revenues are total revenues of the U.S. government in each fiscal year. Expenditures are total spending of the U.S. government in each fiscal year. The difference between the two curves equals the U.S. budget deficit (when expenditures exceed revenues) or surplus (when revenues exceed expenditures).

Source: Data are drawn from *Economic Report of the President*, 2013.

by plotting U.S. government spending as a percentage of gross domestic product over time. Before the Great Depression, federal spending was approximately 3 percent of the GDP; by the end of the Depression, it had risen to about 10 percent. The ratio of spending to GDP reached its peak during World War II, when federal spending hit 44 percent of the GDP. After the war, the ratio fell dramatically and then slowly increased to a peak of about 24 percent in 1983. In recent years, the ratio has been around 20 percent.

Fiscal policy has two components: discretionary fiscal policy and automatic stabilizers. **Discretionary fiscal policy** refers to changes in government spending and taxation that are aimed at achieving a policy goal. **Automatic stabilizers** are elements of fiscal policy that automatically change in value as national income changes. Figure 3 and Figure 4 suggest that government spending is dominated by growth over time. But there is no indication here of

discretionary fiscal policy
Changes in government · spending and taxation that are aimed at achieving a policy goal.

automatic stabilizer
An element of fiscal policy that changes automatically as national income changes.

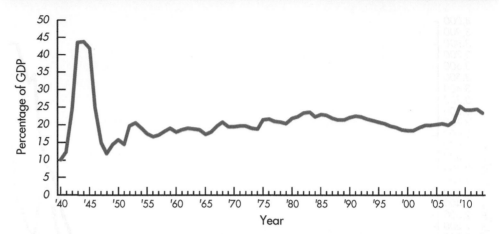

FIGURE 4   U.S. Government Expenditures as a Percentage of Gross Domestic Product

U.S. federal government spending as a percentage of the GDP reached a high of 44 percent in 1943 and 1944. Discounting wartime spending and cutbacks after the war, you can see the upward trend in U.S. government spending, which constituted a larger and larger share of the GDP until the early 1980s.

ECONOMIC INSIGHT

The Taxpayer's Federal Government Credit Card Statement

Suppose the U.S. government's expenditures and revenues were accounted for annually to each individual income tax-payer like a credit card statement. For 2013, the statement would look like the accompanying table.

Statement for 2013 Budget Year	
Previous balance	$ 48,988.89
New purchases	
Defense	$ 5,021.64
Social Security	$ 6,587.31
Medicare	$ 3,932.12
Medicaid	$ 2,106.49
Other	$ 12,839.52
Total Spending	$ 28,380.60
Payments received	
Individual income and social security taxes	$ 17,298.51
Corporate income taxes	$ 2,597.01
Other	$ 1,761.19
Total payments	$ 21,656.71
Finance charge	$ 1,835.82
New balance due	$ 51,067.70

Source: Table created from data drawn from the Office of Management and Budget at budget.gov

discretionary changes in fiscal policy, changes in government spending and taxation that are aimed at meeting specific policy goals. Perhaps a better way to evaluate the fiscal policy record is in terms of the budget deficit. Government expenditures can rise, but the effect on aggregate demand could be offset by a simultaneous increase in taxes so that there is no expansionary effect on the equilibrium level of national income. By looking at the deficit, we see the combined spending and tax policy results, which are missing if only government expenditures are considered.

Figure 5 illustrates the pattern of the U.S. federal deficit and the deficit as a percentage of GDP over time. Figure 5(a) shows that the United States ran close to a balanced budget for much of the 1950s and 1960s. There were large deficits associated with financing World War II, and then large deficits resulting from fiscal policy decisions in recent decades. However, from 1998 to 2001, the first surpluses since 1969 were recorded. Figure 5(b) shows that the deficit as a percentage of GDP was much larger during World War II than it was in the 1980s and 1990s.

Historically, aside from wartime, budget deficits increase the most during recessions. When real GDP falls, tax revenues go down, and government spending on unemployment and welfare benefits goes up. These are examples of automatic stabilizers in action. As income falls, taxes fall and personal benefit payments rise to partially offset the effect of the drop in income. The rapid growth of the deficit in the 1980s involved more than the recessions in 1980 and 1982, however. The economy grew rapidly after the 1982 recession ended,

FIGURE 5 The U.S. Deficit

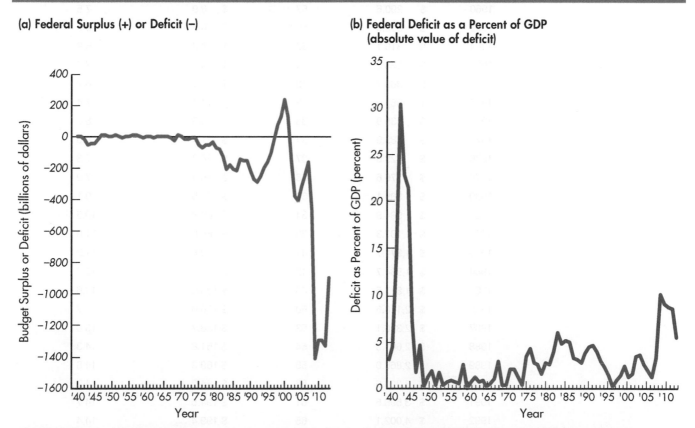

(a) Federal Surplus (+) or Deficit (–)

(b) Federal Deficit as a Percent of GDP (absolute value of deficit)

5(a) Since 1940 the U.S. government has rarely shown a surplus. For much of the 1950s and 1960s, the United States was close to a balanced budget. 5(b) The federal deficit as a percentage of GDP. The deficits during the 1950s and 1960s generally were small. The early 1980s were a time of rapid growth in the federal budget deficit, and this is reflected in the growth of the deficit as a percentage of GDP.

but so did the fiscal deficit. The increase in the deficit was the product of a rapid increase in government spending to fund new programs and enlarge existing programs while taxes were held constant. In the late 1990s, the deficit decreased. This was the result of surprisingly large tax revenue gains, generated by strong economic growth, combined with only moderate government spending increases. The deficit is unlikely to fall significantly in the next few years, however, as government spending for health care along with defense and homeland security rises.

3. What are the effects of budget deficits?

11-2b Deficits and the National Debt

The large federal deficits of the 1980s and 1990s led many observers to question whether a deficit can harm the economy. Figure 5 shows how the fiscal deficit has changed over time. One major implication of a large deficit is the resulting increase in the national debt, the total stock of government bonds outstanding. Table 1 lists data on the debt of the United States. Notice that the total debt doubled between 1981 ($994.8 billion) and 1986

TABLE 1 Debt of the U.S. Government (Dollar Amounts in Billions)				
(1) **Year**	**(2)** **Total Debt**	**(3)** **Debt/GDP** **(percent)**	**(4)** **Net Interest**	**(5)** **Interest/Government** **Spending (percent)**
1958	$ 279.7	63	$ 5.6	6.8
1960	$ 290.5	57	$ 6.9	7.5
1962	$ 302.9	55	$ 6.9	6.5
1964	$ 316.1	50	$ 8.2	6.9
1966	$ 328.5	44	$ 9.4	7.0
1968	$ 368.7	43	$ 11.1	6.2
1970	$ 380.9	39	$ 14.4	7.4
1972	$ 435.9	38	$ 15.5	6.7
1974	$ 483.9	34	$ 21.4	8.0
1976	$ 629.0	37	$ 26.7	7.3
1978	$ 776.6	36	$ 35.4	7.9
1980	$ 909.1	34	$ 52.5	9.1
1981	$ 994.8	34	$ 68.8	10.5
1982	$ 1,137.3	36	$ 85.0	11.6
1983	$ 1,371.7	41	$ 89.8	11.2
1984	$ 1,564.7	42	$ 111.1	13.2
1985	$ 1,817.5	46	$ 129.5	13.6
1986	$ 2,120.6	50	$ 136.0	13.7
1987	$ 2,396.1	53	$ 138.7	13.8
1988	$ 2,601.3	54	$ 151.8	14.3
1989	$ 2,868.0	55	$ 169.3	14.8
1990	$ 3,206.6	56	$ 184.2	14.7
1991	$ 3,598.5	61	$ 194.5	14.7
1992	$ 4,002.1	65	$ 199.4	14.4
1993	$ 4,351.4	67	$ 198.8	14.1
1994	$ 4,643.7	66	$ 203.0	13.9

(continued)

TABLE 1	Debt of the U.S. Government (Dollar Amounts in Billions) *(continued)*			
(1) Year	**(2)** Total Debt	**(3)** Debt/GDP (percent)	**(4)** Net Interest	**(5)** Interest/Government Spending (percent)
1995	$ 4,921.0	66	$ 232.2	15.3
1996	$ 5,181.9	66	$ 241.1	15.5
1997	$ 5,369.7	65	$ 244.0	15.2
1998	$ 5,478.7	63	$ 241.2	14.6
1999	$ 5,606.1	57	$ 229.7	13.5
2000	$ 5,628.7	57	$ 222.9	12.5
2001	$ 5,769. 9	57	$ 206.2	11.1
2002	$ 6,198.4	59	$ 171.0	8.5
2003	$ 6,760.0	63	$ 153.1	7.1
2004	$ 7,354.7	64	$ 160.2	7.0
2005	$ 7,905.3	64	$ 184.0	7.4
2006	$ 8,451.4	64	$ 226.6	8.5
2007	$ 8,950.7	65	$ 237.1	8.7
2008	$ 9,986.1	70	$ 252.8	8.4
2009	$ 11,875.9	85	$ 186.9	5.3
2010	$ 13,528.8	94	$ 196.2	5.7
2011	$ 14,764.2	99	$ 230	6.3
2012	$ 16,350.9	104	$ 222.5	5.9
2013	$ 17,547.9	107	$ 228.6	6

($2,120.6 billion), and then doubled again between 1986 and 1993. Column 3 shows debt as a percentage of GDP. In the late 1990s, the debt was falling as a percentage of GDP. During World War II, the debt was greater than the GDP for five years. Despite the talk of "unprecedented" federal deficits in the 1980s and 1990s, clearly the ratio of the debt to GDP was by no means unprecedented.

We have not yet answered the question of whether deficits are bad. To do so, we have to consider their potential effects.

11-2b-1 Deficits, Interest Rates, and Investment Because government deficits mean government borrowing and debt, many economists argue that deficits raise interest rates as lenders require a higher interest rate to induce them to hold more government debt. Increased government borrowing raises interest rates; this, in turn, can depress investment. (Remember that as interest rates rise, the rate of return on investment drops, along with the incentive to invest.) What happens when government borrowing crowds out private investment? Lower investment means fewer capital goods in the future. So deficits lower the level of output in the economy, both today and in the future. In this sense, deficits are potentially bad.

11-2b-2 Deficits and International Trade If government deficits raise real interest rates (the nominal interest rate minus the expected inflation rate), they also may have an effect on international trade. A higher real return on U.S. securities makes those securities more attractive to foreign investors. As the foreign demand for U.S. securities increases, so does the demand for U.S. dollars in exchange for Japanese yen, British pounds, and other foreign

Through their effects on investment, deficits can lower the level of output in the economy.

currencies. As the demand for dollars increases, the dollar *appreciates* in value on the foreign exchange market. This means that the dollar becomes more expensive to foreigners, while foreign currency becomes cheaper to U.S. residents. This kind of change in the exchange rate encourages U.S. residents to buy more foreign goods and encourages foreign residents to buy fewer U.S. goods. Ultimately, then, as deficits and government debt increase, U.S. net exports tend to fall. Such foreign trade effects are another potentially bad effect of deficits.

11-2b-3 Interest Payments on the National Debt

The national debt is the stock of government bonds outstanding. It is the product of past and current budget deficits. As the size of the debt increases, the amount of interest that must be paid on the debt tends to rise. Column 4 of Table 1 lists the amount of interest paid on the debt; column 5 lists the interest as a percentage of government expenditures. The numbers in both columns have risen steadily over time and only recently started to drop.

The increase in the interest cost of the national debt is an aspect of fiscal deficits that worries some people. However, to the extent that U.S. citizens hold government bonds, we owe the debt to ourselves. The tax liability of funding the interest payments is offset by the interest income that bondholders earn. In this case there is no net change in national wealth when the national debt changes.

Of course, we do not owe the national debt just to ourselves. The United States is the world's largest national financial market, and many U.S. securities, including government bonds, are held by foreign residents. Today, foreign holdings of the U.S. national debt amount to about 28 percent of the outstanding debt. Because the tax liability for paying the interest on the debt falls on U.S. taxpayers, the greater the payments made to foreigners, the lower the wealth of U.S. residents, other things being equal.

Other things are not equal, however. To understand the real impact of foreign holdings on the economy, we have to evaluate what the economy would have been like if the debt had not been sold to foreign investors. If the foreign savings placed in U.S. bonds allowed the United States to increase investment and its productive capacity beyond what would have been possible in the absence of foreign lending, then the country could very well be better off for having sold government bonds to foreigners. The presence of foreign funds may keep interest rates lower than they would otherwise be, preventing the substantial crowding out associated with an increase in the national debt.

So while deficits are potentially bad as a result of the crowding out of investment, larger trade deficits with the rest of the world, and greater interest costs of the debt, we cannot generally say that all deficits are bad. It depends on what benefit the deficit provides. If the deficit spending allowed for greater productivity than would have occurred otherwise, the benefits may outweigh the costs. The financial crisis of 2008 provides a great example: Fiscal policy around the world involved governments increasing spending dramatically so that budget deficits increased substantially. However, the thinking was that the cost of not having government stimulate the economy would have been a much worse recession with many more people unemployed and incomes falling even more, so that the benefits of the deficits were widely thought to outweigh the costs.

11-2c Automatic Stabilizers

We have largely been talking about discretionary fiscal policy, the changes in government spending and taxing that policymakers make consciously. *Automatic stabilizers* are the elements of fiscal policy that change automatically as income changes. Automatic stabilizers partially offset changes in income: As income falls, automatic stabilizers increase spending; as income rises, automatic stabilizers decrease spending. Any program that responds to fluctuations in the business cycle in a way that moderates the effect of those fluctuations is an automatic stabilizer. Examples are progressive income taxes and transfer payments.

In our examples of tax changes, we have been using *lump-sum taxes*—taxes that are a flat dollar amount regardless of income. However, income taxes are determined as a percentage of income. In the United States, the federal income tax is a **progressive tax**: As income rises, so does the rate of taxation. A person with a very low income pays no income tax, while a person with a high income can pay more than a third of that income in taxes. Countries use different rates of taxation on income. Taxes can be regressive (the tax rate falls as income rises) or proportional (the tax rate is constant as income rises) as well as progressive. But most countries, including the United States, use a progressive tax, with the percentage of income paid as taxes rising as taxable income rises.

Progressive income taxes act as an automatic stabilizer. As income falls, so does the average tax rate. Suppose a household earning $60,000 must pay 30 percent of its income ($18,000) in taxes, leaving 70 percent of its income ($42,000) for spending. If that household's income drops to $40,000 and the tax rate falls to 25 percent, the household has 75 percent of its income ($30,000) available for spending. But if the tax rate is 30 percent at all levels of income, the household earning $40,000 would have only 70 percent of its income ($28,000) to spend. By allowing a greater percentage of earned income to be spent, progressive taxes help offset the effect of lower income on spending.

All industrial countries have progressive federal income tax systems. For instance, the tax rate in Japan starts at 5 percent for low-income households and rises to a maximum of 40 percent for high-income households. In the United States, individual income tax rates start at 10 percent and rise to a maximum of 35 percent. In the U.K. tax system, rates rise from 10 percent to 50 percent, while tax rates in Germany rise from 15 to 45 percent and those in France, from 5.5 to 40 percent.

A **transfer payment** is a payment to one person that is funded by taxing others. Food stamps, welfare benefits, and unemployment benefits are all government transfer payments: Current taxpayers provide the funds to pay those who qualify for the programs. Transfer payments that use income to establish eligibility act as automatic stabilizers. In a recession, as income falls, more people qualify for food stamps or welfare benefits, raising the level of transfer payments.

Unemployment insurance is also an automatic stabilizer. As unemployment rises, more workers receive unemployment benefits. Unemployment benefits tend to rise in a recession and fall during an expansion. This countercyclical pattern of benefit payments offsets the effect of business-cycle fluctuations on consumption.

progressive tax
A tax whose rate rises as income rises.

transfer payment
A payment to one person that is funded by taxing others.

RECAP

1. Fiscal policy in the United States is a product of the budget process.

2. Federal spending in the United States has grown rapidly over time, from just 3 percent of GDP before the Great Depression to about 20 percent of GDP today.

3. Government budget deficits can hurt the economy through their effect on interest rates and private investment, net exports, and the tax burden on current and future taxpayers.

4. Automatic stabilizers are government programs that are already in place and that respond automatically to fluctuations in the business cycle, moderating the effect of those fluctuations.

11-3 Fiscal Policy in Different Countries

4. How does fiscal policy differ across countries?

A country's fiscal policy reflects its philosophy toward government spending and taxation. In this section we present comparative data that demonstrate the variety of fiscal policies in the world.

11-3a Government Spending

Our discussion up to this point has centered on U.S. fiscal policy. But fiscal policy and the role of government in the economy can be very different across countries. Government has played an increasingly larger role in the major industrial countries over time. Table 2 shows how government spending has gone up as a percentage of output in five industrial nations. In every case, government spending accounted for a larger percentage of output in 2008 than it did 100 years earlier. For instance, in 1880, government spending was only 6 percent of the GNP in Sweden. By 1929 it had risen to 8 percent, and by 2008, to 26 percent.

Government spending has grown over time as a fraction of GNP in all industrial countries.

Historically, in industrial countries, the growth of government spending has been matched by growth in revenues. But in the 1960s, government spending began to grow faster than revenues, creating increasingly larger debtor nations.

Developing countries have not shown the uniform growth in government spending found in industrial countries. In fact, in some developing countries (e.g., Chile, the Dominican Republic, and Peru), government spending is a smaller percentage of GDP today than it was 20 years ago. And we find a greater variation in the role of government in developing countries.

One important difference between the typical developed country and the typical developing country is that government plays a larger role in investment spending in the developing country. One reason for this difference is that state-owned enterprises account for a larger percentage of economic activity in developing countries than they do in developed countries. Also, developing countries usually rely more on government to build their infrastructure—schools, roads, hospitals—than do developed countries.

How a government spends its money is a function of its income. Here we find differences not only between industrial and developing countries, but also among developing countries. Figure 6 reports central government spending for the United States, an industrial country, and a large developing country, China.

This figure clearly illustrates the relative importance of social welfare spending in industrial and developing countries. Although standards of living are lowest in the poorest countries, these countries do not have the resources to spend on social services (education, health, housing, social security, welfare). The United States spends 43 percent of its budget on social security, health, and education programs. China spends 31 percent of its budget on these programs, and that is substantially more than most developing countries.

TABLE 2 Share of Government Spending in GNP in Selected Industrial Countries, 1880, 1929, and 2008 (Percent)

Year	France	Germany	Sweden	United Kingdom	United States
1880	15	10[1]	6	10	8
1929	19	31	8	24	10
2008	23	18	26	21	16

[1]1881

Source: Data are drawn from World Bank, *World Development Report 1996* and *2006* and OECD. StatExtracts.

FIGURE 6 Central Government Spending by Functional Category

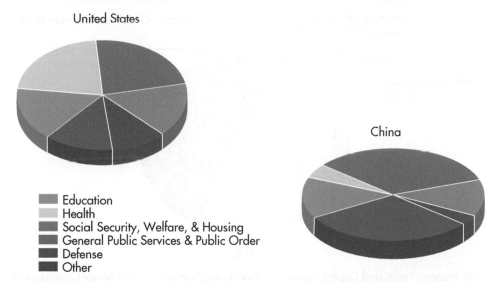

The charts show the pattern of government spending in an industrial country, the United States, and a low-income developing country, China. Social programs (education, health, and social security) account for 43 percent of federal government expenditures in the United States, but only 31 percent in China.

Source: Data are drawn from International Monetary Fund, *Government Finance Statistics Yearbook*, 2013.

11-3b Taxation

There are two different types of taxes: *direct taxes* (on individuals and firms) and *indirect taxes* (on goods and services). Figure 7 compares the importance of different sources of central government tax revenue for an industrial country, the United States, and a developing country, China. The most obvious difference is that personal income taxes are much more important in industrial countries than in developing countries. Why? Because personal taxes are hard to collect in agricultural nations, where a large percentage of household production is for personal consumption. Taxes on goods and services are easier to collect and thus are more important in developing countries.

That industrial countries are better able to afford social programs is reflected in social security taxes typically being higher in industrial countries than developing countries. With so many workers living near the subsistence level in the poorest countries, their governments simply cannot tax workers very much for retirement and health security programs.

Taxes on international trade are typically more important in developing countries. Because goods arriving in or leaving a country must pass through customs inspection, export and import taxes are relatively easy to collect compared to income taxes.

Figure 7 lists "Goods and Services" taxes. For most countries, the majority of these taxes are **value-added taxes (VATs)**. A value-added tax is an indirect tax imposed on each sale at each stage of production. Each seller from the first stage of production on collects the VAT from the buyer, then deducts any VATs it has paid in buying its inputs. The difference is remitted to the government. From time to time, Congress has debated the merits of a VAT in the United States, but it has never approved this kind of tax. The Global Business Insight "Value-Added Tax" provides further discussion.

value-added tax (VAT)
A general sales tax collected at each stage of production.

FIGURE 7 Central Government Tax Composition by Income Group

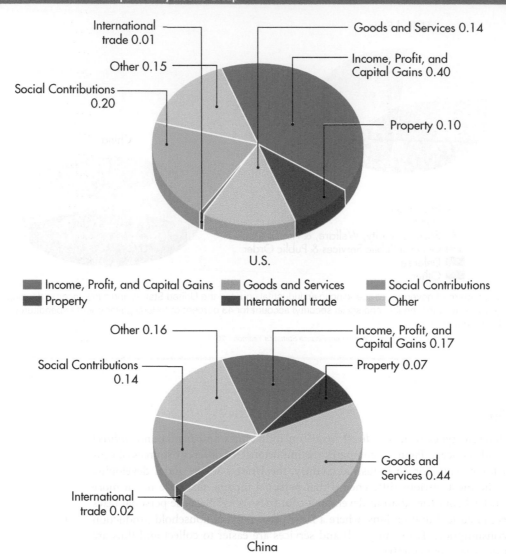

When we group countries by income level, the importance of different sources of tax revenue is obvious. Domestic income taxes account for 40 percent of government revenue in the United States and just 17 percent in China. Sales taxes on goods and services are more important in China, 44 percent of revenue, than in the U.S., 14 percent of revenue. (Note: Percentages do not total 100 because of rounding.)

Source: Data are drawn from International Monetary Fund, *Government Finance Statistics Yearbook*, 2013.

RECAP

1. Over time, government spending has become more important in industrial countries.

2. Governments in developing countries typically play a larger role in investment spending in their economies than do the governments of developed countries.

3. Developing countries depend more on taxes on goods and services as a source of revenue than on income taxes on individuals and businesses.

4. Value-added taxes are general sales taxes that are collected at every stage of production.

GLOBAL BUSINESS INSIGHT

Value-Added Tax

A value-added tax (VAT) is a tax levied on all sales of goods and services at each stage of production. As implied by the name, the tax applies only to the value added at each stage, and so a firm that pays value-added taxes will pay tax only on the value that it added to the good or service that it sells. If a firm sells melons at a fruit stand, the VAT it pays is based on the difference between the cost the firm paid for the melons and the sales price it charges to its customers who buy the fruit. Of course, the customers bear the cost of the VAT, as it is built into the price they must pay.

As the accompanying map indicates, VATs are very popular around the world. Many countries adopted VATs in the 1990s. It is clear that more countries use VATs than do not. Such a tax has its advantages. One important consideration is that a VAT is a tax on consumption. Anyone who buys goods and services will contribute to the government's VAT revenue. Thus, VATs are very powerful revenue generators. Those individuals who evade income taxes and pay less than their legal obligation will not escape the VAT. For instance, a criminal who earns income illegally and pays no tax on that income will still be taxed on all legal goods and services that he or she purchases. In this sense, there is a certain attractiveness to taxing consumption rather than income. But a VAT also acts as a regressive tax in that a poor person would tend to pay a higher fraction of income as VAT than a rich person. It is important to realize that no country relies strictly on a VAT for government revenue. VATs are part of an overall government tax policy that attempts to incorporate fairness along with a need to raise sufficient revenue to finance public expenditures.

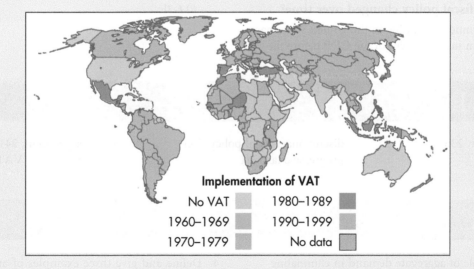

Implementation of VAT

No VAT
1960–1969
1970–1979
1980–1989
1990–1999
No data

Source: International Monetary Fund, VATs are Appropriate for Wide Range of Economies, but Certain Preconditions are Vital for Success, *IMF Survey*, Volume 29, Number 9, May 2000.

SUMMARY

1. How can fiscal policy eliminate a GDP gap?

- A GDP gap can be closed by increasing government spending or by cutting taxes. *§11-1*

- Government spending affects aggregate expenditures directly; taxes affect aggregate expenditures indirectly through their effect on consumption. *§11-1*

- Aggregate expenditures must rise to bring equilibrium real GDP up to potential real GDP to eliminate the GDP gap. *§11-1*

- An increase in government spending that is matched by an increase in taxes raises equilibrium spending and real GDP. *§11-1c*

- If the public expects to pay higher taxes as a result of government borrowing, then the expansionary effects of government deficits may be reduced. *§11-1d*

- Government borrowing can crowd out private spending by raising interest rates and reducing investments. *§11-1e*

2. How has U.S. fiscal policy changed over time?

- Federal government spending in the United States has increased from just 3 percent of the GDP before the Great Depression to around 20 percent of the GDP today. *§11-2a*

- Fiscal policy has two components: discretionary fiscal policy and automatic stabilizers. *§11-2c*

3. What are the effects of budget deficits?

- Budget deficits, through their effects on interest rates, international trade, and the national debt, can reduce investment, output, net exports, and national wealth. *§11-2b*

- Progressive taxes and transfer payments are automatic stabilizers, elements of fiscal policy that change automatically as national income changes. *§11-2c*

4. How does fiscal policy differ across countries?

- Industrial countries spend a much larger percentage of their government budget for social programs than developing countries do. *§11-3a*

- Industrial countries depend more on direct taxes and less on indirect taxes than developing countries do. *§11-3b*

KEY TERMS

automatic stabilizer, 235
crowding out, 233

discretionary fiscal policy, 235
progressive tax, 241

transfer payment, 241
value-added tax (VAT), 243

EXERCISES

1. What is the role of aggregate demand in eliminating the GDP gap? How does the slope of the *AS* curve affect the fiscal policy actions necessary to eliminate the GDP gap?
2. What is the "government budget constraint"? In other words, what are the sources of financing government spending?
3. In what ways are government deficits harmful to the economy?
4. Define and give three examples of automatic stabilizers.
5. Briefly describe the major differences between fiscal policy in industrial countries and that in developing countries.
6. Why will real GDP tend to rise when government spending and taxes rise by the same amount?
7. How can a larger government fiscal deficit cause a larger international trade deficit?

8. Why do government budget deficits grow during recessions?
9. Taxes can be progressive, regressive, or proportional. Define each, and briefly offer an argument for why income taxes are usually progressive.
10. What is a value-added tax (VAT), and what is an advantage of such a tax relative to an income tax?

The following exercises are based on the Appendix to this chapter.

Answer exercises 11–14 on the basis of the following information. Assume that equilibrium real GDP is $800 billion, potential real GDP is $950 billion, the *MPC* is .80, and the *MPI* is .40.

11. What is the size of the GDP gap?
12. How much must government spending increase to eliminate the GDP gap?
13. How much must taxes fall to eliminate the GDP gap?
14. If government spending and taxes both change by the same amount, how much must they change to eliminate the recessionary gap?
15. Suppose the *MPC* is .90 and the *MPI* is .10. If government expenditures go up $100 billion while taxes fall

$10 billion, what happens to the equilibrium level of real GDP?

Use the following equations for exercises 16–18.

$$C = \$100 + .8Y$$
$$I = \$200$$
$$G = \$250$$
$$X = \$100 - .2Y$$

16. What is the equilibrium level of real GDP?
17. What is the new equilibrium level of real GDP if government spending increases by $150?
18. What is the new equilibrium level of real GDP if government spending and taxes both increase by $150?
19. Make a graph showing the spending and tax revenue of your state government for as many years as you can find (use the government of your home country if you are not from the United States). What trends do you notice? What spending categories make up the largest share of the state budget? What are the largest sources of revenue?

ECONOMICALLY SPEAKING

AGREEMENT REACHED ON EURO PACT: EU PRESIDENT

The Times of India Online, March 2011

BRUSSELS: European Union president Herman Van Rompuy announced on Friday via Twitter that the 17 eurozone nations had reached agreement on a pact to coordinate economic policy more centrally.

"We have an agreement on the pact for the euro," said Van Rompuy, who was tasked with piloting through proposals put to a summit to bolster the eurozone's defences against a persistent and damaging debt crisis.

His Twitter site was later amended to say it was "an agreement in principle" with "other elements of the package" still being discussed.

All aspects of economic policy are covered in the pact with the aim of ensuring greater policy coordination so that the eurozone economies prove more competitive and better able to manage their public finances.

If that is achieved, then the debt crisis can be controlled and resolved, avoiding the need for further costly bailouts after Greece and Ireland had to be rescued last year.

The agreement will need to be endorsed at a March 24–25 summit of all 27 EU states.

A draft of the 'Pact for the Euro,' as seen earlier by AFP, sets out four areas for closer cooperation—competitiveness, employment, sustainable public finances and reinforcing financial stability.

Individual states will be responsible for specific measures, but all are supposed to work towards these same goals.

The objective is "to achieve a new quality of economic policy coordination in the euro area, improve competitiveness, thereby leading to a higher degree of convergence," the document states.

The logic is that if eurozone states have the same goals and obey the same rules, then the huge debt burdens and public deficits straining public finances and threatening the euro will ultimately be brought under control.

Eurozone leaders are also looking at how they can bolster the eurozone debt rescue system set up after the Greek bailout last May.

The three-year European Financial Stability Facility is worth notionally 440 billion euros ($610 billion) but in practice it can only provide half that amount. Making its full capacity available is still an issue.

Its 2013 replacement, the permanent European Stability Mechanism, will have double the firepower but there are difficult debates over its ultimate size and powers, especially whether it will be able to buy up eurozone government debt.

COMMENTARY

Government budget deficits are a global concern. While we usually think in terms of internal political and economic pressures on a nation to keep its government budget from generating large and unsustainable deficits, the article discusses the case of the European Union (EU), where member countries face multinational pressure to comply with the EU *stability pact*. When the euro was in the planning stage, it was decided that every country that wanted to use the euro as its currency would have to have a stable, sustainable fiscal policy. The EU created the stability pact to explicitly state the limits on national governments' flexibility with regard to debt and deficits. The stability pact requires all euroland countries to maintain budget deficits of less than 3 percent of GDP and government debt of less than 60 percent of GDP. Crises in Greece and Ireland drew increased attention to the interconnectedness of eurozone economies. In 2010, The Van Rompuy report and legislative initiatives by the European Commission addressed areas for improvement in economic governance:

* Greater focus on public debt levels and satisfactory path of debt reduction
* Effective enforcement through sanctions, including deposits, and tighter voting rules
* Better regulation to enforce reliable and timely statistics
* Surveillance mechanisms for excessive macroeconomic imbalances

For the countries that share the same currency, the euro, it makes sense that they maintain similar fiscal policies in order to maintain a stable value for the euro against external currencies like the dollar. However, should other countries that have their own national money, like the United States or Japan, worry about maintaining a small deficit?

You may have heard arguments concerning the effects of a budget deficit that proceed by means of an analogy between the government's budget and a family's budget. Just as a family cannot spend more than it earns, so the argument goes, the government cannot follow this practice without bringing itself to ruin. The problem with this analogy is that the government has the ability to raise money through taxes and bond sales, options that are not open to a family.

A more appropriate analogy is to compare the government's budget to that of a large corporation. Large corporations run persistent deficits that are never paid back. Instead, when corporate debt comes due, the corporations "roll over" their debt by selling new debt. They are able to do this because they use their debt to finance investment that enables them to increase their worth. To the extent that the government is investing in projects like road repairs and building the nation's infrastructure, it is increasing the productive capacity of the economy, which widens the tax base and increases potential future tax receipts.

There are, of course, legitimate problems associated with a budget deficit. The government has two options if it cannot pay for its expenditures with tax receipts. One method of financing the budget deficit is by creating money. This is an unattractive option because it leads to inflation. Another method is to borrow funds by selling government bonds. A problem with this option is that the government must compete with private investment for scarce loanable funds. Unless saving increases at the same time, interest rates rise and government borrowing crowds out private investment. This results in a lower capital stock and diminished prospects for future economic growth.

So while the euroland countries face pressure, and potential fines, from the European Union if they exceed the limits of the stability pact, there are pressures from financial markets on all countries. The financial markets punish those countries that have excessive budget deficits. A country with big budget deficits will find its interest rates rising as investors buying the bonds sold by a country that borrows ever larger amounts of money will demand a higher and higher return. Those countries that resort to printing money to finance a budget deficit end up with higher and higher inflation rates. Such a policy has brought down more than one government in the past. Good government, as measured by careful management of the budget, is rewarded with good economic conditions (other things equal) and political survival.

An Algebraic Examination of the Balanced-Budget Change in Fiscal Policy

What would happen if government spending and taxes went up by the same amount?

We can analyze such a change by expanding the analysis begun in the Appendix to earlier chaper.

The spending multiplier is the simple multiplier defined in the earlier chapter:

$$\text{Spending multiplier} = \frac{1}{MPS + MPI}$$

In the earlier chapter example, because the MPS equals .30 and the MPI equals .10, the spending multiplier equals 2.5:

$$\text{Spending multiplier} = \frac{1}{MPS + MPI} = \frac{1}{.30 + .10}$$
$$= \frac{1}{.40} = 2.5$$

When government spending increases by $20, the equilibrium level of real GDP increases by 2.5 times $20, or $50.

We also can define a tax multiplier, a measure of the effect of a change in taxes on equilibrium real GDP. Because a percentage of any change in income is saved and spent on imports, we know that a tax cut increases expenditures by less than the amount of the cut. The percentage of the tax cut that actually is spent is the marginal propensity to consume minus the marginal propensity to import ($MPC - MPI$). If consumers save 30 percent of any extra income, they spend 70 percent, the MPC. But the domestic economy does not realize 70 percent of the extra income because 10 percent of the extra income is spent on imports. The percentage of any extra income that actually is spent at home is the MPC minus the MPI. In our example, 60 percent (.70 − .10) of any extra income is spent in the domestic economy.

With this information, we can define the tax multiplier like this:

$$\text{Tax multiplier} = -(MPC - MPI)\frac{1}{MPS + MPI}$$

In our example, the tax multiplier is −1.5:

$$\text{Tax multiplier} = -(.70 - .10)\frac{1}{.30 + .10}$$
$$= -(.60)(2.5) = -1.5$$

A tax cut increases equilibrium real GDP by 1.5 times the amount of the cut. Notice that the tax multiplier is always a *negative* number because a change in taxes moves income and expenditures in the opposite direction. Higher taxes lower income and expenditures; lower taxes raise income and expenditures.

Now that we have reviewed the spending and tax multipliers, we can examine the effect of a balanced-budget change in fiscal policy, where government spending and taxes change by the same amount. To simplify the analysis, we assume that taxes are lump-sum taxes (taxpayers must pay a certain amount of dollars as tax) rather than income taxes (where the tax rises with income). We can use the algebraic model presented in the Appendix to the earlier chapter to illustrate the effect of a balanced-budget change in government spending. Here are the model equations:

$$C = \$30 + .70Y$$
$$I = \$50$$
$$G = \$70$$
$$X = \$50 - .10Y$$

Solving for the equilibrium level of Y (as we did in the Appendix to the earlier chapter), Y equals $500, where Y equals aggregate expenditures.

Now suppose that G increases by $10 and that this increase is funded by taxes of $10. The increase in G changes autonomous government spending to $80. The increase in taxes affects the levels of C and X. The new model equations are:

$$C = \$30 + .70(Y - \$10) = \$23 + .70Y$$
$$X = \$50 - .10(Y - \$10) = \$51 - .10Y$$

Using the new G, C, and X functions, we can find the new equilibrium level of real GDP by setting Y equal to AE $(C + I + G + X)$:

$$Y = C + I + G + X$$
$$Y = \$23 + .70Y + \$50 + \$80 + \$51 - .10Y$$
$$Y = \$204 + .60Y$$
$$Y - .60Y = \$204$$
$$.40Y = \$204$$
$$Y = \$510$$

Increasing government spending and taxes by $10 each raises the equilibrium level of real GDP by $10. A balanced-budget increase in G increases Y by the change in G. If government spending and taxes both fall by the same amount, then real GDP will also fall by an amount equal to the change in government spending and taxes.

CHAPTER 12
Money and Banking

Ju-dangoy/Dreamstime.com

FUNDAMENTAL QUESTIONS

1. What is money?

2. How is the U.S. money supply defined?

3. How do countries pay for international transactions?

4. Why are banks considered intermediaries?

5. How does international banking differ from domestic banking?

6. How do banks create money?

Preview

Up to this point, we have been talking about aggregate expenditures, aggregate demand and supply, and fiscal policy without explicitly discussing money. Yet money is used by every sector of the economy in all nations and plays a crucial role in every economy. In this chapter, we discuss what money is, how the quantity of money is determined, and the role of banks in determining this quantity. In the next chapter, we examine the role of money in the aggregate demand and supply model.

As you will see in the next two chapters, the quantity of money has a major impact on interest rates, inflation, and the amount of spending in the economy. Thus, money is

top: © Carsten Reisinger/Shutterstock

253

important for macroeconomic policymaking, and government officials use both monetary and fiscal policy to influence the equilibrium level of real GDP and prices.

Banks and the banking system also play key roles, both at home and abroad, in the determination of the amount of money in circulation and the movement of money between nations. After we define money and its functions, we look at the banking system. We begin with banking in the United States, and then discuss international banking. Someone once joked that banks follow the rule of 3-6-3: They borrow at 3 percent interest, lend at 6 percent interest, and close at 3 p.m. If those days ever existed, clearly they no longer do today. The banking industry in the United States and the rest of the world has undergone tremendous change in recent years. New technology and government deregulation are allowing banks to respond to changing economic conditions in ways that were unthinkable only a few years ago, and these changes have had dramatic effects on the economy.

12-1 What Is Money?

Money is anything that is generally acceptable to sellers in exchange for goods and services. The cash in your wallet can be used to buy groceries or a movie ticket. You simply present your cash to the cashier, who readily accepts it. If you wanted to use your car to buy groceries or a movie ticket, the exchange would be more complicated. You would probably have to sell the car before you could use it to buy other goods and services. Cars are seldom exchanged directly for goods and services (except for other cars). Because cars are not a generally acceptable means of paying for other goods and services, we do not consider them to be money. Money is the most liquid asset. A **liquid asset** is an asset that can easily be exchanged for goods and services. Cash is a liquid asset; a car is not. How liquid must an asset be before we consider it money? To answer this question, we must first consider the functions of money.

12-1a Functions of Money

Money serves four basic functions: It is a *medium of exchange*, a *unit of account*, a *store of value*, and a *standard of deferred payment*. Not all monies serve all of these functions equally well, as will be apparent in the following discussion. But to be money, an item must perform enough of these functions to induce people to use it.

12-1a-1 Medium of Exchange
Money is a medium of exchange; it is given in exchange for goods and services. Sellers willingly accept money as payment for the products and services that they produce. Without money, we would have to resort to *barter*, the direct exchange of goods and services for other goods and services.

For a barter system to work, there must be a *double coincidence of wants*. Suppose Bill is a carpenter and Jane is a plumber. In a monetary economy, when Bill needs plumbing repairs in his home, he simply pays Jane for the repairs, using money. Because everyone wants money, money is an acceptable means of payment. In a barter economy, Bill must offer his services as a carpenter in exchange for Jane's work. If Jane does not want any carpentry work done, Bill and Jane cannot enter into a mutually beneficial transaction. Bill has to find a person who can do what he wants and who also wants what he can do—there must be a double coincidence of wants.

The example of Bill and Jane illustrates the fact that barter is a lot less efficient than using money. This means that the cost of a transaction in a barter economy is higher than the cost of a transaction in a monetary economy.

1. What is money?

money
Anything that is generally acceptable to sellers in exchange for goods and services.

liquid asset
An asset that can easily be exchanged for goods and services.

The use of money as a medium of exchange lowers transaction costs.

The people of Yap Island highly value, and thus accept as their medium of exchange, giant stones. In most cultures, however, money must be *portable* in order to be an effective medium of exchange—a property that the stone money of Yap Island clearly lacks. Another important property of money is *divisibility*. Money must be measurable in both small units (for low-value goods and services) and large units (for high-value goods and services). Yap stone money is not divisible, so it is not a good medium of exchange for the majority of goods that are bought and sold.

12-1a-2 Unit of Account

Money is a unit of account: We price goods and services in terms of money. This common unit of measurement allows us to compare relative values easily. If whole-wheat bread sells for a dollar a loaf and white bread sells for 50 cents, we know that whole-wheat bread is twice as expensive as white bread.

Using money as a unit of account is efficient. It reduces the costs of gathering information on what things are worth. The use of money as a unit of account lowers information costs relative to barter. In a barter economy, people constantly have to evaluate the worth of the goods and services being offered. When money prices are placed on goods and services, their relative value is obvious.

12-1a-3 Store of Value

Money functions as a store of value or purchasing power. If you are paid today, you do not have to hurry out to spend your money. It will still have value next week or next month. Some monies retain their value better than others. In colonial New England, both fish and furs served as money. But because fish does not store as well as furs, its usefulness as a store of value was limited. An important property of a money is its *durability*, its ability to retain its value over time.

Inflation plays a major role in determining the effectiveness of a money as a store of value. The higher the rate of inflation, the faster the purchasing power of money falls. In high-inflation countries, workers spend their pay as quickly as possible because the purchasing power of their money is falling rapidly. It makes no sense to hold on to a money that is quickly losing value. In countries where the domestic money does not serve as a good store of value, it ceases to fulfill this function of money, and people begin to use something else as money, like the currency of another nation. For instance, U.S. dollars have long been a favorite store of value in Latin American countries that have experienced high inflation. This phenomenon—**currency substitution**—has been documented in Argentina, Bolivia, Mexico, and other countries during times of high inflation.

12-1a-4 Standard of Deferred Payment

Finally, money is a standard of deferred payment. Debt obligations are written in terms of money values. If you have a credit card bill that is due in 30 days, the value you owe is stated in monetary units—for example, dollars in the United States and yen in Japan. We use money values to state amounts of debt, and we use money to pay our debts.

We should make a distinction here between money and credit. Money is what we use to pay for goods and services. **Credit** is available savings that are lent to borrowers to spend. If you use your Visa or MasterCard to buy a shirt, you are not buying the shirt with your money. You are taking out a loan from the bank that issued the credit card in order to buy the shirt. Credit and money are different. Money is an asset, something you own. Credit is *debt*, something you owe.

12-1b The U.S. Money Supply

The quantity of money that is available for spending is an important determinant of many key macroeconomic variables, since changes in the money supply affect interest rates, inflation, and other indicators of economic health. When economists measure the money supply,

The use of money as a unit of account lowers information costs.

currency substitution
The use of foreign money as a substitute for domestic money when the domestic economy has a high rate of inflation.

2. How is the U.S. money supply defined?

credit
Available savings that are lent to borrowers to spend.

they measure spendable assets. Identifying those assets, however, can be difficult. Although it would seem that *all* bank deposits are money, some bank deposits are held for spending, while others are held for saving. In defining the money supply, then, economists must differentiate among assets on the basis of their liquidity and the likelihood of their being used for spending.

The problem of distinguishing among assets has produced more than one definition of the money supply. Today in the United States, the Federal Reserve uses M1 and M2.[1] Economists and policymakers use both definitions to evaluate the availability of funds for spending. Although economists have tried to identify a single measure that best influences the business cycle and changes in interest rates and inflation, research indicates that different definitions work better to explain changes in macroeconomic variables at different times.

12-1b-1 M1 Money Supply

M1 money supply

The financial assets that are the most liquid.

transactions account

A checking account at a bank or other financial institution that can be drawn on to make payments.

The narrowest and most liquid measure of the money supply is the **M1 money supply**, or financial assets that are immediately available for spending. This definition emphasizes the use of money as a medium of exchange. The M1 money supply consists of currency held by the nonbank public, traveler's checks, demand deposits, and other checkable deposits. Demand deposits and other checkable deposits are **transactions accounts**; they can be used to make direct payments to a third party.

Surveys find that families use their checking account for about 30 percent of purchases. Cash transactions account for about 44 percent of purchases.

The components of the M1 money supply are used for about 74 percent of family purchases. This is one reason why the M1 money supply may be a useful variable in formulating macroeconomic policy.

* *Currency* includes coins and paper money in circulation (in the hands of the public). In 2014, currency represented 43 percent of the M1 money supply. A common misconception about currency today is that it is backed by gold or silver. This is not true. There is nothing backing the U.S. dollar except the confidence of the public. This kind of monetary system is called a *fiduciary monetary system*. *Fiduciary* comes from the Latin *fiducia*, which means "trust." Our monetary system is based on trust. As long as we believe that our money is an acceptable form of payment for goods and services, the system works. It is not necessary for money to be backed by any precious object. As long as people believe that a money has value, it will serve as money.

    The United States has not always operated under a fiduciary monetary system. At one time, the U.S. government issued gold and silver coins and paper money that could be exchanged for silver. In 1967, Congress authorized the U.S. Treasury to stop redeeming "silver certificate" paper money for silver. Coins with an intrinsic value are known as *commodity money;* they have value as a commodity in addition to their face value. The problem with commodity money is that as the value of the commodity increases, the money stops being circulated. People hoard coins when their commodity value exceeds their face value. For example, no one would take an old $20 gold piece to the grocery store to buy $20 worth of groceries because the gold is worth much more than $20 today.

    The tendency to hoard money when its commodity value increases is called *Gresham's Law*. Thomas Gresham was a successful businessman and financial adviser to Queen Elizabeth I. He insisted that if two coins have the same face value but different intrinsic values—perhaps one coin is silver and the other brass—the cheaper coin will be used in exchange, while the more expensive coin will be hoarded. People sometimes state Gresham's Law as "bad money drives out good money," meaning that the money

---

[1] Until March 2006, the Federal Reserve also published a broader measure of the money supply known as M3.

with the low commodity value will be used in exchange, while the money with the high commodity value will be driven out of hand-to-hand use and be hoarded.[2]

- *Traveler's checks.* Outstanding U.S. dollar–denominated traveler's checks issued by non-bank institutions are counted as part of the M1 money supply. There are several nonbank issuers, among them American Express and Cook's. (Traveler's checks issued by banks are included in demand deposits. When a bank issues its own traveler's checks, it deposits the amount paid by the purchaser in a special account that is used to redeem the checks. Because this amount is counted as part of demand deposits, it is not counted again as part of outstanding traveler's checks.) Traveler's checks account for less than 1 percent of the M1 money supply.

- *Demand deposits.* Demand deposits are checking account deposits at a commercial bank. These deposits pay no interest. They are called *demand deposits* because the bank must pay the amount of the check immediately upon the demand of the depositor. Demand deposits accounted for 39 percent of the M1 money supply in 2014.

- *Other checkable deposits.* Until the 1980s, demand deposits were the only kind of checking account. Today there are many different kinds of checking accounts, known as *other checkable deposits (OCDs)*. These OCDs are accounts at financial institutions that pay interest and also give the depositor check-writing privileges. Among the OCDs included in the M1 money supply are the following:
  - *Negotiable orders of withdrawal (NOW) accounts* are interest-bearing checking accounts offered by savings and loan institutions.
  - *Automatic transfer system (ATS) accounts* are accounts at commercial banks that combine an interest-bearing savings account with a non-interest-bearing checking account. The depositor keeps a small balance in the checking account; any time the checking account balance is overdrawn, funds are automatically transferred from the savings account.
  - *Credit union share draft accounts* are interest-bearing checking accounts that credit unions offer their members.
  - *Demand deposits at mutual savings banks* are checking account deposits at non-profit savings and loan organizations. Any profits after operating expenses have been paid may be distributed to depositors.

12-1b-2 M2 Money Supply The components of the M1 money supply are the most liquid assets, the assets that are most likely to be used for transactions. The **M2 money supply** is a broader definition of the money supply that includes assets in somewhat less liquid forms. The M2 money supply includes the M1 money supply plus savings deposits, small-denomination time deposits, and balances in retail money market mutual funds.

- *Savings deposits* are accounts at banks and savings and loan associations that earn interest but offer no check-writing privileges.
- *Small-denomination time deposits* are often called *certificates of deposit*. Funds in these accounts must be deposited for a specified period of time. (Small means less than $100,000.)
- *Retail money market mutual fund balances* combine the *deposits of many* individuals and invest them in government Treasury bills and other short-term securities. Many money market mutual funds grant check-writing privileges but limit the size and number of checks.

Figure 1 summarizes the two definitions of the money supply.

According to Gresham's Law, bad money drives out good money.

M2 money supply
M1 plus less liquid assets.

---

[2] Actually, Gresham was not the first to recognize that bad money drives out good money. A fourteenth-century French theologian, Nicholas Oresme, made the same argument in his book *A Treatise on the Origin, Nature, Law, and Alterations of Money,* written almost 200 years before Gresham was born.

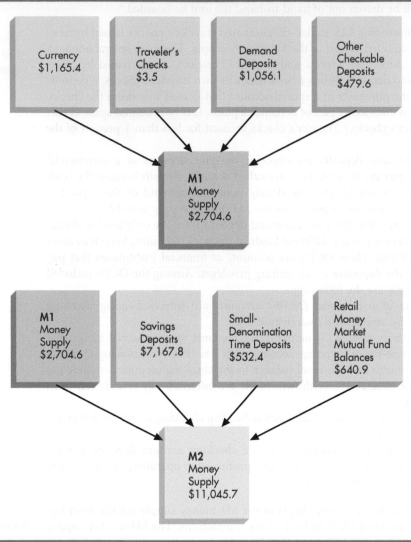

FIGURE 1   The U.S. Money Supply: M1 and M2 (billions of dollars)

12-1c Global Money

3. How do countries pay for international transactions?

So far we have discussed the money supply in a domestic context. Just as the United States uses dollars as its domestic money, every nation has its own monetary unit of account. Japan has the yen, Mexico the peso, Canada the Canadian dollar, and so on. Since each nation uses a different money, how do countries pay for transactions that involve residents of other countries? As you saw in the chapter titled "An Introduction to the Foreign Exchange Market and the Balance of Payments," the foreign exchange market links national monies together so that transactions can be made across national borders. If Target in the United States buys a home entertainment system from Sony in Japan, Target can exchange dollars for yen in order to pay Sony in yen. The exchange rate between the dollar and the yen determines how many dollars are needed to purchase the required number of yen. For instance, if Sony wants 1,000,000 yen for the system and the exchange rate is ¥100 = $1, Target needs $10,000 (1,000,000/100) to buy the yen.

Sales contracts between developed countries usually are written (invoiced) in the national currency of the exporter. To complete the transaction, the importer buys the exporter's currency on the foreign exchange market. Trade between developing and developed nations typically is invoiced in the currency of the developed country, whether the developed country is the exporter or the importer, because the currency of the developed country is usually more stable and more widely traded on the foreign exchange market than the currency of the developing country. As a result, the currencies of the major developed countries tend to dominate the international medium-of-exchange and unit-of-account functions of money.

> *The currencies of the major developed countries tend to dominate the international medium-of-exchange and unit-of-account functions of money.*

12-1c-1 International Reserve Currencies

Governments hold monies as a temporary store of value until money is needed to settle international debts. At one time, gold was the primary **international reserve asset**, an asset used to settle debts between governments. Although gold still serves as an international reserve asset, its role is unimportant relative to that of currencies. Today national currencies function as international reserves. The currencies that are held for this purpose are called **international reserve currencies**.

Table 1 shows the importance of the major international reserve currencies over time. In the mid-1970s, the U.S. dollar made up almost 80 percent of international reserve holdings. By 1990, its share had fallen to less than 50 percent, but that share has risen again recently.

Prior to the euro, there was an artificial currency in Europe, the **European currency unit (ECU)**. The industrial nations of western Europe used ECUs to settle debts between them. The ECU was a **composite currency**; its value was an average of the values of several different national currencies: the Austrian schilling, the Belgian franc, the Danish krone, the Finnish markka, the French franc, the German mark, the Greek drachma, the Irish pound, the Italian lira, the Luxembourg franc, the Netherlands guilder, the Spanish peseta, and the Portuguese escudo (the U.K. pound was withdrawn from the system in September 1992).

The ECU was not an actual money but an accounting entry that was transferred between two parties. It was a step along the way to a new actual money, the *euro*, which replaced the ECU and circulates throughout the member countries as a real European money.

Another composite currency used in international financial transactions is the **special drawing right (SDR)**. The value of the SDR is an average of the values of the currencies of the major industrial countries: the U.S. dollar, the euro, the Japanese yen, and the U.K. pound. This currency was created in 1970 by the International Monetary Fund, an international organization that oversees the monetary relationships among countries. The SDRs are an international reserve asset; they are used to settle international debts by transferring

international reserve asset
An asset used to settle debts between governments.

international reserve currency
A currency held by a government to settle international debts.

European currency unit (ECU)
A unit of account formerly used by Western European nations as their official reserve asset.

composite currency
An artificial unit of account that is an average of the values of several national currencies.

special drawing right (SDR)
A composite currency whose value is the average of the values of the U.S. dollar, the euro, the Japanese yen, and the U.K. pound.

TABLE 1 International Reserve Currencies (Percentage Shares of National Currencies in Total Official Holdings of Foreign Exchange)

Year	U.S. Dollar	Pound Sterling	Deutsche Mark	French Franc	Japanese Yen	Swiss Franc	Netherlands Guilder	Euro	ECU	Unspecified Currencies
1976	78.8	1.0	8.7	1.5	1.9	2.1	0.8	–	–	5.2
1980	56.6	2.5	12.8	1.5	3.7	2.8	1.1	–	16.4	2.7
1990	47.8	2.8	16.5	2.2	7.7	1.2	1.0	–	9.7	11.1
2000	70.5	2.8	–	–	6.3	0.3	–	18.8	–	1.4
2004	65.9	3.3	–	–	3.9	0.2	–	24.9	–	1.9
2008	64.0	4.0	–	–	3.3	0.1	–	26.5	–	2.0
2012	61.9	4.0	–	–	3.9	0.1	–	23.9	–	6.1

Source: Data are drawn from International Monetary Fund, *Annual Report*, various issues.

governments' accounts held at the International Monetary Fund. We discuss the role of the International Monetary Fund in later chapters.

Prior to the actual introduction of the euro, there was much discussion about its potential popularity as a reserve currency. In fact, some analysts were asserting that we should expect the euro to replace the U.S. dollar as the world's dominant currency. As Table 1 shows, the euro is now the second most popular reserve currency, but it has a much lower share of reserve currency use than the dollar does. The dominant world currency evolves over time as business firms and individuals find one currency more useful than another. Prior to the dominance of the dollar, the British pound was the world's most important reserve currency. As the U.S. economy grew in importance and U.S. financial markets developed to the huge size they now are, the growing use of the dollar emerged naturally as a result of the large volume of financial transactions involving the United States. Perhaps over time, the euro will someday replace the dollar as the world's dominant money.

RECAP

1. Money is the most liquid asset.

2. Money serves as a medium of exchange, a unit of account, a store of value, and a standard of deferred payment.

3. The use of money lowers transaction and information costs relative to barter.

4. To be used as money, an asset should be portable, divisible, and durable.

5. The M1 money supply is the most liquid definition of money and equals the sum of currency, traveler's checks, demand deposits, and other checkable deposits.

6. The M2 money supply equals the sum of the M1 money supply, savings deposits, small-denomination time deposits, and retail money market mutual fund balances.

7. International reserve currencies are held by governments to settle international debts.

8. Composite currencies have their value determined as an average of the values of several national currencies.

12-2 Banking

Commercial banks are financial institutions that offer deposits on which checks can be written. In the United States and most other countries, commercial banks are privately owned. *Thrift institutions* are financial institutions that historically offered just savings accounts, not checking accounts. Savings and loan associations, credit unions, and mutual savings banks are all thrift institutions. Prior to 1980, the differences between commercial banks and thrift institutions were much greater than they are today. For example, only commercial banks could offer checking accounts, and those accounts earned no interest. The law also regulated maximum interest rates. In 1980, Congress passed the Depository Institutions Deregulation and Monetary Control Act, in part to stimulate competition among financial institutions. Now thrift institutions and even brokerage houses offer many of the same services as commercial banks. In 1999, Congress passed the Gramm-Leach-Bliley Act, which allowed commercial banks to expand their business into other areas of finance, including insurance and selling securities. This permitted greater integration of financial products under one umbrella known as a financial holding company. During the financial crisis of 2008, some of these large banks suffered dramatically as a result of aggressive risk-taking in financial products that turned out to be unsuccessful.

12-2a Financial Intermediaries

Both commercial banks and thrift institutions are *financial intermediaries*, middlemen between savers and borrowers. Banks accept deposits from individuals and firms, then use those deposits to make loans to individuals and firms. The borrowers are likely to be different individuals or firms from the depositors, although it is not uncommon for a household or business to be both a depositor and a borrower at the same institution. Of course, depositors and borrowers have very different interests. For instance, depositors typically prefer short-term deposits; they don't want to tie up their money for a long time. Borrowers, on the other hand, usually want more time for repayment. Banks typically package short-term deposits into longer-term loans. To function as intermediaries, banks must serve the interests of both depositors and borrowers.

A bank is willing to serve as an intermediary because it hopes to earn a profit from this activity. It pays a lower interest rate on deposits than it charges on loans; the difference is a source of profit for the bank. Islamic banks are prohibited by holy law from charging interest on loans; thus, they use a different system for making a profit (see the Global Business Insight "Islamic Banking").

4. Why are banks considered intermediaries?

12-2b U.S. Banking

12-2b-1 Current Structure If you add together all the pieces of the bar graph in Figure 2, you see that there were 103,271 depository institution offices operating in the United States in 2013. Roughly 90 percent of these offices were operated by banks and 10 percent by savings institutions.

Historically, U.S. banks were allowed to operate in just one state. In some states, banks could operate in only one location. This is known as *unit banking*. Today there are still many unit banks, but these are typically small community banks.

FIGURE 2 U.S. Depository Institutions

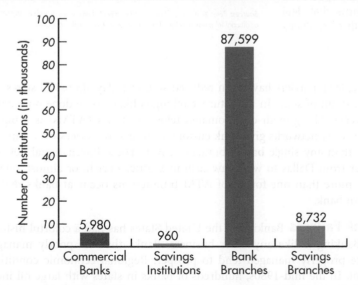

There are many more banks and bank branches than there are savings institutions and savings branches.

Source: Data are drawn from *Federal Deposit Insurance Corporation*, Statistics on Banking; www.fdic.gov.

GLOBAL BUSINESS INSIGHT

Islamic Banking

According to the Muslim holy book, the Koran, Islamic law prohibits interest charges on loans. Banks that operate under Islamic law still act as intermediaries between borrowers and lenders. However, they do not charge interest on loans or pay interest on deposits. Instead, they take a predetermined percentage of the borrowing firm's profits until the loan is repaid, then share those profits with depositors.

Since the mid-1970s, over a hundred Islamic banks have opened, most of them in Arab nations. Deposits in these banks have grown rapidly. In fact, in some banks, deposits have grown faster than good loan opportunities, forcing the banks to refuse new deposits until their loan portfolio could grow to match the available deposits. One bank in Bahrain claimed that over 60 percent of deposits during its first two years in operation were made by people who had never made a bank deposit before. In addition to profit-sharing deposits, Islamic banks typically offer checking accounts, traveler's checks, and trade-related services on a fee basis.

Because the growth of deposits has usually exceeded the growth of local investment opportunities, Islamic banks have been lending money to traditional banks to fund investments that satisfy the moral and commercial needs of both, such as lending to private firms. These funds cannot be used to invest in interest-bearing securities or in firms that deal in alcohol, pork, gambling, or arms. The growth of mutually

profitable investment opportunities suggests that Islamic banks are meeting both the dictates of Muslim depositors and the profitability requirements of modern banking.

The potential for expansion and profitability of Islamic financial services has led major banks to create units dedicated to providing Islamic banking services. In addition, there are stock mutual funds that screen firms for compliance with Islamic law before buying their stock. For instance, since most financial institutions earn and pay large amounts of interest, such firms would tend to be excluded from an Islamic mutual fund.

The most popular instrument for financing Islamic investments is *murabaha*. This is essentially cost-plus financing, where the financial institution purchases goods or services for a client and then, over time, is repaid an amount that equals the original cost plus an additional amount of profit. Such an arrangement is even used for financing mortgages on property in the United States. A financial institution will buy a property and then charge a client rent until the rent payments equal the purchase price plus some profit. After the full payment is received, the title to the property is passed to the client.

Sources: Peter Koh, "The Shari'ah Alternative," *Euromoney* (October 2002). A good source of additional information is found on the website www.failaka.com.

Over time, legal barriers have been reduced so that today almost all states permit entry to banks located out of state. In the future, banking is likely to be done on a national rather than a local scale. The growth of automated teller machines (ATMs) is a big step in this direction. The ATM networks give bank customers access to services over a much wider geographic area than any single bank's branches cover. These international networks allow a bank customer from Dallas to withdraw cash in Seattle, Zurich, or almost anywhere in the world. Today more than one-fourth of ATM transactions occur at banks that are not the customer's own bank.

12-2b-2 Bank Failures Banking in the United States has had a colorful history of booms and panics. Banking is like any other business. Banks that are poorly managed can fail; banks that are properly managed tend to prosper. Regional economic conditions are also very important. In the mid-1980s, hundreds of banks in states with large oil industries, like Texas and Oklahoma, and in farming states, like Kansas and Nebraska, could not collect many of their loans as a result of falling oil and agricultural prices. Those states that were heavily dependent on the oil industry and on farming had significantly more banks fail than did other states. The problem was not so much bad management as it was a matter of unexpectedly bad business conditions. The lesson here is simple: Commercial banks, like other profit-making enterprises, are not exempt from failure.

At one time, a bank panic could close a bank. A bank panic occurs when depositors, fearing that a bank will close, rush to withdraw their funds. Banks keep only a fraction of their deposits on reserve, so bank panics often resulted in bank closings as depositors tried to withdraw more money than the banks had on hand on a given day. In the United States today, this is no longer true. The **Federal Deposit Insurance Corporation (FDIC)** was created in 1933. The FDIC is a federal agency that insures bank deposits in commercial banks so that depositors do not lose their deposits if a bank fails. FDIC insurance covers depositors against losses up to $250,000 in a bank account. Figure 3 shows the number of failed banks. In the 1930s, many of the banks that failed were not insured by the FDIC. In this environment, it made sense for depositors to worry about losing their money. In the 1980s, the number of bank failures increased dramatically, but none of the failed banks were uninsured. Deposits in those banks were protected by the federal government. Even though large banks have failed in recent times, the depositors have not lost their deposits.

Figure 3 shows a rise in the number of bank failures associated with the financial crisis of 2008 (which actually began in 2007). We see that from 0 bank failures in 2006, there were 1 in 2007, 23 in 2008, 126 in 2009, and peaking at 132 in 2010. The financial crisis resulted in many banks experiencing large losses on loans due to businesses and households who were unable to repay their debts.

Deposit insurance exists today in most of the world's countries. Africa is the only continent where deposit insurance is not found widely. Looking at the countries that are neighbors of the United States, Canada insures deposits up to 100,000 Canadian dollars (worth about 91,066 U.S. dollars at the time this text was revised), while Mexico insures deposits up to 1,567,000 pesos (worth about 118,000 U.S. dollars at the time this text was revised).

A bank panic occurs when depositors become frightened and rush to withdraw their funds.

Federal Deposit Insurance Corporation (FDIC)
A federal agency that insures deposits in commercial banks.

FIGURE 3 **Number of Failed Banks**

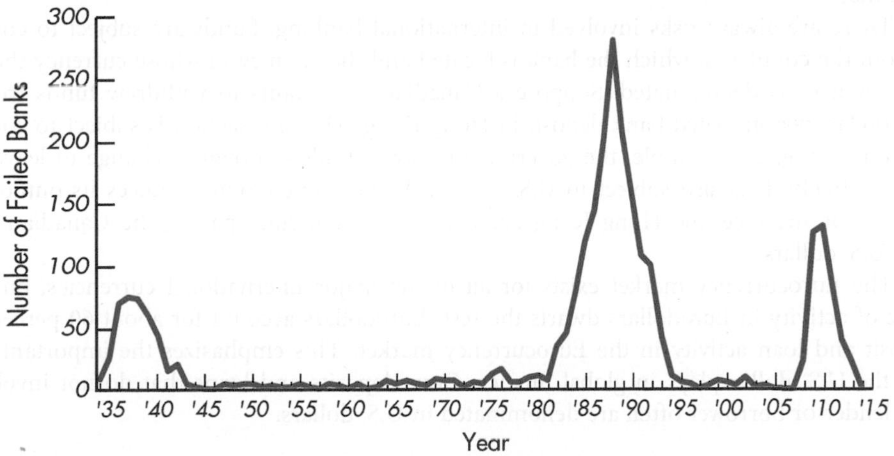

The number of banks that went out of business in the 1980s was the highest it had been since the Depression. Unlike the banks that failed in the 1930s, however, the banks that closed in the 1980s and 2000s were covered by deposit insurance, so depositors did not lose their money.

Source: Data are from *Federal Deposit Insurance Corporation, Statistics on Banking;* www.fdic.gov.

12-2c International Banking

5. How does international banking differ from domestic banking?

Large banks today are truly transnational enterprises. International banks, like domestic banks, act as financial intermediaries, but they operate in a different legal environment. The laws regulating domestic banking in each nation are typically very restrictive, yet many nations allow international banking to operate largely unregulated. Because they are not hampered by regulations, international banks typically can offer depositors and borrowers better terms than could be negotiated at a domestic bank.

12-2c-1 Eurocurrency Market

Eurocurrency market or offshore banking

The market for deposits and loans generally denominated in a currency other than the currency of the country in which the transaction occurs.

Because of the competitive interest rates offered on loans and deposits, there is a large market for deposits and loans at international banks. For instance, a bank in London, Tokyo, or the Bahamas may accept deposits and make loans denominated in U.S. dollars. The international deposit and loan market often is called the **Eurocurrency market**, or **offshore banking**. In the Eurocurrency market, the currency used in a banking transaction generally is not the domestic currency of the country in which the bank is located. (The prefix "Euro-" is misleading here. Although the market originated in Europe, today it is global and operates with different foreign currencies; it is in no way limited to European currencies or European banks.) There are deposits and loans in Eurodollars, Euroyen, Euroeuro, and any other major currency.

In those countries that allow offshore banking, we find two sets of banking rules: restrictive regulations for banking in the domestic market, and little or no regulation for offshore banking activities. Domestic banks are required to hold reserves against deposits and to carry deposit insurance, and they often face government-mandated credit or interest rate restrictions. The Eurocurrency market operates with few or no costly restrictions, and international banks generally pay lower taxes than domestic banks. Because offshore banks operate with lower costs, they are able to offer their customers better terms than domestic banks can.

Offshore banks are able to offer a higher rate on dollar deposits and a lower rate on dollar loans than their domestic competitors. Without these differences, the Eurodollar market probably would not exist because Eurodollar transactions are riskier than domestic transactions in the United States as a result of the lack of government regulation and deposit insurance.

There are always risks involved in international banking. Funds are subject to control by both the country in which the bank is located and the country in whose currency the deposit or loan is denominated. Suppose a Canadian firm wants to withdraw funds from a U.S. dollar–denominated bank deposit in Hong Kong. This transaction is subject to control in Hong Kong. For example, the government may not allow foreign exchange to leave the country freely. It is also subject to U.S. control. If the United States reduces its outflow of dollars, for instance, the Hong Kong bank may have difficulty paying the Canadian firm with U.S. dollars.

The Eurocurrency market exists for all of the major international currencies, but the value of activity in Eurodollars dwarfs the rest. Eurodollars account for about 60 percent of deposit and loan activity in the Eurocurrency market. This emphasizes the important role that the U.S. dollar plays in global finance. Even deposits and loans that do not involve a U.S. lender or borrower often are denominated in U.S. dollars.

12-2c-2 International Banking Facilities

The term *offshore banking is* somewhat misleading in the United States today. Prior to December 1981, U.S. banks were forced to process international deposits and loans through their offshore branches. Many of the branches in places like the Cayman Islands and the Bahamas were little more than "shells," small offices with a telephone. Yet these branches allowed U.S. banks to avoid the reserve requirements and interest rate regulations that restricted domestic banking activities.

In December 1981, the Federal Reserve Board legalized **international banking facilities (IBFs)**, allowing domestic banks to take part in international banking on U.S. soil. The IBFs are not physical entities; they are bookkeeping systems set up in existing bank offices to record international banking transactions. The IBFs can receive deposits from and make loans to nonresidents of the United States and other IBFs.. These deposits and loans must be kept separate from other transactions because IBFs are not subject to the reserve requirements, interest rate regulations, or FDIC deposit insurance premiums that apply to domestic U.S. banking. The goal of permitting IBFs was to allow banking offices in the United States to compete with offshore banks without having to use offshore banking offices.

international banking facility (IBF)
A division of a U.S. bank that is allowed to receive deposits from and make loans to nonresidents of the United States without the restrictions that apply to domestic U.S. banks.

12-2d Informal Financial Markets in Developing Countries

In many developing countries, a sizable portion of the population has no access to formal financial institutions like banks. In these cases, it is common for informal financial markets to develop. Such markets may take many different forms. Sometimes they take the form of an individual making small loans to local residents. Sometimes groups of individuals form a self-help group where they pool their resources to provide loans to each other. To give some idea of the nature of these sorts of arrangements, a few common types are reviewed here.

A common form of informal financial arrangement is rotating savings and associations, or **ROSCAs**. These tend to go by different names in different countries, such as *tandas* in Mexico, *susu* in Ghana, *hui* in China, and *chits* in India. ROSCAs are like savings clubs; members contribute money every week or month into a common fund, and then each month one member of the group receives the full amount contributed by everyone. This usually operates for a cycle of as many months as there are members in the group. For instance, if there are 12 members in the group contributing $10 a month, then a cycle would last 12 months, and each month a different member of the group would receive the $120 available. Thus the ROSCA is a vehicle for saving in which only the last member of the group to receive the funds has saved over the full 12-month period before having the use of $120. The determination of who receives the funds in which month is typically made by a random drawing at the beginning of the cycle. So a ROSCA is a means of saving that allows all but one member in each cycle to receive funds faster than the members could save on their own.

ROSCA
A rotating savings and credit association popular in developing countries.

The informal market in many countries is dominated by individual lenders, who tend to specialize in a local area and make loans primarily for the acquisition of seeds, fertilizer, or mechanical equipment needed by farmers. Surveys in China indicate that about two-thirds of farm loans to poor rural households are made by informal lenders. Such informal lenders are distinct from friends and relatives, who can also be important in lending to poor households. The interest rate charged by informal lenders is typically significantly higher than that charged by banks or government lending institutions. The higher interest rates may reflect the higher risk associated with the borrower, who may have no collateral (goods or possessions that can be transferred to the lender if the borrower does not repay).

Informal loans among friends or relatives are typically one-time loans for purposes like financing weddings or home construction. If your cousin lends you money today in your time of need, then you are expected to lend to him at some later time if he has a need. Repeat loans, like those to a farmer in advance of the harvest each year, tend to be made by individuals who are unrelated to the borrower and are in the business of providing such financing.

A form of informal financial market that gained much publicity after the September 11, 2001, terrorist attacks on New York City's World Trade Center is the **hawala** network. In much of the developing world with heavy Muslim populations, people can send money all over the world using the hawala network. Let us say that a Pakistani immigrant who is working as a taxi driver in New York wants to send money to a relative in a remote village of

hawala
An international informal financial market used by Muslims.

Pakistan. He can go to a hawala agent and give the money to the agent, who writes down the destination location and the amount of money to be sent. The agent then gives the taxi driver a code number and the location of an agent in Pakistan, which the driver passes along to his relative. The agent in the United States then calls a counterpart agent in Pakistan and informs that person of the amount of money and the code number. The Pakistani agent will pay the money to whoever walks in his door with the right code number. Since no records of the name or address of either the source of the money or the recipient are kept, it is easy to see how such a network can be an effective source of financing for terrorist activities. For this reason, the hawala network was a source of much investigation following the 2001 terrorist attacks in the United States. Of course, such a network serves many more than just terrorists, and it is an important part of the informal financial market operating in many countries. For poor people without bank accounts, such informal markets allow some access to financial services.

RECAP

1. The Depository Institutions Deregulation and Monetary Control Act (1980) eliminated many of the differences between commercial banks and thrift institutions.

2. Banks are financial intermediaries.

3. The deregulation act also eliminated many of the differences between national and state banks.

4. Since the FDIC insures bank deposits in commercial banks, bank panics are no longer a threat to the banking system.

5. The international deposit and loan market is called the Eurocurrency market or offshore banking.

6. With the legalization of international banking facilities in 1981, the Federal Reserve allowed international banking activities on U.S. soil.

7. Informal financial markets play an important role in developing countries.

12-3 Banks and the Money Supply

fractional reserve banking system
A system in which banks keep less than 100 percent of their deposits available for withdrawal.

Banks create money by lending money. They take deposits, then lend a portion of those deposits in order to earn interest income. The portion of their deposits that banks keep on hand is a *reserve* to meet the demand for withdrawals. In a **fractional reserve banking system**, banks keep less than 100 percent of their deposits as reserves. If all banks hold 10 percent of their deposits as a reserve, for example, then 90 percent of their deposits are available for loans. When they loan these deposits, money is created.

12-3a Deposits and Loans

Figure 4 shows a simple balance sheet for First National Bank. A *balance sheet* is a financial statement that records a firm's assets (what the firm owns) and liabilities (what the firm owes). The bank has cash assets ($100,000) and loan assets ($900,000). The deposits placed in the bank ($1,000,000) are a liability (they are an asset of the depositors).[3] Total assets always equal total liabilities on a balance sheet.

Banks keep a percentage of their deposits on reserve. In the United States, the reserve requirement is set by the Federal Reserve Board (which will be discussed in detail in the next chapter). Banks can keep more than the minimum reserve if they choose. Let us assume that

6. How do banks create money?

---

[3] In our simplified balance sheet, we assume that there is no net worth, or owner's equity. Net worth is the value of the owner's claim on the firm (the owner's equity) and is found as the difference between the value of assets and the value of nonequity liabilities.

FIGURE 4 First National Bank Balance Sheet, Initial Position

First National Bank

Assets		Liabilities	
Cash	$ 100,000	Deposits	$1,000,000
Loans	900,000		
Total	$1,000,000	Total	$1,000,000

Total reserves = $100,000

Required reserves = 0.1($1,000,000) = $100,000

Excess reserves = 0

The bank has cash totaling $100,000 and loans totaling $900,000, for total assets of $1,000,000. Deposits of $1,000,000 make up its total liabilities. With a reserve requirement of 10 percent, the bank must hold required reserves of 10 percent of its deposits, or $100,000. Because the bank is holding cash of $100,000, its total reserves equal its required reserves. Because it has no excess reserves, the bank cannot make new loans

the reserve requirement is set at 10 percent and that banks always hold actual reserves equal to 10 percent of deposits. With deposits of $1,000,000, the bank must keep $100,000 (0.1 × $1,000,000) in cash reserves held its vault. This $100,000 is the bank's **required reserves**, as the Federal Reserve requires the banks to keep 10 percent of deposits on reserve. This is exactly what First National Bank has on hand in Figure 4. Any cash held in excess of $100,000 would represent **excess reserves**. Excess reserves can be loaned by the bank. A bank is *loaned up* when it has zero excess reserves. Because its total reserves equal its required reserves, First National Bank has no excess reserves and is loaned up. The bank cannot make any new loans.

What happens if the bank receives a new deposit of $100,000? Figure 5 shows the bank's balance sheet right after the deposit is made. Its cash reserves are now $200,000, and its

required reserves
The cash reserves (a percentage of deposits) that a bank must keep on hand or on deposit with the Federal Reserve.

excess reserves
The cash reserves beyond those required, which can be loaned.

FIGURE 5 First National Bank Balance Sheet after $100,000 Deposit

First National Bank

Assets		Liabilities	
Cash	$ 200,000	Deposits	$1,100,000
Loans	900,000		
Total	$1,1000,000	Total	$1,100,000

Total reserves = $200,000

Required reserves = 0.1($1,000,000) = $110,000

Excess reserves = $90,000

A $100,000 deposit increases the bank's cash reserves to $200,000 and its deposits to $1,100,000. The bank must hold 10 percent of deposits, or $110,000, on reserve. The difference between total reserves ($200,000) and required reserves ($110,000) is excess reserves ($90,000). The bank now has $90,000 available for lending.

deposits are now $1,100,000. With the additional deposit, the bank's total reserves equal $200,000. Its required reserves are $110,000 (0.1 × $1,100,000). So its excess reserves are $90,000 ($200,000 − $110,000). Since a bank can lend its excess reserves, First National Bank can loan an additional $90,000.

Suppose the bank lends someone $90,000 by depositing $90,000 in the borrower's First National account. At the time the loan is made, the money supply increases by the amount of the loan, $90,000. By making the loan, the bank has increased the money supply. But this is not the end of the story. The borrower spends the $90,000, and it winds up being deposited in the Second National Bank.

Figure 6 shows the balance sheets of both banks after the loan has been made and the money has been spent and deposited at Second National Bank. First National Bank now has loans of $990,000 and no excess reserves (the required reserves of $110,000 equal total reserves). So First National Bank can make no more loans until a new deposit is made. However, Second National Bank has a new deposit of $90,000 (to simplify the analysis, we assume that this is the first transaction at Second National Bank). Its required reserves are 10 percent of $90,000, or $9,000. With total reserves of $90,000, Second National Bank has excess reserves of $81,000. It can make loans up to $81,000.

Notice what has happened to the banks' deposits as a result of the initial $100,000 deposit in First National Bank. Deposits at First National Bank have increased by $100,000.

FIGURE 6   Balance Sheets after a $90,000 Loan Made by First National Bank Is Spent and Deposited at Second National Bank

First National Bank

Assets		Liabilities	
Cash	$ 110,000	Deposits	$1,100,000
Loans	990,000		
Total	$1,100,000	Total	$1,100,000

Total reserves = $110,000

Required reserves = 0.1($1,100,000) = $110,000

Excess reserves = 0

Second National Bank

Assets		Liabilities	
Cash	$90,000	Deposits	$90,000
Total	$90,000	Total	$90,000

Total reserves = $90,000

Required reserves = 0.1($90,000) = $9,000

Excess reserves = $81,000

Once First National Bank makes the $90,000 loan, its cash reserves fall to $110,000 and its loans increase to $990,000. At this point, the bank's total reserves ($110,000) equal its required reserves (10 percent of deposits). Because it has no excess reserves, the bank cannot make new loans. Second National Bank receives a deposit of $90,000. It must hold 10 percent, or $9,000, on reserve. Its excess reserves equal total reserves ($90,000) minus required reserves ($9,000), or $81,000. Second National Bank can make a maximum loan of $81,000.

Second National Bank has a new deposit of $90,000, and the loans it makes will increase the money supply even more. Table 2 shows how the initial deposit of $100,000 is multiplied through the banking system. Each time a new loan is made, the money is spent and redeposited in the banking system. But each bank keeps 10 percent of the deposit on reserve, lending only 90 percent. So the amount of money loaned decreases by 10 percent each time it goes through another bank. If we carried the calculations out, you would see that the total increase in deposits associated with the initial $100,000 deposit is $1,000,000. Required reserves would increase by $100,000, and new loans would increase by $900,000.

12-3b Deposit Expansion Multiplier

Rather than calculate the excess reserves at each bank, as we did in Table 2, we can use a simple formula to find the maximum increase in deposits given a new deposit. The **deposit expansion multiplier** equals the reciprocal of the reserve requirement:

deposit expansion multiplier
The reciprocal of the reserve requirement.

$$\text{Deposit expansion multiplier} = \frac{1}{\text{reserve requirement}}$$

In our example, the reserve requirement is 10 percent, or 0.1. So the deposit expansion multiplier equals 1/0.1, or 10. An initial increase in deposits of $100,000 expands deposits in the banking system by 10 times $100,000, or $1,000,000. This is because the new $100,000 deposit creates $90,000 in excess reserves and $10 \times \$90,000 = \$900,000$, which when added to the initial deposit of $100,000 equals $1,000,000. The maximum increase in deposits is found by multiplying the deposit expansion multiplier by the amount of the new deposit.

With no new deposits, the banking system can increase the money supply only by the multiplier times excess reserves:

$$\text{Deposit expansion multiplier} \times \text{excess reserves} = \text{maximum increase in deposits}$$

The deposit expansion multiplier indicates the *maximum* possible change in total deposits when a new deposit is made. For the effect to be that large, all excess reserves must be loaned out, and all of the money that is deposited must stay in the banking system.

If banks hold more reserves than the minimum required, they lend a smaller fraction of any new deposits, and this reduces the effect of the deposit expansion multiplier. For instance, if the reserve requirement is 10 percent, we know that the deposit expansion

TABLE 2 The Effect on Bank Deposits of an Initial Bank Deposit of $100,000

Bank	New Deposit	Required Reserves	Excess Reserves (new loans)
First National	$ 100,000	$ 10,000	$ 90,000
Second National	90,000	9,000	81,000
Third National	81,000	8,100	72,900
Fourth National	72,900	7,290	65,610
Fifth National	65,610	6,561	59,049
Sixth National	59,049	5,905	53,144
...	...	...	...
Total	$1,000,000	$100,000	$900,000

A single bank increases the money supply by lending its excess reserves; the banking system increases the money supply by the deposit expansion multiplier times the excess reserves of the system.

NOW YOU TRY IT

What is the deposit expansion multiplier if the reserve requirement is each of the following?

a. 5 percent
b. 25 percent
c. 33 percent
d. 50 percent

multiplier is 10. If a bank chooses to hold 20 percent of its deposits on reserve, the deposit expansion multiplier is only 5 (1/.20).

If money (currency and coin) is withdrawn from the banking system and kept as cash, deposits and bank reserves are smaller, and there is less money to loan out. This *currency drain*—removal of money—reduces the deposit expansion multiplier. The greater the currency drain, the smaller the multiplier. There is always some currency drain, as people carry currency to pay for day-to-day transactions. However, during historical periods of bank panic, where people lost confidence in banks, large currency withdrawals contributed to declines in the money supply.

Remember that the deposit expansion multiplier measures the *maximum* expansion of the money supply by the banking system. Any single bank can lend only its excess reserves, but the whole banking system can expand the money supply by a multiple of the initial excess reserves. Thus, the banking system as a whole can increase the money supply by the deposit expansion multiplier times the excess reserves of the system. The initial bank is limited to its initial loan; the banking system generates loan after loan based on that initial loan. A new deposit can increase the money supply by the deposit expansion multiplier times the new deposit.

In the next chapter, we discuss how changes in the reserve requirement affect the money supply and the economy. This area of policymaking is controlled by the Federal Reserve.

R E C A P

1. The fractional reserve banking system allows banks to expand the money supply by making loans.

2. Banks must keep a fraction of their deposits on reserve; their excess reserves are available for lending.

3. The deposit expansion multiplier measures the maximum increase in the money supply given a new deposit; it is the reciprocal of the reserve requirement.

4. A single bank increases the money supply by lending its excess reserves.

5. The banking system can increase the money supply by the deposit expansion multiplier times the excess reserves in the banking system.

SUMMARY

1. What is money?

- Money is anything that is generally acceptable to sellers in exchange for goods and services. §12-1

- Money serves as a medium of exchange, a unit of account, a store of value, and a standard of deferred payment. §12-1a

- Money, because it is more efficient than barter, lowers transaction costs. §12-1a

- Money should be portable, divisible, and durable. §12-1a

2. How is the U.S. money supply defined?

- There are two definitions of money based on its liquidity. §12-1b

- The M1 money supply equals the sum of currency plus traveler's checks plus demand deposits plus other checkable deposits. §12-1b

- The M2 money supply equals the M1 money supply plus savings deposits, small-denomination time deposits, and retail money market mutual fund balances. §12-1b

3. How do countries pay for international transactions?

- Using the foreign exchange market, governments (along with individuals and firms) are able to convert national currencies to pay for trade. *§12-1c*
- The U.S. dollar is the world's major international reserve currency. *§12-1c*
- The European currency unit (ECU) was a composite currency whose value was an average of the values of several Western European currencies. *§12-1c*

4. Why are banks considered intermediaries?

- Banks serve as middlemen between savers and borrowers. *§12-2a*

5. How does international banking differ from domestic banking?

- Domestic banking in most nations is strictly regulated; international banking is not. *§12-2c*
- The Eurocurrency market is the international deposit and loan market. *§12-2c*

- International banking facilities (IBFs) allow U.S. domestic banks to carry on international banking activities on U.S. soil. *§12-2c*
- Informal financial markets are important in developing countries. *§12-2d*

6. How do banks create money?

- Banks can make loans up to the amount of their excess reserves, their total reserves minus their required reserves. *§12-3a*
- The deposit expansion multiplier is the reciprocal of the reserve requirement. *§12-3b*
- A single bank expands the money supply by lending its excess reserves. *§12-3b*
- The banking system can increase the money supply by the deposit expansion multiplier times the excess reserves in the system. *§12-3*

KEY TERMS

composite currency, 261
credit, 257
currency substitution, 260
deposit expansion multiplier, 271
Eurocurrency market, or offshore banking, 266
European currency unit (ECU), 261
excess reserves, 269

Federal Deposit Insurance Corporation (FDIC), 265
fractional reserve banking system, 268
hawala, 267
international banking facility (IBF), 267
international reserve asset, 261
international reserve currency, 261

liquid asset, 256
M1 money supply, 258
M2 money supply, 259
money, 256
required reserves, 269
ROSCA, 267
special drawing right (SDR), 261
transactions accounts, 258

EXERCISES

1. Describe the four functions of money, using the U.S. dollar to provide an example of how dollars serve each function.
2. During World War II, cigarettes were used as money in prisoner of war camps. Considering the attributes that a good money should possess, why would cigarettes emerge as money among prisoners?
3. What is a financial intermediary? Give an example of how your bank or credit union serves as a financial intermediary between you and the rest of the economy.
4. What is the Eurocurrency market, and how is banking in the Eurocurrency market different from domestic banking?

5. What are IBFs? Why do you think they were legalized?
6. First Bank has cash reserves of $200,000, loans of $800,000, and deposits of $1,000,000.
   a. Prepare a balance sheet for the bank.
   b. If the bank maintains a reserve requirement of 15 percent, what is the largest loan it can make?
   c. What is the maximum amount by which the money supply can be increased as a result of First Bank's new loan?
   d. If the reserve requirement is reduced to 12 per cent, how much more can the bank lend? How much more can the money supply be increased?

7. Yesterday Bank A had no excess reserves. Today it received a new deposit of $4,000.
   a. If the bank maintains a reserve requirement of 2 percent, what is the maximum loan that Bank A can make?
   b. What is the maximum amount by which the money supply can be increased as a result of Bank A's new loan?
8. "M2 is a better definition of the money supply than M1." Agree or disagree with this statement. In your argument, clearly state the criteria on which you are basing your decision.
9. The deposit expansion multiplier measures the maximum possible expansion of the money supply in the banking system. What factors could cause the actual expansion of the money supply to differ from that given by the deposit expansion multiplier?
10. What is liquidity? Rank the following assets in order of their liquidity: $10 bill, personal check for $20, savings account with $400 in it, stereo, car, house, traveler's check.

Use the following table on the components of money in a hypothetical economy to do exercises 11 and 12.

Money Component	Amount
Traveler's checks	$ 100
Currency	$ 2,500
Small-denomination time deposits	$ 2,500
Savings deposits	$ 6,000
Demand deposits	$ 5,000
Other checkable deposits	$ 9,000
Retail money market mutual funds	$ 7,500

11. What is the value of M1 in the preceding table?
12. What is the value of M2 in the preceding table?
13. The deposit expansion multiplier has been defined as the reciprocal of the reserve requirement. Suppose that banks must hold 10 percent of their deposits in reserve. However, banks also lose 10 percent of their deposits through cash drains out of the banking system.
    a. What would the deposit expansion multiplier be if there were no cash drain?
    b. With the cash drain, what is the value of the deposit expansion multiplier?

ECONOMICALLY SPEAKING
INTERNATIONAL DEMAND FOR THE DOLLAR

Because of its relative stability and near-universal recognition and acceptance, USD [U.S. dollars] function as both a store of value and a medium of exchange when other stable or convenient assets (for example, national currencies) are not available. Thus, during times of economic or political crisis, a stable and familiar currency, such as USD, often is sought as a portable and liquid hedge against possible devaluation. Similarly, USD are a popular medium of exchange in regional or cross-border trade when credit markets are undeveloped or banks are underdeveloped or unreliable.

U.S. currency in the form of banknotes (paper currency) in circulation outside the U.S. Treasury and the Federal Reserve System was about $759 billion by the end of 2005. Current estimates indicate that the proportion of U.S. currency held abroad is as much as 60 percent of the amount in circulation, or roughly $450 billion. The accompanying table shows the total amount of U.S. banknotes in circulation as well as the share attributed to the $100 denomination. In value terms, the share of USD held as $100s has increased from around 21 percent at the end of 1965 to nearly 72 percent at the end of 2005. In addition, the share of $100 notes estimated to be held outside the United States has also increased. As shown in the right-hand column of the table, the share of $100 notes held outside the United States rose sharply over the period from 1975 to 1995 and then remained relatively stable at around two-thirds of all $100 notes since 1999.

The international circulation of U.S. currency in Europe expanded after World War I in the wake of the hyperinflation induced by the obligations arising from the Treaty of Versailles. At that time, U.S. currency was viewed favorably because the United States was still on the gold standard, while Great Britain, whose currency was the leading alternative to U.S. currency, remained off the gold standard until May 1925. Other countries, such as Panama, adopted U.S. currency as their official currency. In the past two decades, the international usage of U.S. banknotes expanded largely because of two events: the breakup of the Soviet Union and episodes of high and volatile inflation in Latin America.

During a period of instability, the magnitude of the inflows of U.S. banknotes depends on a country's experience with U.S. currency in the past and its economic circumstances. In particular, demand for USD appears to depend on two factors. The first factor is the ability of people to purchase U.S. banknotes, and the second factor is their confidence in the domestic banking system. The less confidence people have that the value of their bank holdings will be protected, the more likely they are to want to hold U.S. banknotes. Similarly, the more developed the banking system, the more likely it is that people will have a wide variety of options for saving and for making transactions.

Because many holders of U.S. currency view it as a form of insurance against future instability, they are reluctant to alter their usage patterns for USD during periods of economic stability by either shifting out of U.S. banknotes or by switching to another currency, such as the euro. Since the introduction of euro banknotes in the beginning of 2002, it appeared that demand for USD waned somewhat in countries in and near the eurozone. However, responses to International Currency Awareness Program (ICAP) team inquiries indicated that USD holders have moved to holding euros in addition to, rather than instead of, USD. It is likely that underlying patterns of U.S. currency usage will change slowly in countries that already use USD. In countries that do not now use USD to a significant degree, it is difficult to predict if and when a crisis prompting demand for a second currency might develop.

Source: U.S. Treasury Dept., The Use and Counterfeiting of U.S. Currency Abroad, Part 3, Section 1.3, 2006. http://www.federalreserve.gov/boarddocs/rptcongress/counterfeit/counterfeit2006.pdf.

TABLE 3 U.S. Banknotes in Circulation, $100s in Circulation, and $100s Held Abroad (Billions of Dollars, Except as Noted, at Year-Ends)

Year	(1) Total	(2) $100s	(3) Share of $100s in Total (percent)	(4) Estimates of $100s Held Abroad, Wholesale	(5) Estimates of Share of $100s Held Abroad Wholesale (percent)
1965	38.0	8.1	21.4	3.9	48.3
1970	50.8	12.1	23.8	5.7	47.5
1975	77.6	23.1	29.8	10.0	43.2
1980	124.8	49.3	39.5	23.8	48.4
1985	182.0	81.2	44.6	45.8	56.4
1990	268.2	140.2	52.3	85.7	61.1
1995	401.5	241.5	60.2	169.2	70.1
1999	601.2	386.2	64.2	254.6	65.9
2000	563.9	377.7	67.0	256.0	67.7
2001	611.7	421.0	68.8	279.8	66.4
2002	654.8	458.7	70.1	301.3	65.7
2003	690.2	487.8	70.7	317.9	65.2
2004	719.9	516.7	71.8	332.7	64.4
2005	758.8	545.0	71.8	352.0	64.6
2010	914.1	684.8	74.9	389.8	56.9
2013	1,134.7	874.6	77.1	481.3	55

Source: Columns 1 and 2: *Treasury Bulletin,* various issues, Table USCC-2. Figures include vault cash but exclude coin. Column 4: Federal Reserve Board Flow of Funds Accounts (Z.1. Statistical Release, Table L. 204, line 22).

COMMENTARY

There is considerable evidence that U.S. dollars are held in large amounts in many developing countries. Residents of these countries hold dollars because their domestic inflation rate is (or has been) very high, and by holding dollars, they can avoid the rapid erosion of purchasing power that is associated with holding the domestic currency. This "dollarization" of a country begins with people's holding dollars rather than domestic currency as savings (the store-of-value function of money). But if high inflation continues, dollars, rather than domestic currency, come to be used in day-to-day transactions as the medium of exchange. In the late 1980s, as the Polish economy became heavily dollarized, a common joke in Poland was: "What do America and Poland have in common? In America, you can buy everything for dollars and nothing for zlotys [the Polish currency]. In Poland, it is exactly the same." In 2009, one could have made the same comment about Zimbabwe, where the economy was officially dollarized after hyperinflation that eventually led to the issue of a 100 trillion Zimbabwe dollar bill. These were soon selling on eBay for less than 1 U.S. dollar each.

One implication of the demand for dollars in developing countries is that dollar currency leaves the United States. This currency drain will affect the size of the deposit expansion multiplier. In the chapter, the deposit expansion multiplier was defined as

$$\text{Deposit expansion multiplier} = \frac{1}{\text{reserve requirement}}$$

This definition was based on the assumption that when a bank receives a deposit, all of the deposit will be loaned except for the fraction that the bank is required to keep as the legal reserve requirement set by the Federal Reserve. With a currency drain, some of the deposit is withdrawn from the banking system as cash. As a result, the deposit expansion multiplier is now

$$\text{Deposit expansion multiplier} = \frac{1}{\text{reserve requirement} + \text{currency drain}}$$

For instance, if the reserve requirement equals 10 percent, our original definition of the deposit expansion multiplier would provide a multiplier equal to $1/.10 = 10$. But if people withdraw 10 percent of their deposits as cash, then the 10 percent currency drain is added to the 10 percent reserve requirement to yield a deposit expansion multiplier of $1/.20 = 5$. So the larger the currency drain, the smaller the money-creating potential of the banking system.

An additional interesting aspect of the foreign demand for dollars is the *seigniorage*, or revenue earned by the government from creating money. If it costs about 7 cents to print a dollar bill, but the exchange value is a dollar's worth of goods and services, then the government earns about 93 cents for each dollar put into circulation. If foreigners hold U.S. currency, then the government earns a profit from providing a stable-valued dollar that people want to hold. However, we should not overestimate the value of this in terms of the U.S. government budget. Even if all the new currency issued by the U.S. government flowed out to the rest of the world, the seigniorage earned by the United States over the past decade would have averaged less than 1.7 percent of federal government revenue. Given the relatively insignificant revenue earned from seigniorage, it is not surprising that U.S. policy with regard to the dollarization of developing countries has largely been one of disinterest.

CHAPTER 13
Monetary Policy

FUNDAMENTAL QUESTIONS

1. What does the Federal Reserve do?

2. How is monetary policy set?

3. What are the tools of monetary policy?

4. What role do central banks play in the foreign exchange market?

5. What are the determinants of the demand for money?

6. How does monetary policy affect the equilibrium level of real GDP?

Preview

In the previous chapter, we saw how banks "create" money by making loans. However, that money must get into the system to begin with. Most of us never think about how money enters the economy. All we worry about is having money available when we need it. But there is a government body that controls the U.S. money supply, and in this chapter we will learn about this agency—the Federal Reserve System and the Board of Governors that oversees monetary policy.

The amount of money that is available for spending by individuals or businesses affects prices, interest rates, foreign exchange rates, and the level of income in the economy. Thus, having control of the money supply gives the Federal Reserve powerful

277

influence over these important economic variables. As we learned in the chapter titled "Fiscal Policy," the control of government spending and taxes is one of two ways by which government can change the equilibrium level of real GDP.

Monetary policy as carried out by the Federal Reserve is the other mechanism through which attempts are made to manage the economy. In this chapter we will also explore the tools of monetary policy and see how changes in the money supply affect the equilibrium level of real GDP.

13-1 The Federal Reserve System

The Federal Reserve is the central bank of the United States. A *central bank* performs several functions: accepting deposits from and making loans to commercial banks, acting as a banker for the federal government, and controlling the money supply. We discuss these functions in greater detail later on, but first we look at the structure of the Federal Reserve System, or the Fed.

1. What does the Federal Reserve do?

13-1a Structure of the Fed

Congress created the Federal Reserve System in 1913, through the Federal Reserve Act. Bank panics and failures had convinced lawmakers that the United States needed an agency that could control the money supply and make loans to commercial banks when those banks found themselves without sufficient reserves. Because Americans tended to distrust large banking interests, Congress called for a decentralized central bank. The Federal Reserve System divides the nation into 12 districts, each with its own Federal Reserve Bank (Figure 1).

13-1a-1 Board of Governors
Although Congress created a decentralized system so that each district bank would represent the special interests of its own region, in practice the Fed is much more centralized than its creators intended. Monetary policy is largely set by the Board of Governors in Washington, D.C. This board is made up of seven members, who are appointed by the president and confirmed by the Senate.

The most visible and powerful member of the board is the chairman. In fact, the chairman of the Board of Governors has been called *the second most powerful person in the United States*. This individual serves as a leader and spokesperson for the board and typically exercises more authority in determining the course of monetary policy than do the other governors.

The chairman is appointed by the president to a four-year term. In recent years, most chairmen have been reappointed to one or more additional terms (Table 1). The governors serve 14-year terms, with the terms staggered so that a new position comes up for appointment every two years. This system allows continuity in the policymaking process and is intended to place the board above politics. Congress created the Fed as an independent agency: Monetary policy is supposed to be formulated independent of Congress and the president. Of course, this is impossible in practice because the president appoints and the Senate approves the members of the board. But because the governors serve 14-year terms, they outlast the president who appointed them.

13-1a-2 District Banks
Each of the Fed's 12 district banks is formally directed by a nine-person board of directors. Three directors represent commercial banks in the district, and three represent nonbanking business interests. These six individuals are elected by the Federal Reserve System member banks in the district. The three remaining directors are appointed by the Fed's Board of Governors. District bank directors are not involved in the

FIGURE 1 The Federal Reserve System

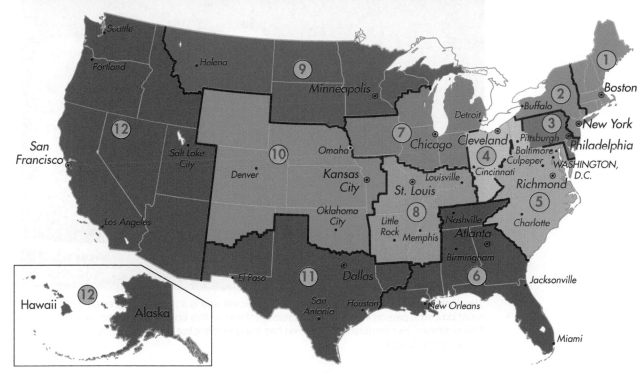

The Federal Reserve System divides the country into 12 districts. Each district has its own Federal Reserve bank, headquarters for Fed operations in that district. For example, the first district bank is in Boston; the twelfth is in San Francisco. There are also branch banks in Los Angeles, Miami, and other cities.

Source: Federal Reserve Bulletin.

TABLE 1 Recent Chairmen of the Federal Reserve Board

Name	Age at Appointment	Term Began	Term Ended	Years of Tenure
William McChesney Martin	44	4/2/51	1/31/70	18.8
Arthur Burns	65	1/31/70	2/1/78	8.0
G. William Miller	52	3/8/78	8/6/79	1.4
Paul Volcker	51	8/6/79	8/5/87	8.0
Alan Greenspan	61	8/11/87	1/31/06	18.4
Ben Bernanke	52	2/1/06	1/31/14	8
Janet Yellen	67	2/3/14		

day-to-day operations of the district banks, but they meet regularly to oversee bank operations. They also choose the president of the bank. The president, who is in charge of operations, participates in monetary policymaking with the Board of Governors in Washington, D.C.

13-1a-3 The Federal Open Market Committee The **Federal Open Market Committee (FOMC)** is the official policymaking body of the Federal Reserve System. The committee is made up of the seven members of the Board of Governors plus five of the 12 district bank presidents. All of the district bank presidents except the president of the Federal Reserve

Federal Open Market Committee (FOMC)
The official policymaking body of the Federal Reserve System.

Drew Angerer/Getty Images

The chairman of the Federal Reserve Board of Governors is sometimes referred to as the second most powerful person in the United States. At the time this book was written, Janet Yellen was the Fed chairman. Her leadership of the Fed has important implications for money and credit conditions in the United States.

Bank of New York take turns serving on the FOMC. Because the New York Fed actually carries out monetary policy, that bank's president is always on the committee. In section 13-2 we talk more about the FOMC's role and the tactics it uses.

13-1b Functions of the Fed

The Federal Reserve System offers banking services to the banking community and the U.S. Treasury and supervises the nation's banking system. The Fed also regulates the U.S. money supply.

13-1b-1 Banking Services and Supervision

The Fed provides several basic services to the banking community: It supplies currency to banks, holds their reserves, and clears checks. The Fed supplies U.S. currency (Federal Reserve notes) to the banking community through its 12 district banks. (See the Economic Insight "What's on a 20-Dollar Bill?")

Commercial banks in each district also hold reserves in the form of deposits at their district bank. In addition, the Fed makes loans to banks. In this sense, the Fed is a *banker's bank*. And the Fed clears checks, transferring funds to the banks where checks are deposited from the banks on which the checks are drawn.

The Fed also supervises the nation's banks, ensuring that they operate in a sound and prudent manner. And it acts as the banker for the U.S. government, selling U.S. government securities for the U.S. Treasury.

13-1b-2 Controlling the Money Supply

All of the functions that the Federal Reserve carries out are important, but none is more important than managing the nation's money supply. Before 1913, when the Fed was created, the money supply did not change to meet fluctuations in the demand for money. These fluctuations can stem from changes in income or from seasonal patterns of demand. For example, every year during the Christmas season,

ECONOMIC INSIGHT

What's on a 20-Dollar Bill?

The figure shows both sides of a 20-dollar bill. We have numbered several elements for identification.

1. **Watermark**
   A watermark, created during the paper-making process, depicts the same historical figure as the portrait. It is visible from both sides when the bill is held up to a light.

2. **Security thread**
   An embedded polymer strip, positioned in a unique spot for each denomination, guards against counterfeiting. The thread itself, which is visible when the bill is held up to a bright light, contains microprinting—the letters *USA*, the denomination of the bill, and a flag. When viewed under ultraviolet light, the thread glows a distinctive color for each denomination.

3. **Color-shifting ink**
   The ink used in the numeral in the lower right-hand corner on the front of the bill looks green when viewed straight on but copper when viewed at an angle.

4. **Serial number**
   No two notes of the same kind, denomination, and series have the same serial number. This fact can be important in detecting counterfeit notes, as many counterfeiters make large batches of a particular note with the same number.

   Notes are numbered in lots of 100 million. Each lot has a different suffix letter, beginning with A and following in alphabetical order through Z, omitting O because of its similarity to the numerical zero.

   Serial numbers consist of two prefix letters, eight numerals, and a one-letter suffix. The first letter of the prefix designates the series. The second letter of the prefix designates the Federal Reserve Bank to which the note was issued, with A designating the first district, or the Boston Fed, and L, the twelfth letter in the alphabet, designating the twelfth district, or the San Francisco Fed.

5. **"In God We Trust"**
   Secretary of the Treasury Salmon P. Chase first authorized the use of "In God We Trust" on U.S. money on the 2-cent coin in 1864. In 1955, Congress mandated the use of this phrase on all currency and coins.

Bureau of Engraving and Printing

Sources: Federal Reserve Bank of Atlanta and Bureau of Engraving and Printing.

the demand for currency rises because people carry more money to buy gifts. During the holiday season, the Fed increases the supply of currency to meet the demand for cash withdrawals from banks. After the holiday season, the demand for currency drops and the public deposits currency in banks, which then return the currency to the Fed.

The Fed controls the money supply to achieve the policy goals set by the FOMC. It does this largely through its ability to influence bank reserves and the money creating power of commercial banks that we talked about in the chapter titled "Money and Banking."

RECAP

1. As the central bank of the United States, the Federal Reserve accepts deposits from and makes loans to commercial banks, acts as a banker for the federal government, and controls the money supply.

2. The Federal Reserve System is made up of the Board of Governors in Washington, D.C., and 12 district banks.

3. The most visible and powerful member of the Board of Governors is the chairman.

4. The governors are appointed by the president and confirmed by the Senate to serve 14-year terms.

5. Monetary policy is made by the Federal Open Market Committee, whose members include the seven governors and five of the 12 district bank presidents.

6. The Fed provides currency, holds reserves, clears checks, and supervises commercial banks.

7. The most important function that the Fed performs is controlling the U.S. money supply.

13-2 Implementing Monetary Policy

2. How is monetary policy set?

The objective of monetary policy is economic growth with stable prices.

Changes in the amount of money in an economy affect the inflation rate, the interest rate, and the equilibrium level of national income. Throughout history, incorrect monetary policy has made currencies worthless and toppled governments. This is why controlling the money supply is so important.

13-2a Policy Goals

The ultimate goal of monetary policy is much like that of fiscal policy: economic growth with stable prices. *Economic growth* means greater output; *stable prices* mean a low, steady rate of inflation.

13-2a-1 Intermediate Targets The Fed does not control GDP or the price level directly. Instead, it controls the money supply, which in turn affects GDP and the level of prices. The money supply, or the growth of the money supply, is an **intermediate target**, an objective that helps the Fed achieve its ultimate policy objective—economic growth with stable prices.

Using the growth of the money supply as an intermediate target assumes that there is a fairly stable relationship between changes in the money supply and changes in income and prices. The bases for this assumption are the equation of exchange and the quantity theory of money. The **equation of exchange** is a definition that relates the quantity of money to nominal GDP:

$$MV = PQ$$

intermediate target
An objective used to achieve some ultimate policy goal.

equation of exchange
An equation that relates the quantity of money to nominal GDP.

where:

$M =$ quantity of money
$V =$ velocity of money
$P =$ price level
$Q =$ the quantity of output, like real income or real GDP

This equation is true by definition: Money times the velocity of money will always be equal to nominal GDP.

The **velocity of money** is the average number of times each dollar is spent on final goods and services in a year. If P is the price level and Q is real GDP (the quantity of goods and services produced in the economy), then PQ equals nominal GDP. If

$$MV = PQ$$

then

$$V = \frac{PQ}{M}$$

velocity of money
The average number of times each dollar is spent on final goods and services in a year.

Suppose the price level is 2 and real GDP is $500; PQ, or nominal GDP, is $1,000. If the money supply is $200, then velocity is 5 ($1,000/$200). A velocity of 5 means that each dollar must be spent an average of five times during the year if a money supply of $200 is going to support the purchase of $1,000 worth of new goods and services.

The **quantity theory of money** uses the equation of exchange to relate changes in the money supply to changes in prices and output. If the money supply (M) increases and velocity (V) is constant, then nominal GDP (PQ) must increase. If the economy is operating at maximum capacity (producing at the maximum level of Q), an increase in M causes an increase in P. And if there is substantial unemployment, so that Q can increase, the increase in M may mean a higher price level (P) as well as higher real GDP (Q).

quantity theory of money
The theory that, with constant velocity, changes in the quantity of money change nominal GDP.

The Fed attempts to set money growth targets that are consistent with rising output and low inflation. In terms of the quantity theory of money, the Fed wants to increase M at a rate that supports steadily rising Q with slow and steady increases in P. The assumption that there is a reasonably stable relationship among M, P, and Q is what motivates the Fed to use money supply growth rates as an intermediate target to achieve its ultimate goal—higher Q with slow increases in P.

Of course, other central banks may have different goals. An example of a central bank that pursues inflation targeting is given in the Global Business Insight "The European Central Bank."

The FOMC used to set explicit ranges for money growth targets; however, in 2000 it stopped doing so. Although it no longer publicly announces a range for money growth, the FOMC still monitors the money supply growth rates. This shift away from announced targets reflects the belief that in recent years, money growth has become an unreliable indicator of monetary conditions as a result of unpredictable changes in velocity.

From the late 1950s to the mid-1970s, the velocity of the M1 money supply grew at a steady pace, from 3.5 in 1959 to 5.5 in 1975. Knowing that V was growing at a steady pace, the Fed was able to set a target growth rate for the M1 money supply and be confident that this would produce a fairly predictable growth in nominal GDP. But when velocity is not constant, there can be problems with using money growth rates as an intermediate target. This is exactly what happened starting in the late 1970s. Figure 2 plots the velocity of the M1 and M2 money supplies from 1959. Although the M2 velocity continued to indicate a stable pattern of growth, M1 velocity behaved erratically. With the breakdown of the relationship between the M1 money supply and GDP, the Fed shifted its emphasis from the M1 money supply, concentrating instead on achieving targeted growth in the M2 money supply. More recently, the velocity of M2 has also become less predictable.

FIGURE 2 Velocity of the M1 and M2 Money Supplies

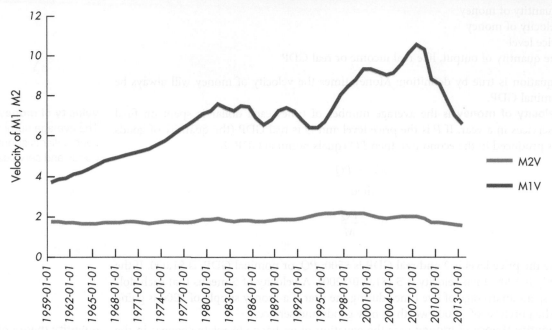

The velocity of money is the ratio of nominal GDP to the money supply. The narrower the definition of money, the higher its velocity. So M1, the narrowest definition, has a higher velocity than M2. In recent years, the velocity of M1 has been much less stable than the velocity of the broader money definitions.

Economists are still debating the reason for the fluctuations in velocity. Some argue that new deposits and innovations in banking have led to fluctuations in the money held as traditional demand deposits, with bank customers switching to different types of financial assets. These unpredictable changes in financial asset holdings affect the various money supplies and their velocities.

In addition to its interest in money growth, the Fed monitors other key variables that are used to indicate the future course of the economy. These include commodity prices, interest rates, and foreign exchange rates. The Fed may not set formal targets for all of them, but it considers them in setting policy. At the time of this edition, the FOMC had an explicit target for the *federal funds rate* of interest—the interest rate that banks pay for borrowing overnight from other banks. We will discuss this interest rate in more detail in the next section.

13-2a-2 Inflation Targeting Some countries have moved away from pursuing intermediate targets like money growth rates and have instead focused on an ultimate goal: a low inflation rate. In part, these countries realize that using monetary policy to support economic growth, low unemployment, and also low inflation has often resulted in an inflationary bias. The public generally likes to see policies supporting faster economic growth, like lower interest rates, whereas fighting inflation may mean unpopular higher interest rates and slower growth. Thus, a central bank may find it politically attractive to stimulate the economy, meaning that inflation takes a secondary position. In addition, if the central bank always considers multiple goals like low unemployment and low inflation, the public may not be able to understand the central bank's decision-making process easily, with the result that there is great uncertainty regarding monetary policy, and business firms and households have more difficulty making economic plans for the future. Commitment to a target inflation rate greatly reduces that uncertainty.

GLOBAL BUSINESS INSIGHT

The European Central Bank

The European Central Bank (ECB) began operations on June 1, 1998, in Frankfurt, Germany, and now conducts monetary policy for the euro-area countries. The national central banks like the Bank of Italy and the German Bundesbank are still operating and perform many of the functions that they had prior to the ECB, such as bank regulation and supervision and facilitating payments systems in each nation. In some sense, they are like the regional banks of the Federal Reserve System in the United States. Monetary policy for the euro area is conducted by the ECB in Frankfurt, just as monetary policy for the United States is conducted by the Federal Reserve in Washington, D.C. Yet the national central banks of the euro area play an important role in their respective countries. The entire network of national central banks and the ECB is called the European System of Central Banks. Monetary policy for the euro area is determined by

the *Governing Council* of the ECB. This council is composed of the heads of the national central banks of the euro-area countries plus the members of the ECB *Executive Board*. The board is made up of the ECB president and vice president and four others chosen by the heads of the governments of the euro-area nations.

The ECB pursues a primary goal of price stability, defined as an inflation rate of less than 2 percent per year. Subject to the achievement of this primary goal, additional issues, such as economic growth, may be addressed. A benefit of a stated policy goal is that people can more easily form expectations of future ECB policy. This builds public confidence in the central bank and allows for greater stability than if the public were always trying to guess what the central bank really cares about and how policy will be changed as market conditions change.

Inflation targeting has been adopted in several countries, including New Zealand, Canada, the United Kingdom, Australia, Switzerland, Chile, Korea, South Africa, and Europe (by the European Central Bank). It is important to realize that in order to use inflation targeting, a central bank must be independent from fiscal policy. It is not enough to announce a target for the inflation rate. The central bank must not be in the position of having to help finance government spending. Only with this independence can a central bank truly have a credible inflation target.

13-2b Operating Procedures

The FOMC sets federal funds rate targets and then implements them through the Federal Reserve Bank of New York. The mechanism for translating policy into action is an **FOMC directive**. At the conclusion of each FOMC meeting, a policy statement is issued to the public that indicates the contents of the directive. The statement and associated directive outline the conduct of monetary policy over the six-week period until the FOMC meets again to reconsider its targets and specify policy tools.

Figure 3 contains the statement issued by the FOMC meeting of January 29, 2014. The FOMC directed the bond traders at the Federal Reserve Bank of New York to buy or sell government bonds as needed to keep the **federal funds rate**, or the interest rate that one bank charges another for overnight lending, between 0 and 0.25 percent. If the rate starts to rise above 0.25 percent, then the New York Fed will buy bonds from bond dealers. The dealers are paid with funds drawn on the Federal Reserve, which are then deposited in the dealers' accounts in commercial banks. This will inject money into the banking system. It will increase bank excess reserves, giving the banks more money to lend; as a result, the cost of these funds, the federal funds rate, will fall. Due to the financial crisis, the lower bound on interest rates was set at zero. The FOMC was intent on stimulating the economy to help end

NOW YOU TRY IT

If $M = \$100$, $V = 4$, $P = 2$,
a. what is the value of Q?
b. what is the value of nominal GDP?
c. If the central bank raises M to $\$105$ and V is unchanged, what will happen to the value of nominal GDP?

FOMC directive
Instructions issued by the FOMC to the Federal Reserve Bank of New York to implement monetary policy.

federal funds rate
The interest rate that a bank charges when it lends excess reserves to another bank.

FIGURE 3   FOMC Directive and Policy Statement

FEDERAL RESERVE press release

Release Date: January 29, 2014

For immediate release

Information received since the Federal Open Market Committee met in December indicates that growth in economic activity picked up in recent quarters. Labor market indicators were mixed but on balance showed further improvement. The unemployment rate declined but remains elevated. Household spending and business fixed investment advanced more quickly in recent months, while the recovery in the housing sector slowed somewhat. Fiscal policy is restraining economic growth, although the extent of restraint is diminishing. Inflation has been running below the Committee's longer-run objective, but longer-term inflation expectations have remained stable.

Consistent with its statutory mandate, the Committee seeks to foster maximum employment and price stability. The Committee expects that, with appropriate policy accommodation, economic activity will expand at a moderate pace and the unemployment rate will gradually decline toward levels the Committee judges consistent with its dual mandate. The Committee sees the risks to the outlook for the economy and the labor market as having become more nearly balanced. The Committee recognizes that inflation persistently below its 2 percent objective could pose risks to economic performance, and it is monitoring inflation developments carefully for evidence that inflation will move back toward its objective over the medium term. Taking into account the extent of federal fiscal retrenchment since the inception of its current asset purchase program, the Committee continues to see the improvement in economic activity and labor market conditions over that period as consistent with growing underlying strength in the broader economy. In light of the cumulative progress toward maximum employment and the improvement in the outlook for labor market conditions, the Committee decided to make a further measured reduction in the pace of its asset purchases. Beginning in February, the Committee will add to its holdings of agency mortgage-backed securities at a pace of $30 billion per month rather than $35 billion per month, and will add to its holdings of longer-term Treasury securities at a pace of $35 billion per month rather than $40 billion per month. The Committee is maintaining its existing policy of reinvesting principal payments from its holdings of agency debt and agency mortgage-backed securities in agency mortgage-backed securities and of rolling over maturing Treasury securities at auction. The Committee's sizable and still-increasing holdings of longer-term securities should maintain downward pressure on longer-term interest rates, support mortgage markets, and help to make broader financial conditions more accommodative, which in turn should promote a stronger economic recovery and help to ensure that inflation, over time, is at the rate most consistent with the Committee's dual mandate.

The Committee will closely monitor incoming information on economic and financial developments in coming months and will continue its purchases of Treasury and agency mortgage-backed securities, and employ its other policy tools as appropriate, until the outlook for the labor market has improved substantially in a context of price stability. If incoming information broadly supports the Committee's expectation of ongoing improvement in labor market conditions and inflation moving back toward its longer-run objective, the Committee will likely reduce the pace of asset purchases in further measured steps at future meetings. However, asset purchases are not on a preset course, and the Committee's decisions about their pace will remain contingent on the Committee's outlook for the labor market and inflation as well as its assessment of the likely efficacy and costs of such purchases.

To support continued progress toward maximum employment and price stability, the Committee today reaffirmed its view that a highly accommodative stance of monetary policy will remain appropriate for a considerable time after the asset purchase program ends and the economic recovery strengthens. The Committee also reaffirmed its expectation that the current exceptionally low target range for the federal funds rate of 0 to 1/4 percent will be appropriate at least as long as the unemployment rate remains above 6-1/2 percent, inflation between one and two years ahead is projected to be no more than a half percentage point above the Committee's 2 percent longer-run goal, and longer-term inflation expectations continue to be well anchored. In determining how long to maintain a highly accommodative stance of monetary policy, the Committee will also consider other information, including additional measures of labor market conditions, indicators of inflation pressures and inflation expectations, and readings on financial developments. The Committee continues to anticipate, based on its assessment of these factors, that it likely will be appropriate to maintain the current target range for the federal funds rate well past the time that the unemployment rate declines below 6-1/2 percent, especially if projected inflation continues to run below the Committee's 2 percent longer-run goal. When the Committee decides to begin to remove policy accommodation, it will take a balanced approach consistent with its longer-run goals of maximum employment and inflation of 2 percent.

Voting for the FOMC monetary policy action were: Ben S. Bernanke, Chairman; William C. Dudley, Vice Chairman; Richard W. Fisher; Narayana Kocherlakota; Sandra Pianalto; Charles I. Plosser; Jerome H. Powell; Jeremy C. Stein; Daniel K. Tarullo; and Janet L. Yellen.

The FOMC always issues a directive to guide the conduct of monetary policy between meetings. In addition, a press statement at the conclusion of the meeting indicates the committee's view regarding the likely course of policy in the near future and offers guidance as to the contents of the directive. At the meeting that took place on January 29, 2014, the policy statement shown here was issued.

the recession. In normal times, the lower bound is set at some positive interest rate. If the rate drops below that rate, then the New York Fed will sell bonds to bond dealers. The dealers pay for the bonds with funds drawn on commercial banks. This drains money from the banking system. Bank excess reserves will fall, and since banks will have less money to lend, the cost of these funds, the federal funds rate, will rise. So the actual federal funds rate fluctuates around the target rate set by the FOMC directive.

In Figure 3, the policy statement issued at the conclusion of the meeting held on January 29, 2014 is given. A key part of this statement is the phrase: "Information received since the Federal Open Market Committee met in December indicates that growth in economic activity picked up in recent quarters." Then in the next paragraph the statement says, "… inflation persistently below its 2 percent objective could pose risks to economic performance." Thus, the Fed saw inflation as being too low and in need of further support. The goals are stable prices and economic growth. The concern over a weak economy in the wake of the financial crisis led the FOMC to maintain the historically low interest rate target for federal funds between 0 and 0.25 percent. In addition, the lack of high inflation has encouraged the FOMC to maintain low rates to encourage the recovery in growth. Going forward, as there are more signs of recovery well under way and the inflation rate picks up, we would expect the FOMC to raise the target interest rate to ensure that spending does not rise too quickly and contribute to inflation.

13-2b-1 Tools of Monetary Policy The Fed controls the money supply and interest rates by changing bank reserves. There are three tools that the Fed can use to change reserves: the *reserve requirement*, the *discount rate*, and *open market operations*. In the last chapter, you saw that banks can expand the money supply by a multiple of their excess reserves—the deposit expansion multiplier, the reciprocal of the reserve requirement.

Reserve Requirement The Fed requires banks to hold a fraction of their transaction deposits as reserves. This fraction is the reserve requirement. *Transaction deposits* are checking accounts and other deposits that can be used to pay third parties. Large banks hold a greater percentage of deposits in reserve than small banks do (the reserve requirement increases from 0 for the first $10.7 million of deposits to 3 percent for deposits from $10.7 to $58.8 million, and then to 10 percent for deposits in excess of $58.8 million).

Remember from the chapter titled "Money and Banking" that required reserves are the dollar amount of reserves that a bank must hold to meet its reserve requirement. There are two ways in which required reserves may be held: vault cash at the bank or a deposit in the Fed. The sum of a bank's *vault cash* (coin and currency in the bank's vault) and its deposit in the Fed is called its **legal reserves**. When legal reserves equal required reserves, the bank has no excess reserves and can make no new loans. When legal reserves exceed required reserves, the bank has excess reserves available for lending.

As bank excess reserves change, the lending and money-creating potential of the banking system changes. One way in which the Fed can alter excess reserves is by changing the reserve requirement. If it lowers the reserve requirement, a portion of what was previously required reserves becomes excess reserves, which can be used to make loans and expand the money supply. A lower reserve requirement also increases the deposit expansion multiplier. By raising the reserve requirement, the Fed reduces the money-creating potential of the banking system and tends to reduce the money supply. A higher reserve requirement also lowers the deposit expansion multiplier.

Consider the example in Table 2. If First National Bank's balance sheet shows vault cash of $100,000 and a deposit in the Fed of $200,000, the bank has legal reserves of $300,000. The amount of money that the bank can lend is determined by its excess reserves. Excess reserves (*ER*) equal legal reserves (*LR*) minus required reserves (*RR*):

$$ER = LR - RR$$

3. What are the tools of monetary policy?

legal reserves
The cash a bank holds in its vault plus its deposit in the Fed.

TABLE 2   The Effect of a Change in the Reserve Requirement

Balance Sheet of First National Bank

Assets		Liabilities	
Vault cash	$ 100,000	Deposits	$1,000,000
Deposits in Fed	200,000		
Loans	700,000		
Total	$ 1,000,000	Total	$1,000,000

Legal reserves (*LR*) equal vault cash plus the deposit in the Fed, or $300,000:

$$LR = \$100,000 + \$200,000$$
$$= \$300,000$$

Excess reserves (*ER*) equal legal reserves minus required reserves (*RR*)

$$ER = LR - RR$$

Required reserves equal the reserve requirement (*r*) times deposits (*D*)

$$RR = rD$$

If the reserve requirement is 10 percent:

$$RR = (.10)(\$1,000,000)$$
$$= \$100,000$$
$$ER = \$300,000 = \$100,000$$
$$= \$200,000$$

First National Bank can make a maximum loan of $200,000.

$$(1/.10)(\$200,000) = 10(\$200,000)$$
$$= \$2,000,000$$

The banking system can expand the money supply by the deposit expansion multiplier (1/*r*) times the excess reserves of the bank, or $2,000,000:

If the reserve requirement is 20 percent:

$$RR = (.20)(\$1,000,000)$$
$$= \$200,000$$
$$ER = \$300,000 - \$200,000$$
$$= \$100,000$$

First National Bank can make a maximum loan of $100,000.

The banking system can expand the money supply by the deposit expansion multiplier (1/*r*) times the excess reserves of the bank, or $500,000:

$$(1/.20)(\$100,000) = 5(\$100,000)$$
$$= \$500,000$$

If the reserve requirement (*r*) is 10 percent (.10), the bank must keep 10 percent of its deposits (*D*) as required reserves:

$$RR = rD$$
$$= .10 \ (\$1,000,000)$$
$$= \$100,000$$

In this case, the bank has excess reserves of $200,000 ($300,000 − $100,000). The bank can make a maximum loan of $200,000. The banking system can expand the money supply by the deposit expansion multiplier (1/*r*) times the excess reserves of the bank, or $2,000,000 (1/10 × $200,000).

If the reserve requirement goes up to 20 percent (.20), required reserves are now 20 percent of $1,000,000, or $200,000. Excess reserves are now $100,000, which is the maximum loan that the bank can make. The banking system can expand the money supply by $500,000:

$$\frac{1}{.20}(\$100{,}000) = 5(\$100{,}000)$$

$$= \$500{,}000$$

By raising the reserve requirement, the Fed can reduce the money-creating potential of the banking system and the money supply. And by lowering the reserve requirement, the Fed can increase the money-creating potential of the banking system and the money supply.

Discount Rate If a bank needs more reserves in order to make new loans, it typically borrows from other banks in the federal funds market. The market is called the *federal funds market* because the funds are being loaned from one commercial bank's excess reserves on deposit with the Federal Reserve to another commercial bank's deposit account at the Fed. For instance, if First National Bank has excess reserves of $1 million, it can lend the excess to Second National Bank. When a bank borrows in the federal funds market, it pays a rate of interest called the federal funds rate.

At times, however, banks borrow directly from the Fed. The **discount rate** is the rate of interest that the Fed charges banks. (In other countries, the rate of interest the central bank charges commercial banks is often called the *bank rate*.) Another way in which the Fed controls the level of bank reserves and the money supply is by changing the discount rate.

When the Fed raises the discount rate, it raises the cost of borrowing reserves, reducing the amount of reserves borrowed. Lower levels of reserves limit bank lending and the expansion of the money supply. When the Fed lowers the discount rate, it lowers the cost of borrowing reserves, increasing the amount of borrowing. As bank reserves increase, so do loans and the money supply.

There are actually two different discount rates, both set above the federal funds target rate. The rate on *primary credit* is for loans made to banks that are in good financial condition. At the time this edition was revised, the interest rate on primary credit was set at .75 percent. In addition to the discount rate for primary credit loans, there is another discount rate for *secondary credit*. This rate is for banks that are having financial difficulties. At the time of this edition, the secondary credit rate was set at 1.25 percent. Loans made at these discount rates are for very short terms, typically overnight.

Open Market Operations The major tool of monetary policy is the Fed's **open market operations**, the buying and selling of U.S. government and federal agency bonds. Suppose the FOMC wants to increase bank reserves to lower the federal funds rate. The committee issues a directive to the bond-trading desk at the Federal Reserve Bank of New York to change the federal funds rate to a lower level. In order to accomplish this, the Fed buys bonds, with the results described earlier. If the higher reserves that result lead to increased bank lending to the public, then the new loans in turn expand the money supply through the deposit expansion multiplier process.

If the Fed wants to increase the federal funds rate, it sells bonds. As a result, the money supply decreases through the deposit expansion multiplier process.

Its open market operations allow the Fed to control the federal funds rate and the money supply. To lower the federal funds rate and increase the money supply, the Fed buys U.S. government bonds. To raise the federal funds rate and decrease the money supply, it sells U.S. government bonds. The effect of selling these bonds, however, varies, depending on whether there are excess reserves in the banking system. If there are excess reserves, the money supply does not necessarily decrease when the Fed sells bonds. The open market sale may simply reduce the level of excess reserves, reducing the rate at which the money supply increases.

Table 3 shows how open market operations change bank reserves and illustrates the money-creating power of the banking system. First National Bank's initial balance sheet shows excess reserves of $100,000 with a 20 percent reserve requirement.

discount rate
The interest rate that the Fed charges commercial banks when they borrow from it.

open market operations
The buying and selling of government and federal agency bonds by the Fed to control bank reserves, the federal funds rate, and the money supply.

To lower the federal funds rate and increase the money supply, the Fed buys U.S. government bonds. To increase the federal funds rate and decrease the money supply, it sells U.S. government bonds.

TABLE 3 The Effect of an Open Market Operation

Balance Sheet of First National Bank

Assets		Liabilities	
Vault cash	$ 100,000	Deposits	$1,000,000
Deposits in Fed	200,000		
Loans	700,000		
Total	$ 1,000,000	Total	$1,000,000

Initially, legal reserves (*LR*) equal vault cash plus the deposit in the Fed, or $300,000:

$$LR = \$100,000 + \$200,000$$
$$= \$300,000$$

If the reserve requirement (*r*) is 20 percent (.20), required reserves (*RR*) equal $200,000:

$$.20(\$1,000,000) = \$200,000$$

Excess reserves (*ER*), then, equal $100,000 ($300,000 − $200,000). The bank can make a maximum loan of $100,000. The banking system can expand the money supply by the deposit expansion multiplier (1/*r*) times the excess reserves of the bank, or $500,000:

$$(1/.20)(\$100,000) = 5(\$100,000)$$
$$= \$500,000$$

Open market purchase:

The Fed purchases $100,000 worth of bonds from a dealer, who deposits the $100,000 in an account at First National. At this point the bank has legal reserves of $400,000, required reserves of $220,000, and excess reserves of $180,000. It can make a maximum loan of $180,000, which can expand the money supply by $900,000 [(1/.20)($180,000)].

Open market sale:

The Fed sells $100,000 worth of bonds to a dealer, who pays with a check drawn on an account at First National. At this point, the bank has legal reserves of $200,000, required reserves of $180,000 (its deposits now equal $900,000), and excess reserves of $20,000. It can make a maximum loan of $20,000, which can expand the money supply by $100,000 [(1/.20)($20,000)].

Therefore, the bank can make a maximum loan of $100,000. On the basis of the bank's reserve position, the banking system can increase the money supply by a maximum of $500,000.

If the Fed purchases $100,000 worth of bonds from a private dealer, who deposits the $100,000 in an account at First National Bank, the excess reserves of First National Bank increase to $180,000. These reserves can generate a maximum increase in the money supply of $900,000. The open market purchase increases the excess reserves of the banking system, stimulating the growth of money and, eventually, nominal GDP.

What happens when an open market sale takes place? If the Fed sells $100,000 worth of bonds to a private bond dealer, the dealer pays for the bonds using a check drawn on First National Bank. First National's deposits drop from $1,000,000 to $900,000, and its legal reserves drop from $300,000 to $200,000. With excess reserves of $20,000, the banking system can increase the money supply by only $100,000. The open market sale reduces the money-creating potential of the banking system from $500,000 initially to $100,000.

quantitative easing
Buying financial assets to stimulate the economy when the central bank target interest rate is near or at zero and the interest rate cannot be lowered further.

Quantitative Easing   What if a central bank has moved its target interest rate near to zero so that interest rates cannot fall further? If the central bank wants additional stimulus for the economy it can employ a policy known as **quantitative easing**. Quantitative easing is a policy of buying financial assets in order to ease credit conditions and make loans more readily available to the public. These financial assets can be government bonds, private corporate bonds, or any other financial asset the central bank chooses. The idea is to flood the economy with money to try to stimulate spending and provide a boost to GDP growth.

The Bank of Japan employed quantitative easing from March 2001 to March 2006 as the policy interest rate was set at zero, yet the economy was in recession with deflation. During the financial crisis of 2008, several central banks, including the Federal Reserve and the Bank of England, employed quantitative easing since they had cut interest rates almost to zero, and still the recession continued. In November 2010, the Fed announced plans to buy 600 billion dollars in government bonds in a second round of quantitative easing. Once the economy starts to recover, the additional purchases of assets ends, and the central bank raises interest rates to avoid creating inflation by overstimulating the economy. In Figure 3 you can see the FOMC voted to continue to decrease, or taper, its asset purchases. The FOMC viewed current signs of the recovery as strong enough to warrant the reduction of its quantitative easing.

Forward Guidance   Beyond quantitative easing, the aftermath of the financial crisis saw the introduction of another new tool of monetary policy, **forward guidance**. This involves making statements that commit policy to low interest rates for a prolonged period of time. The intent is to shape the expectations of the public so that they believe that interest rates will stay low and the central bank will continue to pursue expansionary policies well into the future. The Federal Reserve, Bank of England, and European Central Bank all engaged in a form of forward guidance. In the case of the Federal Reserve, the guidance was that the Fed would keep the federal funds rate near zero until the unemployment rate reached 6.5 percent. The FOMC apparently believed that once the unemployment rate reached that level, there would be sufficient strength in the U.S. economy to warrant consideration of interest rate increases.

However, in this particular case, the Fed ultimately decided to drop the unemployment rate condition in their forward guidance as they decided that the economy would require more stimulus warranting near-zero interest rates even when the unemployment rate reached 6.5 percent. This illustrates that when employing a new instrument of monetary policy, central banks may need to make adjustments as they gain experience with the instrument.

13-2b-2 FOMC Directives When it sets monetary policy, the FOMC begins with its *ultimate goal:* economic growth at stable prices. It defines that goal in terms of GDP and inflation. Then it works backwards to identify its *intermediate target*, the rate at which the money supply must grow to achieve the desired growth in GDP. Then it must decide how to achieve its intermediate target. In Figure 4, as is usually the case in real life, the Fed uses open market operations. But to know whether it should buy or sell bonds, the FOMC must have some indication of whether the money supply is growing too fast or too slowly. The committee relies on a *short-run operating target* for this information. The short-run target indicates how the money supply should change. Both the quantity of excess reserves in the banking system and the federal funds rate can serve as short-run operating targets.

The FOMC carries out its policies through directives to the bond trading desk at the Federal Reserve Bank of New York. The directives specify a short-run operating target that the trading desk must use in its day-to-day operations. In recent years, the target has been the federal funds rate.

13-2c Foreign Exchange Market Intervention

In the mid-1980s, conditions in the foreign exchange market took on a high priority in FOMC directives. There was concern that the value of the dollar in relation to other currencies was contributing to a large U.S. international trade deficit. Furthermore, the governments of the major industrial countries had decided to work together to maintain more stable exchange rates. This meant that the Federal Reserve and the central banks of the other developed countries had to devote more attention to maintaining exchange rates within a certain target band of values. Although more recently exchange rates have had less of a role in FOMC meetings, it is still important to understand how central banks may intervene to change exchange rates. Other central banks have made exchange rates a focus of their policy.

forward guidance
Announcing a commitment by the central bank to maintain policy for a period of time until certain conditions are met.

4. What role do central banks play in the foreign exchange market?

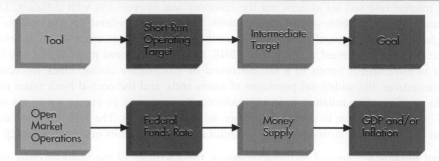

FIGURE 4   Monetary Policy: Tools, Targets, and Goals

The Fed primarily uses open market operations to implement monetary policy. The decision to buy or sell bonds is based on a short-run operating target, like the federal funds rate. The short-run operating target is set to achieve an intermediate target, a certain level of money supply. The intermediate target is set to achieve the ultimate goal, a certain level of gross domestic product and/or inflation.

For example, in 2009 the Swiss National Bank announced that the Swiss franc had appreciated in value too much and that this was "an inappropriate tightening of monetary conditions." As a result, the bank sold Swiss francs in the foreign exchange market and stated that they stood ready to do this to ensure that the currency would not appreciate further.

foreign exchange market intervention

The buying and selling of currencies by a central bank to achieve a specified exchange rate.

13-2c-1 Mechanics of Intervention Foreign exchange market intervention is the buying and selling of foreign exchange by a central bank in order to move exchange rates up or down. We can use a simple supply and demand diagram to illustrate the role of intervention. Figure 5 shows the U.S. dollar-Japanese yen exchange market. The demand curve is the

FIGURE 5   The Dollar–Yen Foreign Exchange Market

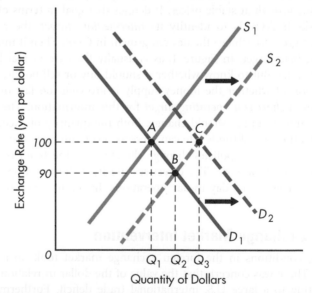

The demand is the demand for dollars arising out of the Japanese demand for U.S. goods and services. The supply is the supply of dollars arising out of the U.S. demand for Japanese goods and services. Initially, the equilibrium exchange rate is at the intersection of the demand curve (D_1) and the supply curve (S_1), at point A where the exchange rate is ¥100 = $1. An increase in the U.S. demand for Japanese goods increases S_1 to S_2 and pushes the equilibrium exchange rate down to point B, where ¥90 = $1. If the Fed's target exchange rate is ¥100 = $1, the Fed must intervene and buy dollars in the foreign exchange market. This increases demand to D_2 and raises the equilibrium exchange rate to point C, where ¥100 = $1.

demand for dollars produced by the demand for U.S. goods and financial assets. The supply curve is the supply of dollars generated by U.S. residents' demand for the products and financial assets of other countries. Here, the supply of dollars to the dollar–yen market comes from the U.S. demand to buy Japanese products.

The initial equilibrium exchange rate is at point A, where the demand curve (D_1) and the supply curve (S_1) intersect. At point A, the exchange rate is ¥100 = $1, and Q_1 dollars are exchanged for yen. Suppose that over time, U.S. residents buy more from Japan than Japanese residents buy from the United States. As the supply of dollars increases in relation to the demand for dollars, equilibrium shifts to point B. At point B, Q_2 dollars are exchanged at a rate of ¥90 = $1. The dollar has *depreciated* against the yen, or, conversely, the yen has *appreciated* against the dollar.

When the dollar depreciates, U.S. goods are cheaper to Japanese buyers (it takes fewer yen to buy each dollar). The depreciated dollar stimulates U.S. exports to Japan. It also raises the price of Japanese goods to U.S. buyers, reducing U.S. imports from Japan. Rather than allowing exchange rates to change, with the subsequent changes in trade, central banks often seek to maintain fixed exchange rates because of international agreements or desired trade in goods or financial assets.

Suppose the Fed sets a target range for the dollar at a minimum exchange rate of ¥100 = $1. If the exchange rate falls below the minimum, the Fed must intervene in the foreign exchange market to increase the value of the dollar. In Figure 5, you can see that the only way to increase the dollar's value is to increase the demand for dollars. The Fed intervenes in the foreign exchange market by buying dollars in exchange for yen. It uses its holdings of Japanese yen to purchase $Q_3 - Q_1$ dollars, shifting the demand curve to D_2. Now equilibrium is at point C, where Q_3 dollars are exchanged at the rate of ¥100 = $1.

The kind of intervention shown in Figure 5 is only temporary because the Fed has a limited supply of yen. Under another intervention plan, the Bank of Japan would support the ¥100 = $1 exchange rate by using yen to buy dollars. The Bank of Japan could carry on this kind of policy indefinitely because it has the power to create yen. A third alternative is *coordinated intervention*, in which both the Fed and the Bank of Japan sell yen in exchange for dollars to support the minimum yen–dollar exchange rate. Following the Japanese earthquake in March 2011, there was a coordinated intervention involving the Bank of Japan, the Fed, and central banks of other developed economies aimed at lowering the value of the yen to make Japanese products cheaper to the rest of the world.

Coordinated intervention involves more than one central bank in attempts to shift the equilibrium exchange rate.

13-2c-2 Effects of Intervention

Intervention can be used to shift the demand and supply for currency and thereby change the exchange rate. Foreign exchange market intervention also has effects on the money supply. If the Federal Reserve wanted to increase the dollar price of the euro, it would create dollars to purchase euro. Thus, when foreign exchange market intervention involves the use of domestic currency to buy foreign currency, it increases the domestic money supply. The expansionary effect of this intervention can be offset by a domestic open market operation in a process called **sterilization** If the Fed creates dollars to buy euro, for example, it increases the money supply, as we have just seen. To reduce the money supply, the Fed can direct an open market bond sale. The bond sale sterilizes the effect of the intervention on the domestic money supply.

sterilization
The use of domestic open market operations to offset the effects of a foreign exchange market intervention on the domestic money supply.

RECAP

1. The ultimate goal of monetary policy is economic growth with stable prices.

2. The Fed controls GDP indirectly, through its control of the money supply.

3. The equation of exchange ($MV = PQ$) relates the quantity of money to nominal GDP.

4. The quantity theory of money states that with constant velocity, changes in the quantity of money change nominal GDP.

5. Every six weeks, the Federal Open Market Committee issues a directive to the Federal Reserve Bank of New York that defines the FOMC's monetary targets and policy tools.

6. The Fed controls the nation's money supply by changing bank excess reserves.

7. The tools of monetary policy are reserve requirements, the discount rate, open market operations, quantitative easing, and forward guidance.

8. The money supply tends to increase (decrease) as the reserve requirement falls (rises), the discount rate falls (rises), and the Fed buys (sells) bonds.

9. If the policy interest rate is lowered near zero, quantitative easing and forward guidance can be used to further stimulate the economy.

10. Each FOMC directive defines its short-run operating target in terms of the federal funds rate.

11. Foreign exchange market intervention is the buying and selling of foreign exchange by a central bank to achieve a targeted exchange rate.

12. Sterilization is the use of domestic open market operations to offset the money supply effects of foreign exchange market intervention.

13-3 Monetary Policy and Equilibrium Income

To see how changes in the money supply affect the equilibrium level of real GDP, we incorporate monetary policy into the aggregate demand and supply model. The first step in understanding monetary policy is understanding the demand for money. If you know what determines money demand, you can see how monetary policy is used to shift aggregate demand and change the equilibrium level of real GDP.

5. What are the determinants of the demand for money?

13-3a Money Demand

Why do you hold money? What does it do for you? What determines how much money you will hold? These questions are addressed in this section. Wanting to hold more money is not the same as wanting more income. You can decide to carry more cash or keep more dollars in your checking account even though your income has not changed. The quantity of dollars that you want to hold is your demand for money. By summing the quantity of money demanded by each individual, we can find the money demand for the entire economy. Once we understand what determines money demand, we can put that demand together with the money supply and examine how money influences the interest rate and the equilibrium level of income.

In the chapter titled "Money and Banking," we discussed the functions of money— that is, what money is used for. People use money as a unit of account, a medium of exchange, a store of value, and a standard of deferred payment. These last functions help explain the demand for money.

People use money for transactions, to buy goods and services. The **transactions demand for money** is a demand to hold money in order to spend it on goods and services. Holding money in your pocket or checking account is a demand for money. Spending money is not demanding it; by spending it, you are getting rid of it.

If your boss paid you the same instant that you wanted to buy something, the timing of your receipts and expenditures would match perfectly. You would not have to hold money for transactions. But because receipts typically occur much less often than expenditures, money is necessary to cover transactions between paychecks.

People also hold money to take care of emergencies. The **precautionary demand for money** exists because emergencies happen. People never know when an unexpected expense

transactions demand for money
The demand to hold money to buy goods and services.

precautionary demand for money
The demand for money to cover unplanned transactions or emergencies.

will crop up or when actual expenditures will exceed planned expenditures. So they hold money as a precaution.

Finally, there is a **speculative demand for money**, a demand created by uncertainty about the value of other assets. This demand exists because money is the most liquid store of value. If you want to buy a stock, but you believe the price is going to fall in the next few days, you hold the money until you are ready to buy the stock.

The speculative demand for money is not necessarily tied to a particular use of funds. People hold money because they expect the price of any asset to fall. Holding money is less risky than buying the asset today if the price of the asset seems likely to fall. For example, suppose you buy and sell fine art. The price of art fluctuates over time. You try to buy when prices are low and sell when prices are high. If you expect prices to fall in the short term, you hold money rather than art until the prices do fall. Then you use money to buy art for resale when the prices go up again.

speculative demand for money
The demand for money created by uncertainty about the value of other assets.

13-3a-1 The Money Demand Function
If you understand why people hold money, you can understand what changes the amount of money that they hold. As you have just seen, people hold money in order to (1) carry out transactions (transactions demand), (2) be prepared for emergencies (precautionary demand), and (3) speculate on purchases of various assets (speculative demand). The interest rate and nominal income (income measured in current dollars) influence how much money people hold in order to carry out these three activities.

The interest rate is the opportunity cost of holding money.

The Interest Rate   There is an inverse relationship between the interest rate and the quantity of money demanded (see Figure 6). The interest rate is the *opportunity cost* of holding money. If you bury one thousand dollar bills in your backyard, that currency is earning no interest—you are forgoing the interest. At a low interest rate, the cost of the forgone interest is small. At a higher interest rate, however, the cost of holding wealth in the form of money

---

FIGURE 6   The Money Demand Function

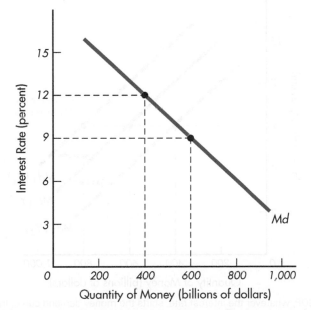

Money demand (*Md*) is a negative function of the rate of interest. The interest rate is the opportunity cost of holding money. The higher the interest rate, the lower the quantity of money demanded. At an interest rate of 9 percent, the quantity of money demanded is $600 billion. At an interest rate of 12 percent, the quantity of money demanded falls to $400 billion.

means giving up more interest. The higher the rate of interest, the greater the interest forgone by holding money, so the less money held. The costs of holding money limit the amount of money held.

Some components of the money supply pay interest to the depositor. Here the opportunity cost of holding money is the difference between the interest rate on a bond or some other nonmonetary asset and the interest rate on money. If a bond pays 9 percent interest a year and a bank deposit pays 5 percent, the opportunity cost of holding the deposit is 4 percent.

Figure 6 shows a money demand function, where the demand for money depends on the interest rate. The downward slope of the money demand curve (Md) shows the inverse relation between the interest rate and the quantity of money demanded. For instance, at an interest rate of 12 percent, the quantity of money demanded is $400 billion. If the interest rate falls to 9 percent, the quantity of money demanded increases to $600 billion.

Nominal Income   The demand for money also depends on nominal income. Money demand varies directly with nominal income because as income increases, more transactions are carried out and more money is required for those transactions.

The transactions demand for money rises with nominal income.

The greater nominal income is, the greater the demand for money. This is true whether the increase in nominal income is a product of a higher price level or an increase in real income. Both generate a greater dollar volume of transactions. If the prices of all goods increase, then more money must be used to purchase goods and services. And as real income increases, more goods and services are being produced and sold and living standards rise; this means that more money is being demanded to execute the higher level of transactions.

A change in nominal income changes the demand for money at any given interest rate. Figure 7 shows the effect of changes in nominal income on the money demand curve. If income rises from Y_0 to Y_1, money demand increases from Md to Md_1. If income falls from

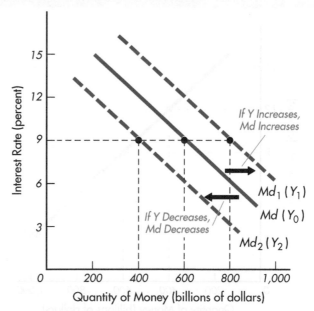

FIGURE 7   The Effect of a Change in Income on Money Demand

A change in real GDP, whatever the interest rate, shifts the money demand curve. Initially real GDP is Y_0; the money demand curve at that level of income is Md. At an interest rate of 9 percent, the quantity of money demanded is $600 billion. If income increases to Y_1, the money demand shifts to Md_1. Here $800 billion is demanded at 9 percent. If income falls to Y_2, the money demand curve falls to Md_2, where $400 billion is demanded at 9 percent.

Y_0 to Y_2, money demand falls from Md to Md_2. When the money demand function shifts from Md to Md_1, the quantity of money demanded at an interest rate of 9 percent increases from $600 billion to $800 billion.

When the money demand function shifts from Md to Md_2, the quantity of money demanded at 9 percent interest falls from $600 billion to $400 billion.

13-3a-2 The Money Supply Function

The Federal Reserve is responsible for setting the money supply. The fact that the Fed can choose the money supply means that the money supply function is independent of the current interest rate and income. Figure 8 illustrates the money supply function (Ms). In the figure, the money supply is $600 billion at all interest rate levels. If the Fed increases the money supply, the vertical money supply function shifts to the right. If the Fed decreases the money supply, the function shifts to the left.

13-3a-3 Equilibrium in the Money Market

To find the equilibrium interest rate and quantity of money, we have to combine the money demand and money supply functions in one diagram. Figure 9 graphs equilibrium in the money market. Equilibrium, point e, is at the intersection of the money demand and money supply functions. In the figure, the equilibrium interest rate is 9 percent, and the quantity of money is $600 billion.

What forces work to ensure that the economy tends toward the equilibrium rate of interest? Let us look at Figure 9 again to understand what happens if the interest rate is not at equilibrium. If the interest rate falls below 9 percent, there will be an excess demand for money. People will want more money than the Fed is supplying. But because the supply of money does not change, the demand for more money just forces the interest rate to rise. How? Suppose people try to increase their money holdings by converting bonds and other nonmonetary assets into money. As bonds and other nonmonetary assets are sold for money, the interest rate goes up.

FIGURE 8 The Money Supply Function

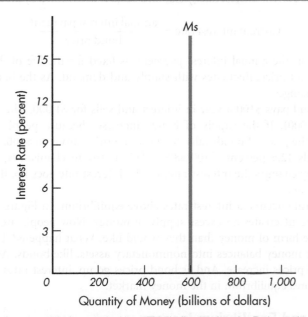

The money supply function (Ms) is a vertical line. This indicates that the Fed can choose any money supply it wants, independent of the interest rate (and real GDP). In the figure, the money supply is set at $600 billion at all interest rates. The Fed can increase or decrease the money supply, shifting the curve to the right or left, but the curve remains vertical.

FIGURE 9   Equilibrium in the Money Market

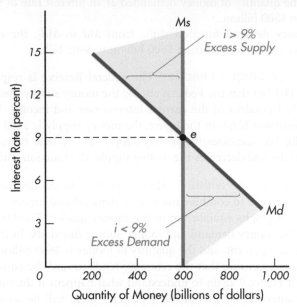

Equilibrium is at point *e*, where the money demand and money supply curves intersect. At equilibrium, the interest rate is 9 percent and the money supply is $600 billion. An interest rate above 9 percent would create an excess supply of money because the quantity of money demanded falls as the interest rate rises. An interest rate below 9 percent would create an excess demand for money because the quantity of money demanded rises as the interest rate falls.

To understand the connection between the rate of interest and buying and selling bonds, you must realize that the current interest rate (yield) on a bond is determined by the bond price:

$$\text{Current interest rate} = \frac{\text{annual interest payment}}{\text{bond price}}$$

The numerator, the annual interest payment, is fixed for the life of the bond. The denominator, the bond price, fluctuates with supply and demand. As the bond price changes, the interest rate changes.

Suppose a bond pays $100 a year in interest and sells for $1,000. The interest rate is 10 percent ($100/$1,000). If the supply of bonds increases because people want to convert bonds to money, the price of bonds falls. Suppose the price drops to $800. At that price, the interest rate equals 12.5 percent ($100/$800). This is the mechanism by which an excess demand for money changes the interest rate. As the interest rate goes up, the excess demand for money disappears.

Just the opposite occurs at interest rates above equilibrium. In Figure 9, any rate of interest above 9 percent creates an excess supply of money. Now people are holding more of their wealth in the form of money than they would like. What happens? They want to convert some of their money balances into nonmonetary assets, like bonds. As the demand for bonds rises, bond prices increase. And as bond prices go up, interest rates fall. This drop in interest rates restores equilibrium in the money market.

6. How does monetary policy affect the equilibrium level of real GDP?

13-3b Money and Equilibrium Income

Now we are ready to relate monetary policy to the equilibrium level of real GDP. We use Figure 10 to show how a change in the money supply affects real GDP. In Figure 10(a), as the money supply increases from Ms_1 to Ms_2, the equilibrium rate of interest falls from i_1 to i_2.

FIGURE 10 Monetary Policy and Equilibrium Income

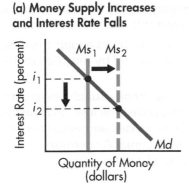

(a) Money Supply Increases and Interest Rate Falls

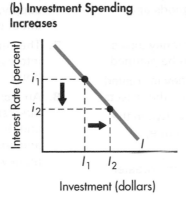

(b) Investment Spending Increases

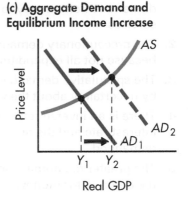

(c) Aggregate Demand and Equilibrium Income Increase

The three diagrams show the sequence of events by which a change in the money supply affects the equilibrium level of real GDP. 10(a) The money supply increases, lowering the equilibrium interest rate. 10(b) The lower interest rate pushes the level of investment up. 10(c) The increase in investment increases aggregate demand and equilibrium real GDP.

Remember that investment (business spending on capital goods) declines as the rate of interest increases. The interest rate is the cost of borrowed funds. As the interest rate rises, the return on investment falls, and with it the level of investment. As the interest rate falls, the return on investment rises, and with it the level of investment. In Figure 10(a), the interest rate falls. In Figure 10(b), you can see the effect of the lower interest rate on investment spending. As the interest rate falls from i_1 to i_2, investment increases from I_1 to I_2. Figure 10(c) is the aggregate demand and supply equilibrium diagram. When investment spending increases, aggregate expenditures are higher at every price level, so the aggregate demand curve shifts to the right, from AD_1 to AD_2. The increase in aggregate demand increases equilibrium income from Y_1 to Y_2.

How does monetary policy affect equilibrium income? As the money supply increases, the equilibrium interest rate falls. As the interest rate falls, the equilibrium level of investment rises. Increased investment increases aggregate demand and equilibrium income. A decrease in the money supply works in reverse: As the interest rate rises, investment falls; as investment falls, aggregate demand and equilibrium income go down.

The mechanism we have just described is an oversimplification because the only element of aggregate expenditures that changes in this model is investment. But an excess demand for or supply of money involves more than simply selling or buying bonds. An excess supply of money probably would be reflected in increased consumption as well. If households are holding more money than they want to hold, they buy not only bonds but also goods and services, so that consumption increases. If they are holding less money than they want to hold, they will both sell bonds and consume less. So the effect of monetary policy on aggregate demand is a product of a change in both investment and consumption. We discuss this in the chapter titled "Macroeconomic Policy: Trade-offs, Expectations, Credibility, and Sources of Business Cycles," where we also examine the important role that expected policy changes can play.

An excess supply of (demand for) money can increase (decrease) consumption as well as investment.

1. The transactions demand for money is a demand to hold money to buy goods and services.

2. The precautionary demand for money exists because not all expenditures can be planned.

3. The speculative demand for money is created by uncertainty about the value of other assets.

4. There is an inverse relationship between the interest rate and the quantity of money demanded.

5. The greater the nominal income, the greater the demand for money.

6. Because the Federal Reserve sets the money supply, the money supply function is independent of the interest rate and nominal income.

7. The current yield on a bond equals the annual interest payment divided by the price of the bond.

8. An increase in the money supply lowers the interest rate; this raises the level of investment, and this in turn increases aggregate demand and equilibrium income. A decrease in the money supply works in reverse.

SUMMARY

1. What does the Federal Reserve do?

- The Federal Reserve is the central bank of the United States. §13-1

- The Federal Reserve System is operated by 12 district banks and a Board of Governors in Washington, D.C. §13-1a

- The Fed services and supervises the banking system, acts as the banker for the U.S. Treasury, and controls the money supply. §13-1b

2. How is monetary policy set?

- The Fed controls nominal GDP indirectly by controlling the quantity of money in the nation's economy. §13-2a

- The Fed uses the growth of the money supply as an intermediate target to help it achieve its ultimate goal—economic growth with stable prices. §13-2a

- Some countries have adopted inflation targeting to guide their monetary policy. §13-2a

3. What are the tools of monetary policy?

- The tools of monetary policy are the reserve requirement, the discount rate, open market operations, quantitative easing, and forward guidance. §13-2b

- The Fed buys bonds to increase the money supply and sells bonds to decrease the money supply. §13-2b

- If the policy interest rate is near zero, a central bank may use quantitative easing to further stimulate the economy and buy financial assets to flood the market with money. §13-2b

- The Federal Open Market Committee (FOMC) issues directives to the Federal Reserve Bank of New York outlining the conduct of monetary policy. §13-2b

4. What role do central banks play in the foreign exchange market?

- Central banks intervene in the foreign exchange market when it is necessary to maintain a targeted exchange rate. §13-2c

5. What are the determinants of the demand for money?

- The demand for money stems from the need to buy goods and services, to prepare for emergencies, and to retain a store of value. §13-3a

- There is an inverse relationship between the quantity of money demanded and the interest rate. §13-3a

- The greater the nominal income, the greater the demand for money. §13-3a

- Because the Fed sets the money supply, the money supply function is independent of the interest rate and real GDP. §13-3a

6. How does monetary policy affect the equilibrium level of real GDP?

- By altering the money supply, the Fed changes the interest rate and the level of investment, shifting aggregate demand and the equilibrium level of real GDP. §13-3

KEY TERMS

discount rate, 289
equation of exchange, 282
federal funds rate, 285
Federal Open Market Committee
 (FOMC), 279
FOMC directive, 285

foreign exchange market
 intervention, 292
forward guidance, 291
intermediate target, 282
legal reserves, 287
open market operations, 289
precautionary demand for money, 294

quantitative easing, 290
quantity theory of money, 283
speculative demand for money, 295
sterilization, 293
transactions demand for money, 294
velocity of money, 283

EXERCISES

1. The Federal Reserve System divides the nation into 12 districts.
   a. List the 12 cities in which the district banks are located.
   b. Which Federal Reserve district do you live in?
2. Briefly describe the functions that the Fed performs for the banking community. In what sense is the Fed a banker's bank?
3. Draw a graph showing equilibrium in the money market. Carefully label all curves and axes, and explain why the curves have the slopes that they do.
4. Using the graph you prepared for exercise 3, illustrate and explain what happens when the Fed increases the money supply.
5. When the Fed decreases the money supply, the equilibrium level of income changes. Illustrate and explain how.
6. Describe the quantity theory of money, defining each variable. Explain how changes in the money supply can affect real GDP and the price level. Under what circumstances could an increase in the money supply have *no* effect on nominal GDP?
7. There are several tools that the Fed uses to implement monetary policy.
   a. Briefly describe these tools.
   b. Explain how the Fed would use each tool in order to increase the money supply.
   c. Suppose the federal funds rate equals zero. Does that mean the Fed can do nothing more to stimulate the economy? Explain your answer.
8. First Bank has total deposits of $2,000,000 and legal reserves of $220,000.
   a. If the reserve requirement is 10 percent, what is the maximum loan that First Bank can make, and what is the maximum increase in the money supply based on First Bank's reserve position?

   b. If the reserve requirement is changed to 5 percent, how much can First Bank lend, and by how much can the money supply be expanded?
9. Suppose you are a member of the FOMC and the U.S. economy is entering a recession. Write a directive to the New York Fed about the conduct of monetary policy over the next two months. Your directive should address a target for the rate of growth of the M2 money supply, the federal funds rate, the rate of inflation, and the foreign exchange value of the dollar versus the Japanese yen and euro. You may refer to the Board of Governors website, **www.federalreserve.gov/monetarypolicy**, for examples, since this site posts FOMC directives.
10. Suppose the Fed has a target range for the yen–dollar exchange rate. How would it keep the exchange rate within the target range if free-market forces push the exchange rate out of the range? Use a graph to help explain your answer.
11. Why do you demand money? What determines how much money you keep in your pocket, purse, or bank accounts?
12. What is the current yield on a bond? Why do interest rates change when bond prices change?
13. If the Fed increases the money supply, what will happen to each of the following (other things being equal)?
    a. Interest rates
    b. Money demand
    c. Investment spending
    d. Aggregate demand
    e. The equilibrium level of national income
14. It is sometimes said that the Federal Reserve System is a nonpolitical agency. In what sense is this true? Why might you doubt that politics have no effect on Fed decisions?

15. Suppose the banking system has vault cash of $1,000, deposits at the Fed of $2,000, and demand deposits of $10,000.

    a. If the reserve requirement is 20 percent, what is the maximum potential increase in the money supply, given the banks' reserve position?

    b. If the Fed now purchases $100 worth of government bonds from private bond dealers, what are the excess reserves of the banking system? (Assume that the bond dealers deposit the $100 in demand deposits.) How much can the banking system increase the money supply, given the new reserve position?

16. What does ECB stand for? Where is the ECB located? In what way is central banking in the euro-area countries similar to the Federal Reserve System?

ECONOMICALLY SPEAKING
THE BANK OF ENGLAND DURING THE FINANCIAL CRISIS

Bank of England Maintains Bank Rate at 5%
September 4, 2008

The Bank of England's Monetary Policy Committee today voted to maintain the official Bank Rate paid on commercial bank reserves at 5.0%.

Bank of England Reduces Bank Rate by 0.5 Percentage Points to 4.5%
October 8, 2008

The Bank of England's Monetary Policy Committee today voted at a special meeting to reduce the official Bank Rate paid on commercial bank reserves to 4.5%.

The Monetary Policy Committee held a special meeting on Wednesday 8 October, some hours in advance of its normal schedule. After that meeting, the Bank of England, in conjunction with the Bank of Canada, the European Central Bank, the US Federal Reserve, Sveriges Riksbank, the Swiss National Bank, and the Bank of Japan, released the following statement:

> Throughout the current financial crisis, central bankers have engaged in continuous close consultation and have cooperated in unprecedented joint actions such as the provision of liquidity to reduce strains in financial markets.

Inflationary pressures have started to moderate in a number of countries, partly reflecting a marked decline in energy and commodity prices. Inflation expectations are diminishing and remain anchored to price stability. The recent intensification of the financial crisis has augmented the downside risks to growth and thus has diminished further the upside risks to price stability.

Some easing of the global monetary conditions is therefore warranted. Accordingly, the Bank of Canada, the Bank of England, the European Central Bank, the Federal Reserve, the Sveriges Riskbank, and the Swiss National Bank are today announcing reductions in policy interest rates. The Bank of Japan expresses its strong support of these policy actions.

In conjunction with the above statement, the Bank of England's Monetary Policy Committee released the following statement:

> In the United Kingdom, CPI inflation rose to 4.7% in August, reflecting increases in food and energy prices. Inflation is likely to rise further to above 5% in the next month or two, in large part as the full effects of already announced increases in the price of domestic energy are felt. But inflation should then drop back, as the contribution from retail energy prices wanes and the margin of spare capacity in the economy increases. Pay growth has so far remained subdued and commodity price pressures have eased, with oil prices down substantially from their mid-summer peak.

Conditions in international credit and money markets have deteriorated very markedly. Many markets are closed. In the United Kingdom, the supply of credit to households and businesses is clearly tightening further as banks seek to adjust their balance sheets. The Committee noted that cuts in official rates could not be expected to resolve the current problems in financial markets and that a significant increase in the capital of the banking sector would be required. The Committee therefore welcomed this morning's announcement of a Government programme to recapitalize the major UK banks.

Data released over the past month indicate that the outlook for economic activity in the United Kingdom has deteriorated substantially, reflecting a sharp monetary contraction. Output growth slowed to a halt in the second quarter, business surveys point to further weakening during the second half of this year, and the labour market has softened. Consumer spending growth has slowed, in part as a result of the squeeze on real incomes, while business and dwellings investment have declined. Equity prices have fallen, and the further tightening in credit conditions will also weigh on domestic demand growth. The depreciation in sterling over the past year should support net exports, but the prospects for demand growth in the UK's main export markets have worsened. The weakness in output growth at home will open up a growing margin of spare capacity that will over time bear down on inflation.

The Committee remains focussed [sic] on setting Bank Rate in order to meet the 2% inflation target. In doing so it continues to balance two risks. On the downside, there is a risk that a sharp slowdown in the economy associated with weak real income growth and the tightening the supply of credit, pulls inflation materially below the target. On the upside, there is a risk that above-target inflation this year and the next raises inflation expectations so that inflation persists above the target for a sustained period. During the past month, the balance of those risks to inflation in the medium term has shifted decisively to the downside. In the light of that outlook, the Committee judged at its October meeting that an immediate reduction in the Bank Rate of 0.5 percentage points to 4.5% was necessary to meet the 2% target for CPI inflation in the medium term.

Source: News Release, The Bank of England. http://www.bankofengland.co.uk/publications/news/

COMMENTARY

Just as the Board of Governors of the Federal Reserve System sets U.S. monetary policy, the Monetary Policy Committee (MPC) of the Bank of England sets U.K. monetary policy. If a monetary policymaker believes that economic growth is too slow and inflation is not likely to increase, then it tries to increase aggregate demand by increasing money growth. As we learned in this chapter, when the Fed increases the money supply, interest rates fall, aggregate demand rises, and real GDP growth increases. The same holds for other central banks.

Here you see two statements from the MPC about the Bank Rate, issued in consecutive months in September and October of 2008. The U.K. Bank Rate is the equivalent of the federal funds rate in the United States. It is the key target for monetary policy. The September statement, which is only one sentence, announces that the MPC decided to leave rates unchanged. There is no discussion of the motivation for this decision or potential changes. One month later the MPC not only decided to reduce the MPC by 0.5 percentage points but also decided to issue a joint statement with other major central bank as well as a discussion of why it thought a reduction in rates was appropriate. In subsequent months the MPC would go on to reduce rates even further and at a faster pace.

What changed to make the MPC go from keeping rates constant and saying essentially nothing to a large decrease in rates along with multiple statements? In between the two months the financial crisis worsened drastically. The financial institution Lehman Brothers filed for bankruptcy, which proceeded to send shock waves through the financial industry across the globe. Massive institutions across the world experienced difficulties finding the funding to continue operating, and the supply of credit came to a near standstill. The MPC recognized that "there is a risk that a sharp slowdown in the economy associated with weak real income growth and the tightening the supply of credit, pulls inflation materially below the target." However, the MPC also mentioned the risk "that inflation persists above the target for a sustained period."

It is important to realize that policymakers do not have very much information at the time when they must make policy decisions. For instance, the consumer price index is available only with a one-month lag, so our knowledge of inflation is always running a month behind the actual economy. The GDP data are even worse. The GDP data are available only quarterly, and we do not find out about GDP until well after a quarter ends, and even then substantial revisions to the numbers often occur many months after the quarter. The point is simply that the Federal Reserve, the MPC, and other policymaking institutions must formulate policy today on the basis of less than complete knowledge of the *current* situation, and the policy must be addressed to a best guess of the *future* situation. It is like trying to drive a car looking only in the rearview mirror. You can see where you have been, but you must make decisions about where you will go next without knowing exactly where you are currently.

For these reasons, policymakers often find themselves the target of critics who dispute their current and future outlook on inflation and other key economic variables. Central banks want to act in advance of rising inflation or slowing GDP growth to avoid a bad economic outcome. However, even central banks cannot always clearly determine the state of the economy and, consequently, the best course of action.

CHAPTER 14

Macroeconomic Policy: Tradeoffs, Expectations, Credibility, and Sources of Business Cycles

©Chuck Rausin/Shutterstock.com

FUNDAMENTAL QUESTIONS

1. Is there a tradeoff between inflation and the unemployment rate?

2. How does the tradeoff between inflation and the unemployment rate vary from the short to the long run?

3. What is the relationship between unexpected inflation and the unemployment rate?

4. How are macroeconomic expectations formed?

5. What makes government policies credible?

6. Are business cycles related to political elections?

7. How do real shocks to the economy affect business cycles?

8. How is inflationary monetary policy related to government fiscal policy?

Preview

Macroeconomics is a dynamic discipline. Monetary and fiscal policies change over time. And so does our understanding of those policies. Economists debate the nature of business cycles—what causes them and what, if anything, government can do about them. Some economists argue that policies that lower the unemployment rate tend to raise the rate of inflation. Others insist that only unexpected inflation can influence real GDP and employment. If the latter economists are right, does government always have to surprise the public in order to improve economic conditions?

top: © Carsten Reisinger/Shutterstock

Some economists claim that politicians manipulate the business cycle to increase their chances of reelection. If they are right, we should expect economic growth just before national elections. But what happens after the elections? What are the long-term effects of political business cycles? Because of these issues, the material in this chapter should be considered somewhat controversial. In the chapter titled "Macroeconomic Viewpoints: New Keynesian, Monetarist, and New Classical," we will examine the controversies in more detail, and it will be more apparent where the sources of controversy lie.

Those who were around in the 1970s can remember the long lines and shortages at gas stations and the rapid increase in the price of oil that resulted from the oil embargo imposed by the Organization of Petroleum Exporting Countries. There was another effect of the oil price shock—the aggregate supply curve in the United States and other oil-importing nations shifted to the left, lowering the equilibrium level of real GDP while raising the price level. Such real sources of business cycles can explain why national output can rise or fall in the absence of any discretionary government macroeconomic policy.

14-1 The Phillips Curve

In 1958, a New Zealand economist, A. W. Phillips, published a study of the relationship between the unemployment rate and the rate of change in wages in England. He found that, over the period from 1826 to 1957, there had been an inverse relationship between the unemployment rate and the rate of change in wages: The unemployment rate fell in years when there were relatively large increases in wages and rose in years when wages increased relatively little. Phillips's study started other economists searching for similar relationships in other countries. In those subsequent studies, it became common to substitute the rate of inflation for the rate of change in wages.

Early studies in the United States found an inverse relationship between inflation and the unemployment rate. The graph that illustrates this relationship is called a **Phillips curve**. Figure 1 shows a Phillips curve for the United States in the 1960s. Over this period, lower inflation rates were associated with higher unemployment rates, as shown by the downward-sloping curve.

The slope of the curve in Figure 1 depicts an inverse relationship between the rate of inflation and the unemployment rate: As the inflation rate falls, the unemployment rate rises. In 1969,

Phillips curve
A graph that illustrates the relationship between inflation and the unemployment rate.

FIGURE 1   A Phillips Curve, United States, 1961–1969

In the 1960s, as the rate of inflation rose, the unemployment rate fell. This inverse relationship suggests a tradeoff between the rate of inflation and the unemployment rate.

the inflation rate was relatively high, at 5.5 percent, while the unemployment rate was relatively low, at 3.5 percent. In 1967, an inflation rate of 3.1 percent was consistent with an unemployment rate of 3.8 percent; and in 1961, 1 percent inflation occurred with 6.7 percent unemployment.

The downward-sloping Phillips curve seems to indicate that there is a tradeoff between unemployment and inflation. A country can have a lower unemployment rate by accepting higher inflation, or a lower rate of inflation by accepting higher unemployment. Certainly this was the case in the United States in the 1960s. But is the curve depicted in Figure 1 representative of the tradeoff over long periods of time?

14-1a An Inflation-Unemployment Tradeoff?

Figure 2 shows unemployment and inflation rates in the United States for several years from 1955 to 2010. The points in the figure do not lie along a downward-sloping curve like the one shown in Figure 1. For example, in 1955, the unemployment rate was 4.4 percent and the inflation rate was −0.4 percent. In 1960, the unemployment rate was 5.5 percent and the inflation rate was 1.7 percent. Both the unemployment rate and the inflation rate had increased since 1955. Moving through time, you can see that the inflation rate tended to increase along with the unemployment rate through the 1960s and 1970s. By 1980, the unemployment rate was 7.1 percent and the inflation rate was 13.5 percent. The scattered points in Figure 2 show no evidence of a tradeoff between unemployment and inflation. A downward-sloping Phillips curve does not seem to exist over the long term.

14-1b Short-Run versus Long-Run Tradeoffs

Most economists believe that the downward-sloping Phillips curve and the tradeoff between inflation and unemployment that it implies are short-term phenomena. Think of a series of Phillips curves, one for each of the points in Figure 2. From 1955 to 1980, the curves shifted out to the right. In the early 1980s, they shifted in to the left.

Figure 3 shows a series of Phillips curves that could account for the data in Figure 2. At any point in time, a downward-sloping Phillips curve indicates a tradeoff between inflation

1. Is there a tradeoff between inflation and the unemployment rate?

2. How does the tradeoff between inflation and the unemployment rate vary from the short to the long run?

FIGURE 2   **Unemployment and Inflation in the United States, 1955–2010**

The data on inflation and unemployment rates in the United States between 1955 and 2010 show no particular relationship between inflation and unemployment over the long run. There is no evidence here of a downward-sloping Phillips curve.

FIGURE 3   **The Shifting Phillips Curve**

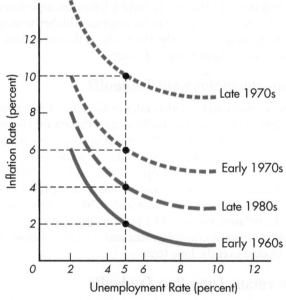

We can reconcile the long-run data on unemployment and inflation with the downward-sloping Phillips curve by using a series of Phillips curves. (In effect, we treat the long run as a series of short-run curves.) The Phillips curve for the early 1960s shows 5 percent unemployment and 2 percent inflation. Over time, the short-run curve shifted out to the right. The early 1970s curve shows 5 percent unemployment and 6 percent inflation. And the short-run curve for the late 1970s shows 5 percent unemployment and 10 percent inflation. In the early 1980s, the short-run Phillips curve began to shift down toward the origin. By the late 1980s, 5 percent unemployment was consistent with 4 percent inflation.

and unemployment. Many economists believe that this kind of tradeoff is just a short-term phenomenon. Over time, the Phillips curve shifts so that the short-run tradeoff between inflation and unemployment disappears in the long run.

On the early 1960s curve in Figure 3, 5 percent unemployment is consistent with 2 percent inflation. By the early 1970s, the curve had shifted up. Here 5 percent unemployment is associated with 6 percent inflation. On the late 1970s curve, 5 percent unemployment is consistent with 10 percent inflation. For more than two decades, the tradeoff between inflation and unemployment worsened as the Phillips curves shifted up, so that higher and higher inflation rates were associated with any given level of unemployment. Then in the 1980s, the tradeoff seemed to improve as the Phillips curve shifted down. On the late 1980s curve, 5 percent unemployment is consistent with 4 percent inflation.

The data indicate that the Phillips curve may have shifted out in the 1960s and 1970s and shifted in during the 1980s.

The Phillips curves in Figure 3 represent changes that took place over time in the United States. We cannot be sure of the actual shape of a Phillips curve at any time, but an outward shift of the curve in the 1960s and 1970s and an inward shift during the 1980s are consistent with the data. Later in this chapter, we describe how changing government policy and the public's expectations about that policy may have shifted aggregate demand and aggregate supply and produced these shifts in the Phillips curves.

14-1b-1 In the Short Run Figure 4 uses the aggregate demand and supply analysis we developed in the chapter titled "Macroeconomic Equilibrium: Aggregate Demand and Supply" to explain the Phillips curve. Initially the economy is operating at point 1 in both diagrams. In Figure 4(a), the aggregate demand curve (AD_1) and the aggregate supply curve (AS_1) intersect at price level P_1 and real GDP level Y_p, the level of potential real GDP. Remember that potential real GDP is the level of income and output generated at the natural rate of unemployment, the unemployment rate that exists in the absence of cyclical unemployment. In Figure 4(b), point 1 lies on Phillips curve I, where the inflation rate is 3 percent and the unemployment rate is 5 percent. We assume that the 5 percent unemployment rate at the level of potential real GDP is the natural rate of unemployment (U_n). A discussion of the natural rate of unemployment and its determinants is given in the Economic Insight, "The Natural Rate of Unemployment."

What happens when aggregate demand goes up from AD_1 to AD_2? A new equilibrium is established along the short-run aggregate supply curve (AS_1) at point 2. Here the price level (P_2) is higher, as is the level of real GDP (Y_2). In part (b), the increase in price and income is reflected in the movement along Phillips curve I to point 2. At point 2, the inflation rate is 6 percent and the unemployment rate is 3 percent. The increase in expenditures raises the inflation rate and lowers the unemployment rate (because national output has surpassed potential output).

Notice that there appears to be a tradeoff between inflation and unemployment on Phillips curve I. The increase in spending increases output and stimulates employment so that the unemployment rate falls. And the higher spending pushes the rate of inflation up. But this tradeoff is only temporary. Point 2 in both diagrams is only a short-run equilibrium.

14-1b-2 In the Long Run As we discussed in the chapter titled "Macroeconomic Equilibrium: Aggregate Demand and Supply," the short-run aggregate supply curve shifts over time as production costs rise in response to higher prices. Once the aggregate supply curve shifts to AS_2, long-run equilibrium occurs at point 3, where AS_2 intersects AD_2. Here, the price level is P_3 and real GDP returns to its potential level, Y_p.

The shift in aggregate supply lowers real GDP. As income falls, the unemployment rate goes up. The decrease in aggregate supply is reflected in the movement from point 2 on Phillips curve I to point 3 on Phillips curve II. As real GDP returns to its potential level (Y_p), unemployment returns to the natural rate (U_n), 5 percent. In the long run, as the economy

FIGURE 4   Aggregate Demand and Supply and the Phillips Curve

(a) Aggregate Demand and Supply

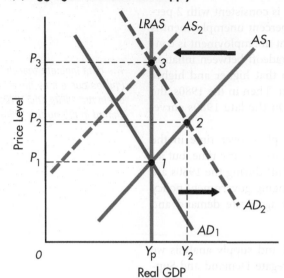

(b) Phillips Curve

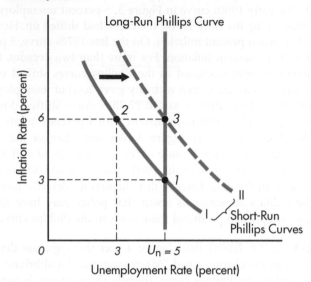

The movement from point 1 to point 2 to point 3 traces the adjustment of the economy to an increase in aggregate demand. Point 1 is initial equilibrium in both diagrams. At this point, potential real GDP is Y_p and the price level is P_1 in the aggregate demand and supply diagram, and the inflation rate is 3 percent with an unemployment rate of 5 percent (the natural rate) along short-run curve I in the Phillips curve diagram.

If the aggregate demand curve shifts from AD_1 to AD_2, equilibrium real GDP goes up to Y_2 and the price level rises to P_2 in the aggregate demand and supply diagram. The increase in aggregate demand pushes the inflation rate up to 6 percent and the unemployment rate down to 3 percent along Phillips curve I. The movement from point 1 to point 2 along the curve indicates a tradeoff between inflation and the unemployment rate.

Over time, the AS curve shifts in response to rising production costs at the higher rate of inflation. Along AS_2, equilibrium is at point 3, where real GDP falls back to Y_p and the price level rises to P_3. As we move from point 2 to point 3 in (b), we shift to short-run Phillips curve II. Here the inflation rate remains high (at 6 percent), while the unemployment rate goes back up to 5 percent, the rate consistent with production at Y_p. In the long run, then, there is no tradeoff between inflation and unemployment. The vertical long-run aggregate supply curve at the potential level of real GDP is associated with the vertical long-run Phillips curve at the natural rate of unemployment.

The long-run Phillips curve is a vertical line at the natural rate of unemployment.

adjusts to an increase in aggregate demand and expectations adjust to the new inflation rate, there is a period in which real GDP falls and the price level rises.

Over time, there is no relationship between the price level and the level of real GDP. You can see this in the aggregate demand and supply diagram. Points 1 and 3 both lie along the long-run aggregate supply curve (*LRAS*) at potential real GDP. The *LRAS* curve has its analogue in the long-run Phillips curve, a vertical line at the natural rate of unemployment. Points 1 and 3 both lie along this curve.

RECAP

1. The Phillips curve shows an inverse relationship between inflation and unemployment.

2. The downward slope of the Phillips curve indicates a tradeoff between inflation and unemployment.

3. Over the long run, that tradeoff disappears.

4. The long-run Phillips curve is a vertical line at the natural rate of unemployment, analogous to the long-run aggregate supply curve at potential real GDP.

ECONOMIC INSIGHT

The Natural Rate of Unemployment

The natural rate of unemployment is defined as the unemployment rate that exists in the absence of cyclical unemployment. As we discussed in the chapter titled "Unemployment and Inflation," the natural rate of unemployment reflects the normal amount of frictional unemployment (people who are temporarily between jobs), structural unemployment (people who have lost jobs because of technological change), and seasonal unemployment (people who have lost jobs because the jobs are available only at certain times of the year). What factors determine the normal amount of frictional and structural unemployment?

One of the most important factors is demographic change. As the age, gender, and racial makeup of the labor force changes, the natural rate of unemployment also changes. For instance, when the baby boom generation entered the labor force, the natural rate of unemployment increased because new workers typically have the highest unemployment rates. Between 1956 and 1979, the proportion of young adults (ages 16 to 24) in the labor force increased, increasing the natural rate of unemployment. Since 1980, the average age of U.S. workers has been rising. As workers age, employers can more easily evaluate a worker's ability based upon that worker's job history. In addition, younger workers are more likely to have difficulty finding a good job match for their skills and so are likely to have higher frictional unemployment, whereas older workers are more likely to have a long-term job with a single employer. As the labor force ages, therefore, we should expect the natural rate of unemployment to fall.

In addition to the composition of the labor force, several other factors affect the natural rate of unemployment:

- In the early 1990s, structural changes in the economy, such as the shift from manufacturing to service jobs and the downsizing and restructuring of firms throughout the economy, contributed to a higher natural rate of unemployment. Related to these structural changes is a decline in the demand for low-skilled workers, so that rising unemployment is overwhelmingly concentrated among workers with limited education and skills.

- Increases in the legal minimum wage tend to raise the natural rate of unemployment. When the government mandates that employers pay some workers a higher wage than a freely competitive labor market would pay, fewer workers are employed.

- The more generous the unemployment benefits, the higher the natural rate of unemployment. Increased benefits reduce the cost of being out of work and allow unemployed workers to take their time finding a new job. For these reasons, we observe higher natural rates of unemployment in European countries, where unemployed workers receive higher benefits.

- Income taxes can also affect the natural rate of unemployment. Higher taxes mean that workers keep less of their earned income and so have less incentive to work.

The effect of these factors on the unemployment rate is complex, so it is difficult to state exactly what the natural rate of unemployment is. But as these factors change over time, the natural rate of unemployment also changes.

One last thing: It is not clear that minimizing the natural rate of unemployment is a universal goal. Minimum wages, unemployment benefits, and taxes have other important implications besides their effect on the natural rate of unemployment. We cannot expect these variables to be set solely in terms of their effect on unemployment.

14-2 The Role of Expectations

The data and analysis in the previous section indicate that there is no long-run tradeoff between inflation and unemployment. But they do not explain the movement of the Phillips curve in the 1960s, 1970s, and 1980s. To understand why the short-run curve shifts, you must understand the role that unexpected inflation plays in the economy.

3. What is the relationship between unexpected inflation and the unemployment rate?

14-2a Expected versus Unexpected Inflation

Figure 5 shows two short-run Phillips curves like those in Figure 4. Each curve is drawn for a particular expected rate of inflation. Curve I shows the tradeoff between inflation and unemployment when the inflation rate is expected to be 3 percent. If the actual rate of inflation (measured along the vertical axis) is 3 percent, the economy is operating at point 1, with an unemployment rate of 5 percent (the natural rate). If the inflation rate unexpectedly increases to 6 percent, the economy moves from point 1 to point 2 along Phillips curve I. Obviously, unexpected inflation can affect the unemployment rate. There are three factors at work here: wage expectations, inventory fluctuations, and wage contracts.

14-2a-1 Wage Expectations and Unemployment

reservation wage
The minimum wage that a worker is willing to accept.

Unemployed workers who are looking for a job choose a **reservation wage**, the minimum wage that they are willing to accept. They continue to look for work until they receive an offer that equals or exceeds their reservation wage.

Wages are not the only factor that workers take into consideration before accepting a job offer. A firm that offers good working conditions and fringe benefits can pay a lower wage than a firm that does not offer these advantages. But other things being equal, workers choose higher wages over lower wages. We simplify our analysis here by assuming that the only variable that affects the unemployed worker who is looking for a job is the reservation wage.

The link between unexpected inflation and the unemployment rate stems from the fact that wage offers are surprisingly high when the rate of inflation is surprisingly high. An unexpected increase in inflation means that prices are higher than anticipated, as are nominal income and wages. If aggregate demand increases unexpectedly, then prices, output, employment, and wages go up. Unemployed workers with a constant reservation wage find it easier to obtain a satisfactory wage offer during a period when wages are rising

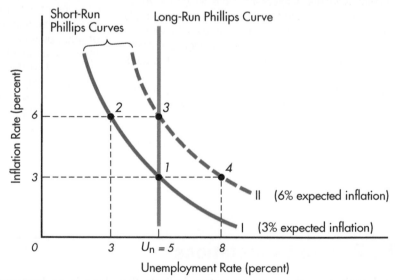

FIGURE 5   Expectations and the Phillips Curve

Short-run Phillips curve I shows the tradeoff between inflation and the unemployment rate as long as people expect 3 percent inflation. When the actual rate of inflation is 3 percent, the rate of unemployment (U_n) is 5 percent (point 1). Short-run Phillips curve II shows the tradeoff as long as people expect 6 percent inflation. When the actual rate of inflation is 6 percent, the unemployment rate is 5 percent (point 3).

faster than the workers expected. This means that more unemployed workers find jobs, and they find those jobs more quickly than they do in a period when the rate of inflation is expected. So the unemployment rate falls during a period of unexpectedly high inflation (Figure 6).

Consider an example. Suppose an accountant named Jason determines that he must find a job that pays at least $105 a day. Jason's reservation wage is $105. Furthermore, Jason expects prices and wages to be fairly stable across the economy; he expects no inflation. Jason looks for a job and finds that the jobs he qualifies for are offering wages of only $100 a day. Because his job offers are all paying less than his reservation wage, he keeps on looking. Let us say that aggregate demand rises unexpectedly. Firms increase production and raise prices. To hire more workers, they increase the wages they offer. Suppose wages go up 5 percent. Now the jobs that Jason qualifies for are offering 5 percent higher wages, $105 a day instead of $100 a day. At this higher wage rate, Jason quickly accepts a job and starts working. This example explains why the move from point 1 to point 2 in Figure 5 occurs.

The short-run Phillips curve assumes a constant *expected* rate of inflation. It also assumes that every unemployed worker who is looking for a job has a constant reservation wage. When inflation rises unexpectedly, then, wages rise faster than expected and the unemployment rate falls. The element of surprise is critical here. If the increase in inflation is *expected*, unemployed workers who are looking for a job will revise their reservation wage to match the expected change in the level of prices. If reservation wages go up with the rate of inflation, there is no tradeoff between inflation and the unemployment rate. Higher inflation is associated with the original unemployment rate.

> If the reservation wage goes up with the rate of inflation, there is no tradeoff between inflation and the unemployment rate.

Let's go back to Jason, the accountant who wants a job that pays $105 a day. Previously we said that if wages increased to $105 because of an unexpected increase in aggregate demand, he would quickly find an acceptable job. However, if Jason knows that the price level is going to go up 5 percent, then he knows that a wage increase from $100 to $105 is not a real wage increase because he will need $105 in order to buy what $100 would buy before. The *nominal wage* is the number of dollars earned; the *real wage* is the purchasing power of those dollars. If the nominal wage increases 5 percent at the same time that prices have gone up 5 percent, it takes 5 percent more money to buy the same goods and services. The real wage has not changed. What happens? Jason revises his reservation wage to account for the higher price level. If he wants a 5 percent higher real wage, his reservation wage goes up to $110.25 (5 percent more than $105). Now if employers offer him $105, he refuses and keeps searching.

FIGURE 6 Inflation, Unemployment, and Wage Expectations

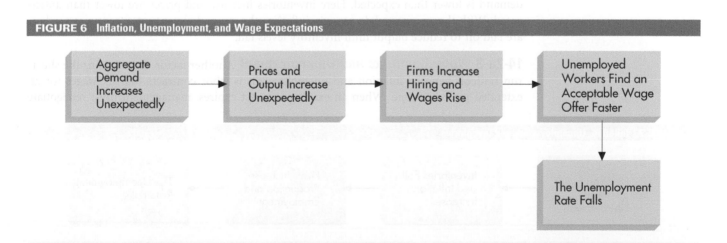

In Figure 5, an expected increase in inflation moves us from point 1 on curve I to point 3 on curve II. When increased inflation is expected, the reservation wage reflects the higher rate of inflation, and there is no tradeoff between inflation and the unemployment rate. Instead, the economy moves along the long-run Phillips curve, with unemployment at its natural rate. The clockwise movement from point 1 to point 2 to point 3 is the pattern that follows an unexpected increase in aggregate demand.

What if the inflation rate is lower than expected? Here we find a reservation wage that reflects higher expected inflation. This means that those people who are looking for jobs are going to have a difficult time finding acceptable wage offers, the number of unemployed workers is going to increase, and the unemployment rate is going to rise. This sequence is shown in Figure 5 as the economy moves from point 3 to point 4. When the actual inflation rate is 6 percent and the expected inflation rate is also 6 percent, the economy is operating at the natural rate of unemployment. When the inflation rate falls to 3 percent but workers still expect 6 percent inflation, the unemployment rate rises (at point 4 along curve II). Eventually, if the inflation rate remains at 3 percent, workers adjust their expectations to the lower rate and the economy moves to point 1 on curve I. The short-run effect of unexpected *disinflation* is rising unemployment. Over time, the short-run increase in the unemployment rate is eliminated.

> *As long as the actual rate of inflation equals the expected rate, the economy operates at the natural rate of unemployment.*

As long as the actual rate of inflation equals the expected rate, the economy remains at the natural rate of unemployment. The tradeoff between inflation and the unemployment rate comes from unexpected inflation.

14-2a-2 Inventory Fluctuations and Unemployment

Businesses hold inventories based on what they expect their sales to be. When aggregate demand is greater than expected, inventories fall below the targeted levels. To restore inventories to the levels wanted, production is increased. Increased production leads to increased employment. If aggregate demand is lower than expected, inventories rise above the targeted levels. To reduce inventories, production is cut back and workers are laid off from their jobs until sales have lowered the unwanted inventories. Once production increases, employment rises again.

> *When aggregate demand is higher than expected, inventories are lower than expected and prices are higher than expected, so the unemployment rate falls. When aggregate demand is lower than expected, inventories are higher than expected and prices are lower than expected, so the unemployment rate rises.*

Inventory, production, and employment all play a part in the Phillips curve analysis (Figure 7). Expected sales and inventory levels are based on an expected level of aggregate demand. If aggregate demand is greater than expected, inventories fall and prices of the remaining goods in stock rise. With the unexpected increase in inflation, the unemployment rate falls as businesses hire more workers to increase output to offset falling inventories. This sequence represents movement along a short-run Phillips curve because there is a tradeoff between inflation and the unemployment rate. We find the same tradeoff if aggregate demand is lower than expected. Here inventories increase and prices are lower than anticipated. With the unexpected decrease in inflation, the unemployment rate goes up as workers are laid off to reduce output until inventory levels fall.

14-2a-3 Wage Contracts and Unemployment

Another factor that explains the short-run tradeoff between inflation and unemployment is labor contracts that fix wages for an extended period of time. When an existing contract expires, management must renegotiate

FIGURE 7   Inflation, Unemployment, and Inventories

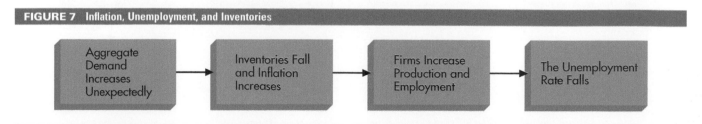

with labor. A firm that is facing lower demand for its products may negotiate lower wages in order to keep as many workers employed as before. If the demand for a firm's products falls while a wage contract is in force, the firm must maintain wages; this means that it is going to have to lay off workers.

For example, a pizza restaurant with $1,000 a day in revenues employs four workers at $40 a day each. The firm's total labor costs are $160 a day. Suppose revenues fall to $500 a day. If the firm wants to cut its labor costs in half, to $80, it has two choices: It can maintain wages at $40 a day and lay off two workers, or it can lower wages to $20 a day and keep all four workers. If the restaurant has a contract with the employees that sets wages at $40 a day, it must lay off two workers.

If demand increases while a wage contract is in force, a business hires more workers at the fixed wage. Once the contract expires, the firm's workers will negotiate higher wages, to reflect the increased demand. For instance, suppose prices in the economy, including the price of pizzas, go up 10 percent. If the pizza restaurant can raise its prices 10 percent and sell as many pizzas as before (because the price of every other food also has gone up 10 percent), its daily revenues increase from $1,000 to $1,100. If the restaurant has a labor contract that fixes wages at $40 a day, its profits are going to go up, reflecting the higher price of pizzas. With its increased profits, the restaurant may be willing to hire more workers. Once the labor contract expires, the workers ask for a 10 percent wage increase to match the price level increase. If wages go up to $44 a day (10 percent higher than $40), the firm cannot hire more workers because wages have gone up in proportion to the increase in prices. If the costs of doing business rise at the same rate as prices, both profits and employment remain the same.

In the national economy, wage contracts are staggered; they expire at different times. Only 30 to 40 percent of all contracts expire each year across the entire economy. As economic conditions change, firms with expiring wage contracts can adjust *wages* to those conditions, whereas firms with existing contracts must adjust *employment* to those conditions.

How do long-term wage contracts tie in with the Phillips curve analysis? The expected rate of inflation is based on expected aggregate demand and is reflected in the wage that is agreed on in the contract. When the actual rate of inflation equals the expected rate, businesses retain the same number of workers that they had planned on when they signed the contract. For the economy overall, when actual and expected inflation rates are the same, the economy is operating at the natural rate of unemployment. That is, businesses are not hiring new workers because of an unexpected increase in aggregate demand, and they are not laying off workers because of an unexpected decrease in aggregate demand.

When aggregate demand is higher than expected, those firms with unexpired wage contracts hire more workers at the fixed wage, reducing unemployment (Figure 8). Those firms with expiring contracts have to offer higher wages in order to maintain the existing level of employment at the new demand condition. When aggregate demand is lower than expected, those firms with unexpired contracts have to lay off workers because they cannot lower the wage, while those firms with expiring contracts negotiate lower wages in order to keep their workers.

Wage contracts force businesses to adjust employment rather than wages in response to an unexpected change in aggregate demand.

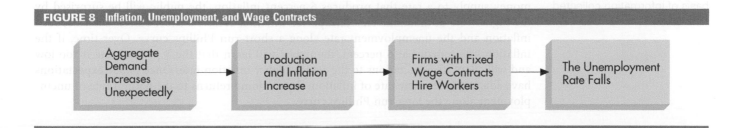

FIGURE 8 Inflation, Unemployment, and Wage Contracts

ECONOMIC INSIGHT

Why Wages Don't Fall During Recessions

A look at macroeconomic data across countries reveals that when economies experience recessions, unemployment rates rise, but wages fall very little, if at all. If we think of a supply and demand diagram for labor, we would think that as demand for labor falls in a recession, both the equilibrium quantity of labor and the equilibrium price, the wage rate, would fall. We do see the quantity effect, as workers lose their jobs and the unemployment rate rises. Why do we not see wages falling also?

The text discusses long-term labor contracts as one reason why wages may be relatively inflexible over time. Beyond the presence of contracts, recent research points to human behavior as a contributing factor. Surveys of firms and workers indicate that worker morale is a major reason why wages are not reduced during recessions. Workers would view a wage cut as an indication that the firm does not value their work as much, and they might, therefore, suffer lower

morale, with the result being lower effort. When some workers are laid off, those workers suffer from the job loss, but they are no longer at the firm and thus cannot harm morale and work effort. Only in cases where the very survival of the firm is clearly at stake do wage cuts appear to be acceptable to workers.

So wages are "sticky downwards" because this promotes good worker effort and ensures that workers and firms share the same goals of efficient production and profit maximization. Rather than keep all workers when demand falls by paying lower wages to all, it may be better for the firm to lay off some workers and keep paying the remaining employees the same wage as before.

Sources: Truman F. Bewley, *Why Wages Don't Fall During a Recession* (Cambridge: Harvard University Press, 1999), and Peter Howitt, "Looking Inside the Labor Market: A Review Article," *Journal of Economic Literature*, March 2002.

If wages were always flexible, unexpected changes in aggregate demand might be reflected largely in *wage* rather than *employment adjustments*. Wage contracts force businesses to adjust employment when aggregate demand changes unexpectedly. The Economic Insight "Why Wages Don't Fall During Recessions" addresses this issue further.

14-2b Forming Expectations

Expectations play a key role in explaining the short-run Phillips curve, the tradeoff between inflation and the unemployment rate. How are these expectations formed?

4. *How are macroeconomic expectations formed?*

adaptive expectation
An expectation formed on the basis of information collected in the past.

14-2b-1 Adaptive Expectations Expectations can be formed solely on the basis of experience. **Adaptive expectations** are expectations that are determined by what has happened in the recent past.

People learn from their experiences. For example, suppose the inflation rate has been 3 percent for the past few years. Based on past experience, then, people expect the inflation rate in the future to remain at 3 percent. If the Federal Reserve increases the growth of the money supply to a rate that produces 6 percent inflation, the public will be surprised by the higher rate of inflation. This unexpected inflation creates a short-run tradeoff between inflation and the unemployment rate along a short-run Phillips curve. Over time, if the inflation rate remains at 6 percent, the public will learn that the 3 percent rate is too low and will adapt its expectations to the actual, higher inflation rate. Once public expectations have adapted to the new rate of inflation, the economy returns to the natural rate of unemployment along the long-run Phillips curve.

14-2b-2 Rational Expectations Many economists believe that adaptive expectations are too narrow. If people look only at past information, they are ignoring what could be important information in the current period. **Rational expectations** are based on all available relevant information.

We are not saying that people have to know everything in order to form expectations. Rational expectations require only that people consider all the information that they believe to be relevant. This information includes their past experience, but also what is currently happening and what they expect to happen in the future. For instance, in forming expectations about inflation, people consider rates in the recent past, current policy, and anticipated shifts in aggregate demand and supply that could affect the future rate of inflation.

If the inflation rate has been 3 percent over the past few years, adaptive expectations suggest that the future inflation rate will be 3 percent. No other information is considered. Rational expectations are based on more than the historical rate. Suppose the Fed announces a new policy that everyone believes will increase inflation in the future. With rational expectations, the effect of this announcement will be considered. Thus, when the actual rate of inflation turns out to be more than 3 percent, there is no short-run tradeoff between inflation and the unemployment rate. The economy moves directly along the long-run Phillips curve to the higher inflation rate, while unemployment remains at the natural rate.

rational expectation
An expectation that is formed using all available relevant information.

RECAP

1. Wage expectations, inventory fluctuations, and wage contracts help explain the short-run tradeoff between inflation and the unemployment rate.

2. The reservation wage is the minimum wage that a worker is willing to accept.

3. Because wage expectations reflect expected inflation, when the inflation rate is surprisingly high, unemployed workers find jobs faster and the unemployment rate falls.

4. Unexpected increases in aggregate demand lower inventories and raise prices. To increase output (to replenish shrinking inventories), businesses hire more workers, which reduces the unemployment rate.

5. When aggregate demand is higher than expected, those businesses with wage contracts hire more workers at the fixed wage, lowering unemployment.

6. If wages were always flexible, unexpected changes in aggregate demand would be reflected in wage adjustments rather than employment adjustments.

7. Adaptive expectations are formed on the basis of information about the past.

8. Rational expectations are formed using all available relevant information.

14-3 Credibility and Time Inconsistency

The rate of inflation is a product of growth in the money supply. That growth is controlled by the country's central bank. If the Federal Reserve follows a policy of rapidly increasing the money supply, one consequence is rapid inflation. If it follows a policy of slow growth, it keeps inflation down.

To help the public predict the future course of monetary policy, Congress passed the Federal Reserve Reform Act (1977) and the Full Employment and Balanced Growth Act (1978). The Full Employment Act requires that the chairman of the Board of Governors of the Federal Reserve System testify before Congress semiannually about the Fed's targets for money growth, along with other policy plans.

time inconsistent
A characteristic of a policy or plan that changes over time in response to changing conditions.

Of course, the Fed's plans are only plans. There is no requirement that the central bank actually follow the plans it announces to Congress. During the course of the year, the Fed may decide that a new policy is necessary in light of economic developments. Changing conditions mean that plans can be **time inconsistent**. A plan is time inconsistent when it is changed over time in response to changed conditions.

14-3a The Policymaker's Problem

Time inconsistency gives the Fed a credibility problem and the public the problem of guessing where monetary policy and the inflation rate are actually heading. Figure 9 shows an example of how announced monetary policy can turn out to be time inconsistent. The Fed,

FIGURE 9 Time Inconsistency: An Example

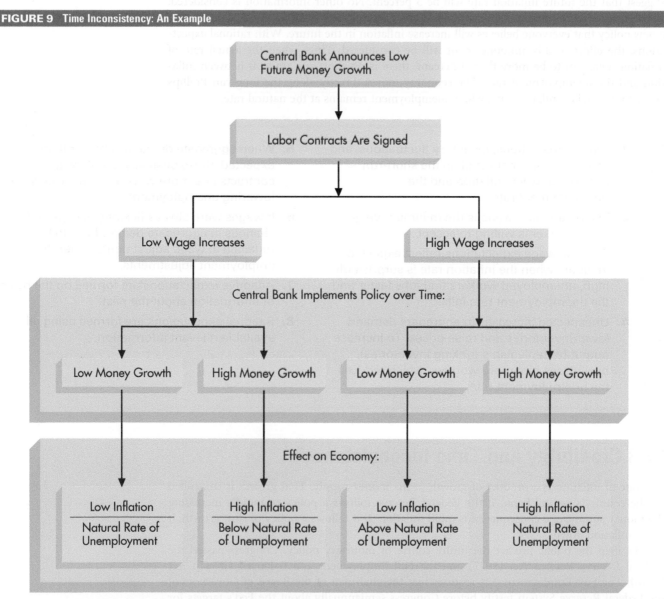

Regardless of which labor contract is signed, the central bank achieves the lowest unemployment rate by following the highmoney-growth policy—the opposite of its announced policy.

like all central banks, always announces that it plans to follow a low-money-growth policy to promote a low rate of inflation. (It is unlikely that a central bank would ever state that it intends to follow an inflationary monetary policy.) Yet we know that the world is often characterized by higher rates of inflation. Because the actual inflation rate often ends up being higher than the intended inflation rate, low-inflation plans often are time inconsistent.

In Figure 9, labor contracts are signed following the central bank's announcement. The contracts call for either low wage increases or high wage increases. If everyone believes that the money supply is going to grow at the announced low rate, then the low-wage contracts are signed. However, if there is reason to believe that the announced policy is time inconsistent, the high-wage contracts are signed.

Over time, the central bank either follows the announced low-money-growth policy or implements a high-money-growth policy. If the low-wage contract is in force and the central bank follows the low-money-growth policy, the actual inflation rate will match the low rate that people expected, and the unemployment rate will equal the natural rate. If the central bank follows a high-money-growth policy, the rate of inflation will be higher than expected, and the unemployment rate will fall below the natural rate.

If the high-wage contract is in force and the low-money-growth policy is followed, the inflation rate will be lower than expected, and the unemployment rate will exceed the natural rate. If the high-money-growth policy is followed, the inflation rate will be as expected, and the unemployment rate will be at the natural rate.

Look at what happens to unemployment. Regardless of which labor contract is signed, if the central bank wants to keep unemployment as low as possible, it must deviate from its announced plan. The plan turns out to be time inconsistent. Because the public knows that unemployment, like the rate of inflation, is a factor in the Fed's policymaking, the central bank's announced plan is not credible.

14-3b Credibility

If the public does not believe the low-money-growth plans of the central bank, high-wage contracts will always be signed, and the central bank will always have to follow a high-money-growth policy to maintain the natural rate of unemployment. This cycle creates an economy in which high inflation persists year after year. If the central bank always followed its announced plan of low money growth and low inflation, the public would believe the plan, low-wage contracts would always be signed, and the natural rate of unemployment would exist at the low rate of inflation. In either case, high or low inflation, if the inflation rate is at the expected level, the unemployment rate does not change. If the central bank eliminates the goal of reducing unemployment below the natural rate, the problem of inflation disappears. However, the public must be convinced that the central bank intends to pursue low money growth in the long run, avoiding the temptation to reduce the unemployment rate in the short run.

How does the central bank achieve credibility? One way is to fix the growth rate of the money supply by law. Congress could pass a law requiring that the Fed maintain a growth rate of, say, 3 to 5 percent a year. There would be problems in defining the money supply, but this kind of law would give the Fed's policies credibility.

In the past decade, central banks around the world have increasingly turned to inflation targeting as a manner of achieving credibility. By establishing a publicly announced target for inflation, the public can anticipate what policy will be by knowing whether the inflation rate is above or below the target. For instance, some banks target a particular inflation rate—for example, the Bank of England targets a rate of 2 percent. Other banks target a range for inflation—for example, the European Central Bank's target of near or below 2 percent, as well as the Bank of Canada's 1 to 3 percent. The Federal Reserve does not announce an official inflation target, but it is believed by many that an inflation rate in the range of 1 to 2 percent is implicit in Fed policy.

5. What makes government policies credible?

A key for establishing credibility is to create incentives for monetary authorities to take a long-term view of monetary policy. In the long run, the economy is better off if policymakers do not try to exploit the short-run tradeoff between inflation and the unemployment rate. The central bank can achieve a lower rate of inflation at the natural rate of unemployment by avoiding unexpected increases in the rate at which money and inflation grow.

Reputation is a key factor here. If the central bank considers the effects of its actual policy on public expectations, it will find it easier to achieve low inflation by establishing a reputation for low-inflation policies. A central bank with a reputation for time-consistent plans will find that labor contracts will call for low wage increases because people believe that the bank is going to follow its announced plans and generate a low rate of inflation. In other words, by maintaining a reputation for following through on its announced policy, the Fed can earn the public confidence necessary to produce a low rate of inflation in the long run.

1. A plan is time inconsistent when it changes over time in response to changing conditions.

2. If the public believes that an announced policy is time inconsistent, policymakers have a credibility problem that can limit the success of their plans.

3. Credibility can be achieved by fixing the growth rate of the money supply by law or by creating incentives for policymakers to follow through on their announced plans.

14-4 Sources of Business Cycles

In the chapter titled "Fiscal Policy," we examined the effect of fiscal policy on the equilibrium level of real GDP. Changes in government spending and taxes can expand or contract the economy. In the chapter titled "Monetary Policy,"we described how monetary policy affects the equilibrium level of real GDP. Changes in the money supply can also produce booms and recessions. In addition to the policy-induced sources of business cycles covered in earlier chapters, there are other sources of economic fluctuations that economists have studied. One is the election campaign of incumbent politicians; when a business cycle results from this action, it is called a *political business cycle*. Macroeconomic policy may be used to promote the reelection of incumbent politicians. We also examine another source of business cycles that is not related to discretionary policy actions, the *real business cycle*.

14-4a The Political Business Cycle

6. *Are business cycles related to political elections?*

If a short-run tradeoff exists between inflation and unemployment, an incumbent administration could stimulate the economy just before an election to lower the unemployment rate, making voters happy and increasing the probability of reelection. Of course, after the election, the long-run adjustment to the expansionary policy would lead to higher inflation and move unemployment back to the natural rate.

Figure 10 illustrates the pattern. Before the election, the economy is initially at point 1 in Figure 10(a) and Figure 10(b). The incumbent administration stimulates the economy by increasing government spending or increasing the growth of the money supply. Aggregate demand shifts from AD_1 to AD_2 in Figure 10(a). In the short run, the increase in aggregate demand is unexpected, so the economy moves along the initial aggregate supply curve (AS_1) to point 2. This movement is reflected in Figure 10(b), in the movement from point 1 to point 2 along short-run Phillips curve I. The pre-election expansionary policy increases real

FIGURE 10   The Political Business Cycle

(a) Aggregate Demand and Supply

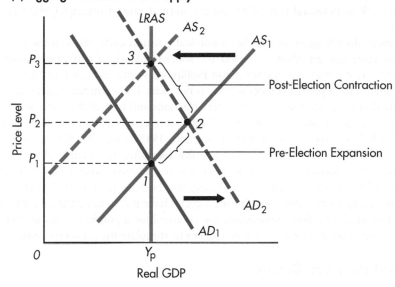

(b) Phillips Curve

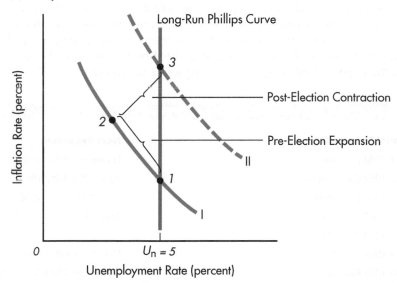

Before the election, the government stimulates the economy, unexpectedly increasing aggregate demand. The economy moves from point 1 to point 2, pushing equilibrium real GDP above Y_p 10(a) and the unemployment rate below U_n 10(b). The incumbent politicians hope that rising incomes and lower unemployment will translate into votes. After the election comes adjustment to the higher aggregate demand, as the economy moves from point 2 to point 3. The aggregate supply curve shifts to the left, and equilibrium real GDP falls back to Y_p. Unemployment goes back up to U_n, and the rate of inflation rises.

GDP and lowers the unemployment rate. Once the public adjusts its expectations to the higher inflation rate, the economy experiences a recession. Real GDP falls back to its potential level (Y_p), and the unemployment rate goes back up to the natural rate (U_n), as shown by the movement from point 2 to point 3 in both parts of the figure.

An unexpected increase in government spending or money growth temporarily stimulates the economy. If an election comes during the period of expansion, higher incomes and lower unemployment may increase support for the incumbent administration. The long-run adjustment back to potential real GDP and the natural rate of unemployment comes after the election.

Economists do not agree on whether a political business cycle exists in the United States. But they do agree that an effort to exploit the short-run tradeoff between inflation and the unemployment rate would shift the short-run Phillips curve out, as shown in Figure 10(b).

The evidence for a political business cycle is not clear. If government macroeconomic policy is designed to stimulate the economy before elections and to bear the costs of rising unemployment and inflation after elections, we should see recessions regularly following national elections. Table 1 lists the presidential elections since 1948 along with the recessions that followed them. In six cases, a recession occurred the year after an election. A recession began before President Kennedy's election, and there was no recession during the Johnson, second Reagan, and Clinton administrations. Of course, just because recessions do not follow every election does not guarantee that some business cycles have not stemmed from political manipulation. If a short-run Phillips curve exists, the potential for a political business cycle exists as long as the public does not expect the government to stimulate the economy before elections.

14-4b Real Business Cycles

In recent years, economists have paid increasing attention to real **shocks**—unexpected changes—to the economy as a source of business cycles. Many believe that it is not only fiscal or monetary policy that triggers expansion or contraction in the economy, but also technological change, change in tastes, labor strikes, weather, war, terrorism, or other real changes. A real business cycle is one that is generated by a change in one of those real variables.

Interest in the real business cycle was stimulated by the oil price shocks in the early 1970s and the important role they played in triggering the recession of 1973–1975. At that

7. *How do real shocks to the economy affect business cycles?*

shock
An unexpected change in a variable.

TABLE 1 Presidential Elections and U.S. Recessions, 1948–2009	
Presidential Election (Winner)	**Next Recession**
November 1948 (Truman)	November 1948–October 1949
November 1952 (Eisenhower)	June 1953–May 1954
November 1956 (Eisenhower)	June 1957–April 1958
November 1960 (Kennedy)	April 1960–February 1961
November 1964 (Johnson)	
November 1968 (Nixon)	October 1969–November 1970
November 1972 (Nixon)	December 1973–March 1975
November 1976 (Carter)	January 1980–July 1980
November 1980 (Reagan)	May 1981–November 1982
November 1984 (Reagan)	
November 1988 (G. H. W. Bush)	July 1990–March 1991
November 1992 (Clinton)	
November 1996 (Clinton)	
November 2000 (G. W. Bush)	March 2001–November 2001
November 2004 (G. W. Bush)	December 2007–June 2009
November 2008 (Obama)	

time, many economists were focusing on the role of unexpected changes in monetary policy in generating business cycles. They argued that these kinds of policy changes (changes in a nominal variable, the money supply) were responsible for the shifts in aggregate demand that led to expansions and contractions. When OPEC raised oil prices, it caused major shifts in aggregate supply. Higher oil prices in 1973 and 1974, and in 1979 and 1980, reduced aggregate supply, pushing the equilibrium level of real GDP down. Lower oil prices in 1986 raised aggregate supply and equilibrium real GDP.

An economy-wide real shock, like a substantial change in the price of oil, can affect output and employment across all sectors of the economy. Even an industry-specific shock can generate a recession or expansion in the entire economy if the industry produces a product used by a substantial number of other industries. For example, a labor strike in the steel industry would have major recessionary implications for the economy as a whole. If the output of steel fell, the price of steel would be bid up by all the industries that use steel as an input. This would shift the short-run aggregate supply curve to the left, as shown in Figure 11(a), and would move equilibrium real GDP from Y_1 down to Y_2.

Real shocks can also have expansionary effects on the economy. Suppose that the weather is particularly good one year, so that harvests are surprisingly large. What happens? The price of food, cotton, and other agricultural output tends to fall, and the short-run aggregate supply curve shifts to the right, as shown in Figure 11(b), raising equilibrium real GDP from Y_1 to Y_2.

Extreme weather can be a source of real business-cycle fluctuations. Hurricane Katrina destroyed some of the capital stock of the nation along the Gulf Coast and was associated with a temporary reduction in output. If good weather leads to a banner harvest, the aggregate supply curve shifts to the right, like the shift from AS_1 to AS_2, raising equilibrium real GDP from Y_1 to Y_2.

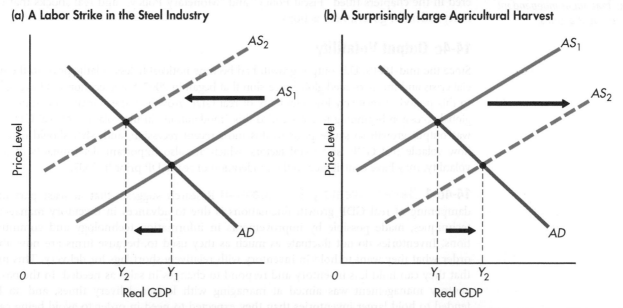

FIGURE 11 The Impact of Real Shocks on Equilibrium Real GDP

(a) A Labor Strike in the Steel Industry

(b) A Surprisingly Large Agricultural Harvest

A labor strike in a key industry can shift the aggregate supply curve to the left, like the shift from AS_1 to AS_2. This pushes equilibrium real GDP down from Y_1 to Y_2. If good weather leads to a banner harvest, the aggregate supply curve shifts to the right, like the shift from AS_1 to AS_2, raising equilibrium real GDP from Y_1 to Y_2.

Extreme weather can be a source of real business-cycle fluctuations. Hurricane Katrina destroyed some of the capital stock of the nation along the Gulf Coast and was associated with a temporary reduction in output

A business cycle can be the product of discretionary government policy or of real shocks that occur independent of government actions.

Real business cycles explain why national output can expand or contract in the absence of a discretionary macroeconomic policy that would shift aggregate demand. To fully understand business cycles, we must consider both policy-induced changes in real GDP, as covered in the chapters titled "Fiscal Policy" and "Monetary Policy," and real shocks that occur independent of government actions.

14-4c Output Volatility

Since the mid-1980s, U.S. output growth had become noticeably less volatile prior to the financial crisis and the associated global recession that began in 2007. Some economists have referred to this period of relatively low variability of real GDP growth as the "Great Moderation." The global recession beginning in 2007 ended this "moderation" in the volatility of real GDP. Why was output growth so stable prior to this most recent recession, and what should determine how volatile real GDP is? Several factors, which are also important determinants of output volatility, may have contributed to the moderation of real GDP prior to 2007.

14-4c-1 Better Inventory Management Research suggests that at least part of the dampening of real GDP growth fluctuations is due to advances in inventory management techniques, made possible by improvements in information technology and communications. Inventories do not fluctuate as much as they used to, because firms are now able to order what they want to hold in inventory with relatively short lags for delivery. This means that they can hold less inventory and respond to changes in sales as needed. In the past, inventory management was aimed at managing with longer delivery times, and so firms tended to hold larger inventories than they expected to need in order to avoid being caught short if sales were greater than expected. In this earlier environment, if sales were lower than expected, then orders for new goods, and consequently production, dropped dramatically in order to allow inventories to be reduced over time to match the lower level of sales. If sales were much higher than expected, inventories dropped to very low levels until firms could restock to catch up with sales. Today, firms are able to receive shipments of new inventory with a much shorter delay; "just in time" inventory management allows firms to adjust inventories to changing business conditions quickly. This has helped level out both inventories and the overall production of goods and has contributed to lower real output volatility.

14-4c-2 Changes in Financial Markets Prior to the early 1980s, the maximum rate of interest that U.S. banks could pay on deposits was limited by a Federal Reserve regulation known as *Regulation Q*. Thus, when interest rates rose above what banks could pay, people would withdraw money from banks and seek higher interest rates elsewhere. This forced banks to reduce their lending on things like home mortgages. As a result, investment in residential housing was much more volatile during the era prior to the removal of the ceiling on interest rates. In addition to changes in financial market regulations, which contribute to less output volatility, more and better financial products have become available to help people smooth their consumption across fluctuations in income. The greater availability of financial products for saving and borrowing has resulted in less variability in consumer spending over time, which in turn contributes to less variability in real output.

The financial crisis beginning in 2007 revealed that some financial products and lending practices, which had been developed during the good times in the earlier part of the decade, created excessive borrowing and risk taking. This tendency was sharply reversed during the financial crisis: Banks dramatically reduced credit availability, cut lending, and tightened credit policies in an attempt to improve the quality of their loans. Financial innovation can help business firms and households smooth consumption against income fluctuations and reduce volatility. However, prudent regulation of financial institutions and adequate controls on lending practices are necessary to avoid financial crises that lead to greater volatility.

14-4c-3 Improved Macroeconomic Policy The belief in a tradeoff between inflation and unemployment, as suggested by the Phillips curve of the 1960s in Figure 1, led policymakers to try to exploit this tradeoff. Their attempts to stimulate the economy resulted in higher inflation, and when they tightened policy to restrain inflation, real output contracted. In the 1980s, it was generally acknowledged that such a tradeoff was probably not easily exploitable, if it was exploitable at all. This realization led to more stable macroeconomic policy, which contributed to less variability in real output.

14-4c-4 Good Luck The real-business-cycle approach emphasizes real shocks to the economy as an important catalyst of business-cycle fluctuations. From the mid-1980s, real economic shocks tended to be less severe than in earlier times. For instance, the oil price shocks of the 1970s were much more destabilizing than more recent oil price shocks. In addition, shifts in productivity were much more pronounced in earlier decades than during the last 20 years. If good luck with regard to the size and impact of real shocks was important in explaining the Great Moderation, such luck does not continue forever: It is not surprising that, eventually, the variability of real output growth increased in 2007–2009.

It is important to realize that there is disagreement among economists as to the causes of the reduction in the variability of real output growth that occurred prior to the financial crisis. It is also possible that all the explanations offered are not independent, and that each has been partly affected by the others. For instance, if monetary policy has become better over time and has contributed to low and stable inflation, then even major real economic shocks should not lead to big changes in inflation, which means that the effects of the shocks could be more moderate than in earlier times. Only time will tell whether the reduction in the growth of real output volatility is a permanent or a temporary economic phenomenon.

1. The political business cycle is a short-term expansion stimulated by an administration before an election to earn votes. After the election comes the long-term adjustment (rising unemployment and inflation).

2. A real business cycle is an expansion and contraction caused by a change in tastes or technology, strikes, weather, or other real factors.

3. Prior to the recent financial crisis, the growth rate of real output was much less volatile in the 1980s and 1990s than in earlier decades. Reasons given include better inventory management, development of financial markets, better macroeconomic policy, and smaller real shocks.

14-5 The Link between Monetary and Fiscal Policies

In earlier chapters, we described how monetary and fiscal policies determine the equilibrium level of prices and national income. In our discussions, we have talked about monetary policy and fiscal policy individually. Here we consider the relationship between them.

In some countries, monetary and fiscal policies are carried out by a single central authority. Even in the United States, where the Federal Reserve was created as an independent agency, monetary policy and fiscal policy are always related. The actions of the central bank have an impact on the proper role of fiscal policy, and the actions of fiscal policymakers have an impact on the proper role of monetary policy.

For example, suppose the central bank follows a monetary policy that raises interest rates. That policy raises the interest cost of new government debt, in the process increasing government expenditures. On the other hand, a fiscal policy that generates large fiscal deficits could contribute to higher interest rates. If the central bank has targeted an interest rate that lies below the current rate, the central bank could be drawn into an expansionary monetary policy. This interdependence of monetary and fiscal policy is important to policymakers, and also to businesspeople and others who seek to understand current economic developments.

14-5a The Government Budget Constraint

The *government budget constraint* clarifies the relationship between monetary and fiscal policies:

$$G = T + B + \Delta M$$

where:

8. How is inflationary monetary policy related to government fiscal policy?

G = government spending
T = tax revenue
B = government borrowing
ΔM = change in the money supply[1]

The government budget constraint always holds because there are only three ways for the government to finance its spending: by taxing, by borrowing, and by creating money.

---

[1] The M in the government budget constraint is government-issued money (usually called base money or high-powered money). It is easiest to think of this kind of money as currency, although in practice base money includes more than currency.

We can rewrite the government budget constraint with the change in M on the left-hand side of the equation:

$$\Delta M = (G - T) - B$$

In this form, you can see that the change in government-issued money equals the government fiscal deficit $(G - T)$ minus borrowing. This equation is always true. A government that has the ability to borrow at reasonable costs will not have the incentive to create rapid money growth and the consequent inflation that results in order to finance its budget deficit.

14-5b Monetary Reforms

In the United States and other industrial nations, monetary and fiscal policies are conducted by separate, independent agencies. Fiscal authorities (Congress and the president in the United States) cannot impose monetary policy on the central bank. But in some developing countries, monetary and fiscal policies are controlled by a central political authority. Here monetary policy is often an extension of fiscal policy. Fiscal policy can impose an inflationary burden on monetary policy. If a country is running a large fiscal deficit and much of this deficit cannot be financed by government borrowing, monetary authorities must create money to finance the deficit.

Creating money to finance fiscal deficits has produced very rapid rates of inflation in several countries. As prices reach astronomical levels, currency with very large face values must be issued. For instance, when Bolivia faced a sharp drop in the availability of willing lenders in the mid-1980s, the government began to create money to finance its fiscal deficit. As the money supply increased in relation to the output of goods and services, prices rose. In 1985, the government was creating money so fast that the rate of inflation reached 8,170 percent. Lunch in a La Paz hotel could cost 10 million Bolivian pesos. You can imagine the problem of counting money and recording money values with cash registers and calculators. As the rate of inflation increased, Bolivians had to carry stacks of currency to pay for goods and services. Eventually the government issued a 1 million peso note, then 5 million and 10 million peso notes.

This extremely high inflation, or hyperinflation, ended when a new government introduced its economic program in August 1985. The program reduced government spending dramatically, which slowed the growth of the fiscal deficit. At the same time, a monetary reform was introduced. A **monetary reform** is a new monetary policy that includes the introduction of a new monetary unit. The central bank of Bolivia announced that it would restrict money creation and introduced a new currency, the boliviano, in January 1987. It set 1 boliviano equal to 1 million Bolivian pesos.

The new monetary unit, the boliviano, did not lower prices; it lowered the units in which prices were quoted. Lunch now cost 10 bolivianos instead of 10 million pesos. More important, the rate of inflation dropped abruptly.

Did the new unit of currency end the hyperinflation? No. The rate of inflation dropped because the new fiscal policy controls introduced by the government relieved the pressure on the central bank to create money in order to finance government spending. Remember the government budget constraint: The only way to reduce the amount of money being created is to reduce the fiscal deficit $(G - T)$ minus borrowing (B). Once fiscal policy is under control, monetary reform is possible. If a government introduces a new monetary unit without changing its fiscal policy, the new monetary unit by itself has no lasting effect on the rate of inflation.

The most dramatic hyperinflation in recent years, and one of the most dramatic ever, occurred in Zimbabwe in 2007–2008. While the government was not forthcoming about inflation data, research[2] indicates that the price index rose from a value of 1.00 in

NOW YOU TRY IT

Rewrite the government budget constraint with *B*, government borrowing on the left-hand-side of the equation. What does this tell you that government borrowing must equal?

monetary reform
A new monetary policy that includes the introduction of a new monetary unit.

The introduction of a new monetary unit without a change in fiscal policy has no lasting effect on the rate of inflation.

[2] Steve H. Hanke, "R.I.P. Zimbabwe Dollar," www.cato.org/Zimbabwe

January 2007 to 853,000,000,000,000,000,000,000 by mid-November 2008, when the price level was doubling every 24 hours. As prices rose, the government issued larger and larger units of paper money as people had to carry huge stacks of old currency to buy anything. A 100 trillion Zimbabwe dollar bill was issued in January 2009. Then in the same month, the government sanctioned the use of U.S. dollars as a substitute currency in Zimbabwe as the local currency had become essentially worthless.

Table 2 lists monetary reforms enacted in recent years. Argentina had a monetary reform in June 1983. Yet by June 1985, another reform was needed. The inflationary problems that Argentina faced could not be solved just by issuing a new unit of currency. Fiscal reform also was needed, and none was made. In any circumstances involving inflationary monetary policy, monetary reform by itself is not enough. It must be coupled with a reduction in the fiscal deficit or an increase in government borrowing to produce a permanent change in the rate of inflation.

TABLE 2	**Recent Monetary Reforms**			
Country	**Old Currency**	**New Currency**	**Date of Change**	**Change**
Angola	Readjusted kwanza	Kwanza	December 1999	1 kwanza = 1,000,000 readjusted kwanza
Argentina	Peso	Peso argentino	June 1983	1 peso argentine = 10,000 pesos
	Peso argentino	Austral	June 1985	1 austra = 1,000 pesos argentino
	Austral	Peso argentino	January 1992	1 peso argentino = 10,000 australes
Bolivia	Peso	Boliviano	January 1987	1 boliviano = 1,000,000 pesos
Brazil	Cruzeiro	Cruzado	February 1986	1 cruzado = 1,000 cruzeiros
	Cruzado	New cruzado	January 1989	1 new cruzado = 1,000,000 cruzados
	New cruzado	Cruzeiro	March 1990	1 cruzeiro = 1 new cruzado
	Cruzeiro	Real	July 1994	1 real = 2,700 cruzeiros
Chile	Peso	Escudo	January 1969	1 escudo = 1,000 pesos
	Escudo	Peso	September 1975	1 peso = 1,000 escudos
Congo, D.R.	New Zaire	Congolese franc	June 1998	1 Congolese franc = 100,000 new Zaire
Georgia	Kuponi	Lari	September 1995	1 lari = 1,000,000 kuponi
Israel	Pound	Shekel	February 1980	1 shekel = 10 pounds
	Old shekel	New shekel	September 1985	1 new shekel = 1,000 old shekels
Mexico	Peso	New peso	January 1993	1 new peso = 1,000 pesos
Peru	Sol	Inti	February 1985	1 inti = 1,000 soles
	Inti	New Sol	July 1991	1 new sol = 1,000,000 intis
Poland	Zloty	New zloty	January 1995	1 new zloty = 10,000 zlotys
Russia	Ruble	New ruble	January 1998	1 new ruble = 1,000 rubles
Turkey	Lira	New Lira	January 2005	1 new lira = 1,000,000 lira
Ukraine	Karbovanets	Hryvnia	September 1996	1 hryvnia = 100,000 karbovanets
Uruguay	Old peso	New peso	July 1975	1 new peso = 1,000 old pesos
Yugoslavia	Dinar	New dinar	January 1994	1 new dinar = 13,000,000 dinars

Monetary policy is tied to fiscal policy through the government budget constraint. Although money creation is not an important source of deficit financing in developed countries, it has been and still is a significant source of revenue for developing countries, where taxes are difficult to collect and borrowing is limited.

1. The government budget constraint ($G = T + B + \Delta M$) defines the relationship between fiscal and monetary policies.

2. The implications of fiscal policy for the growth of the money supply can be seen by rewriting the government budget constraint this way:

$$\Delta M = (G - T) - B$$

3. A monetary reform is a new monetary policy that includes the introduction of a new unit of currency.

4. A government can end an inflationary monetary policy only with a fiscal reform that lowers the fiscal deficit ($G - T$) minus borrowing (B).

SUMMARY

1. Is there a tradeoff between inflation and the unemployment rate?

- The Phillips curve shows the relationship between inflation and the unemployment rate. *§14-1*

2. How does the tradeoff between inflation and the unemployment rate vary from the short to the long run?

- In the long run, there is no tradeoff between inflation and the unemployment rate. *§14-1b*
- The long-run Phillips curve is a vertical line at the natural rate of unemployment. *§14-1b*

3. What is the relationship between unexpected inflation and the unemployment rate?

- Unexpected inflation can affect the unemployment rate through wage expectations, inventory fluctuations, and wage contracts. *§14-2a*

4. How are macroeconomic expectations formed?

- Adaptive expectations are formed on the basis of past experience; rational expectations are formed on the basis of all available relevant information. *§14-2b*

5. What makes government policies credible?

- A policy is credible only if it is time consistent. *§14-3b*

6. Are business cycles related to political elections?

- A political business cycle is created by politicians who want to improve their chances of reelection by stimulating the economy just before an election. *§14-4a*

7. How do real shocks to the economy affect business cycles?

- Real business cycles are the product of an unexpected change in technology, weather, or some other real variable. *§14-4b*

8. How is inflationary monetary policy related to government fiscal policy?

- The government budget constraint defines the relationship between monetary and fiscal policies. *§14-5a*
- When government-issued money is used to finance fiscal deficits, inflationary monetary policy can be a product of fiscal policy. *§14-5b*

KEY TERMS

EXERCISES

1. What is the difference between the short-run Phillips curve and the long-run Phillips curve? Use an aggregate supply and demand diagram to explain why there is a difference between them.

2. Give two reasons why there may be a short-run tradeoff between unexpected inflation and the unemployment rate.

3. "Unexpected increases in the money supply cause clockwise movements in the Phillips curve diagram; unexpected decreases in the money supply cause counterclockwise movements in the Phillips curve diagram." Evaluate this statement, using a graph to illustrate your answer.

4. Economists have identified two kinds of macroeconomic expectations.
   a. Define them.
   b. What are the implications for macroeconomic policy of these two forms of expectations?

5. Write down the government budget constraint and explain how it can be used to understand the relationship between fiscal and monetary policies.

6. Using the government budget constraint, explain:
   a. Why some countries experience hyperinflation.
   b. How fiscal policy must change in order to implement a noninflationary monetary policy.

7. Parents, like governments, establish credibility by seeing to it that their "policies" (the rules that they outline for their children) are time consistent. Analyze the potential for time consistency of these rules:
   a. If you don't eat the squash, you'll go to bed 30 minutes early tonight!
   b. If you get any grades below a C, you won't be allowed to watch television on school nights!
   c. If you don't go to my alma mater, I won't pay for your college education!
   d. If you marry that disgusting person, I'll disinherit you!

8. Suppose an economy has witnessed an 8 percent rate of growth in its money supply and prices over the last few years. How do you think the public will respond to an announced plan to increase the money supply by 4 percent over the next year if:
   a. The central bank has a reputation for always meeting its announced policy goals.
   b. The central bank rarely does what it says it will do.

9. What are the implications for the timing of business cycle fluctuations over the years if all business cycles are:
   a. Manipulated by incumbent administrations.
   b. A product of real shocks to the economy.

10. Suppose the Federal Reserve System were abolished and Congress assumed responsibility for monetary policy along with fiscal policy. What potential harm to the economy could result from such a change?

11. Suppose tax revenues equal $200 billion, government spending equals $330 billion, and the government borrows $25 billion. How much do you expect the money supply to increase, given the government budget constraint?

12. If the government budget deficit equals $240 billion and the money supply increases by $200 billion, how much must the government borrow?

13. Discuss how each of the following sources of real business cycles would affect the economy.
   a. Farmers go on strike for six months.
   b. Oil prices fall substantially.
   c. Particularly favorable weather increases agricultural output nationwide.

14. Using an aggregate demand and aggregate supply diagram, illustrate and explain how a political business cycle is created.

15. Use a Phillips curve diagram to illustrate and explain how a political business cycle is created.

16. What is the natural rate of unemployment? What can cause it to change over time?

17. Many developing countries have experienced high money growth rates and, consequently, high inflation. Use the government budget constraint to explain how a poor country that wants to increase government spending can get into an inflationary situation.

18. What factors should affect the variability of the growth rate of real output? Which do you think could provide for more stability going forward, and which are likely to be less important?

19. Starting in 2011, the Federal Reserve chairman began participating in a quarterly press conference as part of a new strategy to increase communication with the public. Discuss the rationale behind such policy in light of expectations, expected versus unexpected inflation, and credibility.

ECONOMICALLY SPEAKING

SEMIANNUAL MONETARY POLICY REPORT TO THE CONGRESS

Chair Janet L. Yellen
Before the Committee on Financial Services, U.S. House of Representatives,
Washington, D.C. February 11, 2014

Chairman Hensarling, Ranking Member Waters and other members of the Committee, I am pleased to present the Federal Reserve's semiannual *Monetary Policy Report* to the Congress. In my remarks today, I will discuss the current economic situation and outlook before turning to monetary policy. I will conclude with an update on our continuing work on regulatory reform.

Current Economic Situation and Outlook

The economic recovery gained greater traction in the second half of last year. Real gross domestic product (GDP) is currently estimated to have risen at an average annual rate of more than 3-1/2 percent in the third and fourth quarters, up from a 1-3/4 percent pace in the first half. The pickup in economic activity has fueled further progress in the labor market. About 1-1/4 million jobs have been added to payrolls since the previous *Monetary Policy Report* last July, and 3-1/4 million have been added since August 2012, the month before the Federal Reserve began a new round of asset purchases to add momentum to the recovery. The unemployment rate has fallen nearly a percentage point since the middle

of last year and 1-1/2 percentage points since the beginning of the current asset purchase program. Nevertheless, the recovery in the labor market is far from complete. The unemployment rate is still well above levels that Federal Open Market Committee (FOMC) participants estimate is consistent with maximum sustainable employment. Those out of a job for more than six months continue to make up an unusually large fraction of the unemployed, and the number of people who are working part time but would prefer a full-time job remains very high. These observations underscore the importance of considering more than the unemployment rate when evaluating the condition of the U.S. labor market.

Among the major components of GDP, household and business spending growth stepped up during the second half of last year. Early in 2013, growth in consumer spending was restrained by changes in fiscal policy. As this restraint abated during the second half of the year, household spending accelerated, supported by job gains and by rising home values and equity prices. Similarly, growth in business investment started off slowly last year but then picked up during the second half, reflecting improving sales prospects, greater confidence, and still-favorable financing condi-

tions. In contrast, the recovery in the housing sector slowed in the wake of last year's increase in mortgage rates.

Inflation remained low as the economy picked up strength, with both the headline and core personal consumption expenditures, or PCE, price indexes rising only about 1 percent last year, well below the FOMC's 2 percent objective for inflation over the longer run. Some of the recent softness reflects factors that seem likely to prove transitory, including falling prices for crude oil and declines in non-oil import prices.

...

Monetary Policy

Turning to monetary policy, let me emphasize that I expect a great deal of continuity in the FOMC's approach to monetary policy. I served on the Committee as we formulated our current policy strategy and I strongly support that strategy, which is designed to fulfill the Federal Reserve's statutory mandate of maximum employment and price stability.

The Committee has emphasized that a highly accommodative policy will remain appropriate for a considerable time after asset purchases end. In addition, the Committee has said since December 2012 that it expects the current low target range for the federal funds rate to be appropriate at least as long as the unemployment rate remains above 6-1/2 percent, inflation is projected to be no more than a half percentage point above our 2 percent longer-run goal, and longer-term inflation expectations remain well anchored. Crossing one of these thresholds will not automatically prompt an increase in the federal funds rate, but will instead indicate only that it had become appropriate for the Committee to consider whether the broader economic outlook would justify such an increase. In December of last year and again this January, the Committee said that its current expectation—based on its assessment of a broad range of measures of labor market conditions, indicators of inflation pressures and inflation expectations, and readings on financial developments—that it likely will be appropriate to maintain the current target range for the federal funds rate well past the time that the unemployment rate declines below 6-1/2 percent, especially if projected inflation continues to run below the 2 percent goal. I am committed to achieving both parts of our dual mandate: helping the economy return to full employment and returning inflation to 2 percent while ensuring that it does not run persistently above or below that level.

...

Source: Chair Yellen submitted identical remarks to the Committee on Banking, Housing, and Urban Affairs, U.S. Senate, on February 27, 2014

COMMENTARY

acroeconomic policy in the United States is determined by Congress, the presidential administration, and the Federal Reserve. Twice a year, the chairman of the Federal Reserve Board must testify before Congress on Fed monetary policy. The article reports an appearance in 2014 by Federal Reserve Chair Janet Yellen, which highlights some of the issues raised in this chapter.

The U.S. economy was still recovering from the deepest recession since the 1930s at the time of Yellen's testimony. Unemployment was falling slowly and inflation had been persistently low since the recession. The issue of government credibility was highlighted by Yellen's statement, "let me emphasize that I expect a great deal of continuity in the FOMC's approach to monetary policy." The previous chair Ben Bernanke had worked very hard to convince the market the Fed was going to follow a set of specific policies. When Yellen replaced him it was important that the Fed's position be more substantial than one individual's statements. So Yellen made sure to state that the Fed would remain on the policy path it had committed itself to previously.

Yellen highlighted the source of business cycles, saying, "growth in consumer spending was restrained by changes in fiscal policy." This period saw the expiration of some fiscal policies taken to counteract the deep recession. As taxes increased and government expenditures declined, households cut their spending somewhat. However, later "household spending accelerated, supported by job gains and by rising home values and equity prices." The wealth destruction associated with the large drop in housing prices during the recession is thought to have had a significant negative effect on household expenditures. The most valuable asset for most households is the home. When home values dropped dramatically, household wealth dropped dramatically as well. Much of the government's policy during the crisis was aimed at stimulating the housing market and making home mortgage lending more affordable. Here, Yellen notes that as housing prices recover, household expenditures are also recovering.

Of course, there is no guarantee that government policy aimed at minimizing business-cycle fluctuations will be successful. Since the policy is set today, yet is aimed at bettering economic conditions in the future, there is always the possibility that an activist policy will aggravate business-cycle fluctuations rather than moderate them. For instance, suppose the Fed lowers the federal funds rate today because of a belief that the economy needs to be stimulated in order to increase spending. If the economy is already starting to improve without the Fed's intervention (perhaps because of some earlier Fed action), the new stimulus may cause spending to grow too much and generate inflation that otherwise would not have occurred. Economic policymaking is always done with some degree of uncertainty. Although policymakers such as Janet Yellen may support policy changes aimed at growing the economy with low inflation, there is always a chance that their policies will have unintended consequences.

CHAPTER 15

Macroeconomic Viewpoints: New Keynesian, Monetarist, and New Classical

NsOmniak/Dreamstime.com

FUNDAMENTAL QUESTIONS

1. What do Keynesian economists believe about macroeconomic policy?

2. What role do monetarists believe the government should play in the economy?

3. What is new classical economics?

4. How do theories of economics change over time?

Preview

Economists do not all agree on macroeconomic policy. Sometimes disagreements are due to normative differences, or differences in personal values, regarding what the truly pressing needs are that should be addressed. Other disagreements are based on different views of how the economy operates and what determines the equilibrium level of real GDP.

It would be very easy to classify economists, to call them liberals or conservatives, for example. But an economist who believes that the government should not intervene in social decisions (abortion, censorship) may favor an active role for government in economic decisions (trade protection, unemployment insurance, welfare benefits). Another

top: © Carsten Reisinger/Shutterstock

economist may support an active role for government in regulating the social behavior of individuals, yet believe that government should allow free markets to operate without interference.

In this chapter, an overview of important differences among schools of macroeconomic thought is presented. Most economists probably do not align themselves solely with any one theory of macroeconomics, choosing instead to incorporate pieces of various schools of thought. But the three approaches we discuss in this chapter—Keynesian, monetarist, and new classical —have had enormous impact on macroeconomic thinking and policy. Economic thinking has evolved over time as economists develop new economic theories to fit the realities of a changing world.

15-1 Keynesian Economics

Keynesian macroeconomics (named after the English economist John Maynard Keynes) dominated the economics profession from the 1940s through the 1960s. Some economists today refer to themselves as "new Keynesians." The common thread that pervades Keynesian economics is an emphasis on the inflexibility of wages and prices. This leads many Keynesians to recommend an activist government macroeconomic policy aimed at achieving a satisfactory rate of economic growth.

15-1a The Keynesian Model

Keynesian economics grew out of the Great Depression, when inflation was not a problem but output was falling. As a result, the Keynesian model of macroeconomic equilibrium assumes that prices are constant and that changes in aggregate expenditures determine equilibrium real GDP. In an aggregate demand and supply analysis, the simple Keynesian model looks like the graph in Figure 1. The aggregate supply curve is a horizontal line at a fixed level of prices, P_1. Changes in aggregate demand, such as from AD_1 to AD_2, cause changes in real GDP with no change in the price level.

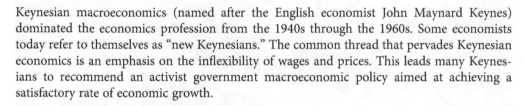

FIGURE 1 The Fixed-Price Keynesian Model

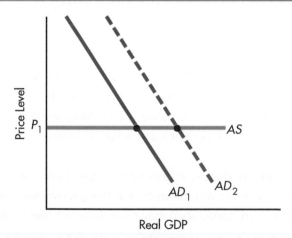

In the simple Keynesian model, prices are fixed at P_1 by the horizontal aggregate supply curve, so that changes in aggregate demand determine equilibrium real GDP.

FIGURE 2   The Modern Keynesian Model

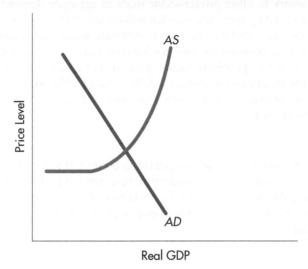

Modern Keynesians typically believe that the aggregate supply curve is horizontal only at relatively low levels of real GDP. As real GDP increases, more and more industries reach their capacity level of output, and the aggregate supply curve becomes positively sloped.

Figure 1 reflects the traditional Keynesian emphasis on aggregate demand as a determinant of equilibrium real GDP. But no economist today would argue that the aggregate supply curve is always horizontal at every level of real GDP. More representative of Keynesian economics today is the aggregate supply curve shown in Figure 2. At low levels of real GDP, the curve is flat. In this region (the Keynesian region), increases in aggregate demand are associated with increases in output, but not with increases in prices. This flat region of the aggregate supply curve reflects the Keynesian belief that inflation is not a problem when unemployment is high. As the level of real GDP increases, and more and more industries reach their capacity level of output, the aggregate supply curve becomes positively sloped.

The economic theories that John Maynard Keynes proposed in the 1930s have given way to new theories. Today **Keynesian economics** focuses on the role the government plays in stabilizing the economy by managing aggregate demand. *New Keynesians* believe that wages and prices are not flexible in the short run. They use their analysis of business behavior to explain the Keynesian region on the aggregate supply curve of Figure 2. They believe that the economy is not always in equilibrium. For instance, if the demand for labor falls, we would expect the equilibrium price of labor (the wage) to fall and, because fewer people want to work at a lower wage, the number of people employed to fall. New Keynesians argue that wages do not tend to fall, because firms choose to lay off workers rather than decrease wages. Businesses retain high wages for their remaining employees in order to maintain morale and productivity. As a result, wages are quite rigid. This wage rigidity is reflected in price rigidity in goods markets, according to new Keynesian economics.

Keynesian economics
A school of thought that emphasizes the role government plays in stabilizing the economy by managing aggregate demand.

New Keynesian macroeconomists argue that wages and prices are not flexible in the short run.

15-1b The Policymakers' Role

Keynesians believe that the government must take an active role in the economy to restore equilibrium. Traditional Keynesians identified the private sector as an important source of shifts in aggregate demand. For example, they argued that investment is susceptible to sudden changes. If business spending falls, the argument continued, monetary and fiscal policies should be used to stimulate spending and offset the drop in business spending. Government intervention is necessary to offset private-sector shifts in aggregate demand and avoid recession. And if private spending increases, creating inflationary pressure, then monetary and fiscal policies should restrain spending, again to offset private-sector shifts in aggregate demand.

New Keynesian macroeconomics does not focus on fluctuations in aggregate demand as the primary source of the problems facing policymakers. Keynesian economists realize that aggregate supply shocks can be substantial. But whatever the source of the instability—aggregate demand or aggregate supply—they emphasize active government policy to return the economy to equilibrium.

RECAP

1. Keynesian economists today reject the simple fixed-price model in favor of a model in which the aggregate supply curve is relatively flat at low levels of real GDP and slopes upward as real GDP approaches its potential level.

2. Keynesians believe that the tendency for the economy to experience disequilibrium in labor and goods markets requires the government to intervene in the economy.

15-2 Monetarist Economics

monetarist economics
A school of thought that emphasizes the role changes in the money supply play in determining equilibrium real GDP and price level.

The Keynesian view dominated macroeconomics in the 1940s, the 1950s, and most of the 1960s. In the late 1960s and the 1970s, Keynesian economics faced a challenge from **monetarist economics**, a school of thought that emphasizes the role that changes in the money supply play in determining equilibrium real GDP and prices. The leading monetarist, Milton Friedman, had been developing monetarist theory since the 1940s, but it took several decades for his ideas to become popular. In part, the shift was a product of the forcefulness of Friedman's arguments, but the relatively poor macroeconomic performance of the United States in the 1970s probably contributed to a growing disenchantment with Keynesian economics, creating an environment that was ripe for new ideas. The Economic Insight "Milton Friedman" describes how Friedman's monetarist theories became popular.

15-2a The Monetarist Model

Monetarists focus on the role of the money supply in determining the equilibrium level of real GDP and prices. In the chapter titled "Monetary Policy," we discussed monetary policy and equilibrium income. We showed that monetary policy is linked to changes in the equilibrium level of real GDP through changes in investment (and consumption). Keynesians traditionally assumed that monetary policy affects aggregate demand by changing the interest rate and, consequently, investment spending. Monetarists believe that changes in the money supply have broad effects on expenditures through both investment and consumption. An increase in the money supply pushes aggregate demand up by increasing both business and household spending and raises the equilibrium level of real GDP. A decrease in the money supply does the opposite.

Monetarists believe that accelerating inflation is a product of efforts to increase real GDP through expansionary monetary policy.

Monetarists believe that changes in monetary policy (or fiscal policy, for that matter) have only a short-term effect on real GDP. In the long run, they expect real GDP to be at a level consistent with the natural rate of unemployment. As a result, the long-run effect of a change in the money supply is fully reflected in a change in the price level. Attempts to exploit the short-run effects of expansionary monetary policy produce an inflationary spiral, in which the level of GDP increases temporarily, then falls back to the potential level while prices rise. This is the rightward shift of the Phillips curve that was described in an earlier chapter.

ECONOMIC INSIGHT

Milton Friedman

Milton Friedman is widely considered to be the father of monetarism. Born in 1912 in New York City, Friedman spent most of his career at the University of Chicago. Early in his professional life, he recognized the importance of developing economics as an empirical science—that is, using data to test the applicability of economic theory.

In 1957, Friedman published *A Theory of the Consumption Function*. In this book, he discussed the importance *of permanent income*, rather than current income, in understanding consumer spending. His analysis of consumption won widespread acclaim, an acclaim that would be a long time coming for his work relating monetary policy to real output and prices.

In the 1950s, Keynesian theory dominated economics. Most macroeconomists believed that the supply of money in the economy was of little importance. In 1963, with the publication of *A Monetary History of the United States, 1867–1960* (coauthored with Anna Schwartz of the National Bureau of Economic Research), Friedman focused attention on the monetarist argument. Still, Keynesian economics dominated scholarly and policy debate.

In the late 1960s and early 1970s, the rate of inflation and the rate of unemployment increased simultaneously. This was a situation that Keynesian economics could not explain. The timing was right for a new theory of macroeconomic behavior, and monetarism, with Milton Friedman as its most influential advocate, grew in popularity. The new stature of monetarism was clearly visible in 1979, when the Fed adopted a monetarist approach to targeting the money supply.

In 1976, Milton Friedman was awarded the Nobel Prize for economics. By this time he had become a public figure. He wrote a column for *Newsweek* from 1966 to 1984, and in 1980 he developed a popular public television series, *Free to Choose*, based on his book of the same title. Through the popular media, Friedman became the most effective and well-known supporter of free markets in the United States and much of the rest of the world until his death in 2006. Many would argue that only Keynes has had as much influence on scholarly literature and public policy in economics as Milton Friedman.

15-2b The Policymakers' Role

Unlike Keynesian economists, monetarists do not believe that the economy is subject to a disequilibrium that must be offset by government action. Most monetarists believe that the economy tends toward equilibrium at the level of potential real GDP. Their faith in the free market (price) system leads them to favor minimal government intervention.

Monetarists often argue that government policy heightens the effects of the business cycle. This is especially true of monetary policy. To prove their point, monetarists link changes in the growth of the money supply to business-cycle fluctuations. Specifically, they suggest that periods of relatively fast money growth are followed by booms and inflation, whereas periods of relatively slow money growth are followed by recessions. The link between money growth, real GDP, and inflation has not been as visible in recent years as it was in the 1970s–1990s. The Federal Reserve used to formulate policy in terms of money growth targets, but stopped doing that a few years ago. This was a sign that the link between money growth, inflation, and real output was not a strong as it used to be. At some times there seem to be closer relationships than at other times. This makes it difficult to predict the effect of a particular change in monetary policy on prices or real GDP. In addition, a number of other variables influence GDP.

Monetarists favor nonactivist government policy because they believe that the government's attempts to make the economy better off by aiming monetary and fiscal policies at low inflation and low unemployment often make things worse. Why? Because economic policy, which is very powerful, operates with a long and variable lag. First, policymakers have to

2. *What role do monetarists believe the government should play in the economy?*

Economic policy operates with a long and variable lag.

recognize that a problem exists. This is the *recognition lag*. Then they must formulate an appropriate policy. This is the *reaction lag*. Then the effects of the policy must work through the economy. This is the *effect lag*.

When the Federal Reserve changes the rate of growth of the money supply, real GDP and inflation do not change immediately. In fact, studies show that as much as two years can pass between a change in policy and the effect of that change on real GDP. This means that when policymakers institute a change targeted at a particular level of real GDP or rate of inflation, the effect of the policy is not felt for a long time. And it is possible that the economy could be facing an entirely different set of problems in a year or two from those that policymakers are addressing today. But today's policy will still have effects next year, and those effects may aggravate next year's problems.

Because of the long and variable lag in the effect of fiscal and monetary policies, monetarists argue that policymakers should set policy according to rules that do not change from month to month or even year to year. What kinds of rules? A fiscal policy rule might be to balance the budget annually; a monetary policy rule might be to require that the money supply grow at a fixed rate over time or that the central bank commit to following an inflation target. These kinds of rules restrict policymakers from formulating discretionary policy. Monetarists believe that when discretionary shifts in policy are reduced, economic growth is steadier than it is when government consciously sets out to achieve full employment and low inflation.

RECAP

1. Monetarists emphasize the role that changes in the money supply play in determining equilibrium real GDP and the level of prices.

2. Monetarists do not believe that the economy is subject to disequilibrium in the labor and goods markets or that government should take an active role in the economy.

3. Because economic policy operates with a long and variable lag, attempts by government to stabilize the economy may, in fact, make matters worse.

4. Monetarists believe that formal rules, rather than the discretion of policymakers, should govern economic policymaking.

15-3 What Is New Classical Economics?

In the 1970s, an alternative to Keynesian and monetarist economics was developed: new classical economics. But before we discuss the new classical theory, let us look at the old one.

classical economics
A school of thought that assumes that real GDP is determined by aggregate supply, while the equilibrium price level is determined by aggregate demand.

Classical economics is the theory that was popular before Keynes changed the face of economics in the 1930s. According to classical economics, real GDP is determined by aggregate supply, while the equilibrium price level is determined by aggregate demand. Figure 3, the classical aggregate demand and supply diagram, shows the classical economist's view of the world. The vertical aggregate supply curve means that the equilibrium level of output (income) is a product only of the determinants of aggregate supply: the price of resources, technology, and expectations (see the chapter titled "Macroeconomic Equilibrium: Aggregate Demand and Supply").

If the aggregate supply curve is vertical, then changes in aggregate demand, such as from AD_1 to AD_2, change only the price level; they do not affect the equilibrium level of output. Classical economics assumes that prices and wages are perfectly flexible. This rules out contracts that fix prices or wages for periods of time. It also rules out the possibility that people are not aware of all prices and wages. They know when prices have gone up and ask for wage increases to compensate.

Both Keynesians and monetarists would argue that information about the economy, including prices and wages, is not perfect. When workers and businesses negotiate wages,

FIGURE 3 The Classical Model

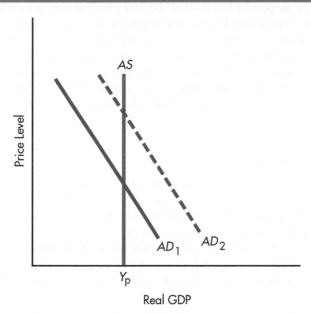

The vertical aggregate supply curve indicates that equilibrium real GDP is determined strictly by the determinants of aggregate supply.

they may not know what current prices are, and they certainly do not know what future prices will be. Furthermore, many labor contracts fix wages for long periods of time. This means that wages are not flexible; they cannot adjust immediately to new price levels.

15-3a The New Classical Model

New classical economics was a response to the problems of meeting economic policy goals in the 1970s. New classical economists questioned some of the assumptions on which Keynesian economics was based. For instance, new classical economists believe wages are flexible, while both traditional Keynesian and new Keynesian economists assume that wages can be fixed in the short run.

New classical economics does not assume that people know everything that is happening, as the old theory did. People make mistakes because their expectations of prices or some other critical variable are different from the future reality. New classical economists emphasize rational expectations. As defined in the last chapter, *rational expectations* are based on all available relevant information. This was a new way of thinking about expectations. Earlier theories assumed that people formed adaptive expectations—that their expectations were based only on their past experience. With rational expectations, people learn not only from their past experience, but also from any other information that helps them predict the future.

Suppose the chairman of the Federal Reserve Board announces a new monetary policy. Price-level expectations that are formed rationally take this announcement into consideration; those that are formed adaptively do not. It is much easier for policymakers to make unexpected changes in policy if expectations are formed adaptively rather than rationally.

Another element of new classical economics is the belief that markets are in equilibrium. Keynesian economics argues that disequilibrium in markets demands government

3. What is new classical economics?

new classical economics
A school of thought that holds that changes in real GDP are a product of unexpected changes in the level of prices.

intervention. For instance, Keynesian economists define a recession as a disequilibrium in the labor market—a surplus of labor—that requires expansionary government policy. New classical economists believe that because real wages are lower during a recession, people are more willing to substitute nonlabor activities (going back to school, early retirement, work at home, or leisure) for work. As the economy recovers and wages go up, people substitute away from nonlabor activities toward more working hours. The substitution of labor for leisure and leisure for labor, over time, suggests that much of observed unemployment is voluntary in the sense that those who are unemployed choose not to take a job at a wage below their reservation wage.

15-3b The Policymakers' Role

New classical economics emphasizes expectations. Its basic tenet is that changes in monetary policy can change the equilibrium level of real GDP only if those changes are *unexpected*. Fiscal policy can change equilibrium real GDP only if it *unexpectedly* changes the level of prices or one of the determinants of aggregate supply.

Figure 4 (which is the same as Figure 4 in the last chapter) illustrates the new classical view of the effect of an unexpected increase in the money supply. Suppose initially the expected rate of inflation is 3 percent and the actual rate of inflation is also 3 percent. The

FIGURE 4   New Classical Economics

(a) Aggregate Demand and Supply

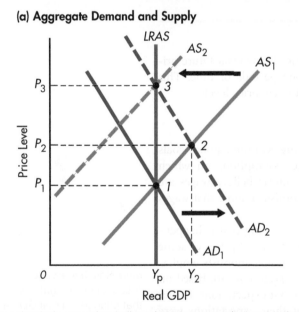

(b) Phillips Curve

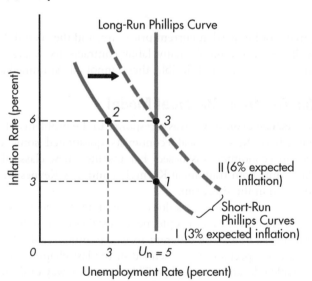

New classical economists believe that government-induced shifts in aggregate demand affect real GDP only if they are unexpected. 4(a) The economy initially is operating at point 1, with real GDP at Y_p, the potential level. An unexpected increase in aggregate demand shifts the economy to point 2, where both real GDP (Y_2) and prices (P_2) are higher. Over time, as sellers adjust to higher prices and higher costs of doing business, aggregate supply shifts from AS_1 to AS_2. This shift moves the economy to point 3. Here GDP is back at the potential level, and prices are even higher. In the long run, an increase in aggregate demand does not increase output. The long-run aggregate supply curve (LRAS) is a vertical line at the potential level of real GDP. 4(b) If the expected rate of inflation is 3 percent and actual inflation is 3 percent, the economy is operating at point 1, at the natural rate of unemployment (U_n). If aggregate demand increases, there is an unexpected increase in inflation from 3 percent to 6 percent. This moves the economy from point 1 to point 2 along short-run Phillips curve I. Here the unemployment rate is 3 percent. As people learn to expect 6 percent inflation, they adjust to the higher rate and the economy moves back to the natural rate of unemployment, at point 3. If the increase in inflation is expected, then the economy moves directly from point 1 to point 3 with no temporary decrease in the unemployment rate.

economy is operating at point 1 in Figure 4(b), the Phillips curve diagram, with unemployment at 5 percent, which is assumed to be the natural rate of unemployment. At the natural rate of unemployment, the economy is producing the potential level of real GDP (Y_p) at price level P_1. If the central bank unexpectedly increases the money supply, pushing the inflation rate up from 3 percent to 6 percent, the economy moves from point 1 to point 2 along short-run Phillips curve I, which is based on 3 percent expected inflation. The unemployment rate is now 3 percent, which is less than the natural rate. In part a, real GDP rises above potential income to Y_2.

Over time, people come to expect 6 percent inflation. They adjust to the higher inflation rate, and the economy moves back to the natural rate of unemployment. At the expected rate of inflation, 6 percent, the economy is operating at point 3 on short-run Phillips curve II. As the expected rate of inflation increases from 3 percent to 6 percent, workers negotiate higher wages and the aggregate supply curve shifts to the left, from AS_1 to AS_2. A new equilibrium exists at point 3 in the aggregate demand and supply diagram, and real GDP drops back to its potential level.

The analysis changes dramatically if the change in the money supply is expected. Now the economy moves not from point 1 to point 2 to point 3 but from point 1 directly to point 3. This is because the shift from point 1 to point 2 is temporary, based on unexpected inflation. If the inflation is expected, the economy is on short-run Phillips curve II, where inflation is 6 percent, unemployment is at the natural rate, and real GDP is at the potential level.

The lesson of new classical economics for policymakers is that managing aggregate demand has an effect on real GDP only if change is unexpected. Any predictable policy simply affects prices. As a result, new classical economists argue that monetary and fiscal policies should be aimed at maintaining a low, stable rate of inflation and should not attempt to alter real national output and unemployment. This brings new classical economists close to the monetarists, who would choose policy rules over discretionary policy.

New classical economists believe that wages and prices are flexible and that people form expectations rationally, so that only unexpected changes in the price level can affect real GDP.

RECAP

1. New classical economics holds that wages are flexible and that expectations are formed rationally, so that only unexpected changes in prices have an effect on real GDP.

2. New classical economists believe that markets are always in equilibrium.

3. According to new classical economic theory, any predictable macroeconomic policy has an effect only on prices.

4. New classical economists argue that monetary and fiscal policies should try to achieve a low, stable rate of inflation rather than changes in real GDP or unemployment.

15-4 Comparison and Influence

The three theories of macroeconomics we have been talking about are often treated as though they are different in every way. Yet at times they overlap and even share conclusions. Moreover, as we mentioned at the beginning of the chapter, it is an oversimplification to categorize economists by a single school of thought. Many if not most economists do not classify themselves by economic theory. Typically they take elements of each, so that their approach to macroeconomics is more a synthesis of the various theories than strict adherence to any one theory.

4. How do theories of economics change over time?

Macroeconomic theories have developed over time in response to the economy's performance and the shortcomings of existing theories. Keynesian economics became popular in the 1930s because classical economics did not explain or help resolve the Great Depression. Monetarist economics offered an explanation for rising unemployment and rising inflation in the United States in the 1960s and 1970s. New classical economics suggested an alternative explanation for rising unemployment and inflation that the static Phillips curve analysis used by traditional Keynesians could not explain. Each of these theories, then, was developed or became popular because an existing theory did not answer pressing new questions.

All of these theories have influenced government policy. A by-product of Keynes's work in the 1930s was the wide acceptance and practice of activist government fiscal policy. Monetarist influence was dramatically apparent in the change in monetary policy announced by the Federal Reserve in 1979. Monetarists had criticized the Fed's policy of targeting interest rates. They argued that money-growth targets would stabilize income and prices. In October 1979, Chairman Paul Volcker announced that the Fed would concentrate more on achieving money-growth targets and less on controlling interest rates. This change in policy reflected the Fed's concern over rising inflation and the belief that the monetarists were right, that a low rate of money growth would bring about a low rate of inflation. The new policy led to an abrupt drop in the rate of inflation, from more than 13 percent in 1979 to less than 4 percent in 1982.

The new classical economists' emphasis on expectations calls for more information from policymakers to allow private citizens to incorporate government plans into their outlook for the future. The Federal Reserve Reform Act (1977) and the Full Employment and Balanced Growth Act (1978) require the Board of Governors to report to Congress semiannually on its goals and money targets for the next 12 months. New classical economists also believe that only credible government policies can affect expectations. In the last chapter we discussed the time consistency of plans. For plans to be credible, to influence private expectations, they must be time consistent.

Table 1 summarizes the three approaches to macroeconomics, describing the major source of problems facing policymakers and the proper role of government policy according to each view. Only Keynesian economics supports an active role for government; the other two theories suggest that government should not intervene in the economy.

The government policy response to the financial crisis that began in 2007 incorporated ideas from the different approaches to macroeconomics. There was a huge increase in government spending financed by borrowing, a very Keynesian approach to stimulating aggregate demand. There was also an emphasis on shaping expectations of the public that fiscal and monetary policy were addressing declining incomes and output, as well as

TABLE 1 Major Approaches to Macroeconomic Policy		
Approach	**Major Source of Problems**	**Proper Role for Government**
New Keynesian	Disequilibrium in private labor and goods markets	To actively manage monetary and fiscal policies to restore equilibrium
Monetarist	Government's discretionary policies that increase and decrease aggregate demand	To follow fixed rules for money growth and to minimize fiscal policy shocks
New classical	Government's attempt to manipulate aggregate demand, even though government policies have effect on real GDP only if unexpected	To follow predictable monetary and fiscal policies for long-run stability

falling prices. If the public believes that their incomes are only temporarily depressed, they will spend more now. If the public believes that deflation will be avoided, they will be more willing to spend rather than hold on to their cash (money rises in value as prices fall), and they will not write contracts that build in expectations of falling prices and wages and further contribute to such price and wage declines. Finally, central banks around the world greatly increased the supply of money to support credit availability and spending by business firms and households. In fact, the global policy response to the financial crisis was unprecedented—which serves to emphasize the macroeconomic lessons learned by economists and government policymakers from past history and macroeconomic theory.

NOW YOU TRY IT

Which of the approaches to macroeconomic policy would be associated with the following quote: "the government has a responsibility to actively change taxes and government spending to provide economic growth."

RECAP

1. Different economic theories developed over time as changing economic conditions pointed out the shortcomings of existing theories.

2. Keynesian, monetarist, and new classical economics have each influenced macroeconomic policy.

3. Only Keynesian economists believe that government should actively intervene to stabilize the economy.

SUMMARY

- Economists do not all agree on the determinants of economic equilibrium or the appropriate role of government policy. *Preview*

1. What do Keynesian economists believe about macroeconomic policy?

- Keynesian economists believe that the government should take an active role in stabilizing the economy by managing aggregate demand. *§15-1a, 15-1b*

2. What role do monetarists believe the government should play in the economy?

- Monetarists do not believe that the economy is subject to serious disequilibrium, which means that they favor minimal government intervention in the economy. *§15-2b*

- Monetarists believe that a government that takes an active role in the economy may do more harm than good because economic policy operates with a long and variable lag. *§15-2b*

3. What is new classical economics?

- New classical economics holds that only unexpected changes in policy can influence real GDP, so government policy should target a low, stable rate of inflation. *§15-3b*

4. How do theories of economics change over time?

- New economic theories are a response to changing economic conditions that reveal the shortcomings of existing theories. *§15-4*

KEY TERMS

classical economics, 344
Keynesian economics, 341

monetarist economics, 342
new classical economics, 345

EXERCISES

1. What is the difference between traditional Keynesian and new Keynesian economics?

2. Why does monetary policy operate with a long and variable lag? Give an example to illustrate your explanation.

3. What is the difference between old classical and new classical economics?

4. Draw an aggregate demand and supply diagram for each theory of macroeconomics. Use the diagrams to explain how the government can influence equilibrium real GDP and prices.

5. What, if any, similarities are there among the theories of economics discussed in this chapter regarding the use of fiscal and monetary policies to stimulate real GDP?

6. If unexpected increases in the growth rate of the money supply can increase real GDP, why does the Fed not follow a policy of unexpectedly increasing the money supply to increase the growth of real GDP?

7. "The popular macroeconomic theories have evolved over time as economic conditions have changed to reveal shortcomings of existing theory." Evaluate this quote in terms of the emergence of the three theories discussed in this chapter.

8. Has the recent financial crisis and recession supported or discredited any of the macroeconomic theories discussed in this chapter? If it was a result of excessive credit creation associated with central banks keeping interest rates too low for too long, what might you answer?

9. Do sticky wages seem realistic? If you wanted to research the stickiness of wages, how might you design your study?

For exercises 10–17, tell which school of thought would most likely be associated with the following quotes:

10. "Changes in prices and wages are too slow to support the new classical assumption of persistent macroeconomic equilibrium."

11. "The best monetary policy is to keep the money supply growing at a slow and steady rate."

12. "Frictional unemployment is a result of workers voluntarily substituting leisure for labor when wages fall."

13. "A change in the money supply will affect GDP after a long and variable lag, so it is difficult to predict the effects of money on output."

14. "Government policymakers should use fiscal policy to adjust aggregate demand in response to aggregate supply shocks."

15. "The economy is subject to recurring disequilibrium in labor and goods markets, so government can serve a useful function of helping the economy adjust to equilibrium."

16. "Since the aggregate supply curve is horizontal, aggregate demand will determine the equilibrium level of real GDP."

17. "If everyone believed that the monetary authority was going to cut the inflation rate from 6 percent to 3 percent, such a reduction in inflation could be achieved without any significant increase in unemployment."

ECONOMICALLY SPEAKING

THE GHOSTS OF CHRISTMAS PAST HAUNT ECONOMISTS

J. Bradford Delong
Africa News, January 10, 2003

Financial crises have come back because policymakers fail to learn earlier lessons. In Charles Dickens' great novel, *A Christmas Carol*, the soulless businessman Ebenezer Scrooge is tormented by a visit from the Spirit of Christmas Past. Today, economists are similarly troubled by unwanted ghosts, as they ponder the reappearance of economic ills long thought buried and dead.

From Stephen Roach at Morgan Stanley to Paul Krugman at Princeton, to the governors of the US Federal Reserve and the senior staff at the European Central Bank, to almost everyone in Japan, economists all over the world are worrying about deflation. Their thoughts retrace the economic thinking of more than 50 years ago, a time when economists concluded that the thing to do with deflation was to avoid it like the plague.

Back in 1933 Irving Fisher—Milton Friedman's predecessor atop the US's monetarist school of economists—announced that governments could prevent deep depressions by avoiding deflation. Deflation—a steady, continuing decline in prices—gave businesses and consumers powerful incentives to cut spending and hoard cash.

It reduced the ability of businesses and banks to service their debt, and might trigger a chain of big bankruptcies that would destroy confidence in the financial system, providing further incentives to hoard. Such strong incentives to hoard rather than spend can keep demand low and falling, and unemployment high and rising, for a much longer time than even the most laissez-faire-oriented politician or economist had ever dared contemplate. Hence the Keynesian solution: use monetary policy (lower interest rates) and fiscal policy (expanded government spending and reduced taxes) to keep the economy from ever approaching the precipice where deflation becomes possible.

But if this is an issue solved more than 50 years ago, why is it haunting us now? Why is this menace a matter of grave concern in Japan today, and a threat worth worrying about in the US? ...

The truth is that economic policymakers are juggling sets of potential disasters, exchanging the one that appears most threatening for a threat that seems more distant.

In the US, the Bush administration is sceptical of the stimulative power of monetary policy and wants bigger fiscal deficits to reduce unemployment, hoping that the future dangers posed by persistent deficits—low investment, slow growth, loss of confidence, uncontrolled inflation and exchange rate depreciation—can be finessed, or will not become visible until after the Bush team leaves office.

In Europe, the European Central Bank believes the danger of uncontrolled inflation following a loss of public confidence in its commitment to low inflation outweighs the costs of European unemployment that is far too high ...

The ghosts of economics' past return because the lessons of the present are always oversold. Politicians and policymakers advance their approach to economics as the One True Doctrine. What they are doing, however, is dealing with the biggest problem of the moment, but at the price of removing institutions and policies that policymakers before them had put into place to control problems they felt to be the most pressing.

Ebenezer Scrooge's nocturnal visitors were able to convince him of the errors of his ways. Let us hope today's economists also learn the lessons of their unwanted ghosts.

Source: Excerpt from *The Ghosts of Christmas Past Haunt Economists*. January 10, 2003 by J. Bradford Delong p. 36. © Project Syndicate, January 10, 2003.

COMMENTARY

Macroeconomics has always been a lively field, filled with controversy over the proper approach to modeling the economy, the correct interpretation of experience, and the role that government policy can and should play. Indeed, debate in macroeconomics is as old as the field itself. The views of John Maynard Keynes, the founder of macroeconomics, were challenged by his colleague at Cambridge University, Arthur Pigou. This debate focused on the importance of the "real balance effect," whereby a fall in the price level raises real money balances (or the purchasing power of the money supply), increases wealth, and thus increases consumption. Like most debates in macroeconomics, this was more than an ivory tower exercise, since the real balance effect provides a channel by which the economy can bring itself out of a slump without government intervention.

The article indicates that, in early 2003, the issue of falling prices was back again as a policy concern. The Japanese economy had experienced deflation in recent years, and some were worried that the United States could also move from low inflation to deflation. In the global recession that started in 2007, there were renewed fears of deflation, so this issue does not go away. The author claims that economists knew long ago that deflation could be avoided by expansionary fiscal and monetary policies. A monetarist-type solution would be central bank targeting of inflation. In the early 2000s, some economists were suggesting that this is what the central bank of Japan should do: Set an inflation target and aim monetary policy solely at the achievement of such a target. A Keynesian-type solution would be to increase government spending and/or reduce taxes. The Bush administration in the United States was proposing a Keynesian approach, with tax cuts to stimulate the U.S. economy. The European Central Bank was utilizing a monetarist approach of inflation targeting to achieve public confidence in its commitment to low inflation. Both of these policies may avoid deflation. However, we can never be sure of the effects of a tax cut on important variables like unemployment, interest rates, and real GDP, and the inflation target achieves only the inflation goal and may have undesirable consequences for unemployment and real GDP growth. In short, there is no magic economic solution that always provides the best mix of macroeconomic outcomes. This is a major reason for the debates that have raged in macroeconomics.

The debate between the Keynesians and the monetarists dominated the macroeconomic discourse of the 1950s and 1960s. During this period, those who identified themselves as Keynesians gave primacy to the role of fiscal policy and to the issue of unemployment; these economists had great faith in the ability of the government to fine-tune the economy through the proper application of policy, thereby ensuring stability and growth. Keynesians of this vintage also believed that changes in the money supply had little effect on the economy. In contrast, monetarists were very concerned about inflation, which they believed to be a purely monetary phenomenon. These economists also doubted that active government intervention could stabilize the economy, for they believed that policy operated only with long and variable lags.

Although outside observers may view the debate within macroeconomics as evidence of confusion, a more accurate appraisal is that the debate is a healthy intellectual response to a world in which few things are certain and much is unknown—and perhaps unknowable. The differences seen between schools of thought mask the fact that there is a great deal of consensus about a number of issues in macroeconomics. This consensus is a product of lessons learned from past debates. In a similar fashion, the controversies of today will yield tomorrow's consensus, and our knowledge of the real workings of the economy will grow.

CHAPTER 16

Economic Growth

© Pavel L Photo and Video/Shutterstock.com

FUNDAMENTAL QUESTIONS

1. What is economic growth?

2. How are economic growth rates determined?

3. What is productivity?

4. What explains productivity changes?

Preview

Modern economies tend to raise living standards for the population generation after generation. This is economic growth. However, this was not always the case. Prior to the seventeenth century, economic activity involved a constant struggle to avoid starvation. Only in recent centuries has the idea of living standards being improved within a generation become common. Economist Angus Maddison has estimated that GDP grew at about a rate of 1.0 percent per year between the years 500 and 1500. Yet, since population growth was about the same at 1.0 percent per year, there was no increase in GDP per capita. He estimates that between 1500 and 1700, growth of per capita GDP

351

increased to 1.0 percent per year, and between 1700 and 1820, it increased to about 1.6 percent per year, not too different from recent growth rates for the major industrial countries. Understanding why and how economic growth happens is a very important part of macroeconomics.

Although much of macroeconomics is aimed at understanding business cycles—recurring periods of prosperity and recession—the fact is that, over the long run, most economies do grow wealthier. The long-run trend of real GDP in the United States and most other countries is positive. Yet the rate at which real GDP grows is very different across countries. Why? What factors cause economies to grow and living standards to rise?

In this chapter we focus on the long-term picture. We begin by defining economic growth and discussing its importance. Then we examine the determinants of economic growth to understand what accounts for the different rates of growth across countries.

16-1 Defining Economic Growth

1. What is economic growth?

economic growth
An increase in real GDP.

What do we mean by economic growth? Economists use two measures of growth—real GDP and per capita real GDP—to compare how economies grow over time.

16-1a Real GDP

Basically, **economic growth** is an increase in real GDP. As more goods and services are produced, the real GDP increases and people are able to consume more.

To calculate the percentage change in real GDP over a year, we simply divide the change in GDP by the value of GDP at the beginning of the year, and then multiply the quotient by 100. For instance, the real GDP of Singapore was approximately 57,450 million Singapore dollars in 2012 and approximately 58,191 million in 2013. This was after the global recession, and the economy grew at a rate of 1.2 percent over that year:

$$\text{Percentage change in real GDP} = (\text{change over year/beginning value}) \times 100$$
$$= [(58,191 - 57,450)/57,450] \times 100$$
$$= 12.5\%$$

Small changes in rates of growth produce big changes in real GDP over a period of many years.

16-1a-1 Compound Growth From 2000 to 2007 (prior to the start of the global recession in 2008), the industrial countries of the world showed an average annual growth rate of real GDP of 2.5 percent. Over the same period, the average annual growth rate of real GDP for developing countries was 6.5 percent. The difference between a growth rate of 2.5 percent and one of 6.5 percent may not seem substantial, but in fact it is. Growth is compounded over time. This means that any given rate of growth is applied every year to a growing base of real GDP, so any difference is magnified over time.

Figure 1 shows the effects of compounding growth rates. The upper line in the figure represents the path of real GDP if the economy grows at a rate of 6.5 percent a year. The lower line shows real GDP growing at a rate of 2.5 percent a year.

Suppose that in each case the economy originally is producing a real GDP of $1 billion. After five years, there is some difference: a GDP of $1.13 billion at 2.5 percent growth versus $1.34 at 6.5 percent growth. However, the effect of compounding becomes more visible over long periods of time. After 40 years, the difference between 2.5 and 6.5 percent growth, a seemingly small difference, represents a substantial difference in output: A

FIGURE 1 **Comparing GDP Growth Rates of 2.5 Percent and 6.5 Percent**

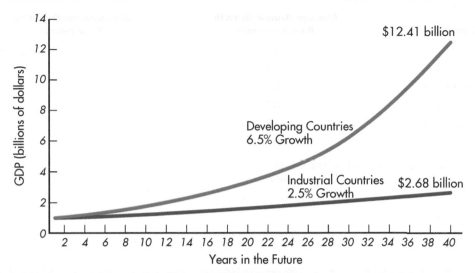

Between 2000 and 2007, real GDP in the industrial countries grew at an average annual rate of 2.5 percent, while real GDP in developing countries grew at an average annual rate of 6.5 percent. The difference seems small, but the graph shows how even a small difference is compounded over time, producing a substantial difference in real GDP.

2.5 percent rate of growth yields an output of $2.68 billion; at 6.5 percent, output is $12.41 billion. After 40 years, the level of output is approximately six times larger at the higher growth rate.

16-1a-2 The Rule of 72 Compound growth explains why countries are so concerned about maintaining positive high rates of growth. If growth is maintained at a constant rate, we can estimate the number of years required for output to double by using the **rule of 72**. If we divide 72 by the growth rate, we find the approximate time that it takes for any value to double.

Suppose you deposit $100 in a bank account that pays a constant 6 percent annual interest. If you allow the interest to accumulate over time, the amount of money in the account grows at a rate of 6 percent. At this rate of interest, the rule of 72 tells us that your account will have a value of approximately $200 (double its initial value) after 12 years:

$$\frac{72}{6} = 12$$

The interest rate gives the rate of growth of the amount deposited if earned interest is allowed to accumulate in the account. If the interest rate is 3 percent, the amount will double in 24 (72/3) years. The rule of 72 applies to any value. If real GDP is growing at a rate of 6 percent a year, then real GDP doubles every 12 years. At a 3 percent annual rate, real GDP doubles every 24 years.

Table 1 lists the average annual rate of growth of GDP between 1990 and 2013 and the approximate doubling times for six countries. The countries listed have growth rates ranging from a high of 10.3 percent in China to a low of 0.9 percent in Japan. If these growth rates are maintained over time, it would take just seven years for the GDP in China to double and 76 years for the GDP in Japan to double.

rule of 72
The number of years required for an amount to double in value is 72 divided by the annual rate of growth.

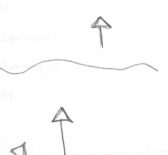

TABLE 1 GDP Growth Rates and Doubling Times

Country	Average Annual Growth Rate (percent)*	Approximate Doubling Time (years)
China	10.3	7
South Korea	5.2	14
Bangladesh	5.5	13
Australia	3.2	22
United States	2.5	29
Japan	0.9	76

* Average annual growth rates from 1990 to 2013.
Source: IMF, World Economic Outlook Database, January 2014.

FIGURE 2 Differences in Per Capita Income Around the World

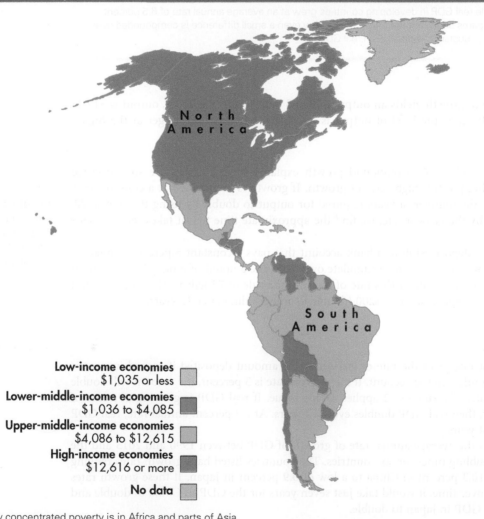

Low-income economies
$1,035 or less

Lower-middle-income economies
$1,036 to $4,085

Upper-middle-income economies
$4,086 to $12,615

High-income economies
$12,616 or more

No data

The map shows how concentrated poverty is in Africa and parts of Asia.

16-1b Per Capita Real GDP

We have defined economic growth as an increase in real GDP. But if growth is supposed to be associated with higher standards of living, our definition may be misleading. A country could show positive growth in real GDP, but if the population is growing at an even higher rate, output per person can actually fall. Economists, therefore, often adjust the growth rate of output for changes in population. **Per capita real GDP** is real GDP divided by the population. If we define economic growth as rising per capita real GDP, then growth requires a nation's output of goods and services to increase faster than its population.

Per capita GDP is often used as an indicator of economic development. In 2007, African countries had an average per capita GDP of $2,413, while the countries of the euro-zone had an average of $33,296. Although there are great differences in the levels of per capita GDP, the difference in per capita real GDP growth between low-income developing and industrial countries is much smaller than the difference in real GDP growth. The difference in growth rates between the level of output and per capita output points out the danger of just looking at real GDP as an indicator of change in the economic well-being of the citizens in developing countries. Population growth rates are considerably higher in developing countries than they are in industrial countries, so real GDP must grow at a faster rate in developing countries than it does in industrial countries just to maintain a similar growth rate in per capita real GDP. Figure 2 depicts how per capita income differs

Economic growth is sometimes defined as an increase in per capita real GDP.

per capita real GDP
Real GDP divided by the population.

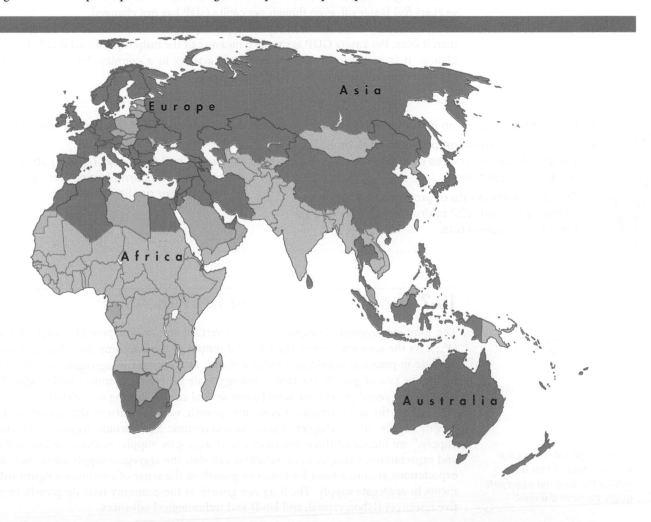

around the world. The map shows how poverty is concentrated around the world and found largely in Africa and parts of Asia.

16-1c The Problems with Definitions of Growth

Economic growth is considered to be good because it allows people to have a higher standard of living, to have more material goods. But an increase in real GDP or per capita real GDP does not tell us whether the average citizen is better off. One problem is that these measures say nothing about how income is distributed. The national economy may be growing, yet the poor may be staying poor while the rich get richer.

Per capita real GDP is a questionable indicator of the typical citizen's standard of living or quality of life.

The lesson here is simple: Economic growth may benefit some groups more than others. And it is entirely possible that, despite national economic growth, some groups can be worse off than they were before. Clearly, neither per capita real GDP nor real GDP accurately measures the standard of living for all of a nation's citizens.

Another reason that real GDP and per capita real GDP are misleading is that neither says anything about the quality of life. People have nonmonetary needs—they care about personal freedom, the environment, and their leisure time. If a rising per capita GDP goes hand in hand with a repressive political regime or a rapidly deteriorating environmental quality, people are not going to feel better off. By the same token, a country could have no economic growth, yet reduce the hours worked each week. More leisure time could make workers feel better off, even though per capita GDP has not changed.

Once again, be careful in interpreting per capita GDP. Do not allow it to represent more than it does. Per capita GDP is simply a measure of the output produced divided by the population. It is a useful measure of economic activity in a country, but it is a questionable measure of the typical citizen's standard of living or quality of life.

R E C A P

1. Economic growth is an increase in real GDP.

2. Because growth is compounded over time, small differences in rates of growth are magnified over time.

3. For any constant rate of growth, the time required for real GDP to double is 72 divided by the annual growth rate.

4. Per capita real GDP is real GDP divided by the population.

5. Per capita real GDP says nothing about the distribution of income in a country or the non-monetary quality of life.

16-2 The Determinants of Growth

2. How are economic growth rates determined?

Economic growth raises the potential level of real GDP, shifting the long-run aggregate supply curve to the right.

The long-run aggregate supply curve is a vertical line at the potential level of real GDP (Y_{p1}). As the economy grows, the potential output of the economy rises. Figure 3 shows the increase in potential output as a rightward shift in the long-run aggregate supply curve. The higher the rate of growth, the farther the aggregate supply curve moves to the right. To illustrate several years' growth, we would show several curves shifting to the right.

To find the determinants of economic growth, we must turn to the determinants of aggregate supply. In the chapter titled "Macroeconomic Equilibrium: Aggregate Demand and Supply," we identified three determinants of aggregate supply: resource prices, technology, and expectations. Changes in expectations can shift the aggregate supply curve, but changing expectations are not a basis for long-run growth in the sense of continuous rightward movements in aggregate supply. The long-run growth of the economy rests on growth in productive resources (labor, capital, and land) and technological advances.

FIGURE 3 Economic Growth

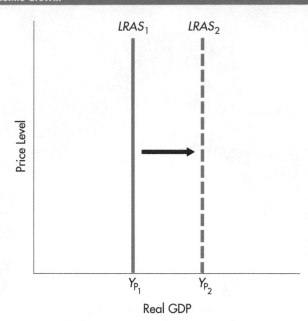

As the economy grows, the long-run aggregate supply curve shifts to the right. This represents an increase in the potential level of real GDP.

16-2a Labor

Economic growth depends on the size and quality of the labor force. The size of the labor force is a function of the size of the working-age population (16 years and older in the United States) and the percentage of that population that is in the labor force. The labor force typically grows more rapidly in developing countries than in industrial countries because birthrates are higher in developing countries. Figure 4 shows the annual growth rates of the population for low-income, middle-income, and high-income countries. Between 1995 and 2010, the population grew at an average annual rate of 1.5 percent in low-income countries, 1.2 percent in middle income countries, and 0.4 percent in high-income countries.

Based solely on growth in the labor force, it would seem that poor countries are growing faster than rich countries. But the size of the labor force is not all that matters; changes in productivity can compensate for lower growth in the labor force, as we discuss in section 3.

The U.S. labor force has changed considerably in recent decades. The most notable event of the post–World War II period was the baby boom. The children born between the late 1940s and the early 1960s made up more than a third of the total U.S. population in the early 1960s and have significantly altered the age structure of the population. In 1950, 41 percent of the population was 24 years old or younger, and 59 percent was 25 years old or older. By 1970, 46 percent of the population was in the younger group, with 54 percent in the older group. By 1990, this bulge in the age distribution had moved to where about 36 percent of the U.S. population was 24 years or younger. Over time, the bulge will move to older ranges of the population. By 2000, 35 percent of the population was 24 years or younger, with 65 percent 25 years or older.

Developing countries are playing an increasing role in the "outsourcing" of labor for firms in the industrial world. Here, workers in Bangalore, India, process data for 24/7 customers.

FIGURE 4 *Average Annual Population Growth in Low-, Middle-, and High-Income Countries (percent)*

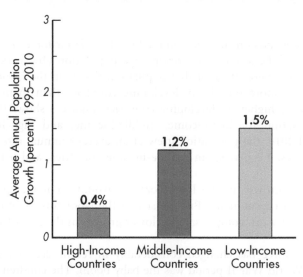

Population growth rates across countries vary considerably. Generally, population grows at a much higher rate in developing countries.

Source: Data are from World Bank; http://devdata.worldbank.org/hnpstats/query/default.html.

The initial pressure of the baby boom fell on school systems, which were faced with rapidly expanding enrollments. Over time, as these children aged and entered the labor market, they had a large impact on potential output. The U.S. labor force grew at an average rate of about 2.5 percent a year in the 1970s, approximately twice the rate of growth experienced in the 1950s. The growth of the labor force slowed in the 1980s and 1990s as the baby boom population aged. On the basis of the size of the labor force, the 1970s should have been a time of greater economic growth than the 1950s and 1960s or the 1980s and 1990s. It was not. More important than the size of the labor force is its productivity.

16-2b Capital

Labor is combined with capital to produce goods and services. A rapidly growing labor force by itself is no guarantee of economic growth. Workers need machines, tools, and factories in order to work. If a country has lots of workers but few machines, then the typical worker cannot be very productive. Capital is a critical resource in growing economies.

The ability of a country to invest in capital goods is tied to its ability to save. A lack of current saving can be offset by borrowing, but the availability of borrowing is limited by the prospects for future saving. Debt incurred today must be repaid by not consuming all output in the future. If lenders believe that a nation is going to consume all of its output in the future, they will not make loans today.

The lower the standard of living in a country, the harder it is to forgo current consumption in order to save. It is difficult for a population that is living at or near subsistence level to do without current consumption. This in large part explains the low level of saving in the poorest countries.

16-2c Land

Land surface, water, forests, minerals, and other natural resources are called *land*. Land can be combined with labor and capital to produce goods and services. Abundant natural resources can contribute to economic growth, but natural resources alone do not generate growth. Several developing countries, such as Argentina and Brazil, are relatively rich in natural resources but have not been very successful in exploiting these resources to produce goods and services. Japan, on the other hand, has relatively few natural resources but showed dramatic economic growth until a recession in the late 1990s. The experience of Japan makes it clear that abundant natural resources are not a necessary condition for economic growth.

Abundant natural resources are not a necessary condition for economic growth.

16-2d Technology

A key determinant of economic growth is **technology**, or ways of combining resources to produce goods and services. New management techniques, scientific discoveries, and other innovations improve technology. Technological advances allow the production of more output from a given amount of resources. This means that technological progress accelerates economic growth for any given rate of growth in the labor force and the capital stock. A particularly dramatic example of technological change is provided in the Economic Insight "Technological Advance: The Change in the Price of Light."

technology
Ways of combining resources to produce output.

Technological change depends on the scientific community. The more educated a population, the greater its potential for technological advances. Industrial countries have better-educated populations than developing countries do. Education gives industrial countries a substantial advantage over developing countries in creating and implementing innovations. In addition, the richest industrial countries traditionally have spent 2 to 3 percent of their GNP on research and development, an investment that developing countries cannot afford. The greater the funding for research and development, the greater the likelihood of technological advances.

Technological advances allow the production of more output from a given amount of resources.

ECONOMIC INSIGHT

Technological Advance: The Change in the Price of Light

A particularly striking example of the role of technological change is provided by the change in the labor cost of providing light. An economist, William Nordhaus, estimated the effects of technological change on the labor cost of providing lighting. Light can be measured in *lumen hours*, where a lumen is the amount of light provided by one candle. Nordhaus estimated the number of hours of work required to produce 1,000 lumen-hours of light. His estimates of the cost of providing 1,000 lumen hours of light are shown in the accompanying table.

Time	Light Source	Labor Price
500,000 BC	Open fire	58 hours
1750 BC	Babylonian lamp	41.5 hours
1800	Tallow candle	5.4 hours
1900	Filament lamp	0.2 hour
1990	Filament lamp	0.0006 hour

The choice of light is appropriate as the desirable service provided by light, illumination, is essentially unchanged over time. What has changed dramatically is the manner in which light is produced and the cost of producing it. The example shows not only how changing technology has increased the productivity of light production, but also how the pace of technological advance has quickened in recent times. The faster technology progresses, the faster the cost of production falls.

Impeded by low levels of education and limited funds for research and development, the developing countries lag behind the industrial countries in developing and implementing new technology. Typically these countries follow the lead of the industrial world, adopting new technology developed in that world once it is affordable and feasible, given their capital and labor resources. In the next chapter we discuss the role of foreign aid, including technological assistance, in promoting economic growth in developing countries.

Source: William Nordhaus, "Do Real-Output and Real-Wage Measures Capture Reality? The History of Lighting Suggests Not," in *The Economics of New Goods*, ed. Timothy Bresnahan and Robert Gordon (Chicago: University of Chicago Press, 1997).

RECAP

1. Economic growth raises the potential level of real GDP, shifting the long-run aggregate supply curve to the right.

2. The long-run growth of the economy is a product of growth in labor, capital, and natural resources and advances in technology.

3. The size of the labor force is determined by the working-age population and the percentage of that population that is in the labor force.

4. The post-World War II baby boom created a bulge in the age distribution of the U.S. population.

5. Growth in capital stock is tied to current and future saving.

6. Abundant natural resources contribute to economic growth but are not essential to that growth.

7. Technology is the way in which resources are combined to produce output.

8. Hampered by low levels of education and limited financial resources, developing countries lag behind the industrial nations in developing and implementing new technology.

16-3 Productivity

In the last section, we described how output depends on resource inputs like labor and capital. One way to assess the contribution that a resource makes to output is its productivity. *Productivity* is the ratio of the output produced to the amount of input. We can measure the productivity of a single resource—say, labor or capital—or the overall productivity of all resources. **Total factor productivity *(TFP)*** is the term that economists use to describe the overall productivity of an economy. It is the ratio of the economy's output to its stock of labor and capital.

16-3a Productivity and Economic Growth

Economic growth depends on both the growth of resources and technological progress. Advances in technology allow resources to be more productive. If the quantity of resources is growing and each resource is more productive, then output grows even faster than the quantity of resources. Economic growth, then, is the sum of the growth rate of total factor productivity and the growth rate of resources:

Economic growth = growth rate of TFP + growth rate of resources

The amount by which output grows because the labor force is growing depends on how much labor contributes to the production of output. Similarly, the amount by which output grows because capital is growing depends on how much capital contributes to the production of output. To relate the growth of labor and capital to the growth of output (we assume no change in natural resources), the growth of labor and the growth of capital must be multiplied by their relative contributions to the production of output. The most straightforward way to measure those contributions is to use the share of real GDP received by each resource. For instance, in the United States, labor receives about 70 percent (.70) of real GDP and capital receives about 30 percent (.30). So we can determine the growth of output by using this formula:

$$\%\Delta Y = \%\Delta TFP + .70(\%\Delta L) + .30(\%\Delta K)$$

where

$$\%\Delta = \text{percentage change in}$$
$$Y = \text{real GDP}$$
$$TFP = \text{total factor productivity}$$
$$L = \text{size of the labor force}$$
$$K = \text{capital stock}$$

The equation shows how economic growth depends on changes in productivity ($\%\Delta TFP$) as well as changes in resources ($\%\Delta L$ and $\%\Delta K$). Even if labor (L) and capital stock (K) are constant, technological innovation will generate economic growth through changes in total factor productivity (TFP).

For example, suppose *TFP* is growing at a rate of 2 percent a year. Then, even with labor and capital stock held constant, the economy grows at a rate of 2 percent a year. If labor and capital stock also grow at a rate of 2 percent a year, output grows by the sum of the growth rates of all three components (*TFP*, .70 times labor growth, and .30 times the capital stock growth), or 4 percent.

How do we account for differences in growth rates across countries? Because almost all countries have experienced growth in the labor force, percentage increases in labor forces

3. What is productivity?

total factor productivity (*TFP*)
The ratio of the economy's output to its stock of labor and capital.

NOW YOU TRY IT

What is the growth rate of real GDP for an economy in which TFP grows at a rate of 4 percent, the labor force grows at a rate of 1 percent, the capital stock has zero growth, labor receives 70 percent of output, and capital receives 30 percent?

4. What explains productivity changes?

have generally supported economic growth. But growth in the capital stock has been steadier in the industrial countries than in the developing countries, so differences in capital growth rates may explain some of the differences in economic growth across countries. Yet differences in resource growth rates alone cannot explain the major differences we find across countries. In recent years, those differences seem to be related to productivity.

16-3b Determinants of Productivity

Productivity in the United States has fluctuated considerably in recent years. From 1948 to 1965, *TFP* grew at an annual average rate of 2.02 percent. In the 1970s, *TFP* growth averaged 0.7 percent per year; in the 1980s, 0.6 percent; and by the late 1990s, 1 percent. If the pre-1965 rate of growth had been maintained, output in the United States would be an estimated 39 percent higher today than it actually is. What caused this dramatic change in productivity—first down in the 1970s and 1980s, and then up in the 1990s? More generally, what determines the productivity changes for any country?

Several factors determine productivity growth. They include the quality of the labor force, technological innovations, energy prices, and a shift from manufacturing to service industries.

16-3b-1 Labor Quality Labor productivity is measured as output per hour of labor. Figure 5 shows how the productivity of labor in the United States and four other countries changed between 1979 and 2011. We see that Korea generally has had the fastest rate of labor productivity growth and Canada the lowest over this time period. Although changes in the productivity of labor can stem from technological innovation and changes in the capital stock, they can also come from changes in the quality of labor. These changes may be a product of the level and quality of education, demographic change, and changing attitudes toward work.

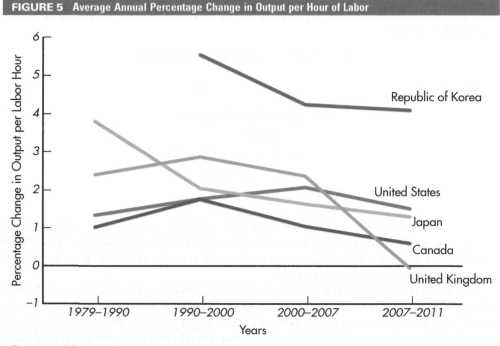

FIGURE 5 Average Annual Percentage Change in Output per Hour of Labor

Output per labor hour is a measure of productivity.

Source: Data from *Bureau of Labor Statistics*; www.bls.gov/fls/home/htm.

Education Level The average level of education in the world has gone up over time. Table 2 lists three measures of education level for the United States.

The first measure, median school years completed, increased from 8.6 years in 1940 to 12.9 years in 2000. From 1940 to 2012, the percentage of adults with at least a high school education rose from more than 24 percent to 87.6 percent, and the percentage of those with a college education rose from less than 5 percent to 32.6 percent. The figures seem to indicate that the level of education supports increases in U.S. productivity.

Demographic Change Changes in the size and composition of the population have an impact on the labor market. As the baby boom generation entered the labor force in the late 1960s and early 1970s, a large pool of inexperienced, unskilled workers was created. The average quality of the labor force may have fallen at this time, as reflected in some large drops in output per hour of labor. In the 1980s, the baby boom segment of the labor force had more experience, skills, and education, thus pushing the quality of the labor force up.

Another important demographic change that has affected the quality of the labor force is the participation rates of women. As more and more women entered the labor force in the 1980s, the pool of untrained workers increased, probably reducing the average quality of labor. Over time, as female participation rates have stabilized, the average quality of labor should rise as the skills and experience of female workers rise.

Finally, immigration can play a role in labor force quality. For instance, the 1970s and 1980s saw a change in the pattern of U.S. immigration. Although many highly skilled professionals immigrate to the United States as part of the "brain drain" from developing countries, recent immigrants, both legal and illegal, have generally added to the supply of unskilled labor and reduced the average quality of the labor force.

16-3b-2 Technological Innovation

New technology alters total factor productivity. Innovations increase productivity, so when productivity falls, it is natural to look at technological developments to see whether they are a factor in the change. The pace of technological innovation is difficult to measure. Expenditures on research and development are related to the discovery of new knowledge, but actual changes in technology do not proceed as evenly as those expenditures. We expect a long lag between funding and operating a laboratory and the discovery of useful technology. Still, a decline in spending on research and development may indicate less of a commitment to increasing productivity.

The most notable technological innovation in recent decades has been the widespread availability of cheaper and faster computers. The information technology (IT) revolution has played an important role in enhancing productivity.

One may think of the purchase of computer hardware or software as investment. The capital stock increases with such purchases. However, researchers have also found that there are increases in total factor productivity associated with the development and spread of information technology. Such gains have not been realized by all countries. Poor countries lag far behind the

TABLE 2 The Average Level of Education, United States, 1940–2012*									
	1940	**1950**	**1960**	**1970**	**1980**	**1950**	**2000**	**2009**	**2012**
Median school years completed	8.6	9.3	10.6	12.1	12.5	12.7	12.9	N/A	N/A
People with at least a high school education (percent)	24.5	34.3	41.1	52.3	66.5	75.2	84.1	86.7	87.6
People with at least four years of college (percent)	4.6	6.2	7.7	10.7	16.2	20.3	25.6	29.5	32.6

*People 25 years of age and over.

Source: http://www.census.gov/hhes/socdemo/education/data/cps/.

rich in the implementation of IT. Table 3 provides data on the number of broadband users per 100 people in selected countries. Clearly, the productivity-enhancing benefits of IT have been realized in countries like Switzerland, the Netherlands, and the other countries at the top of the table, where the number of broadband users per 100 people is 39.89 and 39.81 respectively.

However, in developing countries, the benefits of IT innovations are not being fully exploited as a result of poverty and lack of skills. In Table 3, the lowest level of broadband use is 1.21 in India. However, in poorer countries that are not listed in the table, the level of usage is even less. This indicates an inability to implement IT widely across the economy.

TABLE 3	Broadband Users per 100 People	
Rank	**Country**	**Broadband Users per 100 People**
1	Switzerland	39.89
2	Netherlands	39.81
3	Denmark	38.78
4	France	37.47
5	Korea, Rep.	37.25
6	Norway	36.33
7	United Kingdom	34.04
8	Germany	33.7
9	Belgium	33.27
10	Canada	32.48
11	Sweden	32.28
12	Hong Kong SAR, China	31.17
13	Finland	30.26
14	United States	28.35
15	Japan	27.73
16	Israel	25.34
17	Austria	25.02
18	Spain	24.37
19	Australia	24.34
19	Portugal	22.55
21	Italy	22.14
22	Poland	15.54
23	Russian Federation	14.46
24	China	12.72
25	Chile	12.41
26	Argentina	10.89
27	Turkey	10.62
28	Mexico	10.52
29	Brazil	9.15
30	India	1.21

Source: World Bank: World Development Indicators 2012.

IT is just one example of how productivity may differ across countries as a result of differing uses of modern technology.

16-3b-3 Other Factors

We have seen how changing labor quality and technological innovation are related to changes in productivity. Other reasons have been offered to explain the changes in productivity across countries and over time. We examine three of them: the cost of energy, the shift from a manufacturing to a service-oriented economy, and the development of financial markets.

Energy Prices In 1973, 1974, and 1979, OPEC succeeded in raising the price of oil substantially. The timing of the dramatic increase in oil prices coincided with a drop in productivity growth in the United States. U.S. output per labor hour actually fell in 1974 and 1979. Higher energy prices resulting from restricted oil output should directly decrease aggregate supply because energy is an important input across industries. As the price of energy increases, the costs of production rise and aggregate supply decreases.

Higher energy prices can affect productivity through their impact on the capital stock. As energy prices go up, energy-inefficient capital goods become obsolete. Like any other decline in the value of the capital stock, this change reduces economic growth. Standard measures of capital stock do not account for energy obsolescence, so they suggest that total factor productivity fell in the 1970s. However, if the stock of usable capital actually did go down, it was the growth rate of capital, not *TFP*, that fell.

Manufacturing versus Services In recent decades, the industrial economies have seen a shift away from manufacturing toward services. Some economists believe that productivity grows more slowly in service industries than in manufacturing because of the less capital-intensive nature of providing services. Therefore, the movement into services reduces the overall growth rate of the economy.

Although a greater emphasis on service industries may explain a drop in productivity, we must be careful with this kind of generalization. It is more difficult to measure changes in the quality of services than changes in the quality of goods. If prices in an industry rise with no change in the quantity of output, it makes sense to conclude that the real level of output in the industry has fallen. However, if prices have gone up because the quality of the service has increased, then output actually has changed. Suppose a hotel remodels its rooms. In effect, it is improving the quality of its service. Increased prices here would reflect this change in output.

Service industries—fast-food restaurants, airlines, hotels, banks—are not all alike. One way in which service firms compete is on the basis of the quality of service that they provide. Because productivity is measured by the amount of output per unit of input, if we do not adjust for quality changes, we may underestimate the amount of output and so underestimate the productivity of the industry. The issue of productivity measurement in the service industries is an important topic of discussion among economists today.

Financial Market Development The evidence across countries suggests that economic growth is related to the development of financial markets. For any given amount of labor and capital, the more developed an economy's financial markets are, the more efficient should be the allocation of resources and, therefore, the greater the productivity. A nation may have a high rate of saving and investment and a sizable capital stock, but the key to efficient production is the allocation of resources to their best use.

Financial markets facilitate the allocation of resources. This occurs through the following mechanisms:

- Financial institutions act as intermediaries between savers and borrowers and screen borrowers so that the best projects are more likely to be funded.
- Financial institutions monitor the behavior of borrowers to ensure that the borrowed funds are used as intended.

- Financial institutions lower the risk of providing funds for investment purposes, as they provide loans to different individuals and firms, and through this diversification of loans reduce the likelihood of suffering a catastrophic loss. If one borrower defaults on a loan, the financial institution does not fail as it still has many other loans that are being repaid. This is a far different situation from the one that an individual making a single large loan may face. If you lend a large amount of your wealth to a single borrower and that borrower defaults on the loan, your living standard may be at great risk. Because of the "risk sharing" that takes place in financial institutions, the cost of borrowed funds, the interest rate, will be lower than in an environment in which there is no such pooling of loan risks.

- The more developed the financial sector of an economy, the more types of financing alternatives there are for funding investment. For instance, the typical poor country has a banking sector and a very limited stock market, if any at all. Firms in such a country must rely on bank loans. The governments in such countries often determine where banks are allowed to lend based on political considerations. As economies develop, the financial sector evolves so that alternatives to bank financing come into being. Firms in economies with well-developed financial markets can raise funds by selling shares of ownership in the stock market, by issuing debt in the form of bonds to nonbank lenders, or by borrowing from banks. The more developed a country's financial markets, the more efficient the funding sources for borrowers and the more productive the economy.

16-3c Growth and Development

Economic growth depends on the growth of productivity and resources. Productivity grows unevenly, and its rate of growth is reflected in economic growth. Although the labor force seems to grow faster in developing countries than in industrial countries, lower rates of saving have limited the growth of the capital stock in developing countries. Without capital, workers cannot be very productive. This means that the relatively high rate of growth in the labor force in the developing world does not translate into a high rate of economic growth. We use this information on economic growth in the chapter titled "Development Economics" to explain and analyze the strategies used by developing countries to stimulate output and increase standards of living.

RECAP

1. Productivity is the ratio of the output produced to the amount of input.

2. Total factor productivity is the nation's real GDP (output) divided by its stock of labor and capital.

3. Economic growth is the sum of the growth rate of total factor productivity and the growth rate of resources (labor and capital).

4. Changes in productivity may be explained by the quality of the labor force, technological innovations, energy prices, a shift from manufacturing to service industries, and financial market development.

SUMMARY

1. What is economic growth?

- Economic growth is an increase in real GDP. *§16-1.a*
- Economic growth is compounded over time. *§16-1a*
- Per capita real GDP is real GDP divided by the population. *§16-1b*
- The definitions of economic growth are misleading because they do not indicate anything about the distribution of income or the quality of life. *§16-1c*

2. How are economic growth rates determined?

- The growth of the economy is tied to the growth of productive resources and technological advances. *§16-2*
- Because their populations tend to grow more rapidly, developing countries typically experience faster growth in the labor force than do industrial countries. *§16-2a*
- The inability to save limits the growth of the capital stock in developing countries. *§16-2b*

- Abundant natural resources are not necessary for rapid economic growth. *§16-2c*
- Technology defines the ways in which resources can be combined to produce goods and services. *§16-2d*

3. What is productivity?

- Productivity is the ratio of the output produced to the amount of input. *§16-3*
- Total factor productivity is the overall productivity of an economy. *§16-3*
- The percentage change in real GDP equals the percentage change in total factor productivity plus the percentage changes in labor and capital multiplied by the share of GDP taken by labor and capital. *§16-3a*

4. What explains productivity changes?

- Productivity changes with changes in the quality of the labor force, technological innovations, changes in energy prices, a shift from manufacturing to service industries, and financial market development. *§16-3b*

KEY TERMS

economic growth, 352
per capita real GDP, 355

rule of 72, 353
technology, 359

total factor productivity (*TFP*), 361

EXERCISES

1. Why is the growth of per capita real GDP a better measure of economic growth than the growth of real GDP?
2. What is the level of output after four years if initial output equals $1,000 and the economy grows at a rate of 8 percent a year?
3. Use the data in the following table to determine the average annual growth rate for each country in terms of real GDP growth and per capita real GDP growth (real GDP is in billions of U.S. dollars, and population is in millions of people). Which country grew at the faster rate?

	1999		2001	
Country	Real GDP	Population	Real GDP	Population
Morocco	108.0	30.1	112.0	31.2
Australia	416.2	19.2	528.0	19.5

4. Suppose labor's share of GDP is 70 percent and capital's is 30 percent, real GDP is growing at a rate of 4 percent a year, the labor force is growing at 2 percent, and the capital stock is growing at 3 percent. What is the growth rate of total factor productivity?

5. Suppose labor's share of GDP is 70 percent and capital's is 30 percent, total factor productivity is growing at an annual rate of 2 percent, the labor force is growing at a rate of 1 percent, and the capital stock is growing at a rate of 4 percent. What is the annual growth rate of real GDP?

6. Discuss possible reasons for the slowdown in U.S. productivity growth that occurred in the 1970s and 1980s, and relate each reason to the equation for economic growth. Does the growth of *TFP* or of resources change?

7. How did the post–World War II baby boom affect the growth of the U.S. labor force? What effect is this baby boom likely to have on the future U.S. labor force?

8. How do developing and industrial countries differ in their use of technological change, labor, capital, and natural resources to produce economic growth? Why do these differences exist?

9. How would an aging population affect economic growth?

10. If real GDP for China was 10,312 billion yuan at the end of 2002 and 9,593 billion yuan at the end of 2001, what is the annual rate of growth of the Chinese economy?

11. If Botswana's economy grew at a rate of 1 percent during 2006 and real GDP at the beginning of the year was 44 billion pula, then what is real GDP at the end of the year?

12. Suppose a country has a real GDP equal to $1 billion today. If this economy grows at a rate of 4 percent a year, what will be the value of real GDP after five years?

13. Is the following statement true or false? Explain your answer. "Abundant natural resources are a necessary condition for economic growth."

14. What is the difference between total factor productivity and the productivity of labor? Why do you suppose that people often measure a nation's productivity using labor productivity only?

15. How would each of the following affect productivity in the United States?
    a. The quality of education in high schools increases.
    b. A cutback in oil production by oil-exporting nations raises oil prices.
    c. A large number of unskilled immigrant laborers move into the country.

16. How does the development of financial markets enhance the productivity of a country?

ECONOMICALLY SPEAKING
RIDING A SURGE OF TECHNOLOGY

Federal Reserve Bank of Dallas 2003 Annual Report

Because productivity determines how well we live, Americans want to know how they're doing. In an economy as large and diverse as ours, it's a Herculean task to calculate a productivity number that sums up the efforts of 130 million workers, employed in millions of establishments that produce more than $11 trillion in output. The Bureau of Labor Statistics (BLS) does the best it can in producing quarterly estimates of output per hour, derived largely from surveys of businesses.

BLS data show that U.S. productivity has grown steadily over the long haul, with output per hour rising an average 2.3 percent annually since 1870. A few percentage points a year might not sound like much, but this historical rate doubles per capita income every three decades or so.

The productivity path has been choppy due to business-cycle upturns and slowdowns as well as longer-term economic trends. From 1950 to 1973, for example, output per hour rose a healthy 2.7 percent annually. Over the next 22 years, productivity sank below its long-term trend, rising just 1.5 percent a year. The slowdown remains something of a mystery, although some economists suggest that early investments in computers and information technology didn't provide a big enough payoff.

Productivity broke out of its two-decade doldrums in the mid-1990s as computers, scanners, the Internet and other innovations finally reached critical mass in America's workplaces. Average annual productivity gains have surged at 3.2 percent since 1995.

The revival shows every sign of continuing. The economy emerged from the 2001 recession with productivity growth well above the average of the seven significant business cycles since 1960. In the first 11 quarters after employment peaked, productivity jumped 13 percent, compared with the historical norm of 8 percent. In another break with the past, the gains spread beyond manufacturing, the traditional productivity leader, and into the whole economy, including retailing and services.

Productivity's postrecession surge has been strong enough to spark controversy. The labor market has languished, with no net job creation two years into the recovery. Some see productivity as a millstone that allows companies to expand without hiring more workers. But viewing productivity as a drag on employment is myopic. Americans don't face a choice between having work and working a better way. Higher productivity raises incomes and profits, which fuels demand, boosts investment and puts more people to work, usually at new jobs.

We could dismantle our factory robots and farm equipment with the idea of hiring lots of busy hands to build cars and till the soil. We could junk our backhoes and dig ditches with shovels. Doing so would be absurd. We'd immediately see that renouncing productivity would do us great harm. Prices would be higher, wages lower and the economy smaller. Work would be harder. Living standards would be dragged backward in time, sacrificed to the false god of more jobs.

Rather than shunning productivity, we should embrace it and move forward. As the economic recovery continues, the United States may not be able to sustain the same pace of productivity growth it has the past two years. Even with a slowdown, the nation will likely build on recent years' strong productivity growth, rather than relapse into the post-1973 slump.

The bullish case for future productivity centers on the technologies that have made U.S. workplaces more efficient in recent years. The microchip revolution still has plenty of kick left in it. And as world markets integrate, we should add to our productivity gains from trade.

Further out, new generations of world-shaking technologies will impact the way we work. Take nanotechnology, the science of rearranging atoms and molecules. It promises to create new materials that are stronger, lighter and more flexible and substances with perfect insulating, lubricating and conducting properties. Biotechnology will emerge, too, as a potent force for progress.

When combined with America's entrepreneurial bent and open markets, the inventory of cutting-edge technologies should deliver rapid productivity growth for years. Healthy gains in output per hour may restore the luster of the New Economy, a concept tarnished by the dotcom implosion. The New Economy carries a powerful policy implication: With stronger productivity, the economy can grow faster without fueling inflation.

369

COMMENTARY

Measuring a nation's productivity has never been an easy task. As the article says, it is "a Herculean task to calculate a productivity number that sums up the efforts of 130 million workers, employed in millions of establishments that produce more than $11 trillion in output." Since business and government policymakers make important decisions on the basis of the economic data provided by government, accurate measurement is crucial.

An example of the controversy related to the measurement problems is the issue of the "New Economy." As mentioned at the end of the article, the New Economy means that, with strong increases in productivity, the economy can grow faster without higher inflation. This is a world in which technological advances in computers and information technology are driving increased productivity and output.

To estimate the contribution of computers to growth, one can modify the growth equation presented in section 16-3a of this chapter to allow computers to be treated apart from the rest of the capital stock:

$$\%\Delta Y = \%\Delta TFP + .70(\%\Delta L) + .29(\%\Delta K)$$
$$+ .01\ (\%\Delta COMP)$$

Note that this equation has computers accounting for 1 percent of the real GDP, and other capital for 29 percent.

The growth equation with computers treated separately from the rest of the capital stock allows us to estimate the effect of computers on growth (the product of their GDP share, .01, and the percentage change in the stock of computers).

A study conducted by Dale Jorgensen, Mun Ho, and Kevin Stiroh[1] estimated that a little less than half of the change in *TFP* over the period 1995–2003 can be explained by IT, compared with less than .10 over the earlier period 1959–1973. The U.S. evidence thus indicates a clear role for IT in increasing *TFP*.

The article points out that productivity advances allow higher living standards and create new jobs. Countries that develop and employ new technology will have faster economic growth, less poverty, and less inflation than they would otherwise.

---

[1] Dale W. Jorgensen, Mun S. Ho, and Kevin J. Stiroh, "Will the U.S. Productivity Resurgency Continue?" Federal Reserve Bank of New York, Current Issues in Economics and Finance, December 2004.

CHAPTER 17
Development Economics

©hikrcn/Shutterstock.com

FUNDAMENTAL QUESTIONS

1. How is poverty measured?

2. Why are some countries poorer than others?

3. What strategies can a nation use to increase its economic growth?

4. How are savings in one nation used to speed development in other nations?

Preview

There is an enormous difference between the standards of living in the poorest and the richest countries in the world. In Botswana, the average life expectancy at birth is 61 years, 17 years less than in the United States. In Cambodia, only an estimated 65 percent of the population has access to safe water. In Ghana, 30 percent of the population exists on less than $1.25 per day. And in Chad, only 35 percent of women and 53 percent of men between 15 and 24 years of age can read.

The plight of developing countries is our focus in this chapter. We begin by discussing the extent of poverty and how it is measured across countries. Then we turn to the reasons why developing countries are poor and look at strategies for stimulating growth and development. The reasons for poverty are many, and the remedies often are rooted

top: © Carsten Reisinger/Shutterstock

more in politics than in economics. Still, economics has much to say about how to improve the living standards of the world's poorest citizens.

17-1 The Developing World

Three-fourths of the world's population lives in developing countries. These countries are often called *less-developed countries* (*LDCs*).

The common link among developing countries is low per capita GNP or GDP, which implies a relatively low standard of living for the typical citizen. In other respects, the developing countries are a diverse group, with their cultures, their politics, and even their geography varying enormously. Although we have used GDP throughout the text as the popular measure of a nation's output, in this chapter we frequently refer to GNP, as this is the measure used by the World Bank in classifying countries in terms of stage of development.

The developing countries are located primarily in South and East Asia, Africa, the Middle East, and Latin America (Figure 1). The total population of developing countries is over

FIGURE 1   The World by Stage of Development

Low-income economies
$1,035 or less

Lower-middle-income economies
$1,036 to $4,086

Upper-middle-income economies
$4,087 to $12,616

High-income economies
$12,616 or more

No data

The map of the world is colored to show each country's income level as measured by per capita GNP.

Source: World Bank, http://go.worldbank.org/7EIAD6CKO0.

5.6 billion people. Of this population, 23 percent live in China and 20 percent live in India. The next largest concentration of people is in Indonesia (4 percent), followed by Brazil, Pakistan, Bangladesh, and Nigeria. Except for Latin America, where 74 percent of the population lives in cities, most Third World citizens live in rural areas and are largely dependent on agriculture.

17-1a Measuring Poverty

Poverty is not easy to measure. Typically, poverty is defined in an *absolute* sense: A family is poor if its income falls below a certain level. For example, the poverty level for a family of four in the United States in 2014 was an income of $23,850. The World Bank uses per capita Gross National Income (GNI) of $1,035 or less as its criterion for a low-income country. The countries in gold in Figure 1 meet this absolute definition of poverty.

Poverty is also a *relative* concept. A family's income in relation to the incomes of other families in the country or region is important in determining whether that family feels poor. The poverty level in the United States would represent a substantial increase in the living

1. How is poverty measured?

Poverty typically is defined in absolute terms.

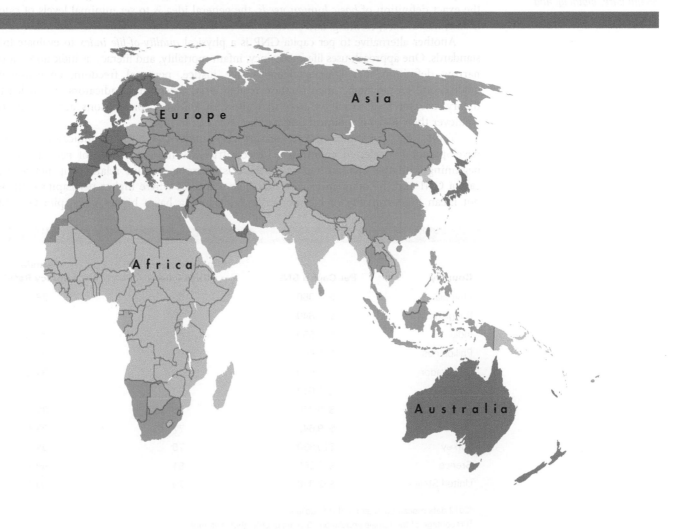

standard of most of the people in the world. Yet a poor family in the United States does not feel less poor because it has more money than poor families in other countries. In a nation where the median income of a family of four is more than $65,000, a family with an income of $20,000 clearly feels poorer.

Because poverty is also a relative concept, using a particular level of income to distinguish the poor from the not poor is often controversial. Besides the obvious problem of where to draw the poverty line, there is the more difficult problem of comparing poverty across countries with different currencies, customs, and living arrangements. Also, data are often limited and difficult to obtain because many of the poor in developing countries live in isolated areas. This makes it difficult to draw a comprehensive picture of the typical poor household in the Third World.

17-1b Basic Human Needs

Basic human needs are a minimal level of caloric intake, health care, clothing, and shelter.

Some economists and other social scientists, recognizing the limitations of an absolute definition of poverty (like the per capita GNP measure that is most commonly used), suggest using indicators of how well basic human needs are being met. Although they disagree on the exact definition of *basic human needs*, the general idea is to set minimal levels of caloric intake, health care, clothing, and shelter.

Another alternative to per capita GNP is a physical *quality-of-life index* to evaluate living standards. One approach uses life expectancy, infant mortality, and literacy as indicators—a very narrow definition that ignores elements like justice, personal freedom, environmental quality, and employment opportunities. Nonetheless, these three indicators are, at least in theory, measures of social progress that allow meaningful comparisons across countries, whatever their social or political orientation.

Table 1 lists per capita GNI (a measure very similar to GNP) and indicators of human development for selected countries. The countries are listed in order of per capita GNI, beginning with the smallest. Generally there is a strong positive relationship between per capita GNI and the other measures. But there are cases where higher per capita GNI does not mean higher quality of life. For instance, Namibia has a higher per capita GNI than

TABLE 1 Quality-of-Life Measures, Selected Countries

Country	Per Capita GNI*	Life Expectancy at Birth (years)	Female Literacy Rate[†]
Ethiopia	$ 380	63	28%
Bangladesh	$ 840	70	73%
India	$ 1,550	66	77%
Philippines	$ 2,500	69	95%
El Salvador	$ 3,590	72	94%
Namibia	$ 5,610	64	94%
China	$ 5,720	75	99%
Mexico	$ 9,640	77	98%
Turkey	$10,830	75	94%
Greece	$23,660	81	99%
United States	$52,340	79	100%

*2012 data measured in terms of U.S. dollars.
[†]Percentage of the female population 15 years or older that is literate.
Source: World Bank, http://web.worldbank.org 2012.

China or the Philippines, but life expectancy and literacy are lower in Namibia than in the other two countries. Remember the limitations of per capita output: It is not a measure of everyone's standard of living in a particular country. However, as the table shows, it is a fairly reliable indicator of differences in living standards across countries. Ethiopia has the lowest per capita GNI and is clearly one of the world's poorest nations. Usually, as per capita GNI increases, living standards increase as well.

Per capita GNP (or GNI) and quality-of-life measures are not the only ways to determine a country's level of economic development—we could consider the number of households with running water, televisions, or any other good that varies with living standards. Recognizing that there is no perfect measure of economic development, economists and other social scientists often use several indicators to assess economic progress.

NOW YOU TRY IT

How might measures of output like per capita GNP be misleading as indicators of how well off people are?

RECAP

1. Usually poverty is defined in an absolute sense as a specific level of family income or per capita GNP or GDP.

2. Within a country or region, poverty is a relative concept.

3. Human development indexes based on indicators of basic human needs incorporate nonmonetary measures of well-being that are an alternative to per capita GDP for measuring economic development.

17-2 Obstacles to Growth

Every country is unique. Each nation's history, both political and cultural, helps economists understand why a particular nation has not developed and what policies offer the best hope for its development. Generally the factors that impede development are political or social. The political factors include a lack of administrative skills, instability, corruption, and the ability of special interest groups to block changes in economic policy. The social obstacles include a lack of entrepreneurs and rapid population growth.

2. Why are some countries poorer than others?

17-2a Political Obstacles

17-2a-1 Lack of Administrative Skills
Government support is essential to economic development. Whether support means allowing private enterprise to flourish and develop or actively managing the allocation of resources, a poorly organized or corrupt government can present an obstacle to economic growth. Some developing countries have suffered from well-meaning but inept government management. This is most obvious in countries with a long history of colonialization. For example, when the Democratic Republic of the Congo won independence from Belgium, few of its native citizens were college educated. Moreover, Belgians had run most of the important government offices. Independence brought a large group of inexperienced and unskilled workers to important positions of power. At first there was a period of "learning by doing."

17-2a-2 Political Instability and Risk
One of the most important functions that a government performs in stimulating economic growth is providing a political environment that encourages saving and investment. People do not want to do business in an economy that has been weakened by wars, demonstrations, or uncertainty. For instance, since becoming an independent nation in 1825, Bolivia has had more than 150 changes in government. This kind of instability forces citizens to take a short-run view of the economy. Long-term planning is impossible when people do not know what the attitudes and policies of the government that is going to be in power next year or even next month will be.

A country must be able to guarantee the rights of private property if it is going to create an environment that encourages private investment.

expropriation
The government seizure of assets, typically without adequate compensation to the owners.

The key issue here is *property rights*. A country that guarantees the right of private property encourages private investment and development. Where ownership rights may be changed by revolution or political decree, there is little incentive for private investment and development. People will not start new businesses or build new factories if they believe that a change in government or a change in the political will of the current government could result in the confiscation of their property.

This confiscation is called **expropriation**. Countries with a history of expropriating foreign-owned property without compensating the owners (paying them the property's market value) have difficulty encouraging foreign investment. An example is Uganda. In 1973, a successful revolution by Idi Amin was followed by the expropriation of over 500 foreign-owned (mostly British) firms. Foreign and domestic investment in Uganda fell dramatically as a result.

The loss of foreign investment is particularly important in developing countries. In the chapter titled "Economic Growth," we pointed out that developing countries suffer from a lack of saving. If domestic residents are not able to save because they are living at or below subsistence level, foreign saving is a crucial source of investment. Without that investment, the economies of developing countries cannot grow.

17-2a-3 Corruption Corrupt practices by government officials have long reduced economic growth. Payment of money or gifts in order to receive a government service or benefit is quite widespread in many countries. Research shows that there is a definite negative relationship between the level of corruption in a country and both investment and growth.

Research also shows that corruption thrives in countries where government regulations create distortions between the economic outcomes that would exist with free markets and the actual outcomes. For instance, a country where government permission is required in order to buy or sell foreign currency will have a thriving black market in foreign exchange, and the black market exchange rate of a U.S. dollar will cost much more domestic currency than the official rate offered by the government. This distortion allows government officials an opportunity for personal gain by providing access to the official rate.

Generally speaking, the more competitive a country's markets are, the fewer the opportunities for corruption. So policies aimed at reducing corruption typically involve reducing the discretion that public officials have in granting benefits or imposing costs on others. This may include greater transparency of government practices and the introduction of merit-based competition for government employment.

Corruption reduces growth most directly through government investment in projects with low productivity. The evidence indicates that corrupt governments spend more on capital goods than governments that are less corrupt, but that the investment projects of corrupt governments probably reduce the productivity of the country. In addition, those countries in which corrupt governments engage in large amounts of capital expenditures have relatively small amounts of private investment. Since private investment is aimed at earning a profit, such investment tends to increase the productivity of a nation. Private firms do not undertake risky projects unless they expect to earn a profit. It is possible, however, that a corrupt government may award large construction projects in order to receive financial rewards from the contractors that are hired. The projects chosen may turn out to be inefficient uses of government funds that retard economic growth rather than increase it.

17-2a-4 Good Economics as Bad Politics Every Third World politician wants to maximize economic growth, all things being equal. But all things are rarely equal. Political pressures may force a government to work toward more immediate objectives than economic growth.

For example, maximizing growth may mean reducing the size of government in order to lower taxes and increase investment. However, in many developing countries, the strongest supporters of the political leaders are those working for the current government. Obviously, it is not good political strategy to fire those workers. So the government remains overstaffed and inefficient, and the potential for economic growth falls.

The governments in developing countries often subsidize purchases of food and other basic necessities. Rather than artificially lower some food prices, it is better to move toward free market pricing of food, energy, and other items to better reflect relative scarcity and then give subsidies to the poor to enable them to buy an adequate diet.

In 1977, the Egyptian government lowered its food subsidies in order to use those funds for development. What happened? There was widespread rioting that ended only when the government reinstituted the subsidies. In 1989, Venezuela lowered government subsidies of public transportation and petroleum products. Public transit fares went up 30 percent, to the equivalent of 7 U.S. cents, and gasoline prices went from 16 to 26 cents a gallon. (One official said that the prices were raised "from the cheapest in the world to the cheapest in the world.")[1] The resulting rioting in Caracas led to 50 deaths, over 500 injuries, and more than 1,000 arrests. Lowering government expenditures and reducing the role of government in the economy can be both politically and physically dangerous.

What we are saying here is that seemingly good economics can make for bad politics. Because any change in policy aimed at increasing growth is going to hurt some group in the short run, there always is opposition to change. Often the continued rule of the existing regime depends on not alienating a certain group. Only a government that is stabilized by military force (a dictatorship), popular support (a democracy), or party support (a Communist or socialist country) has the power to implement needed economic change. A government that lacks this power is handicapped by political constraints in its efforts to stimulate economic growth.

The Global Business Insight "Economic Development in the Americas" points out how history plays a role in shaping the institutions and economic framework in which development takes place. The more rapid development of Canada and the United States than of Latin America may be traced back to colonial times and the institutions that evolved from the conditions that existed then.

17-2b Social Obstacles

Cultural traditions and attitudes can work against economic development. In traditional societies, children follow in their parents' footsteps. If your father is a carpenter, there is a good chance that you will be a carpenter. Moreover, production is carried out in the same way generation after generation. For an economy to grow, it must be willing to change.

17-2b-1 Lack of Entrepreneurs A society that answers the questions *What to produce? How to produce?* and *For whom to produce?* by doing things as they were done by the previous generation lacks a key ingredient for economic growth: entrepreneurs. Entrepreneurs are risk takers; they bring innovation and new technology into use. Understanding why some societies are better at producing entrepreneurs than others may help explain why some nations have remained poor, while others have grown rapidly.

One theory is that entrepreneurs often come from *blocked minorities*. Some individuals in the traditional society are blocked from holding prestigious jobs or political office because of discrimination. This discrimination can be based on race, religion, or immigrant status. Because discrimination keeps them from the best traditional occupations, these minority groups can achieve wealth and status only through entrepreneurship. The Chinese in Southeast Asia, the Jews in Europe, and the Indians in Africa were all blocked minorities, forced to turn to entrepreneurship to advance themselves.

Entrepreneurs are more likely to develop among minority groups that have been blocked from traditional high-paying jobs.

[1] See "Venezuela Rumblings: Riots and Debt Crisis," *New York Times*, March 2, 1989, p. A13.

GLOBAL BUSINESS INSIGHT

Economic Development in the Americas

It is not well known that, at one time, the United States and Canada were not the richest countries in North and South America. The accompanying table shows how per capita GDP relative to that of the United States has changed over time for several countries.

Per Capita GDP Relative to the United States (percent)

County	1700	1800	1900	2000
Argentina	–	102	52	36
Barbados	150	–	–	44
Brazil	–	50	10	22
Chile	–	46	38	28
Cuba	167	112	–	–
Mexico	89	50	35	26
Peru	–	41	20	14
U.S. Real GDP per capita (1985 dollars)	550	807	3,859	34,260

One can see that some of what were then European colonies, such as Barbados and Cuba, were much richer in 1700 than the group of colonies in North America that eventually became the United States. Cuban per capita GDP was 167 percent of U.S. per capita GDP, while Barbados was 150 percent. Others, like Mexico, were about as rich as the colonies that became the United States. In 1800, Argentina was slightly richer than the United States, as was Cuba. But by 1900, per capita GDP had risen much faster in the United States than in these other countries. What happened?

As we have learned, abundant natural resources are not sufficient to ensure economic growth. The industrialization that occurred in the United States in the early 1800s was not duplicated in the Latin American countries. This became a point of divergence for the growth rates of the United States and Latin America. Researchers have suggested that an important difference contributing to the differential rates of development was the provision of government policies, including laws and institutions, in the United States and Canada that encouraged widespread participation in economic development.* Through investment in human capital via education and skills training, workers could experience upward mobility. By saving and investing, individual entrepreneurs could turn small businesses into large, successful enterprises.

In Latin America, institutions developed that blocked opportunities for economic advancement for a large portion of the population. The agriculture and mining industries of Latin America were conducted on a relatively large scale so that there were few entrepreneurs and managers and many poor workers. Even after slavery was ended and these countries achieved their independence from their European colonizers, the institutions of Latin American countries worked against individual investment in human capital and upward mobility. The class of individual entrepreneurs found in Canada and the United States did not emerge in Latin America. The upwardly mobile workers of Canada and the United States provided the opportunities for mass-market consumer goods that drove the industrialization process. But in Latin America, such mass markets of consumers with income to spend did not emerge.

Most poor countries may be characterized as having a small number of very rich individuals and a large number of very poor people. The members of the rich elite want to maintain their position and so support institutions that restrict the opportunities for advancement of the masses of poor people. So the initial development of an environment with a few rich and many poor was carried forward through time. In this way we can see the importance of institutions and government policies for charting a path of high growth and rapid development or low growth and relative stagnation.

*Drawn from World Bank, World Development Report, 2003, and Stanley L. Engerman and Kenneth L. Sokoloff, "Factor Endowments, Institutions, and Differential Paths of Growth among New World Economies: A View from Economic Historians of the United States," in Stephen H. Haber, ed., How Latin America Fell Behind: Essays in the Economic Histories of Brazil and Mexico, 1800–1914 (Stanford, CA: Stanford University Press, 1997).

In developing countries, entrepreneurship tends to be concentrated among immigrants who have skills and experience that do not exist in poor countries. Many leaders of industry in Latin America, for example, are Italian, German, Arab, or Basque immigrants or the descendants of immigrants; they are not part of the dominant Spanish or native Indian population. The success of these immigrants is less a product of their being discriminated against than of their expertise in commerce. They know the foreign suppliers of goods. They have business skills that are lacking in developing regions. And they have the traditions—among them, the work ethic—and training instilled in their home country.

Immigrants provide a pool of entrepreneurs who have skills and knowledge that often are lacking in the developing country.

Motivation also plays a role in the level of entrepreneurship that exists in developing countries. In some societies, traditional values may be an obstacle to development because they do not encourage high achievement. A good example is provided by the tribal culture in sub-Saharan Africa. In this tribal culture, economic success does not result in upward social mobility if the success is obtained outside of the tribe. Instead, it could result in the person being shunned by the rest of the tribe. So incentives work against individual saving and investment or entrepreneurship. The social pressure is to share communally any riches that one obtains and not to rise above the group in any important way. In this sort of environment, development is hindered by the lack of incentives for wealth accumulation and risk taking.

Societies in which the culture supports individual achievement produce more entrepreneurs. It is difficult to identify the specific values in a society that account for a lack of motivation. In the past, researchers have pointed to factors that are not always valid across different societies. For instance, at one time many argued that the Protestant work ethic was responsible for the large number of entrepreneurs in the industrial world. According to this argument, some religions are more supportive of the accumulation of wealth than others. Today this argument is difficult to make because we find economic development in nations with vastly different cultures and religions.

17-2b-2 Rapid Population Growth Remember that per capita real GNP is real GNP divided by the population. Although labor is a factor of production, and labor force growth may increase output, when population rises faster than GNP, the standard of living of the average citizen does not improve. One very real problem for many developing countries is the growth of their populations. With the exception of China and India (where population growth is controlled), population growth in the developing countries is proceeding at a pace that will double the Third World population every 25 years. In large part, the rate at which the population of the Third World is growing is a product of lower death rates. Death rates have fallen, but birthrates have not.

Social scientists do not all agree on the effects of population growth on development. A growing labor force can serve as an important factor in increasing growth. But those who believe that population growth has a negative effect cite three reasons:

Capital shallowing. Rapid population growth may reduce the amount of capital per worker, lowering the productivity of labor.

Age dependency. Rapid population growth produces a large number of dependent children, whose consumption requirements lower the ability of the economy to save.

Investment diversion. Rapid population growth shifts government expenditures from the country's infrastructure (roads, communication systems) to education and health care.

Population growth may have had a negative effect on development in many countries, but the magnitude of this effect is difficult to assess. And in some cases, population growth probably has stimulated development. For instance, the fact that children consume goods and services and thus lower the ability of a nation to save ignores the fact that the children grow up and become productive adults. Furthermore, any diversion of investment from infrastructure to education and health care is not necessarily a loss, as education and health care will build up the productivity of the labor force. The harmful effect of population growth should be most pronounced in countries where usable land and water are relatively scarce. Although generalizations about acceptable levels of population growth do not fit all circumstances, the World Bank has stated that population growth rates above 2 percent a year act as a brake on economic development.

The GNP can grow steadily year after year, but if the population grows at a faster rate, the standard of living of the average individual falls. The simple answer to reducing population growth seems to be education: programs that teach methods of birth control and family planning. But reducing birthrates is not simply a matter of education. People have to choose to limit the size of their families. It must be socially acceptable and economically advantageous for families to use birth control, and for many families it is neither.

Remember that what is good for society as a whole may not be good for the individual. Children are a source of labor in rural families and a support for parents in their old age. How many children are enough? That depends on the expected infant mortality rate. Although infant mortality rates in developing countries have fallen in recent years, they are still quite high relative to those in the developed countries. Families still tend to follow tradition and so keep having lots of children.

RECAP

1. In some countries, especially those that once were colonies, economic growth has been slow because government officials lack the necessary skills.

2. Countries that are unable to protect private property rights have difficulty attracting investors.

3. Expropriation is the seizure of assets by a government without adequate compensation.

4. Government corruption reduces investment and growth.

5. Often government officials know the right economic policies to follow but are constrained by political considerations from implementing those policies.

6. Immigrants are often the entrepreneurs in developing countries.

7. Rapid population growth may slow development because of the effects of capital shallowing, age dependency, and investment diversion.

17-3 Development Strategies

Different countries follow different strategies to stimulate economic development. There are two basic types of development strategies: inward-oriented and outward-oriented.

17-3a Inward-Oriented Strategies

The typical developing country has a comparative advantage over other countries in the production of certain primary products. Having a comparative advantage means that a country has the lowest opportunity cost of producing a good. A **primary product** is a product in the first stage of production, which often serves as an input in the production of some other good. Agricultural produce and minerals are examples of primary products. In the absence of a conscious government policy that directs production, we expect countries to concentrate on the production of that thing in which they have a comparative advantage. For example, we expect Cuba to focus on sugar production, Colombia to focus on coffee production, and

3. What strategies can a nation use to increase its economic growth?

primary product
A product in the first stage of production, which often serves as an input in the production of another product.

the Ivory Coast to focus on cocoa production, with each country selling the output of its primary product to the rest of the world.

Today many developing countries have shifted their resources away from producing primary products for export. Inward-oriented development strategies focus on production for the domestic market rather than exports of goods and services. For these countries, development means industrialization. The objective of this kind of inward-oriented strategy is **import substitution**, or replacing imported manufactured goods with domestic goods.

Import-substitution policies dominate the strategies of the developing world. The basic idea is to identify domestic markets that are being supplied in large part by imports. Those markets that require a level of technology that is available to the domestic economy are candidates for import substitution. Industrialization goes hand in hand with tariffs or quotas on imports that protect the newly developing domestic industry from its more efficient foreign competition. As a result, production and international trade are not based solely on comparative advantages but are affected primarily by these countries' import-substitution policy activities.

Because the domestic industry can survive only through protection from foreign competition, with import-substitution policies, the price of the domestically produced goods is typically higher than that of the imported goods. In addition, the quality of the domestically produced goods may not be as high (at least at first) as the quality of the imported goods. Ideally, as the industry grows and becomes more experienced, price and quality become competitive with those of foreign goods. Once this happens, the import barriers are no longer needed, and the domestic industry may even become an export industry. Unfortunately, this ideal is seldom realized. The Third World is full of inefficient manufacturing companies that are unlikely ever to improve enough to be able to survive without protection from foreign competitors.

import substitution
The substitution of domestically produced manufactured goods for imported manufactured goods.

17-3b Outward-Oriented Strategies

The inward-oriented strategy of developing domestic industry to supply domestic markets is the most popular development strategy, but it is not the only one. Beginning in the 1960s, a small group of countries (notably South Korea, Hong Kong, Singapore, and Taiwan) chose to focus on the growth of exports. These countries started to follow an outward-oriented strategy, utilizing their most abundant resource to produce those products that they could produce better than others.

The abundant resource in these countries is labor, and the goods they produce are labor-intensive products. This kind of outward-oriented policy is called **export substitution**. These countries use labor to produce manufactured goods for export rather than agricultural products for domestic use.

Outward-oriented development strategies are based on efficient, low-cost production. Their success depends on being able to compete effectively with producers in the rest of the world. Most governments using this strategy attempt to stimulate exports. This can mean subsidizing

export substitution
The use of resources to produce manufactured products for export rather than agricultural products for the domestic market.

Foreign firms in developing countries can utilize technology, which depends in part on having a supply of engineers and technical personnel in the country. India has a large number of technical personnel, and much outsourcing is done there by U.S. firms.

domestic producers to produce goods for export rather than for domestic consumption. International competition is often more intense than the competition at home—producers face stiffer price competition, higher quality standards, and greater marketing expertise in the global marketplace. This means that domestic producers may have to be induced to compete internationally. Inducements can take the form of government assistance in international marketing, tax reductions, low-interest-rate loans, or cash payments.

Another inducement of sorts is to make domestic sales less attractive. This means implementing policies that are just the opposite of import substitution. The government reduces or eliminates domestic tariffs that keep domestic price levels above international levels. As profits from domestic sales fall, domestic industry turns to producing goods for export.

17-3c Comparing Strategies

Import-substitution policies are enacted by countries that believe that industrialization is the key to economic development. In the 1950s and 1960s, economists argued that specializing in the production and export of primary products does not encourage the rapid growth rates that developing countries are looking for. This argument—the *deteriorating-terms-of-trade argument*—was based on the assumption that the real value of primary products would fall over time. If the prices of primary products fall in relation to the prices of manufactured products, then countries that export primary products and import manufactured goods find the cost of manufactured goods rising in terms of the primary products required to buy them. The amount of exports that must be exchanged for some quantity of imports is often called the **terms of trade**.

terms of trade
The amount of an exported good that must be given up to obtain an imported good.

The deteriorating-terms-of-trade argument in the 1950s and 1960s led policymakers in developing countries to fear that the terms of trade would become increasingly unfavorable. One product of that fear was the choice of an inward-oriented strategy, a focus on domestic industrialization rather than production for export.

At the root of the pessimism about the export of primary products was the belief that technological change would slow the growth of demand for primary products over time. That theory ignored the fact that if the supply of natural resources is fixed, those resources could become more valuable over time, even if demand for them grows slowly or not at all. And even if the real value of primary products does fall over time, this does not necessarily mean that an inward-oriented policy is required. Critics of inward-oriented policies argue that nations should exploit their comparative advantage—that resources should be free to move to their highest valued use. And they argue that market-driven resource allocation is unlikely to occur in an inward-oriented economy where government has imposed restrictions aimed at maximizing the rate of growth of industrial output.

The growth rates of outward-oriented economies are significantly higher than those of inward-oriented economies.

Other economists believe that developing countries have unique problems that call for active government intervention and regulation of economic activity. These economists often favor inward-oriented strategies. They focus on the structure of developing countries in terms of uneven industrial development. Some countries have modern manufacturing industries paying relatively high wages that operate alongside traditional agricultural industries paying low wages. A single economy with industries at very different levels of development is called a **dual economy**. Some insist that, in a dual economy, the markets for goods and resources do not work well. If resources could move freely between industries, then wages would not differ by the huge amounts that are observed in certain developing countries. These economists support active government direction of the economy in countries where markets are not functioning well, believing that resources in these countries are unlikely to move freely to their highest valued use if free markets are allowed.

dual economy
An economy in which two sectors (typically manufacturing and agriculture) show very different levels of development.

The growth rates of the outward-oriented economies are significantly higher than those of the inward-oriented economies. The success of the outward-oriented economies is likely to continue in light of a strong increase in saving in those economies. In 1963, domestic saving as a fraction of GDP was only 13 percent in the strongly outward-oriented economies. After more than two decades of economic growth driven by export-promotion policies, the rate of saving in these countries had increased to 31.4 percent of GDP. This high rate of saving increases investment expenditures, which increase the productivity of labor, further stimulating the growth of per capita real GDP.

Why are outward-oriented strategies more successful than inward-oriented strategies? The primary advantage of an outward orientation is the efficient utilization of resources. Import-substitution policies do not allocate resources on the basis of cost minimization. In addition, an outward-oriented strategy allows the economy to grow beyond the scale of the domestic market. Foreign demand creates additional markets for exports, beyond the domestic market.

RECAP

1. Inward-oriented strategies concentrate on building a domestic industrial sector.

2. Outward-oriented strategies utilize a country's comparative advantage in exporting.

3. The deteriorating-terms-of-trade argument has been used to justify import substitution policies.

4. Evidence indicates that outward-oriented policies have been more successful than inward-oriented policies at generating economic growth.

17-4 Foreign Investment and Aid

Developing countries rely on savings in the rest of the world to finance much of their investment needs. Foreign savings may come from industrial countries in many different ways. In this section we describe the ways in which savings are transferred from industrial to developing countries and the benefits of foreign investment and aid to developing countries.

4. How are savings in one nation used to speed development in other nations?

17-4a Foreign Savings Flows

Poor countries that are unable to save enough to invest in capital stock must rely on the savings of other countries to help them develop economically. Foreign savings come from both private sources and official government sources.

Private sources of foreign savings can take the form of direct investment, portfolio investment, commercial bank loans, and trade credit. **Foreign direct investment** is the purchase of a physical operating unit, like a factory, or an ownership position in a foreign country that gives the domestic firm making the investment ownership of more than 10 percent of the foreign firm. This is different from **portfolio investment**, which is the purchase of securities, like stocks and bonds. In the case of direct investment, the foreign investor may actually operate the business. Portfolio investment helps finance a business, but host-country managers operate the firm; foreign investors simply hold pieces of paper that represent a share of the ownership or the debt of the firm. **Commercial bank loans** are loans made at market rates of interest to either foreign governments or business firms. These loans are often made by a *bank syndicate*, a group of several banks, to share the risk associated with lending to a single country. Finally, exporting firms and commercial banks offer **trade credit**, allowing importers a period of time before the payment for the goods or services purchased is due. Extension of trade credit usually involves payment in 30 days (or some other term) after the goods are received.

foreign direct investment
The purchase of a physical operating unit or more than 10 percent ownership of a firm in a foreign country.

portfolio investment
The purchase of securities.

commercial bank loan
A bank loan at market rates of interest, often involving a bank syndicate.

trade credit
Allowing an importer a period of time before it must pay for goods or services purchased.

The relative importance of direct investment and bank lending have changed over time. In 1970, direct investment in developing countries was greater than bank loans. By the late 1970s and early 1980s, however, bank loans far exceeded direct investment. Bank lending gives the borrowing country greater flexibility in deciding how to use funds. Direct investment carries with it an element of foreign control over domestic resources. Nationalist sentiment combined with the fear of exploitation by foreign owners and managers led many developing countries to pass laws restricting direct investment. By the early 1990s, however, as more nations were emphasizing the development of free markets, direct investment was again growing in importance as a source of funds for developing countries, and by the late 1990s it was these countries' most important source of funds.

17-4b Benefits of Foreign Investment

Not all developing countries discourage foreign direct investment. In fact, many countries have benefited from foreign investment. Those benefits fall into three categories: new jobs, new technology, and foreign exchange earnings.

17-4b-1 New Jobs Foreign investment should stimulate growth and create new jobs in developing countries. But the number of new jobs created directly by foreign investment is often limited by the nature of the industries in which foreign investment is allowed.

Usually foreign investment is invited in capital-intensive industries, like chemicals or mineral extraction. Because capital goods are expensive and often require advanced technology to operate, foreign firms can build a capital-intensive industry faster than the developing country can. One product of this emphasis on capital-intensive industries is that foreign investment often has little effect on employment in developing countries. A $500 million oil refinery may employ just a few hundred workers, yet the creation of these few hundred jobs, along with other expenditures by the refinery, will stimulate domestic income by raising incomes across the economy.

Many countries have benefited from foreign investment, which can stimulate growth and create new jobs. McDonald's is one such investor, and in China, it has well over 900 restaurants with more than 60,000 employees.

17-4b-2 Technology Transfer In the chapter titled "Economic Growth," we said that economic growth depends on the growth of resources and technological change. Most expenditures on research and development are made in the major industrial countries. These are also the countries that develop most of the innovations that make production more efficient. For a Third World country with limited scientific resources, the industrial nations are a critical source of information, technology, and expertise.

The ability of foreign firms to utilize modern technology in a developing country depends in part on having a supply of engineers and technical personnel in the host country. India and Mexico have a fairly large number of technical personnel, which means that new technology can be adapted relatively quickly. On the other hand, countries in which a large fraction of the population has less than an elementary-level education must train workers and then keep those workers from migrating to industrial countries, where their salaries are likely to be much higher.

17-4b-3 Foreign Exchange Earnings Developing countries expect foreign investment to improve their balance of payments. The assumption is that multinational firms located inside the developing country will increase exports and thus generate greater foreign currency earnings that can be used for imports or for repaying foreign debt. But this scenario does not unfold if the foreign investment is used to produce goods primarily for domestic consumption. In fact, the presence of a foreign firm can create a larger deficit in the balance of payments if the firm sends profits back to its industrial country headquarters from the developing country and the value of those profits exceeds the value of the foreign exchange earned by exports.

17-4c Foreign Aid

Official foreign savings are usually available as either outright gifts or low-interest-rate loans. These funds are called **foreign aid**. Large countries, like the United States, provide much more funding in terms of the dollar value of aid than do small countries. However, some small countries—for example, the Netherlands and Norway—commit a much larger percentage of their GNP to foreign aid.

Foreign aid can take the form of cash grants or transfers of goods or technology, with nothing given in return by the developing country. Often foreign aid is used to reward political allies, particularly when those allies hold a strategic military location. Examples of this politically inspired aid are the former Soviet support of Cuba and U.S. support of Turkey.

Foreign aid that flows from one country to another is called **bilateral aid**. Governments typically have an agency that coordinates and plans foreign aid programs and expenditures. The U.S. Agency for International Development (USAID) performs these functions in the United States. Most of the time, bilateral aid is project-oriented, given to fund a specific project (such as an educational facility or an irrigation project).

Food makes up a substantial portion of bilateral aid. After a bad harvest or a natural disaster (drought in the Sudan, floods in Bangladesh), major food-producing nations help feed the hungry. Egypt and Bangladesh were the leading recipients of food aid during the late 1980s. In the early 1990s, attention shifted to Somalia. The major recipients of food aid change over time, as nature and political events combine to change the pattern of hunger and need in the world.

The economics of food aid illustrates a major problem with many kinds of charity. Aid is intended to help those who need it without interfering with domestic production. But when food flows into a developing country, food prices tend to fall, pushing farm income down and discouraging local production. Ideally, food aid should go to the very poor, who are less likely to have the income necessary to purchase domestic production anyway.

foreign aid
Gifts or low cost loans made to developing countries from official sources.

bilateral aid
Foreign aid that flows from one country to another.

Foreign aid does not flow directly from the donors to the needy. It goes through the government of the recipient country. Here we find another problem: the inefficient and sometimes corrupt bureaucracies in recipient nations. There have been cases where recipient governments have sold products that were intended for free distribution to the poor. In other cases, food aid was not distributed because the recipient government had created the conditions leading to starvation. The U.S. intervention in Somalia in 1993 was aimed at helping food aid reach the starving population. In still other cases, a well-intentioned recipient government simply did not have the resources to distribute the aid, so the products ended up largely going to waste. One response to these problems is to rely on voluntary agencies to distribute aid. Another is to rely on multilateral agencies.

multilateral aid
Aid provided by international organizations that are supported by many nations.

Multilateral aid is provided by international organizations that are supported by many nations. The largest and most important multilateral aid institution is the World Bank. The World Bank makes loans to developing countries at below-market rates of interest and oversees projects in developing countries that it has funded. As an international organization, the World Bank is not controlled by any single country. This allows the organization to advise and help developing countries in a nonpolitical way that is usually not possible with bilateral aid.

RECAP

1. Private sources of foreign savings include direct investment, portfolio investment, commercial bank loans, and trade credit.

2. Developing countries can benefit from foreign investment through new jobs, the transfer of technology, and foreign exchange earnings.

3. Foreign aid involves gifts or low-cost loans that are made available to developing countries by official sources.

4. Foreign aid can be provided bilaterally or multilaterally.

SUMMARY

1. How is poverty measured?

- Poverty usually is defined in an absolute sense as the minimum income needed to purchase a minimal standard of living and is measured by per capita GNP or GDP. *§17-1a*

- Some economists and social scientists use a quality-of-life index to evaluate standards of living. *§17-1b*

2. Why are some countries poorer than others?

- Both political obstacles (lack of skilled officials, instability, corruption, and constraints imposed by special interest groups) and social obstacles (cultural attitudes that discourage entrepreneurial activity and encourage rapid population growth) limit economic growth in developing countries. *§17-2a, 17-2b*

3. What strategies can a nation use to increase its economic growth?

- Inward-oriented development strategies focus on developing a domestic manufacturing sector to produce goods that can substitute for imported manufactured goods. *§17-3a*

- Outward-oriented development strategies focus on producing manufactured goods for export. *§17-3b*

- The growth rates of outward-oriented economies are significantly higher than those of inward-oriented economies. *§17-3c*

4. How are savings in one nation used to speed development in other nations?

- Private sources of foreign savings include direct investment, portfolio investment, commercial bank loans, and trade credit. *§17-4a*

- Foreign investment in developing countries can increase their economic growth by creating jobs, transferring modern technology, and stimulating exports to increase foreign exchange earnings. *§17-4b*

- Official gifts or low-cost loans made to developing countries by official sources are called foreign aid. *§17-4c*

- Foreign aid can be distributed bilaterally or multilaterally. *§17-4c*

KEY TERMS

bilateral aid, 385
commercial bank loan, 383
dual economy, 382
export substitution, 381
expropriation, 376

foreign aid, 385
foreign direct investment, 383
import substitution, 381
multilateral aid, 386
portfolio investment, 383

primary product, 380
terms of trade, 382
trade credit, 383

EXERCISES

1. What are basic human needs? Can you list additional needs besides those considered in the chapter?
2. Per capita GNP or GDP is used as an absolute measure of poverty.
   a. What are some criticisms of using per capita GNP as a measure of standard of living?
   b. Do any of these criticisms also apply to a quality-of-life index?
3. In many developing countries, there are economists and politicians who were educated in industrial countries. These individuals know what policies would maximize the growth of their countries, but they do not implement them. Why not?
4. Suppose you are a benevolent dictator who can impose any policy you choose in your country. If your goal is to accelerate economic development, how would you respond to the following problems?
   a. Foreign firms are afraid to invest in your country because your predecessor expropriated many foreign-owned factories.
   b. There are few entrepreneurs in the country.
   c. The dominant domestic religion teaches that the accumulation of wealth is sinful.
   d. It is customary for families to have at least six children.
5. What effect does population growth have on economic development?
6. Why have most developing countries followed inward-oriented development strategies?
7. Why is an outward-oriented development strategy likely to allocate resources more efficiently than an inward-oriented strategy?

8. Who benefits from an import-substitution strategy? Who is harmed?
9. If poverty is a relative concept, why do we not define it in relative terms?
10. "The poor will always be with us." Does this statement have different meanings depending on whether poverty is interpreted as an absolute or a relative concept?
11. How do traditional societies answer the questions *What to produce? How to produce?* and *For whom to produce?*
12. What are the most important sources of foreign savings for developing countries? Why do developing countries not save more so that they do not have to rely on foreign savings for investment?
13. Private foreign investment and foreign aid are sources of savings to developing countries. Yet each has been controversial at times. What are the potential negative effects of private foreign investment and foreign aid for developing countries?
14. Why do immigrants often play an important role in developing the economies of poor nations? What role did immigrants play in developing the economy of the early United States?
15. How does a nation go about instituting a policy of import substitution? What is a likely result of such a policy?
16. In what ways might development harm the environment? In what ways might development be beneficial for the environment?
17. Search online for information about microfinance in developing countries. What are the potential benefits? What criticism has it received?

ECONOMICALLY SPEAKING
DOES INTERNATIONAL FOOD AID HARM THE POOR?

Carlos Lozada

The delivery of food aid to developing countries seems like an uncontroversial policy—a straightforward effort that helps the poor and underscores the generosity of donor nations. Yet economists have long debated the merits of food aid. By increasing the local supply of food, such aid may depress prices and thus undercut the income of rural farmers in the recipient nations, for example; it also may discourage local production. And, since the poor often are concentrated in rural areas, food aid in fact may disproportionately hurt the poor.

NBER researchers James Levinsohn and Margaret McMillan tackle this debate in "Does Food Aid Harm the Poor? Household Evidence from Ethiopia." The impact of lower food prices on the poor, they reason, hinges on whether poor households tend to be net buyers or net sellers of food. The authors seek to answer this question by examining consumption and expenditures survey data from both urban and rural households in Ethiopia. They focus on Ethiopia because it receives more food aid than almost any other nation in the world, but also because it is widely recognized that raising the productivity and profitability of small-scale

Ethiopian farmers is essential to reducing poverty in the country.

Food aid can take several forms, but some portion of all types of food aid (including emergency relief aid) is eventually sold in local markets and thus competes with domestic producers. Therefore, food aid will benefit Ethiopia's net food buyers and hurt its net food sellers. To carry out their study, Levinsohn and McMillan merge data from two nationally representative surveys and create a data set of 8,212 urban and 8,308 rural Ethiopian households.

Since wheat is the only cereal imported in the form of food aid, it is the 12 percent of rural households that report income from wheat that stand to gain most from price increases and lose most from price declines.

The authors classify households as either net buyers of wheat (if they buy more than they sell) or net sellers. To determine the poverty impact of food aid, they also classify the households by expenditure per capita and assess whether the poor households are net buyers or sellers of food. Finally, they estimate the magnitude of the price changes caused by food aid and hence the welfare effects of an increase in the price of food.

Levinsohn and McMillan offer several conclusions. First, net buyers of wheat are poorer than net sellers of wheat in Ethiopia. Indeed, roughly 85 percent of the poorest households are net buyers of wheat. Second, there are more buyers of wheat in Ethiopia than sellers of wheat at all levels of income—an important result because it means that at all levels of living standards, more households benefit from food aid (and the subsequent reduction in wheat prices) than are hurt by it. Third, the proportion of net sellers is increasing in living standards, and fourth, poorer households (in rural and in urban areas) benefit proportionately more from a drop in the price of wheat. "In light of this evidence," the authors conclude, "it appears that households at all levels of income benefit from food aid and that—somewhat surprisingly—the benefits go disproportionately to the poorest households."

Levinsohn and McMillan estimate that, in the absence of food aid, the price of wheat in Ethiopia would be $295 per metric ton, compared to an actual price of $193 per metric ton ...

COMMENTARY

Hunger is a serious global problem that has long commanded economists' attention. One approach to reducing hunger in poor countries has been shipments of food from rich countries. Yet simply delivering free food to countries suffering from famine may not be the best solution.

Famines do not necessarily imply a shortage of food. Instead, famines sometimes represent shortfalls in the purchasing power of the poorest sectors of society. In many cases, grants of income are a better means of alleviating famines than grants of food.

We can understand this argument using demand and supply analysis. In the following two diagrams, we represent the demand for food and the supply of food in a famine-stricken country that is receiving aid. In each diagram, the demand curve D_1 intersects the supply curve S_1 at an equilibrium quantity of food Q_1, which represents a subsistence level of food consumption. The equilibrium depicted in each graph is one in which, in the absence of aid, a famine would occur.

The first graph illustrates the effects of providing aid in the form of food. The food aid increases the available supply of food, which is shown by an outward shift of the supply curve to S_2. The effect of this aid is to increase the equilibrium quantity of food (Q_2) and lower the equilibrium price (P_2). The lower price of food will adversely affect the income of domestic producers. Domestic producers will thus attempt to grow other crops or to search for sources of income other than growing food if they cannot receive enough money for their produce. As the amount of domestic food production falls, the country becomes more dependent on imports of food. In the article, we are told that wheat prices would have been about $100 a ton higher if Ethiopia had not received shipments of free wheat to help alleviate hunger. Such higher wheat prices would surely have resulted in more farmers growing wheat.

The second graph illustrates the effect of income aid for the famine-stricken country. The aid is depicted by a shift in the demand curve to D_2. As with food aid, this relief allows consumption to rise to a point above the subsistence level. The effects of this aid on domestic food producers, however, are quite different. The price of food rises, and thus domestic food producers are not hurt by the aid package. As a result, aid in the form of income does not cause disincentives for production. An increase in domestic food production also serves to make a country less dependent on food imports.

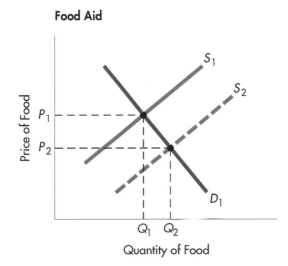

Food Aid

Income Aid

CHAPTER 18
Globalization

FUNDAMENTAL QUESTIONS

1. **What is globalization?**

2. **What are the arguments against globalization?**

3. **What are the arguments in support of globalization?**

4. **How has globalization affected economic growth and poverty?**

5. **Can recent financial crises be linked to globalization?**

Preview

In every chapter, we have discussed the international aspects of the topics covered. However, we have not yet considered the implications of closer links between economies internationally. The so-called *globalization* of the world's economies has become an issue that is rich in controversy. Thousands have gathered to protest globalization in Washington, D.C., and Seattle in the United States; in Johannesburg, South Africa; in Davos, Switzerland; and in many other places. This chapter will provide an introduction to the potential costs and benefits of globalization and offer an analysis of the historical record regarding the effects of globalization.

It is important to recognize that the debate over globalization continues and that it has political and social as well as economic dimensions. Intelligent people disagree about the impact of globalization on rich as well as poor countries. The reader should keep in mind that the issue is unsettled, and much can change in the coming years.

18-1 The Meaning of Globalization

1. What is globalization?

Globalization is characterized by an increased cross-border flow of trade in goods, services, and financial assets, along with an increased international mobility of technology, information, and individuals. As globalization progresses, countries become less isolated so that we can think more in terms of a global economy and its implications for individuals and nations.

18-1a Globalization Is Neither New nor Widespread

Globalization is not new. The forces that drive globalization have existed as long as humans have been around. Everyone has a natural desire to improve his or her well-being, so interest in trade has always existed. As we learned in earlier chapters, trade based on comparative advantage raises living standards. Even primitive societies engaged in trade so that their living standards would be higher than would otherwise have been possible. As circumstances permitted a greater range of travel, trade with more remote regions became possible. International trade is not a new phenomenon. World trade as a fraction of world GDP was about the same at the end of the nineteenth century as it is today. However, between World War I and World War II, the value of international trade plummeted. Then, in the postwar era, international trade rose substantially. Thus, the view that the growth of world trade is something new is true only in the shortsighted view of the world since the 1950s.

Globalization is not yet a truly global phenomenon. Some countries have remained largely closed to the rest of the world. These are mostly the world's poorest countries. If a government follows policies that work against economic integration with other countries, international trade and investment will not materialize. Former UN Secretary General Kofi Annan stated, "The main losers in today's very unequal world are not those that are too exposed to globalization, but those who have been left out." Yet, as we shall see, globalization is controversial, as not everyone benefits and some groups are made worse off than they were when they were more shielded from integration with the rest of the world.

The movement of people across international borders is greatly limited by government policies. There was much more immigration in the nineteenth and early twentieth centuries than there is at the present time. Barriers to immigration are high today, and workers generally cannot move freely from country to country. This was not always the case. In 1900, 14 percent of the U.S. population was born in a foreign country. Today that number is 12 percent. However, there are some multinational agreements that permit international movements of workers. An important example is the European Union (EU). Within the EU, there is free mobility of labor. Of course, this does not mean that there are widespread relocations of workers from, say, Germany to Italy. Family, language, and customs tie people to particular areas, so that the fact that people have the right to move does not mean that large numbers of them will actually do so. This is analogous to workers in the United States, who have the right to move anywhere in the country but many of whom choose to stay in a particular area because they have personal ties to that area.

18-1b The Role of Technological Change

The pace of globalization has been driven by technological change. International trade and the movement of people are facilitated by falling transportation costs. It is estimated that the real cost of ocean freight transport fell by 70 percent between 1920 and 1990.

International communication is enhanced by reductions in the cost of communications. Measured in terms of the value of a U.S. dollar in the year 2000, a three-minute telephone call from New York to London cost $60.42 in 1960 and $.40 in 2000. Now such a call can be made for free using Voice over Internet Protocol (VoIP) technology. The reduction in communication costs has made possible global interactions that were at best a dream just a few decades ago.

The development of fast, modern computers allows information to be processed at speeds that were unimaginable just a generation ago. As a result, technology is shared more efficiently, so that management of business operations can extend more easily to far-flung locations, and complex transactions can be completed in a fraction of the time that was once required. Technological progress in the computer industry is truly amazing. A computer that would sell for $1,000 today would have cost $1,869,004 in 1960.

The fact that globalization has progressed at an uneven rate over time is due to the uneven pace of technological change, in addition to important events, such as war, that disrupt relationships among nations.

18-1c Measuring Globalization

There are many alternatives for measuring how globalized the world and individual nations are. One useful ranking is provided by the KOF Swiss Economic Institute. It ranks countries in terms of three broad categories:

Economic globalization: long-distance flows of goods, capital, and services as well as information and perceptions that accompany market exchanges;

Social globalization: spread of ideas, information, images, and people;

Political globalization: diffusion of government policies (measured by things like number of embassies in a country, membership in international organizations, participation in UN peace missions, and similar concepts).

Table 1 shows the rankings for several countries. Note that poor countries tend to be missing from the top rank of globalized countries. These countries have few foreign workers and relatively low amounts of international communications and contact. They also have relatively low levels of Internet use, as a large segment of the population does not have access to computers or the training to use computers in daily life.

The more globalized an economy, the greater its links with the rest of the world. The aftermath of the terrorist attacks in the United States on September 11, 2001, showed how measures of globalization may be affected by important events. World trade fell after the attacks, as did global foreign direct investment. International travel and tourism dropped in 2002 for the first time since 1945. However, political engagement increased as a result of multinational efforts aimed at combating terrorism. The number of countries participating in UN peacekeeping missions increased. The volume of international telephone calls increased substantially. The increase in telephone use may have been partly due to the drop in international travel. If people choose not to travel for personal or business reasons because of safety concerns, they may be more likely to have telephone conversations with the parties they otherwise would have visited in person. In addition, the number of Internet users grew 22 percent in 2002, with China alone adding 11 million new users. So major events like the terrorist attacks of September 11, 2001, may suppress some measures of globalization while increasing others. This serves as a good reminder to take a broad view when measuring globalization rather than narrowly focusing on one or two measures.

TABLE 1 Globalization Rankings

Country	Index of Globalization	Country	Economic Globalization	Country	Social Globalization	Country	Political Globalization
Ireland	92.17	Singapore	96.09	Singapore	91.61	France	97.76
Belgium	91.61	Ireland	93.69	Ireland	91.55	Italy	97.71
Netherlands	91.33	Luxembourg	92.53	Austria	91.47	Belgium	96.75
Austria	90.48	Malta	91.78	Switzerland	90.86	Austria	96.54
Singapore	88.63	Netherlands	91.17	Netherlands	90.32	United Kingdom	96.19
Denmark	87.43	Belgium	89.43	Cyprus	90.26	Spain	96.18
Sweden	87.39	Estonia	88.04	Belgium	90.17	Sweden	94.92
Portugal	87.01	Bahrain	87.18	Canada	88.91	Brazil	94.72
Hungary	85.91	Hungary	86.82	Denmark	86.84	Portugal	94.37
Finland	85.87	Finland	85.80	France	86.70	Egypt, Arab Rep.	94.16
Switzerland	85.74	Austria	85.10	United Kingdom	86.07	Canada	94.12
Canada	85.63	Sweden	85.09	Portugal	84.75	Denmark	93.91
Cyprus	85.27	United Arab Emirates	85.00	Norway	84.56	Switzerland	93.15
Spain	84.66	Slovak Republic	84.58	Sweden	84.41	Argentina	93.06
Luxembourg	84.57	Cyprus	84.51	Germany	83.71	Netherlands	93.01
Czech Republic	83.97	Portugal	84.09	Finland	83.51	Turkey	92.74
United Kingdom	83.72	Mauritius	83.91	Spain	82.60	India	92.52
Slovak Republic	83.55	Czech Republic	83.71	Australia	82.24	United States	92.47
Australia	82.93	Denmark	83.39	Czech Republic	82.22	Germany	92.44
Norway	82.83	New Zealand	82.14	United Arab Emirates	81.69	Greece	91.83

Source: KOF Index of Globalization; http://globalization.kof.ethz.ch/static/pdf/rankings_2010.pdf.

RECAP

1. Globalization is characterized by an increased flow of trade in goods, services, and financial assets across national borders, along with increased international mobility of technology, information, and individuals.

2. The process of globalization is not new, but it accelerated after World War II.

3. Technological advances play an important role in determining the pace of globalization.

4. Measuring globalization involves measurement of the international movements of goods, services, financial assets, people, ideas, and technology.

---

2. *What are the arguments against globalization?*

18-2 Globalization Controversy

Globalization has stimulated much controversy in recent years. Massive demonstrations have been held to coincide with meetings of the World Trade Organization (WTO), the International Monetary Fund (IMF), the World Bank, and other gatherings of government and business leaders dealing with the process of developing international trade and investment. The two sides see globalization in a very different light. On one side are the critics of globalization, who believe that free international trade in goods and financial assets does more harm than good. On the other side are the supporters of free international trade, who believe that globalization holds the key to increasing the living standards of all the world's people. We will review the arguments on both sides.

18-2a Arguments Against Globalization

Critics of globalization view it as a vehicle for enriching corporate elites, to the detriment of poor people and the environment. In this view, the major international organizations are tools of corporations, whose aim is to increase corporate profits at the expense of people and the environment. Rather than being a democratic system in which the majority of people are involved in economic decision making, globalization is seen by critics as a force that reduces the influence of people at the local level, with power being taken by the global elites, represented by rich corporations and their government supporters. A few specific criticisms associated with the antiglobalization movement follow.

18-2a-1 "Fair," Not "Free," Trade Critics argue that free trade agreements put people out of jobs. When goods are produced by the lowest-cost producer, people working in that industry in less competitive countries will no longer be employed. If foreign competition were limited, then these jobs would be saved. In addition, free trade may encourage governments to participate in a **"race to the bottom,"** with environmental safeguards and workers' rights being ignored in order to attract the investment and jobs that come from a concentration of production based upon comparative advantage. International trade agreements are seen as roadblocks to democratic decision making at the local level, as they transfer power away from local authorities to multinational authorities.

"race to the bottom"
The argument that, with globalization, countries compete for international investment by offering low or no environmental regulations or labor standards.

18-2a-2 International Organizations Serve Only the Interests of Corporations An example of this argument is the assertion that the WTO is a tool of corporations, and that international trade agreements negotiated and enforced through the WTO are used to generate corporate profits against the interests of the citizens of the world. The Global Business Insight "The World Trade Organization" provides background information on the nature of this organization and its duties. International organizations like the WTO are used as platforms for instituting rules for international trade. Thus, an individual who is against free international trade would also be critical of organizations whose aim is the promotion of free trade. The WTO, the IMF, and the World Bank are viewed as undemocratic organizations that have assumed powers over economic decision making that rightly belong to local authorities.

18-2a-3 Globalization Occurs at the Cost of Environmental Quality As stated earlier, critics of globalization fear a "race to the bottom," in which governments block costly regulations related to environmental quality in order to provide a cheaper location for large global firms seeking manufacturing facilities. If the rich countries impose costly regulations on manufacturers, then these firms will shift production to poor countries that are willing to trade environmental degradation for jobs and higher incomes. Related to this issue is World Bank financing for resource extraction projects, such as mining or oil and gas extraction. Such projects are seen as benefiting the corporations that receive contracts for work related to the projects, while environmental destruction is a little-considered by-product. World Bank funding for large dams is also seen as harmful, as these projects frequently involve the relocation of large numbers of poor people, who lose what modest living arrangements they had.

GLOBAL BUSINESS INSIGHT

The World Trade Organization

The World Trade Organization (WTO) is an international organization with 153 member countries, established in 1995 and headquartered in Geneva, Switzerland. The job of the WTO is to provide a venue for negotiating international trade agreements and then to enforce these global rules of international trade. The WTO trade agreements are negotiated and signed by a large majority of the world's nations. These agreements are contracts covering the proper conduct of international trade. An important role of the WTO is the settlement of trade disputes between countries. An example of such a dispute involved bananas and the European Union (EU). The EU restricted banana imports to bananas from only a few

countries that were former European colonies. As a result, the price paid for bananas in European markets was about twice the price of bananas in the United States. The world's largest banana companies, Dole, Chiquita, and Del Monte, headquartered in the United States, complained that they were being harmed because their bananas, which came from other countries in Central and South America, were excluded from the EU system, which favored a few former colonies. The WTO ruled that the EU restrictions on banana imports were harmful and against the rules of trade to which all nations had agreed. This is but one example of the role of the WTO in promoting fair and free international trade.

18-2a-4 Globalization Encourages Harmful Labor Practices This argument is based upon a belief that multinational corporations will locate where wages are cheapest and workers' rights weakest. In these settings, on-the-job safety is ignored, and workers who are injured or ill are likely to be dismissed without any compensation. Furthermore, critics believe that globalization may result in the worst employment practices, such as child labor or prisoner labor. If such practices are allowed in poor countries, then the industrial countries will suffer follow-on effects as workers in rich countries lose their jobs to workers in countries where there are no worker protection regulations, no minimum wages, and no retirement plans, and where employers must pay nothing more than the minimum necessary to attract an employee.

18-2b Arguments in Favor of Globalization

3. What are the arguments in support of globalization?

Globalization's supporters believe that free trade and international investment result in an increase in living standards in all countries. Of course, some individuals and firms are harmed by the globalization process. Those industries that exist in a country only as a result of protection from foreign competitors will suffer when that country's markets are opened to the rest of the world. Yet the few who suffer are small in number relative to the many who benefit from the advantages that globalization provides. This section will consider each of the criticisms mentioned in the prior section and present the alternative view of those who support globalization.

18-2b-1 Free Trade Helps Developing Countries As just discussed, opening markets to free trade will usually harm some individuals and firms. But supporters of globalization believe that the benefits of globalization for all consumers greatly outweigh the costs of providing a social safety net for those who lose their jobs as a result of opening markets to global competitors. Developing countries have much to gain from free trade. Restrictions on trade in rich countries are often aimed at the products that poor countries can produce most efficiently. For instance, textile imports are restricted by the United States, and this harms many developing countries that could provide clothing and fabrics to the United States at a lower cost than U.S. producers can. The European Union restricts imports of agricultural products in order to increase the incomes of European farmers. If such restrictions were lifted, incomes in poor countries would rise substantially. Supporters of globalization believe that free trade agreements administered by the WTO can offer great benefits to poor countries.

18-2b-2 International Organizations Represent Governments and People
Supporters of globalization argue that international organizations offer all countries a platform for expressing their dissatisfaction with economic and social conditions and provide a mechanism for change. Without organizations like the IMF, World Bank, United Nations, and WTO, there would be no opportunities for representatives of all nations to come together to discuss needed changes in the global economy. These organizations also provide for transfers of funds from rich to poor countries that would not occur in an ongoing manner in the absence of such organizations. International organizations are funded by governments, not corporations. Representatives of the government of each member nation participate in the decision making at each organization. This suggests that if international organizations have followed unwise policies, the most effective path for change would be putting political pressure on national governments to support policies that open markets for the goods of poor countries as well as rich countries.

18-2b-3 The Connection between Globalization and Environmental Harm Is Weak
Supporters of globalization argue that there is no evidence of a "race to the bottom" in which multinational firms move production to countries with lax environmental standards. Looking at the globalization rankings in Table 1, the countries at the top of the list tend to have more stringent environmental regulations than do less open economies. Figure 1 plots a country's globalization score against a ranking of environmental quality, where the country's environmental performance is determined by its rankings in terms of the quality of its air and water, its protection of land, and its impact on climate change through carbon dioxide emissions. The figure plots data for those countries ranked in the top 30 and bottom 30 on the environmental quality scale that also have globalization rankings. The higher the number for a country, the better its environmental ranking or the greater its globalization. Figure 1 indicates that, in general, the more globalized the country, the better its environmental quality. For instance, Switzerland has the highest ranking in terms of environmental quality, and it is also the most globalized economy. Niger is the lowest ranked in environmental quality and is also ranked low in terms of globalization. The scatter of the countries plotted in Figure 1 suggests that an upward-sloping line would represent the relationship between globalization and environmental quality well.

In addition, there are many cases of environmental degradation associated with countries that are closed to economic relations with the rest of the world. The governments of the former Communist countries of Eastern Europe displayed the greatest disregard of the environment of any group of nations in modern times. As these nations globalize as part of the transition away from socialism, they are attracting foreign direct investment from rich countries, which has transferred cleaner technology to Eastern Europe and improved environmental quality.

AP Images/Keystone, Salvatore Di Nolfi

FIGURE 1   Globalization and Environmental Quality

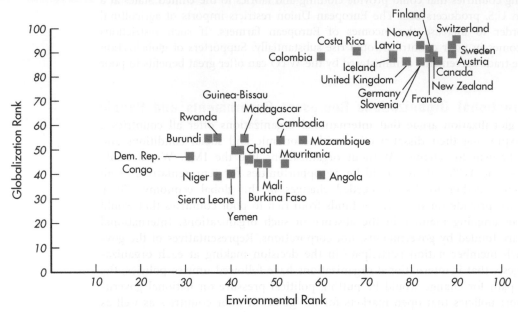

Source: Globalization data are drawn from *KOF Index of Globalization;* http://www.kof.ethz.ch/globalization. Environmental quality rankings are from the "Environmental Performance Index" from www.yale.edu/epi.

One of the major assumptions made by critics of globalization is that multinational firms will locate production units in developing countries, employ local resources, and then sell the products in the rich countries. This may be typical of certain industries, such as the production of shoes or clothing. However, increasingly, multinational firms' production is aimed at supplying local markets. The U.S. Department of Commerce found that more than 60 percent of the production of U.S. firms' subsidiaries in developing countries was sold in the local market where the production occurred. A look at the global firms that have raced to invest in China indicates that the prospect of selling to the massive Chinese market is the attraction for much of this investment. In this situation, governments do not need to offer a lack of environmental standards in order to attract multinational firms.

18-2b-4 Does Globalization Encourage Harmful Labor Practices? Supporters of globalization argue that there is no evidence of a "race to the bottom" in labor standards. In fact, multinational firms tend to pay higher wages than local firms and tend to provide greater benefits for workers than existed in the country prior to globalization. At a basic level, if a worker freely accepts employment, that worker must be better off than he or she would be with the next best alternative. So even though wages in, for instance, Vietnam may be much lower than those in western Europe or North America, this is not evidence that workers are being exploited. The local wages across the Vietnamese economy are lower than those in, say, France or Canada. The workers who accept employment at a factory in Vietnam operated by a multinational firm prefer such work to working in agriculture at much lower wages. It is common to find long waiting lists of workers who want jobs at multinational firms' factories in developing countries. Rather than exploitation, this suggests that globalization is raising living standards and making people better off.

1. Arguments against globalization include a concern that free trade is harmful to people, that international organizations serve only the interests of corporations, and that there is a "race to the bottom," with countries offering lax regulation of environmental quality and labor standards in order to offer multinational firms better opportunities for profit.

2. Supporters of globalization argue that trade based on comparative advantage raises living standards everywhere; that international organizations are funded by governments, not corporations, and provide a formal mechanism for all governments to be represented and to push for change; and that environmental quality and the welfare of workers actually improve with globalization.

18-3 Globalization, Economic Growth, and Incomes

The increased integration of the world's economies has been associated with economic growth and reduction of poverty in most countries. The so-called **Asian tigers**—Hong Kong, Korea, Singapore, and Taiwan—underwent the process of opening their economies in the 1960s and 1970s and experienced rapid growth and dramatic increases in their living standards. Nowadays, these countries are sometimes referred to as "newly industrialized countries," or **NICs**. More recently, several other countries have been through the globalization process. Figure 2 shows the NICs and the post-1980 globalizers. The 24 post-1980 globalizers are spread around the world. One World Bank study tracked the performance of all of these countries over time to measure how globalization has affected them.[1] The major conclusions of the study are as follows:

- *Economic growth has increased with globalization.* Average growth of per capita GDP increased from 1.4 percent per year in the 1960s to 2.9 percent in the 1970s to 3.5 percent in the 1980s to 5.0 percent in the 1990s. At the same time that these countries were increasing their growth rates, average annual per capita GDP growth in the rich countries fell from 4.7 percent in the 1960s to 2.2 percent in the 1990s. What makes this even more dramatic is the fact that nonglobalizing developing countries had average annual growth rates of only 1.4 percent during the 1990s.

- *Income inequality has not increased.* The benefits of increased economic growth are widely shared in globalizing countries. An important exception to this finding is China, where income inequality has increased. However, government policies in China that resulted in moving to free markets from socialism while restricting internal migration may have played a much bigger role in causing changes in the Chinese income distribution than globalization did.

- *The gap between rich countries and globalized developing countries has shrunk.* Some of the countries listed in Figure 2 were among the poorest countries in the world 25 years ago. The higher growth rates experienced by these countries have allowed them to gain ground on the rich countries.

- *Poverty has been reduced.* The fraction of the very poor, those who live on less than $1 per day, declined in the newly globalized economies. For instance, between the 1980s and the 1990s, the fraction of the population living on less than $1 per day fell from 43 percent to 36 percent in Bangladesh, from 20 percent to 15 percent in China, and from 13 percent to 10 percent in Costa Rica.

4. *How has globalization affected economic growth and poverty?*

Asian tigers
Hong Kong, Korea, Singapore, and Taiwan, countries that globalized in the 1960s and 1970s and experienced fast economic growth.

NICs
Newly industrialized countries.

---

[1] David Dollar and Aart Kraay, "Trade, Growth, and Poverty," World Bank Policy Research Department Working Paper No. 2615, 2001. For additional evidence and discussion, see "Globalization: Threat or Opportunity," *IMF Issues Brief,* January 2002, and the articles on the IMF Web site: http://www.imf.org/external/np/exr/key/global.htm.

FIGURE 2   NICS and Post-1980 Globalizers

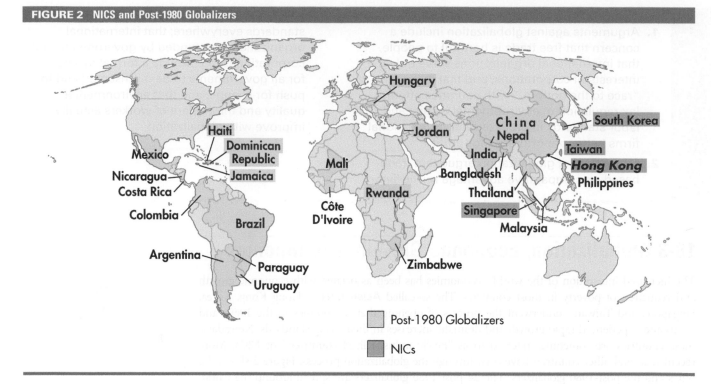

Post-1980 Globalizers

NICs

The evidence from around the world indicates that the real losers in the globalization of the world economy are those countries that have not participated. They tend to be mired in a low-growth path, with enduring poverty and none of the benefits that globalization has conferred.

R E C A P

1. Some studies have shown that globalization increases economic growth without increasing income inequality within nations.

2. Some studies have shown that globalization narrows the income gap between rich and poor nations and reduces poverty.

18-4 Financial Crises and Globalization

5. Can recent financial crises be linked to globalization?

The 1990s provided several dramatic episodes of financial crises in developing countries, in which investors in these countries were punished with substantial losses and local businesses also suffered. In 2007–2008, a global financial crisis struck the developed countries and led to the worst recession since the Great Depression of the 1930s. To understand the nature of the developing market crises of the 1990s, we will first look at some data that illustrate the severity of the crises. Then we will analyze the reasons for the crises. It will be seen that globalization may have played a contributing role in these recent crises. Then we will extend the analysis to the global crisis of 2007–2008 and consider what role globalization played.

18-4a Crises of the 1990s

Table 2 provides summary data on some key economic indicators for countries that underwent severe crises. Crises occurred in Mexico in 1994–1995 and in Southeast Asia—Indonesia, Korea, Malaysia, the Philippines, and Thailand—in 1997. The table shows that in

TABLE 2	Economic Conditions in Crisis Countries			
Country	Short-Term External Debt/Reserves (year)	Bank Loans/GDP (year)	Stock Market Returns (%)	Exchange Rate (month/year)
Mexico	230% (1993)	24% (1993)	−29%	3.88 (12/94); 6.71 (3/95)
Indonesia	226% (1996)	55% (1996)	−40%	2,368 (1/97); 9,743 (1/98)
Korea	300% (1996)	59% (1996)	−26%	850 (1/97); 1,694 (1/98)
Malaysia	42% (1996)	93% (1996)	−57%	2.49 (1/97); 4.38 (1/98)
Philippines	126% (1996)	49% (1996)	−29%	26.3 (1/97); 42.7 (1/98)
Thailand	103% (1996)	99% (1996)	−30%	25.7 (1/97); 52.6 (1/98)

Source: Data on short-term debt/reserves and bank loans/GDP come from Steven B. Kamin, "The Current International Financial Crisis: How Much Is New?" *Journal of International Money and Finance*, August 1999. Stock market returns and exchange rates are drawn from Yahoo! Finance, yahoo.com. Stock market returns are calculated for the six-month period following the onset of the crisis in each country. Exchange rates are the price of local currency per 1 U.S. dollar.

the year prior to the crises, each of these countries except Malaysia owed substantial short-term debt to foreigners. Short-term debt is debt that is due in less than one year. The table lists short-term debt as a fraction of reserves. International reserves were discussed in the chapter titled "Money and Banking," where it was stated that these are assets that countries hold that can be used to settle international payments. The primary international reserve asset is foreign currency, mainly U.S. dollars. So except for Malaysia, all the countries affected by these crises owed more short-term debt to foreigners than the value of their international reserves.

Table 2 also shows that bank loans were a sizable fraction of GDP in all the crisis countries except Mexico. This becomes a problem when business turns bad. If the incomes of individuals and business firms are falling, then they will be less able to repay their loans to banks. As a result, the banks are also in trouble, and the result may be an economic crisis.

In each country, the stock market dropped dramatically. This is seen in Table 2 as the percentage change in stock prices over the first six months following the onset of the crisis. Stock prices dropped by an amount ranging from 26 percent in Korea to 57 percent in Malaysia. Investors in each country lost huge amounts of wealth as a result of the rapid drop in the values of local firms.

Finally, Table 2 shows that the exchange rate against the U.S. dollar dropped substantially in each country. Exchange rates played a particularly large role in these financial crises and pointed out a vulnerability of small developing countries to globalization in terms of international capital flows.

18-4b Exchange Rates and Financial Crises

Each of the countries in Table 2 had a fixed exchange rate prior to the crisis period. The chapter titled "Monetary Policy" included a discussion of how central banks must intervene in the foreign exchange market to maintain a fixed exchange rate. Here we can apply the same analysis to understand how a fixed exchange rate may contribute to financial crises. Figure 3 illustrates the situation for Mexico. The demand in this figure is the demand for dollars arising out of the Mexican demand for U.S. goods, services, and financial assets. The supply is the supply of dollars arising out of the U.S. demand for Mexican goods, services, and financial assets. Initially, the equilibrium is located at point A, where the exchange rate is 4 pesos per dollar and $10 billion are traded for pesos each day. If there is concern that Mexican financial assets will fall in value, then investors will start to sell peso-denominated assets; they will then sell their pesos for dollars in order to buy dollar-denominated assets. This shifts the demand curve for dollars from D_1 to D_2. The new equilibrium would be at

FIGURE 3 **Foreign Exchange Market Intervention with a Fixed Exchange Rate**

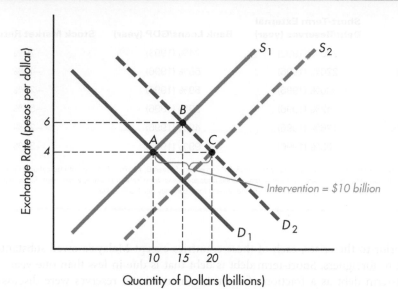

The demand is the demand for dollars arising out of the Mexican demand for U.S. goods, services, and financial assets. The supply is the supply of dollars arising out of the U.S. demand for Mexican goods, services, and financial assets. Initially, the equilibrium is located at point A, where the exchange rate is 4 pesos per dollar and $10 billion are traded for pesos each day. If there is concern that Mexican financial assets will fall in value, then investors will start to sell peso-denominated assets and then will sell their pesos for dollars in order to buy dollar-denominated assets. This shifts the demand curve for dollars from D_1 to D_2. The new equilibrium would then be at point B, with a depreciated peso exchange rate of 6 pesos per dollar and $15 billion per day being traded. To maintain a fixed exchange rate of 4 pesos per dollar and avoid private traders' shifting the equilibrium to point B, the central bank (Banco de Mexico) must intervene in the foreign exchange market, selling dollars equal to the private market demand for dollars in excess of the amount that would yield an equilibrium at point A. In the figure, we see that the new equilibrium with central bank intervention is a point C where the central bank is selling $10 billion per day ($20 − $10 billion) in order to maintain the exchange rate at 4 pesos per dollar.

point B, with a depreciated peso exchange rate of 6 pesos per dollar and $15 billion per day being traded. To maintain a fixed exchange rate of 4 pesos per dollar and keep the private traders from shifting the equilibrium to point B, the central bank (Banco de Mexico) must intervene in the foreign exchange market by selling an amount of dollars equal to the excess of the private market demand for dollars over the amount that would yield equilibrium at point A. In the figure, we see that the new equilibrium with central bank intervention is at point C, where the central bank is selling $10 billion per day ($20 − $10 billion) in order to maintain the exchange rate at 4 pesos per dollar.

If the shift in private investors' demand from D_1 to D_2 is not a temporary phenomenon, then this creates a problem for Banco de Mexico: It has a limited supply of international reserves, including U.S. dollars. The intervention to support the fixed exchange rate involves selling dollars and buying pesos. Eventually Banco de Mexico will exhaust its supply of dollars, and it will then be forced to devalue the currency, letting the exchange rate adjust to the free-market equilibrium of 6 pesos per dollar. Once speculators realize that the central bank is losing a substantial fraction of its international reserves, a **speculative attack** may occur. This is the term given to a situation in which private speculators start selling even

speculative attack
A situation in which private investors sell domestic currency and buy foreign currency, betting that the domestic currency will be devalued.

more pesos for dollars, expecting that the central bank will be forced to devalue the currency. If a speculator sells pesos and buys dollars for a price of 4 pesos per dollar, and then the peso is devalued to 6 pesos per dollar, that speculator can turn around and sell the dollars for pesos, receiving $6 - 4 = 2$ pesos in profit for each dollar invested in the speculative activity. Of course, once a speculative attack occurs, the demand for dollars shifts out even further, and the central bank will have to spend even more of its international reserves to defend the fixed exchange rate.

Each of the international financial crises of the 1980s and 1990s involved a fixed exchange rate. In each case, once it became clear that the domestic currency was overvalued relative to its true free-market value, speculative attacks occurred, and the central bank lost a sizable amount of its international reserves. With floating or flexible exchange rates, the exchange rate changes every day with the free-market forces of supply and demand, so countries are not forced to intervene and spend their international reserves to maintain a fixed exchange rate. In this situation, a speculative attack cannot occur.

Once the currency has been devalued, it is common for some local business firms to be driven into bankruptcy as a result of the effect of the devaluation on the value of their debt. This is because much borrowing is done in U.S. dollars. In Thailand, for instance, prior to the crisis of 1997, the Thai government had repeatedly stated that under no circumstances would it ever change the fixed exchange rate. Business firms, believing that the exchange rate between the Thai baht and the U.S. dollar would not change, borrowed in U.S. dollars, expecting that the dollars they borrowed and the dollars they would have to repay would be worth the same amount of baht. Imagine a firm that had a debt of $1 million. Prior to the financial crisis that started in the summer of 1997, the exchange rate was about 25 baht to 1 U.S. dollar. At this exchange rate, it would cost 25 million baht to repay $1 million. By January 1998, the exchange rate was about 52 baht per dollar. Thus, the firm would find that the baht price of repaying $1 million had risen to 52 million baht. The cost of repaying the dollar loan had more than doubled as a result of the currency devaluation. Because of such exchange rate changes, the financial crises of the 1990s had devastating effects on local businesses in each country. As business firms in these countries lost value, foreign investors who had invested in these firms also suffered large losses. The 1990s financial crises imposed huge costs on the global economy.

NOW YOU TRY IT

How might a fixed exchange rate contribute to a financial crisis?

18-4c What Caused the Crises?

The prior section showed how a fixed exchange rate could contribute to a crisis. The crises of the 1990s taught economists some lessons regarding exchange rates and other factors that increased countries' vulnerability to crises. Considerable resources have been devoted to understanding the nature and causes of financial crises in hopes of avoiding future crises and forecasting those crises that do occur. Forecasting is always difficult in economics, and it is safe to say that there will always be surprises that no economic forecaster anticipates. Yet there are certain variables that are so obviously related to past crises that they may serve as warning indicators of potential future crises. The list includes the following:

- *Fixed exchange rates.* All of the countries involved in recent crises, including Mexico in 1993–1994, the southeast Asian countries in 1997, and Argentina in 2002, had fixed exchange rates prior to the onset of the crisis. Generally, these countries' macroeconomic policies were inconsistent with the maintenance of the fixed exchange rate, and when large devaluations ultimately occurred, domestic residents holding loans denominated in foreign currency suffered huge losses.

- *Falling international reserves.* The maintenance of fixed exchange rates may not be a problem. One way to tell if the exchange rate is no longer an equilibrium rate is to monitor the country's international reserve holdings (largely the foreign currency held by the central bank and the treasury). If the stock of international reserves is falling steadily over time, that is a good indicator that the fixed-exchange-rate regime is under pressure and that there is likely to be a devaluation.

- *Lack of transparency.* Many countries in which there is a financial crisis suffer from a lack of transparency in government activities and a lack of public disclosure of business conditions. Investors need to know the financial situation of firms in order to make informed investment decisions. If accounting rules allow firms to hide the financial impact of actions that would harm investors, then investors may not be able to adequately judge when the risk of investing in a firm rises. In such cases, a financial crisis may come as a surprise to all but the insiders in a troubled firm. Similarly, if the government does not disclose its international reserve position in a timely and informative manner, investors may be taken by surprise when a devaluation occurs. The lack of good information on government and business activities serves as a warning sign of potential future problems.

This short list of warning signs provides an indication of the sorts of variables that an international investor must consider when evaluating the risks of investing in a foreign country. This list is also useful to international organizations like the International Monetary Fund when monitoring countries and advising them on recommended changes in policy.

So far we have not explicitly considered how globalization may contribute to crises. The analysis of Figure 3 provides a hint. If there is free trading in a country's currency and the country has globalized financial markets, so that foreign investors trade domestic financial assets, there is a greater likelihood of a crisis than in a country that is not globalized. The money that comes into the developing country from foreign investors can also flow back out. This points out an additional factor to be considered:

- *Short-term international investment.* The greater the amount of short-term money invested in a country, the greater the potential for a crisis if investors lose confidence in that country. So if foreigners buy large amounts of domestic stocks, bonds, or other financial assets, they can turn around and sell these assets quickly. These asset sales will depress the value of the country's financial markets, and as foreigners sell local currency for foreign currency, like U.S. dollars, the local currency will also fall in value. Too much short-term foreign investment may serve as another warning sign for a financial crisis.

Of course, a country can always avoid financial crises by not globalizing—keeping its domestic markets closed to foreigners. However, such a policy costs more than it is worth. As discussed earlier in this chapter, globalization has paid off by providing faster economic growth and reductions in poverty. To avoid globalization in order to avoid financial crises is to remain in poverty as the rest of the world grows richer. We should think of globalization and financial crises in these terms: A closed economy can follow very bad economic policies for a long time, and the rest of the world will have no influence in bringing about change for the better. A country with a globalized economy will be punished for bad economic policy as foreign investors move money out of the country, contributing to financial market crises in that country. It is not globalization that brings about the crisis. Instead, globalization allows the rest of the world to respond to bad economic policies in a way that highlights the bad policies and imposes costs on the country for following such policies. In this sense, globalization acts to discipline countries. A country with a sound economic policy and good investment opportunities is rewarded with large flows of savings from the rest of the world to lower the cost of developing the local economy.

18-4d The Global Financial Crisis of 2007–2008

While the crises of the 1980s and 1990s were concentrated in developing countries, the global crisis that began in 2007 was concentrated in the developed countries. In fact, the crisis was initially referred to as the "sub-prime crisis," a reference to the fact that defaults on high-risk mortgage loans in the United States were the first wave of the crisis. These were mortgages offered to customers with inadequate income or poor credit histories, but the institutions that made the loans sold the mortgages to others, and the true risk associated with the loans was not well understood. How did bad loans on U.S. mortgages translate into a global crisis? These mortgages were originally made by banks in the United States, but they were then packaged into bundles containing a large number of such mortgages, and these bundles, called "securitized mortgages," were then sold to other investors. The globalization of financial markets played a major role. In recent years, there has been more and more international investment, which includes investments by European banks in U.S. mortgages. So when the U.S. borrowers began to default in large numbers, not only were U.S. financial institutions incurring losses on the mortgages, but so were financial institutions in Europe. So the crisis that began in the U.S. home mortgage industry was transmitted across international borders.

The financial crisis of 2007–2008 illustrated how important the integration of international financial markets could be in contributing to the spread of financial problems from one country to another. The answer is not less international investment, but better regulation of financial institutions to ensure that prudent risk taking exists in the future. We want investment to flow where it is most productive, and this means that money should flow across international borders to find the best opportunities. There was much more than just international investment in U.S. mortgages, and when the crisis began, such investment was cut back dramatically as financial institutions tried to reduce their losses.

Once losses were sustained by financial institutions, they began to cut back their lending in other areas. This is referred to as *deleveraging*—reducing exposure to risk associated with investments. The deleveraging of financial institutions led to the financial crisis sometimes being referred to as the *credit crisis*, as credit was restricted and more difficult to obtain. Not only were banks less willing to lend to their household and business customers, they were also less willing to lend to other banks as they were not sure whether other banks would be able to repay loans. As lending was reduced, spending by households and business firms fell, and a global recession resulted. Of course, as jobs were lost and incomes fell, the recession resulted in more loan defaults as more and more households and businesses were unable to repay their debts.

Table 3 provides measures of the magnitude of the losses suffered by financial institutions due to the crisis. The table reports data for the United States, Europe, and Japan, and shows total loans outstanding and losses sustained by banks, insurance companies, and other firms for loans of different types. For the United States, we see that more than 14 percent of the value of consumer loans will not be repaid and almost 8 percent of the total value of all loans will not be repaid. The numbers are a bit better for Europe and Japan, with a little more than 4 percent of loans unpaid in Europe and only 2 percent in Japan. One can see that the crisis hit U.S. financial institutions the worst, while Japanese institutions were not very exposed to the crisis.

TABLE 3	Estimates of Loan Losses Suffered by Financial Institutions, 2007–2010 (in billions of U.S. dollars)				
	Outstanding Insurer Loan Values	Bank Losses	Insurer Losses	Other Losses	Percent Loss
U.S.					
Residential mortgages	5,117	206	22	204	8.4%
Commercial mortgages	1,913	116	9	62	9.8%
Consumer loans	1,914	169	14	89	14.2%
Corporate loans	1,895	61	5	32	5.2%
Municipal	2,669	50	4	26	3.0%
Total loans	*13,508*	*602*	*54*	*413*	*7.9%*
Europe					
Residential mortgages	4,632	119	10	63	4.1%
Commercial mortgages	2,137	65	5	34	4.9%
Consumer loans	2,467	109	9	58	7.1%
Corporate loans	11,523	258	21	137	3.6%
Total loans	*20,759*	*551*	*45*	*292*	*4.3%*
Japan					
Consumer loans	3,230	58	3	3	2.0%
Corporate loans	3,339	60	3	3	2.0%
Total loans	*6,569*	*118*	*6*	*6*	*2.0%*

RECAP

1. The 1990s saw financial crises in Mexico, Indonesia, Korea, Malaysia, the Philippines, and Thailand.

2. Fixed exchange rates encouraged speculative attacks and ultimate devaluations of the currencies of the countries involved in the 1990s crises.

3. Exchange-rate devaluations raised the cost of debts that were denominated in foreign currency and imposed large losses on debtor firms.

4. Factors contributing to the 1990s financial crises included fixed exchange rates, falling international reserves, a lack of transparency to investors, and a high level of short-term international investment.

5. Globalization works to discipline countries that follow bad economic policies as foreign investors reduce their investments in those countries. Countries that follow good economic policies are rewarded with greater access to the savings of the rest of the world to help finance growth and development.

6. The financial crisis of 2007–2008 was global and began in the developed countries.

7. The global financial crisis pointed out the need for better regulation of financial institutions to ensure prudent lending and credit management policies.

8. The globalization of financial markets with associated international investment facilitates the transmission of financial shocks from one country to another, so a debt crisis originating in one country affects other countries that have invested in those assets.

SUMMARY

1. What is globalization?

- Globalization involves an increased cross-border flow of trade in goods, services, and financial assets, along with increased international mobility of technology, information, and individuals. *§18-1*

- The process of globalization has always existed because of its potential to raise living standards. *§18-1a*

- The rapid pace of globalization in recent decades has been made possible by technological advances. *§18-1b*

2. What are the arguments against globalization?

- Free trade increases corporate profits but harms people. *§18-2a*

- International organizations and the agreements they are associated with serve corporate interests and harm people. *§18-2a*

- Globalization occurs at the cost of environmental quality. *§18-2a*

- Globalization encourages harmful labor practices. *§18-2a*

3. What are the arguments in support of globalization?

- Those who lose their jobs to more efficient producers in other countries will be harmed, but the benefits to all consumers far outweigh the losses of those firms and workers that are harmed by globalization. *§18-2b*

- International organizations are funded by governments, not firms, and such organizations serve the interests of all nations in that they provide a setting where grievances must be heard and policy changes can be implemented. *§18-2b*

- Globalization has not resulted in a "race to the bottom," in which labor practices suffer and environmental decay results. *§18-2b*

4. How has globalization affected economic growth and poverty?

- Globalizers have faster economic growth and less poverty than nonglobalizers. *§18-3*

5. Can recent financial crises be linked to globalization?

- Globalization allows for international financial flows that punish countries that follow bad economic policy. *§18-4c*

KEY TERMS

Asian tigers, 399
NICs, 399

"race to the bottom", 395

speculative attack, 402

EXERCISES

1. What is globalization?
2. Comment on the following statement: "Globalization is an event of the post-1980s. Prior to this time, we never had to worry about globalization and its effects."
3. Write a script for two speakers arguing about globalization and its effects. Give each speaker a name, and then write a script for a debate between the two. The debate should be no longer than two pages, double-spaced. Each speaker should make a few key points, and the other speaker should offer a reply to each point the first speaker makes.
4. Why has the pace of globalization quickened since the 1950s?
5. If you wanted to compare countries on the basis of how globalized they are, how could you construct some numerical measures that would allow a cross-country comparison?
6. What are the major arguments against globalization?
7. What are the major arguments in favor of globalization?
8. What is the difference between "fair" and "free" trade?
9. What is the WTO? Where is it located, and what does it do?

10. Suppose we find that multinational firms are paying much lower wages in some poor countries than they would have to pay in the United States. Would this be sufficient evidence that these firms are exploiting the workers in the poor countries? Why or why not?

11. How can globalization reduce poverty? What does the evidence suggest about globalization and poverty?

12. There were several major international financial crises in the 1990s. What role did globalization play in these crises?

13. Using a supply and demand diagram, explain how central banks maintain a fixed exchange rate. What can cause an end to the fixed-exchange-rate regime?

14. Using a supply and demand diagram, explain how speculative attacks occur in the foreign exchange market.

15. If you were employed by a major international bank to forecast the likelihood of a financial crisis, what key variables would you want to monitor for the countries you are studying? Why would you want to monitor these variables?

16. What was the role of globalization in the global financial crisis of 2007–2008?

17. What is the role of technology in globalization? Explain several ways that the Internet has increased the pace of globalization and several ways that it has decreased the pace of globalization.

18. Have there been any "setbacks" to globalization?

ECONOMICALLY SPEAKING
RESHAPING THE GLOBAL ECONOMY

Jean Pisani-Ferry and Indhira Santos
The Economic and Financial Crisis Marks the End (for Now) of a Rapid Expansion of Globalization

The economic and financial turmoil engulfing the world marks the first crisis of the current era of globalization. Considerable country experience has been accumulated on financial crises in individual countries or regions—which policymakers can use to design remedial policies. But there has not been a world financial crisis in most people's living memory. And the experience of the 1930s is frightening because governments at that time proved unable to preserve economic integration and develop cooperative responses.

Even before this crisis, globalization was already being challenged. Despite exceptionally favorable global economic conditions, not everyone bought into the benefits of global free trade and movement of capital and jobs. Although economists, corporations, and some politicians were supportive, critics argued that globalization favored capital rather than labor and the wealthy rather than the poor.

Now the crisis and the national responses to it have started to reshape the global economy and shift the balance between the political and economic forces at play in the process of globalization. The drivers of the recent globalization wave—open markets, the global supply chain, globally integrated companies, and private ownership—are being undermined, and the spirit of protectionism has reemerged. And once-footloose global companies are returning to their national roots.

Globalization: Reshaping or Unmaking?

... To start with, *public participation in the private sector has increased significantly in the past few months* ... Of the 50 largest banks in the United States and the European Union, 23 and 15, respectively, have received public capital injections; that is, banks representing respectively 76 and 40 percent of pre-crisis market capitalization depend today on taxpayers. Other sectors, such as the automobile and insurance industries, have also received public assistance. Whatever the governments' intention, public support is bound to affect the behavior of once-footloose global firms.

Second, *this crisis challenges globally integrated companies*. Economic integration in the past quarter century has been driven largely by companies' search for cost cutting and talent. Yet globally integrated companies were first put to the test early on in the crisis, with the collapse of banks that acted across international borders. Once-mighty transnational institutions were suddenly at pains to identify which government would support them ... Public aid risks turning global companies into national champions ...

Third, *national responses to the crisis can lead to economic and financial fragmentation*. There is initial evidence that, as governments ask banks to continue lending to domestic customers, credit is being rationed disproportionately in foreign markets. This was what happened recently when the Dutch government asked ING Bank to expand domestic lending while reducing its overall balance sheet. Because companies in emerging and less developed economies depend largely on foreign credit, this leaves them especially vulnerable to financial protectionism. Furthermore, government aid—driven by a legitimate concern with jobs—often, implicitly at least, shows preferences for the local economy. The French bias toward domestic employment in its auto industry's plan, the U.S. "Buy American" provision in the stimulus bill, and U.K. Prime Minister Gordon Brown's now infamous "British jobs for British workers" slogan are but a few examples.

Last but not least, *despite the G-20's commitment last November not to increase tariffs, these have gone up since the start of the crisis in several countries, from India and China to Ecuador and Argentina.*

This follows a similar move one year ago when export restraints were introduced as countries tried to isolate domestic consumers from increasing international food prices.

It is hard to say whether these changes are merely short-term reactions to a major shock or amount to new and worrisome trends. At the very least, the balance between political and economic forces has been significantly altered. Because political support for globalization was at best shallow while the global economy was in a buoyant state, this suggests the pendulum is now swinging in the opposite direction. Against this background, two lessons from history are worth keeping in mind. One, dismantling protections takes time. It took several decades for many of the trade barriers erected during the interwar period to be brought down. Second, even if a significant part of the progress in liberalizing trade in recent times has been institutionalized and strong reversals á la 1930s are not likely, the downward spiral of protectionism acts fast.

Taken together, these risks pose a significant challenge for global integration. This is true also at the regional level. Economic divergence is rising within Europe, and cooperation within East Asia has been limited to say the least, in spite of the violent shock affecting the region.

Source: Excerpts from "Reshaping the Global Economy," *Finance and Development,* International Monetary Fund, March 2009.

COMMENTARY

This chapter has discussed the benefits and costs of globalization and documented the extent to which globalization has progressed. As pointed out in this article, the global financial crisis halted the process of globalization. One point made in the article is that political support for globalization has always been mixed, and it has been business firms that have led the drive for integration across national borders. The current reversal of globalization has important implications for productivity and living standards going forward.

In a globalized world, competition punishes the relatively unproductive or high-cost producers and rewards the relatively more productive or lower-cost producers. This means that in the industrial countries of Western Europe, North America, and Asia, foreign competition will put some domestic firms out of business, and some workers will lose their jobs. These workers typically do not find new jobs that pay as well as their old jobs. As a result, in the face of increasing competition from foreign firms, a natural response from those who are threatened is to fight change. This typically is reflected in calls by labor unions and firms that are losing money for trade restrictions on foreign goods so that the local firms and workers can keep their jobs. Some of the international demonstrations against globalization have been supported by labor unions from rich countries. Their goal is to slow or even stop the globalization process in order to protect jobs in the rich countries. This is one reason why officials in poor countries complain that so far the globalization process has not resulted in the large gains that could be realized if the rich countries truly opened their markets to the products that the developing countries produce best.

The rich countries are slow to open their markets to the poor countries because of political pressure at home to protect the workers and firms that would be displaced by the foreign competitors. Of course, the cost of such protection is lower living standards for all consumers in the country. The data presented in the chapter suggest that those countries that have not globalized have become poorer as the rest of the world has become richer. If the reversal of globalization that occurred with the global financial crisis continues in the post-crisis period, some will benefit (typically relatively high-cost producers who can only exist if protected by government trade restrictions), but the majority of households should expect to pay a price in terms of a lower standard of living.

CHAPTER 19
World Trade Equilibrium

FUNDAMENTAL QUESTIONS

1. What are the prevailing patterns of trade between countries? What goods are traded?

2. What determines the goods that a nation will export?

3. How are the equilibrium price and the quantity of goods traded determined?

4. What are the sources of comparative advantage?

Preview

The United States' once-dominant position as an exporter of color television sets has since been claimed by nations like Japan and Taiwan. What caused this change? Is it because Japan specializes in the export of high-tech equipment? If countries tend to specialize in the export of particular kinds of goods, why does the United States import Heineken beer at the same time it exports Budweiser? This chapter will examine the volume of world trade and the nature of trade linkages between countries. As you saw in the chapter "Scarcity and Opportunity Costs," trade occurs because of specialization in production. No single individual or country can produce everything better than anyone else can. The result is specialization of production based on comparative advantage. Remember that comparative advantage is in turn based on relative opportunity costs: A country will specialize in the production of those goods for which its opportunity costs of production are lower than the costs in other countries. Nations then trade what they produce in excess of their own consumption to acquire other things that they want to consume. In this chapter, we will go a step further and discuss the sources of comparative advantage. We will look at why one country has a comparative advantage in, say, automobile production, while another country has a comparative advantage in wheat production.

The world equilibrium price and quantity traded are derived from individual countries' demand and supply curves. This relationship between the world trade equilibrium and individual country markets will be utilized in the chapter "International Trade Restrictions" to discuss the ways in which countries can interfere with free international trade to achieve their own economic or political goals.

19-1 An Overview of World Trade

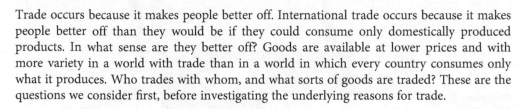

1. *What are the prevailing patterns of trade between countries? What goods are traded?*

Trade occurs because it makes people better off. International trade occurs because it makes people better off than they would be if they could consume only domestically produced products. In what sense are they better off? Goods are available at lower prices and with more variety in a world with trade than in a world in which every country consumes only what it produces. Who trades with whom, and what sorts of goods are traded? These are the questions we consider first, before investigating the underlying reasons for trade.

19-1a The Direction of Trade

Table 1 shows patterns of trade between two large groups of countries: the advanced or industrial countries and the emerging or developing countries. The industrial countries include all of Western Europe, Japan, Australia, New Zealand, Canada, and the United States. The developing countries are, essentially, the rest of the world. Table 1 shows the dollar values and percentages of total trade between these groups of countries as of 2012. The column at the left lists the origin of exports, and the row at the top lists the destination of imports.

As Table 1 shows, trade between industrial countries accounts for the bulk of international trade. Trade between industrial countries is a little more than $6.8 trillion in value and amounts to 38 percent of world trade. Exports from industrial countries to developing countries represent 20 percent of total world trade. Exports from developing countries to industrial countries account for 24 percent of total trade, while exports from developing countries to other developing countries currently represent only 17 percent of international trade.

TABLE 1 The Direction of Trade (in billions of dollars and percentages of world trade)		
	Destination	
Origin	**Industrial Countries**	**Developing Countries**
Industrial countries	$6,822	$3,596
	38%	20%
Developing countries	$4,355	$3,099
	24%	17%

Source: *IMF, Direction of Trade Statistics Quarterly,* February 2011.

Table 2 lists the major trading partners of selected countries and the percentage of total exports and imports accounted for by each country's top trading partners. For instance, 19 percent of U.S. exports went to Canada, and 6 percent of U.S. imports came from Japan. From a glance at the other countries listed in Table 2, it is clear that the United States is a major trading partner for many nations. This is true because of both the size of the U.S. economy and the nation's relatively high level of income. It is also apparent that Canada and Mexico are very dependent on trade with the United States: 75 percent of Canada's exports and 51 percent of its imports involve the United States, as do 78 percent of Mexico's exports and 50 percent of its imports. The dollar value of trade among the three North American nations is shown in Figure 1.

Trade between industrial countries accounts for the bulk of international trade.

The volume of trade in fuels exceeds that of any other category of goods.

19-1b What Goods Are Traded?

Because countries differ in their comparative advantages, they will tend to export different goods. Countries also have different tastes and technological needs, and thus tend to differ in what they will import. Some goods are more widely traded than others, as Table 3 shows. Fuels like crude petroleum are the most heavily traded category of goods in the world, accounting for almost 19 percent of the total volume of world trade. Office and telecom equipment and chemicals are essentially tied for second place in share of world trade. The importance of a few major categories in international trade should not obscure the fact that international trade involves all sorts of products from all over the world.

TABLE 2 Major Trading Partners of Selected Countries

United States

Exports		Imports	
Canada	19%	China	19%
Mexico	14%	Canada	14%
China	7%	Mexico	12%
Japan	5%	Japan	6%
U.K.	4%	Germany	5%

Canada

Exports		Imports	
U.S.	75%	U.S.	51%
China	4%	China	11%
U.K.	4%	Mexico	6%
Japan	2%	Japan	3%
Mexico	1%	Germany	3%

Germany

Exports		Imports	
France	10%	Netherlands	14%
U.K.	7%	France	7%
Netherlands	7%	China	7%
U.S.	6%	Belgium	6%
Austria	6%	Italy	5%

Mexico

Exports		Imports	
U.S.	78%	U.S.	50%
Canada	3%	China	15%
Spain	2%	Japan	5%
China	2%	Germany	4%
Brazil	2%	Korea	4%

Japan

Exports		Imports	
China	18%	China	21%
U.S.	18%	U.S.	9%
Korea	8%	Australia	6%
Taiwan	6%	Saudi Arabia	6%
Thailand	5%	United Arab Emirates	5%

United Kingdom

Exports		Imports	
Germany	11%	Germany	13%
U.S.	11%	China	8%
Netherlands	9%	Netherlands	7%
France	7%	U.S.	7%
Ireland	6%	France	5%

Source: IMF, *Direction of Trade Statistics*, April 2014.

FIGURE 1 Merchandise Trade Flows in North America (billions of dollars)

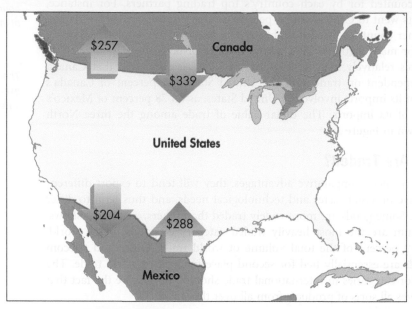

In 2012, the United States exported $257 billion worth of goods to Canada and imported $339 billion of goods from Canada. The same year, U.S. merchandise exports to Mexico were $204 billion, while merchandise imports from Mexico were $288 billion.

TABLE 3 World Merchandise Exports by Major Product Groups

Product Category	Value (billion dollars)	Percentage of World Merchandise Trade
Agricultural products	1,657	9.2
Fuels & mining products	4,139	23.1
Fuels	3,375	18.8
Manufactures (total)	11,490	64.1
Iron & steel	486	2.7
Chemicals	1,957	10.9
Office & telecom equipment	1,647	9.3
Automotive products	1,295	7.2
Textiles	286	1.6
Clothing	423	2.4

Note: Values in this table may not total 100 due to rounding.

Source: World Trade Organization, *International Trade Statistics 2014*; http://www.wto.org/english/res_e/statis_e/its2010_e/its2010_e.pdf.

RECAP

1. Trade between industrial countries accounts for the bulk of international trade.

2. The most important trading partners of the United States are Canada, Mexico, China, and Japan.

3. Fuels are the most heavily traded category of goods in the world, in terms of value of exports.

4. World trade is distributed across a great variety of products.

19-2 An Example of International Trade Equilibrium

The international economy is very complex. Each country has a unique pattern of trade, in terms both of trading partners and of goods traded. Some countries trade a great deal, and others trade very little. We already know that countries specialize and trade according to comparative advantage, but what are the fundamental determinants of international trade that explain the pattern of comparative advantage?

The answer to this question will in turn provide a better understanding of some basic questions about how international trade functions: What goods will be traded? How much will be traded? What prices will prevail for traded goods?

2. *What determines the goods that a nation will export?*

19-2a Comparative Advantage

Comparative advantage is found by comparing the relative costs of production in each country. We measure the cost of producing a particular good in two countries in terms of opportunity costs—what other goods must be given up in order to produce more of the good in question.

Table 4 presents a hypothetical example of two countries, the United States and India, that both produce two goods, wheat and cloth. The table lists the amounts of each good that can be produced by each worker. This example assumes that labor productivity differences alone determine comparative advantage. In the United States, a worker can produce either eight units of wheat or four units of cloth. In India, a worker can produce four units of wheat or three units of cloth.

The United States has an **absolute advantage**—greater productivity—in producing both wheat and cloth. Absolute advantage is determined by comparing the absolute productivity of workers producing each good in different countries. Since one worker can produce more of either good in the United States than in India, the United States is the more efficient producer of both goods.

absolute advantage
An advantage derived from one country having a lower absolute input cost of producing a particular good than another country.

Comparative advantage is based on what a country can do relatively better than other countries. This photo shows a sheep in Canterbury, New Zealand. New Zealand has a comparative advantage in sheep raising and wool production.

TABLE 4 An Example of Comparative Advantage		
	Output per Worker per Day in Either Wheat or Cloth	
	United States	**India**
Wheat	8	4
Cloth	4	3

comparative advantage
An advantage derived from comparing the opportunity costs of production in two countries.

It might seem that, since the United States is the more efficient producer of both goods, there would be no need for it to trade with India. But absolute advantage is not the critical consideration. What matters in determining the benefits of international trade is comparative advantage, as originally discussed in the chapter "Scarcity and Opportunity Costs." To find the **comparative advantage**—the lower opportunity cost—we must compare the opportunity cost of producing each good in each country.

The opportunity cost of producing wheat is what must be given up in cloth using the same resources, like one worker per day. Look again at Table 4 to see the production of wheat and cloth in the two countries. Since one U.S. worker can produce eight units of wheat or four units of cloth, if we take a worker from cloth production and move him to wheat production, we gain eight units of wheat and lose four units of cloth.

The opportunity cost of producing wheat equals $4/8$, or $1/2$, unit of cloth:

$$\frac{\text{Output of cloth given up}}{\text{Output of wheat gained}} = \begin{array}{l} \text{opportunity cost of producing 1 unit of} \\ \text{wheat (in terms of cloth given up)} \end{array}$$

$$\frac{4}{8} = \frac{1}{2}$$

Applying the same thinking to India, we find that one worker can produce four units of wheat or three units of cloth. The opportunity cost of producing one unit of wheat in India is $3/4$ unit of cloth.

A comparison of the domestic opportunity costs in each country will reveal which one has the comparative advantage in producing each good. The U.S. opportunity cost of producing one unit of wheat is $1/2$ unit of cloth; the Indian opportunity cost is $3/4$ unit of cloth. Because the United States has a lower domestic opportunity cost, it has the comparative advantage in wheat production and will export wheat. Since wheat production costs are lower in the United States, India is better off trading for wheat rather than trying to produce it domestically.

The comparative advantage in cloth is found the same way. Taking a worker in the United States from wheat production and putting her in cloth production, we gain four units of cloth but lose eight units of wheat per day. So the opportunity cost is

$$\frac{\text{Output of wheat given up}}{\text{Output of cloth gained}} = \begin{array}{l} \text{opportunity cost of producing 1 unit of} \\ \text{cloth (in terms of wheat given up)} \end{array}$$

$$\frac{8}{4} = 2$$

In India, moving a worker from wheat to cloth production means that we gain three units of cloth but lose four units of wheat, so the opportunity cost is $4/3$, or $1^1/3$ units of wheat for one unit of cloth. Comparing the U.S. opportunity cost of two units of wheat with the Indian opportunity cost of $1^1/3$ units, we see that India has the comparative advantage in cloth production and will therefore export cloth. In this case, the United States is better off trading for cloth rather than producing it, since India's costs of production are lower.

In international trade, as in other areas of economic decision making, it is opportunity cost that matters—and opportunity costs are reflected in comparative advantage. Absolute advantage is irrelevant, because knowing the absolute number of labor hours required to produce a good does not tell us if we can benefit from trade.

We benefit from trade if we are able to obtain a good from a foreign country by giving up less than we would have to give up to obtain the good at home. Because only opportunity cost can allow us to make such comparisons, international trade proceeds on the basis of comparative advantage.

19-2b Terms of Trade

On the basis of comparative advantage, India will specialize in cloth production, and the United States will specialize in wheat production. The two countries will then trade with each other to satisfy the domestic demand for both goods. International trade permits greater consumption than would be possible from domestic production alone. Since countries trade when they can obtain a good more cheaply from a foreign producer than they can obtain it at home, international trade allows all traders to consume more. This is evident when we examine the terms of trade.

The **terms of trade** are the amount of an exported good that must be given up to obtain one unit of an imported good. The Global Business Insight "The Dutch Disease" provides a popular example of a dramatic shift in the terms of trade. As you saw earlier, comparative advantage dictates that the United States will specialize in wheat production and export wheat to India in exchange for Indian cloth. But the amount of wheat that the United States will exchange for a unit of cloth is limited by the domestic trade-offs. If a unit of cloth can be obtained domestically for two units of wheat, the United States will be willing to trade with India only if the terms of trade are less than two units of wheat for a unit of cloth. India, in turn, will be willing to trade its cloth for U.S. wheat only if it can receive a better price than its domestic opportunity costs. Since a unit of cloth in India costs $1\frac{1}{3}$ units of wheat, India will gain from trade if it can obtain more than $1\frac{1}{3}$ units of wheat for its cloth.

The limits of the terms of trade are determined by the opportunity costs in each country:

1 unit of cloth for more than $1\frac{1}{3}$ but less than 2 units of wheat

Within this range, the actual terms of trade will be decided by the bargaining power of the two countries. The closer the United States can come to giving up only $1\frac{1}{3}$ units of wheat for cloth, the better the terms of trade for the United States. The closer India can come to receiving two units of wheat for its cloth, the better the terms of trade for India.

Though each country would like to push the other as close to the limits of the terms of trade as possible, any terms within the limits set by domestic opportunity costs will be mutually beneficial. Both countries benefit because they are able to consume goods at a cost that is less than their domestic opportunity costs. To illustrate the *gains from trade*, let us assume that the actual terms of trade are one unit of cloth for $1\frac{1}{2}$ units of wheat.

Suppose the United States has two workers, one of whom goes to wheat production and the other to cloth production. This would result in U.S. production of eight units of wheat and four units of cloth. Without international trade, the United States can produce and consume eight units of wheat and four units of cloth. If the United States, with its comparative advantage in wheat production, chooses to produce only wheat, it can use both workers in wheat production and produce 16 units. If the terms of trade are $1\frac{1}{2}$ units of wheat per unit of cloth, the United States can keep eight units of wheat and trade the other eight for $5\frac{1}{3}$ units of cloth (8 divided by $1\frac{1}{2}$). By trading U.S. wheat for Indian cloth, the United States is able to consume more than it could without trade. With no trade and half its labor devoted to each good, the United States could consume eight units of wheat and four units of cloth. After trade, the

Countries export goods in which they have a comparative advantage.

terms of trade
The amount of an exported good that must be given up to obtain an imported good.

GLOBAL BUSINESS INSIGHT

The Dutch Disease

The terms of trade are the amount of an export that must be given up to obtain a certain quantity of an import. The price of an import will be equal to its price in the foreign country of origin multiplied by the exchange rate (the domestic-currency price of foreign currency). As the exchange rate changes, the terms of trade will change. This can have important consequences for international trade.

A problem can arise when one export industry in an economy is booming relative to others. In the 1970s, for instance, the Netherlands experienced a boom in its natural gas industry. The dramatic energy price increases of the 1970s resulted in large Dutch exports of natural gas. Increased demand for exports from the Netherlands caused the Dutch currency to

appreciate, making Dutch goods more expensive for foreign buyers. This situation caused the terms of trade to worsen for the Netherlands. Although the natural gas sector was booming, Dutch manufacturers were finding it difficult to compete in the world market.

This phenomenon of a boom in one industry causing declines in the rest of the economy is popularly called the Dutch Disease. It is usually associated with dramatic increases in the demand for a primary commodity, and it can afflict any nation experiencing such a boom. For instance, a rapid rise in the demand for coffee could lead to a Dutch Disease problem for Colombia, where a coffee boom would be accompanied by a decline in other sectors of the economy.

The gain from trade is increased consumption.

United States consumes eight units of wheat and $5\frac{1}{3}$ units of cloth. By devoting all its labor hours to wheat production and trading wheat for cloth, the United States gains $1\frac{1}{3}$ units of cloth. This is the gain from trade—an increase in consumption, as summarized in Table 5.

19-2c Export Supply and Import Demand

The preceding example suggests that countries benefit from specialization and trade. Realistically, however, countries do not completely specialize. Typically, domestic industries satisfy part of the domestic demand for goods that are also imported. To understand how the quantity of goods traded is determined, we must construct demand and supply curves for each country and use them to create export supply and import demand curves.

The proportion of domestic demand for a good that is satisfied by domestic production and the proportion that will be satisfied by imports are determined by the domestic supply and demand curves and the international equilibrium price of a good. The international equilibrium price and quantity may be determined once we know the export supply and import demand curves for each country. These curves are derived from the domestic supply and demand in each country. Figure 2 illustrates the derivation of the export supply and import demand curves.

TABLE 5   Hypothetical Example of U.S. Gains from Specialization and Trade
Without International Trade
1 worker in wheat production: produce and consume 8 wheat
1 worker in cloth production: produce and consume 4 cloth
With Specialization and Trade
2 workers in wheat production: produce 16 wheat and consume 8; trade 8 wheat for $5\frac{1}{3}$ cloth
Before Trade: consume 8 wheat and 4 cloth
After Trade: consume 8 wheat and $5\frac{1}{3}$ cloth; gain $1\frac{1}{3}$ cloth by specialization and trade

FIGURE 2 The Import Demand and Export Supply Curves

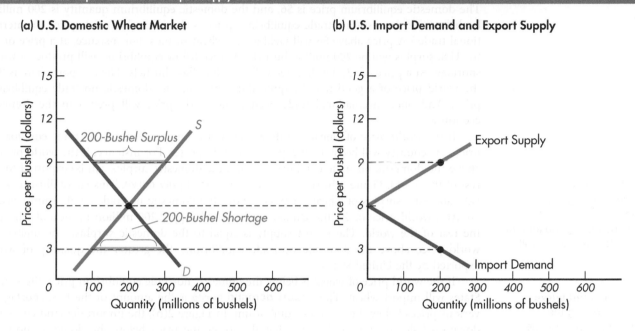

(a) U.S. Domestic Wheat Market

(b) U.S. Import Demand and Export Supply

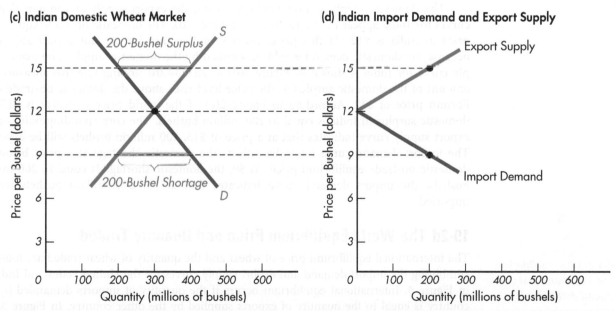

(c) Indian Domestic Wheat Market

(d) Indian Import Demand and Export Supply

Figures 2(a) and 2(c) show the domestic demand and supply curves for wheat in the United States and India, respectively. The domestic no-trade equilibrium price is $6 in the United States and $12 in India. Any price above the domestic no-trade equilibrium prices will create domestic surpluses, which are reflected in the export supply curves in 2(b) and 2(d). Any price below the domestic no-trade equilibrium prices will create domestic shortages, which are reflected in the import demand curves in 2(b) and 2(d).

Figure 2(a) shows the domestic supply and demand curves for the U.S. wheat market. The domestic equilibrium price is $6, and the domestic equilibrium quantity is 200 million bushels. (The domestic no-trade equilibrium price is the price that exists prior to international trade.) A price above $6 will yield a U.S. wheat surplus. For instance, at a price of $9, the U.S. surplus will be 200 million bushels. A price below equilibrium will produce a wheat shortage: At a price of $3, the shortage will be 200 million bushels. The key point here is that the world price of a good may be quite different from the domestic no-trade equilibrium price. And once international trade occurs, the world price will prevail in the domestic economy.

If the world price of wheat is different from a country's domestic no-trade equilibrium price, the country will become an exporter or an importer. For instance, if the world price is above the domestic no-trade equilibrium price, the domestic surplus can be exported to the rest of the world. Figure 2(b) shows the U.S. **export supply curve**. This curve illustrates the U.S. domestic surplus of wheat for prices above the domestic no-trade equilibrium price of $6. At a world price of $9, the United States would supply 200 million bushels of wheat to the rest of the world. The export supply is equal to the domestic surplus. The higher the world price above the domestic no-trade equilibrium, the greater the quantity of wheat exported by the United States.

If the world price of wheat is below the domestic no-trade equilibrium price, the United States will import wheat. The **import demand curve** is the amount of the U.S. shortage at various prices below the no-trade equilibrium. In Figure 2(b), the import demand curve is a downward-sloping line, indicating that the lower the price below the domestic no-trade equilibrium of $6, the greater the quantity of wheat imported by the United States. At a price of $3, the United States will import 200 million bushels.

The domestic supply and demand curves and the export supply and import demand curves for India appear in Figure 2(c) and Figure 2(d). The domestic no-trade equilibrium price in India is $12. At this price, India would neither import nor export any wheat because the domestic demand would be satisfied by the domestic supply. The export supply curve for India is shown in Figure 2(d) as an upward-sloping line that measures the amount of the domestic surplus as the price level rises above the domestic no-trade equilibrium price of $12. According to Figure 2(c), if the world price of wheat is $15, the domestic surplus in India is equal to 200 million bushels. The corresponding point on the export supply curve indicates that at a price of $15, 200 million bushels will be exported. The import demand curve for India reflects the domestic shortage at a price below the domestic no-trade equilibrium price. At $9, the domestic shortage is equal to 200 million bushels; the import demand curve indicates that at $9, 200 million bushels will be imported.

19-2d The World Equilibrium Price and Quantity Traded

The international equilibrium price of wheat and the quantity of wheat traded are found by combining the import demand and export supply curves for the United States and India, as in Figure 3. International equilibrium occurs if the quantity of imports demanded by one country is equal to the quantity of exports supplied by the other country. In Figure 3, this equilibrium occurs at the point labeled *e*. At this point, the import demand curve for India indicates that India wants to import 200 million bushels at a price of $9. The export supply curve for the United States indicates that the United States wants to export 200 million bushels at a price of $9. Only at $9 will the quantity of wheat demanded by the importing nation equal the quantity of wheat supplied by the exporting nation. So the equilibrium world price of wheat is $9, and the equilibrium quantity of wheat traded is 200 million bushels.

export supply curve
A curve showing the relationship between the world price of a good and the amount that a country will export.

import demand curve
A curve showing the relationship between the world price of a good and the amount that a country will import.

3. How are the equilibrium price and the quantity of goods traded determined?

International equilibrium occurs at the point where the quantity of imports demanded by one country is equal to the quantity of exports supplied by the other country.

FIGURE 3 International Equilibrium Price and Quantity

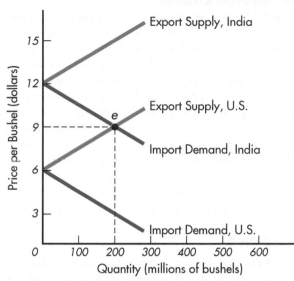

The international equilibrium price is the price at which the export supply curve of the United States intersects the import demand curve of India. At the equilibrium price of $9, the United States will export 200 million bushels to India.

RECAP

1. Comparative advantage is based on the relative opportunity costs of producing goods in different countries.

2. A country has an absolute advantage when it can produce a good more efficiently than can other nations.

3. A country has a comparative advantage when the opportunity cost of producing a good, in terms of forgone output of other goods, is lower than that of other nations.

4. The terms of trade are the amount of an export good that must be given up to obtain one unit of an import good.

5. The limits of the terms of trade are determined by the domestic opportunity costs of production in each country.

6. The export supply and import demand curves measure the domestic surplus and shortage, respectively, at different world prices.

7. International equilibrium occurs at the point where one country's import demand curve intersects with the export supply curve of another country.

19-3 Sources of Comparative Advantage

We know that countries specialize and trade in accordance with comparative advantage, but what gives a country a comparative advantage? Economists have suggested several theories of the source of comparative advantage. Let us review these theories.

19-3a Productivity Differences

The example of comparative advantage given earlier in this chapter showed the United States to have a comparative advantage in wheat production and India to have a comparative advantage in cloth production. Comparative advantage was determined by differences in the number

4. What are the sources of comparative advantage?

of labor hours required to produce each good. In this example, differences in the *productivity* of labor accounted for comparative advantage.

For over two hundred years, economists have argued that productivity differences account for comparative advantage. In fact, this theory of comparative advantage is often called the *Ricardian model,* after David Ricardo, a nineteenth-century English economist who explained and analyzed the idea of productivity-based comparative advantage. Variations in the productivity of labor can explain many observed trade patterns in the world.

Although we know that labor productivity differs across countries, and that this can help explain why countries produce the goods they do, there are factors other than labor productivity that determine comparative advantage. Furthermore, even if labor productivity were all that mattered, we would still want to know why some countries have more productive workers than others. The standard interpretation of the Ricardian model is that technological differences between countries account for differences in labor productivity. The countries with the most advanced technology would have a comparative advantage with regard to those goods that can be produced most efficiently with modern technology.

Comparative advantage due to productivity differences between countries is often called the Ricardian model of comparative advantage.

19-3b Factor Abundance

Goods differ in terms of the resources, or factors of production, required for their production. Countries differ in terms of the abundance of different factors of production: land, labor, capital, and entrepreneurial ability. It seems self-evident that countries would have an advantage in producing those goods that use relatively large amounts of their most abundant factor of production. Certainly countries with a relatively large amount of farmland would have a comparative advantage in agriculture, and countries with a relatively large amount of capital would tend to specialize in the production of manufactured goods.

The idea that comparative advantage is based on the relative abundance of factors of production is sometimes called the *Heckscher-Ohlin model,* after the two Swedish economists, Eli Heckscher and Bertil Ohlin, who developed the original argument. The original model assumed that countries possess only two factors of production: labor and capital. Thus, researchers have examined the labor and capital requirements of various industries to see whether labor-abundant countries export goods whose production is relatively labor intensive, and capital-abundant countries export goods that are relatively capital intensive. In many cases, factor abundance has served well as an explanation of observed trade patterns. However, there are cases in which comparative advantage seems to run counter to the predictions of the factor-abundance theory. In response, economists have suggested other explanations for comparative advantage.

Comparative advantage based on differences in the abundance of factors of production across countries is described in the Heckscher-Ohlin model.

19-3c Other Theories of Comparative Advantage

New theories of comparative advantage have typically been developed in an effort to explain the trade pattern in some narrow category of products. They are not intended to serve as general explanations of comparative advantage, as do factor abundance and productivity. These supplementary theories emphasize human skills, product life cycles, and preferences.

19-3c-1 Human Skills This approach emphasizes differences across countries in the availability of skilled and unskilled labor. The basic idea is that countries with a relatively abundant stock of highly skilled labor will have a comparative advantage in producing goods that require relatively large amounts of skilled labor. This theory is similar to the factor-abundance theory, except that here the analysis rests on two segments (skilled and unskilled) of the labor factor.

The human skills argument is consistent with the observation that most U.S. exports are produced in high-wage (skilled labor) industries and most U.S. imports are products produced in relatively low-wage industries. Since the United States has a well-educated labor force, relative to many other countries, we would expect the United States to have a comparative advantage in industries requiring a large amount of skilled labor. Developing countries would be expected to have a comparative advantage in industries requiring a relatively large amount of unskilled labor.

19-3c-2 Product Life Cycles

This theory explains how comparative advantage in a specific good can shift from one country to another over time. This occurs because goods experience a *product life cycle*. At the outset, development and testing are required to conceptualize and design the product. For this reason, the early production will be undertaken by an innovative firm. Over time, however, a successful product tends to become standardized, in the sense that many manufacturers can produce it. The mature product may be produced by firms that do little or no research and development, specializing instead in copying successful products that were invented and developed by others.

The product life cycle theory is related to international comparative advantage in that a new product will first be produced and exported by the nation in which it was invented. As the product is exported elsewhere and foreign firms become familiar with it, the technology is copied in other countries by foreign firms seeking to produce a competing version. As the product matures, comparative advantage shifts away from the country of origin if other countries have lower manufacturing costs using the now-standardized technology.

The history of color television production shows how comparative advantage can shift over the product life cycle. Color television was invented in the United States, and U.S. firms initially produced and exported color TVs. Over time, as the technology of color television manufacturing became well known, countries like Japan and Taiwan came to dominate the business. Firms in these countries had a comparative advantage over U.S. firms in the manufacture of color televisions. Once the technology is widely available, countries with lower production costs, due to lower wages, can compete effectively against the higher-wage nation that developed the technology.

Manufactured goods have life cycles. At first they are produced by the firm that invented them. Later, they may be produced by firms in other countries that copy the technology of the innovator.

19-3c-3 Preferences

The theories of comparative advantage that we have looked at so far have all been based on supply factors. It may be, though, that the demand side of the market can explain some of the patterns observed in international trade. Different producers' goods are seldom exactly identical. Consumers may prefer the goods of one firm to those of another firm. Domestic firms usually produce goods to satisfy domestic consumers. But since different consumers have different preferences, some consumers will prefer goods produced by foreign firms. International trade allows consumers to expand their consumption opportunities.

Consumers who live in countries with similar levels of development can be expected to have similar consumption patterns. The consumption patterns of consumers in countries at quite different levels of development are much less similar. This would suggest that firms in industrial countries will find a larger market for their goods in other industrial countries than in developing countries.

As you saw earlier in this chapter, industrial countries tend to trade with other industrial countries. This pattern runs counter to the factor-abundance theory of comparative advantage, which would suggest that countries with the most dissimilar endowments of resources would find trade most beneficial. Yet rich countries, with large supplies of capital and skilled labor forces, trade more actively with other rich countries than they do with poor countries. Firms in industrial countries tend to produce goods that relatively wealthy consumers will buy. The key point here is that we do not live in a world based on simple comparative advantage, in which all cloth is identical, regardless of the producer. We inhabit a world of differentiated products, and consumers want choices between different brands or styles of a seemingly similar good.

Another feature of international trade that may be explained by consumer preference is **intraindustry trade**, a circumstance in which a country both exports and imports goods in the same industry. The fact that the United States exports Budweiser beer and imports Heineken beer is not surprising when preferences are taken into account. Supply-side theories of comparative advantage rarely provide an explanation of intraindustry trade, since they would expect each

intraindustry trade
The simultaneous import and export of goods in the same industry by a particular country.

country to export only those goods produced by industries in which a comparative advantage exists. Yet the real world is characterized by a great deal of intraindustry trade.

We have discussed several potential sources of comparative advantage: labor productivity, factor abundance, human skills, product life cycles, and preferences. Each of these theories, which are summarized in Figure 4, has proven useful in understanding certain trade

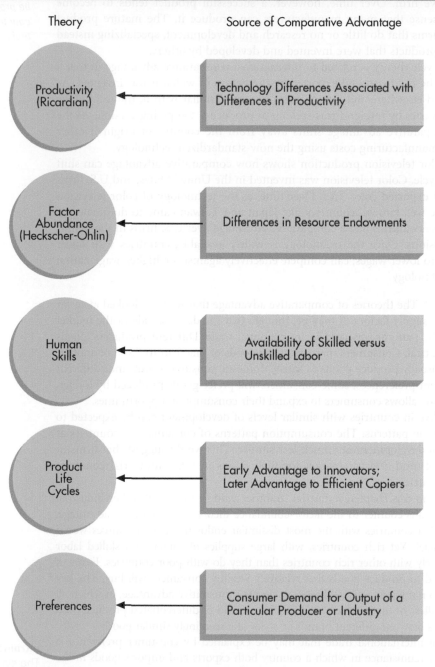

FIGURE 4 Theories of Comparative Advantage

Theory	Source of Comparative Advantage
Productivity (Ricardian)	Technology Differences Associated with Differences in Productivity
Factor Abundance (Heckscher-Ohlin)	Differences in Resource Endowments
Human Skills	Availability of Skilled versus Unskilled Labor
Product Life Cycles	Early Advantage to Innovators; Later Advantage to Efficient Copiers
Preferences	Consumer Demand for Output of a Particular Producer or Industry

Several theories exist that explain comparative advantage: labor productivity, factor abundance, human skills, product life cycles, and preferences.

patterns. Each has also been shown to have limitations as a general theory that is applicable to all cases. Once again we are reminded that the world is a very complicated place. Theories are simpler than reality. Nevertheless, they help us to understand how comparative advantage arises.

RECAP

1. Comparative advantage can arise because of differences in labor productivity.

2. Countries differ in their resource endowments, and a given country may enjoy a comparative advantage in products that use its most abundant factor of production intensively.

3. Industrial countries may have a comparative advantage in products requiring a large amount of skilled labor. Developing countries may have a comparative advantage in products requiring a large amount of unskilled labor.

4. Comparative advantage in a new good initially resides in the country that invented the good. Over time, other nations learn the technology and may gain a comparative advantage in producing the good.

5. In some industries, consumer preferences for differentiated goods may explain international trade flows, including industry trade.

SUMMARY

1. What are the prevailing patterns of trade between countries? What goods are traded?

- International trade flows largely between industrial countries. §19-1a

- International trade involves many diverse products. §19-1b

2. What determines the goods that a nation will export?

- Comparative advantage is based on the opportunity costs of production. §19-2a

- Domestic opportunity costs determine the limits of the terms of trade between two countries—that is, the amount of exports that must be given up to obtain imports. §19-2b

- The export supply curve shows the domestic surplus and amount of exports available at alternative world prices. §19-2c

- The import demand curve shows the domestic shortage and amount of imports demanded at alternative world prices. §19-2c

3. How are the equilibrium price and the quantity of goods traded determined?

- The international equilibrium price and quantity of a good traded are determined by the intersection of the export supply curve of one country with the import demand curve of another country. §19-2d

4. What are the sources of comparative advantage?

- The productivity-differences and factor-abundance theories of comparative advantage are general theories that seek to explain patterns of international trade flow. §19-3a, 19-3b

- Other theories of comparative advantage aimed at explaining trade in particular kinds of goods focus on human skills, product life cycles, and consumer preferences. §19-3c

KEY TERMS

absolute advantage, 413
comparative advantage, 418
export supply curve, 422
import demand curve, 422
intraindustry trade, 425
terms of trade, 419

EXERCISES

1. Why must voluntary trade between two countries be mutually beneficial?

    Use the following table for exercises 2–6.

Amount of Beef or Computers Produced by One Worker in a Day

	Canada	Japan
Beef	8	5
Computers	3	4

2. Which country has the absolute advantage in beef production?
3. Which country has the absolute advantage in computer production?
4. Which country has the comparative advantage in beef production?
5. Which country has the comparative advantage in computer production?
6. What are the limits of the terms of trade? Specifically, when is Canada willing to trade with Japan, and when is Japan willing to trade with Canada?
7. Use the following supply and demand schedule for two countries to determine the international equilibrium price of shoes. How many shoes will be traded?

Demand and Supply of Shoes (in thousands)

	Mexico		Chile	
Price	Qty. Demanded	Qty. Supplied	Qty. Demanded	Qty. Supplied
$10	40	0	55	0
$20	35	20	44	10
$30	30	40	33	20
$40	25	60	22	30
$50	20	0	11	40

8. How would each of the following theories of comparative advantage explain the fact that the United States exports computers?
    a. Productivity differences
    b. Factor abundance
    c. Human skills
    d. Product life cycle
    e. Preferences
9. Which of the theories of comparative advantage could explain why the United States exports computers to Japan at the same time that it imports computers from Japan? Explain.
10. Developing countries have complained that the terms of trade they face are unfavorable. If they voluntarily engage in international trade, what do you suppose they mean by "unfavorable terms of trade"?
11. If two countries reach equilibrium in their domestic markets at the same price, what can be said about their export supply and import demand curves and about the international trade equilibrium?

ECONOMICALLY SPEAKING

LETTER TO SENATE MAJORITY LEADER HARRY REID

January 30, 2008

The Honorable Harry Reid
Majority Leader
United States Senate
U.S. Senate, S-221
Washington, DC 20515

Dear Majority Leader Reid:

We would like to offer our support for prioritizing trade legislation addressing China. We face a host of difficult trade issues with China that require strong action, ranging from currency manipulation and unfair subsidies, to trade law and counterfeit enforcement problems, to imported food and product safety. These issues are hurting American competiveness and expose American consumers to unsafe goods.

The problems facing workers and manufacturers due to unfair trading practices in China and other countries are growing more severe each day. The U.S. trade deficit with China hit $237.5 billion through November 2007, eclipsing the previous year's record of $232.6 billion. This is the highest annual imbalance ever recorded with a single country—and December's figures have yet to be calculated. The deficit with China now accounts for 32.5 percent of the U.S. total trade deficit in goods— and more than half of the U.S. non-petroleum goods deficit.

China is by far the leading violator of international trade rules and its actions continue to harm American workers, industry, and manufacturing. China has done little to address the fundamental misalignment of its currency, a practice that continues to take jobs and wealth from the United States. There is also strong evidence that the massive subsidies the Chinese government provides its producers gives them an unfair advantage in international trade. These factors, in addition to low wages, unsafe working conditions, and the absence of worker rights, have contributed to the loss of millions of manufacturing jobs and our country's reliance on imports.

The American people are demanding action to stop our trading partners from rigging the game. It is time for Congress to meet that demand and take strong action.

It is our belief that any such measure taken to correct this imbalance should ensure that China and other nations float their currencies against the dollar and the other currencies of the world. Should China and other nations fail to do so, an appropriate remedy would treat currency misalignment as a subsidy that is countervailable under U.S. trade law.

We also support provisions that would apply countervailing duties to non-market economies. Current anti-subsidies rules allow the world's largest trade subsidizer, China, to continue its unfair practices without penalty.

Further, we believe it is necessary to ensure that World Trade Organization decisions do not undermine trade law enforcement. We must ensure that U.S. anti-dumping law will work effectively and fairly against China and other trade law violators.

Since Congress granted permanent normal trade relations status to China, intellectual property theft and illegal counterfeiting have increased, costing American businesses billions of dollars annually. We believe a comprehensive approach to China trade issues must include attention to intellectual property enforcement.

Finally, the recent recalls of unsafe toys, food, and other products from China emphasize the need to ensure that our trading system protects public health and safety. While the President's Interagency Working Group on Import Safety has developed recommendations for the federal government and industry to follow, we believe that memoranda of understanding with China alone cannot ensure the safety of products for American consumers. We would like to ensure that increased Customs and Border Patrol surveillance of imported food and products and market-based principles be considered to ensure that importers of products from all countries are liable for their safety and quality.

The challenges facing our nation's manufacturers, farmers, and workers increase with each passing week. We support efforts to address these issues in a comprehensive manner before the consideration of proposed free trade agreements, and we share the view that now is the time to move legislation forward.

Source: Senator Sherrod Brown website listing letter sent by eight senators to Senate Majority Leader Reid: http://brown.senate.gov/newsroom/press_releases/release/?id=45ebb90f-c7be-4e54-815b-eaab5a57a533.

COMMENTARY

There is no lack of stories in the U.S. media on the threat of foreign economic domination. As this letter indicates, officials within the U.S. government were concerned about U.S. trade with China. The United States had experienced a growing trade deficit with China, and some senators wanted action to address what they saw as unfair international trade practices by China.

However, the bilateral trade accounts provide little, if any, information on such issues. Indeed, it is easy to think of an example in which a country has a persistent trade deficit with one of its trading partners but has its overall trade account in balance. Suppose there are three countries that trade among themselves, which we will call countries A, B, and C. The people of each country produce only one type of good and consume only one other type of good. The people of country A produce apples and consume bananas, the people of country B produce bananas and consume cucumbers, and the people of country C produce cucumbers and consume apples. Even when the trade account of each country is balanced, each has a deficit with one of its trading partners and a surplus with the other. Furthermore, a larger trade deficit between countries A and B (with each country retaining balanced trade) implies that the people of country A are better off, since they are consuming more. If the government of country A tried to impose a law forcing bilateral trade balance with country B, citizens of country A could not consume as many bananas as before and would be forced to attempt to sell apples to the uninterested citizens of country B.

This simple example demonstrates that the U.S. trade deficit with China should not in itself be a cause for concern. The United States could have a persistent trade deficit with China and yet maintain an overall balanced trade account. In fact, any country would be expected to have a trade deficit with some countries and a trade surplus with others. This reflects comparative advantage. Trade between countries makes both the exporting and the importing countries better off.

This is not to say that there may not be problems in terms of China failing to allow U.S. exporters access to its consumers, or problems with pirating of intellectual property, or problems in exchange rate management. Also, concern about the overall trade deficit may be well founded. An overall trade deficit indicates that a country is consuming more than it is producing. At any particular time, a country may want to run a trade deficit or a trade surplus, depending on the circumstances it faces. But regardless of the overall trade account of a country, we should expect bilateral trade imbalances among trading partners.

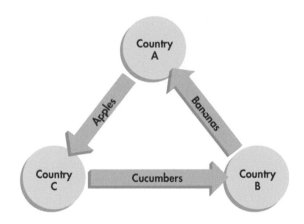

CHAPTER 20
International Trade Restrictions

Pinkcandy/Dreamstime.com

FUNDAMENTAL QUESTIONS

1. Why do countries restrict international trade?

2. How do countries restrict the entry of foreign goods and promote the export of domestic goods?

3. What sorts of agreements do countries enter into to reduce barriers to international trade?

Preview

The Japanese government once announced that foreign-made skis would not be allowed into Japan because they were unsafe. Japanese ski manufacturers were active supporters of the ban. The U.S. government once imposed a tax of almost 50 percent on imports of motorcycles with engines larger than 700 cc. The only U.S.-owned motorcycle manufacturer, Harley-Davidson, produced no motorcycles with engines smaller than 1,000 cc and so did not care about the small-engine market. In the mid-1980s, Britain began replacing the distinctive red steel telephone booths that were used all through the country with new booths. Many U.S. residents were interested in buying an old British phone booth to use as a decorative novelty, so the phone booths were exported to the

top: © Carsten Reisinger/Shutterstock

433

United States. However, when the phone booths arrived, the U.S. Customs Service impounded them because there was a limit on the amount of iron and steel products that could be exported from Britain to the United States. The phone booths would be allowed to enter the country only if British exports of some other iron and steel products were reduced. The British exporters protested the classification of the phone booths as iron and steel products and argued that they should be considered antiques (which have no import restrictions). The phone booths were not reclassified; as a result, few have entered the United States, and prices of old British phone booths have been in the thousands of dollars. There are many examples of government policy influencing the prices and quantities of goods that are traded internationally.

International trade is rarely determined solely by comparative advantage and the free market forces of supply and demand. Governments often find that political pressures favor policies that at least partially offset the prevailing comparative advantages. Government policy aimed at influencing international trade flows is called **commercial policy**. This chapter first examines the arguments in support of commercial policy and then discusses the various tools of commercial policy employed by governments.

commercial policy
Government policy that influences international trade flows.

1. Why do countries restrict international trade?

Protection from foreign competition generally benefits domestic producers at the expense of domestic consumers.

20-1 Arguments for Protection

Governments restrict foreign trade to protect domestic producers from foreign competition. In some cases the protection may be justified; in most cases it harms consumers. Of the arguments used to promote such protection, only a few are valid. We will look first at arguments that are widely considered to have little or no merit, and then at those that may sometimes be valid.

International trade on the basis of comparative advantage maximizes world output and allows consumers access to better-quality products at lower prices than would be available in the domestic market alone. If trade is restricted, consumers pay higher prices for lower-quality goods, and world output declines. Protection from foreign competition imposes costs on the domestic economy as well as on foreign producers. When production does not proceed on the basis of comparative advantage, resources are not expended on their most efficient uses. Whenever government restrictions alter the pattern of trade, we should expect someone to benefit and someone else to suffer. Generally speaking, protection from foreign competition benefits domestic producers at the expense of domestic consumers.

20-1a Creation of Domestic Jobs

If foreign goods are kept out of the domestic economy, it is often argued, jobs will be created at home. This argument holds that domestic firms will produce the goods that otherwise would have been produced abroad, thus employing domestic workers instead of foreign workers. The weakness of this argument is that only the protected industry will benefit in terms of employment. Since domestic consumers will pay higher prices to buy the output of the protected industry, they will have less to spend on other goods and services, which could cause employment in other industries to drop. In addition, if other countries retaliate by restricting the entry of U.S. exports, the output of U.S. firms that produce for export will fall as well. Typically, restrictions to "save domestic jobs" simply redistribute jobs by creating employment in the protected industry and reducing employment elsewhere.

TABLE 1 The Cost of Protecting U.S. Jobs from Foreign Competition

Protected Industry	Jobs Saved	Total Cost (in millions)	Annual Cost per Job Saved
Benzenoid chemicals	216	$ 297	$ 1,376,435
Luggage	226	290	1,285,078
Softwood lumber	605	632	1,044,271
Sugar	2,261	1,868	826,104
Polyethylene resins	298	242	812,928
Dairy products	2,378	1,630	685,323
Frozen concentrated orange juice	609	387	635,103
Ball bearings	146	88	603,368
Maritime services	4,411	2,522	571,668
Ceramic tiles	347	191	551,367
Machine tools	1,556	746	479,452
Ceramic articles	418	140	335,876
Women's handbags	773	204	263,535
Canned tuna	390	100	257,640
Glassware	1,477	366	247,889
Apparel and textiles	168,786	33,629	199,241
Peanuts	397	74	187,223
Rubber footwear	1,701	286	168,312
Women's nonathletic footwear	3,702	518	139,800
Costume jewelry	1,067	142	132,870
Total	191,764	$ 44,262	
Average (weighted)			$ 231,289

Source: Federal Reserve Bank of Dallas 2002 Annual Report, "The Fruits of Free Trade," by W. Michael Cox and Richard Alm, http://dallasfed.org/fed/annual/2002/ar02f.cfm.

Table 1 shows estimates of the cost of saving U.S. jobs from foreign competition. For instance, the cost of saving 226 jobs in the U.S. luggage industry is $290 million, or $1,285,078 per worker. Studies have consistently shown that the costs of protecting domestic jobs typically outweigh the benefits. So while it is possible to erect barriers to foreign competition and save domestic jobs, restricting international trade may impose large costs on an economy. Consumers end up paying much more for the goods they buy in order to subsidize the relatively inefficient domestic producer.

Table 2 shows the annual cost to the United States of import restrictions in terms of reduced GDP as estimated by an agency of the U.S. government. The total estimated amount of $1,126 million means that U.S. GDP would be over $1.1 billion higher without import restrictions. This estimate by the U.S. International Trade Commission incorporates estimates of all gains and losses from labor and capital income, tax revenue changes, and effects on consumption of changes in prices of goods and services. The amount of $1.1 billion is a very small fraction of U.S. GDP but would involve substantial changes for a few industries. For instance, in fabric mills, employment would fall by 14.5 percent and output by about 14 percent, and in the ball bearings sector, employment would fall by 5 percent and output would fall about 2.4 percent. Interestingly, the reduction of some import restrictions are

Saving domestic jobs from foreign competition may cost domestic consumers more than it benefits the protected industries.

TABLE 2 **Annual Gain in U.S. GDP if U.S. Import Restrictions Were Eliminated**

Sector	GDP Gain (millions of dollars)
Simultaneous liberalization of all significant restraints	1,126
Individual liberalization	
Textiles and apparel	483.4
Sugar	276.6
Cigarettes	139.5
Footwear and leather products	114.8
Ceramic and glass products	52.5
Cheese	49.5
Tuna	7.7
Hand and Edge Tools	7.1
Costume Jewelry	5.3
Synthetic organic dyes	−1.4
Pens and mechanical pencils	−2
Ball and roller bearings	−3.5
Residential electric lighting fixtures	−18.6

Source: *The Economic Effects of Significant U.S. Imports Restraints, Eighth Update* (U.S. International Trade Commission, Washington, D.C., 2013).

estimated to actually lower welfare, suggesting that sometimes the employment effects outweigh the price effects.

Table 1 and Table 2 demonstrate the very high cost per job saved by protection. If the costs to consumers are greater than the benefits to the protected industries, you may wonder why government provides any protection aimed at saving jobs. The answer, in a word, is politics. Protection of the U.S. textile and sugar industries means that all consumers pay a higher price for clothing and sugar. But individual consumers do not know how much of the price they pay for clothes and sugar is due to protection, and consumers rarely lobby their political representatives to eliminate protection and reduce prices. Meanwhile, there is a great deal of pressure for protection. Employers and workers in the protected industries know the benefits of protection: higher prices for their output, higher profits for owners, and higher wages for workers. As a result, there will be active lobbying for protection against foreign competition.

20-1b Creation of a "Level Playing Field"

Special interest groups sometimes claim that other nations that export successfully to the home market have unfair advantages over domestic producers. Fairness, however, is often in the eye of the beholder. People who call for creating a "level playing field" believe that the domestic government should take steps to offset the perceived advantage of the foreign firm. They often claim that foreign firms have an unfair advantage because foreign workers are willing to work for very low wages. "Fair trade, not free trade" is the cry that this claim generates. But advocates of fair trade are really claiming that production in accordance with comparative advantage is unfair. This is clearly wrong. A country with relatively low wages is typically a country with an abundance of low-skilled labor. Such a country will have a comparative advantage in products that use low-skilled labor most intensively. To create a "level playing field" by imposing restrictions that eliminate the comparative advantage of foreign firms will make domestic consumers worse off and undermine the basis for specialization and economic efficiency.

Some calls for "fair trade" are based on the notion of reciprocity. If a country imposes import restrictions on goods from a country that does not have similar restrictions, reciprocal tariffs and quotas may be called for in the latter country in order to stimulate a reduction of trade restrictions in the former country. For instance, it has been claimed that U.S. construction firms are discriminated against in Japan, because Japanese construction firms do billions of dollars' worth of business in the United States each year, but U.S. construction companies rarely are seen in Japan. Advocates of fair trade could argue that U.S. restrictions should be imposed on Japanese construction firms.

One danger of calls for fairness based on reciprocity is that calls for fair trade may be invoked in cases where, in fact, foreign restrictions on U.S. imports do not exist. For instance, suppose the U.S. auto industry wanted to restrict the entry of imported autos to help stimulate sales of domestically produced cars. One strategy might be to point out that U.S. auto sales abroad had fallen and to claim that this was due to unfair treatment of U.S. auto exports in other countries. Of course, there are many other possible reasons why foreign sales of U.S. autos might have fallen. But blaming foreign trade restrictions might win political support for restricting imports of foreign cars into the United States.

Calls for "fair trade" are typically aimed at imposing restrictions to match those imposed by other nations.

20-1c Government Revenue Creation

Tariffs on trade generate government revenue. Industrial countries, which find income taxes easy to collect, rarely justify tariffs on the basis of the revenue they generate for government spending. But many developing countries find income taxes difficult to levy and collect, whereas tariffs are easy to collect. Customs agents can be positioned at ports of entry to examine all goods that enter and leave the country. The observability of trade flows makes tariffs a popular tax in developing countries, whose revenue requirements may provide a valid justification for their existence. Table 3 shows that tariffs account for a relatively large fraction of government revenue in many developing countries, and only a small fraction in industrial countries.

Developing countries often justify tariffs as an important source of government revenue.

TABLE 3 Tariffs as a Percentage of Total Government Revenue	
Country	**Tariffs as Percentage of Government Revenue**
European Union	1.55%
United States	2.11%
Canada	.8%
Mexico	1.34%
China	4.2*%
Korea	6%
India	15.01%
Jordan	9.35%
Lesotho	61.99%

Source: World Customs Organization, "Annual Survey to Determine Percentage of National Revenue Represented by Customs Duties, 2013," http://www.wcoomd.org/~/media/WCO/Public/Global/PDF/Topics/Nomenclature/Overview/Surveys/Duties%20Revenue/Duty%20Survey%20Dec2011_E.ashx?db=web

20-1d National Defense

Industries that are truly critical to the national defense should be protected from foreign competition if that is the only way to ensure their existence.

It has long been argued that industries that are crucial to the national defense, such as shipbuilding, should be protected from foreign competition. Even though the United States does not have a comparative advantage in shipbuilding, the argument goes, a domestic shipbuilding industry is necessary, since foreign-made ships may not be available during war. This is a valid argument as long as the protected industry is genuinely critical to the national defense. In some industries, such as copper or other basic metals, it might make more sense to import the crucial products during peacetime and store them for use in the event of war; these products do not require domestic production in order to be useful. Care must be taken to ensure that the national defense argument is not used to protect industries other than those that are truly crucial to the nation's defense.

20-1e Infant Industries

Countries sometimes justify protecting new industries that need time to become competitive with the rest of the world.

Nations are often inclined to protect new industries on the basis that the protection will give those industries adequate time to develop. New industries need time to establish themselves and to become efficient enough that their costs are no higher than those of their foreign rivals. An alternative to protecting young and/or critical domestic industries with tariffs and quotas is to subsidize them. Subsidies allow such firms to charge lower prices and to compete with more-efficient foreign producers, while permitting consumers to pay the world price rather than the higher prices associated with tariffs or quotas on foreign goods.

Protecting an infant industry from foreign competition may make sense, but only until the industry matures. Once the industry achieves sufficient size, protection should be withdrawn, and the industry should be made to compete with its foreign counterparts. Unfortunately, such protection is rarely withdrawn, because the larger and more successful the industry becomes, the more political power it wields. In fact, if an infant industry truly has a good chance to become competitive and produce profitably once it is well established, it is not at all clear that government should even offer protection to reduce short-run losses. New firms typically incur losses, but they are only temporary if the firm is successful.

20-1f Strategic Trade Policy

strategic trade policy
The use of trade restrictions or subsidies to allow domestic firms with decreasing costs to gain a greater share of the world market.

increasing-returns-to-scale industry
An industry in which the costs of producing a unit of output fall as more output is produced.

Government can use trade policy as a strategy to stimulate production by a domestic industry that is capable of achieving increasing returns to scale.

There is another view of international trade that regards the description of comparative advantage presented in the previous chapter as misleading. According to this outlook, called **strategic trade policy**, international trade largely involves firms that pursue economies of scale—that is, firms that achieve lower costs per unit of production the more they produce. In contrast to the constant opportunity costs illustrated in the example of wheat and cloth in the chapter "World Trade Equilibrium," opportunity costs in some industries may fall with the level of output. Such **increasing-returns-to-scale industries** will tend to concentrate production in the hands of a few very large firms, rather than many competitive firms. Proponents of strategic trade policy contend that government can use tariffs or subsidies to give domestic firms with decreasing costs an advantage over their foreign rivals.

A monopoly exists when there is only one producer in an industry and no close substitutes for the product exist. If the average costs of production decline with increases in output, then the larger a firm is, the lower its per unit costs will be. One large producer will be more efficient than many small ones. A simple example of a natural-monopoly industry will indicate how strategic trade policy can make a country better off. Suppose that the production of buses is an industry characterized by increasing returns to scale and that there are only two firms capable of producing buses: Volkswagen in Germany and Ford in the United States. If both firms produce buses, their costs will be so high that both will experience losses. If only one of the two produces buses, however, it will be able to sell buses both at home and abroad, creating a level of output that allows the firm to earn a profit.

Assume further that a monopoly producer will earn $100 million and that if both firms produce, they will each lose $5 million. Obviously, a firm that does not produce earns nothing. Which firm will produce? Because of the decreasing-cost nature of the industry, the firm that is the first to produce will realize lower costs and will be able to prevent the other firm from entering the market. But strategic trade policy can alter the market in favor of the domestic firm.

Suppose Volkswagen is the world's only producer of buses. Ford does not produce them. The U.S. government could offer Ford an $8 million subsidy to produce buses. Ford would then enter the bus market, since the $8 million subsidy would more than offset the $5 million loss it would suffer by entering the market. Volkswagen would sustain losses of $5 million once Ford entered. Ultimately, Volkswagen would stop producing buses to avoid the loss, and Ford would have the entire market and earn $100 million plus the subsidy.

Strategic trade policy is aimed at offsetting the increasing-returns-to-scale advantage enjoyed by foreign producers and at stimulating production in domestic industries that are capable of realizing decreasing costs. One practical problem for government is the need to understand the technology of different industries and to forecast accurately the subsidy needed to induce domestic firms to produce new products. A second problem is the likelihood of retaliation by the foreign government. If the U.S. government subsidizes Ford in its attack on the bus market, the German government is likely to subsidize Volkswagen rather than lose the entire bus market to a U.S. producer. As a result, taxpayers in both nations will be subsidizing two firms, each producing too few buses to earn a profit.

20-2 Tools of Commercial Policy

Commercial policy makes use of several tools, including tariffs, quotas, subsidies, and non-tariff barriers like health and safety regulations that restrict the entry of foreign products. Since 1945, barriers to trade have been reduced. Much of the progress toward free trade may be linked to the *General Agreement on Tariffs and Trade*, or *GATT*, which began in 1947. In 1995, the *World Trade Organization (WTO)* was formed to incorporate the agreements under GATT into a formal permanent international organization to oversee world trade. The WTO has three objectives: to help global trade flow as freely as possible, to achieve reductions in trade restrictions gradually through negotiation, and to provide an impartial means of settling disputes. Nevertheless, restrictions on trade still exist, and this section will review the most commonly used restrictions.

2. How do countries restrict the entry of foreign goods and promote the export of domestic goods?

GLOBAL BUSINESS INSIGHT

Smoot-Hawley Tariff

Many economists believe that the Great Depression of the 1930s was at least partly due to the Smoot-Hawley Tariff Act, signed into law by President Herbert Hoover in 1930. Hoover had promised that, if elected, he would increase tariffs on agricultural products to raise U.S. farm income. Congress began work on the tariff increases in 1928. Congressman Willis Hawley and Senator Reed Smoot conducted the hearings.

In testimony before Congress, manufacturers and other special interest groups also sought protection from foreign competition. The resulting bill increased tariffs on over 12,000 products. Tariffs reached their highest levels ever, about 60 percent of average import values. Only twice before in U.S. history had tariffs approached the levels of the Smoot-Hawley era.

Before President Hoover signed the bill, 38 foreign governments made formal protests, warning that they would retaliate with high tariffs on U.S. products. A petition signed by 1,028 economists warned of the harmful effects of the bill. Nevertheless, Hoover signed the bill into law.

World trade collapsed as other countries raised their tariffs in response. Between 1930 and 1931, U.S. imports fell 29 percent, but U.S. exports fell 33 percent. By 1933, world trade was about one-third of its 1929 level. As the level of trade fell, so did income and prices. In 1934, in an effort to correct the mistakes of Smoot-Hawley, Congress passed the Reciprocal Trade Agreements Act, which allowed the president to lower U.S. tariffs in return for reductions in foreign tariffs on U.S. goods. This act ushered in the modern era of relatively low tariffs. In the United States today, tariffs are about 5 percent of the average value of imports.

Many economists believe that the collapse of world trade and the Depression were linked by a decrease in real income caused by abandoning production based on comparative advantage. Few economists argue that the Great Depression was caused solely by the Smoot-Hawley tariff, but the experience serves as a lesson to those who support higher tariffs to protect domestic producers.

20-2a Tariffs

tariff
A tax on imports or exports.

A **tariff** is a tax on imports or exports. Every country imposes tariffs on at least some imports. Some countries also impose tariffs on selected exports as a means of raising government revenue. Brazil, for instance, taxes coffee exports. The United States does not employ export tariffs, which are forbidden by the U.S. Constitution.

Tariffs are frequently imposed in order to protect domestic producers from foreign competition. The dangers of imposing tariffs are well illustrated in the Global Business Insight "Smoot-Hawley Tariff." The effect of a tariff is illustrated in Figure 1, which shows the domestic market for oranges. Without international trade, the domestic equilibrium price, P_d, and the quantity demanded, Q_d, are determined by the intersection of the domestic demand and supply curves. If the world price of oranges, P_w, is lower than the domestic equilibrium price, this country will import oranges. The quantity imported will be the difference between the quantity Q_1 produced domestically at a price of P_w and the quantity Q_2 demanded domestically at the world price of oranges.

When the world price of the traded good is lower than the domestic equilibrium price without international trade, free trade causes domestic production to fall and domestic consumption to rise. The domestic shortage at the world price is met by imports. Domestic consumers are better off, since they can buy more at a lower price. But domestic producers are worse off, since they now sell fewer oranges and receive a lower price.

Suppose a tariff of T (the dollar value of the tariff) is imposed on orange imports. The price paid by consumers is now $P_w + T$, rather than P_w. At this higher price, domestic producers will produce Q_3 and domestic consumers will purchase Q_4. The tariff has the effect of increasing domestic production and reducing domestic consumption, relative to the free trade equilibrium. Imports fall accordingly, from $Q_2 - Q_1$ to $Q_4 - Q_3$.

FIGURE 1 The Effects of a Tariff

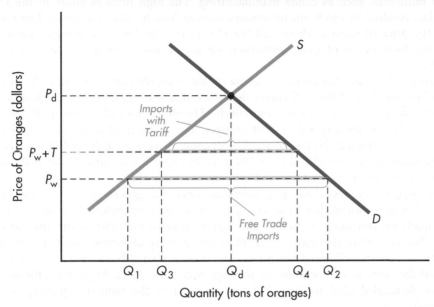

The domestic equilibrium price and quantity with no trade are P_d and Q_d, respectively. The world price is P_w. With free trade, therefore, imports will equal $Q_2 - Q_1$. A tariff added to the world price reduces imports to $Q_4 - Q_3$.

Domestic producers are better off, since the tariff has increased their sales of oranges and raised the price they receive. Domestic consumers pay higher prices for fewer oranges than they would with free trade, but they are still better off than they would be without trade. If the tariff had raised the price paid by consumers to P_d, there would be no trade, and the domestic equilibrium quantity, Q_d, would prevail.

The government earns revenue from imports of oranges. If each ton of oranges generates tariff revenue of T, the total tariff revenue to the government is found by multiplying the tariff by the quantity of oranges imported. In Figure 1, this amount is $T \times (Q_4 - Q_3)$. As the tariff changes, so do the quantity of imports and the government revenue.

20-2b Quotas

Quotas are limits on the quantity or value of goods imported and exported. A **quantity quota** restricts the physical amount of a good. For instance, for 2009, the United States allowed only 1.1 million tons of sugar to be imported. Even though the United States is not a competitive sugar producer compared to other nations like the Dominican Republic or Cuba, the quota allows U.S. firms to produce about 80 percent of the sugar consumed in the United States. A **value quota** restricts the monetary value of a good that may be traded. Instead of a physical quota on sugar, the United States could have limited the dollar value of sugar imports.

Quotas are used to protect domestic producers from foreign competition. By restricting the amount of a good that may be imported, they increase the price of that good and allow domestic producers to sell more at a higher price than they would with free trade. For example, one effect of the U.S. sugar quota is a higher sugar price for U.S. consumers. In the fourth quarter of 2010, the world price of sugar was $0.2952 per pound, but the U.S. price was about 32 percent higher at $0.3883 per pound. Beyond the obvious effect on

quantity quota
A limit on the amount of a good that may be imported.

value quota
A limit on the monetary value of a good that may be imported.

sugar production and consumption in the United States, there are spillover effects in related industries, such as candy manufacturing. The high price of sugar in the United States has resulted in candy manufacturers moving jobs to other countries, like Canada, where the price of sugar is about half the U.S. price. The lesson is that one must think about the total effects of trade restrictions on the economy when evaluating costs and benefits.

Figure 2 illustrates the effect of a quota on the domestic orange market. The domestic equilibrium supply and demand curves determine that the equilibrium price and quantity without trade are P_d and 250 tons, respectively. The world price of oranges is P_w. Since P_w lies below P_d, this country will import oranges. The quantity of imports is equal to the amount of the domestic shortage at P_w. The quantity demanded at P_w is 400 tons, and the quantity supplied domestically at P_w is 100 tons, so imports will equal 300 tons of oranges. With free trade, domestic producers sell 100 tons at a price of P_w.

But suppose domestic orange growers convince the government to restrict orange imports. The government then imposes a quota of 100 tons on imported oranges. The effect of the quota on consumers is to shift the supply curve to the right by the amount of the quota, 100 tons. Since the quota is less than the quantity of imports with free trade, the quantity of imports will equal the quota. The domestic equilibrium price with the quota occurs at the point where the domestic shortage equals the quota. At price P_q, the domestic quantity demanded (300 tons) is 100 tons more than the domestic quantity supplied (200 tons).

Quotas benefit domestic producers in the same way that tariffs do. Domestic producers receive a higher price (P_q instead of P_w) for a greater quantity (200 instead of 100) than they do under free trade. The effect on domestic consumers is also similar to that of a tariff: They pay a higher price for a smaller quantity than they would with free trade.

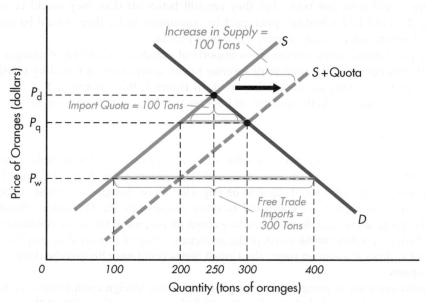

FIGURE 2   The Effects of a Quota

The domestic equilibrium price with no international trade is P_d. At this price, 250 tons of oranges would be produced and consumed at home. With free trade, the price is P_w, and 300 tons will be imported. An import quota of 100 tons will cause the price to be P_q, where the domestic shortage equals the 100 tons allowed by the quota.

A tariff generates government tax revenue; a quota does not (unless the government auctions off the right to import under the quota). Furthermore, a tariff raises the price of the product only in the domestic market. Foreign producers receive the world price, P_w. With a quota, both domestic and foreign producers receive the higher price, P_q, for the goods sold in the domestic market. So foreign producers are hurt by the reduction in the quantity of imports permitted, but they receive a higher price for the amount that they do sell.

20-2c Other Barriers to Trade

Tariffs and quotas are not the only barriers to the free flow of goods across international borders. There are three additional sources of restrictions on free trade: subsidies, government procurement, and health and safety standards. Though these practices are often entered into for reasons other than protection from foreign competition, a careful analysis reveals their import-reducing effect.

Before discussing these three types of barriers, let us note the cultural or institutional barriers to trade that also exist in many countries. Such barriers may exist independently of any conscious government policy. For instance, Japan has frequently been criticized by U.S. officials for informal business practices that discriminate against foreigners. Under the Japanese distribution system, goods typically pass through several layers of middlemen before appearing in a retail store. A foreign firm faces the difficult task of gaining entry to this system to supply goods to the retailer. Furthermore, a foreigner cannot easily open a retail store. Japanese law requires a new retail firm to receive permission from other retailers in the area in order to open a business. A firm that lacks contacts and knowledge of the system cannot penetrate the Japanese market.

The economic stimulus bill that the U.S. Congress passed in February 2009 included a "buy American" provision requiring that any steel or manufactured goods bought with federal government funds must be made in the United States. Many U.S. trade partners expressed concerns over the protectionist aspects of this policy. Such inward-looking policies in response to the financial crisis were not confined just to the United States. The level of international trade fell during the crisis, and there was a fear that if many countries tried to stimulate their domestic economies at the expense of other nations, trade would not recover once the crisis passed.

20-2c-1 Export Subsidies

Export subsidies are payments by a government to an exporter. These subsidies are paid in order to stimulate exports by allowing the exporter to charge a lower price. The amount of a subsidy is determined by the international price of a product relative to the domestic price in the absence of trade. Domestic consumers are harmed by subsidies in that their taxes finance the subsidies. Also, since the subsidy diverts resources from the domestic market toward export production, the increase in the supply of export goods could be associated with a decrease in the supply of domestic goods, causing domestic prices to rise.

export subsidies
Payments made by a government to domestic firms to encourage exports.

Subsidies may take forms other than direct cash payments. These include tax reductions, low-interest loans, low-cost insurance, government-sponsored research funding, and other devices. The U.S. government subsidizes export activity through the U.S. Export-Import Bank, which provides loans and insurance to help U.S. exporters sell their goods to foreign buyers. Subsidies are more common in Europe than in Japan or the United States.

20-2c-2 Government Procurement

Governments are often required by law to buy only from local producers. In the United States, a "buy American" act passed in 1933 required U.S. government agencies to buy U.S. goods and services unless the domestic price was more than 12 percent above the foreign price. This kind of policy allows domestic firms to charge the government a higher price for their products than they charge consumers; the taxpayers bear the burden. The United States is by no means alone in the use of such policies. Many other nations also use such policies to create larger markets for domestic goods. The World Trade Organization has a standing committee working to reduce discrimination against foreign producers and to open government procurement practices to global competition.

20-2c-3 Health and Safety Standards

Government serves as a guardian of the public health and welfare by requiring that products offered to the public be safe and fulfill the use for which they are intended. Government standards for products sold in the domestic marketplace can have the effect (intentional or not) of protecting domestic producers from foreign competition. These effects should be considered in evaluating the full impact of such standards.

As mentioned in the Preview, the government of Japan once threatened to prohibit foreign-made snow skis from entering the country for reasons of safety. Only Japanese-made skis were determined to be suitable for Japanese snow. The government of Japan certifies auto parts that are safe for use by repair shops. U.S.-manufactured parts are not certified for use, so U.S. parts manufacturers are excluded from the Japanese market. Several western European nations once announced that U.S. beef would not be allowed into Europe because the U.S. government had approved the feeding of hormones to U.S. beef cattle. In the late 1960s, France required tractors sold there to have a maximum speed of 17 miles per hour; in Germany, the permissible speed was 13 miles per hour, and in the Netherlands, it was 10 miles per hour. Tractors produced in one country had to be modified to meet the requirements of the other countries. Such modifications raise the prices of goods and discourage international trade.

Product standards may not eliminate foreign competition, but standards different from those of the rest of the world do provide an element of protection to domestic firms.

RECAP

1. The World Trade Organization works to achieve reductions in trade barriers.
2. A tariff is a tax on imports or exports. Tariffs protect domestic firms by raising the prices of foreign goods.
3. Quotas are government-imposed limits on the quantity or value of an imported good. Quotas protect domestic firms by restricting the entry of foreign products to a level less than the quantity demanded.
4. Subsidies are payments by the government to domestic producers. Subsidies lower the price of domestic goods to foreign buyers.
5. Governments are often required by law to buy only domestic products.
6. Health and safety standards can also be used to protect domestic firms.

---

3. What sorts of agreements do countries enter into to reduce barriers to international trade?

20-3 Preferential Trade Agreements

In an effort to stimulate international trade, groups of countries sometimes enter into agreements to abolish most barriers to trade among themselves. Such arrangements between countries are known as preferential trading agreements. The European Union and the North American Free Trade Agreement (NAFTA) are examples of preferential trading agreements.

20-3a Free Trade Areas and Customs Unions

Two common forms of preferential trade agreements are **free trade areas** (FTAs) and **customs unions** (CUs). These two approaches differ with regard to the treatment of countries outside the agreement. In an FTA, member countries eliminate trade barriers among themselves, but each member country chooses its own trade policies toward nonmember countries. Members of a CU agree to both eliminate trade barriers among themselves and maintain common trade barriers against nonmembers.

The best-known CU is the European Union (EU), formerly known as the European Community and still earlier as the European Economic Community (EEC), created in 1957 by France, West Germany, Italy, Belgium, the Netherlands, and Luxembourg. The United Kingdom, Ireland, and Denmark joined in 1973, followed by Greece in 1981 and Spain and Portugal in 1986. In 1992 the EEC was replaced by the EU with an agreement to create a single market for goods and services in western Europe. On May 1, 2004, 10 new members were admitted to the EU: Cyprus, Czech Republic, Estonia, Hungary, Latvia, Lithuania, Malta, Poland, Slovakia, and Slovenia. In 2007, Bulgaria and Romania were admitted to the EU. Turkey is negotiating to be included in future enlargements of the EU. In addition to free trade in goods, European financial markets and institutions will eventually be able to operate across national boundaries. For instance, a bank in any EU country will be permitted to operate in any or all other EU countries.

In 1989, the United States and Canada negotiated a free trade area. The United States, Canada, and Mexico negotiated a free trade area in 1992 that became effective on January 1, 1994. The North American Free Trade Agreement (NAFTA) lowered tariffs on 8,000 different items and opened each nation's financial market to competition from institutions in the other two nations. NAFTA does not eliminate all barriers to trade among the three nations, but it is a significant step in that direction.

free trade area
An organization of nations whose members have no trade barriers among themselves but are free to fashion their own trade policies toward nonmembers.

customs union
An organization of nations whose members have no trade barriers among themselves but impose common trade barriers on nonmembers.

The North American Free Trade Agreement stimulates trade among Mexico, Canada, and the United States. The act results in more container ships from Mexico unloading their cargo at U.S. docks. Similarly, freight from Canada and the United States will increase in volume at Mexican ports.

20-3b Trade Creation and Diversion

Free trade agreements provide for free trade among a group of countries, not worldwide. As a result, a customs union or free trade area may make a nation better off or worse off compared to the free trade equilibrium.

Figure 3 illustrates the effect of a free trade area. With no international trade, the U.S. supply and demand curves for oranges would result in an equilibrium price of $500 per ton and an equilibrium quantity of 425 tons. Suppose there are two other orange-producing countries, Israel and Brazil. Israel, the low-cost producer of oranges, is willing to sell all the oranges the United States can buy for $150 per ton, as represented by the horizontal supply curve SI. Brazil will supply oranges for a price of $200 per ton, as represented by the horizontal supply curve S_B.

With free trade, the United States would import oranges from Israel. The quantity demanded at $150 is 750 tons, and the domestic quantity supplied at this price is 100 tons. The shortage of 650 tons is met by imports from Israel.

Now suppose a 100 percent tariff is imposed on orange imports. The price that domestic consumers pay for foreign oranges is twice as high as before. For oranges from Israel, the new price is $300, twice the old price of $150. The new supply curve for Israel is represented as S_I + Tariff. Oranges from Brazil now sell for $400, twice the old price of $200; the new supply curve for Brazil is shown as S_B + Tariff. After the 100 percent tariff is imposed, oranges are still imported from Israel. But at the new price of $300, the domestic quantity demanded is 600 tons, and the domestic quantity supplied is 250 tons. Thus, only 350 tons will be imported. The tariff reduces the volume of trade relative to the free trade equilibrium, at which 650 tons were imported.

Now suppose that the United States negotiates a free trade agreement with Brazil, eliminating tariffs on imports from Brazil. Israel is not a member of the free trade agreement, so

---

FIGURE 3   Trade Creation and Trade Diversion with a Free Trade Area

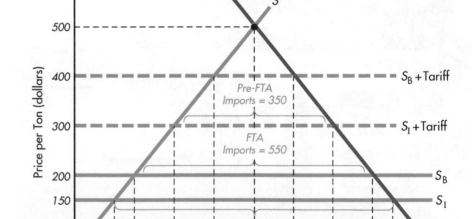

With no trade, the domestic equilibrium price is $500, and the equilibrium quantity is 425 tons. With free trade, the price is $150, and 650 tons would be imported, as indicated by the supply curve for Israel, S_I. A 100 percent tariff on imports would result in imports of 350 tons from Israel, according to the supply curve S_I + Tariff. A free trade agreement that eliminates tariffs on Brazilian oranges only would result in a new equilibrium price of $200 and imports of 550 tons from Brazil, according to supply curve S_B.

imports from Israel are still covered by the 100 percent tariff. The relevant supply curve for Brazil is now S_B, so oranges may be imported from Brazil for $200, a lower price than Israel's price including the tariff. At a price of $200, the domestic quantity demanded is 700 tons and the domestic quantity supplied is 150 tons; 550 tons will be imported.

The effects of the free trade agreement are twofold. First, trade is diverted away from the lowest-cost producer, Israel, to the FTA partner, Brazil. This **trade-diversion** effect of an FTA reduces worldwide economic efficiency, since production is diverted from the country with the comparative advantage. Oranges are not being produced as efficiently as possible. The other effect of the FTA is that the quantity of imports increases relative to the effect of a tariff applicable to all imports. Imports rise from 350 tons (the quantity imported from Israel with the tariff) to 550 tons. The FTA thus has a **trade creation** effect as a result of the lower price that is available after the tariff reduction. Trade creation is a beneficial aspect of the FTA: The expansion of international trade allows this country to realize greater benefits from trade than would be possible without trade.

Countries form preferential trade agreements because they believe that FTAs will make each member country better off. The member countries view the trade creation effects of such agreements as benefiting their exporters by increasing exports to other member countries and as benefiting consumers by making a wider variety of goods available at a lower price. From the point of view of the world as a whole, preferential trade agreements are more desirable the more they stimulate trade creation to allow the benefits of trade to be realized and the less they emphasize trade diversion, so that production occurs on the basis of comparative advantage. This principle suggests that the most successful FTAs or CUs are those that increase trade volume but do not change the patterns of trade in terms of who specializes and exports each good. In the case of Figure 3, a more successful FTA would reduce tariffs on Israeli as well as Brazilian oranges, so that oranges would be imported from the lowest-cost producer, Israel.

trade diversion
An effect of a preferential trade agreement that reduces economic efficiency by shifting production to a higher-cost producer.

trade creation
An effect of a preferential trade agreement that allows a country to obtain goods at a lower cost than is available at home.

RECAP

1. Countries form preferential trade agreements in order to stimulate trade among themselves.

2. The most common forms of preferential trade agreement are free trade areas (FTAs) and customs unions (CUs).

3. Preferential trade agreements have a harmful trade-diversion effect when they cause production to shift from the nation with a comparative advantage to a higher-cost producer.

4. Preferential trade agreements have a beneficial trade-creation effect when they reduce prices for traded goods and stimulate the volume of international trade.

SUMMARY

1. Why do countries restrict international trade?

- Commercial policy is government policy that influences the direction and volume of international trade. *Preview*

- Protecting domestic producers from foreign competition usually imposes costs on domestic consumers. *§20-1*

- Rationales for commercial policy include saving domestic jobs, creating a fair-trade relationship with other countries, raising tariff revenue, ensuring a domestic supply of key defense goods, allowing new industries a chance to become internationally competitive, and giving domestic industries with increasing returns to scale an advantage over foreign competitors. *§20-1a—20-1f*

2. How do countries restrict the entry of foreign goods and promote the export of domestic goods?

- Tariffs protect domestic industry by increasing the price of foreign goods. *§20-2a*

- Quotas protect domestic industry by limiting the quantity of foreign goods allowed into the country. *§20-2b*

- Subsidies allow relatively inefficient domestic producers to compete with foreign firms. *§20-2c1*

- Government procurement practices and health and safety regulations can protect domestic industry from foreign competition. *§20-2c2, 20-2c3*

3. What sorts of agreements do countries enter into to reduce barriers to international trade?

- Free trade areas and customs unions are two types of preferential trade agreements that reduce trade restrictions among member countries. *§20-3a*

- Preferential trade agreements have harmful trade-diversion effects and beneficial trade-creation effects. *§20-3b*

KEY TERMS

commercial policy, 434
customs union, 445
export subsidies, 443
free trade area, 445

increasing-returns-to-scale industries, 438
quantity quota, 441
strategic trade policy, 438

tariff, 440
trade creation, 447
trade diversion, 447
value quota, 441

EXERCISES

1. What are the potential benefits and costs of a commercial policy designed to pursue each of the following goals?
   a. Save domestic jobs
   b. Create a level playing field
   c. Increase government revenue
   d. Provide a strong national defense
   e. Protect an infant industry
   f. Stimulate exports of an industry with increasing returns to scale

2. For each of the goals listed in exercise 1, discuss what the appropriate commercial policy is likely to be (in terms of tariffs, quotas, subsidies, etc.).

3. Tariffs and quotas both raise the price of foreign goods to domestic consumers. What is the difference between the effects of a tariff and the effects of a quota on the following?
   a. The domestic government
   b. Foreign producers
   c. Domestic producers

4. Would trade-diversion and trade-creation effects occur if the whole world became a free trade area? Explain.

5. What is the difference between a customs union and a free trade area?

6. Draw a graph of the U.S. automobile market in which the domestic equilibrium price without trade is P_d and the equilibrium quantity is Q_d. Use this graph to illustrate and explain the effects of a tariff if the United States were an auto importer with free trade. Then use the graph to illustrate and explain the effects of a quota.

7. If commercial policy can benefit U.S. industry, why would any U.S. resident oppose such policies? Find two newspaper articles illustrating opposition to commercial policies and summarize their arguments.

8. Suppose you were asked to assess U.S. commercial policy to determine whether the benefits of protection for U.S. industries are worth the costs. Do Table 1 and Table 2 provide all the information you need? If not, what else would you want to know?

9. How would the effects of international trade on the domestic orange market change if the world price of oranges were above the domestic equilibrium price? Draw a graph to help explain your answer.

10. Suppose the world price of kiwi fruit is $25 per case and the U.S. equilibrium price with no international trade is $40 per case. If the U.S. government had

previously banned the import of kiwi fruit but then imposed a tariff of $5 per case and allowed kiwi imports, what would happen to the equilibrium price and quantity of kiwi fruit consumed in the United States?

11. Think of an industry in your country (if you currently have a job, use that industry). What kind of nontariff barrier could you design that would keep out foreign competitors to the domestic industry? This should be something like a health or safety standard or some other criterion that a government could use as an excuse to protect the domestic industry from foreign competition.

ECONOMICALLY SPEAKING

USDA ANNOUNCES SUGAR TARIFF RATE QUOTAS FOR FISCAL YEAR 2014

United States Department of Agriculture News Release FAS-PR-0105-13

WASHINGTON, Sept. 12, 2013 – The U.S. Department of Agriculture (USDA) today announced the Fiscal Year 2014 raw and refined sugar tariff-rate quotas.

USDA is establishing the FY 2014 TRQ for raw cane sugar at 1,231,497 short tons raw value (STRV) (1,117,195 metric tons raw value, MTRV*), the minimum to which the United States is committed under the World Trade Organization (WTO) Uruguay Round Agreement on Agriculture. Pursuant to Additional U.S. Note 5 to Chapter 17 of the U.S. Harmonized Tariff Schedule (HTS) and Section 359k of the Agricultural Adjustment Act of 1938, as amended, USDA published this decision in the *Federal Register*.

Raw cane sugar under this TRQ must be accompanied by a certificate of quota eligibility and may enter the United States until Sept. 30, 2014. The Office of the U.S. Trade Representative (USTR) will allocate this TRQ among supplying countries and customs areas.

USDA is also establishing the FY 2014 refined sugar TRQ at 134,482 STRV (122,000 MTRV). Of this quantity, 112,057 STRV (101,656 MTRV) is reserved for the importation of specialty sugars as defined by the USTR. The total refined sugar TRQ includes the 24,251 STRV (22,000 MTRV) minimum to which the United States is committed under Uruguay Round Agreement on Agriculture, of which 1,825 STRV (1,656 MTRV) is reserved for specialty sugar.

Because the specialty sugar TRQ is first-come, first-served, tranches are needed to allow for orderly marketing throughout the year. The FY 2014 specialty sugar TRQ will be opened in five tranches. The first tranche, totaling 1,825 STRV (1,656 MTRV), will open Oct. 10, 2013. All specialty sugars are eligible for entry under this tranche. The second tranche will open on Oct. 24, 2013 and be equal to 40,786 STRV (37,000 MTRV). The remaining tranches will each be equal to 23,149 STRV (21,000 MTRV), with the third opening on Jan. 9, 2014; the fourth, on April 10, 2014; and the fifth, on July 10, 2014. The second, third, fourth, and fifth tranches will be reserved for organic sugar and other specialty sugars not currently produced commercially in the United States or reasonably available from domestic sources.

The USTR will allocate the refined TRQ, other than the amount reserved for specialty sugar, among supplying countries and customs areas.

---

*Conversion factor: 1 metric ton = 1.10231125 short tons.

Source: Article online at http://www.usda.gov/wps/portal/usda/usdahome?contentid=2011/06/0265.xml&contentidonly=true

COMMENTARY

This article illustrates some important differences between free and restricted trade. In certain markets, such as the sugar market, domestic firms may seek protection, in the form of quotas or tariffs, from international competition. This is not a unique situation; it is a familiar story worldwide as firms that are threatened with foreign competition seek government protection from that competition. The protectionist measure of imposing quotas or tariffs on imports saves jobs in the domestic import-competing industries, but at a great cost to consumers and, sometimes, to other producers.

Recall that in our supply and demand models, the market clears at a price for which quantity supplied is equal to quantity demanded..In this case of U.S. sugar quotas, the sentence "The Office of the U.S. Trade Representative (USTR) will allocate this TRQ among supplying countries and customs areas" indicates a deviation from market clearing of a free market. This illustrates how trade restrictions complicate the market-equilibrating mechanisms and introduce a need for outside planning that is unnecessary in a free market. Even trade restrictions that are imposed for the sake of "fairness," like the statement that the quota amounts will be allocated across supplier countries, introduce distortions.

The effect of reducing domestic competition with quotas can be understood using supply and demand analysis. Let us analyze the case of quotas on textile imports into the United States. In the diagram, S_1 is the domestic supply of textiles, S_2 is the sum of the domestic supply and the foreign supply allowed in by the quotas, and D is the demand for textiles. Under the quota system, the price of textiles in the United States is represented by P_q, and the quantity of textiles consumed is Q_q. If the quotas were removed, the price of textiles in the United States would equal the world price of P_w, and this lower price would be associated with an increase in the consumption of textiles to Q_w. The quota represents a cost to society in terms of both a loss of consumer welfare and a loss from the inefficient use of resources in an industry in which this country has no comparative advantage, just as Maine has no comparative advantage in the production of pineapples.

Given the costs to society of these quotas, why is there such strong support for them in Congress? An important political aspect of protectionist policies is that their benefits are concentrated among a relatively small number of people—in the case of the article, sugar cane growers—while their costs are diffused and spread across all consumers. Each individual import-competing producer faces very large losses from free trade, whereas the cost of a protectionist policy for each consumer is less dramatic. It is also easier to organize a relatively small number of manufacturers than to mobilize a vast population of consumers. These factors explain the strong lobby for the protection of industries like sugar or textiles and the absence of a legislative lobby that operates specifically in the interest of sugar or textile consumers.

Industrial arguments for trade protection should be seen for what they are: an attempt by an industry to increase its profits at the expense of the general public.

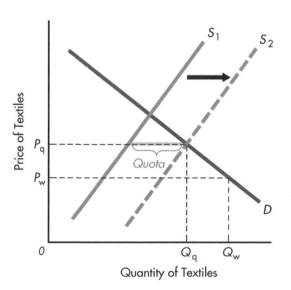

CHAPTER 21

Exchange Rates and Financial Links between Countries

FUNDAMENTAL QUESTIONS

1. How does a commodity standard fix exchange rates between countries?

2. What kinds of exchange-rate arrangements exist today?

3. How is equilibrium determined in the foreign exchange market?

4. How do fixed and floating exchange rates differ in their adjustment to shifts in supply and demand for currencies?

5. What are the advantages and disadvantages of fixed and floating exchange rates?

6. How does a change in the exchange rate affect the prices of goods traded between countries?

7. Why don't similar goods sell for the same price all over the world?

8. How do we find the domestic currency return on a foreign bond?

9. What is the relationship between domestic and foreign interest rates and changes in the exchange rate?

Preview

An exchange rate is the link between two nations' monies. The value of a U.S. dollar in terms of Japanese yen or European euros determines how many dollars a U.S. resident will need in order to buy goods that are priced in yen or euros. Thus, changes in exchange rates can have far-reaching implications. Exchange rates may be determined in free markets, through government intervention in the foreign exchange market, or even by law.

In April 2011, one U.S. dollar was worth about 84 Japanese yen. By April 2014, the dollar was worth 104 yen, a 23 percent appreciation of the dollar against the yen. Why does the dollar fluctuate in value relative to the yen? What are the effects of such

453

changes? Should governments permit exchange rates to change? What can governments do to discourage changes in exchange rates? These are all important questions, and this chapter will help answer them.

The chapter begins with a review of the history of exchange-rate systems. It follows with an overview of exchange-rate practices in the world today, and how exchange rates provide a link between prices and interest rates across countries. Along the way, it introduces terminology and institutions that play a major role in the evolution of exchange rates.

21-1 Past and Current Exchange-Rate Arrangements

21-1a The Gold Standard

1. How does a commodity standard fix exchange rates between countries?

gold standard

A system whereby national currencies are fixed in terms of their value in gold, thus creating fixed exchange rates between currencies.

A commodity money standard exists when exchange rates are fixed based on the values of different currencies in terms of some commodity.

In ancient times, government-produced monies were made of precious metals such as gold. Later, when governments began to issue paper money, that money was usually convertible into a fixed amount of gold. Ensuring the convertibility of paper money into gold was a way to maintain confidence in the currency's value, both at home and abroad. If a unit of currency was worth a fixed amount of gold, its value could be stated in terms of its gold value. The countries that maintained a constant gold value for their currencies were said to be on a **gold standard**.

Some countries had backed their currencies with gold long before 1880; however, the practice became widespread around 1880, so economists typically date the beginning of the gold standard to this period. From roughly 1880 to 1914, currencies had fixed values in terms of gold. For instance, the U.S. dollar's value was fixed at $20.67 per ounce of gold. Any other currency that was fixed in terms of gold also had a fixed exchange rate against the dollar. A simple example will illustrate how this works.

Suppose the price of an ounce of gold is $20 in the United States and £4 in the United Kingdom. The pound is worth five times the value of a dollar, since it takes five times as many dollars as pounds to buy one ounce of gold. Because one pound buys five times as much gold as one dollar, the exchange rate is £1 = $5. Since currency values are linked by gold values, as the supply of gold fluctuates, there will be pressure to alter the prices of goods and services. The gold standard fixes only the current price of gold. As the stock of gold increases, everything else held constant, the gold and currency prices of goods and services will tend to rise (as would occur when the money supply increases).

A gold standard is only one possible *commodity money standard*. Any other highly valued commodity (silver, for instance) could serve as a standard linking monies in a fixed-exchange-rate system.

The gold standard ended with the outbreak of World War I. The war was partially funded by increases in the money supplies of the hostile nations. A gold standard would not permit such a rapid increase in the money supply unless the stock of gold increased dramatically, which it did not. As money supplies grew faster than gold supplies, the link between money and gold had to be broken. During the war years and the Great Depression of the 1930s, and on through World War II, there was no organized system for setting exchange rates. Foreign trade and investment shrank as a result of the war, obviating the need for a well-functioning method of determining exchange rates.

21-1b The Bretton Woods System

At the end of World War II, there was widespread political support for an exchange rate system linking all monies in much the same way as the gold standard had done. It was believed that a system of fixed exchange rates would promote the growth of world trade. In 1944, delegates from 44 nations met in Bretton Woods, New Hampshire, to discuss the creation of such a system. The agreement reached at this conference has had a profound impact on the world.

The exchange-rate arrangement that emerged from the Bretton Woods conference is often called a **gold exchange standard**. Each country was to fix the value of its currency in terms of gold, just as it had under the gold standard. The U.S. dollar price of gold, for instance, was $35 an ounce. However, there were fundamental differences between this system and the old gold standard. The U.S. dollar, rather than gold, served as the focal point of the system. Instead of buying and selling gold, countries bought and sold U.S. dollars to maintain a fixed exchange rate with the dollar. Since the United States had the world's largest financial market and the strongest economy, its currency was the dominant world currency. The United States had the productive capacity to supply much-needed goods to the rest of the world, and these goods were priced in dollars.

The U.S. dollar was the **reserve currency** of the system. International debts were settled with dollars, and international trade contracts were often denominated in dollars. In effect, the world was on a dollar standard following World War II.

21-1c The International Monetary Fund and the World Bank

Two new organizations also emerged from the Bretton Woods conference: the International Monetary Fund and the World Bank. The **International Monetary Fund (IMF)** was created to supervise the exchange-rate practices of member countries and to encourage the free convertibility of any national money into the monies of other countries. The IMF also lends money to countries that are experiencing problems meeting their international payment obligations. The funds available to the IMF come from the annual membership fees (called *quotas*) of the 185 member countries of the IMF. The U.S. quota, for instance, is about $57 billion, or about 17 percent of the total quotas of all member countries. (The term *quota* has a different meaning in this context from the one it has in international trade.)

The **World Bank** was created to help finance economic development in poor countries. It provides loans to developing countries at more favorable terms than are available from commercial lenders, and it also offers technical expertise. The World Bank obtains the funds it lends by selling bonds. It is one of the world's major borrowers. See the Global Business Insight "The IMF and the World Bank" for an explanation of how these institutions work.

21-1d The Transition Years

The Bretton Woods system of fixed exchange rates required countries to actively buy and sell dollars in order to maintain fixed exchange rates when the *free market equilibrium* in the foreign exchange market differed from the fixed rate. The free market equilibrium exchange rate is the rate that would be established in the absence of government intervention. Governmental buying and selling of currencies to achieve a target exchange rate is called **foreign exchange market intervention**. The effectiveness of such intervention is limited to situations in which free-market pressure to deviate from the fixed exchange rate is temporary. For instance, suppose a country has a bad harvest and earns less foreign exchange than usual. This may be only a temporary situation if the next harvest is plentiful and the country resumes its typical export sales. During the period of reduced exports, it will be necessary for the government of this country to intervene to avoid a depreciation of its domestic currency. In the 1960s, however, there were several situations in which permanent rather than temporary changes called for changes in exchange rates rather than government foreign exchange market intervention.

The Bretton Woods agreement established a system of fixed exchange rates.

gold exchange standard
An exchange-rate system in which each nation fixes the value of its currency in terms of gold, but buys and sells the U.S. dollar rather than gold to maintain fixed exchange rates.

reserve currency
A currency that is used to settle international debts and is held by governments to use in foreign exchange market interventions.

International Monetary Fund (IMF)
An international organization that supervises exchange-rate arrangements and lends money to member countries that are experiencing problems meeting their external financial obligations.

World Bank
An international organization that makes loans and provides technical expertise to developing countries.

foreign exchange market intervention
The buying and selling of currencies by a central bank to achieve a specified exchange rate.

GLOBAL BUSINESS INSIGHT

The IMF and the World Bank

The International Monetary Fund (IMF) and the World Bank were both created at the Bretton Woods conference in 1944. The IMF oversees the international monetary system, promoting stable exchange rates and macroeconomic policies. The World Bank promotes the economic development of the poor nations. Both organizations are owned and directed by their 182 member countries.

The IMF provides loans to nations that are having trouble repaying their foreign debts. Before the IMF lends any money, however, the borrower must agree to certain conditions. The IMF *conditionality* usually requires that the country meet targets for key macroeconomic variables like money-supply growth, inflation, tax collections, and subsidies. The conditions attached to IMF loans are aimed at promoting stable economic growth.

The World Bank assists developing countries by providing long-term financing for development projects and pro-

grams. The bank also provides expertise in many areas in which poor nations lack expert knowledge: agriculture, medicine, construction, and education, as well as economics. The IMF primarily employs economists to carry out its mission.

The diversity of World Bank activities results in the employment of about 10,000 people. The IMF has a staff of approximately 2,400. Both organizations post employees around the world, but most work at the organizations' headquarters in Washington, D.C.

World Bank funds are largely acquired by borrowing on the international bond market. The IMF receives its funding from member-country subscription fees, called quotas. A member's quota determines its voting power in setting IMF policies. The United States, whose quota accounts for the largest fraction of the total, has the most votes.

---

devaluation
A deliberate decrease in the official value of a currency.

equilibrium exchange rates
The exchange rates that are established in the absence of government foreign exchange market intervention.

In March 1973, the major industrial countries abandoned fixed exchange rates for floating rates.

2. *What kinds of exchange-rate arrangements exist today?*

The Bretton Woods system was officially dissolved in 1971, at a meeting of the finance ministers of the leading world powers at the Smithsonian Institution in Washington, D.C. The Smithsonian agreement changed the exchange rates set during the Bretton Woods era. One result was a **devaluation** of the U.S. dollar. (A currency is said to be devalued when its value is officially lowered.)

Under the Smithsonian agreement, countries were to maintain fixed exchange rates at newly defined values. It soon became clear, however, that the new exchange rates were not **equilibrium exchange rates** that could be maintained without government intervention and that government intervention could not maintain the disequilibrium fixed exchange rates forever. The U.S. dollar was devalued again in February 1973, when the dollar price of gold was raised to $42.22. This new exchange rate was still not an equilibrium rate, and in March 1973 the major industrial countries abandoned fixed exchange rates.

21-1e Today

When the major industrial countries abandoned fixed exchange rates in March 1973, the world did not move to purely free-market-determined floating exchange rates. Under the system that has been in existence since that time, the major industrial countries intervene to keep their currencies within acceptable ranges, while many smaller countries maintain fixed exchange rates.

The world today consists of some countries with fixed exchange rates, whose governments keep the exchange rates between two or more currencies constant over time; other countries with floating exchange rates, which shift on a daily basis according to the forces of supply and demand; and still others whose exchange-rate systems lie somewhere in between. Table 1, which lists the exchange-rate arrangements of over 180 countries, illustrates the diversity of exchange-rate arrangements currently in effect.

TABLE 1 Exchange Rate Arrangements

	Monetary Policy Framework							
Exchange Rate Arrangement (number of countries)	Exchange Rate Anchor					Monetary Aggregate Target	Inflation Targeting Framework	Other[1]
	U.S. dollar (66)		Euro (27)	Composite (15)	Other (7)	(22)	(44)	(11)
Exchange arrangement with no separate legal tender (10)	Ecuador El Salvador Marshal Islands Micronesia Fed. States of	Palau Panama Timor-Leste Zimbabwe	Kosovo Montenegro San Marino		Kiribati			
Currency Board arrangement (13)	Antigua and Barbuda[2] Djibouti Dominica[2] Grenada[2] ECCU Hong Kong SAR St. Kitts and Nevis[2]	St.Lucia[2] St. Vincent and the Grenadines[2]	Bosnia and Herzegovina Bulgaria Estonia[3] Lithuania[3]		Brunei Darussalam			
Other conventional fixed peg arrangement (68)	Aruba Bahamas Bahrain Bangladesh Barbados Belize Eritrea Guyana Honduras Jordan Kazakhstan Lebanon Malawi Maldives Mongolia Netherlands Antilles Oman Qatar Rwanda Saudi Arabia	Seychelles Sierra Leone Solomon Islands Sri Lanka Suriname Tajikistan Trinidad and Tobago Turkmenistan United Arab Emirates Venezuela Rep Bolivariana de Vietnam Yemen, Rep of	Cameroon[5] Cape Verde Central African Rep.[5] Chad[5] Comoros Congo, Rep. of[5] Côte d'Ivoire[4] Croatia Denmark[3] Equatoria Guinea[5] Gabon[5] Guinea-Bissau[4] Latvia[3] Macedonia, FYR Mali[4] Niger[4] Senegal[4] Togo[4]	Fiji Kuwait Libya Morocco Russian Federation Samoa Tunisia	Bhutan Lesotho Namibia Nepal Swaziland	Argentina Malawi Rwanda Sierra Leone		
Pegged exchange rate within horizontal bands (3)			Slovak Rep.[3]	Syria Tonga Belarus				
Crawling peg (8)	Bolivia China Ethiopia Nicaragua Uzbekistan			Botswana Iran, I.R. of				

(continued)

TABLE 1   Exchange Rate Arrangements (continued)

Exchange Rate Arrangement (number of countries)	Monetary Policy Framework — Exchange Rate Anchor — U.S. dollar (66)	Euro (27)	Composite (15)	Other (7)	Monetary Aggregate Target (22)	Inflation Targeting Framework (44)	Other[1] (11)
Crawling band (2)	Costa Rica		Azerbaijan		Afghanistan, I.R. of, Burundi, Gambia, Georgia, Guinea, Haiti, Jamaica, Kenya, Madagascar		
Managed floating with no predetermined path for the exchange rate (44)	Cambodia, Kyrgyz Rep., Lao P.D.R, Liberia, Mauritania, Mauritius, Myanmar, Ukraine, Algeria, Singapore, Vanuatu		Algeria, Singapore, Vanuatu		Moldova, Mozambique, Nigeria, Papua New Guinea, São Tomé and Príncipe, Sudan, Tanzania, Uganda	Colombia, Ghana, Guatemala, Indonesia, Peru, Romania, Serbia[6], Thailand, Uruguay	Dominican Rep., Egypt, India, Malaysia, Pakistan, Paraguay, Armenia[6]
Independently floating (40)					Zambia	Albania, Australia, Austria[7], Belgium, Brazil, Canada, Chile, Cyprus[7], Czech Rep., Finland[7], France[7], Germany[7], Greece[7], Hungary, Iceland, Ireland[7], Israel, Italy[7], Korea, Rep. of, Luxembourg[7], Malta[7], Mexico, Netherlands[7], New Zealand, Norway, Philippines, Poland, Portugal[7], Slovenia[7], South Africa, Spain[7], Sweden, Turkey, United Kingdom	Congo, Dem. Rep. of, Japan, Somalia[8], Switzerland, United States

[1] Includes countries that have no explicitly stated nominal anchor, but rather monitor various indicators in conducting monetary policy.

[2] The member participates in the Eastern Caribbean Currency Union.

[3] The member participates in the Exchange Rate Mechanism II arrangement to maintain a fixed exchange rate with the euro within the eurozone.

[4] The member participates in the Central African Economic and Monetary Community.

[5] The member participates in the West African Economic and Monetary Union.

[6] The central bank has taken preliminary steps toward inflation targeting and is preparing for the transition to full-fledged inflation targeting.

[7] The member participates in the European Economic and Monetary Union.

[8] As of end-December 1989.

Source: IMF, "De Facto Classification of Exchange Rate Arrangements and Monetary Frameworks," 2013, https://www.imf.org/external/pubs/nft/2013/areaers/ar2013.pdf

We provide a brief description of each:

Crawling pegs The exchange rate is adjusted periodically by small amounts at a fixed, preannounced rate or in response to certain indicators (such as inflation differentials against major trading partners).

Crawling bands The exchange rate is maintained within certain fluctuation margins around a central rate that is periodically adjusted at a fixed, preannounced rate or in response to certain indicators.

Managed floating The monetary authority (usually the central bank) influences the exchange rate through active foreign exchange market intervention with no preannounced path for the exchange rate.

Independently floating The exchange rate is market determined, and any intervention is aimed at moderating fluctuations rather than at determining the level of the exchange rate.

No separate legal tender Either another country's currency circulates as the legal tender or the country belongs to a monetary union where the legal tender is shared by the members (like the euro).

Currency board A fixed exchange rate is established by a legislative commitment to exchange domestic currency for a specified foreign currency at a fixed exchange rate. New issues of domestic currency are typically backed in some fixed ratio (like 1-to-1) by additional holdings of the key foreign currency.

Fixed peg The exchange rate is fixed against a major currency or some basket of currencies. Active intervention may be required to maintain the target pegged rate. *Horizontal bands* The exchange rate fluctuates around a fixed central target rate. Such target zones allow for a moderate amount of exchange-rate fluctuation while tying the currency to the target central rate.

Note that the countries that use the euro as their currency are listed as "Independently floating." The euro floats against other currencies, but each of the member nations of the euro has no separate national money.

Table 2 lists the end-of-year exchange rates for several currencies versus the U.S. dollar beginning in 1950. For most of the currencies, there was little movement in the 1950s and 1960s, the era of the Bretton Woods agreement. In the early 1970s, exchange rates began to fluctuate. More recently, there has been considerable change in the foreign exchange value of a dollar, as Table 2 illustrates.

RECAP

1. Under a gold standard, each currency has a fixed value in terms of gold. This arrangement provides for fixed exchange rates between countries.

2. At the end of World War II, the Bretton Woods agreement established a new system of fixed exchange rates. Two new organizations—the International Monetary Fund (IMF) and the World Bank—also emerged from the Bretton Woods conference.

3. Fixed exchange rates are maintained by government intervention in the foreign exchange market; governments or central banks buy and

sell currencies to keep the equilibrium exchange rate steady.

4. The governments of the major industrial countries adopted floating exchange rates in 1973. In fact, the prevailing system is characterized by managed floating—that is, by occasional government intervention—rather than being a pure free-market-determined exchange-rate system.

5. Some countries choose floating exchange rates; others peg their currencies to a single currency or a composite.

TABLE 2   Exchange Rates of Selected Countries (currency units per U.S. dollar)

Year	Canadian Dollar	Japanese Yen	French Franc	German Mark	Italian Lira	British Pound	Euro
1950	1.06	361	3.5	4.2	625	0.36	—
1955	1	361	3.5	4.22	625	0.36	—
1960	1	358	4.9	4.17	621	0.36	—
1965	1.08	361	4.9	4.01	625	0.36	—
1970	1.01	358	5.52	3.65	623	0.42	—
1975	1.02	305	4.49	2.62	684	0.5	—
1980	1.19	203	4.52	1.96	931	0.42	—
1985	1.4	201	7.56	2.46	1,679	0.69	—
1990	1.16	134	5.13	1.49	1,130	0.52	—
1995	1.36	103	4.9	1.43	1,584	0.65	—
2000	1.49	114	—	—	—	0.67	1.06
2005	1.16	118	—	—	—	0.58	0.84
2010	0.99	81	—	—	—	0.64	0.75
2013	1.06	105	—	—	—	0.60	0.72

Source: End-of-year exchange rates from International Monetary Fund, *International Financial Statistics,* Washington, D.C., various issues, and Pacific Exchange Rate Service, http://fx.sauder.ubc.ca/.

21-2 Fixed or Floating Exchange Rates

3. How is equilibrium determined in the foreign exchange market?

Is the United States better off today with floating exchange rates than it was with the fixed exchange rates of the post–World War II period? The choice of an exchange-rate system has multiple implications for the performance of a nation's economy and, therefore, for the conduct of macroeconomic policy. As with many policy issues in economics, economists often disagree about the merits of fixed versus flexible exchange rates. Let us look at the characteristics of the different exchange-rate systems.

21-2a Equilibrium in the Foreign Exchange Market

An exchange rate is the price of one money in terms of another. Equilibrium is determined by the supply of and demand for the two currencies in the foreign exchange market. Figure 1 contains two supply and demand diagrams for the U.S. dollar–euro foreign exchange market. The downward-sloping demand curve indicates that the higher the dollar price of the euro, the fewer euros will be demanded. The upward-sloping supply curve indicates that the higher the dollar price of the euro, the more euros will be supplied.

In Figure 1(a), the initial equilibrium occurs at the point where the demand curve D_1 intersects the supply curve. At this point, the equilibrium exchange rate is $1 (one euro costs $1), and the quantity of euros bought and sold is Q_1.

Suppose U.S. residents increase their demand for French wine. Because euros are needed to pay for the wine, the greater U.S. demand for French wine generates a greater demand for euros by U.S. citizens who hold dollars. The demand curve in Figure 1(a) thus shifts from D_1 to D_2. This increased demand for euros causes the euro to appreciate relative to the dollar. The new exchange rate is $1.03, and a greater quantity of euros, Q_2, is bought and sold.

Equilibrium in the foreign exchange market occurs at the point where the foreign exchange demand and supply curves intersect.

FIGURE 1 The Supply of and Demand for Foreign Exchange

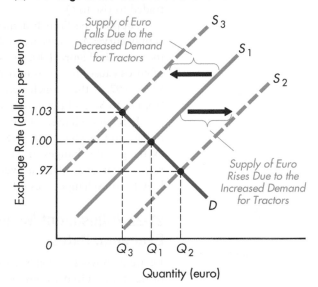

(a) A Change in the U.S. Demand for French Wine

Demand for Euro Rises Due to the Increased Demand for Wine

Demand for Euro Falls Due to the Decreased Demand for Wine

(b) A Change in the French Demand for U.S. Tractors

Supply of Euro Falls Due to the Decreased Demand for Tractors

Supply of Euro Rises Due to the Increased Demand for Tractors

This figure represents the foreign exchange market for euros traded for dollars. The demand curve for euros is based partly on the U.S. demand for French products, and the supply curve of euros is based partly on the French demand for U.S. products. An increase in demand for French wine causes demand for euros to increase from D_1 to D_2. This shift causes an increase from Q_1 to Q_2 in the equilibrium quantity of euros traded and causes the euro to appreciate to $1.03 from the initial equilibrium exchange rate of $1.00. A decrease in demand for French wine causes the demand for euros to fall from D_1 to D_2. This shift leads to a fall in the equilibrium quantity traded to Q_2 and a depreciation of the euro to $.97. If the French demand for U.S. tractors falls, fewer euros are supplied for exchange for dollars, as illustrated by the fall in supply from S_1 to S_3. This shift causes the euro to appreciate to $1.03 and the equilibrium quantity of euros traded to fall to Q_3. If the French demand for U.S. tractors rises, then more euros are supplied for dollars and the supply curve increases from S_1 to S_2. This causes the euro to depreciate and the equilibrium quantity of euros traded to rise to Q_2.

If the U.S. demand for French wine falls, the demand for euros also falls, as illustrated by the shift from D_1 to D_3 in Figure 1(a). The decreased demand for euros causes the euro to depreciate relative to the dollar, so the exchange rate falls to $.97.

So far, we have considered how shifts in the U.S. demand for French goods affect the dollar–euro exchange rate. We can also use the same supply and demand diagram to analyze how changes in the French demand for U.S. goods affect the equilibrium exchange rate. The supply of euros to the foreign exchange market partly originates with French residents who buy goods from the rest of the world. If a French importer buys a tractor from a U.S. firm, the importer must exchange euros for dollars to pay for the tractor. As French residents' demand for foreign goods and services rises and falls, the supply of euros to the foreign exchange market changes.

This figure represents the foreign exchange market for euros traded for dollars. The demand curve for euros is based partly on the U.S. demand for French products, and the supply curve of euros is based partly on the French demand for U.S. products. An increase in demand for French wine causes demand for euros to increase from D_1 to D_2. This shift causes an increase from Q_1 to Q_2 in the equilibrium quantity of euros traded and causes the euro to appreciate to $1.03 from the initial equilibrium exchange rate of $1. A decrease in demand for French wine causes the demand for euros to fall from D_1 to D_2. This shift leads to a fall in the equilibrium quantity traded to Q_2 and a depreciation of the euro to $.97. If the French demand for U.S. tractors falls, fewer euros are supplied for exchange for dollars, as illustrated by the fall in supply from S_1 to S_3. This shift causes the euro to appreciate to

$1.03 and the equilibrium quantity of euros traded to fall to Q_3. If the French demand for U.S. tractors rises, then more euros are supplied for dollars and the supply curve increases from S_1 to S_2. This causes the euro to depreciate and the equilibrium quantity of euros traded to rise to Q_2.

Suppose the French demand for U.S. tractors increases. This brings about a shift of the supply curve: As euros are exchanged for dollars to buy the U.S. tractors, the supply of euros increases. In Figure 1(b), the supply of euros curve shifts from S_1 to S_2. The greater supply of euros causes the euro to depreciate relative to the dollar, and the exchange rate falls from $1 to $.97. If the French demand for U.S. tractors decreases, the supply of euros decreases from S_1 to S_3, and the euro appreciates to $1.03.

Foreign exchange supply and demand curves are affected by changes in tastes and technology and by changing government policy. As demand and supply change, the equilibrium exchange rate changes. In fact, continuous shifts in supply and demand cause the exchange rate to change as often as every day, on the basis of free-market forces. Now let us consider how fixed exchange rates differ from floating exchange rates.

21-2b Adjustment Mechanisms under Fixed and Flexible Exchange Rates

4. *How do fixed and floating exchange rates differ in their adjustment to shifts in supply and demand for currencies?*

Figure 2 shows the dollar–euro foreign exchange market. The exchange rate is the number of dollars required to buy one euro; the quantity is the quantity of euros bought and sold. Suppose that, initially, the equilibrium is at point A, with quantity Q_1 euros traded at $1 per euro.

FIGURE 2 Foreign Exchange Market Equilibrium under Fixed and Flexible Exchange Rates

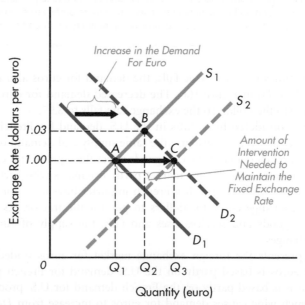

Initially, equilibrium is at point A; the exchange rate is $1 and Q_1 euros are traded. An increase in demand for French wine causes the demand for euros to increase from D_1 to D_2. With flexible exchange rates, the euro appreciates in value to $1.03 and Q_2 euros are traded; equilibrium is at point B. If the government is committed to maintaining a fixed exchange rate of $1, the supply of euros must be increased to S_2 so that a new equilibrium can occur at point C. The government must intervene in the foreign exchange market and sell euros to shift the supply curve to S_2.

Suppose French wine becomes more popular in the United States, and the demand for euros increases from D_1 to D_2. With flexible exchange rates (as in Figure 1), a new equilibrium is established at point B. The exchange rate rises to $1.03 per euro, and the quantity of euros bought and sold is Q_2. The increased demand for euros has caused the euro to **appreciate** (rise in value against the dollar) and the dollar to **depreciate** (fall in value against the euro). This is an example of a freely floating exchange rate, determined by the free-market forces of supply and demand.

Now suppose the Federal Reserve is committed to maintaining a fixed exchange rate of $1 per euro. The increase in demand for euros causes a shortage of euros at the exchange rate of $1. According to the new demand curve, D_2, the quantity of euros demanded at $1 is Q_3. The quantity supplied is found on the original supply curve S_1, at Q_1. The only way to maintain the exchange rate of $1 is for the Federal Reserve to supply euros to meet the shortage of $Q_3 - Q_1$. In other words, the Fed must sell $Q_3 - Q_1$ euros to shift the supply curve to S_2 and thus maintain the fixed exchange rate.

If the increased demand for euros is temporary, the Fed can continue to supply euros for the short time necessary. However, if the increased demand for euros is permanent, the Fed's intervention will eventually end when it runs out of euros. This situation—a permanent change in supply or demand—is referred to as a **fundamental disequilibrium**. The fixed exchange rate is no longer an equilibrium rate. Under the Bretton Woods agreement, a country was supposed to devalue its currency in such cases.

Suppose that the shift to D_2 in Figure 2 is permanent. In this case, the dollar should be devalued. A devaluation to $1.03 per euro would restore equilibrium in the foreign exchange market without requiring further intervention by the government. Sometimes, however, governments try to maintain the old exchange rate ($1 per euro, in this case), even though most people believe the shift in demand to be permanent. When this happens, **speculators** buy the currency that is in greater demand (euros, in our example) in anticipation of the eventual devaluation of the other currency (dollars, in Figure 2). A speculator who purchases the euro for $1 prior to the devaluation and sells them for $1.03 after the devaluation earns $.03 per euro purchased.

appreciate
When the value of a currency increases under floating exchange rates—that is, exchange rates determined by supply and demand.

depreciate
When the value of a currency decreases under floating exchange rates.

fundamental disequilibrium
A permanent shift in the foreign exchange market supply and demand curves such that the fixed exchange rate is no longer an equilibrium rate.

speculators
People who seek to profit from an expected shift in an exchange rate by selling the currency that is expected to depreciate and buying the currency that is expected to appreciate, then exchanging the appreciated currency for the depreciated currency after the exchange-rate adjustment.

Speculators buy and sell currencies in anticipation of future changes in exchange rates.

Speculation puts greater devaluation pressure on the dollar: The speculators sell dollars and buy euros, causing the demand for euros to increase even further. Such speculative activity contributed to the breakdown of the Bretton Woods system of fixed exchange rates. Several countries intervened to support exchange rates that were far out of line with free-market forces. The longer a devaluation was put off, the more obvious it became that the devaluation was forthcoming and the more speculators entered the market. In 1971 and 1973, speculators sold dollars for yen and German marks. They were betting that the dollar would be devalued; both times they were correct. The speculative activity of the early 1970s drew attention to the folly of efforts to maintain fixed exchange rates in the face of a change in the fundamental equilibrium exchange rate.

21-2c Constraints on Economic Policy

5. What are the advantages and disadvantages of fixed and floating exchange rates?

Fixed exchange rates can be maintained over time only between countries with similar economic policies and similar underlying economic conditions. As prices rise within a country, the domestic value of a unit of that country's currency falls, since the currency buys fewer goods and services. In the foreign exchange market too, the value of a unit of domestic currency falls, since it buys relatively fewer goods and services than the foreign currency does. A fixed exchange rate thus requires that the purchasing power of the two currencies change at roughly the same rate over time. Only if two nations have approximately the same inflation experience will they be able to maintain a fixed exchange rate. This condition was a frequent source of problems in the Bretton Woods era of fixed exchange rates. In the late 1960s, for instance, the U.S. government was following a more expansionary macroeconomic policy than was Germany. U.S. government expenditures on the war in Vietnam and domestic antipoverty initiatives led to inflationary pressures that were not matched in Germany. Between 1965 and 1970, price levels rose by 23.2 percent in the United States but by only 12.8 percent in Germany. Since the purchasing power of the dollar was falling faster than that of the mark, the fixed exchange rate could not be maintained. The dollar had to be devalued.

One of the advantages of floating exchange rates is that countries are free to pursue their own macroeconomic policies without worrying about maintaining an exchange-rate commitment. If U.S. policy produces a higher inflation rate than Japanese policy, the dollar will automatically depreciate in value against the yen. The United States can choose the macroeconomic policy it wants, independently of other nations, and let the exchange rate adjust if its inflation rate differs markedly from that of other nations. If the dollar were fixed in value relative to the yen, the two nations could not follow independent policies and expect to maintain the exchange rate.

It became obvious in the late 1960s that many governments considered other issues more important than maintenance of a fixed exchange rate. A nation that puts a high priority on reducing unemployment will typically stimulate the economy to try to increase income and create jobs. This initiative may cause the domestic inflation rate to rise and the domestic currency to depreciate relative to other currencies. If one goal or the other—lower unemployment or a fixed exchange rate—must be given up, it is likely that the exchange-rate goal will be sacrificed.

Floating exchange rates allow countries to formulate their domestic economic policy solely in response to domestic issues; they need not pay attention to the economic policies of the rest of the world. For residents of some countries, this freedom may be more of a problem than a benefit. The freedom to choose a rate of inflation and let the exchange rate adjust itself can have undesirable consequences in countries whose politicians, for whatever reason, follow highly inflationary policies. In these countries, a fixed-exchange-rate system would impose discipline, since maintenance of the exchange rate would not permit policies that diverged sharply from those of its trading partner.

1. Under a fixed-exchange-rate system, governments must sometimes intervene in the foreign exchange market to maintain the exchange rate. A fundamental disequilibrium requires a currency devaluation.

2. Fixed exchange rates can be maintained only between countries with similar macroeconomic policies and similar underlying economic conditions.

3. Fixed exchange rates serve as an anchor to constrain inflationary government policies.

21-3 Prices and Exchange Rates

An exchange rate, as you learned in earlier chapters, is the price of one money in terms of another. The exchange rate does not enter into the purchase and sale of Fords in Michigan and California because each state uses the U.S. dollar. But for goods and services that are traded across national borders, the exchange rate is an important part of the total price. We will assume that currencies are traded freely for each other and that foreign exchange markets respond to supply and demand without government intervention.

Let us look at an example. A U.S. wine importer purchases 1,000,000 euro (€1,000,000) worth of wine from France. The importer demands euros in order to pay the French wine seller. Suppose the initial equilibrium exchange rate is $1 = €1. At this rate, the U.S. importer needs 1,000,000 euros at $1 apiece, or $1,000,000.

6. *How does a change in the exchange rate affect the prices of goods traded between countries?*

21-3a Appreciation and Depreciation

When the exchange rate between two currencies changes, we say that one currency *depreciates* while the other *appreciates*. Suppose the exchange rate goes from $1 = €1 to $1.10 = €1. The euro is now worth $1.10 instead of $1. The dollar has depreciated in value in relation to the euro; dollars are worth less in terms of euros. At the new equilibrium exchange rate, the U.S. importer needs $1,100,000 ($1.10 × 1,000,000) to buy €1,000,000 worth of wine.

Instead of saying that the dollar has depreciated against the euro, we can say that the euro has *appreciated* against the dollar. If the dollar is depreciating against the euro, the euro must be appreciating against the dollar. Whichever way we describe the change in the exchange rate, the result is that euros are now worth more in terms of dollars. The price of a euro has gone from $1 to $1.10.

As exchange rates change, the prices of goods and services traded in international markets also change. Suppose the dollar appreciates against the euro. This means that a euro costs fewer dollars; it also means that French goods cost U.S. buyers less. If the exchange rate falls to $.90 = €1, then €1,000,000 costs $900,000 ($.90 × 1,000,000). The French wine has become less expensive to the U.S. importer.

- When the domestic (home) currency *depreciates*, foreign goods become *more expensive* to domestic buyers.
- When the domestic currency *appreciates*, foreign goods become *less expensive* to domestic buyers.

Let us look at the problem from the French side. When the dollar price of the euro rises, the euro price of the dollar falls; and when the dollar price of the euro falls, the euro price of the dollar rises. If the dollar price of the euro ($/€) is originally $1, the euro price of the dollar (€/$) is the reciprocal (1/1), or €1. If the dollar depreciates against the euro to $1.10, then the euro appreciates against the dollar to 1/1.10, or €.91. As the euro appreciates, U.S. goods become less expensive to French buyers. If the dollar appreciates against the euro to $.90, then the euro depreciates against the dollar to 1/.90, or €1.11. As the euro depreciates, U.S. goods become more expensive to French buyers.

- When the domestic currency *depreciates*, domestic goods become *less expensive* to foreign buyers.
- When the domestic currency *appreciates*, domestic goods become *more expensive* to foreign buyers.

The exchange rate is just one determinant of the demand for goods and services. Income, tastes, the prices of substitutes and complements, expectations, and the exchange rate all determine the demand for U.S. wheat, for example. As the dollar depreciates in relation to other currencies, the demand for U.S. wheat increases (along with foreign demand for all other U.S. goods), even if all the other determinants do not change. Conversely, as the dollar appreciates, the demand for U.S. wheat falls (along with foreign demand for all other U.S. goods), even if all the other determinants do not change.

21-3b Purchasing Power Parity

Within a country, where prices are quoted in terms of a single currency, all we need to know is the price in the domestic currency of an item in two different locations to determine where our money buys more. If Joe's bookstore charges $20 for a book and Pete's bookstore charges $30 for the same book, the purchasing power of our money is greater at Joe's than it is at Pete's.

International comparisons of prices must be made using exchange rates because different countries use different monies. Once we cross national borders, prices are quoted in different currencies. Suppose Joe's bookstore in New York City charges $20 for a book and Pierre's bookstore in Paris charges €30. To compare the prices, we must know the exchange rate between dollars and euros.

purchasing power parity (PPP)
The condition under which monies have the same purchasing power in different markets.

If we find that goods sell for the same price in different markets, our money has the same purchasing power in those markets, which means that we have **purchasing power parity (PPP)**. The PPP reflects a relationship among the domestic price level, the exchange rate, and the foreign price level:

$$P = EP^F$$

where

P = the domestic price
E = the exchange rate (units of domestic currency per unit of foreign currency)
P^F = the foreign price

If the dollar–euro exchange rate is .67 ($.67 = €1), then a book priced at €30 in Pierre's store in Paris costs the same as a book priced at $20 in Joe's New York store:

$$P = EP^F$$
$$= \$.67 \times 30$$
$$= \$20$$

The domestic price (we are assuming that the U.S. dollar is the domestic currency) equals the exchange rate times the foreign price. Because the dollar price of the book in Paris is $20 and the price in the United States is $20, PPP holds. The purchasing power (value) of the dollar is the same in both places.

Realistically, similar goods do not always sell for the same price everywhere. Actually, they do not even sell for the same price within a country. If the same textbook is priced differently at different bookstores, it is unrealistic to expect the price of the book to be identical worldwide. There are several reasons why PPP does not hold. The most important are that goods are not identical, that information is costly, that shipping costs affect prices, and that tariffs and legal restrictions on trade affect prices. If these factors did not exist, we would expect that anytime a price was lower in one market than in another, people would buy in the low-price market (pushing prices up) and simultaneously sell in the high-price market (pushing prices down). This activity, known as *arbitrage*, would ensure that PPP holds.

7. Why don't similar goods sell for the same price all over the world?

RECAP

1. When the exchange rate between two currencies changes, one currency depreciates while the other appreciates.

2. Purchasing power parity means that money has the same purchasing power in different markets.

3. Similar goods do not sell for the same price all over the world because goods are not identical, information is costly, shipping costs affect prices, and tariffs and legal restrictions on international trade affect prices.

21-4 Interest Rates and Exchange Rates

Exchange rates are used to compare international prices of goods and services. They are also used to compare the return on foreign currency–denominated stocks and bonds to the return on domestic assets. For example, suppose you have a choice of buying a U.S. bond or a U.K. bond. The U.S. bond is denominated in dollars and pays 15 percent interest; the U.K. bond is denominated in British pounds and pays 10 percent interest. Because you are a U.S. resident and you ultimately want dollars for household spending, you must compare the dollar return from holding each bond.

21-4a The Domestic Currency Return from Foreign Bonds

The U.S. bond is denominated in dollars, so the 15 percent interest is a dollar return. The U.K. bond, on the other hand, promises to pay 10 percent in terms of British pounds. If you buy the U.K. bond, you exchange dollars for pounds at the time the bond is purchased. When the bond matures, you exchange the principal and interest (the proceeds), trading pounds for dollars. If the exchange rate remains the same, the return on the U.K. bond is 10 percent. But if the exchange rate changes between the time you buy the bond and the time it matures, your return in dollars may be more or less than 10 percent.

Figure 3 shows what happens when a U.S. resident buys a one-year U.K. bond. Suppose the exchange rate is $2 = £1 when the bond is purchased, and the bond sells for £1. The U.S. resident needs $2 to buy the bond. A year later, the bond matures. The bondholder receives the principal of £1 plus 10 percent interest (£.10). Now the U.S. resident wants to convert the pounds into dollars. If the exchange rate has gone up from $2 = £1 to $2.10 = £1, the £1.10 proceeds from the bond are converted into dollars at the rate of 2.10 dollars per pound. The *dollar value* of the proceeds is $2.31 (the exchange rate [2.10] multiplied by the pound proceeds [£1.10]). The *dollar return* from the U.K. bond is the percentage difference between the dollar proceeds received after one year and the initial dollar amount invested, or approximately 15 percent:

$$\text{Dollar return} = \frac{\$2.31 - \$2}{\$2}$$
$$= \frac{\$.31}{\$2}$$
$$= .15$$

FIGURE 3   A U.S. Resident Buys a One-Year U.K. Bond

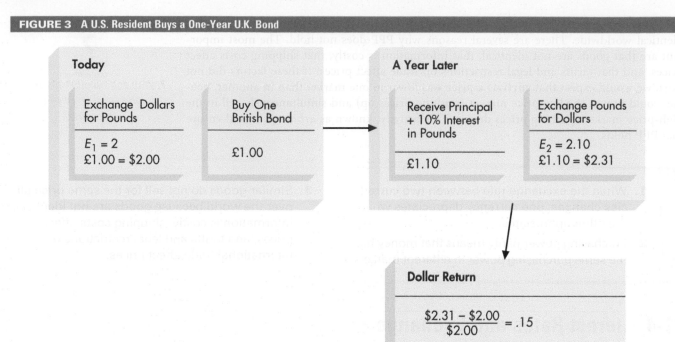

We can also determine the dollar return from the U.K. bond by adding the U.K. interest rate to the percentage change in the exchange rate. The percentage change in the exchange rate is 5 percent:

$$\text{Percentage change in exchange rate} = \frac{\$2.10 - \$2}{\$2}$$
$$= \frac{\$.10}{\$2}$$
$$= .05$$

The dollar return from the U.K. bond equals the 10 percent interest paid in British pounds plus the 5 percent change in the exchange rate, or 15 percent.

In our example, the pound appreciates against the dollar. When the pound increases in value, foreign residents holding pound-denominated bonds earn a higher return on those bonds than the pound interest rate. If the pound depreciates against the dollar, so that the pounds received at maturity are worth less than the pounds originally purchased, then the dollar return from the U.K. bond is lower than the interest rate on the bond. If the pound depreciates 5 percent, the dollar return is just 5 percent (the interest rate [10 percent] *minus* the exchange rate change [5 percent]).

We calculate the domestic currency return on a foreign bond by adding the foreign interest rate (i^F) plus the percentage change in the exchange rate [$(E_2 - E_1)/E_1$], where E_2 is the dollar price of a unit of foreign currency in the next period, when the bond matures, and E_1 is the exchange rate in the current period, when the bond is purchased:

$$\text{Domestic currency return} = \text{foreign interest rate} + \text{percentage change in}$$
$$\text{exchange rate}$$
$$= i^F + \frac{E_2 - E_1}{E_1}$$

21-4b Interest Rate Parity

Because U.S. residents can hold U.S. bonds, U.K. bonds, or the bonds or other securities of any country they choose, they compare the returns from the alternatives when deciding what assets to buy. Foreign investors do the same thing. One product of this process is a close relationship among international interest rates. Specifically, the return, or interest rate, on similar bonds tends to be the same when returns are measured in terms of the domestic currency. This is called **interest rate parity (IRP)**.

Interest rate parity is the financial asset version of purchasing power parity. Similar financial assets have the same percentage return when that return is computed in terms of one currency. Interest rate parity defines a relationship among the domestic interest rate, the foreign interest rate, and the expected change in the exchange rate:

Domestic interest rate = foreign interest rate + expected change in exchange rate

In our example, the U.S. bond pays 15 percent interest; the U.K. bond offers 10 percent interest in pounds. If the pound is expected to appreciate 5 percent, the U.K. bond offers U.S. residents an expected dollar return of 15 percent. Interest rate parity holds in this case. The domestic interest rate is 15 percent, which equals the foreign interest rate (10 percent) plus the expected change in the exchange rate (5 percent).

Interest rate parity is the product of arbitrage in financial markets. If U.S. bonds and U.K. bonds are similar in every respect except for the currency used to pay the principal and interest, then they should yield similar returns to bondholders. If U.S. investors can earn a higher return by buying U.K. bonds, they are going to buy more U.K. bonds and fewer U.S. bonds. This tends to raise the price of U.K. bonds, pushing U.K. interest rates down. At the same time, the price of U.S. bonds drops, raising U.S. interest rates. The initial higher return on U.K. bonds and resulting greater demand for U.K. bonds increases the demand for pounds, increasing the value of the pound versus the dollar today. As the pound appreciates today, if investors expect the same future exchange rate as they did before the current appreciation, the expected appreciation in the future falls. The change in the exchange rate and interest rates equalizes the expected dollar return from holding a U.S. bond or a U.K. bond. U.K. bonds originally offered a higher return than U.S. bonds, but the increase in demand for U.K. bonds relative to U.S. bonds lowers both U.K. interest rates and the expected appreciation of the pound, so the bond returns are equalized.

8. How do we find the domestic currency return on a foreign bond?

9. What is the relationship between domestic and foreign interest rates and changes in the exchange rate?

interest rate parity (IRP)
The condition under which similar financial assets have the same interest rate when measured in the same currency.

R E C A P

1. The domestic currency return from a foreign bond equals the foreign interest rate plus the percentage change in the exchange rate.

2. Interest rate parity exists when similar financial assets have the same interest rate when measured in the same currency or when the domestic interest rate equals the foreign interest rate plus the expected change in the exchange rate.

SUMMARY

1. How does a commodity standard fix exchange rates between countries?

- Between 1880 and 1914, a gold standard provided for fixed exchange rates among countries. *§21-1a*

- The gold standard ended with World War I, and no established international monetary system replaced it until after World War II, when the Bretton Woods agreement created a fixed-exchange-rate system. *§21-1b*

2. What kinds of exchange-rate arrangements exist today?

- Today some countries have fixed exchange rates, others have floating exchange rates, and still others have managed floats or other types of systems. *§21-1e*

3. How is equilibrium determined in the foreign exchange market?

- Foreign exchange market equilibrium is determined by the intersection of the demand and supply curves for foreign exchange. *§21-2a*

4. How do fixed and floating exchange rates differ in their adjustment to shifts in supply and demand for currencies?

- Under fixed exchange rates, central banks must intervene in the foreign exchange market to keep the exchange rate from shifting. *§21-2b*

5. What are the advantages and disadvantages of fixed and floating exchange rates?

- Floating exchange rates permit countries to pursue independent economic policies. A fixed exchange rate requires a country to adopt policies similar to those of the country whose currency it is pegged to. A fixed exchange rate may serve to prevent a country from pursuing inflationary policies. *§21-2c*

6. How does a change in the exchange rate affect the prices of goods traded between countries?

- When the domestic currency depreciates against other currencies, foreign goods become more expensive to domestic buyers and domestic goods become less expensive to foreign buyers. *§21-3a*

- When the domestic currency appreciates against other currencies, foreign goods become less expensive to domestic buyers and domestic goods become more expensive to foreign buyers. *§21-3a*

- Purchasing power parity exists when monies have the same value in different markets. *§21-3b*

7. Why do similar goods not sell for the same price all over the world?

- Deviations from PPP arise because goods are not identical in different countries, information is costly, shipping costs affect prices, and tariffs and restrictions on trade affect prices. *§21-3b*

8. How do we find the domestic currency return on a foreign bond?

- The domestic currency return from holding a foreign bond equals the foreign interest rate plus the percentage change in the exchange rate. *§21-4a*

9. What is the relationship between domestic and foreign interest rates and changes in the exchange rate?

- Interest rate parity exists when the domestic interest rate equals the foreign interest rate plus the expected change in the exchange rate, so that similar financial assets yield the same return when measured in the same currency. *§21-4b*

KEY TERMS

EXERCISES

1. Under a gold standard, if the price of an ounce of gold is 1,400 U.S. dollars and 1,300 Canadian dollars, what is the exchange rate between U.S. and Canadian dollars?
2. What were the three major results of the Bretton Woods conference?
3. What is the difference between the IMF and the World Bank?
4. How can Mexico fix the value of the peso relative to the dollar when the demand for and supply of dollars and pesos changes continuously? Illustrate your explanation with a graph.
5. Draw a foreign exchange market supply and demand diagram to show how the yen–dollar exchange rate is determined. Set the initial equilibrium at a rate of 100 yen per dollar.
6. Using the diagram in exercise 5, illustrate the effect of a change in tastes that prompts Japanese residents to buy more goods from the United States. If the exchange rate is floating, what will happen to the foreign exchange market equilibrium?
7. Using the diagram in exercise 5, illustrate the effect of the change in Japanese tastes if exchange rates are fixed. What will happen to the foreign exchange market equilibrium?
8. When and why should exchange rates change under a fixed-exchange-rate system?
9. Suppose you just returned home from a vacation in Mazatlan, Mexico, where you exchanged U.S. dollars for Mexican pesos. How did your trip to Mexico affect the supply and demand for dollars and the exchange rate (assume that all other things are equal)?
10. What does it mean to say that a currency appreciates or depreciates in value? Give an example of each and briefly mention what might cause such a change.
11. How does a currency speculator profit from exchange-rate changes? Give an example of a profitable speculation.
12. Find the U.S. dollar value of each of the following currencies at the given exchange rates:
   a. $1 = C$.96 (Canadian dollars)
   b. $1 = ¥81 (Japanese yen)
   c. $1 = A$.95 (Australian dollars)
   d. $1 SKr6 (Swedish kronor)
   e. $1 SF.90 (Swiss francs)
13. You are a U.S. importer who buys goods from many different countries. How many U.S. dollars do you need to settle each of the following invoices?
   a. 1,000,000 Australian dollars for wool blankets (exchange rate: A$1 = $.769)
   b. 500,000 British pounds for dishes (exchange rate: £1 = $1.5855)
   c. 100,000 Indian rupees for baskets (exchange rate: Rs1 = $.0602)
   d. 350 million Japanese yen for stereo components (exchange rate: ¥1 = $.0069)
   e. 825,000 euro for German wine (exchange rate: €1 = $1.05)
14. What is the dollar value of the invoices in exercise 13 if the dollar:
   a. depreciates 10 percent against the Australian dollar
   b. appreciates 10 percent against the British pound
   c. depreciates 10 percent against the Indian rupee
   d. appreciates 20 percent against the Japanese yen
   e. depreciates 100 percent against the euro
15. Explain purchasing power parity and why it does not hold perfectly in the real world.
16. Write an equation that describes purchasing power parity and explain the equation.
17. Write an equation that describes interest rate parity and explain the equation.
18. If the interest rate on one-year government bonds is 5 percent in Germany and 8 percent in the United States, what do you think is expected to happen to the dollar value of the euro? Explain your answer.
19. In 1960 a U.S. dollar sold for 620 Italian lire. If PPP held in 1960, what would the PPP value of the exchange rate have been in 1987 if Italian prices rose 12 times and U.S. prices rose 4 times between 1960 and 1987?

ECONOMICALLY SPEAKING

FREQUENTLY ASKED QUESTIONS: EU ENLARGEMENT AND ECONOMIC AND MONETARY UNION (EMU)

1. Which countries have joined the EU since the ECB was established in 1998?

The Czech Republic, Estonia, Cyprus, Latvia, Lithuania, Hungary, Malta, Poland, Slovenia and Slovakia became members of the EU on 1 May 2004. Two other countries, Bulgaria and Romania, joined the EU on 1 January 2007. Croatia joined on 1 July 2013. Iceland, the Former Yugoslav Republic of Macedonia, Montenegro, Serbia and Turkey are official candidates for accession to the EU.

2. Will the new Member States automatically adopt the euro after joining the EU?

No, they don't. However, they are expected to do so when they fulfill the Maastricht convergence criteria. Unlike Denmark and the United Kingdom, new EU Member States do not have a right to opt out of the single currency.

3. Is there a pre-set timetable for the adoption of the euro by new Member States?

There is no such timetable, as the Governing Council of the ECB noted in its "Policy position of the Governing Council of the ECB on exchange rate issues relating to the acceding countries," published on 18 December 2003. In order to adopt the euro, they have to achieve a high degree of sustainable economic convergence. This is assessed by the EU Council on the basis of reports produced by the Commission and the ECB on the degree of these countries' fulfilment

of the Maastricht convergence criteria. These reports are prepared at least once every two years, or at the request of a Member State wishing to adopt the euro.

4. What are the convergence criteria?

In order to adopt the euro, Member States have to achieve a high degree of sustainable economic convergence. This is assessed on the basis of the fulfillment of the convergence criteria set out in Article 140 of the Treaty on the Functioning of the European Union and further detailed in a Protocol attached to the Treaties. The criteria entail the following:

• "The achievement of a high degree of price stability." This means that "a Member State has a price performance that is sustainable and an average rate of inflation, observed over a period of one year before the examination, that does not exceed by more than 1½ percentage points that of, at most, the three

best performing Member States in terms of price stability";

• "The sustainability of the government financial position." This means that, at the time of the examination, the Member State should not be deemed by the Council to have an excessive deficit. The Council decides whether or not an excessive deficit exists by referring to:

1. the ratio of the planned or actual government deficit to GDP at market prices, which should not exceed 3%;

2. the ratio of government debt to GDP at market prices, which should not exceed 60%.

However, the assessment of compliance with the fiscal discipline requirement will also take into account other factors, such as past progress in reducing budgetary imbalances and/or the existence of exceptional and temporary factors contributing to such imbalances. Moreover, in the light of the revisions to the Stability and Growth Pact, in force since end-2011, the assessment will include also the degree of compliance with the enhanced fiscal governance rules. Among other things, Member States with government debt ratios to GDP in excess of 60% are expected to bring them down towards the reference level at a satisfactory pace, i.e., in line with the newly introduced debt reduction benchmark.

- "The observance of the normal fluctuation margins provided for by the exchange-rate mechanism of the European Monetary System, for at least two years, without devaluing against the euro." When assessing compliance with this criterion, the emphasis is placed on the exchange rate being close to its central rate against the euro for a period of at least two years without severe tensions, while also considering factors that may have led to an exchange rate appreciation.

- "The durability of convergence ... being reflected in the long-term interest-rate levels." This means that, "observed over a period of one year before the examination, a Member State has had an average nominal long-term interest rate that does not exceed by more than two percentage points that of, at most, the three best performing Member States in terms of price stability. Interest rates shall be measured on the basis of long-term government bonds or comparable securities, taking into account differences in national definitions."

- The assessment will take several other factors into account, such as "the results of the integration of markets, the situation and development of the balances of payments on current account and an examination of the development of unit labour costs and other price indices."

Source: European Central Bank, http://www.ecb.int/ecb/history/enlargement/html/faqenlarge.en.html#l4.

COMMENTARY

The expansion of the European Union to include the countries from eastern Europe holds much promise for the economic development of these countries. Once in the EU, these countries can trade freely with the other EU countries, just as the states of the United States trade freely with one another. Just as the U.S. states all share a common money to help facilitate interstate trade, it is likely that the Eastern European countries will also welcome the adoption of the euro as their money to further solidify the links between their economies and those of the rest of the EU. The article discusses the criteria that the new accession countries must meet before joining the euro. In general, their macroeconomic policy must converge to that of the current euro-area countries as defined by the "Maastricht convergence criteria" (Maastricht is a town in the Netherlands where the convergence treaty was agreed upon). The criteria include such things as convergence of inflation rates, budget deficits, and government debt to levels near the average existing in the euro area.

A fixed-exchange-rate system represents an agreement among countries to convert their individual currencies from one to another at a given rate. The adoption of one money for Europe is the strongest possible commitment to fixed exchange rates among the EU countries. If every nation uses the same currency, the euro, then all will be linked to the same inflation rate and there will be no fluctuation of the value of the currency across the EU nations using the currency—just as each state in the United States uses the same money, the U.S. dollar. The adoption of a single currency requires that economic policies across EU countries be similar. This means that individual countries must subjugate their monetary policies to the goals of the European Central Bank. If each nation insists on exercising its own monetary and fiscal policies and chooses different interest and inflation rates, there can never be one money. A crisis in the eurozone arose in 2010–2011 due to the divergence of fiscal policy in Greece, Portugal, Ireland, and Spain. This experience just underscores the difficulty of having different nations with different policies sharing one money.

A convergence in inflation rates is necessary for the smooth operation of any fixed exchange rate. Persistent inflation differentials across the members of a fixed-exchange-rate system affect the competitiveness of each member's exports in the world market. Though a fixed-exchange-rate system maintains stable *nominal exchange rates* (the rate observed in the foreign exchange market), the competitiveness of a currency is represented by the *real exchange rate*. The real exchange rate is the nominal exchange rate adjusted for the price level at home compared to the price level abroad:

$$\text{Real exchange rate} = \frac{\text{nominal exchange rate} \times \text{foreign price level}}{\text{domestic price level}}$$

The disruptive changes in competitiveness caused by persistent inflation differentials require a realignment of a fixed-exchange-rate system that adjusts nominal exchange rates to keep real exchange rates from drifting too far from their correct value. For instance, if the Italian price level starts to rise faster than the German price level, Italian goods will be priced out of the German market unless there is an Italian currency that depreciates on the foreign exchange market. According to the equation just presented, if Italy is the domestic country and its price level rises, the real exchange rate falls and Italian goods are, therefore, relatively more expensive unless the nominal exchange rate rises to offset the higher domestic price level. The need for similar inflation rates within a fixed-exchange-rate system indicates that a country can successfully join a fixed-exchange-rate system or a region with one money only when its inflation rate falls to a level close to that of other European countries.

Any countries seeking to join the euro area must align their economic policies with those of the other member countries.

GLOSSARY

A

absolute advantage - An advantage derived from one country having a lower absolute input cost of producing a particular good than another country.

adaptive expectation - An expectation formed on the basis of information collected in the past.

aggregate demand curve - A curve that shows the different equilibrium levels of expenditures on domestic output at different levels of prices.

aggregate supply curve - A curve that shows the quantity of real GDP produced at different price levels.

appreciate - When the value of a currency increases under floating exchange rates—that is, exchange rates determined by supply and demand.

Asian tigers - Hong Kong, Korea, Singapore, and Taiwan, countries that globalized in the 1960s and 1970s and experienced fast economic growth.

automatic stabilizer - An element of fiscal policy that changes automatically as national income changes.

autonomous consumption - Consumption that is independent of income.

average propensity to consume (APC) - The proportion of disposable income spent for consumption.

average propensity to save (APS) - The proportion of disposable income saved.

B

balance of payments - A record of a country's trade in goods, services, and financial assets with the rest of the world.

balance of trade - The balance in the merchandise account in a nation's balance of payments.

barter - The direct exchange of goods and services without the use of money.

base year - The year against which other years are measured.

bilateral aid - Foreign aid that flows from one country to another.

budget deficit - The shortage that results when government spending is greater than tax revenue.

budget surplus - The excess that results when government spending is less than tax revenue.

business cycle - Fluctuations in the economy between growth (expressed in rising real GDP) and stagnation (expressed in falling real GDP).

business firm - A business organization controlled by a single management.

C

capital consumption allowance - The estimated value of depreciation plus the value of accidental damage to capital stock.

capital - Products such as machinery and equipment that are used in production.

classical economics - A school of thought that assumes that real GDP is determined by aggregate supply, while the equilibrium price level is determined by aggregate demand.

coincident indicator - A variable that changes at the same time as real output changes.

commercial bank loan - A bank loan at market rates of interest, often involving a bank syndicate.

commercial policy - Government policy that influences international trade flows.

comparative advantage - An advantage derived from comparing the opportunity costs of production in two countries.

complementary goods - Goods that are used together; as the price of one rises, the demand for the other falls.

composite currency - An artificial unit of account that is an average of the values of several national currencies.

consumer price index (CPI) - A measure of the average price of goods and services purchased by the typical household.

consumer sovereignty - The authority of consumers to determine what is produced through their purchases of goods and services.

consumption function - The relationship between disposable income and consumption.

consumption - Household spending.

corporation - A legal entity owned by shareholders whose liability for the firm's losses is limited to the value of the stock they own.

cost-of-living adjustment (COLA) - An increase in wages that is designed to match increases in the prices of items purchased by the typical household.

cost-push inflation - Inflation caused by rising costs of production.

credit - Available savings that are lent to borrowers to spend.

crowding out - A drop in consumption or investment spending caused by discretionary changes in fiscal policy, changes in government spending and taxation that are aimed at meeting specific policy goals.

currency substitution - The use of foreign money as a substitute for domestic money when the domestic economy has a high rate of inflation.

current account - The sum of the merchandise, services, income, and unilateral transfers accounts in the balance of payments.

customs union - An organization of nations whose members have no trade barriers among themselves but impose common trade barriers on nonmembers.

D

deficit - In a balance of payments account, the amount by which debits exceed credits.

demand curve - A graph of a demand schedule that measures price on the vertical axis and quantity demanded on the horizontal axis.

demand schedule - A table or list of prices and the corresponding quantities demanded for a particular good or service.

demand-pull inflation - Inflation caused by increasing demand for output.

demand - The amount of a product that people are willing and able to purchase at each possible price during a given period of time, everything else held constant.

deposit expansion multiplier - The reciprocal of the reserve requirement.

depreciate - When the value of a currency decreases under floating exchange rates.

depreciation - A reduction in the value of capital goods over time as a result of their use in production.

depression - A severe, prolonged economic contraction.

determinants of demand - Factors other than the price of the good that influence demand—income, tastes, prices of related goods and services, expectations, and number of buyers.

determinants of supply - Factors other than the price of the good that influence supply—prices of resources, technology and productivity, expectations of producers, number of producers, and the prices of related goods and services.

devaluation - A deliberate decrease in the official value of a currency.

discount rate - The interest rate that the Fed charges commercial banks when they borrow from it.

discouraged workers - Workers who have stopped looking for work because they believe that no one will offer them a job.

discretionary fiscal policy - Changes in government spending and taxation that are aimed at achieving a policy goal.

disequilibrium - Prices at which quantity demanded and quantity supplied are not equal at a particular price.

disposable personal income (DPI) - Personal income minus personal taxes.

dissaving - Spending financed by borrowing or using savings.

double coincidence of wants - The situation that exists when A has what B wants and B has what A wants.

double-entry bookkeeping - A system of accounting in which every transaction is recorded in at least two accounts.

dual economy - An economy in which two sectors (typically manufacturing and agriculture) show very different levels of development.

E

economic freedom - The ability to engage in voluntary trade without interference or restrictions by government or outside parties.

economic growth - An increase in real GDP.

equation of exchange - An equation that relates the quantity of money to nominal GDP.

equilibrium exchange rates - The exchange rates that are established in the absence of government foreign exchange market intervention.

equilibrium - The price and quantity at which quantity demanded and quantity supplied are equal.

Eurocurrency market or offshore banking - The market for deposits and loans generally denominated in a currency other than the currency of the country in which the transaction occurs.

European currency unit (ECU) - A unit of account formerly used by Western European nations as their official reserve asset.

excess reserves - The cash reserves beyond those required, which can be loaned.

exchange rate - The price of one country's money in terms of another country's money.

export subsidies - Payments made by a government to domestic firms to encourage exports.

export substitution - The use of resources to produce manufactured products for export rather than agricultural products for the domestic market.

export supply curve - A curve showing the relationship between the world price of a good and the amount that a country will export.

exports - Products that a country sells to other countries.

expropriation - The government seizure of assets, typically without adequate compensation to the owners.

F

Federal Deposit Insurance Corporation (FDIC) - A federal agency that insures deposits in commercial banks.

federal funds rate - The interest rate that a bank charges when it lends excess reserves to another bank.

Federal Open Market Committee (FOMC) - The official policy-making body of the Federal Reserve System.

financial account - The record in the balance of payments of the flow of financial assets into and out of a country.

financial capital - The source of funds used to purchase capital (bonds, stocks).

financial intermediaries - Institutions that accept deposits from savers and make loans to borrowers.

FOMC directive - Instructions issued by the FOMC to the Federal Reserve Bank of New York to implement monetary policy.

foreign aid - Gifts or low-cost loans made to developing countries from official sources.

foreign direct investment - The purchase of a physical operating unit or more than 10 percent ownership of a firm in a foreign country.

foreign exchange market intervention - The buying and selling of currencies by a central bank to achieve a specified exchange rate.

foreign exchange market - A global market in which people trade one currency for another.

foreign exchange - Currency and bank deposits that are denominated in foreign money.

forward guidance - Announcing a commitment by the central bank to maintain policy for a period of time until certain conditions are met.

fractional reserve banking system - A system in which banks keep less than 100 percent of their deposits available for withdrawal.

free trade area - An organization of nations whose members have no trade barriers among themselves but are free to fashion their own trade policies toward nonmembers.

fundamental disequilibrium - A permanent shift in the foreign exchange market supply and demand curves such that the fixed exchange rate is no longer an equilibrium rate.

G

gains from trade - The difference between what can be produced and consumed without specialization and trade and with specialization and trade.

GDP price index (GDPPI) - A broad measure of the prices of goods and services included in the gross domestic product.

gold exchange standard - An exchange-rate system in which each nation fixes the value of its currency in terms of gold, but buys and sells the U.S. dollar rather than gold to maintain fixed exchange rates.

gold standard - A system whereby national currencies are fixed in terms of their value in gold, thus creating fixed exchange rates between currencies.

gross domestic product (GDP) - The market value of all final goods and services produced in a year within a country.

gross investment - Total investment, including investment expenditures required to replace capital goods consumed in current production.

gross national product (GNP) - Gross domestic product plus receipts of factor income from the rest of the world minus payments of factor income to the rest of the world.

H

hawala - An international informal financial market used by Muslims.

household - One or more persons who occupy a unit of housing.

hyperinflation - An extremely high rate of inflation.

I

import demand curve - A curve showing the relationship between the world price of a good and the amount that a country will import.

import substitution - The substitution of domestically produced manufactured goods for imported manufactured goods.

imports - Products that a country buys from other countries.

increasing-returns-to-scale industry - An industry in which the costs of producing a unit of output fall as more output is produced.

indirect business tax - A tax that is collected by businesses for a government agency.

inferior goods - Goods for which demand decreases as income increases.

inflation - A sustained rise in the average level of prices.

interest rate effect - A change in interest rates that causes investment and therefore aggregate expenditures to change as the level of prices changes.

interest rate parity (IRP) - The condition under which similar financial assets have the same interest rate when measured in the same currency.

intermediate good - A good that is used as an input in the production of final goods and services.

intermediate target - An objective used to achieve some ultimate policy goal.

international banking facility (IBF) - A division of a U.S. bank that is allowed to receive deposits from and make loans to nonresidents of the United States without the restrictions that apply to domestic U.S. banks.

International Monetary Fund (IMF) - An international organization that supervises exchange-rate arrangements and lends money to member countries that are experiencing problems meeting their external financial obligations.

international reserve asset - An asset used to settle debts between governments.

international reserve currency - A currency held by a government to settle international debts.

international trade effect - A change in aggregate expenditures resulting from a change in the domestic price level that changes the price of domestic goods relative to that of foreign goods.

intraindustry trade - The simultaneous import and export of goods in the same industry by a particular country.

inventory - The stock of unsold goods held by a firm.

investment - Spending on capital goods to be used in producing goods and services.

K

Keynesian economics - A school of thought that emphasizes the role government plays in stabilizing the economy by managing aggregate demand.

L

labor - The physical and intellectual services of people, including the training, education, and abilities of the individuals in a society.

lagging indicator - A variable that changes after real output changes.

land - All natural resources, such as minerals, timber, and water, as well as the land itself.

law of demand - The quantity of a well-defined good or service that people are willing and able to purchase during a particular period of time decreases as the price of that good or service rises and increases as the price falls, everything else held constant.

law of supply - The quantity of a well-defined good or service that producers are willing and able to offer for sale during a particular period of time increases as the price of the good or service increases and decreases as the price decreases, everything else held constant.

leading indicator - A variable that changes before real output changes.

legal reserves - The cash a bank holds in its vault plus its deposit in the Fed.

liquid asset - An asset that can easily be exchanged for goods and services.

long-run aggregate supply curve (LRAS) - A vertical line at the potential level of real GDP.

M

M1 money supply - The financial assets that are the most liquid.

M2 money supply - M1 plus less liquid assets.

macroeconomics - The study of economics using aggregate sectors – households, businesses, government, and the foreign sector.

marginal propensity to consume (MPC) - The change in consumption as a proportion of the change in disposable income.

marginal propensity to import (MPI) - The change in imports as a proportion of the change in income.

marginal propensity to save (MPS) - The change in saving as a proportion of the change in disposable income.

marginal - Additional, incremental

market - A place or service that enables buyers and sellers to exchange goods and services.

microeconomics - The study of economics using the individual – individual consumer, individual firm.

monetarist economics - A school of thought that emphasizes the role changes in the money supply play in determining equilibrium real GDP and price level.

monetary reform - A new monetary policy that includes the introduction of a new monetary unit.

money - Anything that is generally acceptable to sellers in exchange for goods and services.

multilateral aid - Aid provided by international organizations that are supported by many nations.

multinational business - A firm that owns and operates producing units in foreign countries.

N

national income (NI) - Net national product plus or minus statistical discrepancy.

national income accounting - The framework that summarizes and categorizes productive activity in an economy over a specific period of time, typically a year.

natural rate of unemployment - The unemployment rate that would exist in the absence of cyclical unemployment.

net exports - The difference between the value of exports and the value of imports.

net investment - Gross investment minus capital consumption allowance.

net national product (NNP) - Gross national product minus capital consumption allowance.

new classical economics - A school of thought that holds that changes in real GDP are a product of unexpected changes in the level of prices.

NICs - Newly industrialized countries.

nominal GDP - A measure of national output based on the current prices of goods and services.

nominal interest rate - The observed interest rate in the market.

normal goods - Goods for which demand increases as income increases.

O

open market operations - The buying and selling of government and federal agency bonds by the Fed to control bank reserves, the federal funds rate, and the money supply.

opportunity cost - The highest-valued alternative that must be forgone when a choice is made.

P

partnership - A business with two or more owners who share the firm's profits and losses.

per capita real GDP - Real GDP divided by the population.

personal income (PI) - National income plus income currently received but not earned, minus income currently earned but not received.

Phillips curve - A graph that illustrates the relationship between inflation and the unemployment rate.

portfolio investment - The purchase of securities.

potential real GDP - The output produced at the natural rate of unemployment.

precautionary demand for money - The demand for money to cover unplanned transactions or emergencies.

price index - A measure of the average price level in an economy.

primary product - A product in the first stage of production, which often serves as an input in the production of another product.

private property rights - Ownership; the right to do anything you want with what you own as long as it does not harm the property of others.

private sector - Households, businesses, and the international sector.

producer price index (PPI) - A measure of average prices received by producers.

production possibilities curve (PPC) - A graphical representation showing all possible combinations of quantities of goods and services that can be produced using the existing resources fully and efficiently.

productivity - The quantity of output produced per unit of resource.

progressive tax - A tax whose rate rises as income rises.

public sector - The government.

purchasing power parity (PPP) - The condition under which monies have the same purchasing power in different markets.

Q

quantitative easing - Buying financial assets to stimulate the economy when the central bank target interest rate is near or at zero and the interest rate cannot be lowered further.

quantity demanded - The amount of a product that people are willing and able to purchase at a specific price.

quantity quota - A limit on the amount of a good that may be imported.

quantity supplied - The amount that sellers are willing and able to offer at a given price during a particular period of time, everything else held constant.

quantity theory of money - The theory that, with constant velocity, changes in the quantity of money change nominal GDP.

R

"race to the bottom" - The argument that, with globalization, countries compete for international investment by offering low or no environmental regulations or labor standards.

rational expectation - An expectation that is formed using all available relevant information.

real GDP - A measure of the quantity of final goods and services produced, obtained by eliminating the influence of price changes from the nominal GDP statistics.

real interest rate - The nominal interest rate minus the rate of inflation.

recession - A period in which real GDP falls.

recessionary gap - The increase in expenditures required to reach potential GDP.

required reserves - The cash reserves (a percentage of deposits) that a bank must keep on hand or on deposit with the Federal Reserve.

reservation wage - The minimum wage that a worker is willing to accept.

reserve currency - A currency that is used to settle international debts and is held by governments to use in foreign exchange market interventions.

resources - Goods used to produce other goods, i.e., land, labor, and capital.

ROSCA - A rotating savings and credit association popular in developing countries.

rule of 72 - The number of years required for an amount to double in value is 72 divided by the annual rate of growth.

S

saving function - The relationship between disposable income and saving.

scarcity - The shortage that exists when less of something is available than is wanted at a zero price.

shock - An unexpected change in a variable.

shortage - A quantity supplied that is smaller than the quantity demanded at a given price; it occurs whenever the price is less than the equilibrium price.

sole proprietorship - A business owned by one person who receives all the profits and is responsible for all the debts incurred by the business.

special drawing right (SDR) - A composite currency whose value is the average of the values of the U.S. dollar, the euro, the Japanese yen, and the U.K. pound.

speculative attack - A situation in which private investors sell domestic currency and buy foreign currency, betting that the domestic currency will be devalued.

speculative demand for money - The demand for money created by uncertainty about the value of other assets.

speculators - People who seek to profit from an expected shift in an exchange rate by selling the currency that is expected to depreciate and buying the currency that is expected to appreciate, then exchanging the appreciated currency for the depreciated currency after the exchange-rate adjustment.

spending multiplier - A measure of the change in equilibrium income or real GDP produced by a change in autonomous expenditures.

sterilization - The use of domestic open market operations to offset the effects of a foreign exchange market intervention on the domestic money supply.

strategic trade policy - The use of trade restrictions or subsidies to allow domestic firms with decreasing costs to gain a greater share of the world market.

substitute goods - Goods that can be used in place of each other; as the price of one rises, the demand for the other rises.

supply curve - A graph of a supply schedule that measures price on the vertical axis and quantity supplied on the horizontal axis.

supply schedule - A table or list of prices and the corresponding quantities supplied of a particular good or service.

supply - The amount of a good or service that producers are willing and able to offer for sale at each possible price during a period of time, everything else held constant.

surplus - A quantity supplied that is larger than the quantity demanded at a given price; it occurs whenever the price is greater than the equilibrium price. In a balance of payments account, the amount by which credits exceed debits.

T

tariff - A tax on imports or exports.

technology - Ways of combining resources to produce output.

terms of trade - The amount of an exported good that must be given up to obtain an imported good.

time inconsistent - A characteristic of a policy or plan that changes over time in response to changing conditions.

total factor productivity (*TFP*) - The ratio of the economy's output to its stock of labor and capital.

trade creation - An effect of a preferential trade agreement that allows a country to obtain goods at a lower cost than is available at home.

trade credit - Allowing an importer a period of time before it must pay for goods or services purchased.

trade deficit - The situation that exists when imports exceed exports.

trade diversion - An effect of a preferential trade agreement that reduces economic efficiency by shifting production to a higher-cost producer.

trade surplus - The situation that exists when imports are less than exports.

trade-off - The giving up of one good or activity in order to obtain some other good or activity.

transactions account - A checking account at a bank or other financial institution that can be drawn on to make payments.

transactions demand for money - The demand to hold money to buy goods and services.

transfer payment - Income transferred by the government from a citizen who is earning income to another citizen.

U

underemployment - The employment of workers in jobs that do not utilize their productive potential.

unemployment rate - The percentage of the labor force that is not working.

V

value added - The difference between the value of output and the value of the intermediate goods used in the production of that output.

value quota - A limit on the monetary value of a good that may be imported.

value-added tax (**VAT**) - A general sales tax collected at each stage of production.

velocity of money - The average number of times each dollar is spent on final goods and services in a year.

W

wealth effect - A change in the real value of wealth that causes spending to change when the level of prices changes.

wealth - The value of all assets owned by a household.

World Bank - An international organization that makes loans and provides technical expertise to developing countries.

INDEX

© Carsten Reisinger/Shutterstock

481

U.S. Macroeconomic Data for Selected Years, 1965–2014

Year	Real GDP	Consumption	Investment	Government Spending	Net Exports	Potential GDP	GDP Growth Rate	GDP Price Deflator	Consumer Price Index
				$ billions			%	index	
1965	3,972.9	2,376.1	529.6	1,224.2		3,845.1	6.5	18.7	31.5
1966	4,234.9	2,510.6	577.1	1,331.0		4,013.5	6.6	19.2	32.5
1967	4,351.2	2,585.6	556.9	1,436.4		4,192.4	2.7	19.8	33.4
1968	4,564.7	2,734.1	590.2	1,485.7		4,372.7	4.9	20.6	34.8
1969	4,707.9	2,836.3	623.1	1,488.0		4,552.8	3.1	21.7	36.7
1970	4,717.7	2,903.1	585.2	1,457.7		4,726.5	0.2	22.8	38.8
1971	4,873.0	3,013.9	645.5	1,431.0		4,891.0	3.3	24.0	40.5
1972	5,128.8	3,198.7	718.2	1,424.2		5,054.5	5.2	25.0	41.8
1973	5,418.2	3,357.3	796.8	1,419.6		5,233.2	5.6	26.4	44.4
1974	5,390.2	3,329.6	744.0	1,451.8		5,429.8	−0.5	28.7	49.3
1975	5,379.5	3,405.2	623.5	1,483.8		5,624.6	−0.2	31.4	53.8
1976	5,669.3	3,595.1	742.5	1,491.6		5,808.0	5.4	33.1	56.9
1977	5,930.6	3,746.6	848.4	1,509.2		6,003.8	4.6	35.2	60.6
1978	6,260.4	3,911.3	946.6	1,553.7		6,229.8	5.6	37.6	65.2
1979	6,459.2	4,004.2	979.8	1,582.6		6,456.4	3.2	40.7	72.6
1980	6,443.4	3,991.6	881.2	1,612.5		6,629.7	−0.2	44.4	82.4
1981	6,610.6	4,050.8	958.7	1,628.0		6,780.1	2.6	48.6	90.9
1982	6,484.3	4,108.5	833.7	1,658.0		6,971.7	−1.9	51.6	96.5
1983	6,784.7	4,342.7	911.5	1,721.6		7,180.5	4.6	53.6	99.6
1984	7,277.2	4,571.7	1,160.3	1,783.2		7,402.2	7.3	55.5	103.9
1985	7,585.7	4,812.0	1,159.5	1,904.0		7,650.4	4.2	57.3	107.6
1986	7,852.1	5,014.1	1,161.3	2,007.7		7,914.9	3.5	58.5	109.7
1987	8,123.9	5,183.7	1,194.4	2,066.9		8,179.7	3.5	59.9	113.6
1988	8,465.4	5,400.5	1,223.8	2,094.8		8,440.6	4.2	62.0	118.3
1989	8,777.0	5,558.2	1,273.4	2,155.1		8,702.2	3.7	64.5	123.9
1990	8,945.4	5,672.8	1,240.6	2,224.3		8,965.0	1.9	66.8	130.7
1991	8,938.9	5,685.7	1,158.8	2,250.9		9,223.4	−0.1	69.1	136.2
1992	9,256.7	5,896.6	1,243.7	2,262.1		9,480.5	3.6	70.6	140.3
1993	9,510.8	6,101.5	1,343.1	2,243.3		9,753.1	2.7	72.3	144.5
1994	9,894.7	6,338.1	1,502.3	2,245.5		10,039.3	4.0	73.9	148.2
1995	10,163.7	6,527.7	1,550.8	2,257.5		10,340.8	2.7	75.4	152.4
1996	10,549.5	6,755.7	1,686.7	2,279.2		10,665.5	3.8	76.8	156.9
1997	11,022.9	7,010.0	1,879.0	2,322.0		11,013.3	4.5	78.1	160.5
1998	11,513.4	7,384.9	2,058.3	2,370.5		11,388.3	4.5	78.9	163.0
1999	12,071.4	7,788.2	2,231.4	2,451.7	−382.3	11,790.1	4.8	80.1	166.6
2000	12,565.2	8,182.1	2,375.5	2,498.2	−482.7	12,216.6	4.1	81.9	172.2
2001	12,684.4	8,387.5	2,231.4	2,592.4	−504.2	12,664.8	0.9	83.8	177.0
2002	12,909.7	8,600.3	2,218.2	2,705.8	−584.9	13,106.1	1.8	85.1	179.9
2003	13,270.0	8,866.2	2,308.7	2,764.3	−641.6	13,517.1	2.8	86.7	184.0
2004	13,774.0	9,205.6	2,511.3	2,808.2	−731.9	13,874.4	3.8	89.1	188.9
2005	14,235.6	9,527.8	2,672.6	2,826.2	−777.1	14,207.7	3.4	92.0	195.3
2006	14,615.2	9,814.9	2,730.0	2,869.3	−786.2	14,548.8	2.7	94.8	201.6
2007	14,876.8	10,035.5	2,644.1	2,914.4	−703.6	14,903.9	1.8	97.3	207.3
2008	14,833.6	9,999.3	2,396.0	2,994.8	−546.9	15,248.2	−0.3	99.2	215.3
2009	14,417.9	9,842.9	1,878.1	3,089.1	−392.2	15,527.5	−2.8	100.0	214.6
2010	14,779.4	10,035.9	2,120.4	3,091.4	−462.6	15,747.1	2.5	101.2	218.1
2011	15,052.4	10,291.3	2,224.6	2,992.3	−445.9	15,972.0	1.8	103.2	224.9
2012	15,470.7	10,517.6	2,436.0	2,963.1	−430.8	16,225.4	2.8	105.0	229.6
2013	15,761.3	10,727.9	2,566.4	2,896.9	−412.3	16,496.3	1.9	106.6	233.0
2014	—	—	—	—	—	16,780.3	—	—	—